For Gill

Time is so old
And love so brief,
Love is pure gold
And Time a thief
(Ogden Nash, *One Touch of Venus*)

Acknowledgement

One Touch of Venus
Words by Ogden Nash
Music by Kurt Weill

© 1985 Chappell & Co Inc and Kurt Weill Foundation for Music Inc, USA
Warner/Chappell Music Ltd, London W6 8BS

Reproduced by permission of International Music Publications Ltd

The Pilgrimage
of Grace and the
Politics of the 1530s

R. W. HOYLE

OXFORD
UNIVERSITY PRESS

OXFORD
UNIVERSITY PRESS

Great Clarendon Street, Oxford OX2 6DP

Oxford University Press is a department of the University of Oxford.
It furthers the University's objective of excellence in research, scholarship,
and education by publishing worldwide in

Oxford New York

Athens Auckland Bangkok Bogotá Buenos Aires Cape Town
Chennai Dar es Salaam Delhi Florence Hong Kong Istanbul Karachi
Kolkata Kuala Lumpur Madrid Melbourne Mexico City Mumbai Nairobi
Paris São Paulo Shanghai Taipei Tokyo Toronto Warsaw

Oxford is a registered trade mark of Oxford University Press
in the UK and certain other countries

Published in the United States
by Oxford University Press Inc., New York

© R. W. Hoyle 2001

First published 2001
First published in paperback 2003

British Library Cataloguing in Publication Data

Data available

Library of Congress Cataloging in Publication Data
Hoyle, R. W.
The pilgrimage of grace and the politics of the 1530s / R. W. Hoyle.
p. cm.
Includes bibliographical references (p.).
1. Great Britain—Politics and government—1509–1547. 2. Pilgrimage of Grace,
1536–1537. I. Title.
DA339.H69 2001 942.05′2—dc21 2001016387
ISBN 0–19–820874–X (hbk)
ISBN 0–19–925906–2 (pbk)

1 3 5 7 9 10 8 6 4 2

Typeset by Graphicraft Limited, Hong Kong
Printed in Great Britain
on acid-free paper by
Biddles Ltd, Guildford and King's Lynn

Foreword

This book has been a very long time in the making. There were three events which persuaded me—whilst still a postgraduate in Oxford—that I should write about the Pilgrimage of Grace. The first was the realization that I could not reconcile my understanding of the experience of the first earl of Cumberland during the Pilgrimage with the received orthodoxies of the early 1980s. The second was the discovery on my first day in the archives at Chatsworth of the Clifford letters which I subsequently published in the Camden series: the first to catch my attention was the unknown letter of the council at York asking Cumberland to attend them. That was excitement! The third came from the evening I spent in my bed-and-breakfast in Bakewell reading Darcy's correspondence in *Letters and Papers*. This convinced me that he had been woefully misunderstood. I gave my first papers on the Pilgrimage at the British Agricultural History Society Conference in 1985 (where Chris Hallas's excursion through the Dales probably sticks in the memory of those attending more than my paper) and later that year in Oxford. Later Barbara English invited me to chair an anniversary Conference in Beverley which was great fun and where again some of the arguments were rehearsed and developed. The general direction of the book was decided in the mid-1980s; the first parts were drafted during 1992, and since then I have added to the text when time has permitted. It is a relief that it is now done but it is, I think, a better book for its extended gestation.

The aim of the book which I conceived as a young man was simple. It was to tell a largely unknown history of the Pilgrimage in a way which would be attractive to a history-reading public as well as satisfying an academic audience. The story I wanted to tell was that of how the gentry tamed—and ultimately defeated—a popular movement of the commons, which had been stimulated by rumour and fear of the early Reformation. In the early and mid-1980s there was little interest amongst Tudor historians in the possibility that there were popular movements

and currents in society. Lack of interest in issues of this sort was a curious blind-spot in Sir Geoffrey Elton's historical imagination (which, some
years after his death, we can now see as being extraordinarily limited, at
least in his later years) and so amongst his students too. Indeed, in the
early 1980s it was argued by some that Elton's paper on 'Politics and the
Pilgrimage of Grace'—which I always thought was full of holes—had
solved all the problems concerned with the Pilgrimage. The thesis that
the Pilgrimage of Grace was a popular revolt has lost its novelty as others
entered the field and—all credit to them—wrote and published much faster
than I: but I think that this book tells a story which remains unfamiliar
and which differs in ambition, detail, and emphasis (as well as range) from
the recent work of M. L. Bush and my old friend Steve Gunn.[1]

I also wanted to write a book which was attractive to the reader. I
can quickly state my conviction that historians in universities have a responsibility to communicate to the public outside their profession: I hope
to be read. The importance of producing attractive, approachable books
has, I think, deepened over the past decade for another reason. I went to
university a supplicant, pleased and even relieved to have secured a place
at Birmingham (it was only later I realized how fortunate I was to be
there at that time). Most of us accepted the discipline of being an undergraduate. Those of us who teach undergraduates today have to see them
as mobile, paying customers who exercise their discretion as to what they
will and will not do subjectwise, and, within a module (dread word!) what
they will—and will not—read. Hence this is a book which will, I hope,
attract a general readership as well as an undergraduate readership, that
will bring pleasure as well as inform. As a result, it is neither cluttered
with detail (as is the Dodds' monumental study), not does it spend all
its time cross-referencing its disagreements with other modern writers.

This ambition has also shaped the book in other respects. I have given
all extracts from original records in modernized spelling: my colleagues
can check the originals. Having stressed my desire to be accessible, it
may then seem strange to cite so much manuscript which, by its nature,

[1] I might add that Dr Bush's most recent book appeared after this work was mostly finalized and
I have not been able to take it into account. It tells the story of the post-Pilgrimage in 1537 in great
detail. M. Bush and D. Bownes, *The Defeat of the Pilgrimage of Grace: A Study of the Postpardon Revolts
of December 1536 to March 1537 and Their Effect* (1999).

is less readily accessible than the printed texts in *Letters and Papers of the Reign of Henry VIII*. The ambition of *Letters and Papers* was to publish all the original materials of significance for the reign of Henry VIII: it is both a blessing and a curse. Much of this book has been written with *LP* open: but equally *LP* contains errors, one of which is extremely important for our understanding of the siege of Pontefract Castle: it silently omits significant detail, sometimes whole sections, and it is frequently only a very curtailed paraphrase of the original documents. As far as possible this book is based on the originals of the depositions and examinations and not the printed texts. Quotations are normally taken from the manuscript; where it contains specific information not found in the print, this is indicated. The implications are twofold: that those without access to the manuscripts will not be able to verify all my references (although I give *LP* references so the reader can see what the document is), and that the scholarly apparatus is sometimes excessively complicated.

I ought to add that this is not the last word on the Pilgrimage and, if it were, I should be disappointed. One of the characteristics of this book is that I have tried to tell the story revealed by the documents whilst resisting the temptation to infer too much from them. Some historians have started from what I regard as an untenable assumption: that the Pilgrimage could not have begun without a conspiracy, and in order to find a conspiracy have read into the documents more than they contain, taking inconsistencies and discrepancies as evidence of concealment. Hence (and I leave this unreferenced deliberately): 'Darcy and Hussey were in close contact in November 1536 [actually one exchange of letters, with Hussey's approved by the council] and though the particular messenger used denied that he had ever carried messages to Constable, the very manner of his denial hints that someone else did.' This distinguished author then provides a reference to the printed text of *Letters and Papers*, which is some distance removed from what Creswell actually deposed.[2] Such lax analysis litters writing about the Pilgrimage, past and present. I do not believe that a conspiracy is necessary to explain the rebellion of 1536, nor, I suspect, would any medievalist familiar with the modern literature on 1381. And I have tried to read the surviving evidence for what it says

---

[2] For this episode, below pp. 318–21.

and not what it might say. When Aske says that he did not know Darcy before the fall of Pontefract, I believe him. When he says that he did not send a letter to Beverley calling on the town to rise, I believe him too. I am not above wondering, though, what we might discover if we could question our principles. To give one example, who was the 'friend' who sent an early warning of the Lincolnshire disturbances to Darcy? Why was Darcy coy about naming him in his letter to the king? Is it possible that the man was Aske, and that he sent letters to both Beverley and Temple Hirst, not calling for a rising but warning of disturbances which needed to be countered and resisted?[3] Of course this is speculation, but it shows the sort of deduction I have tried to avoid. Occasionally I point to instances where others have, to my mind, been led astray by this form of deductive reasoning. But this plain fare will not satisfy all, as I know from teaching undergraduates and talking to public groups, for many are wedded to a view of history in which conspiracies are needed to move events along. I look forward to someone trying to revive a thesis of prior planning. And I am sure that someone will.

Otherwise, I might paraphrase Aske, but before I do I ought to say that he puzzled me for years. I now think that I have his measure. I address my reader the way he addressed the king: I too have declared the 'plainness of the premises' so far as I can recall them, and I too am willing that if I have omitted any matter (and I fear I have), then I will declare the truth from time to time, and I beseech my reader for their most merciful pardon in the premises.[4]

The gestation and writing of this book has taken me from Magdalen to Bristol, back to Magdalen, then to the University of Central Lancashire, and comes to completion as I prepare to move on to the University of Reading. As the book comes to an end, so too does a thin period of my professional life. A book which has taken so long to produce has debts which are old: indeed, I cannot offer repayment of some of them. Without overtly engaging in reminiscence, my debts to Rodney Hilton, Joan Thirsk, and Richard Smith are considerable. None of them would have written this book—they would have done it differently and

---

3 'Aske's Examination', 568; For Darcy's letter, *LP* XI, no. 563; and discussion of whether Aske wrote to Beverley, below, p. 184.

4 Loosely based on Aske's conclusion to 'The manner of the taking of Robert Aske', 343.

better—but I hope that they approve of the result even if they cannot see in it anything that I have learnt from them. But their influence is there—somewhere. My career is based on two pieces of generous and fortunate patronage. I am grateful to the President and Fellows of Magdalen College, Oxford, for electing me to a Research Fellowship in 1985 and to the British Academy for appointing me to a Postdoctoral Research Fellowship in 1989. Both appointments allowed me to continue in academic life at a moment when I might otherwise have looked for another trade to ply. At Magdalen I enjoyed the company of Angus Macintyre, sadly no longer with us, Gerald Harriss, Lawrence Brockliss, Michael John, Tessa Webber, and John Nightingale. At that time I learnt a lot from the company of Cliff Davies, George Bernard, Steve Gunn, Peter Gwyn, and others. And I am grateful too to Eric Ives for discussions of the Pilgrimage. More recently books have been a constant problem: Magdalen has been too polite to ask for the return of its copy of volume XI of *Letters and Papers* whilst David Palliser let me have his copy of volume XII (i). For publishers I thank both Virginia Murphy for persuading me to write this book, and Ruth Parr for accepting it for OUP when the original publishing arrangements fell through. Much of the writing was undertaken in Preston whilst I was on the staff of the University of Central Lancashire: I am grateful to my old department for its financial support, which took me on frequent journeys to the Public Record Office.

My most important debts are personal. Dr Margaret Clark, Rosalind Collier, and Dr Henry French all read sections of the text as it was produced and wielded their pencils to my benefit. I am grateful to them for their encouragement and chivvying. George Bernard read the final text and let me have extensive comments: where we disagree (and we do, not least over Anne Boleyn), I am confident that it is for the best of reasons and with the greatest of cheer.

Gill has been with me even longer than the Pilgrimage. I cannot say that she made the book possible by cooking dinner or that she read every page as it was written: but her contribution is immeasureable. She is the best and most precious part of my life and the rock on which I've built these last twenty years. So, this is for her.

Fulwood

July 2000

Afterword to the paperback edition

On the day after the proofs of the index were returned to the Press (not so much a milestone as a full stop for an author's role in a book's production), Dr Angus Winchester sent to me for my comment a late seventeenth-century tract on customary tenure – tenant right – in Cumberland and Westmorland. This work, attributed to Thomas Denton (1637–98) but based on an earlier treatise, contained within it extracts from a number of otherwise unknown letters and documents concerning the rising of 1536 in the north west of England. Some documents which we would love to have before us – an intercepted letter of Robert Aske to John Atkinson, 'captain of the commons in Kendale' for instance – were noticed in passing where others are (selectively) quoted at length. The most significant contribution these new documents make to our knowledge is that they show how general the agitation against landlords was in the Lake Counties in 1536. The peasant mobilisation against them is revealed by the text of other inquests into the ills of the commonwealth to mirror that from around Kirkby Stephen (pp. 251–3 below). They remind us how much is lost to us but also offer hope that more will be found in the future.

The new documents will be published, with a commentary, in R. W. Hoyle and A. J. L. Winchester, 'A new source for the rising of 1536 in north-west England', *English Historical Review*, 118, 2003.

September 2002

Contents

Maps   xiv

Tables   xiv

Abbreviations   xv

1. The Risings of 1536–1537: Retrospect and Prospect   1
2. A Northern Panorama   28
3. 1536: The Year of Three Queens   55
4. Lincolnshire   93
5. The Dynamics of the Lincolnshire Rising   135
6. Fever Days: The Reaction to Lincolnshire   158
7. The Rising in the East Riding   176
8. The 'Captain Poverty' Revolts   209
9. Misunderstanding Darcy   256
10. The Confrontation at Doncaster   282
11. The Benignity of the Prince   306
12. Winding Up the Pilgrimage   339
13. The King's Love For the North   365
14. The Return of the Duke of Norfolk   389
15. The Rebellions as Commons' Revolts   423
16. Epilogue: 'to knit up this tragedy'   448

Select Documents   455

   (i) The Lincoln Articles, 9 October 1536   455
   (ii) Aske's Proclamation to the City of York, 15–16 October 1536   456
   (iii) The Oath, ?24 October 1536   457
   (iv) The Hampole Articles, ?27 October 1536   458
   (v) The Instructions for Sir Thomas Hilton and the Pontefract Articles, 4 December 1536   459
   (vi) The Opinions of the Pseudo-Convocation at Pontefract, 4 December 1536   463

Bibliography of Printed Sources   465

Index   473

Maps

1. The Lincolnshire rising   94
2. The distribution of persons prosecuted for involvement in
   the rising   96
3. The rising in the East Riding   177
4. The Richmondshire movement   211

Tables

5.1. The occupations of known rioters at Louth on Monday,
     2 October   136
5.2. Occupations of men indicted for rebellion at Lincoln,
     6 March 1537   137

Abbreviations

'Aske's Examination'	Printed in paraphrase in *LP* XII (i), nos. 900, 901, 945, 946, and in full by M. Bateson in 'Aske's Examination', *EHR* 5 (1890), 550–73. All page references are to the Bateson edition
BL	British Library
Bodl.,	Bodleian Library, Oxford
Bush, *Pilgrimage of Grace*	M. L. Bush, *The Pilgrimage of Grace: A Study of the Rebel Armies of October 1536* (1996)
'Derby Correspondence',	T. N. Toller (ed.), 'Correspondence of Edward, Third Earl of Derby, during the years 24 to 31 Henry VIII, Preserved in a MS in the Possession of Miss ffarington of Worden Hall', *Chetham Soc.*, NS 19 (1890)
Dodds, *Pilgrimage*	M. H. Dodds and R. Dodds, *The Pilgrimage of Grace, 1536–1537 and the Exeter Conspiracy, 1538*, 2 vols. (1915)
Fletcher and MacCulloch, *Tudor Rebellions*	A. Fletcher and D. MacCulloch, *Tudor Rebellions*, 4th edn. (1997)
Hist. Parl., *1509–1558*	S. T. Bindoff (ed.), *The History of Parliament: The Commons, 1509–1558*, 3 vols. (1982)
HJ	*Historical Journal*
'Letters of the Cliffords'	R. W. Hoyle (ed.), 'Letters of the Cliffords, Lords Clifford and Earls of Cumberland, *c.*1500–*c.*1565', in *Camden Miscellany 31*, Camden 4th ser., 44 (1992), 1–189.
LP	*Letters and Papers, Foreign and Domestic, of the Reign of Henry VIII*, ed. J. S. Brewer *et al.* 21 vols. and *Addenda* (1862–1932)
Moigne	Thomas Moigne's account of the Lincolnshire revolt, SP1/110, fos. 148r–158v, printed in a poor abstract in *LP* XI, no. 971.
NH	*Northern History*
PRO	Public Record Office

SP1	Public Record Office, State Papers Henry VIII (used for citations of original MSS abstracted in *LP*)
St. P.	*State Papers During the Reign of Henry the Eighth*, 11 vols. (1830–52)
Stapleton	'The true confession of William Stapulton . . .', printed in paraphrase in *LP* XII (i), no. 392, and verbatim by J. C. Cox, 'William Stapleton and the Pilgrimage of Grace', *Trans. East Riding Antiquarian Soc.*, 10 (1903). All references are to the Cox transcript.
'The manner of the taking of Robert Aske'	Printed in paraphrase, *LP* XII (i), no. 6, and in full by M. Bateson, 'The Pilgrimage of Grace', *EHR* 5 (1890), 331–43. All page references are to the Bateson edition
'Thomas Master's Narrative'	R. W. Hoyle (ed.), 'Thomas Master's Narrative of the Pilgrimage of Grace', *Northern History*, 21 (1985)
VCH	Victoria County History
YAJ	*Yorkshire Archaeological Journal*
YASRS	*Yorkshire Archaeological Society Record Series*

All references to MSS are, unless otherwise indicated, to collections held in the Public Record Office. The spelling and punctuation of quotations from MSS in the text has been modernized.

The Risings of 1536–1537: Retrospect and Prospect

We may begin with the final act of the Pilgrimage of Grace, for it is not the end which is troublesome to historians, but the beginning. On 18 September 1541 the mayor, aldermen, and the recorder of York, a large party of citizens, and the gentry of the wapentake of the Ainsty gathered at Fulford on the edge of the city's liberties to greet Henry VIII. This was the king's first and only visit to the city: it had been promised for the summer of 1537 but deferred for some years. The original reasons for his visit were now stale, but there was unfinished business to be transacted. For the mayor and his brethren this was certainly not a comfortable moment. A few days before they had been in consultation with the archbishop of York about the tone of their first contact with the king. Did they, in the 'name of the whole body of this city', need to 'confess themselves guilty in anything done in time of the late rebellion against the king's majesty, according as the Lincolnshire men now have done at the coming of the king's said majesty there?' The archbishop must have recommended that it would be prudent to do so. For after writing desperate letters for impossible aid, in October 1536 York had surrendered to the rebels without a siege, witnessed them attend a service in the Minster, and then, at the end of November, played host to

their council of war. And so incriminated, at Fulford, on the approach
of the king, 120 citizens of York and sixty persons drawn from the Ainsty
all fell to their knees. The city's recorder, also prone, addressed the king
and made a humble submission on their behalf, admitting their collective fault for entering rebellion against him and thanking the king
for his pardon, 'whose bountiful heart and liberal grant we of ourselves
are in no wise able to recompense or satisfy, but continually have been
from the bottoms of our hearts repentant, woe[ful] and sorrowful for
our said unnatural and heinous offences.' They declared that nothing like
it would ever happen again, promised their prayers for the king, Queen
Catherine, and Prince Edward, and gave the king a gratuity.[1]

This was one of a sequence of similar humble submissions made to
Henry as he travelled northwards. At Lincoln, where the city had been
successively entered by insurgents and royal troops in October 1536, a
similar submission was enacted. The gentry of Yorkshire, said to be 200
in all, accompanied by 4,000 'tall yeomen and serving men, well
horsed', made their submission at Bawtry when the king entered the
county. Henry first met and addressed those who had remained loyal to
him, whilst some distance apart knelt the rebels, amongst them the archbishop of York. Sir Robert Bowes made a long confession of their treasons and their gratitude for the king's lenience and his pardon.[2] Bowes
was one of the two envoys from the rebels who had travelled to Windsor
to relay their demands to the king five years previously. At Barnsdale, as
the court travelled from Hatfield to Pontefract, the king was met by
Archbishop Lee and 300 or more clergy, who also submitted and gave
the king a cash gift of £600. Lee was the archbishop who had first fled
from the rebels and had then been one of their council (albeit, he claimed,
unwillingly). And whilst he had scandalized the Pilgrims by preaching
against their movement, this was the man who (rather ineptly) wrote to
the king on 7 December 1536 expressing his pleasure that the king had
not only offered the rebels an unconditional pardon but had conceded
their requests (which he had not).[3]

---

[1] For this and the next paragraph, A. G. Dickens, 'The Yorkshire Submissions to Henry VIII,
1541', *EHR* 53 (1938), 267–75.
[2] *LP* XVI, no. 1130.   [3] Hoyle, 'Thomas Master's Narrative', 75.

There were relatively few of the leaders of northern society in 1541 who had not, in some way, been touched by the rebellion of 1536. A few had stories of heroism—of being besieged by rebels or of flight to evade them—which they could tell. The majority were tainted by their association with the rebels: for whatever reason, and for whatever motivation, they had been amongst them, sometimes under duress, sometimes out of sympathy for their objectives, sometimes actively encouraging the rebel host onwards or leading negotiations. A few of the most prominent individuals in the rebellion of 1536 could not be present. The king had long before taken his revenge on the lawyers Robert Aske and Thomas Moigne, the elderly Thomas, Lord Darcy, and Sir Robert Constable, men whose role in the movement was complex but judged to be treasonous.

As their collective submissions were read, the men on their knees doubtless reflected on their own experiences in the last months of 1536. For some the memory was perhaps one of exhilaration, of the pleasure of courting death for a principle devoutly believed in. For others the recollection was probably that of the quiet terror of subterfuge, of being semi-captive amongst the rebels and forced to voice their rejection of royal policy, then in the months after the movement had collapsed, of hoping that no one would enquire too closely into what they had done, and that they (unlike some of their neighbours) would not receive an innocent letter calling them to London for what might be congratulation, or interrogation, imprisonment, and ultimately execution. One doubts whether any of those present could forget the experience, but few committed their recollections to paper. Those who left us accounts normally had them taken down at dictation by John ap Rice, or Drs Layton and Leigh, in the Tower of London. For the rising in Lincolnshire in 1536 and the Pilgrimage of Grace in Yorkshire and the North was a defeat. At the second meeting at Doncaster the king's emissaries were brought to make promises on his behalf—for instance, for a parliament to review the legislation of the Reformation Parliament—which were never honoured. There was no song or ballad written to commemorate a notable victory, for there was no victory. The only work of literature to come out of the North was a denunciation of rebellion and a call for ecclesiastical reform of the sort which would have horrified the

Pilgrims.[4] So for many the submissions of August and September 1541 were a bitter moment. They had tried to save the smaller monasteries, but now all monastic houses had gone. The alteration in religion announced by the articles and injunctions of 1536 had never been reversed: indeed, every man was now entitled to read the Bible in English, which ten years before would have been taken as prima facie evidence of heresy. The shrine of St Hugh in Lincoln Minster had been dismantled during the previous summer and its jewels and silver carted off to the king's coffers.[5] The hated Dr Layton, one of the visitors of the monasteries in 1535–6 and complained about by name in the Pontefract Articles, was now dean of York.[6] In less than ten years Lee's successor as archbishop would be a married man. The penitents prostrate before the king probably recalled 1536 as the year in which the old verities of faith were first challenged and the cause of their defence lost.

I

The events of the last few months of 1536 and the winter of 1537, which form the subject of this book, can be quickly outlined.[7] The year 1536 was the one in which Katherine of Aragon died, Anne Boleyn abruptly fell from the king's favour, and the king took Jane Seymour for his third wife. It was the year in which the smaller monasteries were dissolved. During the summer the first alterations in the religious practice of the laity were announced. These disturbances in the body politic and the

---

[4] Wilfred Holme, *The fall and evil success of rebellion* (written 1537, pub. 1573), discussed at length in A. G. Dickens, *Lollards and Protestants in the Diocese of York* (1959), 114–31. More recently Janice Liedl has suggested that *A dyalogue betwene the playntife and the defendaunt* by William Calverley is another work reflecting on the error of rebellion, but I am not wholly convinced. J. Liedl. 'The Penitant Pilgrim: William Calverley and the Pilgrimage of Grace', *Sixteenth Century Journal*, 25 (1994).

[5] M. Bowker, 'Historical Survey, 1450–1750', in D. M. Owen (ed.), *A History of Lincoln Minster* (1994), 181.

[6] Layton was appointed to the deanship in July 1539. He died whilst on a diplomatic mission to Brussels in June 1544. *DNB, sub nomine.*

[7] The best short account of the 1536 risings is A. Fletcher and D. MacCulloch, *Tudor Rebellions*, 4th edn. (1997), ch. 4. The fullest account remains the Dodds, *Pilgrimage*, whose strengths and weaknesses are discussed below, pp. 12–13.

activism of government in enforcing change (all of which will be considered further in Chapter 3) form the essential background to the rising which began in Lincolnshire and then spread into Yorkshire and the North of England generally. The insurrections—and the flickering into renewed flame of the autumn rising in the New Year—are collectively called the Pilgrimage of Grace. In fact this term was only used in Yorkshire and those areas of the North influenced by the rising led by Robert Aske. We should therefore distinguish between the rising in Lincolnshire, the mature movement in east Yorkshire (though it is argued subsequently that the Pilgrimage was a child of the rising which started in Louth on 2 October), and the rising in Richmondshire which was spread by letter into Westmorland and Cumberland.

On this Monday, 2 October, two officials of the bishop of Lincoln were expected in Louth: his steward, John Hennage, who was attending the town's court to oversee the election of the bailiff, and the bishop's commissary, Dr Frankish, who was to meet with the clergy of Louth Esk deanery. The expectation in Louth on the Sunday evening was that Frankish was coming to confiscate the plate and goods of Louth church. To prevent their seizure, a group of men barricaded themselves in the church overnight. There were no such plans. The fears current in Louth arose out of the fears and anxieties of the autumn of 1536, out of what was rumoured to be intended rather than anything which was planned. On the Monday morning Hennage was seized by a crowd and then released after he promised to discover whether there was any truth in the rumoured confiscation. Frankish narrowly escaped being beaten up by his own clerical colleagues and saw his books and papers publicly burnt. Later in the day two of Cornwall's servants overseeing the dissolution of the nearby nunnery at Legbourne were captured. This was a bit of small-town trouble.

It became more than this when a group of Louth townspeople travelled to Caistor on the following morning. There they expected to find the subsidy commissioners at a meeting to set in train the assessment of the subsidy. Their aim was to seek confirmation from the gentry present there that their church goods were not threatened, but the subsidy commissioners, seeing their approach, scattered, and what might have been a meeting where they defused the rebellion became a fiasco as the commons rode after and captured some of their number. By evening word of the Louth insurrection was spreading widely. The gentry themselves were confined at Louth whilst one of their number rode to the court with a plea that the king rescue his fellow commissioners. This same day—Tuesday, 3 October—there was a copycat rising at Horncastle where a number of gentry were captured and sworn by a crowd from the town. On the following day Dr Rayne, the chancellor of the diocese of Lincoln, whom the rebels found ill at Bolingbroke, was brought to Horncastle and lynched by his own clergy. The Lincolnshire movement was then spread by groups of commons riding about the county swearing the commons, capturing gentry, and calling musters. On Saturday a force of 10,000 men (perhaps more, perhaps less, but a sizeable number) entered Lincoln. It advanced no further, but drew up articles which were sent to the king. The gentry with the rebels then insisted that they would not advance until they had received a reply to their articles: when Lancaster Herald arrived at Lincoln on Wednesday, 11 October, he found it fairly easy to persuade the rebels to disperse back to their homes. The gentry were able to sue for peace with the duke of Suffolk, whose expeditionary force against the movement was gathering around Stamford.

The Lincolnshire rising was over within a fortnight: only the king's retribution on its most prominent activists took longer. The news that the revolt here had petered out was received with great relief at court. Henry, ignorant of developments further north, disbanded the army he was gathering at Ampthill (which he proposed to lead in person) only to learn—too late to recall his troops—that the Lincolnshire rising had spread into Yorkshire.

The first of the Yorkshire movements was simply Lincolnshire abroad. News of the rising there reached Beverley on Sunday, 8 October. The commons of the town rose out of solidarity, then wrote to the Lincolnshire rebels for guidance. From Beverley the rising spread northwards into the Wolds and eastwards into Holderness. Contacts were made with Hull which, initially, was defiant, but which capitulated to the rebels on 19 October. The area around the confluence of the rivers Aire and Don, the Marshland, and Howdenshire rose on 10 October. The movement here came to coalesce around the lawyer Robert Aske, who emerged over the following fortnight as the pivotal figure in the movement. Aske quickly emerged as leader of a group of commons from the Marshland and Howdenshire: he led this force northwards, forging an alliance with the Beverley rising and holding musters as he went. In a clear emulation of the behaviour of the Lincolnshire rebels, he entered York on 16 October after the mayor had judged the town too divided to withstand a siege. Aske also took the initiative and called on the parallel rising in Richmondshire to join him. It was he who gave the moment its name, its oath, and so its purpose:

Ye shall not enter into this our Pilgrimage of Grace for the commonwealth, but only for the love that ye do bear unto Almighty God, his faith and the Holy Church militant and the maintenance thereof, to the preservation of the king's person and his issue, to the purifying of the nobility and to expulse all villain blood and evil councillors against the commonwealth from his grace and his privy council . . .[8]

Aske has always seemed a puzzle to historians; his actions are considered anew and perhaps understood for the first time in Chapter 6.

Aske was also aware that a large number of gentry and senior clerics —including the archbishop of York—had taken refuge in Pontefract Castle about 18 miles south of York. The castle was in the custody of the elderly Thomas, Lord Darcy, a man entirely out of sympathy with the constitutional and religious changes of the early 1530s. Like Aske's, Darcy's behaviour has seemed problematic: whilst he was sending full and accurate accounts of the scale of the rising in Yorkshire to Henry VIII (letters which Henry either never saw or disregarded as being too alarmist to be reliable), he surrendered the castle and its occupants to Aske after a perfunctory siege and then emerged as one of the Pilgrims' leaders. Contemporaries, both theirs and ours, have suspected that by surrendering the castle without a fight and throwing in his own hand with the rebels, Darcy revealed his true colours. In Chapter 8 I will argue that this is an unfair judgement on his behaviour.

At the same time as Aske was spreading the rebellion through the East Riding, a second independent rising was taking place in the northern

---

[8] *LP* XI, no. 705 (4); printed most conveniently in Fletcher and MacCulloch, *Tudor Rebellions*, 132.

part of the county. Before the end of September there had been disturbances in Dentdale: but these appear to have been coincidental with rather than a progenitor of the Pilgrimage. The first rising took place in Richmondshire, or rather in the district around Ripon and running northwards to Richmond. Whether this was a further seedling of the Lincolnshire movement or whether it took place in ignorance of events to the south cannot be established. Richmondshire was an area with a prior history of disturbances: in 1489 the Richmondshire men had marched on York, and in 1513 they had launched a tax strike throughout the upper Yorkshire Dales. In October 1536 they set about capturing the gentry of the district and then, after a meeting in Richmond when letters calling for a general rising were circulated in the name of Captain Poverty, the movement sent out three raiding parties to spread the word and capture additional gentry. One penetrated through the Dales to Skipton; another went into County Durham, where they held musters and sacked the bishop of Durham's palace at Bishop Auckland; and a third travelled into Ryedale towards Scarborough. The Captain Poverty letters spawned risings in the Upper Eden Valley and Penrith, with musters being progressively held throughout Cumberland, and in Northumberland (where the disturbances took more the form of gentry faction-fighting). The Richmondshire rising also spread at second-hand into Westmorland and north Lancashire and through Craven into east Lancashire. The Richmondshire men appear to have advocated social revolution: their risings had a radical anti-landowning edge not generally found elsewhere.

Aske called the Richmondshire men to him and the Pilgrimage of Grace took its final shape at Pontefract. The Pilgrims took up position on the high ground overlooking Doncaster, where they faced a much smaller force under the earl of Shrewsbury who, having first set his face against Lincolnshire, made a pre-emptory (and perhaps incautious) advance northwards to seize the bridges over the Don at Doncaster on 22 or 23 October.

Both Shrewsbury and the duke of Norfolk, who was riding well forward of his scratch army, appreciated that the situation at Doncaster was a full-scale military emergency in which the Crown's hastily assembled army was outnumbered and in danger of being overwhelmed. Norfolk elected to open negotiations with the leadership of the Pilgrims. A truce was struck during Friday, 27 October, when the Pilgrims disbanded in return for the safe passage of two emissaries, Sir Ralph Ellerker and Sir Robert Bowes, to convey their petition to the king in person. The face-saving explanation was that the River Don had risen and that the camps of both armies had been washed away by heavy rain: this may well have been true, but both Aske and Norfolk shared the conviction that in the event of battle, Shrewsbury's men (drawn mostly from the north Midlands) would not have fought the Pilgrims. Norfolk's preference was always to negotiate the rebels out of existence. By Sunday, 29 October, he could report that the Pilgrims had almost entirely dispersed, and that the royal army had broken up and was returning home. Word then circulated throughout the North of the Doncaster truce. It was received in Lancashire in time to prevent the earl of Derby from leading an army from Preston along the Ribble Valley to engage with the Craven commons around Sawley Abbey, and to stop the commons of Cumberland from laying siege to Carlisle.

The magnitude of the Crown's problem was that by the last weekend of October it had lost control of virtually the whole of the North from the rivers Don in Yorkshire and Ribble in Lancashire to the borders of Scotland. All that held out for the king were three castles, Skipton, Scarborough, and Norham, none of which were of any strategic importance. It was an appreciation of the Crown's military inferiority which marked its policy over the following five weeks. The king, as always, was a hawk, reluctant to offer any compromise which might look like weakness. Others, notably Norfolk, advised 'policy'. The duke, though, had disbanded the royal army; yet it quickly became apparent that whilst the Pilgrims had dispersed from Doncaster, their army had only gone into abeyance and the North remained prepared, even enthusiastic, for war if a settlement on their terms could not be achieved.

The Pilgrims had expected the rapid return to them of Ellerker and Bowes. In fact they were held at court and only returned to Pontefract on 18 November. Even then they were not equipped with a conclusive answer, but with an invitation to formulate a fuller set of grievances, the king having found their articles to be 'general, dark and obscure'. Norfolk would return to the North and give the king's answer to a meeting of 300 at Doncaster. Ellerker and Bowes reported to a council of the Pilgrims held at York on 21 November, and whilst they stressed the king's good faith, the council was appalled when an intercepted letter from Cromwell to Sir Ralph Eure, the defender of Scarborough Castle, was read to them. This promised a severe retaliation against the rebels. Despite this authentic insight into the Crown's attitude, the council agreed to convene a fuller representative meeting at Pontefract on 2–4 December. This devised the so-called 'Pontefract articles' from bills of complaint presented to it. Concurrently, a convocation of senior clergy produced its own critique of the king's religious polices after 1529.[9]

When the Pilgrims met Norfolk he sidestepped consideration of the articles by offering a universal free pardon, the promise of a parliament to be held in the North in the future, and a range of minor (and deliberately unwritten) concessions. Norfolk's options were limited. He had no military force beyond his retinue. That a sizeable group of commons had gathered at Pontefract to hear the outcome of the negotiations made Norfolk's expedition much more militarily dangerous than had been anticipated. His instinct (as in October) was to play for more time by giving undertakings to the rebels, whilst avoiding discussion of the highly specific concerns expressed in the Pontefract articles. This satisfied the nobles and gentry who met with Norfolk, but the rank and file gathered at Pontefract were less readily appeased, and it fell to Aske to sell the agreement to them. In fact they only dispersed when Aske showed them the pardon. This done, the way was open for the nobility and gentry to make their formal submission to Norfolk, but it also left a legacy of suspicion in the minds of the commons. Their conviction that the gentry had sold out grew over the following weeks as many of the latter travelled to London to make their private peace with the king. Even Aske was invited to court, where he advised the king about the future treatment of the North. During January there were a number of bids by the commons to revive the movement. There was a deluded and easily repressed attempt by Sir Francis Bigod and one of the leaders of the East Riding commons, John Hallam, to seize Hull and Scarborough.

---

[9] The Pontefract articles are printed below, pp. 460–3, and the articles made by the pseudo-convocation pp. 463–4.

Likewise, attempts were made to revive the Richmondshire movement. With the exception of mavericks like Bigod, most of the Yorkshire gentry remained committed to the Doncaster agreement, and were anxious that discipline should be maintained amongst the commons lest further outbreaks of revolt should undermine the king's adherence to their agreement with Norfolk. Much more serious was the renewed revolt in Cumberland and Westmorland, where a bungled attempt to seize the ringleaders of the autumn rebellion provoked an attack on Carlisle on 17 February. This produced the only real conflict between troops loyal to the king and rebels. The use of borderers by Sir Christopher Dacre was particularly bloody: it was claimed that 700 or 800 men were taken prisoner. Norfolk declared martial law and executed seventy-four prisoners.

Amongst the rebels generally, the number executed was relatively small. One hundred men were tried and thirty-four executed in Lincolnshire in March 1537 and a further twelve in London later in the month.[10] In Yorkshire the pardon precluded large-scale executions. Where rebellion was renewed (as by Bigod) or conspiracy took place after the second Doncaster meeting (as was alleged for Aske, Darcy, and others), the government arrested and interrogated. The majority of those pulled in were senior figures with whom the king had a particular score to settle: very few of the commons were questioned or prosecuted. Darcy was tried on 15 May and executed on 30 June. Aske and fifteen others were tried on 16–17 May for offences committed after the pardon, and executed at the end of the month or in the first few days of June.

II

What happened during the Pilgrimage of Grace is largely uncontentious. As we shall see subsequently, some moments are deeply—and deliberately—obscure. Others, by accident, are ill-documented. The controversies about the risings of 1536 are primarily concerned with motivation. Were the risings the result of conspiracy amongst the gentry and

---

[10] Dodds, *Pilgrimage*, II, 151–4.

nobility, an expression of disaffection amongst the political elite, a last throw of the dice by a disenchanted and failing court faction, who led their tenants into war? Or was it a popular movement in which the initiative was taken by the commons, the lower orders who had no normal role in political society except as passive subjects? And whether conspiracy or a spontaneous outburst of anger, were the movements motivated by fears for religion or by economic and social grievances?

It is a truism to say that historians see the past through the prism of their own times and their own experience of society and social change. At some moments particular views of historical causation have been popular, at other moments less so. The interpretation of the Pilgrimage of Grace has taken markedly different forms over the course of the twentieth century, with the result that there is no real consensus about why the rebellions took place or what were their internal dynamics. The first modern writers on the Pilgrimage, Madeleine Hope Dodds and Ruth Dodds (1915), offered a fine-grained narrative of the risings which remains a valuable work of reference. M. H. Dodds was amongst the early women students to take the Historical Tripos at Cambridge.[11] The Dodds sisters, perhaps because of M. H. Dodds's training, believed that they were writing 'scientific history'.[12] Perhaps for this reason they concentrated on impartial narrative with the minimum of comment or interpretation. One has to turn to their conclusions to discover something of the interpretative framework within which they worked, but not even here do they provide any reflections on the underlying causation of the revolt. Overall, it is clear enough that they inclined towards the view that the rebellion was 'popular'. Their movement was an aspect of the conflict between the free spirit of the English people and forms of tyranny: the Pilgrims were engaged in a struggle between liberty and despotism which was carried through to success only in 1649.[13] Hence the Dodds were against Henry VIII but for Katherine of Aragon; they referred to the 'sinister power' of Thomas Cromwell, and held that Robert Aske

[11] M. H. Dodds died in 1972. See the obituary (by Ruth Dodds) in *Archaeologia Aeliana*, 5th ser., I (1973), 223–4.

[12] See their comments in Dodds, *Pilgrimage*, II, 330.

[13] The Dodds went so far as to trace the involvement of families involved in the Pilgrimage in the Civil War. Ibid., II, 333–4.

was near a saint and deserving of commemoration by the Catholic church.[14] This presented the Dodds with some difficulties, for the Pilgrims were Catholics, engaged in the defence of the unreformed Catholic church with which the Dodds had little sympathy. They revealed their intellectual predicament just once: immediately after printing Aske's oath, they commented that '[t]here is a loftiness in the call—a ring in the words that, even today, sets a calm Protestant heart beating to the tune of the Pilgrims's march'.[15] Hence the Dodds, finding a campaign to defend the Catholic church to be unappealing, ultimately came to stress the importance of non-religious factors in the movement and supposed that the defence of the church was the sole concern of the clerical estate. The higher clergy were 'supine': some fled, the archbishop of York and the abbots 'gave [the Pilgrims] no encouragement'. 'This inaction [by the clergy] to a great extent caused the failure of the most promising attempt to preserve the Church of Rome which was ever made in England.' They argued that the commons wished to secure social reform, notably lower rents and higher wages: the concern of the gentleman was for higher rents and lower wages. For the Dodds the Pilgrimage was a coalition of interest groups, each with its separate concerns and priorities.[16]

The Dodds' book is a fine narrative but weak on analysis and political understanding. Fifty years after it was published A. G. Dickens began the work of reassessment in terms which, in retrospect, look all too Doddsian. He too saw a 'fundamental divergence of interests and attitudes between gentry and commons'. He thought that the Pilgrims had made an early mistake by choosing Aske as their 'Grand Captain' rather than a prince of the royal blood. And, having reviewed the evidence, he found nothing to suggest that the revolt was spiritual or motivated by 'Catholic idealism'.[17] The following year C. S. L. Davies offered an acuter analysis which came to the conclusion that the revolts were essentially movements of religious protest. 'Religious factors, then, were an essential feature of the Pilgrimage: they figured large among the causes, they served to give the movement cohesion, to bind together different classes with widely different interests, providing slogans and scapegoats, in the

[14] Ibid., II, 330, 331.   [15] Ibid., I, 182.   [16] Ibid., II, 330.
[17] A. G. Dickens, 'Secular and Religious Motivation in the Pilgrimage of Grace', most conveniently in Dickens, *Reformation Studies* (1982).

last resort legitimating resistance to the king.' But the mechanics of motivation remained obscure: Davies doubtless held, as Dickens did, that the Pilgrimage, like the Western Rising of 1549, were 'at their grass-roots, peasant-risings which some of the gentle and clerical leaders were trying with varying degrees of success to guide into political and religious courses'.[18] The overall character of the Pilgrimage was therefore clear; and in 1968 J. J. Scarisbrick could write in his biography of Henry VIII that the Pilgrimage was 'a large-scale, spontaneous, authentic indictment of all that Henry obviously stood for: and it passed judgement against him as surely and comprehensively as *Magna Carta* condemned John and the *Grand Remonstrance* the government of Charles I.'[19] M. E. James, writing at much the same time, took a very different approach, seeing the Lincolnshire rising of 1536 as emerging out of the tensions within county society prompted by the duke of Suffolk's plantation as a great regional magnate. His rebellion—until it all went wrong—was a disciplined demonstration which had the aim of petitioning the king.[20]

A considerable stone was thrown into this limpid stream by the late Sir Geoffrey Elton in 1979. Elton had clearly been rereading the literature of the divorce for his textbook *Reform and Reformation*, published in 1977. Here he overturned all the conventional understanding of the movements by assimilating them into the analysis of Henrician politics developed by Professor Ives and Dr Starkey. In this perspective the Henrician court was riven between factions which, by turn, the king might favour or which might secure a temporary influence over him. The Pilgrimage was the consequence of the unexpected overthrow of Anne Boleyn in the spring of 1536 and the consolidation of power at court and in government by Thomas Cromwell.[21] Elton's overall conclusion was that there

---

[18] C. S. L. Davies, 'The Pilgrimage of Grace Reconsidered', repr. in P. Slack (ed.), *Rebellion, Popular Protest and the Social Order in Early Modern England* (1984), from *Past and Present*, 41 (1968); the quotation from p. 36 of the reprint. Dickens, 'Secular and Religious Motivation', p. 82.

[19] J. J. Scarisbrick, *Henry VIII* (1968), 341.

[20] M. E. James, 'Obedience and Dissent in Henrician England: The Lincolnshire Rebellion, 1536', *Past and Present*, 48 (1970), repr. in James, *Society, Politics and Culture: Studies in Early Modern England* (1986).

[21] This will be treated at greater length in the account of the events of 1536 in Chapter 3. It also ought to be said that Elton's interpretation was strongly influenced by Mr James's analysis of northern society and R. B. Smith's *Land and Politics in the Reign of Henry VIII: The West Riding* (1970). James's essays are most conveniently read in his *Society, Politics and Culture*.

was nothing spontaneous about the revolt. 'In fact', he wrote, 'it cannot any longer be seriously doubted that the main part of the rebellion
was led and presumably incited by the northern gentry . . . the pilgrim's
host was brought into existence by the natural rulers of the region . . .'
'The idea of a spontaneous combustion which then brought in the existing inflammatory material to set the whole north ablaze is not in accord
with the facts; it is necessary to regard the evidence of manifest advance
planning.' Having reviewed this evidence, he concluded: '. . . the Pilgrimage originated in a decision by one of the court factions to take the
battle out of the court into the nation, to raise the standard of loyal rebellion as the only way left to them if they were to succeed in reversing
the defeats suffered at court and in parliament, and in forcing the King
to change his policy.'[22] And there was much more. A subsequent paper
firmed up many of Elton's ideas and offered evidence.[23] Elton was satisfied that '[t]he whole course of the rebellion—its inception, its spread, its
avowed and secret purposes, its end—becomes clearer when it is recog-
nised that it was at heart the work of a political faction which utilised
the social, economic and religious grievances to be found in the disaffected north . . .' It was also bungled. Lincolnshire, for instance, went
off prematurely; other rebellions failed to fire.[24] Elton's new analysis achieved
the status of holy writ by being incorporated, wholesale, into the third
edition of Anthony Fletcher's *Tudor Rebellions* in 1983.[25]

   Nonetheless, Elton's account was never watertight. Kevin Sharpe
pointed out that Elton 'never really argued from evidence and [the case]
rests on some questionable assumptions', and suggested that Elton did
not need a conspiracy to explain a popular rising. Anthony Fletcher offered
his own caveat: 'Professor Elton's revisionist interpretation of the rising
is absorbingly interesting but at the same time tantalisingly hard, at some
crucial points, to substantiate.' C. S. L. Davies quickly wrote to restore
religion and so popularity to a place in the Pilgrimage (although he too

---

[22] G. R. Elton, *Reform and Reformation: England, 1509–1558* (1977), 260–70.
[23] G. R. Elton, 'Politics and the Pilgrimage of Grace', first published in B. Malament (ed.), *After
the Reformation* (1979), and repr. in Elton's *Studies in Tudor and Stuart Politics and Government*, 4 vols.
(1974–92), III, 183–215.
[24] Ibid. 214; for Lincolnshire, pp. 198–9 and for other rebellions, p. 214, n. 77.
[25] A. Fletcher, *Tudor Rebellions*, 3rd edn. (1983), 28–36.

was at least partly seduced by Eltonian notions of conspiracy).[26] Elton's article betrayed a lack of understanding of the workings of northern society; it never showed how it was possible to assemble such large bodies of people; and it deliberately disregarded the evidence of the coercion of gentry by their tenants. This Cambridge professor, albeit one who had lived through 1968, found this too improbable for words.[27] Nonetheless, the article showed the need to integrate the echo of the events of 1536 into the history of the North and English society generally. This necessarily involves making a leap of which Elton was incapable. The author of *Policy and Police*—a book concerned to uncover the rich vein of gossip and political criticism which existed in the 1530s—could not envisage the possibility of independent political action by the great majority of the population (the commons), any more than it occurred to the Dodds sisters that it might have been the commons, rather than the higher clergy, who were concerned to protect the practice of the Church from Henrician reformation.

In the past fifteen years opinion has swung away from Elton's perspective. The behaviour of the commons has attracted greater attention. In 1985 and 1986 I offered evidence to suggest that the Pilgrimage needed to be read as a popular revolt, with the commons in the driving seat.[28] This book is the final development of the opinions offered then. At about the same time Dr Steve Gunn was exploring the behaviour of the Lincolnshire commons and establishing their independence of the gentry.[29] Most recently Dr M. L. Bush has published extensively on aspects of the events of late 1536 and has anticipated some of the conclusions of this study.[30]

[26] Sharpe in *History*, 67 (1982), 131–2; Fletcher, *Tudor Rebellions*, 33. For other assessments of the paper see also Simon Adams, 'Politics', and C. Haigh, 'Religion', both in 'The Eltonian Legacy', *Trans. Royal Historical Soc.*, 7 (1997), 254–5, 295–6. C. S. L. Davies, 'Religion and the Pilgrimage of Grace', in A. Fletcher and J. Stevenson (eds.), *Order and Disorder in Early Modern England* (1986).

[27] '. . . the tale rings very false . . . The usual story is really quite odd': 'Politics and the Pilgrimage of Grace', 191.

[28] 'Before the fall of Pontefract: The Pilgrimage of Grace in Yorkshire, 30 September–21 October 1536' (a paper read in Oxford in Oct. 1985 and again at a meeting to celebrate the Pilgrimage in Beverley in 1986): 'Thomas Master's Narrative of the Pilgrimage of Grace', *NH* 21 (1985).

[29] S. J. Gunn, 'Peers, Commons and Gentry in the Lincolnshire Revolt of 1536', *Past and Present*, 123 (1989).

[30] M. L. Bush, *The Pilgrimage of Grace: A Study of the Rebel Armies of October 1536* (1996). See my review in *American Historical Rev.*, 103 (1998), 879–80, and Bush's rejoinder at p. 1763. I have many disagreements with Bush's book, which it would be tedious to itemize. But it is a study of Yorkshire

Historians, then, have failed to come to any consensus about the character of the northern revolt of 1536–7. Some have regarded it as a conspiracy, others as a popular movement. It has been read as a movement of social and economic protest against taxation and the damage which the dissolution wrought on northern society; it has also been made into something holy and spiritual, concerned solely with the defence of the Catholic church.

The interpretation to be advanced in this book may be quickly outlined. The rebellion was overwhelmingly popular and spontaneous. There was no gentry conspiracy—none was found at the time nor can one be discovered now—although the gentry were first coerced into offering leadership and then strove hard to establish their grip over the movement. The dynamic heart of the rising, whether in Lincolnshire, Yorkshire, or the fringes of Lancashire and Cumbria, lay with the commons. Whilst every local movement had its own hue, the determination to rise came from two sources: first, the rumours of the dismemberment of parochial religion which circulated in the summer of 1536 (the culling of parish churches, the confiscation of church goods, the threatened taxation of baptisms); and second, word of the rising elsewhere. The movement in the East Riding and the central area of the West Riding saw itself as being a part of the Lincolnshire rising. The risings in Craven, Lancashire, and Cumbria were a response to the movement in Richmondshire, although it is not possible to say with certainty whether the rising there took place in reaction to news of Lincolnshire. Whilst the gentry secured control of the movement by the end of October and used it to try and buy concessions to assuage the commons, in January the activists in some quarters, convinced that they had been sold out by their notional leaders, attempted to reconstruct the alliances of October. This final efflorescence was quickly stamped out, but the breach of the December agreement gave the Crown its opportunity to exact a retribution on the gentry of the North.

alone which, as will appear, I think is mistaken. I am not clear what Bush believes the relationship of the Lincolnshire to the Yorkshire movements to be. He complains of the Dodds that: 'Their mistake was to regard the Lincolnshire uprising as an integral part of the pilgrimage of grace, so much that they devoted two substantial chapters to it'; but seven pages later he writes that 'a final distinguishing feature of the pilgrimage of grace was its dependence upon the Lincolnshire uprising. In the early stages the Pilgrimage was but an adjunct of the movement south of the Humber.' Bush, *Pilgrimage of Grace*, 6, 13.

The evidence for this interpretation will, it is hoped, emerge from the narrative which forms the remainder of this book. Before turning to that account, it may be helpful to offer some reflections on the problems of writing about rebellions, and on the character of the surviving evidence for the rebellions of 1536-7.

III

Rebellions, riots, and civil disturbances of all sorts hold a particular fascination for historians. The collapse of normal social disciplines and restraints is held to reveal tensions and conflicts embedded but concealed within pre-revolutionary society. The origins of a rising may perhaps be traced deep within society, both in social or economic terms but also chronologically. The fact that such tensions exist—and are perhaps normal—does not make conflict inevitable. For this reason some historians have adopted a division between preconditions—the simmering background to a disturbance—and precipitants—the events which made society fracture along the lines of cleavage established by the preconditions.

Rebellions and riots are, however, deeply abnormal occasions. English society in the later Middle Ages was normally pacific. The majority of the English lived and died without ever becoming involved in any form of violent or civil disturbance. Whilst there were clearly tensions between the commons and elite groups, whether landlords and tenants, clergy and laity, or the 'county community' and the Crown, the number of occasions on which the normal bonds of deference dissolved in violent or mass action is very small. But which bonds of deference? As we have seen from the historiographical account of the previous writings on the 1536 movements, it is possible to adduce two quite different models of rebellion. In the first, the bonds of obedience and deference within regional society remained intact and the conventional leadership of that society—its nobility and gentry, its county community, perhaps too its urban elites—led their tenants and artisans as a body in opposition to the Crown, perhaps with the aim of securing change through petitioning. This view supposes a holistic society either without internal conflicts or with a high level of deference and discipline. Such a view of society informs M. E. James's work. Gunn has already criticized James for his blindness to the violence which the gentry suffered in the first days of 1536, and in general this model does not describe what we see in 1536.[31] Indeed, it may be doubted whether this mode of behaviour ever existed, at least in a pure form. The second model sees rebellion arising, in part at least, and being shaped by fractures within regional society, where one group—the commons—was led to rise in opposition to the Crown, pulling along with it those higher social groups whose instinct was to comply with and perhaps implement unpopular government policies. This is an activists' or commons' rising. In this model the rising can properly be called popular, but it is also sectional within that society. Historians have seen the risings of late 1536 as containing elements of both models, the risings in Lincolnshire and maybe Yorkshire perhaps conforming to the first model, whilst the risings in Richmondshire and the Lake District have always been admitted to contain elements of social conflict.

A rebellion in which the commons are mobilized in a disciplined fashion on the instructions of their social superiors, with authority concentrated within a small elite group, is obviously a relatively simple matter provided the rank and file are compliant with their instructions. A rising launched by activists drawn from outside the local elites is more complicated. It allows for the possibility of disputes amongst the activists over objectives; but it also has implicit within it the possibility of conflict between the activist cadre and the displaced elite as the latter try and claw back their grip over society. Such conflicts can be identified both in Lincolnshire and in the Pilgrimage of Grace. They are also found in other movements. In Kett's Revolt (where the hostility of the crowd to the gentry has always been acknowledged), one gentleman tried to make his peace with the camp at Mousehold by arriving with carts laden with food and drink. The rebels found this behaviour all too blatant and beat him up.[32]

All the 1536 movements were, in the first days, activist movements in which the local bonds of deference were severed or, perhaps it is truer

[31] James, 'Obedience and Dissent', Gunn, 'Peers, Commons and Gentry', *passim*.
[32] D. MacCulloch, 'Kett's Rebellion in Context', *Past and Present*, 84 (1979), 58.

to say, inverted: the activists expected the gentry to do their bidding. When he was captured, Sir Stephen Hamerton was told that where he had ruled his captors, now they would rule him.[33] In the second phase of the rebellion the gentry won a competition for leadership with the activists but found themselves saddled with the problem of offering leadership to an enthusiastic rank and file (who would accept elite authority so long as it was advancing their interests), whilst making their own composition with the Crown. The appearance of activists drawn from outside the dominant society is characteristic of revolts, but poses the problem for historians that these people often have little prominence in the earlier historic record: like nova, they have their moment of brilliance before they fade back into parochial obscurity. Take John Eglisfield, bailiff of Leconfield in the East Riding. Twenty years after the events of the Pilgrimage his opponent in a lawsuit explained how, 'in the time of the great commotion in the north parts without compulsion [he] did foresake [his master, the earl of Northumberland] being his sworn servant and went to the disordered commons with all such power as he was able to make, which was not the part of a true subject to go against the king your father . . .'.[34] There is no other reference to Eglisfield's involvement save for this one tantilizing glimpse of him abandoning the earl and mobilizing his neighbours. John Speed heard that the commons had a captain called James Diamond, 'General of the Foot', and another, 'a poor fisherman styled by himself and others the Earl of Poverty'. We know nothing more about these people (if, indeed, they existed).[35]

Just as it would be unrealistic to expect any rebellion to remain under the same command throughout, so it is improbable that it would retain the same aims and objectives. A characteristic of a rebellion is its fluidity or inconsistency of aim. It appears to have been the rebels' practice to circulate letters containing a few key justifications for the rebellion and calling on areas to rise in support of those already risen. Aske's chosen method was to circulate his oath. Formal manifestos, in the shape of articles, appear to have been drawn up only when petitioning the king or dealing with his field commanders, and therefore come from not only

[33] *LP* XII (i), no. 1034.   [34] PRO, Req2/20/118.
[35] J. Speed, *The History of Great Britain*, 3rd edn. (1632), 1018.

a particular stage of the rebellion, but out of a particular social group. The first statements of the Lincolnshire rebels were considerably watered down before they were sent to the king. The Lincoln articles are a statement arising from the mature, gentry-dominated revolt; they tell us little or nothing about why the revolt began only a week previously.[36] Similarly, in important respects the Pontefract articles retreat from some of the demands made earlier in the autumn. None of these manifestos arising out of a mature movement uneasily dominated by the gentry sheds much light on why the commons rose days or weeks before. The Pontefract articles tell us a great deal about the strains within society, the preconditions as it were, but reveal virtually nothing about the *precipitants* which set people mustering. It is simply not methodologically legitimate to employ statements of aims created at the end of the revolt to illuminate the causes of the rising. Similarly, the reflections of gentry on the causes of the revolt made whilst under suspicion in March or April 1537 have to be used very cautiously as evidence of the feelings of the rank and file in the first fortnight of the previous October. Moreover, their professed objectives varied from area to area. The preoccupations of the Cumberland rebels were not the same as those in Westmorland, which, in turn, owed little to the initial rising in Richmondshire. Indeed, the surviving documentation needs to be handled with much greater forensic precision than has sometimes been the case, whilst resisting the temptation to read too much into it. And so it is appropriate to review the nature of that material and some of its pitfalls before turning to the narrative of the 1536 movements.

IV

Compared to the rebellions of 1381, 1450, or 1549, there is a mass of evidence bearing on the movements of 1536–7. It falls into two main parts: contemporary correspondence, and the records of the investigations to determine the culpability of individual rebels whose names had

---

[36] Below pp. 153–7 for some consideration of the development of the Lincolnshire articles.

come to the attention of government. Most of the material has been known since the late nineteenth century, when it was gathered together in volumes XI and XII (part one) of *Letters and Papers of the Reign of Henry VIII*. This great Victorian compilation printed (in English paraphrase, and sometimes faultily) all the material then known to survive in the Public Record Office and the British Museum, together with selected materials from provincial and foreign archives.[37] Since then relatively little material has emerged: some letters concerning the city of Hull in early 1537, three caches of material relating to the first earl of Cumberland, each of which contained Pilgrimage materials, and a seventeenth-century digest of letters, some now lost, made for Thomas, Lord Herbert of Cherbury, whilst he was writing his *Life of Henry VIII*.[38]

Relatively little correspondence survives. Much of the material contained in volume XI of *Letters and Papers* is the 'minutes' (drafts) of outgoing letters from the king and incoming letters from his field commanders (the dukes of Norfolk and Suffolk and the earl of Shrewsbury) and observers (such as Lord Darcy, and the earls of Cumberland and Derby) who attempted to keep the king informed about the rebels' strength and disposition. The public records also contain a significant number of letters which were sent on to the king for his information, for instance, the letters of Sir Brian Hastings at Hatfield.[39] Letters between individuals caught up in the rebellion are extremely rare. One of the very few is a letter of Lady Katherine Scrope to her father, the first earl of Cumberland, detailing the movement of rebels in Richmondshire and asking his advice.[40] Letters sent out by the rebels are even rarer: the contents of the Captain Poverty letter have to be reconstructed from the faded recollections of those who saw it or heard it read.[41] The abstracts of correspondence made by Thomas Masters shows that there was once rather more than now survives.[42]

[37] For the multiple faults of *Letters and Papers*, see above p. ix.

[38] A. G. Dickens, 'New Records of the Pilgrimage of Grace', *YAJ* 33 (1937), 298–308; Dickens (ed.), 'Clifford Letters of the Sixteenth Century', *Surtees Soc.*, 172 (1962); R. W. Hoyle (ed.), 'Letters of the Cliffords, Lords Clifford and Earls of Cumberland, *c.*1500–*c.*1565', *Camden Miscellany 31, Camden* fourth ser., 44 (1992), 1–189; id., 'Thomas Master's Narrative'.

[39] *LP* XI, nos. 662–3, 759, 966, etc.

[40] Dickens, 'Clifford Letters', 111–12.   [41] Below pp. 217–18.

[42] Hoyle, 'Thomas Master's narrative'. There is now very little material relating to the Pilgrimage in the Cotton MSS in the British Library.

Two of the nobles caught up the rebellion kept letter books of their correspondence. The Derby Letter Book is a mixed compilation maintained over some years, of which Pilgrimage letters form but a part.[43] The Darcy Letter Book, of which two copies survive, contains letters sent to Darcy by the king and other correspondents as well as Darcy's outgoing letters.[44] Its aim was quite obviously to vindicate Darcy's conduct in the Pilgrimage: its postscript makes his bitterness at his treatment all too plain. Nonetheless, it does appear to be an accurate record of the letters it contains, but it lacks letters from within Darcy's circle of gentry in the central West Riding.

As a failed rebellion, both the Lincolnshire movement and the Pilgrimage generated substantial quantities of records as authority was restored by the investigation of the rebels to determine their culpability. It needs to be emphasized that the investigation was not conducted as a modern criminal investigation. Government was not interested in discovering what had happened in the round. Statements were generally not sought from witnesses not under suspicion, nor did the major participants make aides-mémoires. For this reason, we have no account from either Norfolk or Shrewsbury of what transpired at either of the Doncaster meetings.[45] If either of them gave evidence against, say, Darcy at his trial, it has not survived.

Government was concerned to secure hanging evidence—mostly by self-admission—against suspects. Hence a large proportion of the statements were given under the pressure of arrest or imprisonment, often (in the case of the Pilgrimage statements) in the Tower of London, and their authors therefore had every reason to conceal their role or place the best possible gloss on their actions. (We will see some examples of this subsequently.) Individuals of less than gentry status were generally not interrogated in Yorkshire, for the pardon granted at Doncaster discouraged the Crown from enquiring too hard into the activities of rebels

---

[43] Lancashire RO, DDF/1, printed in 'Derby Correspondence'. A few of these letters were republished in LP.

[44] LP XI, no. 929 (1), (2).

[45] Two important aides-mémoires were made by heralds: by Lancaster Herald of his meeting with Aske, Darcy, and others at Pontefract on 21 Oct. (LP XI, no. 826, printed in full, St. P., I, 485–7); and Somerset Herald of his meeting with Darcy on 14 Nov., LP XI, no. 1086, printed Dodds, Pilgrimage, I, 300–6.

in October 1536. The duke of Norfolk seems to have declined to follow the rising back into its local roots. A reading of the examinations
of John Hallam or Ninian Staveley, both of whom were arrested for their
attempts to raise a new rebellion, shows little interest in their activities
before the pardon.[46] It is therefore very difficult to reach the voice of
the rank and file in the Pilgrimage of Grace because they largely escaped
scot-free. In Lincolnshire, on the other hand, the government made careful enquiries of the artisans of Louth and Horncastle as to events there
in the first days of October; and these deponents were largely executed.
The work of interrogating suspects in Lincolnshire began within ten days
of the collapse of the rebellion. Their examinations filled a series of numbered books: later in January selected suspects were examined further on
articles in the Tower of London. Their responses filled a twentieth book,
'called the Additions'.[47] Finally, it may be added that some depositions
are lost, including Darcy's interrogation in the Tower. For Robert Aske,
the chief source is his own memoir.[48] Whether he made a further statement whilst in the Tower is unknown, but it would be surprising if he
had not. Again, we have some of the questions put to him when he was
examined and a few of the answers. Other casual references reveal the
existence of additional examinations which are now lost.[49]

   The surviving statements fall into three broad categories. For the first,
there are three accounts by lawyers, Thomas Moigne, Brian Stapleton,
and Robert Aske.[50] These are autobiographical narratives of the author's
role in the rebellion. They appear to have been composed by the writers
without aid. Characteristically, they are detailed, self-justificatory narratives. Each was written by an individual who had a good war and who
was confident that he had little or nothing to fear. Moigne, who was
prominent in the Lincolnshire rising, offers an account of how he had
deflected the commons through policy. Stapleton, who comes over as a
rather simple soul, penned a detailed day-by-day account of the Beverley
rising with all the air of a venture scout at camp. Aske's is the most com-

---

[46] *LP* XII (i), nos. 201 (iv), 1012.   [47] Ibid., no. 70.
[48] Ibid., nos. 900, 901, 945, 946, all published by Mary Bateson in *EHR* 5 (1890), 550–73, and
hereafter referred to as 'Aske's examination'. For Aske's memoir, see subsequently.
[49] *LP* XII (i), no. 1089 mentions (towards the end) examinations which are now lost.
[50] Moigne is very poorly summarized by *LP* at *LP* XI, no. 971. Aske and Stapleton (*LP* XII (i),
nos. 6, 392) have both been printed in full; these transcripts are to be preferred to the *LP* paraphrases.

plicated of the three. It was almost certainly written for the king's own inspection around Christmas 1536, when Aske believed that he had eased himself into the royal service.[51] The account is therefore caught on a painful dilemma: whether to cast Aske as the victim of the rebels, who had skilfully managed their disbandment whilst advocating their programme, or as the rabble-rousing rebel leader who, by force of numbers, had obliged the king to take him into his service and pay attention to a point of view to which he was disinclined. The very title of Aske's memoir ('The manner of the taking of Robert Aske') and his stress on the occasions on which he—single-handed—restrained the rebel host shows him leaning to the former position. On the other hand, the memoir is massively incriminating, as, for instance, when he denounces the nobility for failing to withstand the dissolution of the smaller monasteries.[52] It is boastful, even arrogant. It constantly places Aske in the foreground.[53] But because Aske wished to paint a picture of his accidental capture and his responsible and loyal actions throughout the rebellion, he skips over matters—why he fell in with the rebels, why he set out from York to Pontefract, why he did not attend the first Doncaster meeting—where he was probably incapable of glossing his behaviour in a favourable light. His memoir therefore needs to be read as much for its concealments and silences as for its overt contents.

Secondly, a number of individuals have left statements ('confessions') similar to those for Aske, Moigne, and Stapleton, but at much shorter length. Here the appearance is that the accused were given pen and paper and allowed to draft an account of their involvement in the movement. These personal statements end with an appeal for clemency. Confessions of this sort survive for John, Lord Hussey, John Dakyn, the rector of Kirkby Ravensworth in the North Riding, and Robert Thompson, vicar of Brough in Westmorland.[54] It is possible that more were made which

---

[51] If it is the book 'made for the king' which Aske showed Darcy on his return from the south. *LP* XII (i), no. 1175 (i).

[52] 'The manner of the taking of Robert Aske', 335.

[53] The omission of others may have been to protect them. When he went to the Hambledon Hill muster he travelled with Nicholas Girlington and Robert Ascue (*LP* XI, no. 971). Aske never mentions his companions.

[54] *LP* XI, no. 852 (addressed to the council); *LP* XII (i), no. 785, 687 (4). Dakyn seems to have made his confession before being sent to London: ibid., no. 698.

do not survive. Edward Lee, archbishop of York, and Christopher Aske, brother to Robert, both made declarations in which they itemized their dealings with the Pilgrims and justified their actions: these are similar in appearance to confessions, although they end without a plea for clemency.[55]

Thirdly, there are the examinations. Those for Lincolnshire have already been mentioned. Examinations were made throughout the Spring of 1537 of persons implicated in the Pilgrimage, many of them by the team of John Tregonwell, Dr Richard Layton, and Dr Thomas Leigh, with John ap Rice as clerk. When George Lumley, son and heir to Lord Lumley, was examined on 8 February Thomas Cromwell was also in attendance.[56] Some of the examinations seem to be replies to articles (for example, Sir Thomas Percy's).[57] In this and other examinations the interrogators can be seen prompting the examinee and asking him to clarify points. In others the attending clerk appears to have taken down at dictation speed a statement prepared by the accused. The examination of William Morland, the monk formerly of Louth Park, fills six-and-a-half pages of printed transcript in *Letters and Papers*.[58] As this is a carefully crafted narrative of his activities, it is probably that it incorporates a prepared text which Morland had read into the formal record. The 'confession' of Robert Thompson is reproduced substantially in his examination, but the 'confession' contains additional details which were not read into the examination.[59]

The memoirs and confessions we would expect to be self-exculpatory, the examinations less so. But the process of examination seems to have been less testing, less forensic than one might expect. Some examinations are slight and narrow. They lack dates, they lack names of collaborators, they often contain hearsay about third parties. They is no real evidence of the comparison of examinations and the cross-examination of the accused on points made by others. Whilst some examinations are very substantial indeed, others, perhaps the majority, are rather slight. The deponents most certainly concealed matters. When Sir Stephen

55 Ibid., nos. 1022, 1186. Lee's is called a 'declaration'; Aske's is endorsed 'Aske's confession'.
56 Ibid., no. 369.   57 Ibid., no. 393.   58 Ibid., no. 380.
59 Examination, *LP* XII (i), no. 687 (2) (= SP1/117, fos. 48r–56r): confession (*LP* XII (i), no. 687 (4) (but not printed), (= E36/119, fos. 71r–74v).

Hamerton was examined he completely omitted to mention his role in raising east Lancashire, although this was testified to by his co-captain, Nicholas Tempest.[60]

A heavy reliance on the examinations is unavoidable. A single examination may be our entire evidence for a branch of the movement, as in Kendal and south Westmorland, where our sole authority is William Collins, the bailiff of Kendal.[61] In the majority of cases it is impossible to confirm statements made in the examinations. We must approach all the material made as a part of the process of criminal investigation in the knowledge that the majority of our witnesses were selected because government was confident of their guilt. Where we have digests of evidence produced for trial, we can see that prosecutions were based as much on the accused's own admissions twisted to indicate guilt as on evidence from third parties.[62]

There are significant lacunae in the materials. We have no reports about the attitude of the civic elites of either Lincoln or York to the revolt. Some significant towns—Boston in Lincolnshire, Malton, Richmond, Ripon, and Selby in Yorkshire—have left nothing. There are no accounts of the exchanges between the duke of Norfolk and the Pilgrims' leaders at Doncaster. What remains, though, is marvellously rich: it is from this extensive but incomplete body of evidence that an account of the Lincolnshire Rising and the Pilgrimage of Grace of 1536 and the secondary risings of 1537 can be fashioned.

---

[60] See below p. 231.   [61] *LP* XII (i), no. 914.   [62] Ibid., no. 1087; below pp. 408–10.

2

A Northern Panorama

There is a rather unthinking view which holds that the Pilgrimage was in some way a northern phenomenon and therefore one which contains few lessons for the history of England as a whole. The North, it is maintained, was backward, conservative, lightly governed (a problem solved by the Council of the North), and prone to violence. Its nobility retained a military demeanour at a time when the nobility of southern England had softened into a court or service nobility.[1] Hence, until it was tamed the North was an ideal breeding ground for opposition to the divorce, the royal supremacy, and the dissolution of the monasteries. This view is perhaps odd in the light of the simple fact that the insurrection started in Lincolnshire—not normally counted as a northern county—and was initially expected to spread into East Anglia, where there was an attempt to raise a new revolt in April 1537.[2] Whilst the north Midlands were mustered against the Pilgrims, there was evidently sympathy for the rebels amongst those facing them.[3] We might conclude

---

[1] For an exposition of this view, L. Stone, *The Crisis of the Aristocracy, 1558–1641* (1965), 234–5, 250–3.

[2] *LP* XI, no. 567 shows that the 'gootes' (goites or sluices) were raised to flood the fenland around Spalding and Peterborough. C. E. Morton, 'The Walsingham Conspiracy', *Historical Res.*, 63 (1990). The duke of Norfolk thought that the Lincolnshire rebels would advance into Suffolk to seek the support of the textile trades there: D. MacCulloch, *Suffolk under the Tudors: Politics and Religion in an English County, 1500–1600* (1986), 299.

[3] As the duke of Norfolk admitted, Dodds, *Pilgrimage*, I, 269.

that the risings of 1536 chanced to happen in the North rather than arose out of any ingrained characteristic of northern society.

The view that the risings were the work of geographically marginal and culturally backward minorities was held by contemporaries. Cranmer tried to place the best gloss on the events of 1536 in a letter to Bullinger in Zurich. Having blamed the revolt on 'unlearned priest and monks' whose fulminations had found an audience amongst a misguided laity, he identified a third group who had risen in opposition to 'the return of evangelical teaching from captivity to its rightful place':

added to these was a certain sort of barbarous and savage people, who were ignorant of and turned away from farming and the good arts of peace, and who were so utterly unacquainted with knowledge of sacred matters, that they could not bear to hear anything of culture and more gentle civilisation. In its furthest regions of the Scottish border, England has several peoples of such a kind, who I think should rather be called devastators; in ancient fashion they fight with their neighbouring clans on both sides [of the border] in perpetual battle and brigandage, and they live solely upon the pillage and plunder won from it.[4]

Cranmer's rhetorical association of the rebellion with the disorderly border surnames was a means of denying its real significance. It may well have convinced his Swiss correspondent, but the archbishop knew better. The rebels in Lincolnshire were only 20 or 30 miles from Cranmer's home village in Nottinghamshire; the barbarous and savage people gathered at Pontefract and Doncaster were no more than a day's ride northwards. The border surnames were 150 miles distant to the North: the rebels had little or nothing in common with them. The tendency to treat the North as a homogenous zone characterized by its extremes is both extremely old and very common. Many, if not most parts of the Tudor North were indistinguishable in their economy, wealth, social structure, and doubtless religious practice from southern lowland England.

I

It may be profitable to divide the North into four broad areas, between which traffic was made difficult by the Pennines. The first, Yorkshire

[4] D. MacCulloch, *Thomas Cranmer: A Life* (1996), 178.

and County Durham, contained several prosperous towns (York, Hull,
Beverley, and we might include Newcastle), which acted as entrepôts for
the export trade out of the region: grain from the East Riding, lead from
the Dales, textiles from the West Riding, and, of course, coals from
Newcastle. These areas were well integrated into the national economy.
In a panegyric upon Yorkshire by William Vavasour of Hazelwood, he
recounted how Bishop Tunstall had taken Henry VIII up on to Scausby
Leys during the progress of 1541 and shown him the panorama of the
Vale of York, 'to show his majesty one of the greatest and richest valleys that he ever found in all his travels through Europe'.[5] Yorkshire presented problems of government because of the size of the county, its
fragmented pattern of landownership, and (after 1485) the large expanses
of Crown lands within its boundaries. Government by the commission
of the peace was reinforced by a succession of councils with jurisdiction
over the county (which I will discuss subsequently). The county could be
lawless: government could clearly not make its writ run over large parts
of the county in taxation years such as 1489 and 1513/14.[6] The second
area, Lancashire and Westmorland, was much poorer than Yorkshire, not
least because its location on the west side of the Pennines made access
to the major English and European markets difficult. This may be
enough to explain why there were few large towns in these counties.
Even so, at some periods in the early sixteenth century there was a reg-
ular traffic in Kendal cloth taken overland by packhorse to be exported
through Southampton.[7] It would be wrong to make too much of either
the isolation or backwardness of even Westmorland. We may then identify a third area, the deep border, Cumberland and Northumberland, a
society organized for war, prone to occasional disruptions by border conflicts
and raiding into the lowlands by the border surnames. Northumberland
had particular administrative problems arising from the lack of resident
gentry in the county. At some moments in the early years of Henry VIII

---

[5] J. J. Cartwright, *Chapters of Yorkshire History* (1872), 366, printing an extract from BL, Lansdowne
MS 900.

[6] R. W. Hoyle, 'Resistance and Manipulation in Early Tudor Taxation: Some Evidence From the
North', *Archives*, 20 (1993).

[7] B. C. Jones, 'Westmorland Pack-horse Men in Southampton', *Trans. Cumberland and Westmorland AAS*, 2nd ser., 59 (1960).

the quarter sessions of the county appear to have been in abeyance; and so we have the fascinating contrast of a major town, Newcastle, with a burgeoning trade to London, located on the edge of an area in which the normal processes of law enforcement had ceased to function.[8]

The final area, the narrow border, was a militarized frontier divided into three sectors (the West Marches in Cumberland, the Middle and East in Northumberland) under the control of royal officers (the wardens of the Marches). Here society was organized into kin groups or surnames, and civil society was disturbed by the constant cross-border raiding of the surnames for cattle. Such law as operated was enforced by quasi-military means. The Marches contained two fortified and garrisoned border towns, Carlisle and Berwick, which, together with a number of royal and private castles, were England's first defence against Scottish invasion. It may be conceded that the Borders presented special problems of government: but they were a place apart, even within the North.

In another respect the North as a whole betrayed its origin as a border territory. Three of the northern counties—Cheshire, Lancashire, and County Durham—were all palatinates in which the king's writ did not run. The administration of these counties was therefore exercised in the name of the lord of the palatinate who, in the case of Cheshire and Lancashire, was the king, or the bishop of Durham in his county. These areas were administratively distinct from the English system of lawcourts: in addition, Cheshire and County Durham did not return members to parliament. Neither Cheshire nor Durham contributed to parliamentary taxation, nor did the three most northerly counties, but they were excluded for their poverty rather than their lack of representation.

The clearest evidence that the North was regarded as a problematic area comes from the special arrangements made for its government by councils under a royal lieutenant. Such councils existed—probably intermittently—from the 1480s onwards. From 1537 their existence is continuous, but previous councils appear to have flourished and died with their president's tour of duty. It is, for instance, most likely that no council existed between the death of Archbishop Savage in 1507 and the creation

---

[8] S. G. Ellis, 'Tudor Northumberland: British History in an English County', in S. J. Connolly (ed.), *Kingdoms United? Great Britain and Ireland Since 1500, Integration and Diversity* (1999).

of a new council under the duke of Richmond in 1525.[9] All the northern councils are obscure: the almost total disappearance of their records
makes it impossible to establish exactly what they did or even their area
of geographical competence. Broadly, they seem to have been a variant
on the aristocratic council. A president (who might be called the king's
lieutenant) appointed by the king was given a council of fee'd northern
magnates, gentry, and lawyers which met to hear petitions. The duke of
Richmond's council was a variant on this model because the duke, as a
royal prince (he was Henry VIII's bastard) was given a household at Sheriff
Hutton Castle near York and extensive lands throughout Yorkshire and
Westmorland. Richmond was also made titular warden of the Scottish
Marches, but this arrangement seems to have been abandoned towards
the end of 1527. The pre-1536 councils appear to have been intended
to act as the king's eyes and ears in Yorkshire, a county which was too
large for a single magnate to dominate. Richmond's council was given
a competence in Westmorland, Cumberland, and Northumberland as well
as Yorkshire: this is shown by the incorporation of members of his council in the commission of the peace for these counties in 1525.[10]
Richmond's dispatch to Sheriff Hutton probably owed less to conditions
in the North than to Wolsey's reorganization of government in 1525. A
parallel council was (re)established in Wales under the Princess Mary, and
the possibility ought to be considered that both councils were part of a
strategy to reduce the flow of petitions to Wolsey's Star Chamber jurisdiction by having some business resolved locally.[11] When the council was
reshaped on Richmond's departure from the North in 1530, it returned
to being a purely Yorkshire council.[12]

The jurisdiction of any northern council was compromised by the existence of other competing jurisdictions. The council's writ never

[9] I hope to write further about the government of Yorkshire in this period and expand on some
of the comments made here.

[10] J. Guy, 'Wolsey and the Tudor polity', in S. J. Gunn and P. G. Lindley (eds.), *Cardinal Wolsey:
Church, State and Art* (1991), 69–70.

[11] This was agreed in 1526: J. A. Guy, *The Cardinal's Court: The Impact of Thomas Wolsey in Star
Chamber* (1977), 47.

[12] This is indicated by the council's commission, printed R. R. Reid, The *King's Council in the
North* (1921, repr. 1975), 502–3, and the removal of the Richmond circle from the commissions of
the peace.

extended to Lancashire or Cheshire, both palatinates. Even in Yorkshire
it shared authority with the Duchy of Lancaster. One of the characteristics of the central West Riding was the large areas held by the Duchy
as landlord.[13] This created problems of government to which I will return,
but the duchy maintained its own equity courts for cases arising out of
its estates. There is no sign that either Richmond's council or the councils which followed in the early 1530s attempted to interfere in the disputes between Sir Henry Savile and Sir Richard Tempest over the
jurisdiction of the duchy's manor of Wakefield, of which Tempest was
the steward. When Thomas, Lord Darcy found himself embroiled in 1532–3
with the duchy's tenants of Rothwell over an enclosure dispute, he sought
their indictment at quarter sessions and then further prosecuted them
in the duchy's court at London: the Council of the North was never
involved (although a delegation of tenants had approached the duke of
Richmond in 1526).[14]

Whilst the existence of the Council of the North probably served to
make the North seem much more distinctive than it actually was, it is
also all too readily assumed that power was much more noble and territorial in the North than in the south, and that there was an element
of competition between the Tudors and the northern nobility for
authority. Certainly power over men through the exercise of stewardships was still valued, if only amongst the older generation. William
Constable the elder, writing to his nephew Francis Bigod (barely out of
his teens) in 1527, congratulated him on being in Wolsey's household
for the opportunities it could bring him. With the cardinal's support Bigod
could reclaim the offices held by his father and grandfather. He should
strive to secure the grant of the stewardships of the Percy and Clifford
lands in the East Riding. Constable would secure for them both a number of grants of other stewardships within the East Riding. In this way
a regional hegemony could be created.[15]

Inevitably, the competition for territorial power provoked occasional
conflicts, as between Archbishop Savage and the fifth earl of Northumberland in the dying days of Henry VII's reign, or a generation later between

[13] Smith, *Land and Politics*, ch. 2 *passim*.

[14] R. W. Hoyle, 'Thomas Lord Darcy and the Rothwell Tenants, *c.*1526–1534', *YAJ* 63 (1991).

[15] Dickens, *Lollards and Protestants*, 60, citing *LP* IV (ii), no. 3146.

the first earl of Cumberland and John Norton over the stewardship of Kirkby Malzeard.[16] The Crown's selection of local officers could provoke turf wars, as rivals for an office made it difficult for their opponents to exercise it effectively. This is not the same as individuals challenging the Crown: the appropriate modern analogy is perhaps the kind of bitter complaints which might arise when head office transfers the Preston ice-cream sales area from the district office in Liverpool to that in Manchester, placing reputations as well as commission at stake. There can be little doubt that the Tudors were hostile to any individual who appeared to pose a danger to their regime; but it is a another matter completely to suppose that they had a concerted plan to reduce the authority of the noble estate. There are no grounds to suppose that the northern nobility were culturally different from the nobility as a whole: they were, for instance, well integrated into the nobility by marriage. The first earl of Cumberland (d. 1542), sixth earl of Northumberland (d. 1537), and third Lord Dacre (d. 1563) all married daughters of the fourth earl of Shrewsbury (d. 1538). The third earl of Derby married a daughter of the second duke of Norfolk in about 1530. The fourth earl of Westmorland married a daughter of Henry VIII's victim, the duke of Buckingham. With the possible exception of Dacre, all were familiar figures at court. The fifth earl of Northumberland (d. 1527), who never served as warden of the East and Middle Marches, was employed on ceremonial occasions at court and was present at the Field of the Cloth of Gold in 1520. His heir, the sixth earl, was brought up in Wolsey's household where he may (or may not) have been a suitor for the hand of Anne Boleyn. Perhaps the most telling example of the integration of the northern nobility into the English nobility as a whole is the little-noticed fact that the widow of the third Lord Latimer of Snape in the North Riding (d. 1542–3), who was one of the peers who negotiated on behalf of the Pilgrims at Doncaster, went on to marry Henry VIII. She, of course, was Katherine Parr. The English nobility was one: there were no peers sulking in the

---

[16] R. W. Hoyle, 'The Earl, the Archbishop and the Council: The Affray at Fulford, May 1504', in R. E. Archer and S. Walker (eds.), *Rulers and Ruled in Late Medieval England: Essays Presented to Gerald Harriss* (1995); id., 'The first Earl of Cumberland: A Reputation Reassessed', *NH* 22 (1986), 80–1.

North in cultural or political opposition to the Tudors. Co-operation between the English nobility and the Crown was the norm.[17]

When, however, individual nobles were seen behaving in a fashion which broke the peace or challenged royal authority, or worst of all, raised Henry VIII's suspicions of their loyalty, retribution of one sort or another followed. The fifth earl of Northumberland was repeatedly fined for misdemeanours when a young man. So too was the earl of Derby for laying siege to Furness Abbey in 1514 and trying to depose the abbot.[18] In 1534 Lord Dacre was tried for treasonable communications with the Scots during the war of 1532–3, acquitted, but fined £10,000 and forced to seek the Crown's licence over where he resided.[19] Ill-discipline could be punished by a fine, loss of office, and loss of favour.

When this happened the Crown had to find alternative figures who could fill the role vacated by the disgraced or incompetent noble. The apparent unsuitability of the fifth earl of Northumberland to exercise authority in the East and Middle Marches forced a series of unsatisfactory stopgaps, including the deployment of wardens drawn from elsewhere in the northern counties (amongst whom may be counted Thomas, Lord Darcy from the West Riding). For a period of fourteen years Thomas, third Lord Dacre (d. 1525) was given charge of all three wardenries, a task which he accepted with great reluctance and fulfilled in an increasingly unsatisfactory fashion, not least (as he admitted), because he had no power-base in the East Marches.[20] After his dismissal in 1524, and again following his son's fall from grace in 1534, the king was forced to search for a new figure who could serve in the Dacres' place on the West Marches. In both 1525 and 1534 his choice fell on the first earl of Cumberland, whose estates were mostly in northern Westmorland and Yorkshire: again, Cumberland was a reluctant occupant of the wardenry. His tenure was marked by conflicts over the practical exercise of the warden's authority and control of the lands which formed part of his

---

[17] I consider some of these issues further in a forthcoming paper entitled 'The Decline of the Northern Nobility: A Case of Low Resolution Telescopy?'

[18] Hoyle, 'The Earl, the Archbishop and the Council'; R. W. Hoyle and H. R. T. Summerson, 'The Earl of Derby and the Deposition of the Abbot of Furness, 1514', *NH* 30 (1994).

[19] Steven Ellis, *Tudor Frontiers and Noble Power: The Making of the British State* (1995), ch. 8.

[20] Ellis, *Tudor Frontiers and Noble Power*, ch. 5: for Dacre's inability to manage the East Marches, see his comments on p. 151.

endowment. In 1537, the Cumberland experiment having shown itself to have failed, Henry rejected advice to reinstate Dacre and turned to a lesser figure, Sir Thomas Wharton, whose jostling for position against long-established and entrenched interests in Cumberland and Westmorland led to twenty years of feuding between him, Dacre, and Cumberland.[21] The successful administration of the Borders therefore turned on the Crown being able to trust the locally pre-eminent landowner, Dacre in the west and the Percy earl of Northumberland in the east, and their ability to exercise the office with authority. The ill-health and progressive break-down of the sixth earl of Northumberland (d. 1537) was therefore a dis-aster for the Crown.[22] Northumberland gave away his estates to the benefit of a small circle of intimates, of whom Wharton was one. In 1537, on the eve of his death, he assigned the rump of his estates to the king. He was an unhappy man; his marriage collapsed, he was at loggerheads with his younger brothers (whom he disinherited, then denounced to the coun-cil in January 1537), and he suffered from some sort of incapacitating ill-ness (whether physical or psychological cannot be determined). There is little evidence to support the old view that Northumberland, as a weak and inadequate man, fell victim to an avaricious monarch. On the contrary, his decline produced enormous problems of government in the north-east, which were compounded by the king's impetuous decision to execute the earl's younger brother after he had taken the opportunity of a general breakdown in order to attack the earl's favourites in Nor-thumberland.[23] Again, there was no settled administration of the eastern Borders, merely stopgaps, until the sixth earl's nephew was created seventh earl in 1557 and had the estates returned to him.

The creation of new nobles was occasionally necessary to fill the void left by political failure, disability, or premature death. Whilst it has been argued that Henry VIII selected 'new men' in the aftermath of

---

[21] On the advice received by Henry, M. L. Bush, 'The Problem of the Far North: A Study of the Crisis of 1537 and its Consequences', *NH* 6 (1971), and for the subsequent disputes, R. W. Hoyle, 'Faction, Feud and Reconciliation Amongst the Northern English Nobility, 1525–1569', *History*, 84 (1999).

[22] R. W. Hoyle, 'Henry Percy, Sixth Earl of Northumberland, and the Fall of the House of Percy, 1527–37', in G. W. Bernard (ed.), *The Tudor Nobility* (1992).

[23] For events here, Dodds, *Pilgrimage*, I, 198–201.

the Pilgrimage of Grace,[24] the archetypal new man, of gentry origins, ennobled and endowed with estates to fill a particular gap in regional government, was actually one of the victims of the Pilgrimage. Thomas, Lord Darcy was of gentry stock from Temple Hirst near Selby. He established a reputation as a soldier on the Border in the 1490s: in 1498 he was made constable of Bambrough, captain of Berwick, and Henry, duke of York's deputy in the East and Middle Marches. In 1505 he was ennobled; in 1509 he was made a knight of the garter, a councillor, and had his commission renewed as warden of the East Marches and as captain of Berwick. In 1499–1500 he married Edith, the widow of Ralph Neville, Lord Neville, son and heir of the third earl of Westmorland (which surely indicates considerable royal favour). Darcy was made steward and surveyor of his stepson's extensive lands in County Durham in 1509: this was doubtless a confirmation of a position he already held.[25] He was also granted the key Duchy of Lancaster stewardships in the West Riding. Dacre, however, was made warden in the East and Middle Marches in late 1511, and in 1515 Darcy surrendered the captaincy of Berwick. In the latter years of Henry VII's reign he filled some of the gap left by the minority and then perceived unreliability of the fifth duke of Northumberland; in the first years of Henry VIII's reign he may have fulfilled some of the functions of the late Archbishop Savage's council. But Darcy was excluded from Richmond's council when it was created in 1525, and this may explain his bitterness towards and joy at the fall of Wolsey in 1529.[26] He suffered the misfortune of living too long. He was one of the last survivors of Henry VII's court, a man with first-hand knowledge of Henry VIII's marriage to Katherine of Aragon. At the end of his life he was alienated from Henry VIII, hostile to the divorce, appalled by the royal supremacy, and, as we shall see, he was prepared to talk of treason. That he surrendered Pontefract Castle to Robert Aske

---

[24] A theme of James's study of Thomas Lord Wharton, 'Change and Continuity in the Tudor North: Thomas, First Lord Wharton', in James, *Society, Politics and Culture*; Bush, 'The Problem of the Far North'; also Elton, *Reform and Reformation*, 271. All, to my mind, overstate the novelty of the decisions of the summer of 1537.

[25] *LP* I (i), no. 94 (67).

[26] Darcy took the opportunity of Wolsey's fall to compile a petition calling for Richmond's council to be abolished, *LP* XII (ii), no. 186 (38). He may have been admitted to the refurbished council of 1530. Reid, *King's Council*, 120–1.

has been taken as evidence of his willingness to conspire against the king, but I will subsequently argue that his protestations of continued loyalty to Henry VIII are most likely to be true. Nonetheless, this brief account shows how a 'new man', created to fill a particular combination of circumstances, long outlived his usefulness.[27]

The experience of the Borders in the early sixteenth century is a forceful reminder that power was personal. The Dacres and Percys could mobilize their gentry neighbours and tenants: outsiders could not. This is a dimension of the lineage society described by Mr James for County Durham.[28] The nobleman retained a high level of prestige: his household acted as a social and, doubtless, political focus for regional society. The service of gentry as household or estate officers for a superior lord remained common in the 1530s. These circles of gentry around a nobleman, linked by common interests in the noble family's fortunes and by intermarriage within the circle (and sometimes with the premier family), remained an organizing principle in northern society. The noble estates also had their military aspects. The expectation that tenants would keep horse or harness and undertake service for their lord on the Borders in times of war remained strong. As late as the end of the 1570s the leases (or warrants) issued by the earl of Cumberland required his tenants to serve the earl or monarch when required. In the crisis of 1536 figures such as the earl of Derby in Lancashire or the earl of Shrewsbury in the north Midlands were able to raise large contingents of troops to face the rebels by drawing on their own tenants and the tenants of their gentry supporters.[29] (Other northern noblemen, as we shall see, were unable to mobilize their forces in this way.) When one sees the assertion made that southern nobility no longer had the authority to command their tenants in this way, one wonders how they were ever able to raise an army against the Pilgrims. The comparison between North and south is overdrawn in this respect as in others: it is not clear how the lineage society of the North differed from that of an overtly more economically

[27] Again, I hope to write further about Darcy's life.

[28] M. James, *Family, Lineage and Civil Society: A Study of Society, Politics and Mentality in the Durham Region, 1500–1640* (1974).

[29] Cumberland, R. W. Hoyle, 'Land and Landed Relations in Craven, Yorkshire, *c.*1520–1600', D.Phil thesis, University of Oxford (1986), 259–61; Shrewsbury and Derby, *LP* XI, nos. 930, 1251.

advanced county such as Norfolk, where the earls of Norfolk and their household acted as a similar focus of society.[30] And it is quite wrong to characterize the North as dominated by noble households when there were probably only three such foci of real substance: those of the earl of Derby in Lancashire, the earl of Northumberland in Northumberland and the East Riding, and the earl of Westmorland in County Durham. The households of peers such as the Dacres or the Clifford earls of Cumberland, or first-generation peers such as Thomas, Lord Darcy, were almost certainly much more local in their influence and far less capable of drawing into them figures of independent standing within the county.

All in all, it is hard to see that the northern nobility presented a threat to the Crown, or that the Crown wished to reduce its power. In the 1560s the situation was different: the northern nobility was uniformly conservative and hostile to the 1559 religious settlement. Anxious to see Mary, Queen of Scots made Queen Elizabeth's heir, the Percy and Neville interests rose in a confused and wholly unsuccessful rebellion in the autumn of 1569, probably in the expectation that there were others willing to join with them.[31] In the early 1530s nobles generally, whatever they thought privately of the divorce, exhibited a remarkable solidarity with the king in his marital misadventures. The fracturing of the nobility into religious camps was very much a feature of the middle years of the century.

The nobility could present a threat to the peace of the North. The first and second earls of Cumberland seem to have been especially willing to employ their 'power' either to intimidate or challenge the decisions of the courts. In 1531 the first earl and John Norton had an armed confrontation over the right to hold the manorial court at Kirkby Malzeard. The second earl deployed large groups of men against Lord Wharton in their struggles over Wharton Park in Westmorland in the early 1550s (and vice versa). In a protracted dispute over a house called Friarhead near Malham, in 1557 the earl's servants attacked the house, evicted its tenant's family, and garrisoned it with men drawn from the West Marches. When commissioners from the Duchy of Lancaster court

---

[30] MacCulloch, *Suffolk and the Tudors*, ch. 2a.

[31] We lack a comprehensive study of the 1569 rebellion, but see Fletcher and MacCulloch, *Tudor Rebellions*, ch. 8, for a businesslike account.

appeared at Friarhead to insist that the earl surrender possession, they were fired on. When they withdrew the earl's troops fired their cannon in a victory salute from *inside* the building.[32] Similar cases could be offered, but not very many from the north in the 1530s and later. The more usual perpetrators of malfeasance, riot, or other public-order offences in the 1520s and 1530s were gentry of independent standing such as Sir Richard Tempest of Bracewell and Bowling Hall in Bradford and Sir William Gascoigne of Gawthorpe (a lost house which stood in the park of the modern Harewood House). Tempest, a particularly unpleasant character, had been an esquire to the Body: amongst other Duchy of Lancaster offices, he served as steward for the manors of Bradford and Wakefield in the West Riding and the honour of Clitheroe.[33] He had at least six murders laid against him, including one at Easter 1536 of a Wakefield man who had commenced a suit against him before the council at Westminster. As well as procuring assassins, he was also accused of extortion and maintained a long dispute with Sir Henry Savile over the jurisdiction of the manor of Wakefield.[34] The law, it seemed, was incapable of catching up with Tempest. Arrested on suspicion of disloyalty during the Pilgrimage, he died in August 1537.[35] An anonymous writer on the state of Yorkshire in about 1533 or 1534 does not give the impression of widespread disorder, but he does name JPs (including Gascoigne, Tempest, and Savile) whose removal from the commission would be of benefit to justice.[36] It was individuals of this standing who were accused of illegal retaining in Lancashire in the 1540s and 1550s or of mustering 300 men to attack the earl of Westmorland at Gaterley Moor races in 1554.[37]

One murder does stand out as being of unusual importance. At the end of February 1536 Ralph Carr, a Newcastle merchant, was murdered by a gang led by William Wycliffe esq. of Wycliffe in the North Riding. Carr was no ordinary merchant. He was a member of a prominent Newcastle family which, over a number of generations, provided the city

[32] Hoyle, 'Land and Landed Relations', 270, 276–7.

[33] R. Somerville, *History of the Duchy of Lancaster*, 2 vols. (1953, 1970), I, 501, 522, and other references; R. W. Hoyle, 'The Fortunes of the Tempest Family of Bracewell and Bolling Hall in the Sixteenth Century' (forthcoming).

[34] For Gascoigne and Tempest's abuse of the law, Smith, *Land and Politics*, 144–51.

[35] He begged to be released from the Fleet, but apparently died there. *LP* XII (i), nos. 179, 576.

[36] *LP* VII, no. 1669.

[37] C. Haigh, *Reformation and Resistance in Tudor Lancashire* (1975), 96; Stone, *Crisis of the Aristocracy*, 215.

with mayors. Carr himself had served as sheriff in 1532 and mayor in 1534. The family were also North Riding landowners and had connections with the Richmondshire gentry through marriage. Carr's mother was a daughter and co-heir of Ralph Wycliffe (d. 1536); it has been overlooked that Carr was knifed by his cousin, who represented the heirs male of the Wycliffe family. Carr's social prominence and the domestic nature of the quarrel may have made this a cause célèbre in which Cromwell, amongst others took an interest. Writing from York in March, one of the justices of gaol delivery told Cromwell that at Mrs Carr's request he had moved to have Carr arraigned but that the jury (which was expected to be favourable to the Carrs) had refused to indict. The judge, Christopher Jenny, clearly believed that an injustice had been done, presumably by the jury bringing in a verdict contrary to the evidence, and he bound them to appear in Star Chamber in May, where they were heavily fined. Whatever the rights or wrongs of their actions, their prosecution in the council was thought to be unjust and provoked great anger in the county (although this is by no means a unique example of a jury being fined).[38]

The murder of Ralph Carr hardly proves that the North was more prone to violence than southern England, but the North did contain a few men, like Tempest and Gascoigne, whose manipulation of Crown office for private gain and ready recourse to violence and intimidation looks like behaviour which had largely been stamped out in southern England by closer conciliar discipline over the previous generation. In all of these matters the North may be said to be more distant than different, and in the far North government and society were both coloured by the military requirements of an armed border.

II

What of the religious life of the North? This has been less thoroughly explored than the devotional world of (say) East Anglia or the Western

---

[38] I have examined the case in greater detail in a forthcoming paper. See Aske's comments on the unpopularity of Cromwell, 'The manner of the taking of Robert Aske', 339–40; it was also the subject of hostile comment in the paper attributed to Sir Thomas Tempest, *LP* XI, no. 1244, at p. 505.

Counties, but some preliminary points may be made. In terms of institutions, the church was enormously patchy in its coverage. In some parts of the North there was the familiar association of village and parish. In other areas, notably in the Pennines and much of Lancashire, parishes were enormous, straddling half-a-dozen or more secondary settlements ('townships') over a distance of several miles. Beneficed clergy could be quite thin on the ground, but self-help over several centuries often meant that the individual townships within these larger parishes had their own chapels. Luddenham, in the populous textile parish of Halifax, had sought consecration of its chapel as recently as 1535, whilst the inhabitants of other townships in Halifax were, at about this time, engaged in erecting new chapels.[39] Moreover, benefices were generally poor. In 1535 Archbishop Lee had complained that graduates would not accept northern livings because of their inadequate stipends, and that as a result he was forced to ordain men of little education who were merely honest and competent to administer the sacraments. Preaching, Lee said, had been undertaken by the friars as the secular clergy were rarely capable. Certainly the clergy of the city of York came to exhibit the inbred conservatism of a group trained and recruited locally.[40] But there were benefices, sometimes lucrative ones, in the North, which attracted graduates who tended to be pluralists. A significant benefice like Kendal in Westmorland was held by Thomas Magnus, the pluralist master of St Leonard's Hospital at York, archdeacon of the East Riding, *inter alia* the linchpin of the northern council and occasional diplomat in Anglo-Scottish affairs.[41] Peter Vannes, Henry VIII's Latin secretary, held the vicarage of Kirkby Stephen in Westmorland.[42] The complaint from the Westmorland move-

[39] W. and S. Sheils, 'Textiles and Reform: Halifax and its Hinterland', in P. Collinson and J. Craig (eds.), *The Reformation in English Towns, 1500–1640* (1999), 132–5.

[40] C. Cross, 'Priests into Ministers: The Establishment of Protestant Practice in the City of York, 1530–1630', in P. N. Brooks (ed.), *Reformation Principle and Practice: Essays in Honour of A. G. Dickens* (1980).

[41] For materials—by no means complete—on the life of Magnus, see C. Cross and N. Vickers, 'Monks, Friars and Nuns in Sixteenth-Century Yorkshire', *YASRS* 150 (1995), 512–13. For Magnus as vicar of Kendal, see M. Clark, 'Kendal: The Protestant Exception', *Trans. Cumberland and Westmorland Antiquarian and Arch. Soc.*, 2nd ser., 95 (1995), 142–3.

[42] J. Caley and J. Hunter (eds), *Valor Ecclesiasticus, temp. Henrici VIII, auctoritate regia institutus*, 7 vols. (1810–34), V, 297 (where he appears as 'Peter Bane'), which I owe to Dr Margaret Clark. For his career, see A. B. Emden, *A Biographical Register of the University of Oxford, AD 1501–1540* (1974), 590–1.

ment that Cromwell's chaplains took benefices is a complaint about absenteeism, but does show that well-connected graduate clergy might be appointed to northern livings.[43]

The apparatus of the intercessionary mass was found here as elsewhere: but it seems likely that chantries and, in particular, parish gilds were less frequently encountered in the North than in East Anglia. In assessing the religious practice of the North on the eve of the Reformation one needs to eschew hindsight. By the 1560s the North was certainly back-wards, in that it had been little exposed to reformed preaching and, after the battle-lines had hardened in Mary's reign, was generally inclined to be hostile to the new ideas. This is not evidence that the North in the 1530s was especially backward-looking or unreceptive to reform, for which parts of England outside a limited range of south-eastern counties had much experience of reform-inclined preaching by 1536? The North in the 1530s was not *especially* conservative so much as *typically* conservative. It may well have remained backward for *longer* because of problems of clerical recruitment, but Archbishop Lee (d. 1545) did little to advance the preaching of the New Learning, indeed, was anxious to suppress any contentious debate. Lee's caution may have derived from the preaching war which took place in Doncaster between the priors of the Carmelite and Franciscan friaries in 1534, but one suspects that maintaining pub-lic order by suppressing all preaching suited his own preferences.[44] With Tunstall as bishop of Durham, the North escaped not only the itinerant preaching which men like Bilney were offering in East Anglia in the late 1520s, but also the preaching sponsored by advanced prelates like Cran-mer. It seems unlikely that there was much preaching of reform (as opposed to the royal supremacy) undertaken in the North before Edward's reign.[45] The duke of Norfolk remarked on the lack of preaching before

---

[43] *LP* XI, no. 1080. The complaint may refer to one John Knowles (*Knollis*), vicar of Great Musgrave in Westmorland by 1535 and still in 1539, when he was dispensed to hold another benefice. On this occasion he was called Cromwell's chaplain. *Valor Ecclesiasticus*, V, 294; D. S. Chambers (ed.), *Faculty Office Registers, 1534–1549* (1966), 189. Again, I owe this to the great kindness of Dr Clark. *LP* XI, no. 877 shows one of Cromwell's chaplains had the next presentation to Giggleswick in Craven, but by his surname he was a local man.

[44] Dickens, *Lollards and Protestants*, 143–4.

[45] This comes out plainly from Haigh's detailed account of Lancashire, but I cannot discover any preaching in, say, York. Indeed, I suspect that there was little reformed preaching in the North gen-erally before 1550. Haigh, *Reformation and Resistance*, ch. 11.

the Pilgrimage, and thought that if three or four preachers had been active in the North the Pilgrimage might have been avoided.[46] Likewise, Lee's innate conservatism led him not to take any steps to secure the dismantling of shrines in the late 1530s. Henry VIII was doubtless surprised to discover that they still stood in the northern province, and ordered them to be taken down on his northern progress in September 1541.[47] The Pilgrims' opposition to reform was to something of which they had heard at second hand, but of which they almost certainly had no experience.

Moreover, in describing the religious inclinations of the North at the time of the Pilgrimage, we probably place too great a weight on the preferences of Thomas, Lord Darcy and Robert Aske, the most prominent figures in the Pilgrimage. Darcy's commitment to the mendicant orders is revealed by his acceptance of the nomination by the Dominicans of Beverley as their founder in 1524. The prior of Beverley at this time was Henry Aglionby: it was to him that Darcy turned to be confessed before his execution.[48] He purchased a confraternity of the Austin Friars in 1511, an obit of the Friars Preachers of York in 1525, and another of the Carmelite Friars of York at some time in the 1520s.[49] His accounts for 1529 show that he was paying fees of 66s. 8d. each to the Observant Friars of Newark, Newcastle upon Tyne, Richmond, Greenwich, Hampton, and Canterbury, all houses which hardened into opposition to the divorce and the royal supremacy and were dissolved in 1534.[50] These were old-fashioned tastes in the 1530s, but no more than we would expect of a man nearing 70. The fourth earl of Shrewsbury (d. 1538), a man a decade or so younger than Darcy but who opposed him during the Pilgrimage, was equally conservative. Confronted with the singing-master of Jesus College, Rotherham, who was accused of possessing an English New Testament, Shrewsbury told him 'thou art a heretic and but for shame I should thrust my dagger into thee'.[51] Again, his preferences tell us little of those of younger, more contemporary figures.

[46] *LP* XII (i), no. 1158. Preachers were sent into the North in the spring of 1537, below p. 370.

[47] Sir H. Nicholls (ed.), *Proceedings and Ordinances of the Privy Council of England*, VIII, 1540–42 (1842), 247.

[48] PRO, E42/398; *LP* XII (i), no. 1234.

[49] Victoria County History, *Yorkshire*, III, 264; PRO, E329/455; E326/10257.

[50] SP1/39 fos. 161–5; D. Knowles, *The Religious Orders in England*, 3 vols. (1948–59), III, ch. 17.

[51] Dickens, *Lollards and Protestants*, 37–8.

It is harder to assess the religious tastes of Robert Aske. Aske, the Pilgrims' captain or 'Grand Captain', was the younger son of a family established at Aughton near Selby and was probably aged in his early or mid-thirties.[52] He was a cousin to the first earl of Cumberland, whom his brother Christopher served as receiver.[53] Aske was a common lawyer: in the late 1520s he served the sixth earl of Northumberland as his secretary.[54] He never carried sufficient weight to be admitted to the commission of the peace, but as a lawyer we may suspect that he was both well known locally but also operated in networks which spanned the London courts (and Inns of Court) and the provinces. Lawyers were the ubiquitous brokers between centre and locality: as frequent visitors to London they doubtless knew (and communicated) the best gossip. They were also in daily contact with many individual clients, some gentry, but others of less than gentle status. They doubtless knew everyone's business: indeed, they transacted that business, whether amongst their clients or, for the more senior lawyers, as members of the commission of the peace. The prominence of lawyers in the Pilgrimage comes as no surprise.[55]

Something of Aske's own networks may be discovered from two settlements made in 1536 in which he acted as a feoffee. In May he was named as a feoffee in the settlement of Henry Hamerton, the son and heir of Sir Stephen Hamerton of Wigglesworth in Craven, with Joanne, daughter of Christopher Stapleton of Wighill in the East Riding (and so the niece of Brian Stapleton, who became captain of the Beverley rebels). Amongst the other feoffees of this settlement was Thomas

---

[52] For the family, see the will of Aske's grandfather, Sir John, 'Testamenta Eboracensia', IV, *Surtees Soc.*, 53 (1869), 123–4; of his father, Sir Robert, 'Testamenta Eboracensia', VI, *Surtees Soc.*, 106 (1902), 21–2; and of his elder brother, John, ibid. 178–9. Aske is not named, nor does it appear that his father was married, in Aske's grandfather's will of 1497. I would therefore suggest that he was born after 1497.

[53] Hoyle, 'Land and Landed Society', 247. For Christopher Aske's examination, see *LP* XII (i), no. 1186.

[54] Bush, *Pilgrimage of Grace*, 121. BL, Add. Ms. 38,133, which may have been owned by Aske, contains accounts for money disbursed by Aske on the earl's behalf in 1527 (fo. 9r–v). As much of this was Percy's petty expenses about court, it is quite possible that Cromwell and others, also about court and moving in Wolsey's household, knew Aske from this time onwards. Otherwise, this MS contains disappointingly little about Aske.

[55] For the lawyers, see E. W. Ives, *The Common Lawyers of Pre-Reformation England* (1983), which includes (pp. 13–15) helpful comments on the Wakefield lawyer Thomas Grice, who acted for Darcy. For the idea of lawyers as brokers, C. Holmes, *Seventeenth-Century Lincolnshire* (1980), ch. 5.

Wharton, son of Thomas, Lord Wharton (Joanne's cousin through his mother). On 21 September he was one of the feoffees of the estates of another lawyer, John Lambert of Calton in Craven, along with Henry, Lord Clifford, Sir George Darcy, Sir Arthur Darcy, Sir Thomas Tempest, son of Sir Richard, and Christopher Aske.[56]

A little more than a fortnight after making this deed Aske was to be amongst the rebels in Lincolnshire, but we know virtually nothing about the man until he came to prominence in the Pilgrimage. Most importantly, we have no clue as to whether he was known as a political activist before the rising; but the way in which he is first mentioned in the correspondence between Audeley and Cromwell suggest both a familiarity with his name and a lack of surprise that he should have been involved in insurrection.[57]

Aske was interrogated at length after his arrest and provided detailed and articulate answers. His interrogators were interested not so much in Aske's own beliefs as in his assessment of why the rebellion started, but from Aske's answers some conclusions can be drawn about his convictions. In turn, these shed light on how he tried to shape the rebellion. Whilst he was never monocausal, throughout his depositions he placed a particular emphasis on the dissolution as inciting revolt. Asked about the rumours circulating throughout England in the summer of 1536 (which I will discuss in Chapter 3, and which in my interpretation were a central cause of the rebellion), Aske agreed that he had heard them, but maintained that the dissolution 'was the greatest cause of the insurrection, which the hearts of the commons most grudged at'.[58] To the question of whether there would have been an insurrection if the rumours had been extinguished, he replied that he thought 'that only the suppression of the abbeys and division of preachers had caused the insurrection, though the brutes [rumours] had not been spoken of at all'.[59] When asked what acts of parliament the rebels had objected to, he placed the dissolution

---

[56] For these settlements, Bodl., Ms. Dodsw. 155, fo. 3v; PRO, C54/405 no. 4 (the original of which is in Lancashire RO, DDMa (unlisted)).

[57] *LP* XI, no. 750. Likewise Darcy, who quickly identified Aske as a ringleader. Dodds, *Pilgrimage*, I, 301.

[58] 'Aske's Examination', 558, answ. 7 (and cf. 'The manner of the taking of Robert Aske', 342).

[59] Ibid. 559, answ. 16. 'And division of preachers' is an insertation into the MS text, a point I owe to Dr Bernard.

statute first and the supremacy second; later he returned to blame some of the council for the dissolution statute, 'which statute and other statutes the north parts thought was not for the commonwealth of the realm'.[60]

In a passage which has become famous, Aske expounded at length on the importance of the monasteries to the North:[61]

First, to the statute of suppressions, he did grudge against the same and so did the whole country, because the abbeys in the north parts gave great alms to poor men and laudably served God; in which parts of late days they had but small comport by ghostly [priestly] teaching. And by occasion of the said suppression the divine service of almighty God is much diminished, great number of masses unsaid and the blessed consecration of the sacrament now not used and showed in those places, to the distress of the faith and spiritual comfort to man's soul, the temple of God ruffed and pulled down, the ornaments and relics of the church of God unreverent used, the towns and sepulchres of honourable and noble men pulled down and sold, no hospitality now in those places kept but the farmers for the most part let and taverns [lease] out the farms of the same houses to other farmers, for lucre and advantage to themselves. And the profits of these abbeys yearly goeth out of the country to the king's highness, so that in short space little money by occasion of the said yearly rents, tenths and first fruits shall be left in the same country in consideration of the absence of the king's highness in those parts, want of his law and the frequentation of merchandise. Also divers and many of the said abbeys were in the mountains and desert places where the people be rude of conditions and not well taught the law of God, and when the abbeys stood, the said people not only had wordly refreshing in their bodies but also spiritual refuge both by ghostly living of them and also by spiritual information and preaching; and many tenants were their fee'd servants to them and serving men, well succoured by abbeys: and now not only these tenants and servants wants refreshing there, both of meat, cloth, and wages and knoweth not now where to have any living, but also strangers and badgers of corn as between Yorkshire, Lancashire, Kendal, Westmorland, and the bishopric [Durham] was neither carriage of corn and merchandise greatly succoured both horse and man by the said abbeys, for none was in these parts denied, neither horse meat or man's meat, so that the people was greatly refreshed by the said abbeys, where now they have no such succour: and wherefore the

---

[60] Ibid. 559, answ. 19, again answ. 23; p. 571, answ. 53.

[61] Ibid. 561–2. Chris Haigh has tested this account against the evidence of the Lancashire houses. C. Haigh, 'The last days of the Lancashire monasteries and the Pilgrimage of Grace', *Chetham Soc.*, 3rd ser., 17 (1969), 53–8.

said statute of suppression was greatly to the decay of the commonweal of the country and all those parts of all degrees greatly grudged against the same, and yet their duty of allegiance always saved.

Also the abbeys was [*sic*] one of the beauties of the realm to all men and strangers passing through the same: also all gentlemen much succoured in their needs with money, their young sons there succoured and in nunneries their daughters brought up in virtue: and also their evidences and money left to the uses of infants in abbeys' hands, always sure there; and such abbeys as were near the danger of sea banks [were] great maintainers of sea walls and dikes, maintainers and builders of bridges and highways such other things for the commonwealth.

This requires some commentary. First, apart from the loss of divine service, the reduced number of masses, and Aske's evident distaste for the sacrilegious treatment of church ornaments and fabric, this is an apologia for monasteries couched in utilitarian social and economic terms. There is no challenge to the right of the king to dissolve, or comment on the loss of masses for founders and donors. Secondly, Aske is trying to make an exceptionalist case for the North, perhaps conceding the relative lack of secular clergy: but how many of these functions were not undertaken by abbeys throughout England? Aske's eulogy may be taken to indicate that monastic houses were more closely integrated into northern society than their southern brethren. Communal solidarity with the dispossessed monks might then explain why the North alone saw acts of resistance to the monastic commissioners (at Hexham and Vale Royal), and why some of the recently dissolved houses were reoccupied by their monks in October 1536.

Evidence for Aske's monastophilia being a general northern preference is decidedly lacking. Professor Cross has read the surviving Yorkshire wills for the decade and a half before the commencement of the dissolution and finds that only about a sixth of them mention monasteries. From the examples she offers, it appears that many refer to the houses without affection, but settle unfinished business such as the payment of forgotten tithes or, in the case of monastic tenants, seek the good lordship of the abbot and convent. A few (and it appears to be a very few) left money to monasteries for prayers or masses, and one or two sought burial within the monastic precinct. Professor Cross has made the best case possible, but it amounts to little.[62] One may ask, though, whether wills would have much cause to mention monasteries, and whether this source is capable of proving or disproving Aske's claim that they occupied a central place in northern society. Monasteries offered hospitality, education, and employment: there is no good reason why they should be remembered in wills any more than familiar modern institutions such as churches, libraries, or even universities. Monasteries may well have been a familiar and valued part of the fabric of early sixteenth-century northern society, but the risings of 1536 were not primarily about their defence. Nationally, the fate of the smaller houses provoked little complaint, if that can be measured in the number of acts of violence and resistance which came to the notice of government. The two most notorious cases are both northern. On 28 September the monks of Hexham resisted the commissioners who had come to seize the priory for the king. They withdrew without any acts of violence having taken place. The king, however, was incandescent at this challenge to his authority and instructed the earl of Cumberland to go to Hexham and restore order. The monks may have had right on their side, for it would seem that they had secured a licence for the continuation of the house. A second instance of an abbey mobilizing its tenants to protect it comes from Norton in Cheshire. Here the procedures of dissolution were completed and the commissioners packed up when, on 8 October, they were attacked by the abbot and a crowd or 200 or 300 people and forced to take refuge in a tower whilst the abbot's tenants and clients enjoyed a celebratory ox-roasting. The party was still in swing when the sheriff, Sir Piers Dutton, arrived with a posse which scattered the crowd, arrested the abbot and several monks, and put the king's commissioners back in possession. Whilst Henry wanted the abbot and canons hanged, they escaped the hangman at the cost of several months in gaol.[63]

These two isolated incidents come late in the dissolution of the smaller houses. The Yorkshire houses dissolved by the 1536 statute were surveyed in May and the first half of June: they were dissolved in late

---

[62] C. Cross, 'Monasticism and Society in the Diocese of York, 1520–1540', *TRHS* 5th ser., 38 (1988).

[63] Dodds, *Pilgrimage*, I, 193–5; *LP* XI, no. 504; 'Letters of the Cliffords', 51–2. For events at Norton, VCH *Cheshire*, III, 168–9.

July–August. Disturbances whilst the dissolution was in train would have
been understandable, but by the first week in October it was all over
in Yorkshire.[64] The monks and their households had been dispersed,
the farm stock sold off and tenants installed, the precious metal from the
roofs and bells melted into ingots and carted away. Reoccupation of the
part-demolished buildings was therefore a foolhardy and empty gesture:
the monks of Sawley had an uncomfortable time, lacking both food
and fuel to put away for the winter, and reduced to seeking charity
from their neighbours.[65] We lack precise dates for the dissolution in
Lincolnshire, but it seems to have been completed before trouble
erupted in Louth on 2 October. But the Lincolnshire rebels showed no
interest in supporting the monasteries, never included the dissolution as
a grievance in their articles, nor urged the monks to reoccupy their houses.
Within Yorkshire the commons took the lead in restoring the monks to
Sawley (near Clitheroe), to St Agatha's at Richmond, and to Coverham
in Wensleydale, and it seems likely that most of the Yorkshire houses
dissolved in the summer of 1536 saw some sort of occupation by the
commons or reoccupation by some or all of their former monks. Aske
issued his order restoring the dispossessed religious to their houses on
23 October 'because the commons would needs put them in'.[66]

So, whilst there was a degree of local support for dissolved houses, it
seems most likely that the opposition to the dissolution which forms a
strand of the Pilgrimage was largely the result of Aske's own preoccupations. It may be no coincidence that his brother bought a corrody of
Bolton Priory some months before the Pilgrimage broke out.[67] Rather
than place an emphasis on the Aske brothers' particular brand of conservatism, we might also notice that the North did contain a scattering of
younger individuals who, by the standards of the 1530s, were advanced
in their beliefs and preferences.[68] Professor Dickens has introduced us to
Sir Francis Bigod, who was probably in his late twenties at the time of

---

[64] For these dates, S. Jacks, 'Dissolution Dates for the Monasteries Dissolved Under the Act of
1536', *Bulletin of the Institute of Historical Res.*, 43 (1970), 179.

[65] Below p. 228.   [66] Below, pp. 202–3.

[67] R. W. Hoyle, 'Monastic Leasing Before the Dissolution: The Evidence of Bolton Priory and
Fountains Abbey', *YAJ* 61 (1989), 131.

[68] For what follows, see Dickens, *Lollards and Protestants*, chs. 3 and 4.

the Pilgrimage. Bigod had been in Wolsey's household as a child and had spent time in Oxford as an undergraduate in the late 1520s. Around 1535 he published 'A treatise concerning impropriations of benefices', whose erudite title concealed a concern for the preaching of the gospel and a conviction that monasteries, especially in the way in which they controlled impropriations (parish livings) and took their profits, were a dead weight in achieving the society for which Bigod strove. The monasteries were full of indolent monks, irreconciled to the royal supremacy and practising unspeakable vices. Partial disendowment would allow the creation of a cadre of preaching clergy who could reinvigorate belief. Within Yorkshire he put his scepticism of the monastic vocation into effect and went so far as to preach the royal supremacy in Jervaulx. Bigod was, by the standard of his times, a thoroughly modern man, driven by convictions which were perhaps the direct opposite of Aske's. Darcy, amongst others, was appalled by his heretical chaplain.[69] Another younger gentleman who expressed excitement at the New Learning in London was Edward Plumpton, aged about 20 at the time of the Pilgrimage. In two letters written to his mother from the Inner Temple, Plumpton shows how he had drunk deeply at the well of evangelism. Not satisfied with persuading her to read the New Testament, he expressed his satisfaction that 'the gospel of Christ was never so truly preached as it is now'. A third younger gentleman who also leant towards the New Learning was Wilfred Holme of Huntington near York, who wrote a verse treatise on 'The fall and evil success of rebellion' in which he offered not only an account of the Pilgrimage but a much longer and elaborate rumination on the principles of the Henrician Reformation. Holme displayed the same distaste for monasticism that coloured Bigod's tract, but he also denounced purgatory, works, and relics, and thought auricular confession to be without scriptural foundation. None of these three gentry survived to see the Edwardian Reformation. There is no way of knowing how their beliefs might have matured, nor of establishing how representative their views were of other younger northern gentry being educated within the court and the Inns of Court. What makes these individuals exceptional is not their existence, but the depth of our knowledge of their views.

[69] Ibid. 75.

III

In 1914 Dr Rachel Reid, the historian of the northern council, having summarized a whole range of political and social problems in the North, wrote that a rebellion in the North was inevitable in the mid-1530s. In 1996 Dr Bush referred on several occasions to a northern rebellion of 1535, the year preceding the Pilgrimage.[70] Was the Pilgrimage merely waiting to happen, an inevitable adjustment to new realities? And had the Pilgrimage a precursor out of which it developed?

There was a tradition of rebellion in one district of the North.[71] Richmondshire, the area around and between Ripon and Richmond, had risen in 1489. The best interpretation of events is that this year saw a movement against taxation in the North Riding which persuaded the fourth earl of Northumberland to communicate his grievances to Henry VII: when Northumberland had to report the king's rejection of his overtures to a group of rebels at Topcliffe on 28 April, he was assassinated. There were then musters in the North Riding, out of which coalesced a force which moved southwards, joined another contingent of rebels at Sheriff Hutton, and then marched southwards to Doncaster. From there they turned northwards and entered York, then dispersed without confronting any rival force. The geographical coincidence and similarity of behaviour with the Richmondshire movement in the Pilgrimage is most striking. The same area was active, mustering and maintaining protest meetings against taxation, in 1513: a refusal to co-operate with the subsidy commissioners seems to have spilled out into the Yorkshire Dales and perhaps Lancashire and Yorkshire in this and subsequent subsidy years, including 1524–5. In 1536 Richmondshire was the heart of the Yorkshire Pilgrimage. The movement here owed little or nothing to the movement in Lincolnshire, wrote letters in the name of 'Captain Poverty', and sent out expeditions to recruit and spread word of the rising. It had a decided hue of social conflict not found elsewhere.[72]

---

[70] Reid, *King's Council*, 126; Bush, *Pilgrimage of Grace*, 408. And cf. my review and his rejoinder: *American Historical Rev.*, 103 (1998), 879–80, 1763.

[71] For what follows, Hoyle, 'Resistance and Manipulation', and M. A. Hicks, 'The Yorkshire Rebellion of 1489 Reconsidered', *NH* 22 (1986).

[72] Below Ch. 8, pp. 423–5.

The Pilgrimage of Grace was not, to any significant degree, about taxation.[73] Whilst the subsidy was being assessed in early October 1536, the previous assessment made a year earlier had not prompted disturbances. Both collections were, in any case only levied on the very richest taxpayers. The taxation complaint contained in the Lincolnshire petition refers to the collection of the fifteenth scheduled for the following year. All in all, the levying of taxation in 1536 must be regarded as something which coincided with, rather than inspired the Pilgrimage of Grace. The collection of clerical taxation is a different matter: Archbishop Lee (and probably with justice) blamed the rising on the imposition of the clerical tenth and regarded the instruction to recommence its collection in January as potentially inflammatory.[74]

Nonetheless, there were disturbances in the summer of 1535 which the government took extremely seriously. These were mentioned to Cromwell by Sir Richard Tempest as an afterthought to a letter of 13 June: that crowds of 300–400 persons had rioted and thrown down enclosures about Giggleswick near Settle.[75] In fact three separate riots appear to have taken place at about the same time. New enclosures by the earl of Cumberland were destroyed, as were enclosures made by John Catterall of Rathmell. Other, better-documented riots were aimed against enclosures made by John Lambert (the man for whom Aske acted) at Airton in Malhamdale. Cromwell seems to have read much more into Tempest's report than the disturbances warranted. Letters were sent to the earl of Cumberland, Sir Richard Tempest, Sir Stephen Hamerton, Sir Marmaduke Constable, and Lord Monteagle ordering them to investigate and send the ringleaders southwards. By the time this letter was in Tempest's hands some had already been apprehended and imprisoned at York. The Airton rioters were indicted at extraordinary sessions held at Gisburn on 1 July.[76]

For whatever reasons, Tempest's report also came to the notice of the king. A letter of 21 June demanding investigations into disturbances in

---

[73] M. L. Bush, ' "Up for the commonweal": The Significance of Tax Grievances in the English Rebellions of 1536', EHR 106 (1991), and my note of dissent, 'Resistance and Manipulation', 172–4.

[74] Hoyle, 'Thomas Master's Narrative', 75, Dodds, Pilgrimage, II, 33–4.

[75] LP VIII, no. 863. I first outlined these events in 'First Earl of Cumberland', 77–8.

[76] This can be followed through LP VIII, nos. 893, 946, 970, 984, 991, 992–5; Add. I, no. 996; also VII, nos. 1314, 1315.

the North was sent to (at least) the earls of Cumberland, Westmorland, Northumberland, and Lord Monteagle. (The king's letter does not survive, but they all submitted reports in response to it.) Monteagle received the letter on 3 July and immediately travelled into Craven, where he found that Tempest and Robert Chaloner, another lawyer and JP, had matters in hand. He then went into Westmorland, where he encountered the earl of Westmorland at Brough. Westmorland had travelled throughout the northern counties in a great arc, doubtless starting at Brancepeth but passing through Hexham, Haltwhistle, and Carlisle before curving southwards to Brough. Monteagle next attended the sessions held at Shap on 13–14 July, where some anti-enclosure rioting was indicted: but both he and Westmorland had only a thin haul to report for their endeavours.[77]

There was nothing happening in the North in the summer of 1535 with which the normal routine of quarter sessions could not deal. The mobilization of the nobility to deal with agrarian disturbances (the earls of Northumberland and Westmorland *both* proposed to be at the Gisburn special sessions[78]) was an extreme over-reaction reflecting the government's acute nervousness in the season after the execution of the London Carthusians, Bishop Fisher, and Sir Thomas More, the hard kernel of the opponents of the royal supremacy. Events in Craven and elsewhere in the North—enclosure riots were reported from Cleator and Frizington in west Cumberland in late July—and the overthrowing of enclosures in the Eden Valley during the Pilgrimage do point to rampant enclosure in the Dales and Lakes in the mid-1530s.[79] But there is nothing in these disturbances which warrants the title of rebellion. They were entirely local events, which never generated the regional consciousness and solidarities needed in a rebellion; and, this being so, it is hard to see why the Pilgrimage was, in any sense, inevitable.

---

77 *LP* VIII, nos. 984, 1030, 1046.   78 Ibid., no. 991.

79 Ibid., no. 1133; below p. 252. For the Cumberland disturbances, see also PRO, STAC 2/1/44–5, 21/181, 21/218.

3

1536: The Year of Three Queens

In common with all late-medieval monarchs, Henry VIII was no figure-head to government. His preferences permeated every aspect of government, whether its foreign policy, its religious policy, or its deployment of patronage. In late-medieval or Tudor polities the monarch was the key guarantor of good government, of the impartial administration of the law, and of the maintenance of civil peace. A king who was indolent or partial towards his own circle, or worse, incapacitated and unable to set in train the machinery of government by his signature, was a misfortune inflicted upon his kingdom. Equally, kings who were minors presented grave dangers: minorities might be attended by political instability, as factions sought to control the king or jockey for power and influence over him. Fifteenth-century English history—recent history to the Tudors—was punctuated by problem monarchs, from the seizure of the throne by Henry IV onwards: his grandson Henry VI was not merely partial in his selection of councillors but was unable to control the rivalries between nobles; in addition, he was insane and incapacitated for periods. The result was intermittent civil strife, the Wars of the Roses. Edward IV, whatever his other merits, died leaving a child, Edward V, as his heir, who was deposed by his uncle, Richard III, whose rule was tyrannous. He, in his turn, was overthrown by invasion. The Tudors tended to portray themselves as healers, ending a century of civil strife through the marriage of Edward IV's daughter Elizabeth, the heir to the white rose, to Henry VII, the representative of the red rose party.

The worst of all situations occurred when there was no recognized heir. Whilst the Tudors may have brought stability and prosperity, the Tudor dynasty was racked by persistent problems over the succession. Henry VIII finally had three legitimate children (that is, born to women to whom he was married at the time), two of whom (Mary and Elizabeth) were subsequently declared to be illegitimate. Henry and Katherine of Aragon produced a son fairly quickly after their marriage, but the young Prince Henry died only seven weeks after his birth: thereafter there was a further child born to the marriage, the Princess Mary, in 1516, and Katherine's other pregnancies ended in miscarriages. She conceived for the last time in 1518. For the first part of Henry's reign Mary was the king's immediate heir, although there was some doubt as to whether a woman could rule. Certainly the king yearned for a son. Doubts over Mary's ability to rule were perhaps responsible for the decision to push the king's bastard son, Henry Fitzroy (b. 1519), into the limelight: created duke of Richmond in 1525, he may have been seen as a possible heir but he died in 1536. By early 1527 Henry was convinced that his marriage was barren because of its illegality: he had married his elder brother's widow, albeit after the appropriate dispensations had been secured and in the knowledge that the young Prince Arthur had never consummated his marriage. Under the weight of the king's guilt and fear that he was being punished by God, together with the more prosaic reason that the queen's childbearing years were behind her, the marriage collapsed.

Subsequent events can be read in several ways. We might hold that Henry sought an annulment of the marriage on the principled grounds that he was living sinfully with a woman to whom he could not, by God's law, be married; or that the demands of the succession outweighed what residual affection he felt for Katherine, and that it was imperative that he enter a new union which would be blessed in a way which his first marriage had not been; or we might read the annulment as the means by which the king could be released to marry a younger woman around court, Anne Boleyn. It is perhaps fairest to say that the divorce (correctly, the annulment) was launched for all of these reasons. As the king's future wife, Anne Boleyn suffered from a number of disadvantages, not least of which was that the king's intercourse with her elder sister Mary placed Anne within the same affinity as Henry (allegedly) stood to his brother. Anne may or not have been betrothed before; and she was also relatively old (although this was perhaps less of a problem when it was assumed that the divorce would be achieved expeditiously). But both their and our contemporaries are prone to lean to the cynical view that the divorce was driven by a middle-aged man's lust. Certainly, in the popular mind Anne was merely a whore and the subject of a great deal of popular distaste.[1] In 1530 the Imperial ambassador, Chapuys, predicted an uprising if Henry married her, but this contained a large element of wishful thinking.[2] Moreover, she was a far from neutral figure, being an educated and opinionated woman who attracted supporters and detractors in equal measure.

If there was an early belief that the divorce could be achieved quickly, then this was shattered by the failure of the legatine court held at Blackfriars in July 1529 and the granting of the queen's request that her case be heard at Rome. The success of Katherine's plea made it unlikely that the divorce would ever be granted, and forced the development of a new strategy in 1530–1. In the short term, the discovery that the king was not master in his own kingdom but, on a matter as vital as the succession, was at the mercy of an unsympathetic pontiff provoked an angry reaction. The strategy developed in 1530–1 was to separate the English church from the larger Catholic church so that the divorce could be tried within England without any right of appeal to the higher authority. This necessarily involved destroying the independence of the church and demonstrating its political subordination to both king and common law. The process was begun with the Pardon of the Clergy in January 1531, continued with the Submission of the Clergy in May 1532, and was fully completed by the declaration of the royal supremacy by statute in 1534. The key statute which allowed the divorce to be secured was the Act in Restraint of Appeals, enacted in April 1533. This allowed Archbishop

[1] G. R. Elton, *Policy and Police: The Enforcement of the Reformation in the Age of Thomas Cromwell* (1972), index, sub 'Boleyn, Anne, abuse of'.

[2] *Calendar of State Papers Spanish* (hereafter *CSPSp*), IV (i), p. 290.

Cranmer to pronounce the divorce. Confident of the outcome, Henry and Anne finally consummated their relationship towards the end of 1532, and Anne was already pregnant when they married on 24 January 1533. She gave birth to a child, Elizabeth, on 7 September. Thereafter, although pregnant on several occasions, she, like Katherine, lost her pregnancies to miscarriages.

There were certainly those who disliked the principle of the divorce but who, for pragmatic reasons, were prepared to swallow it. After 1529 a much larger group clearly believed that the ends did not justify the means, and found Henry's fracturing of the Catholic church and the erection of the royal supremacy more than they could accept. Some doubtless felt that the schism was an aberration which could be repaired at some future moment (as, indeed, it was in 1555 when Mary returned England to the Roman obedience). Exactly how many were opposed to the royal supremacy cannot be ascertained. The 1534 statute made speaking against the royal supremacy an act of treason: opponents therefore had good reason to be discreet in their criticisms. It seems as though many amongst the clergy were irreconciled to the supremacy. They found it hard to accept that the pope should be reduced to the pejorative title of bishop of Rome, and that they should be forced to preach that he had no greater authority than any other bishop. A few priests salved their consciences by courting martyrdom. One Christopher Michell, curate of Winestead in Holderness, addressed his congregation in June 1535 in these words: 'Neighbours, I pray you pay your duty to St Robert of Knaresborough and I pray you all pray for the spirituality and for me, for I have made my testament, for I am bound to such a journey that I trawe[?] never to see you again, for it is said that there is no pope, but I say there is a pope.' Arrested, he remained defiant, telling his captors that 'if I had the king's commandment here now to show and if the pope's commandment were also come to me, I would show and publish the pope's commandment and leave the king's and there of my head should be stricken off . . .'. Archbishop Lee regarded Michell as an embarrassment, 'a foolish and lewd priest'. His final fate is unknown.[3] Other clergy

---

[3] PRO, KB9/533 m. 45: *LP* VIII, nos. 990, 1011, 1020. Michell was not rector: Richard Hillyard, rector from 1529, fled into Scotland to oppose the Reformation from there. VCH *East Riding*, V, 155.

held their tongues, but when cut, bled anger at their predicament. When a pseudo-convocation was held at Pontefract during the Pilgrimage, the clergy present, all middle-ranking northern clerics, rejected the royal supremacy and called for the statutes creating it to be revoked.[4] Likewise, the main articles of the Pilgrims drawn up at Pontefract demanded that the spiritual headship of the papacy be restored.

The political costs of the divorce were high. After 1529 it was pursued relentlessly, without regard for convention, until an alternative legal framework had been erected which gave the annulment and the king's (re)marriage a veneer of legality, albeit a legality which would be accepted in one nation only. To adapt the words of a modern commentator speaking of our own times, to achieve the divorce 'they had to hobble, crush or uproot the . . . institutions and values which stood in its way [and] sweep away the understandings and practices which had constrained the central executive in the past'.[5]

One of the key 'understandings and practices' which fell casualty to the juggernaut of the divorce was the notion of counsel.[6] The idea of good counsel was that the monarch should gather around him and accept advice from a broadly based group of intimates, some of whom would have been nominated for this role by birth. The king's council should be a body which reflected the broader opinions of the nation: it should be wise but also consensual. Medieval history was littered with examples of monarchs who broke the rules of counsel by surrounding themselves with circles of councillors (or less formally counsellors) who persuaded the king into ruling contrary to the interests of the commonwealth. It might be possible to impose good councillors on wayward monarchs, but ultimately the problem arose of what should be done with monarchs who persisted in taking bad counsel. Edward II, Richard II, and Henry VI were all deposed, but deposition in the public interest only engendered the larger question of how the throne should be transferred to a new monarch,

---

[4] Printed below pp. 463–4 and discussed pp. 355–7.

[5] Professor David Marquand talking of the Thatcherite creation of the free market, quoted in the *Observer*, 22 Nov. 1998.

[6] The following section draws on J. Guy, 'The King's Council and Political Participation', in A. Fox and J. Guy, *Reassessing the Henrician Age: Humanism, Politics and Reform, 1500–1550* (1986), and F. W. Conrad, 'The Problem of Counsel Reconsidered: The Case of Sir Thomas Elyot', in P. A. Fidler and T. F. Mayer (eds.), *Political Thought and the Tudor Commonwealth* (1992).

and who that person should be. It must be admitted that those most concerned with counsel were men for whom (in twentieth-century parlance)
the phone had ceased to ring, who, whilst they considered themselves
entitled to a role in political decision-making, were excluded by their
political opponents. They took refuge in a constitutionalism with which
they could beat their enemies.

The conviction was strong in the years before the Pilgrimage that the
normal processes by which the king took counsel had broken down. To
outsiders, it was obviously the case that the king had pursued a divorce
which was misguided, but moreover, had surrounded himself with partisans of the divorce such as Cranmer and Cromwell. For insiders, the
failure of counsel was also the failure of the council as an institution within
government. The tangled history of the council in the 1520s and early
1530s need not over-concern us; but it is now accepted that Henry found
the council, a large body of changing membership, an unsatisfactory instrument with which to plot the divorce, not least because some if its members were leaking strategy to the queen's party. Henry came to rely on
advice from a smaller 'kitchen cabinet' of intimates committed to the
divorce. This probably met to suit the king's convenience rather than
at the palace of Westminster: it was secret, informal, and committed
to a single policy; and for all these reasons it broke the tenets of good
counsel. Out of this smaller council there emerged, at the time of the
Pilgrimage, a small, private or 'privy' council whose membership was
tightly drawn to include the major officeholders of household and
administration. Inevitably, this was a mix of nobles, bishops, and career
administrators like Cromwell.[7]

From the vantage-point of the mid-1530s it looked to many as through
the king was under the dominance of a sectarian clique who manipulated him in their own self-interest, for the advancement of a woman of
suspect morals and religion, and the promotion of bishops and religious
practices of doubtful orthodoxy. Counsel had failed. Aske criticized the
nobility for not having done its duty by advising the king against the

---

[7] J. A. Guy, 'The Privy Council: Revolution and Evolution', in C. Coleman and D. Starkey (eds.),
Revolution Reassessed: Revisions in the History of Tudor Government and Administration (1986), with his
more recent reflections in 'Thomas Wolsey, Thomas Cromwell and the Reform of Henrician
Government', in D. MacCulloch (ed.), *The Reign of Henry VIII: Politics, Policy and Piety* (1995), 48–53.

dissolution.[8] Parliament was no safeguard against this clique: it too had been packed and suborned by Cromwell.[9] Criticism of the king's choice of counsellors appears in all the petitions from the autumn of 1536. The Lincolnshire rebels submitted that 'we your true subjects think that your grace takes of your counsel and being about you such persons as be of low birth and small reputation . . .'.[10] The king was infuriated by this criticism:

Concerning choosing of councillors, I have never read, heard, nor known that princes' councillors and prelates should be appointed by rude and ignorant common people; nor that they were persons meet, or of ability, to discern and choose meet and sufficient councillors for a prince. How presumptuous then are ye . . . to find fault with your prince, for electing of his councillors and prelates; and to take upon you, contrary to God's law and man's law, to rule your prince . . .[11]

A similar comment on the choice of councillors was contained in the articles carried south by Ellerker and Bowes at the end of October.[12] This drew a more considered answer, where the king compared the membership of the council at his accession with the privy council of the moment, placing a stress on the noble and episcopal members and silently omitting the figures to whom the Pilgrims were most hostile, Cromwell, Lord Chancellor Audeley, and Archbishop Cranmer: 'How how far be ye abused to reckon that there were more noblemen in our privy council then than now?'[13] His bluster did not convince. An unknown writer, but one versed in the political realities of the mid-1530s, submitted a tract to the Pilgrim's conference at Pontefract arguing that if the king would not admit 'virtuous men that loveth the commonwealth' to his counsel, then there was a need for a council for the commonwealth (like the parlement of Paris), 'for princes should choose such virtuous men as would regard the commonwealth above their prince's love'. This writer then turned to the precedents for deposing monarchs who refused good

---

[8] 'The manner of the taking of Robert Aske', 335.
[9] See Sir Thomas Tempest's comments cited below, n. 14.
[10] Fletcher and MacCulloch, *Tudor Rebellions*, 131.
[11] Dodds, *Pilgrimage*, I, 136.   [12] Below, p. 301.
[13] Dodds, *Pilgrimage*, I, 276; discussed in Guy, 'Privy Council: Revolution or Evolution', 77–8 and 'King's Council and Political Participation', 143–5.

counsel. But the figure this writer really had in his sights was Cromwell, and the pernicious influence he exercised over the king.

The false flatterer [Cromwell] says he will make the king the richest prince in Christendom, but a man can have no more of us that we have, which in manner he had already, and yet not satisfied. I think he goes about to make him the poorest prince in Christendom, for when by such pillage he has lost the hearts of his baronage and poor commons, the riches of the realm are spent and his [coronation] oath and faith broken, who will then love or trust him?

This writer argued that Cromwell and his servants believed themselves to be above the law: at the very least they should be exiled. Parliament should seize their goods, which could be profitably spent for the commonwealth.[14]

The demand that the king should choose new councillors was not included in the Pontefract articles: it was perhaps regarded as too inflammatory. The Pilgrims contented themselves by demanding 'condign punishment' for Cromwell, Audeley, and Sir Richard Rich (chancellor of the Court of Augmentations) 'as the subvertors of the good laws of this realm and the maintenance of the false sect of heretics and the first inventors and bringers in of the same'. Cromwell was deliberately kept out of sight during the Pilgrimage. When Percival Creswell visited Lord Darcy in early November, Darcy's household servants asked for news from the court. Had Cromwell and other ill councillors been put from the council? Who were the councillors about the king? Creswell named the duke of Norfolk, the earls of Oxford and Sussex, Sir William Fitzwilliam (lord admiral), Sir William Paulet (the comptroller), and Mr Kingston. Creswell's audience was satisfied: 'God save the king and them all, for as long as such noblemen of true noble blood may reign about the king, all shall be well.'[15]

The tension, as may be seen from these comments, was superficially between the right of *consiliari nati* to participate in politics and exercise a role, almost *ex-officio*, as the king's advisors, and the king's right to choose his councillors from the pool of loyal and capable administrators. But

---

[14] *LP* XI, no. 1244, extracts printed more accessibly in Fletcher and MacCulloch, *Tudor Rebellions*, 134–5. The writer is normally taken to be Sir Thomas Tempest, who had sat for Newcastle upon Tyne in the Reformation Parliament.

[15] *LP* XII (i), no. 1013; Dodds, *Pilgrimage*, I, 290.

the preference for noble councillors was finally a political calculation to strike at non-noble opponents. To look to the nobility as guarantors of the constitution was as much a refuge of the political loser then as now.

The identification of Cromwell, Audeley, and Rich as 'maintainers of the false sort of heretics' brings us to another issue on which the court had become dislocated from the popular opinion of the time. The Lincolnshire petition named six bishops, including Thomas Cranmer, archbishop of Canterbury, whose orthodoxy was suspect.[16] The Lincoln articles sent south from the first Doncaster meeting requested the punishment of subvertors of the laws of God and the realm and specifically named Cranmer, Cromwell, Audeley, and Hugh Latimer, bishop of Worcester. The Pontefract articles, again drawing back from some of the Pilgrims' earlier and wilder demands, merely sought the punishment of heretics, whether bishops or lay persons.

There is something odd about the laity accusing bishops of heresy (although examples may be found in our own times). The middle years of Henry's reign were the moment at which the comfortable unity of the late-medieval church gave way under pressure of a reform movement within the church and the weight of new ideas circulating out of first Lutheran Germany and then the Swiss Reformation. In the 1520s it had been possible to denounce all Luther's works as heretical. In the 1530s there was a tendency to look on the Lutherans as possible allies against the pope and Charles V, a policy which reached its apotheosis in the Cleves marriage. The early 1530s also saw the development of ideas of reform which were largely native and, by Lutheran standards conventional, even old fashioned, but which still appalled English conservatives. Given that this was a period of flux in theological thought, when individual positions could alter with rapidity, it would be wrong to place labels on people even when we have detailed knowledge of their beliefs. In particular, it is impossible to talk of a divide between Catholics and Protestants. The name 'Protestant' had yet to be coined; individuals who had rejected transubstantiation were, in any case, few and far between in England in the 1530s. A threefold distinction may profitably be made

---

[16] Fletcher and MacCulloch, *Tudor Rebellions*, 131. A seventh, Bishop Longland of Lincoln, was blamed as the begetter of the troubles, apparently a reference to a story that Longland had sown the seeds of the divorce in the king's mind during confession. Conrad, 'The Problem of Counsel Reconsidered', 98.

between the conservatives, some of whom supported the divorce and acquiesced in the royal supremacy and dissolution, the reform party or evangelicals, and the extremely small number of Lutherans.

Like the commonwealthmen of the 1540s, it would be a mistake to see the evangelicals, evangelical brethren, or 'gospellers' as a party: on the contrary, they were a loose coalition of individuals drawn together by a desire to advance knowledge and understanding of the English gospels, and who were collectively conscious of their susceptibility to persecution by the conservatives.[17] Their ambition was to 'reconstruct religion out of the scriptural text of the Good News':[18] they therefore emphasized the desirability of every man and woman having access to the vernacular scriptures. From this followed the ideal that every man should achieve a knowledge of the word of God; this, in turn, made the evangelicals value vernacular preaching and education. They also brought to the late-medieval church a scepticism concering its claim to be the sole and necessary mediator between man and God. Some looked to verify the practice of the church in the scriptures and found the evidence for purgatory lacking, whilst the commitment to knowledge led to a devaluation of works, of masses for the dead, of prayers to saints, and pilgrimages. To relics they brought an Erasmian rationality. That is not to claim that every evangelical held to these points in equal measure. Anne Boleyn placed a particular emphasis on education which Cromwell seems not to have shared; but his commitment to the vernacular scriptures cannot be mistaken. Hugh Latimer was particularly scathing about relics and pilgrimage. If the evangelicals had a patron, then whilst she lived it was Anne Boleyn. Had she not fallen in early May 1536, she would doubtless have been included by the Pilgrims amongst the heretics, for her patronage of men of heterodox views was well known.[19]

It was easy to denounce those bishops who, by reputation at least, were unsound in religion. What would have been dangerous would have

---

[17] For the Evangelicals, see MacCulloch, 'Henry VIII and the Reform of the Church', in id. (ed.), *The Reign of Henry VIII*, 169–72, although I offer a broader account of their concerns than he, largely based on what they did (or tried to do) in the later 1530s.

[18] Ibid. 169.

[19] This has been a matter of dispute between Professor Ives and Dr Bernard: G. W. Bernard, 'Anne Boleyn's Religion', *HJ* 36 (1993); E. W. Ives, 'Anne Boleyn and the Early Reformation in England: The Contemporary Evidence', *HJ* 37 (1994). On this occasion I follow Professor Ives.

been direct criticism of the king himself. There is an element of mystery about Henry's beliefs: a recent article on Henry and the reform of the church actually says very little about the king's own preferences.[20] We have been told that he lacked application to work and was easily led: we have also been offered a view of him as a directive chief executive, very much in touch with the direction of policy. He was a competent amateur theologian, able to offer a critique of the formularies of faith drawn up by his bishops or to hold his own in a dispute with Latimer over the existence of purgatory; but he was also capable of trying to rewrite the Ten Commandments. As a young man he was conservative and deeply hostile to Luther. Galvanized by the divorce, he became more sympathetic to Luther's position and during the 1530s surrounded himself with men of a reformed persuasion, such as Cranmer and Cromwell; he courted and married a woman who developed pronounced evangelical tastes. Towards the end of his life he lost his faith in purgatory but never in transubstantiation. He became violently hostile to monks. We can say that his beliefs were eclectic, perhaps inconsistent. But two elements were desperately important to him. Having established the royal supremacy, he was passionately jealous of its authority. And he cared for unity and feared strife.

The beauty of the royal supremacy was that it was not only the tool of control but also of change. The powers of visitation vested in the Supreme Head were first used against the universities and the monasteries in 1535. In 1536 the authority of the supremacy was used to issue the Ten Articles (drawn up by a Henry and a committee of bishops and rubber-stamped by convocation); later in the year Thomas Cromwell, as vice-gerent, issued a set of injunctions to the parochial clergy. These were reforming statements—exactly how much so will be discussed later— which it is impossible to argue did not reflect the king's opinions in mid-1536. At this moment he was prepared to espouse the loose nexus of beliefs called evangelical, even if their implementation was in the name of a more radical and less cautious deputy or 'vice-gerent', Cromwell. Indeed, despite the many inconsistencies in the religious policies of the

[20] MacCulloch, 'Henry VIII and the Reform of the Church'. G. W. Bernard, 'The Making of Religious Policy, 1533–1546: Henry VIII and the Search for the Middleway', *HJ* 41 (1998) makes a clear case for Henry's commitment to reform.

last decade of his life, the king ought to be claimed as a cautious but persistent reformer of the church along Catholic lines.[21]

The Pilgrims' belief that there was something rotten at the heart of government was quite right; but that something was the king as much as his ministers. Unwilling to speak of deposition, they complained instead of the king's choice of councillors, ministers, and bishops rather than the king himself. When in 1967 Scarisbrick wrote that the Pilgrimage was an 'authentic indictment of all that Henry most obviously stood for',[22] he not only launched a thousand exam questions but accurately summarized the range of criticism contained within the Pontefract articles. However, as I argued in Chapter 1, we cannot read the articles compiled at Pontefract as evidence of why the Pilgrimage of Grace broke out. They tell us a great deal about the strains within society, the deep alienation of political society from the Crown's policies over the previous decade. These were all preconditions, as it were, but they reveal virtually nothing about the *precipitants* or triggers which set people mustering at a particular moment in late 1536. In order to understand why bitterness over policy was converted into insurrection, we have to look at the events of the middle months of 1536, and then to focus on the working out of fears and rumours in a single town.

I

Before turning to the events of 1536, we might quickly consider another question: why there was so little opposition to the divorce, the schism from Rome, and the erection of the royal supremacy earlier in the 1530s? There are hints—no more—of parliamentary opposition to Henry, but little can be discovered about them.[23] The Church produced a handful of martyrs—More, Fisher, the Carmelite Friars—whilst a few clergy, like Christopher Mitchell, made pyrrhic gestures. Others, amongst whom we

---

[21] In this I agree with the assessment of Bernard, 'Henry VIII and the Search for the middleway'.

[22] Scarisbrick, *Henry VIII*, 341

[23] G. R. Elton, 'Thomas More and the Opposition to Henry VIII', in id., *Studies*, II; R. W. Hoyle, 'The Origins of the Dissolution of the Monasteries', *HJ* 38 (1995), 300–1.

may count the vicar of Londesborough in Yorkshire, William Thwaites, dragged their feet over preaching the royal supremacy or took refuge in the make-believe world of prophecy, predicting that all would come right and terrible misfortunes would befall the king. Thwaites—if the allegations of which he was acquitted were true—would apparently voice his disgruntlement to anyone who would listen, to the point where he became an embarrassment to his neighbours. It was probably they who, at the end of 1535, drew him to the attention of the local JPs, including John Aske, Robert Aske's elder brother. John Dobson, vicar of Muston (near Filey), stopped praying for the king at the time of the Pilgrimage and only preached on the royal supremacy at the insistence of his parishioners in November 1537. He too quoted prophecies, but where Thwaites was apparently acquitted, Dobson was executed for treason.[24]

The nobility, outwardly at least, remained solidly behind Henry. A few peers were prepared to countenance military action against Henry and Cromwell and sought the aid of Charles V. These conversations, which I am inclined to regard as so much hot air from elderly, embittered men, are worth exploring here, for the two advocates of rebellion, the lords Hussey and Darcy, played a prominent role in the 1536 revolts and their discussions must be considered in any assessment of their motivation.

The imperial ambassador, Chapuys, reported an interview which he had had with Lord Hussey in September 1534.[25] Hussey, like Darcy, was another survivor of Henry VII's circle. Born in the mid-1460s, he served Henry VII as comptroller of the household and Henry VIII as chief butler from 1521. He was ennobled in 1529. In 1533 he was appointed chamberlain of Mary's household. His wife served Mary as one of her attendants, but was deprived of her office in late 1534 for persisting in calling her 'Princess' Mary: in June 1536 she was imprisoned for the same offence. There is little doubt that both Husseys were partisans on Mary's behalf. Again, there can be no question but that Hussey's instincts in religion were conservative: he was amongst those appalled by Bigod's

[24] Thwaites, *LP* IX, no. 791, VIII, no. 457 (misdated by a year). He survived until at least 1549. J. S. Purvis, 'Tudor Crockford' (MS *penes* Borthwick Institute, York), *sub nomine*. For Dobson, see A. G. Dickens, 'Sedition and Conspiracy in Yorkshire During the Later Years of Henry VIII', in his *Reformation Studies*, 1–2.

[25] For what follows, *CSPSp, 1534–5*, no. 257 (= *LP* VII, no. 1206).

chaplain, and once offered the opinion that the nobility were unable to curb heresy without the aid of the commons.[26]

In his discussion with Chapuys, Hussey was concerned that Charles V should intervene in English politics to restore the true faith and to protect Princess Mary: he expressed disappointment that Charles had not already done so. Chapuys was non-committal, seeing a danger in a foreign power intervening in England, but Hussey thought that people would welcome it. Indeed, even a declaration of war on Henry would encourage the English to revolt.

Pressed on the military details of such an intervention, Hussey referred Chapuys to Darcy. Chapuys sent his secretary to confer with Darcy who, it seems, was only too happy to talk of treason. He was, he said, the king's most loyal subject 'in such matters of duty as were not against conscience and honour: but the present affair was such an offence against God and reason that he neither would nor could be called a right honourable gentleman or a good Christian were he to consent to such things against the faith'.

Darcy thought that he could draw on sixteen earls and other gentlemen in the North who shared his opinions, although he had never canvassed them: he had not even shared his views with his sons, Sir George and Sir Arthur.[27] He hoped to secure the king's licence to travel north. There were reports circulating that at the next session of parliament a bill to introduce Lutheranism into England would be presented. Darcy proposed to use the clergy to preach against it and whip the people into resistance. He added that he would like to see some of the nobles who countenanced Lutheranism arrested, specifically mentioning the earl of Northumberland. Then Darcy turned to outlining his military plans. He looked to an invasion by Scotland whilst Henry was distracted elsewhere; he wanted Charles to send a force into the Thames estuary and another into the North. Darcy himself thought that he could put 8,000 men into the field. He also seems to have expected support from the earl of Derby and Lord Dacre, and on this or another occasion he thought

---

[26] Dodds, *Pilgrimage*, I, 21–6; *LP* XII (i), no. 576. For Hussey, see also James, 'Obedience and Dissent', 240–4.

[27] The printed text has '600 earls, knights and other gentlemen', but Dr Bernard tells me that the MS in Vienna reads 16 (*seize*).

he might be assisted by the duke of Norfolk.[28] Darcy had clearly pondered his strategy.

When, at the beginning of 1535, Chapuys had had no news from Darcy for several months (but some gifts), he sent a servant to enquire after him.[29] Darcy, he found, was constant to the cause. Chapuys now believed that Darcy was in alliance with Lord Sandys, the chamberlain of the household and a seasoned soldier:[30] he now suggested that it might be possible to raise 100,000 men. (One wonders whether Darcy exaggerated for effect, or whether there was an element of the fantasist in him.) In March Darcy was still hoping for imperial aid: finally, at the beginning of May, he sent word that he was travelling northwards and that he would set about 'the business'.[31] At this juncture Chapuys seems to have believed that a rebellion was imminent. Later in the month someone out of Darcy's circle brought word to Chapuys that he intended to go abroad to seek an audience with Charles V, at which he might persuade him to come to their aid, or at least return with the knowledge that they should not wait on him. Chapuys cautioned against this because of the jeopardy in which it might place Darcy and his allies. In July there was one last contact between Chapuys and Darcy when, again, he was urging Charles V to send troops and assistance.[32]

In the year before the Pilgrimage there were no further contacts between Darcy and Chapuys. Certainly, when the Pilgrimage broke out Chapuys was not forewarned, nor did he read the Pilgrimage as being Darcy's work.[33] Having contemplated rebellion in 1534, why did he not launch a disturbance? There are two broad answers. For one, in Darcy we see a profoundly troubled man, deeply loyal to his king, but disturbed in his conscience that he was a party to the king's heretical reforms, and that this complicity meant that he could not call himself a good Christian. In the end loyalty won through. Secondly, what Darcy particularly feared was the 'introduction of Lutheranism' in the November 1534 session of parliament. 'Lutheranism', like Lollardy, was merely a pejorative phrase

---

[28] *CSPSp, 1536–8*, 269. Aske said that Darcy had claimed in his hearing that 15 lords had promised to suppress heresy. *LP* XII (i), no. 852.

[29] *LP* VIII, nos. 1, 121.   [30] Lord Sandys was another elderly peer, b. *c.*1470, d. 1540.

[31] *CSPSp, 1534–5*, no. 139 (= *LP* VIII, no. 355); *LP* VIII, no. 666.

[32] *LP* VIII, nos 750, 1018.   [33] See the letter of 7 Oct. 1536, *CSPSp, 1536–8*, 269.

to be used of ones' opponents. It may be suggested that Darcy had wind of plans for a general dissolution of the monasteries which, I have suggested elsewhere, was proposed and lost in the autumn session of 1534.[34] This justifies the phrase 'Lutheran', for the confiscation of monastic lands had been a common feature of the German reformations. As this eventuality never came to pass, Darcy's enthusiasm for rebellion might well have cooled, and he may have been further discouraged by the growing realization that Charles V would not offer any assistance. The practical soldier in Darcy knew that without the intervention of a foreign power Henry could not be defeated. The rebellion, when it came, was not of Darcy's inspiration, nor was it the rebellion he envisaged in his conversations, but a movement of the commons, and his instinct was to offer it not leadership but opposition. Again, the cleavage in his personality, between king and faith, was resolved in favour of his monarch.

II

The Reformation Parliament, which had served Henry so well in legislating for the break with Rome, assembled for what was to be its final sitting on 4 February 1536. For our purposes, the most significant legislation to arise out of this session was the passage of the bill for the dissolution of the smaller monasteries.[35] A confiscation was certainly talked about in 1529: a legislative dissolution was probably sought and refused in 1534. The motivation behind attempts to secure a dissolution were various and sectional. All could agree that the monasteries needed a greater discipline, a closer adherence to their founders' intentions, and a greater spirituality. The royal supremacy was immediately concerned to reduce monks' familiarity with the world and to deny them the comforts which made the monastic life tolerable. A younger, humanist-influenced generation—amongst which Henry VIII may perhaps be counted—certainly doubted the utility of the monastic vocation and saw the resources devoted to its support as misapplied. As modernizers, they believed that the monks'

---

34 Hoyle, 'Origins of the Dissolution', 292–4.   35 For what follows, see ibid.

rents and estates could serve as an endowment for more relevant, contemporary ways of bringing the word of God to the laity—by preaching—and for education and works of charity. Both Cardinal Wolsey and Bishop Fisher (a man of impeccable reputation amongst conservatives in the 1530s) had dissolved failing monastic houses in order to endow their colleges in Oxford and Cambridge. Wolsey had sought powers by papal bull to convert monastic houses into bishoprics, much as was done with a few selected abbeys at the beginning of the 1540s. Thomas Starkey, writing to the king in the summer before the Pilgrimage, thought that if the founders and donors to monasteries could see what they had become, they would 'cry out with one voice . . . to the princes of the world, "alter these foundations which we of long time did institute, and turn them to some better use and commodity"'. Starkey recommended that they should be converted in to schools 'for the education of youth in virtue and religion'. A dissolution could also serve less altruistic ends: a transfer of monastic wealth to the Crown would make the king astonishingly rich by the standards of his predecessors.[36]

All monastic houses were visited by two sets of royal commissioners in 1535 or early 1536. The first, whose work was authorized by commissions issued on 30 January 1535, was to discover the wealth of monastic houses—and bishoprics and individual benefices—so that the extremely onerous and continuous taxation of the church granted by the statute of First Fruits and Tenths might be levied. This was the subject of considerable clerical resentment. When William Thwaites heard of the grant of lay taxation by the parliament of 1534, he expressed himself glad that 'the temporal men [should] be pilled and polled as well as the spiritual men'.[37] The returns of these commissions were gathered together in the great compilation called the *Valor Ecclesiasticus*: they were put to use in 1536 in selecting monastic houses for dissolution. The second commission was a visitation of the monasteries which, although authorized on 21 January, did not begin its work until the middle of the year and was not completed until late February 1536.

[36] S. J. Herrtage (ed.), 'England in the Reign of King Henry the Eighth', part I, *Early English Text Soc.*, extra ser., 22 (1878), pp. lv–lvi (printing extracts from *LP* XI, no. 156).

[37] *LP* XI, no. 791.

This visitation had several aims. It was, obviously enough, intended to confront houses with the reality of the royal supremacy by having the vice-gerents' agents visit and enforce his authority. The commissioners were supplied with an elaborate set of articles on which to quiz the monks, in some instances individually. They investigated the internal conduct of the house in minute and oppressive detail, including questions about the monks' habits, their shaving, and the length of their hair.[38] They were charged with collecting a range of information about each house, in-cluding the name of its founder, the value of its lands, and the character of any shrines or relics which it possessed. As the visitors were viewing two or more houses a day, it must have been impossible for them to press the full range of questions included in the articles. It is hardly surprising that their record, or *comperta*, suggests that they were primarily interested in moral offences, income, and the shrines or relics. The visitors also interfered in the administration of some houses, deposing abbots and replacing them with more tractable placemen. Some at least of the commissioners were corrupt, accepting money for bribes, and this was complained about in the Pontefract articles.[39] Overall, this was not a careful, studied investigation of either the state of monasticism or of individual houses: it was undertaken largely for effect and to gather damaging evidence of the state of monasticism.

One feature has always stood out from the surviving *comperta*: their reporting of apparently high levels of homosexuality, heterosexual contacts by monks, and other sexual activities.[40] Whilst we can now treat this material without too great a prurience, it has generally been regarded as utterly scandalous. In fact, on the evidence of the *Compendium Compertorum*, sexual contacts between monks and men or boys seem to have been relatively rare. The offence admitted with greater frequency was masturbation ('self-abuse'). In the northern province only eighteen monks

---

[38] D. Wilkins (ed.), *Concilia Magnae Britanniae et Hiberniae*, 4 vols. (1737), IV, 786–9.

[39] For the implementation of the royal supremacy in Yorkshire, C. Cross, 'Monks, Friars and the Royal Supremacy in Sixteenth-Century Yorkshire', in D. Wood (ed.), *The Church and Sovereignty, c.590–1918*, Studies in Church History, subsidia 9 (1991). MacCulloch and Fletcher, *Tudor Rebellions*, 136 (art. 11). For Norfolk's discovery of Layton and Lee's corrupt practices, Hoyle, 'Thomas Master's Narrative', 78.

[40] Knowles, *Religious Orders in England*, III, ch. 22. The comperta have recently been reanalysed by Dr Bernard in an unpublished paper and by Mr A. Shaw in an University of Warwick MA thesis: I am grateful to both for sharing their conclusions with me.

admitted to sodomy but 145 to acts of self-abuse, either on its own or in combination with other offences. The overwhelming majority of monks admitted no sexual misdemeanours. We might conclude that the *comperta* discovered no more than we might expect to find in closed male societies: some homosexuality, some liaisons between monks, women, and boys, and rather more confessed instances of masturbation. The crucial point is that this information did not come to the notice of the commissioners by accident. It was sought. Admissions of reprehensible sexual activities are never likely to come to light voluntarily, and are most unlikely to be discovered on the sort of flying inspection which the commissioners made. Whilst the *comperta* place a great weight on these failings, the surviving set of visitation articles only seek information about liaisons with women. They do ask whether any monk has had boys or young men 'lying with him', but the subsequent injunctions make it clear that this condemns the practice of monks having personal servants.[41] As the commissioners for the two circuits with surviving *comperta* were clearly enquiring after evidence of both masturbation and homosexual practices, their questions may be regarded as *ultra vires* and part of a determined effort to gather salacious and damning evidence which could be used to smear the whole monastic estate.

The *comperta*, or an abstract derived from them, was presented to the final session of the Reformation Parliament in March 1536. The preamble of the dissolution statute begins by speaking of the 'manifest sin, vicious, carnal and abominable living [which] is daily used and committed among the little and small abbeys', and later speaks of the Supreme Head's knowledge of this, 'as well by the accounts of his late visitations as well by sundry credible information'. Hugh Latimer recalled that 'when their enormities were first read in the parliament house, they were so great and abominable that there was nothing but "down with them"'. The king's own later advice to the Scottish regent, Arran, was to collect evidence of the 'abominations' of the monks as a way to achieve a dissolution.[42] The king made a reference to the *comperta* in the answer to the Lincolnshire petition written in October: justifying the selective

[41] Wilkins (ed.), *Concilia Magnae*, IV, 787 (arts. 20–2), 790.
[42] Hoyle, 'Origins of the Dissolution', 295–6.

dissolution, he wrote that, 'for there be none houses suppressed where God was well served; but where most vice, mischief and abomination of living was used: and that doth appear by their own confession, subscribed with their own hands, in the time of the visitations'.[43]

Parliament was persuaded by this unpalatable evidence to grant a dissolution of the smaller houses, arbitrarily defined as those with less than £200 in income. The monks of these houses were to be offered the option of transferring to other larger houses or being dispensed to hold benefices: only the heads of houses were to be offered pensions.

The rhetoric of the statute and all the public documents arising out of the dissolution process stressed that the dissolution was a reform. The statute admitted that standards were adequate in the larger houses: the dissolution of the smaller monasteries was not an attack on the monastic vocation as a whole, merely a tidying of its more scandalous corners. Whilst discipline might be better-enforced in the larger houses, reinforced with brethren transferred from the smaller, soon to be defunct, houses, it was a mighty odd reform when the major beneficiary was not the monks but the king, who gained the lands of the dissolved houses. The statute placed no limitation on the uses which the king could make of this land: the estates were merely committed 'unto the king's majesty and to his heirs and assigns forever, to do and use therewith his and their own wills, to the pleasure of Almighty God and to the honour and profit of his realm'.[44] Or, more ominously, as the commissions to dissolve a house began, 'forasmuch as we understand that [the house] is at this part in such state as the same is neither used to the honour of God nor to the benefit of the commonwealth, we late you wit [let you know] that therefore being minded to take the same into our own hands for a better purpose . . .'.[45] Even before the parliament ended, Cromwell was receiving solicitations seeking either the outright grant or the lease of the lands of houses destined to fall under the new legislation.[46]

Parliament was dissolved in 14 April. By the beginning of the month the personnel of the Court of Augmentations was being selected: the

[43] Dodds, *Pilgrimage*, I, 136–7.   [44] 27 Henry VIII c. 28 (*Statutes of the Realm*, III, 575–8).

[45] J. W. Clay (ed.), 'Yorkshire Monasteries Suppression Papers', *YASRS* 48 (1912), 22.

[46] *LP* X, nos. 335, 531, 552, 563, 567, 607, 613, 633, 643, and cf. no. 572, in which Sir Francis Bryan writes of suitors approaching him.

court formally came into being on 24 April.[47] The same day commissions to dissolve houses were issued. That something was wrong, horribly wrong, was apparent when writs were issued for a new parliament on 27 April and from the arrest of Anne Boleyn and members of her circle on 2 May. The queen was executed on 19 May: her alleged paramours followed a few days later. Why parliament should have been recalled within a fortnight of its dismissal has never satisfactorily been resolved. The obvious answer is that it was needed to unscramble the Boleyn succession and vest the inheritance of the Crown in the heirs of Henry VIII and Jane Seymour. In turn, this implies that the decision to depose the queen had been taken by 27 April at the latest. In favour of this argument is the issuing of a commission of oyer and terminer (a judicial commission) on 24 April, but there is little to connect it with the fall of the queen.[48] The new parliament was indeed used to unscramble the Boleyn inheritance, but this is not necessarily why it was called into existence. Some understanding of the queen's fall is vital to an understanding of the Pilgrimage, even though the revolts flowed not from the coup against her, but from the parliament and convocation which met after her death.

There has been much debate about the reasons for Anne's sudden fall. Professor Ives has seen the queen as the victim of a coup by her enemies, executed on perjured allegations of adultery and incest. Dr Bernard has argued for the truth of at least some of these allegations.[49] Both would agree that the queen's fall was shockingly sudden. On 18 April Henry was still trying to persuade the emperor's ambassador, Chapuys, to show the queen the courtesy and recognition which he customarily refused her.[50] Letters to ambassadors drafted on 25 April gave no hint of impending difficulties. Cromwell did take advice about

[47] W. C. Richardson, *History of the Court of Augmentations, 1536–1554* (1961), 32–3.

[48] It might have been issued as a reserve power to be used in the event of disorder arising from the dissolution. The argument against it being solely issued to be employed to try the queen was that it was empowered to deal with offences committed in Middlesex and Kent only, i.e. at some, but not all, of the king's houses (not Windsor, for instance). E. W. Ives, *Anne Boleyn* (1986), 359.

[49] Ibid., chs. 16–17; G. W. Bernard, 'The Fall of Anne Boleyn', *EHR* 106 (1991); Ives, 'The Fall of Anne Boleyn Reconsidered'; Bernard, 'The Fall of Anne Boleyn: A Rejoinder', both in *EHR* 107 (1992). The account which follows is my own and owes elements to both authorities: but it is heterodox.

[50] Ives, *Anne Boleyn*, 351–2.

a possible divorce at the end of April, but we do not know whether this was on the king's instructions or Cromwell's own initiative.[51]

An understanding of the state of the royal marriage in April probably has to begin with the death of Katherine of Aragon on 7 January. Her death, when aged only 51, could never have been envisaged when the king began his proceedings to secure an annulment of his marriage. For those who never accepted the legality of the annulment the king was now a widower, and he may have started the process of recalculation, running over the history of the last decade. By a cruel chance, Anne miscarried of a male foetus on 27 January, the day of Katherine's burial: Henry was heard to say that this was God once again denying him the son he craved. The more immediate cause of the miscarriage may also have been the shock felt by the queen when she heard on 21 January that Henry had fallen from his horse: he was unconscious for two hours before reviving. The king was now 44. This intimation of mortality may have been more important in its consequences than the miscarriage.[52]

Whatever the strength of the relationship between Anne and Henry, it must have altered with the death of Katherine and this further miscarriage. It may have been a result of his disillusionment with Anne that his attention was caught by Jane Seymour. Whether or not she was coached by the queen's opponents (as Chapuys understood), she operated by the same rule as Anne Boleyn: that she would not offer the king her body until she had a promise of marriage. It is quite possible that the king's marriage, already under stress because of its failure to produce a boy and Henry's conviction that it was cursed, should have been further strained by Anne's anger at the king flirting with a woman who overtly threatened her position. But Anne's fall was also a dimension of infighting within the court over policy. There was a struggle to influence Henry's mind over foreign-policy issues.[53] It is equally possible that we should introduce another factor into the coup against Anne, her dissent from the king and Cromwell's line over the dissolution. The achievement of a partial dissolution split the evangelicals into those who wished to see monastic endowments used to the advantage of the commonwealth and those who saw a dividend to be shared out between the king and his circle.

[51] Ibid. 361.   [52] Ibid. 342–3.   [53] Ibid. 350–3.

Writing for the instruction of Anne's daughter, Queen Elizabeth, in about 1559, Anne's former chaplain, William Latymer, was able to offer an eyewitness account of some of the events of April 1536.[54] Latymer explained how, when Anne heard that the smaller monasteries were to be dissolved, she instructed Hugh Latimer to argue in his next sermon before the king that the houses should not be dissolved but converted to better uses. Anne was not an uncritical supporter of monasticism: Latymer reports how she told a delegation of abbots and priors that they kept 'their gates close from the preachers of God's word, and yourselves sit either idle or scarce well occupied in your cloisters, clean void of knowledge', knowledge being here the correct evangelical familiarity with the scriptures. Anne's agenda was not dissolution but transformation:[55] Latimer 'besought [the king] it might please his grace of goodness to convert the abbeys and priories to places of study and good letters and to the continual relief of the poor'. Anne instructed her other preachers to include in their sermons 'continual and earnest petitions for the stay of the same'. One of these sermons partially survives because its preacher, John Skip, the queen's almoner, was heavily censured for interfering in matters of state.[56] The sermon he gave on 2 April shows how Skip (and we must assume his patron) was angry at the plunder of the clergy, of which the dissolution was a part. Skip's text was 'which of you convicts me of sin'; the sermon was written using a patchwork of Old Testament history, carefully manipulated to carry a contemporary political message. Skip plunged into an account of Solomon who, in his declining years, fell into the company of his many wives and concubines, a deliberate rebuke to the king from the queen's mouthpiece. Then Skip took a swipe at Cromwell and the other councillors who attempted 'the innovation or alteration of any old or ancient customs or ceremonies' in religion, but also 'renovations or alterations in civil matters'. Skip attacked the secularization of church wealth: like Latimer, he urged the need to find money for education and especially the universities. He made

---

[54] For the following section, see M. Dowling (ed.), 'William Latymer's chronickille of Anne Bulleyne', in *Camden Miscellany 31*, Camden, 4th ser., 39 (1990), 57–9.

[55] See here Ives's comments on Matthew Parker's transformation of the college at Stoke by Clare for what Anne perhaps had in mind; *Anne Boleyn*, 330.

[56] For Skip's sermon, see the full analysis by Ives, 'Anne Boleyn and the Early Reformation in England', 395–400, which I follow here; also MacCulloch, *Cranmer*, 154–5.

oblique accusations against Cromwell, that he and others were interested in pursuing the reformation for their own private gain.[57] And he portrayed Anne as being a restraining force on the private plunder of a commonwealth asset. The sermon was not a plea for the monasteries per se, but the expression of a fear that the great possibilities the dissolution offered for reform and improvement would be frittered away in acts of patronage. Starkey's letter to Henry VIII (written after the Anne's fall) has a subtext of similar anxieties.[58]

Latymer tells us more. The abbots and priors, thinking that the queen was on their side, approached her with a supplication only to be denounced in the robust terms mentioned earlier. Some were so impressed by her advocacy of preaching and education that they offered money or advowsons for the support of students at the universities and preachers,

wherein her highness seemed to take great pleasure, determining most liberally and willingly to employ the same upon the sincere preachers of God's word . . . but this her godly enterprise and gracious endeavour . . . (although undertaken to the only glory of God) yet was clean cut off by the too lamentable and untimely death of this virtuous princess . . .[59]

Latymer's memoir is a late source, but one written by someone who was well placed to see these events and appreciate something of the politics. His message is that in April 1536 the queen was pursuing her own policy towards the monasteries, arguing that the dissolution was mistaken and, in effect, encouraging houses to buy their survival by soliciting gifts and contributions towards her pet projects. Perhaps her intention was to persuade the king to grant licences to those houses of whom she approved. Her campaign may also have arisen out of one concrete piece of royal patronage, which is worth exploring here because of its bearing on events later in the year during the Pilgrimage.

[57] Alexander Ales, who was around court at the time of the queen's fall, reported that he had heard that the queen had criticized both Cromwell and Wriothesley of 'under the guise of the gospel advancing their own interests', and of corruption in the sale of benefices. *Calendar of State Papers Foreign, 1558–9*, 526. Ives (*Anne Boleyn*, 375) reads this as a dispute over monastic lands, but the source is not so explicit.

[58] Herrtage (ed.), 'England in the reign of Henry VIII', pp. lv–lvi, lxi (printing extracts from *LP* XI, no. 156); also *LP* XI, no. 73.

[59] 'Latymer's Cronickille', 58–9.

Sir Arthur Darcy, who we encountered earlier, was the younger (but apparently more able) son of Thomas, Lord Darcy. That he could expect little from his father probably explains much of his character; an essentially second-rank individual, notably in Edward's reign when he served as captain of the Tower, he was a wheeler-dealer, a man about whom there was always a whiff of sharp practice. In the mid-1530s he evidently had the king's ear or, at least, was so well thought of by him that the king was willing to do him quite extraordinary favours. In 1532 he grumbled to Cromwell that after fourteen years' service to the king he had received only small rewards. In September 1533 he was made captain of Guernsey, but his main concern seems to have been to trade this position for something more attractive.[60] On 17 January 1536 he exchanged the captaincy with Sir Thomas Vaux, Lord Vaux of Harrowden, for manors in Northamptonshire and Buckinghamshire. Vaux covenanted that these manors were worth £300 per annum. This arrangement was then given additional weight by being enacted as a statute in the last session of the Reformation Parliament, the same session that passed the dissolution statute. (Vaux came to believe that he had been worsted in this deal, and complained to the council that the profits of the captaincy fell short of the 800 marks per annum which Darcy had led him to expect.) Behind this arrangement stood the king. By a deed of 1 January 1536, the best part of a month before he acquired them, Darcy sold the Vaux manors to Henry for £1,000 in cash down and the promise of further lands to be granted to Darcy in the future.[61] By a further deed of 28 March the king honoured this undertaking by granting to Darcy monastic lands in Yorkshire. He was first offered the site of St Leonard's Hospital, York, which he declined in favour of the site and lands of Sawley in Yorkshire, two manors of Holy Trinity, York, and messuages belonging to Coverham Abbey.[62] At the time that the indenture was made these houses

---

[60] *LP* V, no. 1288; VI, no. 1195 (17).

[61] 27 Henry VIII c. 29 (*Statutes of the Realm*, III, 578–9): PRO, STAC2/26/20. The strange story of the grant of Sawley has previously been explored by Smith, *Land and Politics*, 228–9, and Bush, *Pilgrimage of Grace*, 220–1.

[62] The deed is recited in the confirmatory statute, 27 Henry VIII c. 54 (*Statutes of the Realm*, III, 624–5). Darcy claimed not to know Sawley's worth at its grant, but whilst willing to present his rentals for inspection, he was circumspect about offering any value. *LP* XIII (i), no. 59 (printed in Clay, 'Yorkshire Monasteries Suppression Papers', 51–2).

still stood: technically there was no legal mechanism to dissolve them until
the assent was given to the statute at the close of the session a fortnight
later. The gift was therefore highly irregular, the more so because Sawley
should not have been dissolved under the 1536 statute. Whilst entered
in the *Valor Ecclesiasticus* at a little under £150,[63] it was probably worth
more than £500 per annum. Whether the king knew this may be doubted:
the appearance is that he made a gift to Darcy of lands worth, say, £200.[64]

This gift was made in anticipation of a statute whilst the Reformation
Parliament was still sitting; it was also based on a mistaken estimate of
Sawley's worth. Sawley itself was not dissolved until 13 May, although
the commissioners were instructed to take the surrender of Sawley as
quickly as possible.[65] Whilst this is all remarkable enough, Darcy proceeded to have his indenture confirmed by a further statute which must
have had the effect of making these arrangements a matter of semi-
public knowledge. In the medium term, the irregularity of the grant to
Darcy may well explain the defence of the house during the Pilgrimage
and the hostility with which Sir Arthur was greeted when he came to
claim his property in the spring of 1537. But we may speculate that the
discovery of this grant was one of the factors which prompted Skip's sermon and its declaration of the queen's dissatisfaction with the secularization of church property.

The preaching campaign which the queen organized must have
marked the beginning of hostilities between Anne and Cromwell. If the
debate over the use of monastic property still raged throughout April,
then it may explain why parliament was suddenly recalled later in the
month: to enact a restraint on the king's disposal of his lands. This is
to make the hypothesis that by the third week of April the king had
been persuaded that he should accept some statutory limitation on or
clarification of his freedom of disposal.

The moves against the queen at the very end of the month may have
come from many directions—Henry's increasing dissatisfaction with the

[63] After deductions: we do not know its real value because of the loss of the full *Valor* for the
Diocese of York. *Valor Ecclesiasticus*, V, 144.

[64] The doubts over the conveyance were settled by the issue of letters patent in 1538: *LP* XIII (i),
no. 1115 (13).

[65] Jack, 'Dissolution Dates', 162, 197.

queen's failure to bear him an heir, the seductions of Jane Seymour—but the crucial impetus may have come from the falling out of Anne and Cromwell over the monastic lands, and Cromwell's determination to preserve the king's freedom of action. Having lost over the recalling of parliament, the queen was then destroyed by Henry's anxieties over his own death and paranoia over the queen's sexual betrayal.[66] On Sunday, 30 April, Anne, perhaps feeling the pressure of sharing a court with a woman manoeuvring to supplant her in her husband's affections, had a highly public row with the king's long-standing friend Henry Norris, the groom of the stool. Anne demanded to know why Norris, a widower, had deferred his marriage to Margaret Shelton. Was this because Norris wanted to be free to claim Anne for himself in the event of the king's death? 'You look for dead men's shoes: for if ought came to the king but good you would look to have me.' When calm was restored, Norris went to the queen's almoner to swear that 'the queen was a good woman', that is, that she and Norris had not engaged in sexual relations, that they were not lovers. As word of this argument spread, there was a further public altercation between Henry and Anne. It may have been the king's jealousy at the thought of Anne and Norris being lovers which stimulated his anger: it may equally have been the *faux pas* of openly discussing what would happen after the king's death, especially when the question was topical after the king's fall from his horse earlier in the year. By the end of the day there was a full-scale crisis, the council was in session late into the evening, and the court's projected progress to Calais, fixed to depart on the following Tuesday, was abruptly cancelled.

It was perhaps this suggestion of immorality in the queen's privy chamber which allowed Cromwell his opening. He arrested for questioning one of the queen's lowlier servants, a musician called Mark Smeaton. We may imagine that the initial point on which evidence was sought was whether Anne and Norris had engaged in improper relations. Smeaton, possibly after torture, admitted that he, Norris, and the queen's brother, Viscount Rochford, had all been the queen's lovers since her marriage to the king. Whilst Smeaton was being examined, probably at Cromwell's house at Stepney, relations between the king and Norris

---

[66] For what follows, see the more detailed narrative in Ives, *Anne Boleyn*, 364–6.

appear to have been cordial at the May Day festivities at Greenwich. The two travelled together back to Whitehall together, when the king took the opportunity to question Norris about his relations with the queen. Norris denied any wrongdoing, and this may have satisfied the king. But Henry was probably told of Smeaton's revelations late the same evening after he returned to Whitehall; he chose to believe these rather than Norris's denials, and Norris was sent to the Tower early on the Tuesday morning. The queen herself was questioned later that morning about Smeaton's allegations and was herself sent to the Tower. Her brother, Rochford, followed. But on Wednesday Sir Edward Baynton admitted that neither the queen, Rochford, or Norris had made any admissions to confirm Smeaton's stories and this probably always remained the case, even after the queen underwent a breakdown in the Tower as she awaited her fate. Certainly we know of no very convincing evidence offered at the queen's trial: all the victims protested their innocence at their executions.[67]

The fall of Anne Boleyn, it may be suggested, came most immediately from the king's reaction to her row with Norris and proximately from the dispute over the use of monastic lands: Cromwell (and perhaps the king too) could see all their painfully secured gains being tied up in annuities for preachers and endowments for undergraduates, a noble aim and one which it was difficult to resist. The usefulness of the allegations of promiscuity was that they gave a court something on which to convict and Cromwell a story to circulate justifying the coup against Anne. The identity of the victims after Norris and Rochford was unimportant. They were bystanders hit by wayward bullets.

The annulment of the Boleyn marriage on 17 May and Anne's execution on 19 May left the king free to marry Jane Seymour, which he did on 30 May. But the events of that month had also left him with two greater problems: what to do with the parliament called for 8 June and the Canterbury convocation which would meet concurrently, and how to show that the execution of the queen did not mean that he was turning his face from either the dissolution or the moderate and cautious reform of religion. One signal was the appointment of Hugh Latimer

---

[67] This is to say that I pay little heed to the 'French poem' on which Bernard places a great deal of weight. One could hardly convict the queen on grounds of the king's paranoia and her altercation with Norris. The French poem outlines a plausible but perjured case against her.

to preach at the opening of convocation: he lampooned and mocked previous convocations in a good knock-about-fashion. The new political realities were made even plainer by the admittance of Cromwell or his representative to sit amongst the bishops in convocation.[68] Then, in mid-June, Mary was crushed and forced to acknowledge her illegitimacy and so the illegality of her parent's marriage.

When both parliament and convocation gathered, the king had no business prepared for them. The revision of the succession act to vest the inheritance of the throne in Henry's heirs by Jane and bastardize Elizabeth was announced in the speaker's opening address, but the bill was only presented to the Lords on the thirteenth day of the session, 30 June. Parliament could be trusted to occupy itself with private legislation and bills left over from previous sessions, but the lower house of convocation avoided idleness by drawing up a list of sixty-seven 'mala dogmata' which were erroneously preached.[69] These varied from complaints of scepticism of a sort found at all periods (that holy water was of no greater efficacy than river water) and superstition (that holy water was a good medicine for horses) to erroneous beliefs which were more Lutheran in hue: that saints did not intercede with God (arts. 39, 41), that there was no purgatory (arts. 44–5), that 'it is sufficient enough to believe though a man do no good works at all' (art. 54), and 'that by preaching, the people have been brought in opinion and belief that nothing is to be bettered except it can be proved expressly by scripture' (art. 56). After these were presented to the upper house of convocation on 23 June, the lower house was found some work to do confirming the annulment of the Boleyn marriage; it was then prorogued and only called back on 11 July to be confronted with the statement of faith known as the Ten Articles which we might see as an answer to their complaints about the circulation of 'mala dogmata'.

The Ten Articles were one of a series of formularies designed to establish key tenets of the faith and so avoid controversial or inflammatory preaching (or, as they would have said, 'diversity' in preaching). The truth was, however, that Henry's statements of faith were never quite

---

[68] For convocation, see S. E. Lehmberg, *The Later Parliaments of Henry VIII* (1977), 37–9; MacCulloch, *Cranmer*, 160–6.

[69] Wilkins (ed.), *Concilia Magna*, IV, 804–7.

orthodox but, in trying to bridge between increasingly entrenched positions, always leant towards reform. It may always have been intended that the convocation which met in June should have written such a statement; but it may also be supposed that it was the lower clergy's submission of their list of 'mala dogmata' which persuaded the king that a formulary needed to be drawn up, and this may have been done whilst the lower house was in recess. The relationship of the Ten Articles to the Augsburg confession of 1530 and the articles drawn up in Wittenberg earlier in the spring in abortive negotiations with the German Lutherans need not be discussed here.[70] What is important is that the king claimed to have had a hand in their production: their title said that they were 'articles devised by the king's majesty to establish Christian quietness and unity amongst us'. In November he went so far as to claim them as his own work.[71] Although one recent author has suggested that they were predominantly conservative in tone,[72] the articles contained a series of key ideas and phrases which would instantly be recognized as owing much to Lutheranism. Their silences—what was not considered necessary for salvation—were equally significant. The articles declared that the primary means of achieving salvation was through faith in the passion of Our Lord: works were necessary but secondary to the 'inward spiritual motions'. The articles discussed three sacraments (baptism, the Eucharist, and penance), whilst omitting the other four sacraments of the Catholic church. The worshipping of images was frowned upon; the laity were warned that the only mediator with God was Christ and that grace, remission of sin, and salvation could not be secured from prayers to saints, no matter how laudable such prayers were. In the final article, purgatory was addressed with considerable coolness. It was conceded that praying for the dead was a good act of charity and so a practice fit to be continued. But as to what happened to the souls of the departed, 'the place where they be, the name thereof, and kind of pains there, also be to us uncertain by scripture: therefore this with all other

---

[70] MacCulloch, *Cranmer*, offers the most convenient account. For their text, C. H. Williams (ed.), *English Historical Documents, 1485–1558* (1967), 795–805, or G. Bray (ed.), *Documents of the English Reformation* (1994), 162–75.

[71] *LP* XI, no. 1110.

[72] R. Rex, *Henry VIII and the English Reformation* (1977), 145–8. The Lutherans considered them to be a grave disappointment. MacCulloch, *Cranmer*, 164.

things were remitted to Almighty God, unto whose mercy it is meet and convenient for us to commend them, trusting that God accepteth our prayers for them, referring the rest wholly to God, to whom is known their estate and condition.' Devices to release souls from the torment of purgatory, including indulgences, masses, and prayers before images, were expressly condemned as abuses. The overall effect was to diminish the role of saints as intercessors to God and his Son.

The reaction of the lower house to these articles is unrecorded: probably, given the list of 'mala dogmata' of the previous month, it was one of absolute horror. Perhaps anticipating trouble, the king suspended all preaching until the end of September so as to give time for the distribution of printed copies of the articles.[73] Convocation then agreed that the number of saint's days celebrated should be curtailed: the feast day of saints removed from the calendar would now be 1 October. This was announced by royal letter in August: Bishop Longland circulated news of the decision within his diocese by a letter of 3 September showing proper, but perhaps ultimately fatal promptitude.[74] Convocation was then dissolved on 20 July.

Convocation had consented to two key statements, the Ten Articles and the act made for the abrogation of saints' days, to both of which most of the members of the lower house were probably irreconciled.[75] Both were then circulated in the king's name. This served to make clear how little a role there was for an independent convocation under the royal supremacy, but it was also a practical consideration given that the Canterbury convocation could not legislate for the northern province: the authority of the royal supremacy was therefore needed to enforce the same measures on both provinces. A set of injunctions was then published, probably after convocation had dispersed, in the name of Cromwell as vice-gerent. The 'First Henrician Injunctions' were instructions for the parish clergy.[76] The clergy were to preach against the bishop of Rome

---

[73] Wilkins, *Concilia Magna*, IV, 807–8.

[74] Ibid. IV, 823–4; M. Bowker, *The Henrician Reformation: The Diocese of Lincoln Under John Longland, 1521–1547* (1981), 150.

[75] Convocation may also have discussed the establishment of parish registers, although the order for the clergy to keep them was not circulated until the second Henrician injunctions of September 1538. The rumours of the taxation of baptisms and burials which were widespread in late 1536 may owe much to the circulation of reports of these discussions. *English Historical Documents, 1485–1558*, 813.

[76] For their text see ibid. 805–8, or Bray, *Documents*, 175–8.

and his usurped power. They were to preach both the Ten Articles and the orders abrogating saints' days. They were forbidden to extol images, relics, miracles, and pilgrimages; they were to preach that the laity would serve God better by providing for their families or the poor than by going on pilgrimage. The clergy were to preach the Lord's Prayer, the Creed, and the Ten Commandments in English. If absent from their parishes, they were to make provision for this teaching to be provided. Then, turning to the behaviour of individual clergy, Cromwell forbade them to frequent alehouses: their leisure should be spent reading the scriptures. Clergy with benefices worth £20 or more were to give one-fortieth to the poor of their parish: those with £100 a year were to support scholars at the universities or at school. All clergy were to spend one-fifth of their income on repairs to their church's chancel or parsonage until repaired. There may have been a further instruction that by 1 August 1537 every parish was to possess an English Bible: but as none was then licensed by the bishops, this provision may have been a case of idealism outstripping practicality.[77]

As the members of convocation returned to their dioceses to report what had been done in the name of the clergy, one may imagine their reports being met with dismay. The long list of 'mala dogmata', much more than the partisan 'via media' of the Ten Articles, surely reflected the instinctive position of most of the clergy. The Ten Articles were bad enough; but the instruction to preach on a document which used such Lutheran buzzwords as 'justification', silently omitted sacraments, discouraged prayers to saints, and disparaged purgatory as unscriptural must have spread anxieties that neither the king nor his bishops were wholly orthodox. Cromwell's injunctions also forced on the clergy a layman's perception of how they should conduct themselves: they should teach and catechize (which the majority of clergy were probably ill-equipped to do); they should eschew socializing with their parishioners in favour of self-instruction; and they should devote a significant proportion of their income to the support of the poor and education. The requirement

---

[77] Printed copies of the injunctions survive both with and without the injunction to procure a Bible, suggesting that it may have been added or withdrawn later. MacCulloch, *Cranmer*, 166, n. 95, but cf. A. W. Pollard, G. R. Redgrave *et al.* (eds.), *A Short Title Catalogue of Books Published in England, Scotland and Ireland, 1475–1640*, 2nd edn., 3 vols. (1986–91), I, at 10084.7, 100085.

to provide English bibles was an abrupt *volte-face* when reading the scripture in the vernacular had, even during the previous decade, been accepted as evidence of heretical leanings.

The summer of 1536 was the moment at which the royal supremacy revealed itself as being concerned as much with doctrine as jurisdiction. What must be emphasized is that the momentous developments of June and July were all unplanned. By the middle of April the government felt that it had achieved all it wished for the moment. Parliament could be dissolved, not prorogued. It was the decision to call a new parliament, for reasons which are unclear but which may be explained by Anne's campaign on behalf of the abbeys, which provided an unexpected opportunity to drive policy forwards and to recapture an initiative which looked as though it might have been surrendered with the fall of Anne.

By early autumn the majority of the parochial clergy were probably aware of—even if they had not read—the three documents introducing novel alterations in both doctrine and observance. Taken together, they were a stark reminder of the subordination of church to state and clergy to laity. The Ten Articles in particular asked the clergy to reverse their teachings in favour of positions which they probably found heterodox, if not heretical. Of course, this placed them in an impossible position vis-à-vis their parishioners. There are one or two cases of ugly confrontations between clergy and parishioners, particularly over saints' days.[78] Whilst they were expected to justify these alterations through their preaching, in truth the majority of the parochial clergy probably lacked the intellectual skill to construe fine points of orthodox theology before their parishioners: to explain and justify arbitrary reformulations of belief was certainly beyond them.[79] At least some beneficed clergy were anxious that their lack of learning might not be held against them at a time when they could so easily be replaced by more highly educated ex-monks. Conversely, some ex-monks looked for the deprivation of the less well-equipped parochial clergy.[80] All probably recognized that as the

---

[78] Nicholas Leach, vicar of Belchford (Lincs.), preached against the pope and persuaded his parishioners that they might work on the days abrogated, for which he feared their revenge: *LP* XII (i), no. 70 (xi, p. 38). For other instances of hostility to priests, below pp. 189, 215, 242.

[79] P. Marshall, *The Catholic Priesthood and the English Reformation* (1994), ch. 3.

[80] Morland was quite clear that it was to his advantage if some of the 'unlettered parsons' were deprived, below p. 104.

Ten Articles cast doubt on purgatory and masses for the dead, the traditional support of the unbeneficed priest—the saying of masses on behalf of the departed—might soon dry up. Whilst deprivation might be a danger, some clergy might also have read into Cromwell's injunctions an attack on pluralism: where they held two or more poor parishes, it was not possible to provide an 'honest, well-learned and expert curate'. Hence, it is not hard to suppose that a familiarity with these instructions produced an environment of fear and anxiety amongst the clergy. Conservative in tone they might be, but this is unlikely to be how they were perceived from the parishes. When some of the clergy of Lincolnshire had their representative in the lower house of convocation in their grasp, they lynched him: and so Dr Rayne became the first casualty of the rebellions of 1536.

Ultimately, though, these were sectional grievances. There is little sign that the laity as a whole shared the clergy's anger. Rather, the laity were energized by a rather different set of rumours which were circulating in the late summer and early autumn of 1536. When John Tregonwell, one of Cromwell's trusted circle of civil lawyers, wrote to his master on 5 September, he reported that the articles and injunctions had provoked little complaint in the West Country but that the district was convulsed by rumours that the purpose of Tregonwell's mission was to confiscate crosses, chalices, 'and other idols of the churches', evangelical-speak for the gold and silver contained in images and shrines. Similar rumours circulated at the Michaelmas fair at Swettuns near Sleaford in Lincolnshire.[81] The Lincolnshire JPs were well aware of their currency: at the meeting at Caistor on 3 October Thomas Moigne explicitly denied the reports. They also circulated in Yorkshire.[82] Broadly speaking, three types of rumour can be distinguished, all of them nervous reports of future royal policy. First, there were reports of penal taxation, including the taxation of animals, wheat-bread, and births and deaths; second, claims that church goods were to be confiscated; and third, a belief that parishes were to be amalgamated.

Of the rumours, those concerning taxation were probably the least important. When a number of prisoners from Lincolnshire held in the

[81] *LP* XI, no. 405; XII (i), no. 828 (iii) (p. 324).   [82] See below, pp. 89, 114, 259.

Tower were asked about the rumours circulating, only two mentioned those concerning taxation, the majority plainly having not heard them. Roger Newe had heard a story that all cattle which were not marked were to be seized for the king, whilst Philip Trotter knew of a rumour that the king would have 8*d.* per score of sheep and other cattle rateably. This is a reference to the Tenth and Fifteenth to be collected in late 1537: concern about the weight of this tax was expressed in the Lincolnshire articles.[83] Whilst preparations were being made for a subsidy to be collected in early October, this touched only the tiniest part of the population and was simply not an issue in the turmoil of September. Rumours of impending taxation might have carried more weight in Yorkshire. A description of the rumours circulating there includes the report that the consumption of white bread, geese, and capons would be taxed and that a fee would be paid to the king on every baptism, marriage, and burial. William Maunsell held that bills had circulated claiming that the king would have 6*s.* 8*d.* of every plough, 6*s.* 8*d.* of every baptism, and 4*d.* a beast; another witness talked of the atmosphere of fear created by reports of a tax on christenings and marriages.[84] This same basket of taxes was described by Wilfred Holme of Huntingdon near York in his poem *The Fall of Rebellion*.[85] Lancaster Herald heard the same stories at Pontefract on 21 October 1536:

And I demanded of them why they were in harness and assembled of such sort and they answered me, that it was for the commonwealth, and said, if they did not so, the commonalty and the church should be destroyed. And I demanded of them, how? And they said that no man should bury, nor christen, nor wed, nor have their beasts unmarked, but that the king would have a certain sum of money for every such thing and the beast unmarked to his own house, which had never been seen.[86]

A variant on the theme of taxation was the belief that a recoinage was to be announced: this had been heard by a couple of deponents in Lincolnshire and was one of the rumours reported to be circulating in Yorkshire.[87]

---

[83] Fletcher and MacCulloch, *Tudor Rebellions*, 131.   [84] *LP* XI, nos. 768 (ii), 1047.
[85] Holme, *The fall and evil success of rebellion*, sig. cijr.
[86] *St. P.*, I, 485 (= *LP* XI, no. 826).   [87] *LP* XI, nos. 854 (ii), 968.

The conviction that church goods were to be confiscated, as reported by Tregonwell, was prevalent throughout Lincolnshire and Yorkshire. Philip Trotter gave a particularly full version of the rumour, showing how so many matters might be rolled into one:

he saith that about one month before the insurrection, it was commonly bruited about in all places that all the abbeys of England should be suppressed save only the monastery of Westminster. And further saith that it was likewise bruited that all jewels of the church, that is to say crosses, chalices, and censers, should be taken away from the churches and chalices, crosses, and censers of tin put in their places and two or three parish churches should be put in one.[88]

These reports sometimes circulated with a great deal of concrete detail as to when and where (and by whom) this confiscation was to be done. It was held in Louth that the city of Hull had sold its church plate and other goods to keep them out of the hands of the king.[89] The expectation in Louth that the church goods would be confiscated on Monday, 2 October, was absolute and, as will be shown, well justified by reports from credible witnesses. At Horncastle, William Leach claimed to have seen the confiscation at Louth take place.[90]

The rumour that church goods were to be seized was probably the most widespread of the changes being rumoured. In both counties there were reports that the number of churches was to be reduced. The details varied: sometimes two or three churches would be made into one, sometimes one church would be left every 6 or however many miles apart. Thomas Yoell, the aged and blind parson of Sotherby who lodged in Louth, claimed that he had heard a letter read at the market cross in Louth on the second day of the rising which announced the king's pleasure that 'there should be but one parish church standing 6 miles from another'.[91] They were probably felt particularly sharply in those long, thin Lincolnshire parishes which stretched between the wold and the fen, where the churches might only be a couple of miles apart, though serving large and populous parishes. Much the same stories circulated within Yorkshire. It was rumoured in Richmondshire that Drs Layton and Lee

---

[88] PRO, E36/119 fo. 14r (= *LP* XII (i), no. 70 (x)).

[89] *LP* XI, no. 828 (iii). The records of Hull are so poor at this period that it is impossible to verify the report.

[90] Ibid., no. 967 (v).   [91] Ibid., no. 973.

would return to pull down all dependent chapels and leave only one parish church standing every 10 miles, and would confiscate all silver chalices and substitute tin ones in their place.[92] William Stapleton reported how the 'common Bruit' was that parishes should be merged and church goods confiscated. When Dr Palmes announced his intention to sit at Tadcaster and required the churchwardens to present him with an inventory of their church goods, everyone's worst fears were confirmed.[93]

Of course, contemporaries were not credulous. They had a considerable appetite for news, but only in retrospect could they distinguish an erroneous rumour from a correct report. In a world gone mad, all these rumours were credible. A divorced queen had died; another had been executed. With the sanction of parliament the king had seized the smaller monasteries, amid accusations of gross sexual impropriety which probably did not ring true of those monks (probably his brother) with whom the peasant in the field was acquainted. Smoke could probably be seen rising from the sites of monasteries in the summer of 1536 as the lead was stripped off roofs and made into ingots, the bells melted down, and the unsaleable timber burnt. The king, even after he had disposed of his whore, was still under the thumb of a group of freewheeling heretics who were now insisting that basic elements of faith were erroneous and should be suppressed. There was nothing unreasonable about these rumours of forthcoming taxation, the seizure of church goods, or the merging of churches in the light of what people could see happening. In the case of the amalgamation of churches, we might admit that their fears were probably well grounded given that there exists a draft bill to bring about this very end.[94] Moreover, they knew these reports to be true because people in authority told them. On the few occasions when we can trace their genesis, these reports lead back to the clergy.

Brian Stanes was told, some time in mid-September, by the vicar of Millingsby that the king's officers were coming to seize corn and cattle. He also heard the story about the amalgamation of churches and the seizure of church plate from the vicar.[95] On the Saturday before the

---

[92] LP XII (i), no. 1011. [93] Stapleton, 82.

[94] LP XIV (i), no. 868 (15). This is placed by the editors of LP under 1539 for no very obvious reason: it could be a bill which failed to find support in 1536.

[95] LP XII (i), no. 70 (ix)

rising Simon Maltby, vicar of Farforth, told his parishioners that he had appeared before Dr Rayne and knew for a fact that their church goods were to be confiscated and chalices of tin substituted. Thomas Yoell heard the reports of the ex-monk William Morland.[96] In Yorkshire William Maunsell blamed the Friars of St Roberts in Knaresborough for writing and circulating bills spreading the rumours. Wilfred Holme is quite adamant that the clergy invented the rumours.[97]

The truth about 1536 is that, through the accident of Anne Boleyn's fall and the need to be seen to be still committed to evangelical reform (and the opportunity which an unexpected parliament and convocation provided), Henry and his ministers tried to do too much too fast. The suppression of the smaller monasteries was clearly unsettling: to then proceed to insist on gross alterations in religious practice of a kind which looked heretical was to force the pace too far. By its alienation of the clergy the government ensured that there was a figure in authority to bad-mouth it in every parish, sometimes every village. The atmosphere was volatile. Perhaps with better luck nothing would have happened. In one Lincolnshire town, however, a few rash men wished to demonstrate their pride in the achievements of their fathers by tilting at a chimera. Rather than surrender their church goods to a straw foe, they sallied forth to defend them. What arose from events at Louth is the proper subject of this book.

[96] *LP* XI, nos. 975 (p. 401), 973.

[97] Ibid., no. 1047; Holme, *The fall and evil success of rebellion*, sig. civ, cijr.

4

Lincolnshire

The most striking feature of the Lincolnshire rebellion was the speed
with which it passed from outbreak to collapse.[1] The rebellion began at
Louth on the morning of Monday, 2 October; the following day,
Tuesday, a body of men from Louth and the surrounding countryside
'captured' a group of the leading county gentry who were arranging the
assessment of the subsidy at Caistor. That same day there was a second
rising at Horncastle prompted by news of the first, and here the commons of the town swiftly 'captured' the sheriff, Sir Edward Dymock,
and several other gentry at his house at Scrivelsby just outside the town.
After several days spent raising the countryside and smaller towns the
two forces of rebels marched on Lincoln, which they entered peacefully,
without disturbance or resistance, on Saturday, 7 October (Map 1). By
the following Friday they had dispersed back to their homes and the
gentry who had seen service as their leaders travelled to Stamford to submit to the duke of Suffolk. Whilst the county remained disturbed for
some weeks longer, the rebellion lasted for less than a fortnight. What

---

[1] For previous (and alternative) accounts of the Lincolnshire revolt, see Dodds, *Pilgrimage of Grace*,
I, chs. 5 and 6, James, 'Obedience and Dissent', and Gunn, 'Peers, Commons and Gentry'. A. Ward,
The Lincolnshire Rising, 1536 (1986), offers a detailed narrative of events.

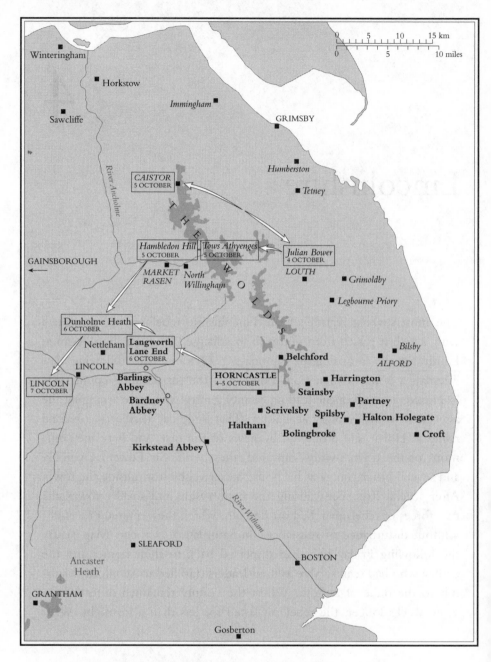

MAP 1. The Lincolnshire rising

Places in *italics* were active in the Louth rising: those in **bold** in the Horncastle rising.

is more, at the time of its disbandment it had achieved none of the objectives declared in its manifestos and articles. Indeed, the requests of the
rebels, sent from Louth on 3 October in the names of the captured gentlemen, had been substantially rejected in a royal letter received at
Lincoln on Tuesday, 10 October. A further petition, only dispatched to
London on Monday, 9 October, remained unanswered at the time that
the rebels returned to their homes. The general pardon which the rebels
sought was never granted, and 100 rebels were tried (and many executed)
in Lincoln in the New Year. The rising was utterly unsuccessful.

The movement simply fizzled out. At its height it attracted perhaps
20,000 men. By numbers alone it posed a fearsome threat to the much
slighter forces gathered by the Crown to defend the road to London.
There is evidence that as late as Friday, 6 October there were plans for
a push south, but having reached the county town the movement failed
to capitalize on its twin advantages of surprise and size and, in the following week, as the insurrectionary fervour was lost, the rank and file
drifted home, encouraged by a herald who addressed the rebel host on
Wednesday, 11 October. Whether by loss of nerve or deliberate policy,
the second week saw a strong hand dissipated by inactivity. As a consequence, there was no confrontation between the royal forces and the
commons. Instead, the earl of Suffolk was able to enter Lincoln and the
smaller towns without opposition. The casualties of the movement were
almost entirely amongst those selected for trial and execution.

The revolt was also extremely localized, and is misnamed as the
'Lincolnshire' revolt, although its exact geographical range is hard to establish with certainty. The rebellion never spread west of Ermine Street or
south and west of the River Witham. If we look at the homes of the
100 men tried for rebellion (which may or may not reflect the composition of the host), we find that the largest number was contributed by
the two towns of Louth and Horncastle. Of the remainder, virtually all
came from Lindsey, and then mostly from the area between the Wolds
and the sea. None came from Kesteven and only a handful from Holland
(Map 2). This, however, is not quite fair. We know, for instance, of a
breakdown of authority in Holland and the seizure of the JPs there by
the commons. It seems likely that if the movement had struck south from
Lincoln, this part of the county would have thrown in its lot with the

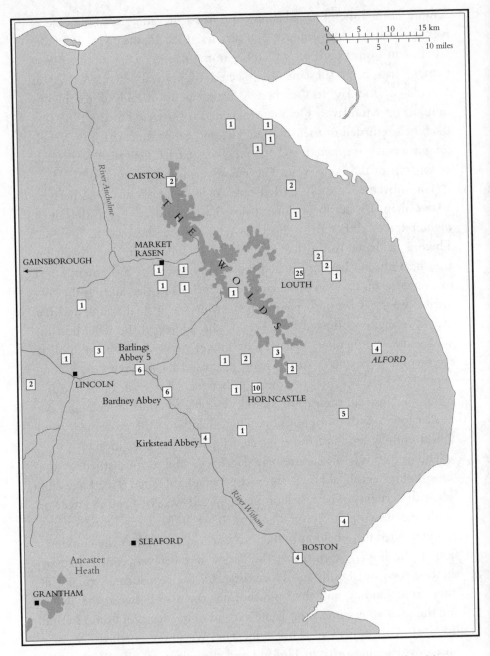

MAP 2. The distribution of persons prosecuted for involvement in the rising

Lindsey insurgents. We know too that the rebels found sympathy in Kesteven—for instance, Lord Hussey found it impossible to raise any large body of men around Sleaford—and elsewhere in the east Midland counties. Here too, if the rebels had advanced beyond Lincoln it seems probable that they could have converted sympathy into hard support.

The rebels at Lincoln had amongst their number, whether willingly or unwillingly, a high proportion of the JPs of Lindsey. Eighteen gentry travelled to Stamford on 12 and 13 October to submit formally to the duke of Suffolk. They included the sheriff, Edward Dymock, and nine other JPs, including two prominent lawyers, Thomas Moigne, recorder of Lincoln, and Thomas Portington. This by no means includes all the gentry who fell into the hands of the rebels or served as captains or petty captains of the rebel host. Other senior figures within county society fled in advance of the rebels—lords Burgh, Clinton, and Hussey—and joined the royal forces marshalling on the borders of the county.

There is undeniably an argument that the gentry were complicit in the rebellion, if not actually its first begetters. Yet, as we have seen, the rebellion abounds in peculiarities, of unfulfilled potential. Previous historians have tended to explain these in terms of conspiracies which either went off at half-cock or which were abandoned when the gentry perceived how slight was the likelihood of success. So Davies can suggest that the vicar of Louth, Thomas Kendall, 'fired the gun too soon' with his 'inflammatory' sermon on Sunday, 1 October, but this is to overlook the fact that the timing of the sermon was determined by the commissary's visitation expected on the Monday morning.[2] And for James, the movement collapsed when its prime movers, the gentry, came to recognize that there were no concessions to be secured from the king.[3] The curious fortunes of the movement certainly suggest that if the gentry brought it to life, then they also conspired at its withering away. An understanding of the gentry's behaviour is essential towards achieving an understanding of the movement, but so too is an understanding of the urban origins of the revolt. It started in Louth and so must we.

[2] Davies, 'Popular Religion and the Pilgrimage of Grace', 90.
[3] James, 'Obedience and Dissent', 266–7.

I

Louth was a second-rank town of some wealth and a greater than local importance. It was a Banbury or a Stratford-upon-Avon: a populous market centre of some prosperity, a local administrative centre equipped with a range of ecclesiastical institutions which probably attracted devotees from outside the town.

Louth is situated 25 miles north-east of Lincoln in a classic position for a market town, between two quite different agricultural regions, the Wolds on the west and the marshland reaching to the sea on the east. The town held two markets each week, a weekly livestock market, and a cycle of annual fairs. A generation after the rebellion one Louth man was a stapler of Calais, which suggests that for some at least the wool trade remained an important source of wealth.[4]

Louth was a manor (and not a borough) of the bishop of Lincoln. It therefore possessed a manorial court, but had no formal institutions of self-government until the ex-chantry lands in the town were granted in fee farm to feoffees for the maintenance of a grammar school in 1551. In 1564 the town also had a grant in fee farm of the manor from the queen.[5] Before then the government of the town was in the hands of the lord's steward, in 1536 John Hennage, who attended to hold the manorial courts.[6] The only elected officer was the reeve who had responsibility for collecting the lord's rents. He was elected at the Michaelmas court by a college of the former reeves and served for a single year.[7] There was also a bailiff, in 1535 William King, but he was appointed by the bishop's patent.[8] Towns in which the government was essentially that of a rural manor are familiar from elsewhere in England, for example,

[4] John Bradley, one of the original assistant governors of the school. *Calendar of Patent Rolls, Edward VI*, IV, 119. The fairs are listed there, pp. 121–2.

[5] Ibid., *Calendar of Patent Rolls, 1563–6*, 106–7.

[6] Hennage has a minor role in the disturbances of 2 October 1536. He was the younger son of a well-connected Lincolnshire gentleman, a lawyer and JP who had sat in the Reformation Parliament as member for Grimsby. *Hist. Parl., 1509–1558*, II, 334–5. He was also active in the dissolution (e.g. *LP* XI, no. 1268), but I cannot discover in what formal capacity, and was quick to take leases of monastic lands, *LP* XIII (i), no. 1520, p. 578. For the Hennage family in general, G. A. J. Hodgett, *Tudor Lincolnshire* (1975), 53–5.

[7] R. W. Goulding, *On the Court Rolls of the Manor of Louth* (?1901), 2.

[8] *Valor Ecclesiasticus*, IV, 6.

Stratford-upon-Avon, and it has been shown how in such places the guilds tended to act as de facto instruments of government as well as holding lands on behalf of the town.[9] Louth had three guilds, whose total income from land was in the region of £77. As elsewhere, we may assume that the property and income of the guilds was under the control of the richer inhabitants of the town.

There certainly were a handful of individuals of some wealth in the town. The lay subsidy of 1524 names 151 taxpayers, of whom forty-five (30%) paid on assessments of 20s. in wages. By contrast there were 625 taxpayers in Lincoln, but only 118 taxpayers in Grimsby, of whom seventy-one (60%) paid on wages. Whilst Grimsby is acknowledged to have been a significant town (and with borough status), it was, on these figures, both smaller and arguably poorer than Louth.[10] The Louth figures suggest a town with a sizeable artisanal population, but they also name nine individuals with more than £20 in goods.[11] Horncastle, to which the rebellion spread, was altogether a smaller town, with only eighty-seven taxpayers in 1524, and its tax payment was less than half of Louth's.[12]

The rector and patron of the living of Louth was the prebendary of Louth in Lincoln Cathedral. The parish was therefore served by a vicar, but one remunerated at a relatively generous rate. In 1526 the vicarage was worth £13 6s. 8d., making its holder the best-salaried (save one) in the deanery of Louth and Ludborough.[13] In the *Valor Ecclesiasticus* the vicarage was assessed at £12, when the average in Lincolnshire as a whole was £8 3s. 0d.[14] It was therefore rich enough to attract graduate clergy. George Thomson, instituted in 1527, had been a fellow of Pembroke Hall, Cambridge, and served as senior proctor of the university in 1511–12. Once appointed to Louth he received a licence to study and was

[9] R. H. Hilton, *The English Peasantry in the Later Middle Ages* (1975), 83, 93–4; also the comments of C. V. Phythian-Adams, 'Urban Decay in Later Medieval England', in P. Abrams and E. A. Wrigley (eds.), *Towns in Societies* (1978), 175–6.

[10] PRO, E179/138/478 (Louth), Phythian-Adams, 'Urban Decay', 171 (Lincoln), 136/311 (Grimsby).

[11] But this is a minimum figure because of the anticipation of the subsidy.

[12] John Sheail, 'The Regional Distribution of Wealth in England as Indicated in the 1524/5 Lay Subsidy Returns', *List and Index Soc.* special ser., 28–9 (1998), II, 196, gives summary details.

[13] H. E. Salter (ed.), 'A Subsidy Collected in the Diocese of Lincoln in 1526', *Oxford Historical Soc.*, 63 (1909), 11–15.

[14] *Valor Ecclesiasticus*, IV, 62; Bowker, *The Henrician Reformation*, 134. The average in the *valor* for Louth Esk deanery is £7 4s. 0d.

presumably an absentee before his resignation during the summer of 1534. His successor was one Thomas Kendall, formerly a fellow of Balliol College, Oxford, and vicar of Earls Colne in Essex. In 1532–3 he had been employed by the bishop of London to rebut the opinions of heretics in Colchester. The indications are that he was a well-trained and well-connected clerical careerist of a conservative hue. He may have seen his transfer to Louth as being more than a promotion within his profession, for there is evidence, itself not quite conclusive, that he was a Louth man whose father had been a member of the Holy Trinity Guild. Indeed, if it is the same man, then the guild lent the young Thomas Kendall money in 1514–15 to assist his education in Oxford.[15]

Kendall was vicar, which made him the senior of the clergy in Louth. The 1526 subsidy records ten other clergy in the town besides the then vicar, of whom eight are described as stipendiary priests.[16] The church was served by the vicar and the 'parish priest'. The latter may have been a curate appointed by the vicar or a stipendiary paid by the churchwardens. The distinction between the two has not always been acknowledged, and it was the parish priest, not the vicar, who accompanied the Louth rebels to Lincoln.[17] At least four priests were employed by the guilds within the town. The point must be made that all these men, with quite different educations, career patterns, and security, were sharing a single church, albeit with several altars, and it is not hard to see that relations between them may not always have been cordial.

Kendall may have been a local man, but he was appointed to Louth and not by Louth, and this distinguishes him from the other priests. Indeed, the speed with which he abandoned his cure after the failure of the rebellion and his attempts to secure a berth in the Coventry Charterhouse illustrates the danger of graduate clergy, here today, gone tomorrow.[18]

---

[15] For vicars of Louth in general, see R. W. Goulding, *The Vicars of the Vicarage of Louth* (Louth, 1906); for Thomson see A. B. Emden, *A Biographical Register of the University of Cambridge to AD 1500* (1963), *sub nomine*; for Kendall, *Biographical Register of the University of Oxford, 1501–1540* (1974), *sub nomine*.

[16] Salter (ed.), '1526 Subsidy', 12.

[17] For the distinction between the two men clearly made, R. W. Dudding (ed.), *The First Churchwarden's Book of Louth, 1500–24* (1941), 13 ('Master Vicar and his parish priest'). The salary of the priest appears not to be included in the churchwarden's accounts. *LP* XI, no. 854 (ii), q. 3; also SP1/110, fo. 145v (not in *LP* XI, no. 970 (14)).

[18] *LP* XI, no. 970 q. 16; XII (i), no. 70 (i) q. 10. (He told the Charterhouse that he came from Oxford and had a benefice near Colchester, which, given that he had been vicar of Earls Colne, was a plausible lie.)

There is a sense in which the vicar was rather an irrelevance within the town. Most aspects of church life were controlled by townsfolk, whether the churchwardens or the wardens of the town's guilds.[19] The two largest guilds were especially important. Both supported priests to sing the masses requested by their founders and donors at altars within the parish church. This, after all, was their primary purpose; but the interesting part of their work was the contribution they made to other aspects of parochial life. The oldest, St Mary's, supported six poor men and women in a bead house and paid 'singing men' to serve in the church. (So did the churchwardens.) Holy Trinity Guild of John Whittingham's foundation supported a similar bead house and also provided a school and schoolmaster for the boys of Louth and the adjoining villages.[20]

Whilst the religious and ceremonial life of the guilds may have offered an alternative focus for the devotions of their members, the spiritual and social life of the majority was focused on the parish church. (Indeed, the lack of craft guilds may have focused the civic pride of the town onto the parish church rather than diffusing it through a variety of institutions.) The previous generation of Louth men and women had given this pride physical form when they raised a spire on the top of the existing tower. At 295 feet, it literally and symbolically looks out over the countryside. What has perhaps not been appreciated is the degree to which it was financed from the ordinary income of the church. R. W. Goulding showed how the total expenditure on the spire from 1501–2 to 1515 was £305 8s. 5d., of which over half (£178) was from the surplus on the churchwardens' ordinary account transferred to the building fund. Of the remainder, only £53 was from gifts specifically made towards the costs of rebuilding, and the balance (£74) was raised as loans from the guilds. It is not certain whether these were ever repaid, but as the guilds took the church goods as pledges, it would be wrong to assume that they were concealed gifts. The topping out of the spire, with the

---

[19] The churchwardens' accounts give the names of 4 churchwardens annually: in about half the instances they provide an occupational designation. Of 27 churchwardens with occupations, 1527–39, there were 6 drapers and 4 mercers, but 4 tailors, 2 each of millers and shoemakers, and single instances of crafts such as barbers, butchers, glovers, sherman, tanners, and weavers. This suggests that quite poor householders might serve as churchwarden. Lincolnshire RO, Louth St James 7/2, *passim*.

[20] See the chantry certificates, C. W. Foster and A. H. Thompson (eds.), 'The Chantry Certificates for Lincoln and Lincolnshire Returned in 1548 Under the Act of Parliament of 1 Edward VI', *Reports and Papers of the Associated Architectural Socs.*, 36 (1922), 277–81.

priests singing the *Te Deum*, the churchwardens ringing the bells, and bread and ale being offered to the parishioners, was clearly a special and proud occasion.[21] If the fabric of the church, and particularly its spire, acted as a focus for civic pride, so too did the church goods. By 1486 the church possessed four silver or gilt crosses, the largest weighing 435 oz. In 1522–3 the parish went so far as to prosecute the then parish priest for damaging (one assumes accidentally) the *third* silver cross. There was, in addition, a whole treasury of ecclesiastical silver, service books, vestments, and altar cloths doubtless acquired over many years.[22] Nor was the work of beautification all in the past. In 1531–2 the church built a new organ which cost £22, of which half was paid by a Louth man who had made a career as a Norfolk clergyman.[23] A rumour that all was to be confiscated produced anxieties which legitimately struck to the very heart of civic and parochial pride.

II

Events in Louth on the first Monday, Tuesday, and Wednesday of October 1536 are documented in copious (although sometimes selective) detail. As we saw earlier, Louth was large enough to support a range of ecclesiastical institutions and a substantial artisan sector. It was the existence of this sector which permitted and shaped the rising which took place there on Monday, 2 October and the following day. The participants in this movement were overwhelmingly drawn from the poorer urban trades—their captain took the name of Captain Cobbler—and the rising arose from the mistrust which they harboured towards their social superiors, the churchwardens and town officers.

We have already seen how rumours of an impending confiscation of church goods, the enforced merger of parishes, and the demolition of

---

[21] R. W. Goulding, *The Building of Louth Spire, 1501–1515* (1908), offers calculations made from the first churchwarden's book.

[22] Inventory of 1486 printed in Dudding (ed.), *First Churchwarden's Book*, 150–7; prosecution of the parish priest, pp. 219–20.

[23] Lincolnshire RO, Louth St James 7/2, fo. 19v.

'surplus' churches were circulating in Lincolnshire in the late summer. In Louth these were made more concrete by a number of specific occurrences. The first was an additional rumour that the men of Hull had sold their church goods at York in advance of their seizure and used the proceeds to pave their streets. This story circulated in Louth, where vicar Kendall heard it; William Morland, the former monk of Louth Park, had it from a shipman of Hull whom he met at Grimsby on the Saturday before the rising.[24] The second was an altercation which had taken place in Louth church between some parishioners and an unknown man who had provoked an argument by saying that the church goods were fitter for the king's use than theirs. The stranger was widely supposed to have been one of Cromwell's servants.[25] The third was the anticipated arrival in Louth on Monday, 2 October of the bishop's commissary, Dr Frankish. Exactly what Frankish's purpose was has never been fully ascertained. He may have been engaged in collecting the clerical tenth;[26] but what was more important were the twin convictions amongst some of the laity that he was going to confiscate church goods, and amongst the clergy that they were to be examined by him and the less qualified of their number deprived of their livings.[27]

Rumours of the impending confiscation appear to have run ahead of Frankish. Morland speaks of them having become rife after two diocesan officials had held a probate court on 23 September.[28] It was reported that Simon Maltby, vicar of Farforth, who attended the commissary's court at Bolingbroke as an observer on the Saturday returned to his parish and told his neighbours that their church goods would be confiscated and tin chalices substituted for silver ones.[29] This, of course, served to

[24] *LP* XII (i), nos 70 (i) q. 1; 481.

[25] Reported by Thomas Mawre, monk of Bardney. *LP* XI, no. 828 (vii).

[26] I favour this explanation. Frankish had a 'book of accounts' which he tried to protect, and some of the clergy were carrying very large sums of money (in the case of the vicars of Belleau and South Somercote, £20 each) which we may take to be their first fruits: both made a show of donating these sums to the commons. For a list of priests who gave money to the commons, *LP* XI, no. 968.

[27] Morland described these fears best: *LP* XII (i), no. 380 (p. 173).

[28] Ibid., no. 380. For the identification of the officials involved, M. Bowker, 'Lincolnshire 1536: Heresy, Schism and Religious Discontent?', in D. Baker (ed.), *Schism, Heresy and Religious Protest*, Studies in Church History, 9 (1972), 198. Morland was pressed on this in his second deposition but was unable to give a specific example of a clergyman spreading such reports. *LP* XII (i), no. 481.

[29] *LP* XI, no. 975 (p. 401).

play on lay fears and to associate the laity with the grievances of the clerical estate. The point must be made that the clergy estate was not at one in opposing the examination of the clergy to weed out the unlettered. When Morland heard that every parson or vicar was to be examined to see if his learning was sufficient to allow him to continue in the cure of souls, he was 'right glad, and thought to himself that it might perchance be his fortune to succeed some of such unlettered parsons or vicars in some of their rooms'.[30] And it may not be unreasonable to suppose that Kendall was also right glad. As a graduate, he had nothing to fear from an elementary test of his literacy and knowledge. And he might well have been favourably inclined towards a device designed to raise clerical standards, albeit at the cost of deprivation of the benefices of the unlettered. But there is no evidence that such a task was intended. Kendall appears to have mentioned the visitation in his sermon on Sunday, 1 October. Unfortunately no direct account of his sermon survives, for neither he nor any of the Louth rioters was questioned about it or thought to mention it in their interrogations. The only account comes from Morland, who heard (but did not himself hear) that Kendall had advised his parishioners to 'look well on such things as should be enquired'.[31] This, contrary to received opinion, was hardly an incitement to riot; rather, it looks like an attempt to reassure, to puncture fears and anxieties.[32]

The seed of the Louth rising was not Kendall's sermon, whatever it said, but idle gossip during the procession which proceeded high mass on Sunday. This was led by a silver cross belonging to the church.[33] Thomas Foster, who was described by Nicholas Melton ('Captain Cobbler') as

---

[30] *LP* XII (i), no. 380.

[31] Ibid., no. 380. Morland enlarged on this in his second deposition, implying that he was puzzled as to why Kendall was excluded from the pardon and was told that it was because of the sermon. But Morland was still unable to point to anything incendiary in what Kendall said. Ibid., no. 481. Melton though thought that he had Kendall's blessing on the Monday evening (SP1/110, fo. 134v (= *LP* XI, no. 968). Kendall came to Henry VIII's notice: he expressed astonishment that Kendall had not been accused of anything, and had him excluded from the pardon (*LP* XI, nos. 843, 1224 (2)). He was amongst those executed on 29 March 1537 (*LP* XII (i), no. 764, citing *Wriothesley's Chronicle*).

[32] Cf. James, 'Obedience and Dissent', 202, which is erroneous.

[33] Little attention has been paid to the ritual significance of processions. They were finally forbidden by injunction in 1547. Nowhere is it indicated whether this procession took place within the church or whether it was a ceremonial entry to the church.

a yeoman with £10 in lands, but who was also employed as a 'singing man' by the church, said out loud what every man believed, that there would be no further opportunities to follow the cross. Melton reports him as saying 'our lord speed you, for I think that ye shall be taken away shortly so that we shall never follow you no more'. Foster admitted that he had said to one Robert Johnson 'go we follow the crosses for and if they are taken from us, we will follow them no more'. This was then spread through the crowd by one John Wilson alias 'Joken Sene' who (according to Melton) was paid 1 d. to do so by Robert Norman, a roper.[34] The procession appears to have passed off without incident: high mass was said and evensong sung.

Then, after evensong, a body of anxious men, said by John Brown to be forty in number, congregated in the church. They included Melton and Wilson (who, according to Melton, was responsible for gathering them together). This group of men was convinced that the churchwardens intended to hand over the jewels of the church on the following day. The churchwardens were confronted and sworn at (one deponent has members of the group swearing 'by George's blood' that they would have the keys and that 'they were more worthy to keep them than the church-wardens were'). The keys having been surrendered by the churchwardens, they came into the hands of Melton who opened up the treasury to be assured that everything was correct. He locked it and took the keys away with him. The common bell was also run for a period.[35] This did not satisfy all, and a party shut themselves in the church to guard the jewels. Vicar Kendall knew of this watch.

When I came home to my house, I perceived them in the church door and said unto them these words, 'Masters, where at do ye rise? Against the wind truly. I do see no other cause why ye should rise.' That by and by one answered up among them and said 'Sir, as for you, ye said that we should be hanged'[36] and so began to pick a quarrel to me and I was glad to send for a potell of good ale for them. And so I went home that night.[37]

[34] *LP* XI, nos. 828 (i); 968; 828 (iii, i) and also the deposition of Brown, no. 854.

[35] The fullest accounts are Foster, *LP* XI, no. 828 (iii, i); Brown, no. 854; SP1/110, fo. 161r (deposition of John Stace, not in ibid., no. 972).

[36] A reference to Kendall's sermon?   [37] SP1/110, fo. 146v (not in *LP* XI, no. 970).

On the Monday morning they would only admit to the church those whom they trusted. Melton, making his deposition on 21 October, implied that the church was still garrisoned.[38]

We are talking here of a small group of artisans who were engaged in the defence of their parochial goods against a contrived and erroneous rumour. The situation was clearly dangerous, but what made it into something more was the way in which it was both born out of, but also caught up in, the violent militancy of the local clergy. On Saturday the chancellor, Dr Rayne, had sat at Bolingbroke. He was reportedly gathering details of the valuation of benefices; but he too was probably levying the clerical tenth. Priests from the deanery of Louth Esk had attended that court to see what was going on, and were disappointed to find that 'the priests of the aforesaid Bolingbroke [deanery] were content and conformable to abide all such order as was then taken by the said chancellor, then the said priests of Louth Esk [said] that they would not be so ordered ne yet examined of their ability in learning or otherwise in the keeping of cure of soul'.[39] Sir Symond Maltby told his parishioners on his return from Bolingbroke that their church goods should be confiscated. Moreover, '[he] said that he with other priests were determined that and [recte if] the chancellor did sit any more, they would strike him down, trusting that their neighbours would take their parts'.[40] On Monday morning there were several dozen fearful and resentful clergy in and about Louth, some of whom were expecting to be deprived of their livings.

It seems probable that the clergy were quite deliberately manufacturing a rumour that the consistory was sitting to inventory and confiscate church goods. The eighty or a hundred men who gathered at Corpus Christi altar in Louth church on the Monday morning were all persuaded of the truth of these reports; they were the clergy's dupes. According to Melton's second deposition, one of their number, called Smith, pointed out that John Hennage, the bishop's steward, would be in Louth that morning and suggested that they 'took him and swore him to their aid'. The common bell was then rung to gather the commons of the town and neighbouring countryside together. Melton left this crowd and, on

---

[38] SP1/109, fo. 1r (= LP XI, no. 821 (i) (1)).
[39] PRO, E36/118, fo. 5v (= LP XI, no. 975, p. 401, sayings of Thomas Taylbois).
[40] PRO, E36/118, fo. 5r.

his way home, met with Hennage who demanded to know what the disturbance was about. Melton claimed that he took Hennage into Proctor's wife's house to talk to him, but that they were seen, and the house was surrounded by a crowd of 200 who demanded that the pair should come out and strike no deals in private. Hennage agreed to go to the church to hear their grievances.[41] There he was told of their fears for their jewels and ornaments; he undertook to ride to the court to discover if the king intended any such thing, and persuaded them to be quiet until he returned. He was then sworn. As others of the 'honest men' of the parish arrived they too were made to swear an oath to God, the king, and the commonalty. The party then left the church with Hennage to go to the market cross, where they intended to proclaim that every man should be at peace until Hennage's return. But the clergy who were congregating there to await their examinations would not allow the proclamation to be made. Melton argued that if it had been, peace would have been restored.[42]

All this doubtless happened, but Melton's two depositions make no reference to his role as the leader of a crowd which went around Louth seizing its social superiors. Thomas Foster describes how, having taken Hennage to the church and sworn him, Melton and the crowd went to the house of William Ashby, constable of the wapentake of Louth Esk, and led him to the church. They then went to the common hall and took those who were there waiting for Hennage to the church, where they too were sworn. As the new bailiff was elected by a college of former bailiffs, it is likely that all the senior men of the town were present. Then Melton and his company went to the Saracen's Head, where they found Dr Frankish, and led him and his clerk to the market cross where Hennage had already been taken.[43]

---

[41] *LP* XI, nos. 828 (i) (= SP1/109, fo. 1r); 968 (a fuller account). Melton makes Hennage's trip to the church seem voluntary, but Morland describes his treatment as being much more violent. He has Hennage being rescued from the mob by the 'honest men of the parish' and locked in the choir. *LP* XII (i), no. 380 (p. 174).

[42] SP1/110, fo. 134r (= *LP* XI, no. 968, p. 390, which omits Melton's comment that the disturbance would have stopped). This was also the opinion of another witness, John Child, SP1/110, fo. 164v (not in *LP* XI, no. 972).

[43] *LP* XI, no. 828 (iii, i) misrepresents this: use the MS, SP1/109, fos. 4v–5r. Brown's account, SP1/109, fo. 76v, is corrupt, but from what can be read of his text it looks as though violence was offered against the 'heads of the town'.

It was at this moment that the artisan rioters found a common purpose with the congregating priests. William Morland, whose capacity to insinuate (or write) himself into the centre of action deserves our admiration, describes how, when Frankish entered Louth, the common bell was rung and he was mobbed by a crowd. His books were taken from him and carried into the market place, where it was intended to burn them. Morland, catching up with this crowd, asked what they proposed to do, and on being told that their purpose was to burn the books, argued that they should not be burnt unread. Kendall was called for, and Morland and six others were each given books to read, but whilst Morland was puzzling over the king's commission other bystanders threw the books on the fire. Then Frankish was brought out to the market cross and forced to climb up a ladder propped against it; as he did so he begged Morland to save the commission and his book of reckonings. Morland did this; the commission was given to Hennage and Frankish was finally forced to burn the remainder of his books himself, save the account book, which Morland managed to preserve for a time despite the suspicions of the crowd.[44]

There is an aspect of the assault on Frankish which passes unnoticed in Morland's narrative. According to Thomas Foster, it was not only his books that were burnt, but a proclamation was made that all English books of the New Testament and other 'new' books should be surrendered up to be burnt. And some, including a copy of 'Fryth his book' were brought to the market cross.[45] None of the principal accounts describe the role of the clergy in this. Two of the rank-and-file participants were emphatic in claiming a decisive role for the priests. John Overey of Louth, woolpacker, said that 'the chief occasion of this business rose by the mean[s] of the priests [he then named priests who offered money] . . . they with many other were there and cried with a loud voice "go to it!", holding up their hands and said they [the commons] should [loose?] nothing if they would go forward and win the holy cross'.[46] And John Child deposed 'that there were on the Monday to his estimation forty priests and they

---

[44] *LP* XII (i), no. 380, pp. 174–5.
[45] *LP* XI, no. 828 (iii, i). 'Fryth his book' is obviously a tract by John Frith (burnt for heresy, 1533); one cannot speculate which, but his works attacked both the papacy and the real presence.
[46] *LP* XI, no. 942.

said with a loud voice "let us go forward and ye shall lack no money" ... and he saith that the priests were the chief occasion of their going forward for and they had not been there, Mr Hennage had stayed the whole town and they were at a good stay until the priests came'.[47]

The afternoon appears to have passed more peacefully. Hennage was allowed to leave Louth. He passed Guy Kyme as he was riding out of the town, saying that he feared the commons would follow him. Kyme continued into Louth and tried to calm matters. Hennage did not go immediately to the king: shaken, he took refuge with his wife in a poor man's house. He only set out for court the following morning, after Guy Kyme had seen him and told him of the plan to travel to Caistor.[48] Frankish was also allowed to leave Louth, but bought Morland some lunch first by way of thanks.[49] Later a party of men sallied forth to Legbourne Nunnery to capture the dissolution commissioners then working there. On the way they met with Cromwell's servant John Bellow. He was taken with violence, and some of the party turned back to Louth with Bellow as their prisoner. En route they encountered Sir William Skipwith, who was sworn and allowed to depart. Bellow was set in the stocks at Louth. The remainder of the party then proceed to Legbourne, where they found one Millicent, one William Gleyn, and the John Brown who was to make a valuable deposition. They too were brought to Louth, sworn, and Millicent was set in the stocks with Bellow. Part of the hostility directed towards Bellow and Millicent was that they were both agents or servants of Cromwell, who was the post-dissolution lessee of Legbourne.[50] One man wanted to knife Bellow and Millicent and there were cries that they should be hanged, but they were not.[51] (They were, however, imprisoned throughout the fortnight of the rising and only released on Suffolk's instructions.)

The capture of Bellow and Millicent was insignificant compared to the plans that were being laid for the following day. Throughout the

[47] SP1/110, fo. 163r, 165r (neither in *LP* XI, no. 972).

[48] *LP* XI, no. 828 (xii).   [49] *LP* XII (i), no. 380 (p. 175).

[50] *LP* XI, no. 854 (= SP1/109, fo. 77r). Cromwell was crown lessee of Legbourne from August, *LP* XIII (i), no. 1520 (p. 578), also XI no. 959. Bellow went on to become a prominent speculator in monastic lands and MP for Grimsby: *Hist. Parl., 1509–1558*, I, 415–6; Hodgett, *Tudor Lincolnshire*, 59–60, 105. For Millicent, *Hist. Parl., 1509–1558*, II, 606–7.

[51] SP1/110, fo. 162v (not in *LP* XI, no. 972); no. 968, p. 390.

afternoon it appears that the priests who were in Louth for their examinations were being sworn in support of the commons' adventure, and
that some at least were promising money.[52] At a meeting at the High
Cross it was decided that all present should return the following morning.[53] The decision was also taken that that the Louth men should travel
en masse to the meeting of the subsidy commissioners which was due
to be held at Caistor on the Tuesday morning. Moreover, the priests
were also sworn that on their return to their parishes they would ring
their common bells to call out their parishioners and have them rendezvous with the Louth men at Orford near Binbrook (between Louth
and Caistor) on the Tuesday morning.[54] In this way a riot by urban artisans was transformed into the rising of a rural canton. A more efficient
means of gathering recruits could not have been found.

As the rising was being spread, a struggle was clearly going on within
Louth between the artisan element and the richer inhabitants of the town.
Even on the Monday morning the richer men may have been surprised
and cowed by the willingness of the mob to offer them violence. Eating
his breakfast at William Hert's, Morland describes how Nicholas, Lord
Burgh's servant, said that if the commons continued in this fashion some
of them would be hanged. He was rebuked by his host: 'hold thy peace
Nicholas, for I think as much as thou dost but if they heard us say so,
then would they hang us.'[55] Both Kendall and Brown said that the commons coerced the rich men of the town into taking the commons' part.[56]
This is not a matter on which the depositions dwell, perhaps because,
apart from Kendall, no higher-status inhabitants were interviewed after
the failure of the rebellion. When William West and others met with
Melton in the evening and counselled him to 'leave his going to Caistor
. . . and make no more business', he answered that it could not be cancelled 'for he had otherwise appointed with the town and country'.[57]
This was certainly true, and it gave the rich no choice but to align
themselves with the movement. Hence the party which set out for

---

[52] See below p. 437.   [53] *LP* XII (i), no. 380 (p. 175).
[54] *LP* XI, no. 970. Orford House is at NGR TF 203949; the meeting was perhaps at the nunnery there (the prioress lent Morland a horse).
[55] *LP* XII (i), no. 380 (p. 174).   [56] *LP* XI, no. 970.
[57] SP1/109, fo. 5r (= *LP* XI, no. 828 (iii) (i)).

Caistor on the Tuesday morning consisted of both rich and poor. John Smythson described how on that morning he was met at the church door by Guy Kyme and William Ashby, who told him to go to Richard a Bawarley and get harness from him. Smythson asked that he should be allowed to remain at home for he was sick and would stay to defend the town, but Kyme and Ashby insisted he went 'because he was a tall fellow'.[58] The significance of this story is that two of the socially significant inhabitants of Louth were acting as muster captains. The captains of Louth who led the town to Caistor were named by George Huddeswell as one Brown, William King, and Richard Curson. Elsewhere King is named as bailiff of Louth and Curson is identified as a scrivener.[59] We may interpret this as an indication that, having lost control on the Monday, the 'honest men' of the town were now trying to re-establish their authority by seizing control of the artisans' movement.

The voyage to Caistor ended with the capture of the fleeing subsidy commissioners and their detention under house arrest at Louth. Whilst the narrative accounts speak of the purpose of the excursion as having been to take the gentry, some of the fuller evidence of the common's actions suggests that this was not the sole aim (although it would be wrong to assume that the several thousand men who travelled to Caistor had a single notion of what they were about). The challenge in providing an account of Tuesday's events is to avoid the assumption that the capture of the gentry was the inevitable or intended outcome of the day.

Morland is our main source for events at Louth on Tuesday morning.[60] The common bell was rung at daylight and Melton and John Tailor made a proclamation for all to be ready to set out at the next ringing of the bell. The Louth men then appointed a delegation of eight to speak with the subsidy commissioners at Caistor: four clergy, Thomas Lincoln, the ubiquitous Morland, William Dicheham, and Thomas More,[61] and

---

[58] SP1/110, fo. 163v (= LP XI, no. 972).

[59] LP XI, no. 853; King, ibid., no. 568; Curson SP1/110, fo. 163r (= LP XI, no. 972, in a section of the deposition of Thomas Noble, which is silently omitted). Curson appears as the bailiff of the former monastery of Louth Park after the dissolution. PRO, SC6/Henry VIII/2006, mm. 43, 44.

[60] The following account is mostly based on LP XII (i), no. 380 (pp. 175–6).

[61] Morland names the last two as priests of Louth: Lincoln and More were stipendiaries at Louth in 1526 (Salter (ed.), '1526 Subsidy', 12).

four laymen, of whom we have only the names of Richard Curson and William King.[62] The Louthmen then set out after hearing mass, travelling in two groups, the 'poor men' first 'because they were footmen and after them the rich men on their horses'. Kendall thought that there were perhaps 100 of the latter.[63] Morland set out on foot, but was loaned a horse by the prioress at Orford. How many men from the wapentake were waiting for them there is unrecorded. Estimates of the size of the force that approached Caistor vary from Melton's bragging 20,000 to Huddeswell's more plausible 3,000.[64] Melton describes how, on the way, they encountered Nicholas, the servant of Lord Burgh's, who advised that not more than twenty or thirty should ride to the commissioners whilst the remainder waited at a distance.[65] Morland reports that above Rothwell it was proposed that only 100 should ride on to to the commissioners, but the body of the crowd would not agree to remain behind, so a dozen mounted men (of whom, of course, Morland was one) were appointed to ride on ahead. Until this moment we appear to have a peaceful, though large, body of men passing through Lincolnshire, from amongst whom a delegation had been chosen to speak to the gentry. And then, above Caistor, everything went wrong.

At Louth we saw how a session of the manorial court had coincided with the sitting of the commissary's court. At Caistor we have an even more unfortunate conjunction between a sitting of the consistory (which the clergy of the deaneries of Yarborough, Grimsby, and Walescroft had been instructed to attend) and a meeting called by the subsidy commissioners at which the charge for the assessing of the subsidy would be delivered to the township assessors.[66] Who was supposed to be conducting the former meeting is unrecorded—perhaps Frankish—but he had made

---

[62] Maddison singled out King (bailiff of Louth), Robert Brown and Melton (both shoemakers), Robert Spencer, and his brother as being 'the persons of most substance and the chief speakers . . .' from Louth at Caistor, together with Huddeswell, Morland, and a number of others. *LP* XI, no. 568.

[63] SP1/110, fo. 143v (= *LP* XI, no. 970. *LP* is misleading: the MS says 100 horsemen which *LP* reads as 100 in total).

[64] *LP* XI, nos. 828 (i); 853. The letter of the gentlemen detained at Louth to Henry VIII says 20,000 men or more.

[65] SP1/110, fo. 134v (= *LP* XI, no. 968). It may be a reasonable hypothesis that Nicholas was acting as a scout for the subsidy commissioners.

[66] For the persons present at these meetings, see below p. 139.

himself scarce, and Dr Rayne was lying ill at Bolingbroke where he had held a meeting of the court on Saturday. The subsidy commissioners were playing a deeply cautious game.[67] They had heard of Hennage's treatment at the hands of the Louth commons. Messengers were sent between them and it was agreed that they should meet a mile outside the town at nine o'clock to test the temper of the commons and decide how to proceed. This they did: news of the events at Louth was shared and a scout was sent into Caistor. When he reported that there was no one there other than the subsidy assessors, the commissioners, unaware of the approach of the Louth men, decided to enter the town.

The only account of events inside Caistor comes from George Huddeswell, a gentleman of Hockstow near Barton on Humber, one of the seven inhabitants of Hockstow who travelled to Caistor. Huddeswell went there expecting trouble (although he never admits it himself). A tenant of Sir Edward Maddison's encountered Huddeswell's band of men making their way there early on Tuesday morning and was sworn by Huddeswell to God, the king, and to 'do as they did'. This was before the meeting with the commissioners.[68]

Huddeswell cannot be taken to be an innocent observer of events. He thought that there were 2,000 men within the town waiting for the subsidy commissioners; 500 seems more reasonable. Within this crowd a number of men spread the rumour that the commissioners were charged with the confiscation of all their harness, which was to be deposited in the royal castle at Bolingbroke. Expressions of defiance were made. Huddeswell was made a captain and the crowd spilled into Caistor church, where 160 or so clergy were awaiting their examination. The commons demanded to know whether the clergy would join them or not: the priests agreed. The priests (including the deans of Grimsby and Rasen) gave Huddeswell 'divers papers' and requested that he burn them. He refused and gave them back. Then the priests with the commons went into the market place, where the priests burnt their own books. Finally, the commons and the clergy left the town to speak to the subsidy commissioners. But they had already fled.[69]

---

[67] The following is based on Moigne's account, SP1/110, fo. 149r–v (= LP XI, no. 971).
[68] LP XI, no. 568.   [69] Ibid., no. 853.

Moigne tells the story from the gentry's point of view.[70] As they moved towards Caistor they heard that 10,000 men were coming towards them from Louth and they decided to abandon their meeting. Mr Dalison proposed that they should explain to the subsidy assessors why they were not sitting and 'get them home before the coming of the said commons of Louth or else our sudden departing should not only encourage the commons but also the meeting of the said commons should make the matter more dangerous'. So the subsidy assessors were called to the commissioners outside Caistor, but they refused to come except for 100 or so. Moigne was asked to explain to them why they were deferring their sitting, but 'I thought that it was not only meet to declare unto them that matter, but also to declare unto them that such tales and slanderous inventions as were put in their heads concerning the taking of their church goods, pulling down of churches and other impositions as the king should demand upon them was false and untrue'. This he did, and after starting with a description of the subsidy, he told the commons that the rumours and tales were false, adding: 'and over and besides they might know by reason that the said rumours were false, for as concerning the taking away of their church goods and pulling down their churches which should be a plain destruction of the church and they might be sure that the king's grace might not do so, he being supreme head of the church, might not of his honour see the same church destroyed.' Then his speech was interrupted by the ringing of church bells in Caistor. The commissioners hurriedly agreed to meet at Spittal the following day at noon, and Moigne was told to write to Lord Hussey for his support.[71] Then they dispersed. Moigne made it back to his house. The others were less fortunate.[72]

Morland describes how he arrived on Caistor Moor to find a thousand people milling about (who we may take to be the priests and subsidy assessors from Caistor). He asked where the commissioners were and was told that they had ridden down Caistor Moor towards Kettleby and Sir William Ascue's house. Ascue, Sir Thomas Missenden, Sir Edward

---

[70] For what follows, SP1/110, fos. 149v–151r (= LP XI, no. 971).

[71] For Hussey's reply to Moigne, below p. 160 and LP XI, no. 532.

[72] This account broadly agrees with Lord Burgh's shorter but contemporary description of events, LP XI, no. 533.

Maddison, and Mr Booth could be seen in the distance and Morland, with eighteen or twenty others, rode after them. Catching them up, Morland, with his cap in his hand, desired them to return and speak to the commons. Ascue asked what was the cause of the assembly. Morland answered that the commons were set on ill opinions and that Ascue and the gentlemen 'should do much good amongst them and set them to some stay and quietness'. Sir William was doubtful. 'Trowest thou that if I should come amongst them I should do any good and be in surety of my life?'[73] On Morland's promise to go into the crowd before Ascue, he, Maddison, and Mr Booth turned back to the commons by whom they were sworn, whilst Sir Thomas Missenden took the opportunity to slip away to the anger of the commons. Then Morland turned to Ascue and said, 'Sir, I trust your lordship will ride over unto yonder company and know their mind', which Ascue agreed to do.[74] Other elements within the commons chased Sir Robert Tyrwhit (who was captured and sworn) and Lord Burgh (who escaped). Having lost Burgh, the commons set about his servant Nicholas and lynched him.[75] The commissioners were then taken back to Louth.

On Monday the Louth commons had agreed that Hennage should take their grievances and fears to the king to seek his reassurance that the reports of impending confiscation were untrue. On Tuesday a large force set out for the meeting of the subsidy commissioners at Caistor. As they appointed a delegation, their purpose seems to have been to seek the further reassurance of the commissioners that the rumours circulating amongst them were false. We might observe that Moigne, for one, recognized this need in the speech he delivered to the small number who would come to hear it. There is no sign that the commons sought in the first instance to seize the commissioners. However, by fleeing (and who could blame them?), the latter showed that they were not aligned with the common's aims and ambitions, for their fear indicated opposition and thereby challenged the legitimacy of the commons' movement. The common's anger at this can be seen in their lynching of the servant,

---

[73] E36/119, fos. 53r–54r (some silently omitted in *LP* XII (i), no. 380).
[74] Ibid., fo. 54r (omitted in *LP*).
[75] The commons may have sent word to Burgh to join them under penalty of having his house fired. He fled into Nottinghamshire. *LP* XI, no. 536.

Nicholas.[76] Flight was not the response that the commons sought or expected. Morland did not approach Ascue and the others as a man who had rejected their authority, for (as he tells us) he came to them cap in hand. Their flight was a disappointment to those elements who were seeking to use the gentry to reassure the commons and so bring about their disbandment. Thus Morland's exchange with Ascue: the commons held erroneous opinions which Ascue could dispel. Ascue was sceptical as to whether he could exercise any influence over a substantial crowd of uncertain temper. Yet Morland's twice-repeated request that Ascue should address the commons must be seen as calling the gentry to their proper responsibilities, and so rebuked, they returned to the commons.

The circumstances in which the Louth commons met the gentry at Caistor served to convince them that the gentry were against them, and it may be for that reason, rather than as the result of any planning, that they were brought back over the Wolds to Louth. There is no sign that they were brutalized: lodged at Guy Kyme's house, they were fed and 'well entertained'.[77] Once there, the gentlemen were asked, as Hennage had been, to seek reassurance from the king that the rumoured attack on parochial goods would not take place. Sir Edward Maddison described to the council how at the request of the 'most substantial persons of the said town of Louth' a letter was drafted during the evening which was then shown to and approved by the 'the rebels', that is, the commons.[78]

Fortunately the letter survives.[79] It opens with a statement that on 3 October the signatories had gathered to arrange the levying of the subsidy at Caistor, where they had found an assembly of 20,000 of the king's subjects.

The cause of their assembly was, as they affirmed to us, that the common voice and fame was that all the jewels and goods of the church of the country should

[76] We are never told whether Nicholas was killed. He tried to hide amongst the horsemen (i.e. the richer inhabitants of Louth), and Morland is quite explicit that he was hunted down and lynched 'by the footmen of Louth and Louth Esk'. He had him carried to Caistor, where he confessed him and had surgeons brought from Louth. *LP* XII (i), no. 380 (p. 176).

[77] SP1/106, fo. 295r (= *LP* XI, no. 568).

[78] Ibid., fo. 295r–v (= *LP* XI, no. 568). Kyme says that Melton would not allow the letter to be dispatched until the commons had read it. SP1/109, fo. 13r (= *LP* XI, no. 828 (xii)).

[79] SP1/106, fo. 250r–v (= *LP* XI, no. 534, printed Dodds, *Pilgrimage*, I, 98–9, where they misread XX^ml for XXII^ml).

be taken from them and brought to your grace's council and also that your said loving and faithful subjects should be put of new to enhancements and other importunate charges which they were not able to bear by reason of extreme poverty.

The commons had sworn them to be true to the king and to take their part in maintaining the commonwealth. They had been brought from Caistor to Louth, where they would remain until they knew further of the king's pleasure. The gentlemen asked for a general pardon for both themselves and the commons, without which they expected never to see the king or their houses again. But they added that the commons wished to express their continued loyalty to the king. Maddison was dispatched after midnight to carry the letter to the king.

The letter clearly expresses the distance between the commons and its gentry signatories. So too does the letter that they wrote to Hussey the following day: 'we have sent to you by these bearers to know whether you will be content to come and aid the commonalty in their service to God, the king, and the commonwealth.'[80] The grievances of the commons were not shared ones. The letter to the king stated the common voice amongst the commons as though it were true, adding that the commons could not afford the threatened impositions, but we know, from Moigne's speech at Caistor, that the gentry knew the rumours to be false. But by treating the reports as though they were true, they invited the king either to rescind the impositions or deny that any such course of action had been intended. Maddison's deposition stressed how the letter was made on behalf of the richer Louth men, who sought not only an authoritative denial of rumours in which they probably never believed, but also a general pardon.[81] No clearer sign of the cleavage between the rich and the poor of the town could be required.

Hennage had already set out for the court on the behalf of the Louth commons to discover whether the circulating rumours were true. Now Sir Edward Maddison rode southwards with a similar invitation to the

---

[80] *LP* XI, no. 539 (= SP1/110, fo. 255r). For a later instance of distance, *LP* XI, no. 618 (the gentry to the earl of Shrewsbury, where the body of the letter is signed in the name of the commonalty and a postscript by the gentry).

[81] SP1/106, fo. 295r (= *LP* XI, no. 568).

king to prick the rumours by making an authoritative denial.[82] Until
that was done the position of the gentry was highly dangerous, not believing the stories, but unable to persuade the commons of their error.
By stressing their own impotence and the need for a royal initiative
to rescue them, they invited the king to defuse the situation. Perhaps
they could do no more. Perhaps too they mistook their monarch. If this
was a miscalculation, so too was their evident confidence that they had
struck a bargain with the commons whereby the latter would be quiescent until the king's reply was received. Ascue told Moigne the following morning that it was business as normal, but by mid-morning
Moigne had been taken captive by a wandering band of rebels who brought
to Louth intercepted letters which destroyed the basis of trust between
gentry and commons.

Neither Wednesday nor Thursday could match Monday or Tuesday for
excitement. Rather, they appear to have been days of consolidation in
which the gentry established a conditional discipline over the commons
whilst the rebellion itself spread further. The most significant events on
Wednesday were perhaps the subsidiary risings in Market Rasen and Alford,
the first of which, in an indirect way, served to undermine the precar-
ious grip on events which the gentry in Louth had established by sending the letter to the king.

The story might best be picked up on Tuesday. Thomas Moigne
successfully made his way from the abortive meeting of the subsidy
commissioners at Caistor to his house at North Willingham, 2 miles east
of Market Rasen, stopping in Usselby to write a letter to Hussey seeking
his aid. When he reached home he found that a dyer of Louth had
ridden through the village and all the men, except Moigne's household
servants and those unable to ride, had followed him to a meeting of
the commons at Binbrook. In his 'Declaration' Moigne describes how
he intended to flee and prepared his harness, but when word of this
(through some incautious talk by a messenger sent by one John Sheffield)
reached a body of Louth men returning from Caistor, they promised to

---

[82] It might be added that Maddison stumbled into the Horncastle rising—there may have been an
attempt to take him there—and he appears to have been the first with news of that disturbance in
London.

return to 'pull down my house or else burn it'. Word reached Moigne
that the other subsidy commissioners had fallen into the hands of the
commons and that the commons were proposing to come for Moigne
the following day. Moigne sent his bailiff to Sir William Ascue at Louth,
asking him to use his influence to keep the commons away from his
house or, if that were impossible, to have them send people to capture
him who would neither terrorize his sick wife nor spoil his house. Still
contemplating escape, he abandoned the idea when told that a watch
was being kept on every road. On his own account he spent a sleepless
night awaiting the return of his bailiff from Louth. At seven in the morning the bailiff returned with word from Ascue that 'the commons were
well contented to stay themselves' until they had a reply from the king
to their letter sent the previous evening. In a spectacular misreading
of the situation, Ascue advised Moigne to go ahead and hold the
Michaelmas court of the Isle of Axholme scheduled for Thursday.[83]

Ascue may have been confident that he and his fellows had established
a sufficient hold over the Louth commons, but they failed to allow for
the fashion in which the impetus had passed to the smaller towns. Both
men and clergy from Market Rasen had been at Caistor on Tuesday;
later that day a proclamation was made there that all men should be in
readiness.[84] On Wednesday morning the bells of both Market Rasen and
the neighbouring villages were rung. A contingent of Rasen commons
came to North Willingham, caused the bells of the church to be rung,
and entered the courtyard of Moigne's house. There 'they made a great
proclamation for me and then I seeing my own ability of resistance did
come out to them with great fear and asked them what they would have.
And they said they would have me. And I asked them to what intent,
and they said I should take their part and do as they did. And then I
told them I was not able to resist them.' As he rode out of the house
with the commons, a butcher stopped him and insisted that he be sworn
to the commons, which he was, on a service book brought from his
own chapel.[85]

[83] SP1/110, fos. 151r–152v (= *LP* XI, no. 971).

[84] Deposition of John Wolson of Linwood, SP1/110, fo. 170r–v (poorly abstracted in *LP* XI,
no. 973).

[85] SP1/110, fos. 152r–v (= *LP* XI, no. 971).

This party of rebels had previously captured two sons of Sir William Ascue and a servant of Lord Hussey called George Gatton. Ascue's sons, it appears, had come close to being murdered and Gatton was threatened with beheading.[86] Gatton had been to Lincoln with a letter for the mayor and carried a reply to Hussey in which the mayor referred to the 'insurrection of the rebellious in Lindsey'. He was intercepted on his way from Lincoln towards Louth, carrying an additional letter from Hussey to Sir Robert Tyrwhit and Sir William Ascue in which Hussey said that 'certain false traitorous knaves' had gathered around Louth, instructing Tyrwhit and Ascue to suppress them, and offering to come to their aid if necessary. The letters were found and read, and their language—that the commons were called rebels—scandalized the commons. Despite Moigne's persuasions, the Rasen commons insisted on having them publicly read when they arrived at Louth.[87]

Both Kyme and Foster say that the Rasen commons arrived with the letters at around 10 a.m. Louth was, at that time, quiet; all the witnesses agree that most of the commons had gone home. The letters were read, the commons were outraged, and despite the efforts of the gentry the common bell was rung and the commons of the town and countryside reassembled.[88] The letter shook the gentry's hold over the commons. 'And thereupon the commons gathered themselves together in such number that the men of worship being there could not be heard in no ways.'[89] Their response, according to Moigne, was to muster the commons in the fields and divide them into wapentakes. No sooner had they started to do this than the commons of Alford arrived with Sir Andrew Bilsby, Mr Fawcett, and other gentlemen in their custody, and a rumour went around that Lord Burgh was approaching with a force of 10,000 men to fight them. Again the gentry lost control; it was agreed that scouts should

---

[86] SP1/110, fos. 152v–153r (= LP XI, no. 971); PRO, E36/118, fo. 8r (= LP XI, no. 975); SP1/109, fos. 70–71r (not reproduced at LP XI, no. 852).

[87] SP1/110, fo. 153r–v (= LP XI, no. 971).

[88] LP XI, no. 828 (iii, i); xii (= SP1/109, fos. 5r, 13r–v); SP1/110, fo. 153v (= LP XI, no. 971). There are discrepancies in the chronology of events on this day. Morland speaks of the alarm but attributes it to the rumour that Burgh was advancing, but he does not talk of the furore created by the intercepted letter, nor does he mention the arrival of Bilsby and Forcett. Other sources say that Bilsby and Forcett were brought to Louth during the afternoon, e.g. William Wilson of Alford, who says they arrived there about 3 p.m. I would assume that Moigne is in error on this particular point.

[89] SP1/110, fo. 153v (= LP XI, no. 971).

be sent out to look for Burgh's approach (amongst those dispatched were Melton and Morland), and until they returned the commons were to have dinner.[90] Morland, with his usual impeccable nose, rode over to Horncastle but saw no sign of Lord Burgh's phantom army. Instead, he stumbled into the Horncastle rising.

The Louth deponents say that the commoners sent messengers on Tuesday instructing Bilsby and Fawcett to come to Louth, but the depositions show that they were brought to Louth, having been forcibly taken by the commons. William Wilson of Alford, miller, and Arthur Washingley of Alford, servingman, were both adamant that the rebellion was spread to Alford by the vicar who had been a witness to events in Louth. The common bell was rung between five and six on Wednesday morning, and when Wilson arrived at around eight o'clock he found Thomas Totheby, gent. trying (and failing) to calm the commons. The crowd then went to Bilsby, only a mile or so away, where they found Sir Andrew Bilsby and Edward Fawcett, gent. James Metcalfe says that he saw the pair in the churchyard surrounded by a crowd of 140 men who were calling out that they were false to the king and the commonwealth. The two gentlemen were taken back to Alford where they were sworn by the vicar at the churchyard stile; then they, with Totheby and others, were taken back to Louth with the commons, where they arrived at about 3 p.m.[91]

The alarm that Burgh was approaching proved to be false, and the afternoon passed in holding musters and appointing captains and petty captains at Julian Bower. Brown says that the commons 'compelled' the gentry to act as captains.[92] Moigne, in a section of his account which we will consider more fully later, described how the gentry began mustering the commons, dividing the wapentakes one from another and appointing themselves as captains, as the means by which the commons could be restrained.[93] Nonetheless, they were unable to prevent the commons calling for further musters on Thursday at Tows Athyenges between Louth and Market Rasen or advancing towards Lincoln. The

[90] Ibid., fos. 153v–154r (= *LP* XI, no. 971).

[91] SP1/109, fos. 77v–78r (= *LP* XI, no. 854); SP1/110, fos. 169v–170r, 128r–129r (= *LP* XI, no. 967 (x, xi)).

[92] SP1/109, fo. 77v (= *LP* XI, no. 854).   [93] This is considered further below, p. 148.

commons also had them write to the mayor of Lincoln and Lord Hussey asking whether they were for or against them.[94] And as they sat at dinner that evening Morland appeared fresh from Horncastle and told them of the murder of Chancellor Rayne and the hanging of Wulcye.[95]

On Thursday the commons mustered at Tows as arranged. Melton and others were sent to Gainsborough to persuade Lord Burgh to throw in his hand with them; they returned empty-handed the following day and met the commons on the road between Market Rasen and Lincoln.[96] From Tows, Moigne and his band of men were called to Hambledon Hill near Market Rasen, where they were joined by the commons of the wapentake of Yarborough.[97]

It was on Hambleton Hill that there occurred the first of the two encounters between Robert Aske and the Lincolnshire rebels.[98] In his account of his role in the Pilgrimage, Aske explained how on Wednesday, 4 October he was travelling southwards to London with his three nephews when, having crossed the Humber, he discovered that Lincolnshire had risen. As he could not recross to the north bank, he decided to strike out for his brother-in-law Thomas Portington's house at Sawcliffe. His party was stopped by one Mr Huddeswell (doubtless George of Horkstow) in the company of fourteen or sixteen others and Aske was unwillingly sworn before being allowed to carry on to Sawcliffe. Arriving there, he found that Portington had already been taken by the commons (he had fallen into their hands at Caistor) and, after an abortive start to take a boat at Winteringham, Aske was forced to go back to Sawcliffe and lodge there on Wednesday night. Before day broke on Thursday morning he was taken by a party of commons. They agreed to allow his nephews to return into Yorkshire, but Aske himself was taken by them to another (unnamed) town. He then spent the morning aiding this party raise townships along the south bank of the Humber in response to Lord Burgh's instruction that these same townships should raise against the rebels. (Aske recalled that this force was without either

---

[94] For the letter to the mayor of Lincoln, *LP* XI, no. 553.
[95] *LP* XII (i), no. 380 (p. 176). For these deaths, see below p. 133.
[96] *LP* XI, no. 968 (p. 390).
[97] SP1/110, fos. 154v–155r (= *LP* XI, no. 971); *LP* XI, no. 853. Hambledon Hill, modern Hamilton Hill, is a prominent hill about half a mile NE of Market Rasen.
[98] For the following section, see 'The manner of the taking of Robert Aske', 331–3.

captain or gentry leadership and that most of them lacked harness. Moigne called them the commons of West Ankome.[99]) The commons then proposed to join the 'host of Caistor' at Hambleton Hill, having heard 'by the common fame' that a muster was going to take place there. Aske volunteered to ride over to see if anyone was there and, if so, to discover what their plans were. This he did, in the company of Nicholas Girlington and Robert Ascue. When word was brought to Moigne that Aske and his companions were at the bottom of the hill, he set out to ride down the hill to speak to him. (Moigne did not know Aske but knew of him; he immediately seems to have thought that he could trust a fellow lawyer.[100]) The commons insisted on hearing what passed between them and so Aske was called up the hill. Aske spoke on behalf of the commons of West Ankome: 'I [Moigne] made answer according to the minds of the commons.'[101] Aske then asked to review the commons, and after remarking that they numbered about 500 he rode back to the commons waiting at Kirton and crossed the Humber back into Yorkshire. The meeting was of no importance to Moigne or the Lincolnshire movement; but it may have been decisive in shaping Aske's understanding of the movement and his ambition to replicate it in Yorkshire.[102]

Thursday night was spent by both the Louth men and the forces collected under Moigne around Market Rasen. On Friday the consolidated force moved to Dunholme Heath,[103] about 5 miles north-east of Lincoln, where they were joined by the commons of Kirton Soke 'without captains or banners', perhaps the same group that Aske had assisted the previous day.[104] Late on Friday afternoon they entered Lincoln. The victuallers of the town had been instructed to sell food to the commons at reasonable prices. The gentlemen went to lodgings with the dean and chapter within the cathedral close.[105] On Saturday the commons mustered outside the city, then settled into a routine of musters whilst their twin advantages of numbers and surprise were dissipated.

[99] SP1/110, fo. 155r.

[100] As Moigne says, 'knowing the said Aske was towards the law and so thinking him to be by reason thereof a man of quietness . . .', SP1/110, fo. 155r.

[101] Ibid.   [102] Aske's behaviour is considered further in Chapter 7.

[103] Some sources name this muster as taking place at Grange de Lings. A glance at the map shows that same place is almost certainly intended.

[104] SP1/109, fos. 1v, 13v (= LP XI, no. 828 (i), (xii)).   [105] LP XI, no. 853.

III

The rising at Horncastle on Tuesday and Wednesday 3–4 October bears a number of superficial resemblances to that at Louth. It was the work of a small group of artisans. The rising within the town moved to capture the neighbouring gentry, including the sheriff of Lincolnshire, Sir Edward Dymock, and the registrar of the diocese, Dr Rayne. The dissimilarities are more telling. Where the Louth rising was spontaneous, the Horncastle rising was an opportunist, copycat adventure, deliberately raised by a single man, William Leach. The commons rose in the absence of the clergy, who seem to have been due in town to meet the commissary on Wednesday.[106] And, compared to the Louth movement, that at Horncastle was much more aggressive and violent. Frankish had left Louth alive; the gentry captured at Caistor were apparently well treated. At Horncastle, where Rayne was beaten to death and another man hanged, the commons exhibited a ready resort to violence not seen in Louth. Unfortunately, events in Horncastle cannot be described in the detail or with the precision of those in Louth. The depositions of a number of principals (especially the Dymocks) do not survive, and William Leach, unlike Nicholas Melton, appears to have evaded capture and so may never have been examined about his role.

We saw earlier how interest in and anxiety over the commissary's court prompted clergy from the deanery of Louth Esk to travel to Bolingbroke on the Saturday to watch the conduct of the court. Events in Horncastle followed from a similar contact. The earliest evidence for trouble brewing in Horncastle comes from Monday evening. Either William Leach or his brother, Nicholas Leach, vicar of Belchford, had been in Louth during the day and had witnessed the events there. William Longbothom, barber, heard a report that Vicar Leach had brought word to William Leach that the Louth men had risen. One Edward Leach (perhaps a further Leach brother) told Longbothom that a man had been killed there.[107] Other deponents testified that it was William Leach

---

[106] It is not clear when the court was to be held: Leach implies Tuesday, but the clergy were obviously present when Rayne was murdered on Wednesday.

[107] SP1/109, fo. 3r–v (omitted by *LP* XI, no. 828 (ii)).

himself who had been in Louth. Thomas Dixson explained how, on the evening of 2 October, Leach went around the town asking men to come to his house. Once there Leach told them that he had been at Louth, that the visitors had taken away the church goods, and that on Tuesday they would be in Horncastle to do the same. Dixson was told that if he 'heard any business in the town, he should resort thither'. A number of others confirmed this story; William Gainsborough, however, told how Leach came to him on Monday night and instructed him (on pain of death) to be with him at nine the following morning.[108]

At about that time next day the common bell was rung by one Davy Bennett, a weaver. Robert Sotheby and William Bywaters, the church-wardens, were going to inspect the work of plumbers employed at the church when it was rung. They asked Davy who had instructed him to ring it and he answered that 'I would thou knowest that I am commanded [by] the commons'.[109] Then Sotherby and Bywater were sworn in the churchyard with many others. Philip Trotter reports that after the swearing of oaths Nicholas Leach reported on the previous day's events in Louth to William Leach; it is possible that he addressed the crowd. Trotter says that at this time 'the whole town of Horncastle was congregate with other and no man spake against the rebellion'.[110] Edward Richardson of Thimbleby, a mile west of Horncastle, deposed that William Leach 'stirred and moved the commons to rise for the saving of the jewels of the church, that the bishop's officers should with them nothing have to do and that Leach forced him and others to take an oath, binding him by the same to take such part as they took'.[111] At some point in the late morning or early afternoon the decision was taken to go to Scrivelsby Hall, 2 miles or so south of Horncastle, the home of the Dymock family. The intentions of the commons in proceeding there are nowhere expressed and have to be inferred from their actions. By the end of the afternoon they had captured and sworn several members of the Dymock family and their

---

[108] *LP* XI, no. 967 (v), (vii). The belief that these men were paid needs knocking on the head. The evidence used to support this claim in fact refers to money paid to poorer members of the Horncastle commons on the Friday as they set out towards Lincoln. James, 'Obedience and Dissent', 198; see *LP* XI, no. 967 (iii) [William Marshall].

[109] SP1/110, fo. 124r (= *LP* XI, no. 967). [110] SP1/109, fo. 2r (= *LP* XI, no. 828 (i) (ii)).

[111] SP1/110, fo. 173r (= *LP* XI, no. 974).

house guests. The circumstances in which the Dymocks allowed themselves to be captured have been substantially misunderstood.

James recognized that two accounts existed of the events at Scrivelsby. In the first, threats were made against the gentry, and Sir William Sandon put up resistance and was roughly handled by the commons. James was sceptical whether these were anything more than ritual gestures on either side: 'the degree of maltreatment to which he [Sandon] was consequently subjected, however, was not such as to confirm the view that the other gentlemen failed to follow his example because their lives were in danger.'[112] The subsequent behaviour of the gentry inclined James to accept another account of their capture, offered by Philip Trotter, in which the gentlemen came from their house to the commons, swore oaths, and assumed the leadership of the rebellion.[113] Trotter's description of events serves James's case well, for it allows him to cast doubt on the account given 'official credence', that the gentry, like those at Caistor, had been overwhelmed.[114] Unfortunately, James's preference for this account is remarkably self-serving. Nowhere does James (or Dr Gunn, in an article which discusses the same evidence) acknowledge that Trotter twice offered a description of the events of that afternoon, and that the account drawn on here, the second of the pair, must be read as an amplification of a small element within the longer and earlier deposition. However, James, unlike Dr Gunn, overlooks the fullest account of events at Scrivelsby. When all the depositions are read an account of events emerges which is substantially different from both of James's options.[115]

Trotter's first account says that at around midday (three hours after the common bell was rung, which other deponents time at about nine o'clock) 500 persons set out from Horncastle to Scrivelsby. This party sent a group of seven or eight, including Trotter and Robert Sotheby, before them to 'command' Sir Robert Dymock, his son Sir Edward (the sheriff), and the other son Sir Arthur 'to come to them'. At Scrivelsby they found the Dymocks, some relatives, and their house guests, including

---

[112] James, 'Obedience and Dissent', 218. Actually, Sandon was roughly handled after the others had been sworn.

[113] Ibid. 220.   [114] Ibid. 218.

[115] Gunn, 'Peers, Commons and Gentry', 54–5. I cannot accept Gunn's assertion that the accounts of events at Scrivelsby are 'almost entirely mutually contradictory'.

Sir William Sandon. All (save Sandon), came 'incontinent' to Leach and company (who were standing about a thousand yards from the house), where they were sworn. There is nothing in this account to say that Leach or the commons actually went to the house, for the contact between them and the Dymocks was made through the delegation. There then appears to have been a pause before Sir William appeared, according to Trotter, 'with his cap in his hand' (a point to which we shall return). After the oath had been sworn, all the gentry save Sandon were allowed to return to Scrivelsby. Sandon, however, was taken to Horncastle and custody.[116] Trotter's other account, made in January and contained in the book called 'The Additions', describes how the Dymocks came to Leach and 100 others a quarter of a mile from the house. Dymock, it is reported, said to the company 'masters, ye be welcome', then Leach said 'ye must be sworn', and so they were. Then, assuming their natural authority, they commanded Leach to bring in other gentry and raise the countryside.[117] The first deposition gives an account of events before the swearing, the second of the circumstance of the swearing. They are complementary, not contradictory.

Trotter supplies an outline of events which is consistent with the reports of all other witnesses. William Marshall of Horncastle said that the rebellious commons sent a messenger to the Dymocks. Thomas Dixson said that as Leach and company went forward to Scrivelsby they sent a number of Horncastle men to Sir Robert and Sir Edward Dymock and such gentlemen as were in the house to come and speak to them in the field. There they caused them to be sworn. Both of these short accounts add pieces of evidence which further detract from the received accounts. Marshall has the commons 'charging them [the gentry] to come to them [the commons] in pain of their lives, and if they would not so to do, they would destroy them and burn down their house over their heads'. Dixson has the Dymocks putting up a show of resistance, 'saying that they would take a time to know wherefore they rose and what was their intent and to know the king's pleasure first'.[118]

Both Marshall and Dixson confirm Trotter's account that a contact was made by the Horncastle commons before the gentry were sworn.

---

[116] *LP* XI, no. 828 (i) (ii) (= SP1/109, fo. 2r–v). [117] *LP* XII (i), no. 70 (p. 37).
[118] SP1/110, fos. 125v, 126r (= *LP* XI, no. 967 (ii), (iii), (v)).

Marshall adds the detail that the messengers went armed with a threat to destroy Scrivelsby Hall, Dixson that the gentry put up at least some resistance, wanting to know why the commons had risen. The swearing of the Dymocks appears more like a reluctant surrender (with a hint of continued defiance) than a prepared and collusive meeting of commons and gentry.

Then there is then the fullest account of the events of this afternoon, made by Robert Sotheby. Sotheby, it will be recalled, was one of those named by Trotter as going to Scrivelsby to call on the Dymocks to meet Leach. Given the importance of his account, it is best given in full.

Further the said deponent saith that Tuesday, 3 October, William Leach accompanied with 100 [men] or thereabouts came unto Sir Robert Dymock's house and said that they would fetch out Edward Dymock sheriff and such gentlemen as was there if they would not come and [...] they did they would pull them all out of the house. And then the said deponent thought if the said misdemeaned [the rebels] presently should come there, they [...] fail to dispoil the house, wherefore the said deponent desired Leach and the rest of the company for to stay. And Richard Talbot, Thomas Tuphom[..] [and] [.....] Newcum would go thither and look what they would have [.....] they would go thither and bring them word again what answer [they] made.

And in the mean season came tidings to Leach and th[..] [.....] that Sir William Sandon should say that they had begun such a bar[...] they should be hanged in the end for their labours. Whereupon they were in such a fury and rage that they called him traitor to the commonweal and to the church of England and swore many great oaths [that] if they had him, they would kill him, wherefore they had much work to stay them.

And so the said deponent with the other three persons went and spoke with them and showed them the sayings of Leach and the residue of the company, showing them how they handled themselves. And so the said sheriff Edward Dymock, Robert [...] and one Sanderson went into the field to the said company and when they came there Leach took the sheriff by the bosom and said that if they would not be sworn to take such part as they did, they would die and live on them and struck his bill upon the ground in a great rage. And then the sheriff desired him to be good to him with his bonnet in his hand for fear of his life. And the said Leach said that he had no good cause to be good to him for he was against him in a matter at the assizes at Lincoln. And then Thomas Dymock of Carleton said, 'Master Leach, you come then of malice and not for the commonwealth.' With that the said Leach to the sheriff took a book and bad him swear and then the sheriff asked him wherefore they rose and what was their intent. Then the said Leach said that the visitors would come and take away their church goods and put down the churches. Then the sheriff said to them that 'you were too hasty to rise seeing that there was no such matter done'. And then Leach swore many great oaths, 'what, shall we stand here all day? Lay your hand on the book.' With that the sheriff answered 'wherefore should I be sworn? I am sworn to the king already.' With that the said Leach said 'make an end, and be sworn to do as we do or else it shall cost you your life and as many as will not swear.' And so the sheriff was sworn. And the rest of the gentlemen for safeguard of their lives [were sworn] that they should be true to God, the king, and the commons and the faith of the church.[119]

There are one or two points in this account which ideally might be clarified. Estimates of the size of the Horncastle commons vary, but a sizeable crowd is indicated. The identities and number of the group which went to parley with the Dymocks is variable: Sotheby says four where Trotter says seven or eight. More mysterious is the fact that we are never told how the commons came to hear of Sandon's denunciation of them. According to Sotheby, news of it came to the commons before he and the others undertook their mission to the gentry. We must suppose that the gentry at Scrivelsby were warned of the common's advance and the commons told of their reaction by an unknown third party, perhaps a household servant. Overall, the account that Sotheby offers is of a piece with the others. The commons agreed to allow messengers to go forwards to Scrivelsby to warn the Dymocks of the common's advance and intentions. It is hard to see that they had much to say except to advise the gentry to accept the common's discipline or risk their anger. It would appear that the gentry were divided in their response, with Sandon advocating a course of defiance. Nonetheless the Dymocks, when they met with the commons, are shown putting up a spirited resistance in the face of Leach's intimidation. Moreover, if Sotheby's account of the exchange is correct, Dymock had to enquire why the commons had risen—he did not know—and when told, he challenged the whole justification for the movement as erroneous. Given that we have four or five gentry being confronted by a much larger group of potentially hostile commons,

[119] Ibid., fos. 124r–v (= *LP* XI, no. 967 (i)), (the latter part printed with the original spelling in Gunn, 'Peers, Commons and Gentry', 55). [...]. indicates sections lost through decay.

Dymock and his fellows deserve some commendation for exhibiting no small amount of physical courage. There is no sign here of a prearranged handover of authority of the kind that James suspected took place.

Sotheby's account offers other clues as to the relationship of gentry and commons. Dymock is mentioned as holding his hat: in another deposition (Longbothom's), Leach is described as meeting Dymock and the other gentry 'with his cap on his head'.[120] Here we see an inversion of the normal rules of social deference and a visible demonstration of the raw realities of power at this meeting.

The price of defiance was paid by Sandon. The accounts all agree that Sandon came out to the commons after the others had been sworn, that he was then sworn himself and taken back to Horncastle. Trotter tells us that Sandon came to the commons 'with his cap in his hand', thus indicating his submission. Some accounts (Trotter, Longbothom) merely say that Sandon was carried to Horncastle, others that he was abused and manhandled by the crowd.[121] Sotheby reports that after Sandon came to the commons, 'they had him by the arms and swore him and harried him forth and [.....] and press of people, he was almost overcome and ever in fear of his life, and they cried "down with him" and so carried him to Horncastle and [put] him in the moot hall'.[122] Two deponents offer the additional observation that during the journey from Scrivelsby to Horncastle, when 'hurt and weariness almost overcame him', Sandon was offered a horse, but one of the rebels struck out at this and said he should go 'a foot' as they did.[123] The assailant is elsewhere named as Thomas Davy of Braytoft who, it is alleged, when he struck at the horse, said to the commons 'let us kill him [Sandon]'.[124] Sandon escaped the fate of Dr Rayne, but his treatment shows how futile were gestures of defiance when confronted by crowds of commons.

Having sworn the Dymocks and their guests and carried Sandon back to Horncastle, the commons set out again to visit and swear other local gentry.[125] According to several depositions, Dymock was asked in the field

---

[120] SP1/109, fo. 3v (not in *LP* XI, no. 828 (ii)).   [121] *LP* XI, no. 828 i (2); 2 (ii).
[122] SP1/110, fo. 124v (not in *LP* XI, no. 967).   [123] Ibid., fo. 126r (not in *LP* XI, no. 967).
[124] *LP* XI, no. 975, fo. 1 (= E36/118, fo. 2v).
[125] It is uncertain what happened to Sandon during the rest of the day. Trotter says that, after a short period in the moot hall, he was taken to William Bywater's house and kept there until the next morning, but then says that Sandon was sent to swear Littlebury and Coppledike. SP1/109, fo. 2v.

near Scrivelsby what the commons should do next. All the witnesses, in slightly different ways, explain how he (in Bernard Fletcher's words) 'commanded the people to go to Mr Littlebury and Sir John Coppledike and to all the gentlemen in Lindsey and the marsh country towards the seaside and to raise them and to will them to be at Horncastle the next Monday [sic] by 8 o'clock'. Trotter adds that when the sheriff was asked whether they should ring the bells, he answered 'yea, and ye will for it is expedient and necessary that the people have knowledge'.[126] This is puzzling. That the commons should suddenly turn to Dymock for advice as to what to do next and that the sheriff should so readily have accepted a guiding role seems quite contrary to the account of events just presented. Of course, it may be held that this ready assumption of authority undermines this account. It may also be that the sheriff's behaviour confirms the previous account, that having been forced into swearing their oath, the gentry had to further confirm the legitimacy of the crowd's cause (and their subscription to it) by offering instructions in the name of all. It may be argued that Dymock was merely fulfilling the expectations placed on him now that he was in the commons' hands. There are, however, grounds for doubting that this exchange ever took place. It is not mentioned in the accounts made in October and November 1536, but it does appear in the depositions made in the Tower in January 1537. As we shall see, deponents were then offering damaging evidence against the gentry, even to the point of contradicting their own previous examinations.

Whether on their own initiatives or by the instructions of Edward Dymock, some of the Louth commons set out in the late afternoon on a circular sweep to swear the gentry living to the east of Horncastle whilst the others went to Bolingbroke. William Longbothom, with a party of sixteen of his neighbours, proceeded first to Thomas Littlebury's house at Stainsby, where he told Littlebury of the events at Scrivelsby and delivered an injunction that Littlebury should be Horncastle the next morning. He and the others then went to Sir John Coppledike's at Harrington and Ralph a Green's at Partney before turning to Bolingbroke, where they met with the main body of the Horncastle commons.[127]

---

[126] E36/119, fo. 11r, 14 [bis]r (= LP XII (i), no. 70 (viii) (p. 36); x (p. 38). Richard Leeds also attributes similar words to the sheriff.
[127] SP1/109, fo. 3v (not in LP).

Roger Newe, on the other hand, seems to have been both there and somewhere else. He went by Leach's commandment (and not Dymock's) to Littlebury's house at Stainsby. Leach went into the house in the company of a large crowd (Newe says 1,000):

> and there took the said Littlebury and swore him against his will and charged him to go with him to Sir John Coppledike's house in pain of his life and when they came there, they [took the] said Coppledike and swore him in like manner upon like pain and set out with them the space of half a mile and then licensed them to go home to their houses when it was night, charging them on their lives to be with them the next day at Horncastle at 8 o'clock.[128]

Whilst this was going on Robert Leach was in Spilsby with a troop of men who rang the bells, swore the master of the college there and the brethren and the parish constables.[129] He may have carried on to Halton Holegate, where the common bell was rung during Tuesday and the commons went to Horncastle on Wednesday.[130]

There was perhaps a prearranged plan to meet at Bolingbroke. The chancellor of the diocese, Dr Rayne, had held a session of the commissary's court there on Saturday, and then falling ill, had remained there in a chantry priest's house where he was found by the Horncastle commons. According to Trotter he was sworn in his bed, after which all the commons save nine or ten and Trotter returned to Horncastle.[131] Thomas Mayhew accused Leach, Longbothom, and Trotter of coming to Bolingbroke with a great company who rang the common bell and cried 'kill him!' Rayne begged Trotter to save him. Trotter agreed to do what he could and Rayne gave him 20s. for drink to buy peace from the crowd. Trotter then swore everyone to be at Horncastle the following morning.[132] On the Wednesday morning Rayne was brought from Bolingbroke, but in the field before Horncastle his party encountered a crowd of whom many were clergy. There was a clamour for him to be killed, Rayne was pulled from his horse, and bludgeoned to death where he fell. It seems that the last thing he heard were his own clergy crying 'kill him! kill him!' Dymock and Coppledike were present and the

---

[128] SP1/110, fo. 127v (= *LP* XI, no. 967 (v)).   [129] *LP* XI, no. 967 (ii).

[130] SP1/110, fo. 170v (not in *LP* XI, no. 973).   [131] *LP* XI, no. 828 (1), (2).

[132] Ibid., no. 975, fo. 2 (= E36/118, fo. 3r). Trotter returned to Horncastle the following morning, and although he says nothing about it, it seems likely that he and his guard took Rayne there.

sheriff distributed the chancellor's money to the poor men in the crowd. Whether they encouraged the murder is unrecorded, but it seems most likely that Rayne's murder was unexpected and almost accidental. Stanes places a special emphasis on the clergy calling for Rayne's murder, and continues by saying that 'after the chancellor was slain, every parson and vicar in the field counselled their parishioners with many comfortable words to proceed in their journey, saying unto them that they should lack neither gold nor silver', an echo of the support offered by the clergy at Louth.[133]

This was the first murder of the day. The second was of a man called Thomas Wulcey or Wolsey. Morland saw Leach go to the gentry and ask them to exchange Wulcey for one Stephen Haggar. This they did, and then Wulcey was hanged. Trotter saw Rayne and Wulcey being buried, but neither he nor anyone else has ever explained who Wulcey or Haggar were, or how Wulcey earned his fate at the hands of a mob.[134]

After this the commons dispersed, having agreed to meet anew the following day between Horncastle and Scrivelsby.[135] Word of this muster was circulated. The vicar of Snelland heard that the whole of the wapentake of Wraggoe was to be there.[136] Word was sent to the monks of Kirkstead that if they did not join the host their house would be burnt down; when the monks assembled during the afternoon to set out for Horncastle they were told that they would not be required until the following morning. But during the night a party of sixty rebels came to the house and took away with them all the monastery's servants.[137] On Friday the Horncastle commons set out for Lincoln, holding a further muster at Langworth Lane End, about 12 miles from Horncastle and 4 from Lincoln. Troops from other districts seem to have met the Horncastle commons there, the vicar of Snelland reporting that his parishioners were called there, out of whom the best men were selected to go forwards.[138] The abbot of Barlings, who had unwillingly entertained a large body of men in the monastic precincts the previous night, was instructed by messengers from the sheriff to bring victuals to commons massing near his

[133] The only account is that by Brian Stanes, *LP* XII (i), no. 70 (ix) (p. 37).
[134] Ibid., no. 380 (pp. 176–7). [135] SP1/109, fo. 2v (not in *LP* XI, no. 828 (ii).
[136] *LP* XI, no. 828 (xi). [137] Ibid., no. 828 (viii).
[138] SP1/109, fo. 12v (not in *LP* XI, no. 828 (xi)).

house and to send his brethren to join the commons.[139] From here it was only a short distance to Lincoln, from where they advanced no further. The sheriff had, however, given instructions for the inhabitants of Boston to meet with the Horncastle commons on Ancaster Heath, 15 miles south of Lincoln, on the Sunday afternoon.[140] The intention was clearly to strike south, perhaps having consolidated forces with the Louth men at Lincoln.

[139] That the abbot supplied the commons with food and drink is not in doubt, nor that his monks joined the rebellion. A reading of the depositions made by him and the junior members of the house (*LP* XI, nos. 805, 828 (v–viii)) can leave no doubt but that the abbot came under appalling pressure to co-operate and did so in the hope that a show of willing aid would persuade the commons to leave his house in peace. James is quite unfair to say that he was wholly committed to the rebel cause ('Obedience and Dissent', 205).

[140] SP1/110, fo. 167r–v (omitted in *LP* XI, no. 973), 169r (in *LP*).

5

The Dynamics of
the Lincolnshire Rising

The rising at Louth was founded on the expectation that the plate and other liturgical gold and silver of the parish church would be confiscated on Monday, 2 October. The rising at Horncastle was founded on the lie that the confiscation had taken place. As Louth had a considerable investment to protect, it is easy to appreciate why these fears should have had a particular resonance amongst its inhabitants; but there is no sign that Horncastle, as the smaller town, had a similar investment in church goods. In both towns the revolutionary vanguard was drawn from the artisans of the town. This may particularly be seen in Louth. Of the twenty-one men whose names and occupations can be gleaned from the depositions made by Melton and John Brown, four were shoemakers, and there were three drawn from amongst the butchers, labourers, and sawyers (Table 5.1). The composition of the insurrectionary vanguard recruited by Leach is less readily discovered. There is uncertainty about Leach's own social standing, but of the individuals who admitted to being warned by him on the Monday night, four were labourers, three shoemakers, and the other two a saddler and a cordever.

If we look at the names and occupations of the 100 Lincolnshire men indicted, tried, and executed, then the preponderance of poorer urban

TABLE 5.1. *The occupations of known rioters at Louth
on Monday, 2 October*

Butcher	3
Husbandman	1
Labourer	3
Plumber	1
Pouchmaker	1
Roper	1
Sawyer	3
Shoemaker	4
Smith	1
Tailor	1
Weaver	2
Woolwinder	1
Yeoman	1
TOTAL	23

Source: 19 names with occupations taken from the deposition
of Nicholas Melton, SP1/109, fos. 1r–2r (= *LP* XI, no. 828 (i)),
supplemented by 4 additional names with occupations (including Melton's) from the deposition of John Brown, SP1/109,
fo. 76r–v (= *LP* XI, no. 854).

trades is striking. It is not certain how these people were selected from
amongst the much larger number who rose out of solidarity (or intimidation), but labourers and shoemakers form the most prominent occupational categories (Table 5.2). In both towns the commons made it their
prime purpose to capture their neighbouring gentry. For some of the
Louth commons this was the purpose which lay behind their voyage to
Caistor. There remain two puzzles about how the rebellion developed.
How did two relatively small groups of urban artisans manage to launch
a rebellion which came to engulf the eastern part of Lincolnshire and
spread, largely by word of mouth, into Yorkshire? And what were the
relations between them and the gentry?

TABLE 5.2. *Occupations of men indicted for rebellion at Lincoln, 6 March 1537*

	Louth	Horncastle	All other places	Total
Urban trades				
Butcher	3		1	4
Carpenter			2	2
Cooper	1			1
Labourer	4	4	10	18
Mercer			3	3
Miller			2	2
Plumber	2			2
Potter			1	1
Sawyer	2			2
Shoemaker	5	4	3	12
Smith	1			1
Tailor	1		1	2
Thatcher	1	1		2
Tinker			1	1
Weaver	1	1	3	5
Clergy				
Seculars	3		4	7
Regulars			14	14
Rural status groups				
Fishermen			2	2
Yeoman	1		9	10
Husbandmen			7	7
Gentleman			2	2
TOTAL	25	10	65	100

Source: PRO, KB9/539 mm. 1–6.

I

Obviously, much of their success turns on the twin advantages of surprise and numbers, but the speed with which the rebellion spread outside the towns indicates the receptivity of Lincolnshire rural society to their message. This may lend credibility to Kendall's report that it was said before the rising that if one would rise, all the people would rise.[1] People were familiar with the rumours of the amalgamation of parishes and the seizure of church goods, and there was also, to a degree which it is hard to establish, a simmering discontent with the other religious reforms propagated in 1536. Even if the message of the Louth rioters, that it was the time to act to save the commonwealth from destruction, was received with enthusiasm, their real secret was that they were able to take advantage of a coincidence of meetings to spread word of their actions.[2]

Their first means of spreading the word was through the clergy gathered at Louth on Monday, 2 October. It is not certain what body of priests had been called there, whether only the priests of Louth and Louth Esk deanery or those of Calcewaith and Candleshoe deaneries as well. Certainly clergy from the latter two deaneries were present (although they could have attended as observers in the same fashion as clergy from Louth deanery had travelled to Bolingbroke). Louth deanery had forty-two parishes, Calcewaith thirty-nine, and Candleshoe twenty-five. John Child said that he saw forty priests in the market place; Kendall placed their number at sixty.[3]

The clergy were ready recruits to the project launched by the artisans. The priests were sworn to ring their common bells on their return to their parishes. Ralph Grey, vicar of Croft (in Candleshoe deanery) was at Louth and caused the common bell to be rung when he reached Croft, 'and assembled the commons of that parish, moving them to take the common's part for they did enter a commonwealth . . . and further

---

[1] PRO, E36/119, fo. 3r (= LP XII (i), no. 70 (i), where it is misleadingly printed).

[2] But it is important to recognize that the rebellion spread out of solidarity rather than knowledge of the Louth rebels' exact grievances.

[3] Parishes counted from Salter (ed.), '1526 Subsidy'; LP XI, no. 972 (p. 398); LP XII (i), no. 70 (i).

said that if they did not assent, they should be hanged and burnt at their own doors and their houses burnt and destroyed'.[4] The common bell of Alford (Calcewaith deanery) was rung by the vicar on Wednesday morning: he too had been at Louth.[5] Kendall thought that the priests were willingly sworn to ring their bells, and offered the further observation that they were under no real compulsion to ring them at their coming home, 'for they might at that time have fled to what part of the realm that they would, for there was no insurrection in no part of Lincolnshire but only at Louth'.[6] Clerical enthusiasm also persuaded many priests to offer significant sums of money to the commons at Louth.[7]

The second means by which the commons of Louth spread word of their insurrection was by their visit to Caistor. Here they were able to tap into two quite different bodies of people, although drawn from much the same geographical area. Clergy had been summoned from the three north-eastern deaneries in Lincolnshire: Grimsby, Yarborough, and Walshcroft. Huddeswell says that 160 clergy were awaiting the commissary in Caistor church: in fact the three deaneries contained just a few short of 100 parishes. The other meeting at Caistor was of the subsidy assessors for the four wapentakes of Yarborough, Walshcroft, Bradley, and Haverstowe. Again, these wapentakes contained, in all, just under 100 villages.[8] Moigne tells us that four subsidy assessors had been called from every township, but Huddeswell is quite specific that he was one of seven called from the township of Hockstowe.[9] Both these bodies of men were witnesses to the 'capture' of the subsidy commissioners. There is no firm statement that the clergy or subsidy assessors were sworn, but the venturing of the Louth men to Caistor surely spread word of their rebellion all over north-eastern Lincolnshire.

The consequences of the fundamentally opportunist use of clergy and subsidy assessors to call out the commons was that the insurrection passed beyond the control of the gentry, and that it permitted many individuals to launch their own initiatives. North Willingham and the surrounding villages were raised by a dyer of Louth whose name is

---

[4] PRO, E36/118, fo. 2v (= *LP* XI, no. 975 (p. 399)).   [5] *LP* XI, nos. 967 (x), 973.

[6] PRO, E36/119, fo. 4r (not printed in *LP* XII (i), no. 70).

[7] Described below, p. 437.   [8] Calculated from PRO, E179/136/311.

[9] SP1/110, fo. 149v (not in *LP* XI, no. 971); *LP* XI, no. 853.

unrecorded.[10] One Robert Dilcock or Dymock of Humberston was said to have raised Tetney on 4 October by riding through the town crying 'ring the common bell!', but his story was that he had travelled to Louth to sell wheat and found himself sworn to raise his own township. Evidently he raised Tetney too on the way back.[11] We know that beacons were lit on the northern Wolds overlooking the Humber, but we do not know by whom or on whose instructions.[12] And Aske, it will be recalled, fell into the hands of a bunch of commons active along the south side of the Humber who lacked gentry direction or leadership.[13] There is every sign that the revolt was unregulated before the gentry at Louth began to arrange co-ordinated musters for Thursday. Huddeswell was called to muster on Yarborough Hill by the head constable of the wapentake, but he omits to say that he had been leading his own group in the extreme north of Lincolnshire and had earlier that day met and sworn Robert Aske.[14]

By comparison, the rebellion appears to have been spread from Horncastle by the deliberate instructions of the gentry, although, as has already been suggested, it is unlikely that they were free agents. We have already seen how two or more parties of commons were sent eastwards from Horncastle on Tuesday afternoon.[15] On Wednesday a messenger went to Boston carrying word that the whole town should be in readiness to serve the king. On Friday Dymock and the other gentry sent a formal warrant (though couched in unusual terms) to Boston instructing them to meet with the Horncastle men at Ancaster Heath on Sunday afternoon.[16] There may have been other similar warrants circulated, for according to a letter written on Saturday the whole of Holland had risen on the sheriff's instruction.[17]

It is not certain to whom the sole surviving warrant is directed.[18] The form of address used is to 'you, the king's true subjects and their faithful friends'. The recipients were 'to prepare yourselves forward' to

---

[10] LP XI, no. 975, fo. 8.

[11] PRO, E36/118, fo. 5v (= LP XI, no. 975, fo. 4); SP1/110, fo. 173v (= LP XI, no. 974).

[12] LP XI, no. 563.   [13] Above pp. 122–3.   [14] Above p. 191.

[15] Above pp. 131–2.

[16] LP XI, nos. 571; 973; SP1/110, fos. 167r, 168v (completely omitted by LP XI, no. 973), 169r.

[17] LP XI, no. 585.

[18] Ibid., no. 571. It may be the copy of the warrant which was sent by the author of the letter to Audeley.

meet the senders at Ancaster Heath on Sunday afternoon and 'raise the country, swearing every man as well gentleman as other, to be true unto God, to the king and the commonwealth'. It was, then, not addressed to the justices, head constables, or constables but to the commons. The result was a rising without noble or gentle leadership which compelled the gentry to be its captains. The sole witness to events here is an anonymous letter (but most likely written by Anthony Irby, a Holland JP and clerk of the peace), to Lord Chancellor Audeley on Saturday, 7 October.[19] Irby reported that he and the other gentlemen of Holland had been forced on the previous day to appear before the commons at Boston, where they had been sworn to God, the king, the commons, and the commonwealth. The threat had been made by the commons that the goods of any gentry who had fled or refused to be sworn would be seized for the maintenance of the army. Amongst those who had fled was one Mr Tamworth: his house was indeed broken into by the commons and his goods and harness rifled.[20] At Boston the writer, Mr Holland, and the other JPs had been instructed to raise the towns around them, serve as their captains, and lead their troops to Ancaster Heath. 'If we should withstand their rebellious commandment, there were no way with us but only death, loss of our goods and destruction of our children. And the sheriff and all other gentlemen who they make their captains are brought in by like compulsion.' One gentlemen who had been sworn as a captain was a Mr Etton. He had subsequently fled and, Irby understood, been murdered by the commons.[21]

The justices were not lacking in spirit. They had called before them the 'honest persons of the towns about us whom we thought would have been advertised by our advice and counsel and did show them the

---

[19] The letter is dated from Gosberton; the writer, himself a JP, is therefore most likely to be Anthony Irby of Gosberton. Irby was assessed at £26 goods in 1525 and £60 in lands in 1541, E179/137/370, m.7; 136/329 rot. 4, m.1. He was clerk of the peace at this time or slightly later. He died in 1548. *Hist Parl., 1509–1558*, II, 436. Irby was named as a captain, but later made his way to join Suffolk's forces. SP1/109, fo. 70v–71r (very poorly reproduced in *LP* XI, no. 852).

[20] PRO, E36/118, fo. 6r (= *LP* XI, no. 975, fo. 5).

[21] I cannot confirm this or even identify Mr Etton to my satisfaction. For a possible identification as John Etton of Firsby, see A. R. Maddison, 'Lincolnshire Pedigrees', *Harleian Soc.*, 50–2, 55 (1902–6), I, 377. Etton did not achieve the seniority of a place on the commission of the peace. I have not been able to locate a will or grant of probate. A Mr Etton 'of Louth' submitted to Suffolk, so perhaps the rumour was erroneous. *LP* XI, no. 672 (2).

danger of this rebellious insurrection, that it should be to their own destruction'. But their advice to their neighbours to give the rebels no aid was received without enthusiasm: 'they would take such part as their neighbours took and they could not die in a better quarrel than in God's and the king's.' The writer was deeply pessimistic for his future: he ended by commending his widow and children to Audeley.

The letter indicates a pattern of behaviour similar in some respects to that seen at Horncastle. The rebels wanted the gentry to lead them, but it was the commons which had called the gentry before them and sworn them to adhere to their cause. In essence, the gentry were superfluous to the common's movement, but the failure to comply with their demands was to invite the commons to seize and destroy property and perhaps person.

The other, and perhaps the most frightening observation of the letter was its remark that the commons were 'trusting to have the aid of all of the commons of this realm'. There are signs that the commons had an alternative political structure based on the solidarity and common understanding of other communities. The instruction to Boston to mobilize came in the name of the sheriff, but it was clearly directed by the commons to the commons of Boston, and not to the mayor or JPs. The commons of North Lincolnshire rose not out of support for the Louth rebellion's objectives, but out of solidarity for the fact that they had risen: as Moigne says of the commons who came to Hambledon Hill with Aske, they came 'for to speak with some of our commons to know what was the cause of their insurrection'.[22] The most chilling moment in the Lincolnshire rebellion was surely that when it became clear that the Lincolnshire commons were finding support amongst the commonalties of other towns. On Sunday morning two messengers from the commons of Beverley were escorted before the gentry and commons in the Chapter House. They carried a letter under the common seal of the commons of Beverley directed to the commons of Lincolnshire, 'the effect whereof was that they, hearing that the commons of Lincolnshire had risen, did write to them to ascertain them that they in likewise were

---

[22] SP1/110, fo. 155r (= *LP* XI, no. 971). Aske says that the rising he encountered on 4–5 October was prompted by Lord Burgh calling these districts out against the Louth rising. This can be paralleled over the Humber, where the rising was prompted by a similar call to mobilize. 'The manner of the taking of Robert Aske', 332.

risen and desired the commons of Lincolnshire to ascertain the commons of Beverley what was the causes of their rising and they would be
ready to help them and aid them at all times'.[23] Remarkably, the letter
from Beverley survives (although dated 10 October), and the text makes
it clear that it was indeed from the commons and, being unsigned, was
written in the name of the commonalty and not of individuals within
it.[24] The response of the Lincolnshire commons was to send messengers
to Beverley, but they carried letters signed by the gentry and not made
in the name of the commons.[25] Then, later on Sunday morning, there
came a messenger from Halifax also declaring that the country had risen
and was ready to aid the commons of Lincolnshire.[26] Whether the support of Halifax was genuine cannot be determined (it seems unlikely),
but Beverley had indeed risen. The commons of Beverley offered their
aid, but also asked what was the cause of the Lincolnshire rebellion. They
did not know: their support was based on a collective solidarity rather
than subscription to a common political programme.

II

By the time the two rebel forces entered Lincoln, the gentry had established a hold over the rebellious commons. The detailed descriptions
presented earlier of the way in which the gentry joined the rising can
leave little doubt that in the first days they were unwilling and coerced
participants, taken by large groups of men who were not unwilling to
back their demand that the gentry should join their cause with threats
of personal violence and the destruction of property. Resistance was
not really a possibility for most gentry. Capture came as a surprise; there
was no time to flee, and in any case flight might merely encourage the
commons to wreak their revenge on property and any members of the
household whom they might be able to secure. The notion advanced

[23] SP1/110, fo. 156r.
[24] *LP* XI, no. 645. It was brought to Lincoln by a servingman, William Woodmansey, and this
may indicate the milieu from which it arose. Ibid., no. 842 (4).
[25] Stapleton, 89, for a description of the letter.   [26] SP1/110, fo. 156v (= *LP* XI, no. 971).

by some historians, that the gentry expected their capture and virtually sat at their doors, coat on, horse saddled, awaiting their prearranged collection, is far from the truth. Even Aske believed that Moigne 'had been enforced' to be the captain of the rebels on Hambleton Hill.[27]

The case of Sir William Sandon illustrates just how little was to be gained from directly opposing the commons. By calling them traitors and saying that they would be hanged for their deeds, Sandon directly challenged their legitimacy as a movement and claimed a superior legitimacy for himself and his own actions. He was loyal, they were traitors, a complete inversion of what the commons themselves believed. Sandon most certainly had an uncomfortable time once he fell into the common's hands, but more important than this, his denunciation of the movement destroyed his credit with them and so his ability to influence their actions.[28] The penalty was to have men like Thomas Tetney of Partney riding around saying that 'if he could get that false churl Sir William Sandon, he would kill him'.[29] It would be unjust to compare his stance with that of the other gentry taken at Scrivelsby, for while his was a heroic but futile gesture, the others were not cowards, but practical men who had no desire to get themselves killed.

The more cautious gentry were playing a long game whose essence was to persuade the commons and onlookers that they were at one with the rank and file whilst looking for the means to restrain and hinder the host. Here they had one advantage. Every enlargement of the scope of the host, whether social, to include the richer townsfolk and gentry, or geographical, to draw more people out of the countryside, diluted the hold of the original rebels and passed the initiative to the gentry and the normal custodians of law and order. It is striking that the examinations of the Louth rebels all tail off after the fourth or fifth day of the rebellion, as they ceased to be leaders and became rank-and-file participants in the rebel host. The enlargement of the revolt was a necessary gentry strategy, forced on the gentry by circumstances which compelled them to be seen to advance the aims of the revolt in order to buy the acquiescence

---

[27] 'The manner of the taking of Robert Aske', 333.

[28] Note too how the commons at Louth were outraged by the reference to them as 'rebels' in Hussey's letters. Above p. 120.

[29] *LP* XI, no. 975, fo. 1.

of its radical supporters. That the gentry were witnessed giving orders is not itself evidence that they were wholly in control.

Hence, if Dymock really did give orders for the bringing in of other gentry and the ringing of church bells immediately after his own capture, then he was doing no more than fulfilling the common's expectations at that moment—he could hardly forbid these actions without revealing himself to be an opponent of the commons—whilst recruiting other gentry who could aid him in taming the rebels. Likewise, when we see him ordering the abbot of Barlings to provide victuals for the commons, we must acknowledge that his actions were determined by the need to maintain order and discipline within the host, and that his actions were conducive towards that end. That which the abbot would not bring willingly, the commons could always take as plunder. But it is also significant that the few letters and warrants issued by the gentry during the Louth movement are written in the name of the commons and with their authority, even though signed by the gentry. We have already seen how the Louth letter to Henry VIII carefully distanced its signatories from the commons. The letter sent to Boston calling out the commons there was signed by the gentry, but with its demand that every man be sworn to the commons it was transparently not the sheriff's work. In Boston it was believed that the 'sheriff and others therein were compelled and put in fear of their lives to make the said letter'.[30]

If the gentry were falsely enthusiastic about the movement, then we enter a world of mirrors. How can we discover what their real intentions were? If we total up the comments made on the gentry's motivation in the depositions taken after the movement had failed, we find that as many thought that the gentry were not involved in the movement out of choice as believed that they were the driving force behind the rebellion. So, a canon of Barlings commented that 'he cannot say whether they [the gentry] were there with all their wills or against their wills, but by [what] he saw in part of them, he thinketh in his conscience that they were there against their wills because he saw divers of them fashion themselves towards the staying of the commons'.[31] Again, William Wilson of Alford, who saw the capture of Sir Andrew Bilsby, said that '[they] were

---

[30] SP1/110, fo. 169r (omitted in *LP* XI, no. 973). John Foster of Boston, kerner.
[31] SP1/109, fo. 9v (omitted in *LP* XI, no. 828).

compelled by force of the country to go forth with them and durst do no other for fear of their lives', and commented 'that for as much as he knows, the gentlemen were taken against their wills and was fain to go with the commons and to do as they did for fear of their lives'.[32] And there is Morland's opinion, when examined about how many of the gentlemen were setters-forth of the rebellion, 'that so far as he could see, both all the gentlemen and honest yeomen of the country were weary of the matter and sorry for it, saying that they dissembled the matter and durst not be known for the time of their opinions amongst the commons for fear of losing their lives'.[33]

All the significant cases of deponents incriminating the gentry come from the depositions made in the Tower in January 1537 by men drawn from the Horncastle branch of the movement. Philip Trotter, who had previously described how the gentlemen had been seized at Scrivelsby and how he, with others, had encouraged them to surrender, came close to contradicting his first deposition in his second.

Item, he saith that gentlemen were the chief setters forward of them and they were in all their proceedings directed by the gentlemen and obedient to their commandment . . .

Item, he saith that he thinketh in his conscience that all the gentlemen were amongst the commons willingly and without constraint of any man, for he did see them at all times busy to set forward their purpose with no less diligence than the commons did themselves.[34]

Nicholas Leach deposed that,

as it appeared unto them, by all the exterior acts and gestures of the gentlemen, they were amongst the commons willingly, for that he did see them always as diligent to set forward every matter as the commons were. And further saith that during all that time of the insurrection, there was not one of the gentlemen that did persuade the people to desist their naughty and abominable enterprise, nor declared unto them that the same was high treason, for if they had, he thought verily that they would not have gone forward in the same.[35]

---

[32] SP1/110, fo. 128v (= LP XI, no. 967 (x)).

[33] PRO, E36/119, fo. 57r (= LP XII (i), no. 380 (reduced by LP to 'but [they] durst not disclose their opinion to the commons for fear of their lives')).

[34] Ibid., fos. 14v, 14 (bis)v. (= LP XII (i), no. 70 (x)).

[35] Ibid., fo. 16v (= LP XII (i), no. 70 (xi)).

Others amongst these deponents made similar points, suggesting, for instance, that the sheriff could have controlled the commons on Wednesday if he had tried (with a white rod, according to Longbothom). The result is a mixture of anecdotes, some unexceptional (that the gentry brought food to the commons), others quite wild. One Bernard Fletcher, who described himself as a servant of Thomas Dymock's, insinuated that the gentry at Scrivelsby had gone there earlier in the day quite deliberately to make themselves available for capture.[36] It is hard to escape the impression that when these deponents were examined in London in January 1537 they conspired to do as much damage as they could to the reputations of the gentry taken at Scrivelsby.

It is in this context that we turn to the only extant account by a gentleman participant in the rebellion. Although Thomas Moigne's deposition was published in a severely curtailed paraphrase over a century ago, it has never attracted the attention from historians of the rebellion that it deserves.[37] Of course, we might regard it as exculpatory and self-seeking, but no more than any other deposition. A close reading suggests that Moigne was actually rather proud of his role in the movement and had no doubt that his actions had been impeccably loyal and proper throughout. The constant theme in his deposition was to show how the gentry had worked to secure control of the movement so that they should be in a position to persuade and divert the commons from adopting an aggressive, forward campaign. The gentry's chosen instrument, adopted even before Moigne's capture, was their refusal to advance until they had received an answer from the king to their letters and petitions, and their unspoken hope was clearly that the king's response would be the means by which the commons would be persuaded home.

We have already seen how Sir William Ascue believed that with the sending of a letter to the king on the evening of Tuesday, 3 October, the gentry at Louth had struck a bargain with the commons whereby the latter would be quiescent until a reply was received. On Wednesday morning he felt confident enough to tell Moigne to hold the great court on the Isle of Axholme as arranged, but this peace was shattered by the

---

[36] *LP* XII (i), no. 70 (iii) (p. 34); (viii) (p. 36). A rod is a symbol of officeholding and responsibility.
[37] *LP* XI, no. 971. I have used the original MS (SP1/110, fos. 149r–158v) throughout this account.

reading of the two letters intercepted by the men of Market Rasen and the rumour that Lord Burgh was approaching.

When the common bell was rung and the commons reassembled in large numbers, the gentlemen sought to muster them in the fields outside Louth, 'to the intent that every gentleman might resort to his wapentake and so to do the most good amongst his own neighbours in [the] staying of them'.[38] This was abandoned until after lunch, when the gentry divided the commons into wapentakes and for each one appointed

to be their captain the [subsidy] commissioner which dwelled in their wapentake and so every one of us went to our own wapentakes and persuaded them that they should not go forward but to depart home unto their own houses to such time as they had answer from the king's highness, but that they would not do in no means, but cried to go forward out of hand or else they would destroy and slay us and choose other captains. And then when we did see them in such obstinate and wilful opinions, we determined ourselves for to follow their minds and to stay them when we came to Lincoln by such policies as we could in our minds invent, to the intent to weary them and make them spend their money and so by such policy compel them to go home again.[39]

That evening the common bell was rung at midnight and Moigne describes the commons discussing in the market place whether they would be better to kill the gentry there and then, for 'the men of worship would surely betray them, and that appeared by them the day before, for they said that every one of us persuaded our companies as much as we might that they should not go forward'.[40]

On the Thursday Moigne went with his company to Hambleton Hill, where there was again a demand that they should press forwards. Moigne told them that there were two urgent reasons why they should not, the first being that it was the season to put land in tillage and sow, and that if they all went they should be short of corn the following year; the second being that if they all went they should lack money and victuals and be forced to spoil the country. Moigne persuaded them only to send on only so many from every village. Whilst men were being appointed, he received word that Aske and Nicholas Girlington, who had come from the commons in Kirton Soke, wished to speak to him. Moigne knew

---

38 SP1/110, fo. 153v.   39 Ibid., fo. 154r.   40 Ibid., fo. 154v.

that Aske was a lawyer, 'and so thinking him to be by reason thereof to be a man of quietness intended clearly to have spoken with them secretly and to have disclosed unto them what we had privily devised to do concerning *the staying of the commons*'.[41] As the commons insisted that they should talk openly before them, this information was never shared.

After the arrival at Lincoln, a meeting was held on Saturday between the 'men of worship' of the two forces and members of the commons. Here it was felt that the articles drawn up by the Horncastle men were 'unreasonable and foolish' and required reform, 'and so sent unto the king's highness to the intent that they might have an occasion to desire the commons to stay there unto such time as they might have an answer of the same articles'.[42] On Sunday the revised articles were read to the commons who, after persuasions made to them, consented not to advance further until they had the king's answer to them. Then two messengers were received in the Chapter House by the gentry and commons, the first from the Beverley commons, saying that they had risen and promising their help to the commons in Lincoln, the second from Halifax, again offering aid and assistance. On each occasion the commons, 'in great fury', wished to recommence their campaign: twice the gentry persuaded them to await their answer from the king, saying that if they went forward before they had an answer, 'we should commit high treason and them that they had comfort upon [Beverley and Halifax] should not be near them to aid them'.[43]

The articles were signed by the gentlemen on Monday morning and dispatched to London. Again the commons wished to set off, and once more the gentry persuaded them to stay at Lincoln, this time promising them the goods of those who had fled from them.

Tuesday brought disaster. At noon the gentlemen, then being in the Chapter House, were visited by 300 commons who escorted a messenger carrying the king's letter in reply to that sent from Louth the previous Tuesday evening. The gentry hoped to read the king's letter secretly; the commons would not allow it and demanded that the letter be openly read. Moigne read it to commons and gentry, but attempted to leave unread a clause 'that we feared would stir the commons'. This

---

[41] Ibid., fo. 155r (my emphasis).   [42] Ibid., fo. 155v.   [43] Ibid., fo. 156v.

omission was noticed by the vicar of Snelland, who called out that the letter was misread. There was a row, and 200 of the commons withdrew into the cloister where they debated what to do with the gentry who were so obviously determined to deceive them. They agreed to murder the gentry if they would not go forward the following morning, then, changing their mind, decided to kill them as they came through the west door. The gentry escaped out of the south door into the chancellor's house, and the commons 'departed to their lodgings in a great fury, determining to kill us the morrow after unless we would go forward with them'.

The inevitable breach with the commons having occurred, the gentry considered what to do next. Moigne's opinion was

that I thought we were driven to such extremities that policies would no more serve us. Wherefore there was no remedy but that every one of us should prove what friends we could make to stay and if we could make our party in any reasonable strength, rather to fight with them that would not be contented to stay than we would go forward. If we could make no power able to make any countenance to fight with them, that then we should keep the [cathedral] close until such time as the king's power might rescue us.[44]

This was adopted by the gentry. Each of them sent for the men they trusted most within their companies and 'opened unto them the danger of our going forward to the displeasure of our prince with the mischief that should ensue thereof. And so moved them to stay until such time as we might hear further of the king's pleasure.' They then stated their fear that if the rest of the commons would not wait in Lincoln any longer, then the gentry proposed to fight them, 'for it was better to be slain in our prince's quarrel [than to] go forward and be destroyed with our prince's power'.[45] They moved their supporters to return in the morning with as many of the commons as could be relied upon to assist them.

When their supporters returned on Wednesday morning with others from the commons, the gentry, dressed for war, went with them into the fields, 'where we declared unto them that we would not in anywise go forwards before we had further answer from the king'.[46] By their persuasion they convinced the majority of the commons to wait for

[44] Ibid., fo. 157v.   [45] Ibid., fo. 158r.   [46] Ibid., fo. 158r.

the king's next letter. After the arrival of Lancaster Herald that evening, and following more persuasions by Moigne and the other gentry, they were able to persuade the majority of the commons to depart on the Thursday and Friday but only on the condition that if they could not obtain their suit from the king, or if the duke of Suffolk's army approached, they would call the commons back to Lincoln.

Moigne ended his description of the rising: 'pleaseth your lordship to understand that I have not here written neither all the circumstances and policies that was used to stay the commons nor all the dangers that we were in ourselves by reason of using the said policies because they be not all in my remembrance and if they were they would contain a volume.'[47] The question is whether the 'policies' that Moigne describes were a genuine strategy employed by the gentry or an exculpatory rationalization by one of their members designed to twist acts of sedition into acts of loyalism. The problem of proof is considerable. Moigne's is the only extant account of the movement's period at Lincoln, for the examinations of the lesser figures are rarely interested in events after the arrival there. Nonetheless, there are grounds for believing that the account he gives is a straightforward description of the strategy that the gentry devised to cope with their own capture and the insurgents. First, it offers a convincing explanation as to why the movement, having successfully entered Lincoln and given notice of its plans to move southwards, remained in and around the town until it dispersed. Secondly, the rumour was circulating on Saturday that whilst the rebels hoped for a letter from the king by noon, they intended to tarry about Lincoln until a letter was received.[48] Thirdly, the letters addressed by the gentry at Lincoln to the duke of Suffolk and Sir Edward Maddison after the reading in the Chapter House of the king's letter both expressly refer to their use of delaying tactics. To Suffolk they said that it would now be harder to stay the rebels by policy, both because of the letter and the comfort that they had from other places now in rebellion. 'And if we had not stayed them there by good policy and making of a petition to the king, they [would] had been this day at Huntingdon.' And in what may be a continuation of this letter, the gentry say that, 'with much peril of our lives [we] have

47 Ibid., fo. 158v.   48 SP1/107, fo. 66r (= LP XI, no. 587 (2)).

brought them to this stay that they shall march no further until they hear again from his majesty'. To Maddison they wrote of the fury with which the king's letter had been received, but that 'nevertheless, we trust, God willing, to find such policy and means to stay them two or three days'.[49] Earlier, on 9 October, when the commons sent a copy of their articles to the earl of Shrewsbury, the gentry added: 'also the said commonalty humbly desireth your lordship to be good lord unto this bearer which is a man of good bearing and hath daily since our business began done the best that he might for the staying of the said commonalty in quietness and rest.'[50] The claim that 'policy' was being used to detain the rebels was not simply an excuse dreamt up *after* the failure of the insurrection.

There is important confirmatory evidence of this strategy. George Huddeswell, the captain of the rebel band which swore Aske, led his irregulars to Hambledon Hill on Thursday, 5 October, to the muster conducted by Thomas Moigne. On Friday, at Market Rasen, he recalled that the gentlemen went into council. Afterwards, Sir Andrew Bilsby 'said the commons [had] been unruly and will not be ruled. Sir William Skipwith said that they shall be ordered whether they will or no, then every gentlemen said that it should be well done that they be ruled and that the said George saith that at that time the commons had submitted themselves to the rule of the said knights and gentlemen.' Unfortunately Huddeswell also believed that the gentry had 'furthered' the insurrection 'to their power'.[51] At this same muster some people were selected to go forwards to Lincoln and others turned back: the intention may, in part, have been to remove firebrands from the host.

What the gentry sought was a free and unconditional pardon. Hussey told a delegation of rebels from Horncastle that he would not lose his head and his lands as they seemed likely to do:[52] the fear of all the gentry (quite justifiably) was that even association with the rebels jeopardized their own lives. A pardon, therefore, was their guarantee, not the commons'. This had been requested in their letter from Louth, but the royal letter received at Lincoln on Tuesday, 10 October made no

---

[49] 'Thomas Master's Narrative', 65–6; *LP* XI, no. 665.
[50] SP1/107, fo. 108r (= *LP* XI, no. 618).
[51] PRO, E36/118, fo. 55r (completely omitted in *LP* XI, no. 853).
[52] SP1/109, fos. 70v–71r (not in *LP* XI, no. 852).

concession of a pardon. Instead, it insisted that unless the commons dispersed and a hundred rebels submitted to Suffolk with halters around their necks, they would be militarily crushed.[53] In their letter to Suffolk the gentry stressed that the means to appease the commons was to announce a pardon, and they particularly asked Maddison to press this on the duke. Suffolk did ask Henry whether he would grant a pardon to allow his forces to advance against the larger and more threatening revolt developing in Yorkshire.[54] The heat went out of the issue as the rebels drifted home, but even then their dispersal might have been encouraged by the gentry's offer to continue to sue for a general pardon.

There is the possibility that the gentry were pursuing contradictory aims, of restraining the commons until boredom and expense forced them home, whilst maintaining the host in the belief that this would best secure them a pardon. This seems not to have happened, and the movement had ceased to be of military significance long before the (conditional) pardon was received.

The gentry, on their own account, sought to control the movement to delay the common's offensive whilst using the petitions as an excuse for procrastination. This justification of their enforced leadership appears to be borne out by whatever sources extra to Moigne's account survive. It seems almost certain that the worst fears of the commons, expressed by the man who said that Sir William Skipwith was false to the movement because he would make no speed therein, were acute. Another man held that the gentry 'would deceive the commons'.[55] If the gentry were employing 'policy' to take the heat out of the rebellion, if they were interested in securing a pardon for themselves and the commons, were they also serious about the articles which were compiled and sent to London, or were these merely fashioned as a further cynical strategy against the commons?

The answer to this question would seem to be that the two independent sectors of the Lincolnshire movement had different approaches to the

[53] *LP* XI, no. 569.

[54] Ibid., no. 672. For the belief that the rebels at Lincoln had a promise from Shrewsbury that he would secure a pardon, see 'Letters of the Cliffords', 143 and cf. *LP* XI, no. 694, which has the commons remaining at Lincoln to await an answer from Suffolk.

[55] PRO, E36/118, fos. 3v, 4v (= *LP* XI, no. 975).

question of petitioning. The Louth gentry made no attempt to formulate their grievances further after they sent their letter to the king with Sir Edward Maddison. The articles sent to London with George Stanes or Stones of Haltham (south of Horncastle) on Monday, 9 October appear to have originated with the Horncastle arm of the rebellion and were sent to London only after the Louth gentry had insisted on their being toned down.[56]

The Horncastle gentry drew up articles (which do not survive) on the evening of Tuesday, 3 October. Richard Leeds recalled that on the Wednesday he heard the sheriff, Mr Deighton, and Thomas Dymock read articles in Horncastle field which they had made the night before: these named Cromwell, Rich (the Chancellor of Augmentations), and a number of bishops as being the devisors of the taking away of church goods and the pulling down of churches.[57] A copy of these articles was taken to Louth by Morland, the ex-monk, on Wednesday, and it is possible that they were also carried to Lord Hussey. Hussey heard on Wednesday morning of the rising and sent two of his servants, Cutler and Dales, to investigate. He also offered a safe passage for three or four of the Horncastle men to attend him at Sleaford. There he was visited by a delegation who carried a letter signed by the gentry; they also requested that Hussey sue for them a conditional pardon, which he declined to do. There is no sign that these articles were sent to the king by the rebels.[58]

Dr Bush has suggested that the demands reported by Anthony Irby on 7 October are a hearsay account of these lost articles. If this is correct (and it seems a reasonable surmise), then they were radical indeed.[59] The first demand was that the church was to have all its traditional privileges restored, meaning that the status quo of 1529 was to be revived. Secondly, all suppressed religious houses were to be restored except for those which the king had suppressed for his own power. Thirdly, a roll-call

---

[56] All the witnesses agree that Stanes was the prime mover in the preparation of the articles, e.g. 'when he [Stanes] had devised his articles, he went from wapentake to wapentake to the people and did set the articles forward to all his power': PRO, E36/119, fo. 5v (= LP XII (i), no. 70 (iii)). This means that he went between the contingents of the rebel host rather than that he rode about Lincolnshire.

[57] PRO, E36/119, fo. 17r (= LP XII (i), no. 70 (xii)).

[58] SP1/110, fo. 154v (Moigne, who says that they were articles to be sent to the king, but makes no comment on their contents); LP XII (i), no. 380 (p. 177). For Hussey, see his deposition, LP XI, no. 852 and below p. 161.

[59] Bush, '"Up for the Commonweal"', 303, n. 4.

of royal servants and bishops, starting with Cranmer and including the trio of Cromwell, Wriothesley (Master of the Rolls), and Rich (Chancellor of Augmentations), were either to be delivered to the rebels or banished. And finally, the king was not to demand further taxes of his subjects except in time of war.[60]

The gentry seized at Scrivelsby together with George Stanes then produced new articles on the Thursday evening or Friday morning which were read to the rebels in Langworth field on Friday. Nicholas Leach recalled Stanes, with other gentlemen, saying to the commons: ' "Masters, ye see that in all the time we have been absent from you, we have not been idle. How like you these articles? If they please you, say yea, if not, ye shall have them amended." And then the commons held up their hands with a loud voice, saying "we like them very well".'[61] This may have been the occasion on which Trotter saw the sheriff and the other Dymocks, Deighton, Saunderson, Stanes, and William Leach ask the commons whether they would have Cromwell, Wriothesley, and Rich and a number of bishops who together were the 'imaginers and devisors of all the false laws' sent to them for punishment. 'And the commons asked the gentlemen "Masters, if ye had them, would that mend the matter anything" and the gentlemen said "yea, for these be the doers of all mischief".'[62] The gentry might have been acute in their assessment. They may equally have been merely pandering to the crowd.

It therefore seems quite satisfactorily evidenced that the Horncastle gentry were responsible for formulating articles for which they sought the assent of the commons.[63] In the particular case of the article against the Statute of Uses, one deponent says quite clearly that Stanes brought to the sheriff a bill condemning the statute. This may well have been on Wednesday, for on Friday we have an account of the sheriff explaining the ill effects of the statute to the crowd at Langworth and seeking their consent to the inclusion of the grievance in the articles.[64]

---

[60] LP XI, no. 585.   [61] PRO, E36/119, fo. 16r (= LP XII (i) no. 70 (xi)).

[62] Ibid., fo. 14 (bis)v–15r (= LP XII (i) no. 70 (x)).

[63] In addition to Leach quoted before, Bernard Fletcher has Stanes reading the articles and asking: ' "Sirs, how like you these articles? Doth they please you or no?" And to that the people held up their staves saying "yea, yea, yea".' LP XII (i), no. 70 (viii).

[64] Ibid., no. 70 (xi, xii).

The text of the Langworth articles cannot fully be established. Certainly there was a clause identifying Cromwell and the bishops as the source of all current woes, another that the subsidy should be remitted, one that the abbeys should stand, and a fourth asking for the repeal of the Statute of Uses. If the demands noted by Irby really are those prepared on Wednesday, then these articles already represent a considerable watering down of the rebels' ambitions. Nonetheless, when the Louth gentry met with those of Horncastle at Netlam on Saturday, they were confronted with a programme with which they could not agree, perhaps because, as it was so confrontational, it undermined their own efforts to secure a pardon. Moigne, our sole witness, was sent to bring in Sir John Sutton and missed the meeting, but says that the Horncastle articles were found to be 'wondrous unreasonable and foolish' and required reformation before they could be sent to the king. He was quite specific, though, that the purpose of sending the articles was 'that they might have an occasion to desire the commons to stay there [Lincoln] unto such time as they might have an answer of the same articles'. The revised articles were read to the commons on Sunday and a promise extracted that they would not stir from Lincoln until the king's answer was received. The articles were signed by the gentry on Monday morning and sent southwards with George Stanes, who was almost immediately captured, sent on to London, and ultimately executed.[65]

Thus it may be seen how the articles originated on the Horncastle side of the rebellion but were watered down once (if not twice) before being dispatched to the king. The articles sent to Henry had ceased to be a series of demands but were transformed into a set of grievances which the rebels drew to the king's attention, and to which was annexed a request for a pardon. Hence, the demand circulating in Holland that the king should demand no more taxes except in time of war was transformed into a request that the subsidy should be rescinded, and finally became an observation about the impossibility of paying the fifteenth due to be collected a year hence.[66] The demand that the liberties of the

---

[65] SP1/110, fos. 155v, 156r, 156v.

[66] Stanes was apparently going around saying that the articles included a demand that the subsidy should be remitted and no more monasteries and churches suppressed as late as Sunday. *LP* XI, no. 828 (v).

church should be re-established became first a request that suppressed religious houses should be re-established, and then an observation that because of the dissolution, the service of God was less well performed and hospitality had decayed. The king was not asked to reverse the dissolution. The demand that the king send to the rebels Cromwell and others to be lynched was replaced by some gentle chiding about the king surrounding himself by counsellors of low birth and reputation who were suspected to be corrupt. The petition only sought the repeal of the Statute of Uses. Every other clause was explanatory. It had ceased to be a platform from which the rebels could negotiate.[67]

What was also lost was the conviction that a confiscation of church goods was imminent and had to be opposed. It is noticeable that on Wednesday Robert Leeds has the sheriff and others appearing before the host and identifying Cromwell and others as the persons responsible for the confiscation of church goods and the pulling down of churches.[68] There can be no doubt that the gentry knew that these reports of confiscation and demolition were false, but at this moment felt unable to confront the convictions of the crowd. The Langworth articles show that they were swinging the rank and file away from their gut fears towards a more general programme, but inevitably this was a case of the gentry shaping the common's fears into more conventional political terms. On Saturday this strategy was adopted by the Louth gentry as a device to delay the commons further and watered down into a series of complaints and request for a pardon. This served to discipline the rebels around a programme and delay their advance, but in doing this the gentry also provided the means by which bloodshed and further conflict could be avoided. The king could defuse the revolt by making minor concessions, promising to consider the rebels' grievances, and offering a pardon. In adopting this strategy the gentry mistook their monarch, but in Lincolnshire this barely mattered, for the rebellion had collapsed before Henry returned his second inflammatory reply.

---

[67] *LP* XI, no. 705 (i), printed Fletcher and MacCulloch, *Tudor Rebellions*, 131, to be read with Bush, ' "Up for the commonweal" ', 303 n. 4.

[68] *LP* XII (i), no. 70 (xii).

6

Fever Days: The Reaction to Lincolnshire

The reaction of the Lincolnshire gentry, faced with a disturbance which they could not control, was to send word of their difficulties to the king and await rescue. So, first John Hennage rode southwards, then Sir Edward Maddison. Lord Burgh, who evaded the rebels at Caistor, fled westwards into Nottinghamshire and wrote to the king on Tuesday night from Saundby giving an outline of the day's events. He also sent word to Thomas, Lord Darcy and the earl of Shrewsbury in Yorkshire, finding Shrewsbury at his house in Sheffield Park. Shrewsbury immediately sent news of the outrage to the king. Other reports, including one from John, Lord Hussey at Sleaford, were received in the following days.[1] The news was also spread by word of mouth. Sir William Fitzwilliam, passing through Guildford on Saturday, heard that everywhere the people prayed God [to] 'speed the rebellious people in Lincolnshire'.[2] On the Sunday following the rising at Louth the duke of Norfolk wrote that there was rejoicing at the rising in Essex, and the following day could report rumours circulating in mid-Suffolk of the capture of Lord Hussey and the fall of Boston.[3]

---

[1] *LP* XI, nos. 533, 536, 538. Saundby is on the Nottinghamshire side of the Trent from Gainsborough.

[2] Ibid., no. 584.   [3] Ibid., nos. 603, 625.

Yet there were also those who remained in blissful ignorance of the great events taking shape in Lincolnshire and Yorkshire. On the fourth day after the Louth rising the earl of Huntingdon wrote to Henry VIII from Ashby de la Zouche, only 75 miles from Louth, saying that he had heard that Shrewsbury was recruiting men to suppress a rebellion, but he knew not who had risen or where.[4] This chapter describes the actions of those not immediately caught up in the Lincolnshire movement but who were touched by it from a distance, first Hussey at Sleaford, then the king and those who were mobilized on his behalf to repress the rebels.

I

John, Lord Hussey had a rotten rebellion. First he saw his local authority disintegrate, then he was forced to flee to Nottingham in disguise. Later in October he was called to London, and whilst confident that he had acted with impeccable loyalty, he was ultimately executed. If this was not enough, his actions have been misconstrued by some modern historians.[5]

As we saw earlier, Hussey was an elderly minor peer of conservative inclinations with close connections with the household of the Princess Mary. He and his wife may have been the object of suspicion for their evident Catholic and pro-Marian sympathies. His house at Sleaford stood on the road south from Lincoln to Peterborough. Horncastle was about 20 miles north-east. It was in recognition of his local pre-eminence that Lord Clinton sent him word of the Louth rising on the Monday evening. Hussey thanked Clinton for his report and made his own fruitless enquiries as to events in Louth. When he tried to get back in contact with Clinton on Wednesday, Clinton had disappeared, doubtless because he had ridden to the king with news of the rising.[6] On Tuesday morning Hussey had word from George Hennage, the dean of Lincoln, of

---

[4] Ibid., no. 560.

[5] James, 'Obedience and Dissent', *passim*. This account was first exploded by Gunn, 'Peers, Commons and Gentry'.

[6] *LP* XI, no. 852; Clinton was riding north on Friday and Saturday with letters for Huntingdon, Shrewsbury, and a number of gentlemen. Ibid., nos. 587, 590.

the same events. He then wrote to the mayor of Lincoln offering the deduction that the rebels would advance there and commanding him to take precautions to close the city against a rebel attack.[7] At some point during the day Hussey also had a letter from Thomas, Lord Burgh seeking his counsel and Hussey agreed to meet with him at Lincoln on Wednesday.[8] A third letter which arrived that evening came from Thomas Moigne, writing on the subsidy commissioners' behalf after they had dispersed at Caistor but in ignorance of the capture of most of his colleagues. It will be recalled that the commissioners had proposed to reconvene at Spittal in the Street on Wednesday morning and wished Hussey to be present to confer with them as to how they should proceed. Hussey, though, thought that Moigne's letter was an attempt to trap him. He demanded to know why Moigne alone had signed it. Rather than being at Spittal (which was inconvenient for Hussey, lying to the north of Lincoln) on Wednesday, he proposed to meet the commissioners at Lincoln on Wednesday evening or Thursday morning.[9] Hussey also wrote at some point during the day to Sir Robert Tyrwhit and Sir William Ascue, almost certainly in response to the letter he had received from the dean of Lincoln and obviously before Moigne's letter reached him. In this letter Hussey called on them to gather their forces and repel the rebels; if they were not able to do so, Hussey himself would come their aid. This letter was entrusted to the same servant who carried his letter to the mayor of Lincoln. During the night of Tuesday/Wednesday the messenger, a man called Gatton, was captured and both letters fell into the commons' hands. The terms in which they were couched mightily angered them and served to inflame the situation further when they were read at Louth on Wednesday morning.[10] Hussey also wrote on Tuesday to the JPs of Kesteven telling them to maintain order. If they could not, then they were to break down bridges and stop the passage of people into East Anglia. It may have been on these instructions that the sluices of the drains and sea defences were opened.[11] When Hussey wrote to Cromwell on Wednesday he was unaware that the movement already encompassed both Louth and Horncastle, that the more prominent

[7] Ibid., no. 531.   [8] Ibid., no. 852 (= SP1/109, fos. 72v–73r).

[9] SP1/110, fo. 151r (= LP XI, no. 971); LP XI, no. 532; SP1/109, fos. 72v–73r (= LP XI, no. 852).

[10] Above p. 120.   [11] LP XI, nos. 852, 567.

Lindsey JPs had been captured and taken to Louth,[12] that Clinton and Burgh had fled from the county, and that his letters, which declared his opposition to the revolt, had been captured and publicly read at Louth.

The scale of the crisis at Louth probably only became clear when Hussey received a letter written on Wednesday morning in the names of the commons but signed by Tyrwhit, Ascue, Moigne, and other gentry then detained at Louth.[13] The letter threatened that if he did not come in, the commons would come to get Hussey as 'their utter enemy'. Most seriously, the letter revealed how the gentry with whom Hussey could have organized resistance were already the prisoners of the commons. The projected meeting at Lincoln never happened because Hussey had no one with whom to confer.

At some other point during Wednesday Hussey became aware of the rising at Horncastle. On his own account he sent two of his servants, Cutler and Dale, to establish the cause of the trouble, offering that 'if the commissioners had put them [the townspeople] to anything further than the king's commission was, I would help to see it redressed'.[14] (His assumption was clearly that the rising arose from the levying of the subsidy.) Hussey offered a safe conduct for three or four of the Horncastle men to come to him to explain their actions. Several did come and carried a letter signed by the gentlemen. They asked that Hussey should sue for their pardon, but on conditions. Hussey bade them 'walk home knaves, for the king is used not to condition with no such rebellious'.

And I showed them that if they would submit themselves to the king's mercy, I would take the pain to ride myself to him for them. And they said that their captains would passing fain have me and my counsel. I told them that I was not ready to lose my head and my lands as they were like to do if they mended not their manners shortly, and bade them to get them home, so they drank and went home.[15]

---

[12] I assume that the letter to Cromwell (*LP* XI, no. 538) was written before Hussey received the letter from Louth (no. 539).

[13] *LP* XI, no. 539.

[14] Cutler left a short account of the journey to Horncastle, making it clear that he travelled with Hussey's offer to join in the repression of the rebels. Ibid., no. 620.

[15] Hence Hussey acknowledges the impossibility of the negotiations James believes he was trying to open towards the end of the week through Shrewsbury. SP1/109, fos. 70v–71r (poorly represented in *LP* XI, no. 852).

He was, he said, encouraged to take this hard line by a letter from the king of which we are otherwise ignorant.[16] A Horncastle man recalled rather less bravado at this meeting, Hussey apparently saying that 'he would not be false to his prince, nor would he be against them, for he said that if he should be against them, he thought not one of his tenants should take his part'.[17]

Hussey appears to have had good evidence to lead him to this view. Robert Carr of Sleaford, who according to tradition was one of Hussey's estate officers, made a deposition in which he implicitly accused Hussey of cowardice. On Wednesday Hussey was taking soundings in the town but was told that he should be telling the townsmen what to do rather than asking them what he should do. On Thursday there were rumours circulating that the Horncastle men were coming to burn Sleaford, having already burnt Gainsborough Hall in revenge for Burgh's flight. A delegation went to Hussey to ask what he would do: he said he would do as he wished. Some thought he would flee. As the townspeople saw him as their guarantee against attack, they refused to allow him to leave and blockaded his house. Carr thought that Hussey could have rallied the townsmen to drive back the rebels, but Carr also went to Lincoln to plead that the town should not be burnt or ransacked, making it clear that he was driven by self-interest rather than any principle.[18] Hussey's own account confirms much of what Carr says. A group of the townsmen came to the gates of his house and called on him to talk to them. They expressed fears that he would flee: Hussey said he would come and go as he wished. He asked them if they would serve the king, but they answered that 'they would die and live with me but they would never strike stroke against them [the rebels], for if they went with me, they would deceive me'.[19]

Hussey was clearly unable to influence events at a distance whilst his control of Sleaford slowly slipped from him. He told Cromwell on Thursday that his countrymen would be glad to defend him, but he did not

---

[16] SP1/109, fos. 70v–71r (= *LP* XI, no. 852).

[17] PRO, E36/119, fo. 6r (= *LP* XII (i), no. 70 (iii)).

[18] For Carr's background, James, 'Obedience and Dissent', 213–4. *LP* XI, no. 969.

[19] SP1/110, fos. 72v–73r (= *LP* XI, no. 852). Cf. the perverse reading of this incident in *LP* XII (i), no. 1012 (4) (i).

trust them to fight the rebels. This is no more than the exchange at the gates of his house indicated: that the commons' support for Hussey was entirely conditional on him bending to their collective will. On Friday Christopher Ayscough, who had been sent into southern Lincolnshire to gather intelligence, believed that Hussey would be taken later that day or Saturday, 'for he dares not stir and none of his tenants will rise for him'.[20] Clinton reported on Saturday that Hussey was trapped in his house. A further mutilated letter, written by Sir Marmaduke Constable (who delivered letters to Hussey on Thursday evening), appears to say much the same.[21] On Thursday or Friday Hussey started to send his servants away with their harness. On Saturday he himself escaped disguised as a priest, and travelled to the earl of Shrewsbury at Nottingham. Even the flight was attended with farce. After he left, his house was visited by a detachment of rebels from Lincoln who had come to get him, and they persuaded his wife, accompanied by Huddeswell, to chase after him to call him back.[22] He would not return with them.

Why did Hussey flee then and not before? After all, both Burgh and Clinton demonstrated their loyalty by flight, the latter serving as a high-class dispatch rider and neither contributing anything very substantial to the collapse of the movement.[23] The simplest explanation is that he fled the very moment before the rebels came to take him. On Friday George Cutler was sent to Lincoln with letters left by Sir Marmaduke Constable the previous night. He had instructions to discover the rebels' intentions but to lie about Hussey's.[24] When, on his return, Cutler told Hussey that the gentlemen were planning to come to get him, his determination to keep out of their hands gave him no choice but to flee.[25]

The circumstances of Hussey's flight have been confused by Dr James's reading of the letter which Hussey sent to Shrewsbury on Friday and

[20] *LP* XI, nos. 547, 567.   [21] Ibid., nos. 590, 578.   [22] Ibid., nos. 852, 853.

[23] Cf. Gunn, 'Peers, Commons and Gentry', 77.

[24] SP1/109, fos. 72v–73r (not in *LP* XI, no. 852). Huddeswell says that Cutler, appearing before the gentry outside Lincoln, was pressed about Hussey's attitude to them. Huddeswell originally reported that Cutler said that Hussey would '"take the same part as you do" and held out his hands all abroad', a marvellously ambiguous gesture. The deposition was then altered to read that 'he and all his servants and his house be at their [the gentry's] and the commons' commandment when they will come to him'. PRO, E36/118, fo. 55v (= *LP* XI, no. 853).

[25] *LP* XI, no. 620; SP1/109, fos. 72v–73r (= *LP* XI, no. 852).

Shrewsbury's reply the following day.[26] He saw the first letter as an attempt to open a channel, through Shrewsbury, to the king, to allow Hussey to speak on the rebel's behalf to secure concessions from Henry.[27] As this overture was rejected, the attempt failed and Hussey was forced to choose between the king and the rebels. Belatedly, he threw in his hand with the earl at Nottingham.

It must be remembered that at this moment Shrewsbury had the largest group of forces in arms against the rebels. There was at Stamford little more than an advance party, nor would any substantial body of men be there for several more days. There is, though, no sign that Hussey had been in contact with Shrewsbury before Friday, for all his extant correspondence is directed to Cromwell. It is not clear how well informed Shrewsbury was of events in Lincolnshire or whether he knew much of Hussey's difficulties.

On Thursday evening Hussey received a letter from the king brought to Sleaford by Tyrwhit, Constable, and Hennage. The contents of this letter are lost but it is unlikely to have been more than a general instruction to repress the rebellion.[28] Hussey clearly understood from them that there were further instructions in letters addressed to Shrewsbury of which Shrewsbury would inform him. He wrote to the earl on Friday saying that he had the king's letter but asking what was in Shrewsbury's letter that he should know. He would have gone to Shrewsbury in person, but 'I am so environed so that I dare not come out of my house'. He therefore wished the earl to 'ascertain me your advice and pleasure . . . which I shall accomplish to the uttermost of my power and to be with you as shortly as I may and where you will appoint me'.

Hussey's letter is about two things. The first is that he understood that Shrewsbury had received instructions denied him, therefore he was placed in a subordinate position under Shrewsbury. He may well have feared that he was excluded from the chain of command because he was compromised by his reputation as a religious conservative, by the capture of his colleagues in the commission of the peace, and by their

---

[26] James, 'Obedience and Dissent', 247–55, followed by Hodgett, *Tudor Lincolnshire*, 34–5. The letters are *LP* XI, nos. 561, 589. For the date of the second letter, see n. 29 below.

[27] Why Hussey should have needed to employ Shrewsbury as an intermediary when he had already written direct to the king requires explanation.

[28] See *LP* XI, no. 557.

calling on him to join them. The second matter was the painful admission that there was little or nothing that Hussey could do. He was stranded in hostile territory—everyone recognized that—and he was seeking his commander's permission to withdraw under the oblique guise of seeking 'his advice and pleasure'.

Shrewsbury's reply, which was written in Saturday, was intended to set Hussey at ease.[29] There was nothing in the king's letters except instructions to suppress the rebels, that is, there was nothing in the letters about Hussey.[30] Then he tried to stiffen Hussey's resolve. Now Shrewsbury may have recognized the need to do this because of the report brought back to him by one Martin Green, Sir John Markham's servant, who had been sent to Lincoln on Friday to gather intelligence. Green had encountered Cutler, who had told him that he expected Hussey to surrender to the rebels.[31] He therefore wrote: 'My very good lord, for all the old acquaintance and familiarity betwixt your good lordship and me as unto him that I entirely love,[32] I will write the plainness of my mind to your lordship. Ye have always been an honourable and true gentlemen and showed yourself and I doubt not but now so will prove yourself according to your bounden duty.' Hussey, Shrewsbury told him, could do the king no greater service than by 'practising to put these misruled persons in some stay by policy' in concert with the gentlemen, or by detaching the gentlemen from the rebels after which the rebels could 'do small hurt' (perhaps because he expected the rebellion to dissolve without gentry leadership). In that way the shedding of blood could be avoided: if not, Shrewsbury had 40,000 men gathering at Nottingham on Saturday. And then the letter continues: 'and I trust undoubtedly to have your good lordship to keep us company which shall be much to my comfort.' Shrewsbury's letter was a call to arms, but it also gave Hussey the option of withdrawing from Sleaford, to be at Nottingham in the company of Shrewsbury and the 40,000-strong force on Sunday night, a clear signal to abandon Sleaford. But, given that the letter was written during

---

[29] The copy of the letter is undated. But Hussey's letter was received after Shrewsbury wrote to the king at 8 p.m. on Friday (*LP* XI, no. 562), but the reply had been written before his letter written at 6 p.m. on Saturday (no. 587). That the letter to Hussey was written during Saturday is further confirmed by the reference to Shrewsbury's intention to be at Nottingham the following evening, that is, Sunday evening, which is Shrewsbury's stated intention in his letters to the king.

[30] The likelihood is that the letters were couched in very general terms; below p. 167.

[31] *LP* XI, no. 587 (2).   [32] The MS reads 'eterely': the reference is to the king.

Saturday and that Hussey fled Sleaford during that same day, spending Saturday night at Sir John Byron's house at Colwick (2¹/₂ miles east of Nottingham), the likelihood is that Hussey had already decamped before the letter reached Sleaford. Indeed, he may never have seen it. His decision to abandon his house was almost certainly taken for the reason he advanced in his examination, that he was determined not to fall into the rebels' hands.[33] The thesis that he was forced to choose between the rebels and his king by Shrewsbury's letter is erroneous.[34]

Whilst we may be sure that Hussey had made the best of a hopeless job, his contemporaries could not be so certain. His decision to remain in Sleaford, contacts with the rebels, and decline into inactivity and impotence had left him compromised. He was called to London with his servant Cutler and apparently was glad to go, believing that he could vindicate his actions before the king and council. Shrewsbury, Huntingdon, and Rutland could point to no disloyal actions since he had joined them. His son was serving with them, with 200 men.[35] Nor can the armchair historian discern what Hussey could have done better to halt the rebellion (though he might have saved his life by an earlier tactical retreat). His execution must be seen as a retribution inflicted on a man in the wrong place at the wrong time.

II

We know nothing of the reception of either Hennage or Maddison at court. Maddison was formally examined by the council on 6 October about the events at Caistor and the treatment of the gentry after they had been conveyed to Louth. Hennage, however, was sent straight back to Lincolnshire with Sir Marmaduke Constable and Robert Tyrwhit, the cousin of the Tyrwhit captured at Caistor. They had reached Stilton,

---

[33] SP1/109, fos. 72v–73r (= *LP* XI, no. 852).

[34] Hussey also said in his declaration that he sent 20 or 30 of his household servants to await him at Colwick on *Thursday or Friday*, indicating that he planned a tactical retreat before the exchange of letters with Shrewsbury. SP1/109, fos. 72v–73r (mangled in *LP* XI, no. 852).

[35] *LP* XI, no. 772.

(Cambs.) about 12 miles north of Huntingdon, by 9 a.m. on Thursday, from where they sent back information gleaned from an unnamed priest who had been at Louth. That evening they reached Ancaster, 15 or so miles short of Lincoln, and again sent intelligence back to Cromwell. By midnight they had reached Hussey at Sleaford and set off back for court in the early hours. As would happen on other occasions, the letters they carried were overtaken by the course of events, for amongst those left with Hussey were letters to the gentry captured at Caistor.[36] Given the letters between Hussey and Shrewsbury, it seems likely that they or someone else carried a letter to Shrewsbury which he received mid-morning on Friday. These letters contained no specific instructions, merely authorizing the recipients to repress the rising.[37] Not far behind this trio was Edward, Lord Clinton who carried letters to the earls of Huntingdon at Ashby de la Zouche (Leics.) and Shrewsbury at Hardwick (Derbs.).[38] On Sunday Sir Edward Maddison was sent back into Lincolnshire with the king's letter to the gentlemen at Louth. As Maddison rode northwards he doubtless passed the first labouring convoys which marked the beginning of the mobilization against the rebellion, and at Huntingdon he overtook the earl of Suffolk who added his own letter to the king's.[39]

The rising at Louth was, from the very first, seen as a problem requiring a military solution. The hope of the captured gentry—that a free pardon might be conceded to secure the disbandment of the rebels—was never an option which the king considered. Indeed, it might be said that the king's categorization of the rising determined his attitude to it and this, in turn, arose from his anger at the challenge to his authority and pride. If we take the letter read at Lincoln on 10 October, we find that Henry first attacks the gentry for putting themselves in the hands of the commons rather than raising a force for their suppression. These criticisms were unjust, unreasonable, and cruel. Then he complained of the 'great unkindness' of the commons in assembling themselves against the king without cause. Here the king denied the rumours circulating, saying

[36] Ibid., nos. 552, 553, 561.
[37] Ibid., no. 557 (1) is endorsed 'the first minute for Lincolnshire', and may be a draft of this letter.
[38] Ibid., no. 590.   [39] Ibid., nos. 615–16.

that the reports of impositions were untrue (although he also constructs an unnecessary argument about the burden of the subsidy). Rather than admit that the assembly was based on false reports, for believing which the commons might be forgiven, the letter demanded that unless they dispersed and sent 100 of their ringleaders with halters around their necks to the king's lieutenant, they would be destroyed by the army of 100,000 men already descending on them. If they advanced out of Lincolnshire the army was ready to invade the country to destroy their goods.[40]

This was, as we shall see, so much bluster. The forces available to be employed against the rebels were still gathering and the policy of Henry's field commanders was to play for time. Yet whilst this crude and furious outburst may have assuaged Henry's temper, how would it be seen at Lincoln? Whilst it offered the comprehensive denial of the rumours which the gentry had sought in their earlier letter, by refusing a pardon it did nothing to help their stand against the rebels for it revealed the bankruptcy of their strategy to secure a pardon. It undermined their assertion that the fault lay within the king's circle rather than with the king himself. Instead, it inflamed matters by its uncompromising line and invited the rebels to continue with their voyage.

The same uncompromising position, with a stress on the humiliating submission of the rebels, appears on two further occasions. The answer to the petition of six articles sent to the king on 9 October rebutted the articles one at a time. It then called on the rebels to withdraw to their houses and to deliver to the king's lieutenant the ringleaders of the rising. The rebels were to choose amongst themselves 100 persons to be delivered into the hands of the lieutenant for punishment, or else see their families, goods, and lands destroyed by the sword. The king's reply to the submission of the rebels taken by Lancaster Herald (and almost certainly drafted after the collapse of the rebellion) contained a long prologue describing how Henry was entitled to destroy the rebels, their wives, and children as a retribution for their treason, but offered clemency if the rebels would deliver their weapons and harness to the king's lieutenant in Lincoln, an act which would serve not only to demilitarize society but would also bring about the emasculation of its members by

---

[40] Ibid., no. 569.

depriving them of their civil status as yeomen within a society still organized for war.[41]

The strategy adopted by Henry therefore had three strands. The first was to deny the rumours circulating in Lincolnshire. The second was to offer clemency if the rebels would disperse and then purge their error by undergoing a ritual humiliation and the surrender of ringleaders to the king's commander. The third, to be invoked if the second did not achieve its aim, was to destroy the rebellion by military force. Of these three, one senses that the royal paranoia demanded that the treason of the commons and their rejection of the benefits of the king's gracious rule could only be purged by a bloodletting. The refusal to offer a pardon to purchase peace made conflict inevitable unless the rebels backed down. It was an incautious game upon which the king embarked.

The mobilization had two aspects. The first, although from our point of view the least important, was the dispatch of the nobility and other locally influential figures from the court into their counties to keep order and guard against further disturbances. Lord Chancellor Audley was sent into Essex. The duke of Norfolk, who received word of the rebellion and mobilization at Easterford (Essex) whilst in the company of the earl of Oxford and duke of Suffolk, was instructed to remain locally and maintain order whilst Suffolk (to Norfolk's considerable disappointment) was told to make his way north to take charge of operations.[42] The importance attached to this may be seen from the fact that we have lists of those gentry who were to supply men for the king's army and 'those appointed by the king to abide in their counties to keep good order in the absence of the rest of the noblemen'.[43] A further dimension of the campaign to prevent the rebellion spreading was the letter sent to Darcy in Yorkshire (and doubtless to others) on 8 October acknowledging that the rebellion in Lincolnshire grew by rumours of the confiscation of church goods and the subsidy, and instructing that these rumours be denied.[44]

---

[41] Ibid., nos. 718 (pr. *St. P.*, I, 468–70); 780 (pr. *St. P.* I, 463–6, Dodds, *Pilgrimage*, I, 136–8). For a similar insistance on humiliation as the price of forgiveness, see Hall's account of the aftermath of Evil May Day in 1517, E. Hall, *The union of the two noble and illustre famelies of Lancastre and Yorke* (1809 edn.), 590–1.

[42] *LP* XI, nos. 559, 601, 602.   [43] Ibid., no. 580 (4).   [44] Ibid., no. 598.

Whilst these steps were being taken, plans were also being laid for the second aspect of the mobilization. Letters were sent out on 6 October (Friday) announcing the fact of the rebellion, ordering the recipients to keep order around them, and instructing them to be ready to move with their forces at an hour's notice. Letters were prepared the following day announcing the king's intention to lead an army towards Lincolnshire or to send some great personage in his place. By 10 October it had been decided that the royal army was to muster at Ampthill near Dunstable on Monday, 16 October, and Norfolk's earlier impatience was rewarded with the instruction that he was to take charge there as high marshall. The king himself intended to be at Ampthill and lead his army against the rebels.[45] But advance parties were already making their way north as the summons to the Ampthill muster was circulated. Richard Cromwell, Thomas Cromwell's nephew, had reached Ware (Hereford) on Sunday, evening with 100 horsemen and forty handgun-men trailing at Waltham. On Monday Sir William Fitzwilliam was at Aylesbury making his way to Stamford, and around dawn on Monday morning Suffolk arrived at Huntingdon, although his retinue was far behind.[46]

These preparations were doubtless very impressive to contemporaries, but there was also a chance that they were too little, too late. Suffolk arrived at Huntingdon intending to lead on to Stamford whomever he found waiting there: but no one was waiting. Sir Francis Bryan was at Kimbolton (Hunts.) with 300 horse, whilst the vanguard of Sir John Russell and Sir William Parr, who were at Stamford, were too few in numbers to withstand any sizeable force. As they reported that the town was sympathetic to the rebels, its walls weak, and its inhabitants opposed to the destruction of its bridges, there was little chance of holding the rebels there if they came. Suffolk's fear that the rebels would be at Stamford on Monday evening would not have been unrealistic if, as was expected, they had advanced to Ancaster on Sunday. Hence his proposal to call back Russell and Parr from Stamford and gather what force he could to stop the commons at Huntingdon was a prudent strategy.[47] When Suffolk reached Stamford on Tuesday, he found that Russell, Bryan, and

---

[45] Ibid., nos. 556, 579, 637, 641, 642, 579 (3) (which must be a few days later than the date assigned by *LP*), 671.

[46] Ibid., nos. 607, 613, 615.   [47] Ibid., nos. 615, 621.

Parr had 900 men but no ordnance or money. By noon on Friday there were still only 5,000 men at Stamford, of whom two-fifths had neither horse nor weapons.[48]

Whilst these forces were gathering to block a southwards advance, a second body of men was being gathered at Nottingham under the earls of Shrewsbury, Huntingdon, and Rutland. Shrewsbury had word from Lord Burgh of the disturbances at Louth and Caistor, and immediately called on his servants and tenants to muster at Mansfield on Thursday evening. By Friday he had moved from Sheffield to his house at Hardwick and called a further muster at Nottingham for Monday evening. This he brought forward to Sunday evening on news that the rebels intended to be at Newark that night.[49] At Nottingham he was joined by the earls of Huntingdon and Rutland. And whilst he could tell Hussey that he expected 40,000 men (an exaggeration) drawn from the north Midlands to be at Nottingham, the fact remained that they were in the wrong place.[50] If the rebels chose to move south, Shrewsbury's forces would, most likely, have had to chase them southwards and attack them in the rear. The small detachment based at Newark was unlikely to resist the commons for long if they passed that way—as was expected on 6 October.[51] The military situation was indeed dire, as Norfolk recognized on 9 October.[52]

That the scratch royal forces were never put to the test was their extreme good fortune. By Wednesday, 11 October the vanguard of royal servants at Stamford—Suffolk, Fitzwilliam, Russell, Bryan, Parr, and Richard Cromwell—clearly understood that the rebels had started to disperse from Lincoln. The report that the rebellion had collapsed at Boston was erroneous but encouraging. Richard Cromwell reported that Fitzwilliam, Russell, Parr, and himself intended to ride on to Lincoln on Saturday.[53] The position in Lincoln itself was not so clear-cut. As we saw, on Wednesday Sir Edward Maddison's servant delivered two letters to the gentry, the first from the king and a second from Suffolk. The king's rejection of the request for a pardon and the requirement that the commons should make the most humbling submission served only to

---

[48] Ibid., no. 808.   [49] Ibid., no. 562.

[50] Shrewsbury had 6,000 men at his disposal around the weekend of 14–15 October. Ibid., no. 771.

[51] Ibid., nos. 562, 644.   [52] Ibid., nos. 644, 625.   [53] Ibid., no. 658.

inflame matters. Suffolk's own letter urged the gentry to follow the king's letters and disband or, if they marched towards him, he was prepared to destroy them with his forces. He wished to be informed of their decision.[54] This was so much posturing. Suffolk wrote to the king requesting instructions as to how to proceed if the commons submitted, as the king's letter required them to do. If they declined to submit, he refused to make any suit on their behalf to the king unless they gave an undertaking not to advance further. The strategy was clearly to play for time to allow the royal forces to mass.[55] There is the possibility that the gentry at Lincoln gave Suffolk the undertaking he sought, perhaps in the letter of 10 October which survives only in a seventeenth-century abstract, and that Suffolk in turn offered to petition the king for their pardon if they put down their arms. Certainly, the Lincoln gentry implored Maddison at Stamford to persuade the duke to do this, and it was understood at Nottingham that Suffolk had agreed to advance their case.[56]

Wednesday and Thursday were therefore days of uncertainty, as the royal forces gathered at Stamford whilst the rebels slowly ebbed away at Lincoln. As Moigne makes clear, the dispersal of the rebels was assisted by the sweet-talking of Lancaster Herald who, it might be noticed, was sent to Lincoln by Shrewsbury and not Suffolk. Lancaster then rode to London carrying their submission to the king.[57] The drift of events is indicated by Shrewsbury's request for instructions as to how to deal with any of the rebels who came to Nottingham to submit, although at the same moment Suffolk was talking of burning Louth, Horncastle, and Caistor should the need require.[58]

At midnight on Thursday Suffolk, Fitzwilliam, and Russell were able to report that the sheriff and the other Dymokes had already surrendered themselves. Fourteen of the gentlemen held captive at Lincoln were waiting at Sir John Thimbleby's house at Burne and intended to

---

[54] Above pp. 149–50 for the king's letter. For Suffolk's letter, *LP* XI, no. 616.

[55] Ibid., no. 615.

[56] 'Thomas Master's Narrative', 65–6; 'Letters of the Cliffords', 143; *LP* XI no. 694.

[57] Ibid., nos. 674, 718; 'Letters of the Cliffords', 143. According to John Browne of Louth, a herald came from the earl of Shrewsbury on Friday with a message that if the commons did not go home, Shrewsbury would fight them on Ancaster Heath. Browne is presumably mistaken as to the day. *LP* XI no. 854.

[58] Ibid., nos. 673, 658, 'Thomas Master's Narrative', 67.

submit to Suffolk on Friday morning, 13 October. On Sunday evening Wriothesley passed this report on to Cromwell, but a letter of later that evening gave Cromwell the appalling news that a post from Darcy had brought word that the rebellion had taken hold in Yorkshire. Satisfaction passed to despair: 'this matter hangeth yet like a fever, one day good, one day bad.'[59]

The course of events in Yorkshire I reserve for later. The submission of the Lincolnshire commons arose from the successful prosecution of the gentry's strategy against the rank and file and had nothing to do with the military forces gathering at Stamford. The collapse of the movement, though, posed two new problems: the need to disband the troops making their way to Ampthill, and the need to provide for the civil government of Lincolnshire. Both came to be subsumed within the greater problem of Yorkshire. Letters cancelling the Ampthill muster had been drawn up on 12 October, rather ahead of the news of the submission reaching London. As over six-dozen of these letters survive in the State Papers, they were probably never dispatched. On 14 October Norfolk was told to hold his son and his troops wherever the letter found them (Cambridge, as it happened), and on 15 October general letters were sent out cancelling the Ampthill musters.[60] Nearly 20,000 troops had assembled there, and all, except for 3,000 with Norfolk, 2,000 with the marquis of Exeter, and some other small contingents, were sent home. The ordnance returned to London. This was a major miscalculation based on an unawareness or underestimation of the danger of the Yorkshire rising, and as the scale of the disturbances there became clear an attempt was made to retrieve some of the returning troops. Time was wasted, for Norfolk was still at Cambridge on 21 October, by which time he had discharged some of his own men.[61]

The arrangements for the civil government of Lincolnshire were probably also based on a failure to appreciate the seriousness of the situation further north. In his letter of Thursday, 12 October Suffolk asked whether the king would grant a pardon in Lincolnshire so that his forces could switch their attention to Yorkshire, or whether they should concentrate on eradicating the rebellion in Lincolnshire.[62] Henry was

[59] *LP* XI, nos. 672, 722–3. [60] Ibid., nos. 701, 727, 720.
[61] Ibid., nos. 803, 825. [62] Ibid., no. 672.

positively for the latter option, and established the future direction of
the campaign in Lincolnshire in a letter of 15 October. After Suffolk had
the gentlemen captive and had entered Lincoln, Shrewsbury was to advance
towards Yorkshire, Suffolk supplying him with ordnance. Within
Lincolnshire Suffolk was to announce that if the commons would voluntarily surrender their weapons and harness, then he would be a suitor
to the king for them. The gentlemen were to be examined to discover
how the movement began. The king had made an answer to the submission of the commons brought him by Lancaster Herald: this was
to be read openly unless the commons had already dispersed. If the
commons and the gentlemen would not co-operate, then Suffolk and
Shrewsbury were to advance and 'set upon them'. Once in Lincoln, Suffolk
was to take the cathedral close for his headquarters. The king had a mind
to establish a garrison there and Suffolk was to advise on its suitability.
If the commons submitted, then Louth, Caistor, and Horncastle were
not to be pillaged but the captains of those towns were to be detained.[63]

These instructions were carefully and progressively implemented.[64] The
advance guard entered Lincoln on Monday, 16 October. The inhabitants
of Louth were probably told to travel to Lincoln on Friday, 20 September to make their submissions, and the opportunity was taken to arrest
the instigators of the disturbances. Melton, making his first deposition
in custody on 21 October, was able to refer to six others from Louth who
were also in prison with him.[65] Horncastle came in on 21 October, and
arrangements were made for the Lincolnshire wapentakes to appear before
Suffolk a few at a time to swear a new oath of allegiance.[66] Although
Suffolk had already written to Louth for the release of Bellow and the
other prisoners, it was not until 28 October that the royal forces entered
the town to disarm the inhabitants. Simultaneously the same was done at
Horncastle and Market Rasen, and finally all the arms in the shire were
deposited at Lincoln.[67] There was clearly much hostility to Suffolk's army,
but a large number of men implicated in the rising were arrested, exam-

---

[63] Ibid., no. 717.

[64] The fullest account of the occupation of Lincolnshire during the autumn of 1536 is S. J. Gunn,
Charles Brandon, Duke of Suffolk, c.1484–1545 (1988), 145–52, on which the following section is based.

[65] *LP* XI, no. 834; SP1/110 fo. 136r; 109 fo. 1r (where the date must be Friday, 20 October).

[66] *LP* XI, no. 838.   [67] Ibid., no. 913.

ined, and imprisoned. Depositions were taken from the gentry, who were found to be willing collaborators in the work of investigation. As early as Sunday, 15 October Dymock the sheriff brought in one of the more prominent rebels (although we are never told his name).[68] This has persuaded some commentators to suppose that the gentry were anxious to earn Suffolk's favour after the failure of their enterprise. It is equally likely that they wished to seek their own revenge on those who had humiliated them and undermined their authority. Certainly Suffolk never appears to have doubted the interpretation of the gentry's role in the movement advanced at greatest length by Moigne. The individuals who continued to believe that the rebellion was gentry-inspired were the king (as may be seen in the articles to be investigated that he sent Suffolk on 23 October[69]) and that self-important and scathing observer of the Lincolnshire gentry, Richard Cromwell.[70] By the last week of November Suffolk was arranging for an army to be raised locally to enter Yorkshire if the need arose.

Suffolk had to proceed with great caution. A bloodbath in Lincolnshire would only have diminished the prospect of achieving a peaceful settlement in Yorkshire. Hence there were no (or very few) summary executions in Lincolnshire and the trials of rebels were postponed until the New Year when the Yorkshire rebellion had been defused.

The maintenance of an army in Lincolnshire when the theatre of action had become south Yorkshire was a wasteful deployment of scarce recourses. By early November the needs of Lincolnshire offered no justification for maintaining an establishment of 4,000 men at a cost of £150 a day. Suffolk's forces, though, came into their own after the first Pontefract conference and the disbandment of the royal forces facing the Pilgrims. As Lincolnshire was excluded from the terms of the truce, Suffolk was able to act as a staging-post for communications with Yorkshire and the North whilst gathering intelligence in Lincolnshire and covertly supporting the king's supporters at Skipton, Hull, and Scarborough with supplies. At the same time the royal army was dispersed along the Trent and Humber coast to prevent incursions from the North. By late November Bryan, Russell, and Cromwell were based at Newark with a garrison of 700 men. The army had been wound down by the end of the year.

---

[68] Ibid., no. 728.   [69] Ibid., no. 843; also 764.   [70] 'Thomas Master's Narrative', 69.

7

The Rising in the East Riding

> As I have passed in these parts, I have communed in divers towns
> with some of the honest sort that were householders and asked them
> upon what ground the people were thus stirred to rebel against their
> prince, and who they were that first did stir them thereunto: and
> they, as men that would excuse themselves, said that they began in
> Lincolnshire and if they had not risen there, no one man would
> have risen in the North.[1]

The rising in the East Riding (Map 3) was nothing more than a northwards extension of the Lincolnshire rebellion. This opinion was not only
held by Sadler's 'honest men', but also by no less a figure than Aske
himself: 'If Lincolnshire had not rebelled, surely Yorkshire had never
rebelled.'[2] News of events in Lincolnshire was carried into the East Riding
by people travelling northwards through Lincolnshire, taking the ferry
over the Humber from Barton-upon-Humber to Hessle, and so passing
to Hull. News may also have spread coastwise through Boston and Grimsby
to Hull. The beacons fired on the Lincolnshire Wolds were readily visible
from the north bank. On 4 October Thomas, Lord Darcy had a letter

---

[1] Sir Ralph Sadler to Cromwell, 23 Jan. 1537. *St. P.* I, 527 (= *LP* XII (i), no. 200).
[2] 'Aske's Examination', 571.

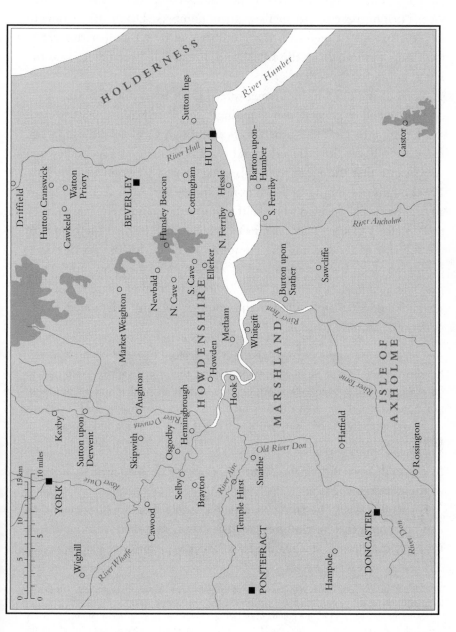

MAP 3. The rising in the East Riding

from 'a friend' in Lincolnshire alerting him to the rising at Louth; that same evening Sir Ralph Ellerker the younger sent word that the rebels were burning beacons to increase their numbers. Darcy urged him to stop the passage of men over the Humber, but by 6 October the fact of the rising was known in the Marshland, the area between Selby and the Humber, and in Beverley.[3]

News of the Lincolnshire rising spread in an irresistible fashion. Word of it spawned a general panic amongst the East Riding gentry, with some fleeing to Hull and others to Scarborough Castle. Archbishop Lee received refugees from Beverley and the East Riding at Cawood; when word came that the rebels were planning to raid Cawood to take him, Lee thought of running to Scarborough for shelter. After seeking Darcy's advice, he finally decided to make the shorter but ultimately fatal journey to Pontefract Castle. These camps of refugees determined the course of the Pilgrimage by drawing the commons to them, for the act of taking refuge was seen by the commons as a hostile act of opposition.[4] Their fear was genuine: whether it was justified is another matter. As Hull surrendered, Sir Ralph Ellerker the younger was still frightened of the commons' attitude to him:

And they brought in the said Sir Ralph and Sir William Constable to the Charter-house [in Hull]. Then Sir Ralph made request that every captain would go to his company and to persuade them neither to hurt them that was commen in, nor none that belonged to them; which was done accordingly and the commons well contented. For he was sore afraid of the commons and especially of Holderness.[5]

In the end, only those who went to Scarborough managed to stay out of the commons' grasp.

For its first week the rising remained a largely spontaneous reaction to news of events in Lincolnshire. For that reason it looked to Lincolnshire for both direction and a manifesto to articulate common grievances. It

---

[3] *LP* XI, no. 563. For Burgh warning Darcy of the debacle at Caistor, ibid., no. 533. For knowledge of the rising in the Marshland and Beverley, below, pp. 183–4, 193.

[4] Stapleton, 91, 92. And cf. the comment of George Bawne on hearing that a number of gentry were holed up at Scarborough: 'he would go win them or else he would hazard his life in the quarrel.' Ibid. 92. *LP* XII (i), no. 1022.

[5] Stapleton, 98 (repunctuated).

therefore came as a severe shock when the Lincolnshire rebellion pre-
cipitately collapsed around 11–12 October. Indeed, when the word
reached the besiegers of Hull on 15 October it was first discounted as a
lie then, in anger, a letter was sent to Lincoln denouncing 'the unkindness of Lincolnshire to them who rose by their motions'. Within a few
days the same men were considering trying to make their peace with
the king through the duke of Suffolk.[6] But if the fall of Lincoln seemed
to some an end, to Aske it was a liberation, and the moment when he
transformed an arm of the Lincolnshire rebellion into the Pilgrimage of
Grace.

I

Beverley, like Louth, was an episcopal town, a manor of the archbishop
of York. It was probably larger than Louth. Four-hundred-and-seventy
men mustered there in 1539, suggesting a population of around 1,200.
The arrangements for its government were correspondingly more elaborate. As at Louth, there was a steward appointed by the archbishop, but
Beverley was also a liberty of the archbishop in which he had the right
to appoint JPs. Internally Beverley had a range of craft guilds (apparently
seventeen in 1535) and a common council of twenty-four, but the government of the town rested in the hands of twelve governors, elected
annually on St Mark's Day (25 April). It was a convention that no governor was drawn from outside the town, and that none held office for two
consecutive years.[7]

There was intermittent conflict between successive archbishops and
the town. In the first decade of the century there had been a contest over
the stewardship of the town between Archbishop Savage and the fifth earl
of Northumberland, at a time when the titular steward was Henry, Prince
of Wales. As the earl maintained a house at Leconfield, only 2 miles away,
it was probably inevitable that he should see Beverley as an extension of
his own estates. The Percys traditionally used Beverley Minster as their

---

[6] Ibid. 96, 99.   [7] See in general VCH *East Riding*, VI, 65, 70.

burial place. Within the town there was a faction which was prepared to wear the Percy crescent in preference to the Tudor roses which Archbishop Savage distributed.[8] A generation later the town was again divided between the supporters of Archbishop Lee and an external landowner, but this time it was Sir Ralph Ellerker the elder. The story of the contested elections of 1534–6 has still to be told in full, but a brief account is necessary to place the Beverley rising in context.[9]

Ellerker lived at Risby, 3 miles south-west of the town.[10] In the early 1530s he launched a campaign to involve himself in the government of Beverley; for a period he divided the town and ruled with the support (apparently) of the commons. Ellerker bought a house there and, having met the residence qualification demanded of the twelve governors, was elected one of their number in 1534. Around Christmas 1534 Archbishop Lee was trying to alter the form of election, probably as a manoeuvre against Ellerker, but at the elections held on St Mark's Day, 1535, Ellerker demanded that he be re-elected as a governor. When objections were raised he embarked on a campaign of intimidation and malfeasance, collecting the bills of nomination brought in by the crafts and substituting his own list. He then secured the re-election of himself and seven of his supporters who had also sat amongst the outgoing governors. So armed, Ellerker withdrew the freedom of the town from his opponents and prevented a commission of JPs, sent by Lee to investigate the contested election, from meeting within Beverley. Ellerker's opponents petitioned first Lee, and then the king's council. Lee also petitioned the council who, towards the end of 1535, overturned the April election. The council also ordered that governors were not to serve in consecutive years, that the ownership of a house was not an adequate qualification

---

[8] I have discussed the conflict between the earl and Archbishop Savage in 'The Earl, the Archbishop, the Council: The Affray at Fulford, May 1504'.

[9] The following account is based on the pleadings before the council, PRO, STAC2/4/181, 19/243, 255, printed in abstract in W. Brown (ed.), 'Yorkshire Star Chamber Proceedings', *YASRS* 41, 45, 51, 70 (1909–27), I, 34–9; II, 99–104, 105–14, together with *LP* VIII, nos. 721, 774. The account in VCH *East Riding*, VI, 63–4 could be considerably expanded.

[10] There is a danger of confusion between Sir Ralph Ellerker the elder (d. 1539) and his son, Sir Ralph the younger (d. 1546). After his first contacts with the Beverley commons, Sir Ralph the elder seems to have laid low. It was his son who took refuge in Hull and later went to Windsor as one of the two representatives of the Pilgrims. See *Hist. Parl., 1509–58*, II, 89–90.

for election, and specifically barred Ellerker and his son in law, Oswin Ogle, from holding office within the town.[11] Lee was permitted to substitute twelve more governors, who were to sit until the next annual election was held in April 1536.

The council also authorized Archbishop Lee to recast the rules regulating the town's elections. In January 1536 140 burgesses agreed to abide his order, and on 1 April he promulgated an order for the conduct of the following election. This drew opposition in the town, and on 19 April Lee was visited at Cawood by fifty dissatisfied burgesses. They apparently believed that Lee wished to manipulate the elections to maintain his authority, which was exercised, they claimed, through the interim governors appointed the previous December. They left threatening disorder if the new elections went ahead as planned. Lee then ordered the election to be deferred whilst he conferred with the council. The twelve retiring governors, expecting trouble on St Mark's Day, put this order into effect by locking both the common hall and the building which housed the common bell, but the disaffected faction rang the bell (which they reached with ladders), held an impromptu election outside the common hall, and then (whether by having forced their way in or through discovering a rear door unlocked depends on whom you believe) entered the common hall, where they swore twelve governors for the following year. Their action was then reported to the council by Lee and litigation ensued. A concordat between Lee and the town was finally signed in November 1536.

How the town divided over these issues is uncertain, partly because we have few names of activists. Why Ellerker involved himself with Beverley is also none too clear, nor is it certain that all the members of his party can be identified with the archbishop's opponents. Some can: John Raffles or Raffellis (alderman of the bakers), John Newcomb (of the walkers, hatters, and cappers craft), Christopher Saunderson (described as one of Ellerker's chief councillors in 1535 and a governor on five occasions), and one William Dent are all found in both contexts. Robert Grey, though, who was also called a chief councillor to Ellerker in 1535, does not feature

---

[11] The decree is published in A. F. Leech, 'Beverley Town Documents', *Selden Soc.*, 14 (1900), 64–5.

amongst those accused of riot in 1536.[12] It was not a simple contest of commons against masters, althrough, given that first Ellerker and then the archbishop's opponents seem to have been able to call on large crowds from amongst the commons, a degree of popular involvement is indicated.

Except on its first day, the character of the rising in Beverley was not a simple repeat of these disputes over town government. On Sunday, 8 October the proclamation that the town should rise was read by one William Endyke (who may be related to Richard Neudyke who had assisted in the illegal election of the previous April). The man swearing the rebels was one Richard Wilson, perhaps the man of that name who had been both a rioter and elected a governor earlier in the year. As the commons assembled, one William Wysse, a notable supporter of the archbishop, was 'almost slain', and there were 'quarrels picked' with Robert Raffles who had been amongst those excluded from the freedom by Ellerker.[13] After William Stapleton was made captain these dissensions were either forgotten or submerged by other imperatives. When Ellerker, whom Lee had called 'a man more meet to be a captain of evil ruled persons than to be a governor of men' appeared, it was to call for calm and not to lead the commons forwards.[14] Nonetheless, the tensions over the government of the town resurfaced in January 1537, when Roger Kitchen and Richard Wilson proposed to go 'a-mumming' to a meeting of 'the most ancient men' of Beverley who were their opponents in the dispute.[15]

Our major source for events at Beverley and Hull is the long account of William Stapleton, a lawyer, who unwittingly became the commons' captain. At the beginning of October Stapleton was lodged at the Greyfriars in Beverley with his elder brother, who suffered from some form of incapacitating illness. He was intending to set out for London and the new law term on Thursday, 5 October when word came that the roads through Lincolnshire were impassable because of the Lincolnshire revolt.[16]

---

[12] For Saunderson, *LP* VIII, no. 721, VCH *East Riding*, VI, 64, 72. Grey was also barred from officeholding by the council, although the order was rescinded.

[13] Stapleton, 85.   [14] Quotation from *LP* VIII, no. 774.   [15] *LP* XII (i), no. 201 (viii).

[16] Stapleton's confession is printed in *LP* XII (i), no. 392: the full transcript by J. C. Cox in *Trans. East Riding Antiquarian Soc.*, 10 (1903), 80–106, is much to be preferred. Page numbers here refer to Cox's transcription.

II

News of the Lincolnshire rising reached Beverley in a number of ways. Archbishop Lee wrote to Robert Craike of Beverley of the setting forward of the earl of Shrewsbury to suppress the rebellion. He asked Craike to pass word to Sir Ralph Ellerker the younger, and required both of them to keep an eye on the town. Robert Aske may also have sent word of events in Lincolnshire to Robert Raffles, one of the twelve governers. William Breyer (who seems to have wandered the countryside dressed in royal livery, and so was taken for the king's servant) implies that Beverley people were talking sympathetically of the rising on the following Saturday, by which time two Lincolnshire canons who spoke treasonable words had arrived there.[17]

Market-place grudging and complaint was turned into action on the morning of Sunday, 8 October by the ringing of the common bell. There are two contradictory accounts of why the town rose that morning. Stapleton recounts how a servant told him of a conversation with Roger Kitchen, a glover. Kitchen maintained that Aske had sent the town a letter calling on it to rise; he was determined that he would ring the common bell to ensure that it did. Stapleton tried to prevent this by sending word of Kitchen's plan to Christopher Saunderson, but his messenger returned to say that the bell was already being rung.[18] The alternative account comes from Kitchen himself, interrogated after the failure of Bigod's revolt in January 1537.[19] Kitchen had heard that there was a letter from Aske to Raffles, which Raffles concealed, but he rather indicates that he did not know this until later, and he certainly does not say that Aske ordered the town to rise. The first that Kitchen knew of the rising in Lincolnshire came from Richard Wilson and William Woodmansey, the last a serving-man who travelled out of Lincolnshire.[20] On Sunday morning Kitchen, Woodmansey, Richard Wilson, Richard

---

[17] Stapleton, 83; *LP* XII (i), no. 1022; 201 (vii); XI, no. 841. The two canons may have been the men for whom a passport was signed by Sir William Sandon: *LP* XI, add., no. 10.

[18] Stapleton, 83–4.   [19] *LP* XII (i), no. 201 (vii).

[20] It is not clear who Woodmansey was. His name is clearly derived from the village just outside Beverley, and there are references which make it clear that he came from there, e.g. *LP* XII (ii), nos. 291 (ii), 481.

Neudyke, and John Turvey, a priest, met together before matins and, having heard Woodmansey's account of events in Lincolnshire, decided to ring the common bell at dinner-time. Once the town had gathered in the market hill Wilson and Neudyke read a bill of articles from Lincolnshire. Breyer claimed that Wilson made a proclamation in the name of Robert Aske.[21]

Stapleton's instinct was to flee, but he decided to remain to protect his ailing brother. The Stapleton brothers instructed all their servants to stay indoors save for one George Bell, whom they sent out into Beverley to reconnoitre. Bell came back to say that Richard Neudyke had made a proclamation for every man to come in, and Richard Wilson was busy swearing them to the commons. Soon afterwards a proclamation was made for every man to assemble at the Hall Garth. Stapleton thought that at this meeting a letter of support for Lincolnshire was drawn up and carried by Woodmansey to Lincoln. The commons then moved to Westwood Green, near the Greyfriars. After some time a proclamation was made for them to reconvene the following day.[22]

Once it fell dark the Stapleton brothers sent for Christopher Saunderson to explain the day's events. Saunderson interpreted the disturbance as being about the settlement of grudges between the pro- and anti-archepiscopal factions within the town, and reported that two of the archbishop's allies had come close to being slain. Some confirmation of this is offered by Archbishop Lee himself. He reported being visited at Cawood by a man impersonating a royal servant—obviously Breyer—who told him of the rising in Beverley and warned him that Kitchen and Wilson were both against him, and had threatened to come and destroy him.[23]

When the commons reassembled on the following morning they followed the pattern of the Lincolnshire towns in looking for leadership

---

[21] *LP* XII (i), no. 201 (vii); 'The manner of the taking of Robert Aske', 333. Breyer claimed that a proclamation was made in Aske's name, *LP* XI, no. 841. It would not surprise me if Aske had sent a warning of events in Lincolnshire to Raffles with his nephews when they were permitted to leave Lincolnshire, but I very much doubt whether this called on Beverley to rise. The timing argues against it. If his nephews returned on Thursday, 5 October, word could have been in Beverley by the end of the day and the town could have risen on the Friday: instead, it rose on Sunday, after the commons had received word of the rising from one of their own, Woodmansey. If Aske told Raffles to rise, he did not act on it.

[22] Stapleton, 83–4.   [23] Ibid. 85; *LP* XII (i), no. 1022.

from outside their own numbers.[24] Stapleton does not say with whom the idea originated, but a delegation made up of the deputy steward, Richard Faircliffe, Richard Wharton of Hull Bridge, Christopher Saunderson, and others was sent to solicit the support of Sir Ralph Ellerker the younger. Ellerker rejected their overtures, but did offer to come to talk to them if they would allow him to pass unsworn. This suggestion was declined. Within a few days Ellerker had taken sanctuary in Hull. It was then that the commons alighted on William Stapleton. It was asked why the Stapletons had not been sworn. Some urged that they be burnt out of the Greyfriars. One of the friars, Thomas Johnson, acted as an intermediary before a delegation entered the Greyfriars, swore Christopher Stapleton in his bed, and led William and Brian Stapleton out to the commons. They too were sworn, then William Stapleton was acclaimed captain.

Stapleton professed to be puzzled by this. He knew virtually no one in Beverley, but this may have been a positive asset.

After which oath, the said William seeing the wild disposition of the said people, the great fear that the honest men were in by reason of the aforesaid dissension amongst themselves and thereby likelihood of great murder, upon all which premises moved to him of the behalf of the said honest men, was much steered thereby to take the governance and rule of the said people and they all continually crying 'Master William Stapleton shall be our captain', which the said William thinketh came by reason of the said observant [Johnson] in setting forth some praises to the said people or else they would never have been so earnest of him who they did not know.

The town was clearly too fractured to accept one of its own as captain and, after the refusal of Sir Ralph Ellerker the younger, they turned to the nearest convenient gentleman, who happened to be Stapleton. He, recognizing that the commons were divided by long-standing feuds, began by insisting that all quarrels be forgotten and that there should be no spoiling of goods. Then he dismissed them for the day. It was then, as they were dispersing, that Roger Kitchen appeared and set himself up in opposition to Stapleton, calling on those that 'were true to the commons' to accompany him to raise Cottingham, Hessle, and other neighbouring

---

[24] Except where indicated, all the following text is based on Stapleton's account.

towns. The majority were persuaded to disband, but a minority refused. During the night they lit fires of hedges and haystacks on Hunsley Beacon.

The fires served their purpose of drawing support from the neighbouring villages. As the Beverley commons were gathered at Westwood Green on Tuesday morning, men appeared from Newbald and Cottingham wanting to know when they should set forwards. (North Cave, also attracted by the beacons, sent representatives on Wednesday morning.) Stapleton 'had great business to stay them from going forward' but, with the aid of Wharton and Faircliffe, persuaded the commons to wait until a reply was received to their letter to Lincoln. In order to strengthen his control over them, Stapleton persuaded the commons to accept Brian Stapleton as his deputy, and Richard Wharton ('who was taken for the most honest and substantial man there and a man both of good age and gratuity and [who] much pains took about the staying of all the business') and Richard Faircliffe as petty captains.[25] His selection of deputies and the reasons for his choice is evidence of the degree to which he saw himself as both in charge of the commons and also in opposition to their aims. Then, having again lectured the commons about their making no spoils, he felt sufficiently confident of his hold over them to send Christopher Saunderson to ask Sir Ralph Ellerker the elder to attend the following day, 'to help to stay the said town'. Stapleton did, though, condone the spreading of the rebellion by giving Sir Robert Esch or Ashton, a friar of Knaresborough, a passport to travel through the Wolds to raise Ryedale and Pickering.[26]

Ellerker agreed to come. At breakfast on Wednesday he met with the two Stapletons, Sir John Milner, and others at Christopher Saunderson's 'to consult of this same stay'. They then went to the Green, where Ellerker exhorted the commons to stay at Beverley. But again events overtook the plans of the captains. Although Stapleton had discussed the desirability of stationing some 'honest men' at Hessle to intercept (and if necessary, amend) any letter coming back from Lincolnshire, nothing had been done. Ellerker was still addressing the commons when Woodmansey returned, followed by a fraternal delegation of the Lincolnshire rebels carrying letters. Whilst Sir Ralph wanted to have the letters scrutinized

---

[25] Quotation from Stapleton, 87.   [26] Ibid. 88.

by the captains before they were read, the commons demanded that they be immediately shared with them. The letter was read by Thomas Dunne, then Guy Kyme expounded the course of the Lincolnshire rising. When Kyme declared that the Lincolnshire rebels could give 'battle to any king christened', 'the hearts of our wild people was set a flutter and then no words but still forward', and after he had finished his oration, 'then no longer stay could not be taken'. With his strategy of delay wrecked, Stapleton allowed Sir Ralph to depart home unsworn (although this drew much criticism from the crowd). 'Then all delays set apart, no remedy but forward.' Hunsley and Tranby beacons were fired and word was sent to Cottingham and Hessle to be at Hunsley the following morning.[27]

Stapleton's own account of events on Thursday traces the spread of the rebellion, the marginalization of Beverley as the countryside rose, and Stapleton's own penchant for becoming sidetracked into kindly and decent works. The country assembled at Hunsley Beacon. A lawyer from Brantingham, called Smytheley, was not present and when a party was sent to bring him it found him ill in bed. The commons believed that he was feigning and wished to carry him to the commons in a cart: 'but with much pain the said William spared him.' Then it was pointed out that Leonard Beckwith's house at South Cave contained money and valuables from the dissolved monasteries of Ferriby and Haltenprice. To prevent the commons from breaking into Beckwith's house Stapleton went there himself, ascertained that all the house contained was coffers of deeds, and arranged for their security.[28]

Of course, Stapleton's willingness to involve himself in this trivia is an illustration of how he offered the Beverley commons *firm* leadership, but denied them any *forward* leadership. As on the previous day, it was events elsewhere which determined what the Beverley commons were to do next. During Thursday word came that Robert Aske had raised all Howdenshire and Marshland and would be around Market Weighton that night. Aske wanted the Beverley men to muster the following day at

---

[27] Ibid. 88–90.

[28] Ibid. 90–1. Beckwith was the newly appointed receiver of the court of augmentations for Yorkshire, knighted 1544, d. 1557. B. A. English and C. B. L. Barr, 'The Records Formerly in St Mary's Tower, York', *YAJ* 42 (1966–70), 366–7. He was amongst the first lessees of the Court of Augmentations, notably of monastic lands in York. *LP* XIII (i), no. 1520 (pp. 577–8).

Market Weighton, where he could see their numbers. Reports also reached the commons that Holderness had risen, but that whilst some of the gentry had been taken, others had sought refuge in Hull. Towards the end of the day a delegation was gathered to go to Hull to discover whether the town was for or against them. They saw the mayor, who promised that Hull would go in with them and undertook to send a fuller answer to Beverley on the following morning. Four Hull representatives did indeed appear before the commons on Friday morning and agreed to yield Hull to them.[29] By the time this had been done in Beverley it was too late for the commons to move as a body to Market Weighton. Stapleton, in the company of a number of gentlemen and the messengers from Lincolnshire, went to meet with Aske.

III

Whilst Stapleton was trying to moderate the Beverley commons, other, less well-documented risings were taking place within the East Riding as an independent response to the rumours of confiscation and the news of the rising in Lincolnshire. In Holderness the rising took place after the common bells were rung. The district then divided along administrative or territorial lines, with musters being held locally, before a general muster was held at Sutton Ings. Here each bailiwick chose a captain. Under the guidance of the three captains (Richard Tenand, William Barker, and William Omler), the massed tenants marched to Beverley.[30] Stapleton records that on 12 October word came to Beverley that Holderness had risen and taken Sir Christopher Hilyard and a number of other gentry (one of whom was hurt), whilst others, including Sir John Constable, his son (also Sir John), Sir William Constable, young Sir Ralph Ellerker, and others had taken refuge in Hull. On Saturday, 14 October Stapleton was told that the Holderness men had come to Beverley and that Sir Christopher Hilyard, with other gentlemen, was requesting an interview

---

[29] Hull subsequently declined to surrender, and Stapleton embarked on a blockade of the town.
[30] William Nicholson of Preston in Holderness is our sole witness: *LP* XII (i), no. 202 (v).

with him. At this meeting the chief subject of discussion appears to have been how to take Hull. The Holderness men, said to number 300, mustered that night on Westwood Green outside the walls of Beverley; on the following day they joined Beverley in a blockade of Hull which lasted for most of the following week. Ultimately the Holderness contingent followed Stapleton to Pontefract, where they were absorbed into the force under the command of Sir Thomas Percy.[31]

Who originally raised the alarm in Holderness, or at whose request it was raised, is never mentioned, but here is the Pilgrimage in microcosm: a peasant rising which owed little to the gentry, but which they came to control as the movement matured. Hence, Sir Christopher Hilyard follows the usual gentry pattern of being taken in one week, while by the end of the next he was accepting the surrender of his neighbours at Hull. The movement in the district immediately to the north of Beverley is better documented. Of all the branches of the 1536 movement in Yorkshire, this was the one which was most clearly an activists' rising rather than a gentry-led affair. It never acquired gentry leadership, remaining under the dominance of John Hallam of Cawkeld, near Watton. Unlike Holderness, it is possible to be fairly specific about what Hallam owed to his contacts with Beverley and Lincolnshire.

When he was examined after the failure of his renewed revolt in January, Hallam began his account of events in October with a description of the outrage caused by the failure of his parish priest to announce the St Wilfred's Day holiday (12 October) on the previous Sunday.[32] When challenged by his parishioners, the priest said that the holiday was abolished by the king's authority and with the consent of the clergy sitting in convocation. On the following Monday or Tuesday (although if we employ Stapleton's chronology it would be Wednesday) Hallam visited Beverley to collect a debt. There was a great deal of talk in the town about Lincolnshire. Hallam encountered Guy Kyme and Thomas Dunne and heard them explain why Lincolnshire had risen. He probably secured a copy of their articles. He allowed himself to be sworn and was given one

---

[31] Stapleton, 91, 93–4, 95, 97–8, 100.
[32] The following account is based on *LP* XII (i), no. 201 (iv), with quotations from the MS, PRO, E36/119, fos. 26v–27r.

of the letters written by Robert Eshe alias Ashton, the friar from
Knaresborough, to take back to his neighbours. What Hallam never admitted was that he used this letter to raise the district about Watton.
William Horsekey of Watton offered hanging evidence against Hallam
when he explained how he had called his neighbours together, told them
that Lincolnshire was up, and forced them to rise in solidarity on pain of
death. In this way Hallam had 'stirred up' Watton, Hutton Cranswick,
and all the country from there to Driffield, 'and he was the ringleader
and captain of them all'.

Hallam wished to suggest that the movement was more spontaneous.
From the time of his visit at Beverley, 'no man could keep his servant
at plough but that every man that was able to bear a staff went forward
toward [the muster at] Hunsley'. And his own position emerged progressively: 'that the commons . . . were without a leader or a captain two
or three days after and then the people named Mr Robert Hotham, Henry
Newark, William Cawrser, and this examinate to be captains of all the
commons from Beverley to Driffield.'[33] And then began the round of
musters, the siege of Hull, and then a further muster at Hunsley 'with
all the gentlemen they had taken out of Hull'. And then to Pontefract.
But, bit by bit, the other captains withdrew, leaving Hallam the undis-
puted leader of this sector of the rising.

IV

For the Miss Dodds, Aske had something in common with Macavity the
mystery cat: a guiding force, but somewhat hard to pin down. Their problems perhaps began with their conviction that it was a conspiracy which
spawned the risings in Lincolnshire and Yorkshire. They therefore read
into Aske's account of his movements in the first few days of October
motives which he certainly never admitted. If we try to read Aske's movements as those of a conspirator, then they simply do not make sense.

---

[33] Stapleton says that Hotham and Hallam (amongst others) with their bands came into Beverley
on 13 October. Stapleton, 92.

When the rising in Lincolnshire broke out, Aske was one of the members of a hunting party at William Ellerker's house at Ellerker.[34] Also there were his brothers John and Christopher, and awaited was Sir Ralph Ellerker the younger. This was a family party. When word came that Sir Ralph was committed to serving as the king's (subsidy) commissioner and would not be attending, the party broke up. Aske set out for London on Wednesday, 4 October, in the company of three of his nephews, crossing the Humber by the ferry from Hessle to Barton-upon-Humber. It was only after they had embarked that Aske learnt that the commons had assembled at Caistor. Unable to get back into Yorkshire by that ferry, he decided to travel westwards along the south bank of the Humber and lodge for the night at the house of his brother-in-law, Thomas Portington, at Sawcliff. But at Ferriby he was stopped by Huddeswell in the company of sixteen or eighteen men, all mounted. They demanded to know who Aske was and, when told, insisted that he should take the oath. Aske enquired what the oath was, decided that it was not incompatible with his oath to the king, and after a token resistance allowed himself to be sworn.[35] Huddeswell, who was an eyewitness to events at Caistor the previous day, told him of the rising at Louth and outlined the causes of the revolt. The rebels then let him travel on to Sawcliff unhindered. At Sawcliff he discovered that Portington had already gone with the rebels. Aske therefore elected to carry on westwards to the ferry at Winteringham to escape back into Yorkshire. Again he was waylaid by the commons and returned to Sawcliff, where his party spent the night. Before daybreak on 5 October he was roused from his bed by a group of commons. At Aske's request, his nephews were allowed to return to Yorkshire whilst he went with the commons to a town (which he does not name) 3 miles inland, where he found a group of 200 commons 'without captain or great gentlemen and most of them without harness'. He agreed to go with them and raise the Soke of Kirton, one party travelling directly to Kirton and Aske, with the other group, taking a more circuitous route along the banks of the Humber. The two parties met again at Kirton at around two o'clock in the afternoon.[36]

---

[34] The following account is based on 'The manner of the taking of Robert Aske', 331–3.
[35] See p. 440 below for this incident.   [36] 'The manner of the taking of Robert Aske', 332–3.

Aske wanted to know what the commons wished to do next. They told him they thought that they should meet with the other Lincolnshire commons at Hambledon Hill near Harkel Rasen. He then asked whether they were certain that there would be others congregated there. They were not, but it was commonly held that there would be. As none of the Kirton commons were willing to reconnoitre, Aske volunteered to ride there himself if the commons would wait for him to return: and he rode over in the company of Nicholas Girlington and Robert Ascue.[37]

At Hambledon Hill, as we have already seen, Aske encountered Thomas Moigne.[38] Moigne briefed Aske on what the commons proposed to do, and having made this contact, Aske rode back to the Kirton commons. From there he was allowed to depart (although he says nothing of any conditions which might have been attached to his liberty). He spent a second night at Sawcliff, and early on the following morning, Friday, 6 October, he crossed the Trent into Yorkshire at Burton upon Strather.

Aske portrays his adventures up to this point as a series of accidents and, although he never emphasizes it, draws an account of himself as a man who had stumbled into a rebellion and tried to take the prudent course of turning his back on it. Is his account plausible? The answer must be that it is. His experience of being sworn and then pressed into leadership finds parallels in both the Lincolnshire and Yorkshire movements. His willingness to swear the oath on the grounds that there was nothing in it that contravened his existing oaths is also a characteristic reaction. Where Aske's experience is different from all the others (and here the contrast with Moigne and Stapleton, also lawyers, is marked) is that he did more than was required of him. The others dragged their feet. Aske volunteered to venture further into Lincolnshire to make contact with the Louth commons at Hambledon Hill. This was reckless. It does not appear that he was compelled to do it; rather, it seems that even at this early stage he welcomed the opportunity to go and see what was happening elsewhere.

On the other hand there is no evidence that Aske and Moigne exchanged confidences at Hambledon Hill. Indeed, quite the opposite:

---

[37] Aske never mentions his companions: their names come from Moigne's account.
[38] Above p. 123.

both their accounts emphasize that their conversation was conducted before the assembled commons. As Moigne admitted, he 'made them answer according to the minds of the commons'.[39] Whatever passed between them doubtless conformed to the rhetoric of feigned enthusiasm which the Lincolnshire gentry employed. There is no indication that on 6 October Aske was recruited to the rebel cause. Nor were his actions when he returned to Yorkshire those of a committed insurgent. Crossing into Marshland, he found the commons 'in a great rumour and ready to rise: and as soon as they perceived the said Aske, having knowledge that he was taken in Lincolnshire and leader there, they were purposed to have rung the bells in those parts'. Aske refused to allow them to do so until they had heard the bells at Howden rung. Then, crossing the Ouse and travelling into Howdenshire, he found the people there equally ready to rise. He reversed his instructions: Howden was not to rise until they had heard the bells of Marshland.[40] He later glossed this to say that they should not rise until they heard the king's answers to the Lincolnshire petition.[41] Aske had constructed a simple device to inhibit the spread of the movement when, if he was serious about stirring rebellion, it was in his own interest to press it forwards. Then, from Howden he went to his brother's house at Aughton but found it deserted. He returned to Howden and took lodgings there for the night.[42]

So Aske could be satisfied. He had escaped Lincolnshire and had done his bit to quieten the East Riding. Then, in an extraordinary about-turn, he decided to return to Lincolnshire. His explanation for this was simply that he heard a rumour that Mr Hennage was expected to bring the king's answers to the petitions.[43] So, on Saturday, 7 October he travelled to Lincoln. The report he had heard was mistaken and anticipated the royal response by several days. Moreover, he was warned in Lincoln that,

[39] SP1/110, fo. 155v (= LP XI, no. 971).

[40] 'The manner of the taking of Robert Aske', 333.   [41] LP XII (i), no. 946 (1), answ. 107.

[42] Bush, on the evidence of Breyer, suggests that Aske stayed with the lawyer, William Babthorpe, and from his house sent a latter to Beverley telling the town to rise. Aske makes no mention of any of this. Breyer says that Raffles told him that Aske had dined at Babthorpe's house. Breyer then claimed to have encountered Christopher Aske making his way to Skipton, who said that he had been at Babthorpe's house the previous Sunday (is 30 September intended?) with his brother (query, John or Robert?). Bush, Pilgrimage of Grace, 28, 81; LP XI, no. 841; I am sceptical.

[43] 'The manner of the taking of Robert Aske', 333. He had also heard that Sir George Darcy was searching for him. LP XII (i), no. 946 (1), answ. 108.

having gone back into Yorkshire, he was a marked man: he changed lodgings and returned to Yorkshire early on the Sunday morning.[44] Aske's own story reveals very clearly how his erratic actions had destroyed his credit with the Lincolnshire rank and file: so why did he go? It seems most likely that for a second time Aske's curiosity and his enthusiastic, interfering personality led him back. His first flight into Yorkshire and the restraints he placed on the commons in the Marshland and How-denshire suggest that he was at that time not committed to rebellion until he knew what the king's reply said: his return to Lincolnshire indicates that he could not resist seeing what was happening there.

Aske appears to have returned north-westwards through Lincolnshire rather than north to the Barton-upon-Humber–Hessle crossing, for he refers to the Trent being too high to cross, and we know that he spent some time at Whitgift. We must assume that he was again heading for Aughton. He was forced to wait two days for the river to abate, that is, Sunday and Monday, and finally crossed at about midnight on Monday.

By his own account, Aske was still avoiding trouble. His description of the rising in the Marshland on Tuesday, 10 October assigns no role whatsoever to himself. Sir Brian Hastings of Stirsthorp, steward of the royal manor of Hatfield, wrote to the gentlemen of the Marshland asking them to assemble a force and come to him. (These were troops destined for the earl of Shrewsbury at Nottingham, which Hastings had been asked to mobilize in a letter from Henry VIII received at Pontefract on Sunday, 8 October.[45]) The gentry convened a meeting, called the com-mons to them and then the bells were rung and answered by those of Howdenshire. Where was Aske? He was hiding in 'a poor man's house, secretly, to the intent not to have been known'. His refuge was discovered by the commons, and at some point in the evening he was called by them into Howdenshire. It was there that Aske intervened to stop the commons burning Sir Thomas Metham's house at Metham and persuaded them to go to their homes.[46] On the following day, Wednesday, the com-mons of Howdenshire mustered at Ringstone Hurst in Howden and the commons of the Marshland on Hook Moor. Aske attended both musters.

---

[44] For the danger he was in, see additionally 'Aske's examination', 559.
[45] *LP* XI, no. 662.   [46] 'The manner of the taking of Robert Aske', 334.

On Thursday the commons of Howdenshire proceeded towards Weighton under Aske's direction, and on Friday he met with Stapleton.

Again, is this account plausible, with its implication that after his second return from Lincolnshire Aske underwent a conversion to the rebel cause? And perhaps most importantly, what caused this conversion?[47] Up to the moment that Aske and Stapleton met on Friday, 13 October, there is only one document which sheds any independent light on Aske's activities. This is an undated letter calling on the recipients to prepare themselves that evening and to assemble on Skipwith Moor (which is only 9 miles from York) the following morning.[48] In effect, it is a letter from the Howdenshire commons (from where the gentry subscribers are all drawn) to those of the Marshland:

Masters, all men to be ready tomorrow and this night and in the morning to ring your bells in every town and to assemble yourselves upon Skipwith Moor and there appoint your captains Master Hussey, Master Babthorpe, and Master Gascoigne and other gentlemen and to give warning to all beyond the water to be ready upon pain of death for the commonwealth and make your proclamation every man to be true to the king's issue and the noble blood, to preserve the church of God from spoiling and to be true to the commons and their wealths and ye shall have tomorrow the articles and causes of your assembly and petition to the king and place of our meeting and all other of power [poure] and commonwealth, in haste, etc.

By me Robert Aske chief captain of Marshland, the Isle and Howdenshire, Thomas Metham, Robert Aske younger, Thomas Saltmarsh, William Monkton, Mr Franke, Master Cawood, captains of the same.

The letter has a number of puzzling aspects. It dates from the moment when Robert Aske assumed authority over the incipient rebellion in the area divided between Lincolnshire (the Isle of Axholme), the West Riding (the Marshland), and the East Riding (Howdenshire). But when was it written, and was Aske actually in the company of his co-signatories? The letter itself is undated, and there appears to be no reliable independent evidence of the date at which the Skipwith Moor muster took place. The account given by Thomas Maunsell, the vicar of Brayton

---

[47] For evidence that his interrogators were puzzled, see the questions put to him, 'Aske's Examination', 556–7, the answers to which do not survive.

[48] *LP* XI, no. 622, printed in Dodds, *Pilgrimage*, I, 148.

near Selby, is chronologically confused, but is best read as saying that the muster happened on Thursday, 12 October, the day after the musters at Ringstone Hurst and Hook Moor.[49] It is therefore plausible that the letter was sent on Wednesday from the Ringstone Hurst muster into the area to the north-west, over the Derwent, calling for a muster on Thursday, and that the signatories were all in the commons' hands at the Wednesday muster, perhaps even before Aske threw in his lot with them.[50] Thomas Metham might have been taken on the Tuesday evening when the commons besieged his father's house. Two of them, Robert Aske the younger and William Monkton, were close relatives, being Aske's nephew and brother-in-law respectively. As for the three gentlemen whom the commons were to take as captains, the lawyer William Babthorpe had already or was soon to flee from his house at Osgodby to the archbishop of York at Cawood, and then to Pontefract.[51]

Whether any of these men, or indeed any of the letter's signatories, attended the Skipwith Moor muster is unknown. Certainly Aske was not there; Thomas Maunsell, who was, never refers to his presence. On Aske's own account, he started Thursday at Howden and ended it camped near Market Weighton.[52]

---

[49] *LP* XI, no. 1402.

[50] The signatories can be identified as follows: Thomas Metham, elder son of Sir Thomas Metham of Metham, b. c.1526, d. 1537; Robert Aske the younger, Robert Aske's nephew as elder son of his elder brother John; Thomas Saltmarsh, elder son of Edward Saltmarsh of Saltmarsh and Thorganby, d. 1545, married Elizabeth, daughter of Thomas Metham of Metham, so uncle by marriage to Thomas Metham previous; William Monkton of Cavill, who was brother-in-law to Robert Aske by his marriage to Aske's sister Anne; Mr Franke = Thomas Franke, rector of Loftus (North Riding) from 1521— and rector of Catton, 1527–1543 (N. A. H. Lawrence in *YASRS* 143 (1985), 21–2; also *LP* XII (i), no. 493); Mr Cawood = Gervais Cawood, the bishop of Durham's receiver of Howdenshire in 1536 and keeper or tenant of Howden Park c.1531 (*Valor Ecclesiasticus*, V, 300, also p. 137, *LP* XII (i), no. 853; *Yorks. Star Chamber Procs.*, I, 55–9). Other genealogical details are taken from J. W. Clay, *Dugdale's Visitation of Yorkshire With Additions*, 3 vols. (1899–1917).

[51] For Babthorpe's flight, *LP* XII (i), no. 1022. For his life, *Hist. Parl., 1509–1558*, I, 357–8, and T. Burton, ed. J. Raine, *The History and Antiquities of Hemingborough* (1888), 312–4. He was a member of the duke of Richmond's council in 1525 and the Council of the North from 1537, knighted 1549, d. 1555. He was at Pontefract by 15 October. *LP* XI, no. 729. The other gentry to be brought in were George Hussey of North Driffield (a nephew of John, Lord Hussey of Sleaford, a point unnoticed by conspiracy theorists) and John Gascoigne of South Driffield, a very obscure figure. See Burton, ed. Raine, *Hemingborough*, 219–20.

[52] *LP* XI, no. 1403; 'Aske's Examination', 334. There is also the question of whether on Wednesday or Thursday he went to the earl of Northumberland at his house at Wressle, which is about 3 miles from Howden. Aske never mentions it, but Sir Thomas Percy, the earl's brother, who was not an eyewitness to events there, heard how Aske had been both there and at Howden. *LP* XII (i), no. 393.

The clue which the letter offers to Aske's purpose is in its reference to the declaration of articles. Aske, it will be recalled, told the Marshland and Howdenshire commons not to mobilize until they had heard the king's answer, and went to Lincoln in the hope of hearing it for himself. Now the answer which was then expected was a reply to the letter sent from Louth on 3 October. This was not received until Tuesday, 10 October. The full Lincoln articles were not drawn up until Monday, 9 October, when George Stanes carried them to the king. What converted Aske to the rebellion was not the king's answer but the sight of the Lincoln articles. In a declaration made after his arrest, Aske said that he first saw them at a poor man's house at Whitgift, a village in Yorkshire on the south side of the Humber opposite Metham.[53] He gives no date, but Whitgift is on the route which one might expect him to have taken back into Yorkshire via Burton on Strather. The date must therefore have been Tuesday, 10 October. If his own account is true, then he spent at least part of that day hiding from the commons; but by the end of the following day he had emerged as chief captain of three wapentakes.

The Skipwith Moor letter makes clear the centrality of the articles to Aske's thought. Those who gathered there were to hear the articles which explained 'the causes of your assembly and petition to the king'. And this is the clue to Aske's behaviour. Access to the articles clarified for him the purpose of the movement. Before seeing them, he was interested but uncommitted. He was probably uncertain as to the movement's aims. He knew, from Moigne, of what the *commons* complained. He too had heard the rumours circulating amongst them about the confiscation of church goods and the suppression of churches, and he knew them to be untrue.[54] He was not interested in lending his weight to a rebellion of the commons based on erroneous gossip. It was after seeing the articles that he understood the rebellion had political objectives to which he could subscribe. It was at this point that he threw his own weight behind it and started to spread the rebellion in Yorkshire. Aske then adopted the Lincolnshire articles as his own. There was no incongruity in this:

---

[53] *LP* XII (i), no. 852 (ii).   [54] 'Aske's examination', pp. 558–9 (answer 10–16).

his movement was not yet a Pilgrimage of Grace but a northwards extension of the Lincolnshire Rising.[55]

It was Aske, and not Stapleton, who took the initiative to bring the Howdenshire and Beverley contingents together. Instead of leading his force directly to York (which is to the north-west of Howden), Aske headed north-east to Market Weighton (on the direct road from Beverley to York) on the Thursday. Aske passes over the events of Thursday and Friday somewhat lightly in his narrative. Stapleton, as usual, offers a full account. Having spent the first part of Friday hearing representatives from Hull, Stapleton and a number of gentlemen set out to meet with Aske at Market Weighton. Amongst those who went with him were the Lincolnshire messengers, who particularly wanted to review Aske's force before they returned home.[56] The Beverley men ran into Aske, Nicholas Rudstone and his brother, and Thomas Metham (a signatory of the letter from the Howdenshire commons), who were coming to look for them. Aske gave an account of his taking in Lincolnshire. Stapleton invited Guy Kyme and the others to deliver their messages again. Then Aske 'asked of them of Lincolnshire if they had any letter for him, as he knew the state of their host as well as they for he had been at their several musters and showed the places. Where they answered that they had no letter but to the town of Beverley.'[57]

Kyme's account of this meeting is fuller, but damaged by damp.[58] When the groups met, Aske and Stapleton with others drew apart, but Kyme overheard Aske insist on Stapleton's subservience to him.[59] Stapleton then introduced Kyme. Aske wanted to know whether they had brought him a letter, to which they replied that they had not, unless he meant their letter to the king. Aske was unimpressed and would not accept their credence by mouth. 'And then they desired licence to depart and so he bade "God be with them", saying they were pilgrims and had a pilgrimage gate to go to.' There is no sign that he took the opportunity to send any message back to Lincoln.

---

[55] The petition to the king referred to in the letter calling the Skipwith Moor muster was that made by the Lincolnshire rebels: there was no intention that another should be made.

[56] Stapleton, 92.   [57] Ibid. 92.   [58] *LP* XI, no. 828 (xii) (= SP1/109, fo. 14r).

[59] 'He heard Aske say "he would be served . . . [remainder lost]"'. SP1/109, fo. 14r.

This seems a crucial meeting. That Aske expected Kyme to be carrying one or more letters for him indicates that on his own estimation he
was a part of the Lincolnshire rising and looked to Lincoln for instructions. But it also suggests that Aske had fundamentally misread the movement there. The Lincolnshire gentry saw the articles not as a means to rally
support but as a device to buy time. The political objectives outlined
there may well have commanded universal support amongst them—we
do not know—but were secondary to the overall objective of restraining and taming the commons. Aske, on the other hand, was drawn to
the rebellion because he supported the articles. Indeed, his behaviour
suggests that although he was no more in favour of a revolt of the commons per se than the Lincolnshire gentry, he saw the enthusiasm of the
commons under gentry leadership as the means to secure the political
ends identified in the Lincoln articles. Hence, after the Lincolnshire gentry disbanded their movement and made peace with the duke of Suffolk
(which was happening at the very moment Aske was talking to Stapleton
and Kyme), there was only one enthusiast left for their political programme,
Aske. He was therefore thrust forwards to a degree he probably neither
envisaged nor sought.

V

From Market Weighton Aske led his company towards York, arriving
on the banks of the River Derwent on Saturday. Here they took and
held the bridges at Sutton upon Derwent and Kexby, it having been
rumoured that Sir Oswold Wilstrop would throw them down to hinder
their passage. At Kexby Lane End a muster was held during Saturday,
where Aske proclaimed the Lincolnshire articles to the commons. On
Sunday a further muster was held outside York itself. On Monday afternoon, 16 October, the rebels made an orderly entry into the city.

In leading his force to York, Aske was traversing countryside already
troubled by rumour and sympathetic to the rebel cause. William Acclom,
gent., of Moreby (an Ouseside parish about 5 miles south of York) explained
how he had been taken on the previous Thursday by one Edwin, a

servant of Sir Robert Constable's. On Friday he had attended a muster arranged by Edwin at a place called Whitmore. On Saturday Acclom, Edwin, and the commons raised by Edwin mustered with Aske at Kexby Lane End. From there, in the company of sixty others, they drove south by way of Leonard Beckwith's house at Stillingfleet (which they plundered), before moving on to the archbishop of York's house at Cawood where they swore the remaining servants (the archbishop himself having fled some days earlier). The party then made its way along the bank of the Ouse to York, 'stirring and moving the people by the way'.[60]

In York itself there was neither the will nor the enthusiasm to resist the rebels (although, as at Lincoln, events within the city are poorly documented). Lancelot Collins, the treasurer of the Minster, later deposed how, on Tuesday, 10 October, it was reported in York that Howdenshire had risen under Aske. (Either Collins is in error or he anticipates events around Howden.) On Wednesday it was said that the commons were up within 3 miles of the city, and on Thursday they were up in the city itself.[61] York sent a last, desperate letter to the king requesting aid on Saturday, 14 October.[62] Despite some attempts to man the walls and bars of the city, the city was amenable to a negotiated surrender or, more strictly, conceded Aske a right of free passage. Again, the details of the negotiations are obscure. Aske says that he sent a letter requesting free passage and offering, if he were refused, to assault the city. He agreed fair prices with the city for victuals and ordered that all provisions and horse meat were to be paid for; and he forbade footmen to enter the city.[63] Richard Bowyer, who had tried to organize the defence of the city, confirms that orders were made for the victualling. He implies that this was done on Sunday, but Aske's forces did not enter until Monday.[64] Bowyer states that the decision to open the city to Aske was taken by the mayor without consulting the commonalty, perhaps implying that Harrington undercut Bowyer and others who were willing to make a fight of it. In fact the city's position was hopeless, with the commons sympathetic to the rebels, whose numbers Darcy estimated at about 20,000 men. Collins thought that 4,000 or 5,000 men entered the city with Aske.

---

[60] *LP* XII (i), no. 536.   [61] *LP* XII (i), no. 1018.   [62] *LP* XI, no. 704.
[63] 'The manner of the taking of Robert Aske', 334.   [64] *LP* XII (i), no. 762.

Aske himself conceded that the city had neither artillery or gunpowder to use in its defence.[65] He was received at the Minster by its clergy and processed with them to the high altar. That evening he and his colleagues dined at Sir George Lawson's.[66]

In entering York, Aske was merely re-enacting the course taken by the Lincolnshire rebels. It will be recalled that after they had entered Lincoln the rebels failed to advance, spending their days mustering, drawing up a new petition to the king, and waiting for a royal answer. These were all delaying tactics of the gentry, designed to buy time in the hope that sufficient concessions could be secured to allow the rebels to disperse satisfied, or that the waiting itself might encourage the commons to drift back to their homes. It has already been suggested that Aske, on the basis of his limited contacts with the Lincolnshire gentry, did not appreciate that they were less concerned with achieving their professed aims than with securing a peaceable end to the rebellion and their own pardon. He sought to emulate the public aims of the Lincolnshire rebels, and not the private strategies of the Lincolnshire gentry. He encouraged where they temporized. Hence, having taken York, Aske could be expected to make contact with the king through petitions reiterating the demands of the Lincolnshire commons. Now if this had ever been his aim (and nothing says directly that it was), then all was thrown out of balance by the disintegration of the Lincolnshire movement. The shock of this betrayal felt by the Beverley rebels has already been described. It can hardly have been less amongst the East Riding men who had followed Aske to York. Aske, therefore, had the alternatives of capitulating himself, of maintaining the movement's momentum by adopting a static petitioning strategy, or of launching an aggressive forward policy. By Wednesday it was clear that he had adopted the latter option.

In assessing what Aske did at York, it is crucial to discover when word of the failure of Lincolnshire reached him. Neither Aske himself, nor any other of the sparse witnesses to events at York, refers to it. The earl

---

[65] *LP* XI, nos. 729, 760 (ii); XII (i), no. 1018; 'The manner of the taking of Robert Aske', 334.

[66] Bowyer names Aske's companions as Rudstone, Cawood, Monkton, Donnington, and others, 14 in all. *LP* XII (i), no. 306. Thomas Strangeways, who met with Aske at Lawson's house later in the evening, says that he was then in the company of Rudstone, Monkton, and Cawood (who he calls Calverd). *LP* XI, no. 762.

of Shrewsbury, at Nottingham, wrote to Darcy on Friday, 13 October saying he expected that the Lincolnshire rebels would soon have dispersed.[67] Darcy may have heard during Saturday that the Lincolnshire movement was winding down, but when news of its dispersal reached Wakefield at one o'clock on Sunday it seems to have been both fresh and unexpected. It was also inaccurate in detail.[68] Stapleton does not clearly state when word reached Hull, but the letter which the rebels wrote back to Lincolnshire included the tidings that, even whilst it was being written, news had come that York was won. This suggests Monday, 16 October.[69] It is likely that Aske knew nothing of the collapse of the Lincolnshire rebellion until Monday. He must certainly have known by the early hours of Tuesday morning, when Darcy's steward, Thomas Strangeways, met with Aske at York in an attempt to discover the rebels' intentions.[70] As Darcy knew of the course of events in Lincolnshire, it is inconceivable that Strangeways would not have told Aske, if he still had not already heard.

The news of the failure in Lincolnshire did not cause Aske to falter. First he convened a council of the gentry then in the commons' hands in York. Amongst those attending were Sir Oswold Wilstrop, Mr Plumpton (who had been brought in by Wilstrop), Thomas Metham, and Thomas Saltmarsh (both of whom had signed the order for the musters at Skipwith Moor the previous Wednesday).[71] The meeting decided that every gentleman should 'take his friends that were gentlemen and bring them in'. They were to do this using an oath which Aske had devised before the meeting. Aske also issued an order forbidding the destruction any man's property unless he had at least twenty-four hours warning to join the commons, and even then spoils were only to be made on the authority of two members of his council.[72]

Secondly, Aske had posted on the doors of the Minster an order permitting the members of suppressed religious houses to re-enter their

---

[67] *LP* XI, no. 694.

[68] Ibid. no. 734. The informant understood that the king (through his herald) had both granted the rebels his pardon and had conceded 'their reasonable desires for certain causes and in especial concerning his churches etc. . . .'. The word then was that the Lincolnshire movement had achieved its objectives, and it is in this light that the expectation that the secondary rising in Yorkshire would now wind down must be seen.

[69] Stapleton, 96.   [70] Below, p. 277.   [71] 'Aske's examination', 560, answ. 28.

[72] 'The manner of the taking of Robert Aske', 334–5.

convents and repossess their goods, requiring the Crown's farmers of their lands to support them during the time of the common's petition-making. (As the surviving copy is on the same paper as a petition for aid from Sawley Abbey, the order may have been drafted as a response to their predicament.)[73] Thirdly, letters were sent announcing the fall of York to the besiegers of Hull. Aske subsequently circulated his oath widely, sending it into Lancashire with a servant of the earl of Derby.[74]

Aske's brief time in York was used for consolidation. The most important of the ways in which he achieved this, though, was through an elaboration of the rhetoric of the movement. This had the effect of distancing the Yorkshire movement from its failed parent in Lincolnshire and giving it a life (though not quite a purpose) of its own. The develop-ment of the language employed by the Yorkshire rebels, and their emer-gence as the Pilgrims of Grace, is worth considering at length.

When Aske reached Kexby on Saturday, he found that he did not have a copy of the Lincoln articles with him. Whilst he says (in his examina-tion) that he published the Lincoln articles at Kexby, he must have done so from memory, for he also wrote to Stapleton asking for the text to be sent to him. As Aske wanted them 'to show to them [the commons] why he had raised [the area] betwixt the rivers of Ouse and Derwent', it may be that he still saw himself as advancing the Lincolnshire move-ment.[75] When he opened negotiations with York by sending three of his petty captains into the city with letters for the mayor, he was almost certainly obliged to formulate something of his own to explain the com-mon's aims.[76] What may be the letter to the city survives in two copies, one of which has the heads of the Lincoln articles on the reverse (it is

---

[73] Ibid. 335; text SP1/108, fos. 180r–181v (= *LP* XI, no. 784 (ii)). The Dodds date the posting of this order to Monday evening after the commons' entry into the Minster, and place the convening of the council to Tuesday morning. I have found no evidence to confirm these timings, which must be regarded as conjecture.

[74] 'Aske's Examination', 560, answer 28, 29. For his oath being employed in Craven, p. 233 below.

[75] It is most likely that the Dodds are wrong when they say that Aske sent a copy of the Lincolnshire articles to the mayor of York. A set of the Lincolnshire articles survives, endorsed with the mayor's name (*LP* XI, no. 705, printed in Dodds, *Pilgrimage*, I, 177). Bowyer says that a Lincolnshire man brought their articles to York, but he doesn't say when. As we know that the Lincolnshire rebels deliberately set out to distribute copies of their articles (one of which Aske saw at Whitgift), it would not be improbable that York had a copy carried to them directly.

[76] The three petty captains are referred to (but unfortunately not named) by Bowyer.

printed below, pp. 456–7).[77] There are grounds for supposing that this document dates from before Tuesday.

The document which survives is addressed to 'lords, knights, masters, kinsmen, and friends', and not to the mayor or the city. It begins by denying reports that 'this assembly or pilgrimage' has come together in opposition to the king's impositions, protesting that they have always been as ready as any other subjects to make payments to the king. This, then, was not a taxation revolt. Rather, as the proclamation explains, (unnamed) members of the king's council had seduced the king with 'many and sundry new inventions, which be contrary [to] the faith of God and honour to the king's majesty and the commonwealth of this realm', and that they thereby intended to destroy both the church of England and its ministers. Moreover, these same councillors had spoiled and robbed and intended to further spoil and rob the whole body of the realm. The proclamation continues:

This pilgrimage, we have [under]taken it for the preservation of Christ's church, of this realm of England, of the king . . . the nobility, and commons of the same, and to the intent to make a petition to the king's highness for the reformation of that which is amiss within this realm and for the punishment of heretics and subvertors of the laws and we neither for money, malice, [or] displeasure to no persons but such as be not worthy to remain nigh about the king our sovereign lord's person.

If the recipients of the letter would not join with them, then they would fight with all those that tried to stop them in their pilgrimage. The proclamation was signed in the name of Robert Aske, 'chief captain of the conventual assembly or pilgrimage for the same, barony and commonalty of the same'.

Two aspects of the language of the proclamation hint at a date before the entry into York. First, it refers to the movement four times (and a fifth time in Aske's title) as a pilgrimage (once as 'this assembly or pilgrimage'), but never as the Pilgrimage of Grace. The name 'Pilgrimage of Grace' appears during the first or second day immediately *after* the entry into York in three undated documents. The first is the Pilgrim's oath, the

---

[77] *LP* XI, 705 (2–3), printed in full, *St. P.* I, 466, and incompletely by the Dodds, *Pilgrimage*, I, 175–6.

second the order for the continuation of monastic houses already mentioned, and the third a letter of protection on behalf of St Mary's Abbey, York.[78]

Aske tells us that the Pilgrim's oath was his own work.[79] It must have been written after the early hours of Tuesday morning. Thomas Strangeways reports that when he met with Aske and sought a copy of their articles on the Monday evening, all Aske could give him was a copy of the Lincolnshire oath.[80] On the other hand, Aske also tells us that the oath was written at the time of the meeting which agreed to seek out and swear in other gentry.[81] It seems most likely that the oath was composed on the Tuesday morning or shortly thereafter. It may be suggested that the other documents which use the phrase 'Pilgrimage of Grace' take their language from the oath, and so follow on from it. As the proclamation describes the movement as a pilgrimage but not a Pilgrimage of Grace, it may be deduced to be earlier in date, but it also shows the key features of Aske's thinking: the defence of the church, the hostility to heretics, and the conviction that the king's councillors were unworthy of their place.

Secondly, the form of the subscription employed by the proclamation, in the name of Aske, chief captain of the 'conventual assembly on Pilgrimage for the same, barony and commonality of the same' does not reappear. The form adopted on the order for monastic houses and the protection of St Mary's Abbey are, respectively, 'whole consent of all the herdsmen of our Pilgrimage of Grace' and Robert Aske and other 'herds of the commonwealth'. The conclusion must be that Aske acted in his own name before the entry into York, but then shared his authority with a committee or council in the days immediately following.

---

[78] The oath, *LP* XI, no. 705 (4), printed in Dodds, *Pilgrimage*, I, 182; the order for the continuation of monastic houses, *LP* XI, no. 784 (ii), printed in Dodds, *Pilgrimage*, I, 178–9; the order for St Mary's, *LP* XI, no. 784 (iii) (and not printed). The oath survives in several contemporary copies. The ur-text would be the copy transmitted to the king with the duke of Norfolk after the first meeting at Doncaster (*LP* XI, no. 902 (2)): this is badly decayed, but reproduced so far as it can be at pp. 458–9 below. This is an extended version of the oath: shorter versions are at ibid., no. 705 (4), and in the earl of Derby's Letter Book, Lancashire RO, DDF/1 (unfoliated), from which printed by HMC, *Sixth Report*, 446, 'Derby Correspondence', 50–1 and below pp. 457–8.

[79] 'Aske's Examination', 572 (answ. 68).

[80] *LP* XI, no. 762. 'Oath of Lincolnshire' is what Strangeways says: he must mean the articles.

[81] 'Aske's Examination', 572 (answ. 68).

The title 'Pilgrimage of Grace', which seems to have been devised by Aske in York on the Tuesday, served two fundamental purposes. For one, it stole the spiritual high ground and declared the Pilgrims to be the arbiters of the true church. It combined the familiar act of Pilgrimage, of travelling to make a devotion, with the political act of making a supplication. For the other, it distinguished the East Riding rebellion from the failed Lincolnshire movement. It gave it a powerful brand-name and a collective identity where Lincolnshire had none, and a powerful oath where the Lincolnshire movement had only a bland and generalized assertion of solidarity with the commons. In doing this, it transformed the revolt from a commons' rising into something much more serious. This was Aske's reaction to the dispersal of the Lincolnshire rebels.

That said, when Aske was examined about the oath on 15 April 1537, he stated that the Pilgrim's oath was put in writing to swear the gentlemen (of the Ainsty), and *'because part of the commons' petition might appear in the same'*.[82] The petition was, of course, that made in Lincoln. Here again, we see how the Lincolnshire movement continued to guide the Pilgrimage. But it was only *part* of the commons' petition which was employed in the oath. The emphasis placed on the individual articles was substantially altered. We have already seen how Aske's proclamation, made before his entry into York, denied that the movement was about taxation grievances. This was carried over into the oath ('you shall not enter into this Pilgrimage of Grace for the commonwealth').[83] The

---

[82] Ibid.

[83] The interpretation I place on the oath will not be universally accepted. It seems to me that the opening line of the oath ('You shall not enter into this our Pilgrimage of Grace for the commonwealth but only for the love that ye do bear unto Almighty God . . .') contains a fundamental ambiguity of meaning which allows it to be read in one of three ways. First, should 'Pilgrimage of Grace for the commonwealth' be read as one phrase, a form of extended title? Or, as the second option, is the Pilgrimage to be understood as 'being on behalf of the commons', which seems to be the sense in which 'commonwealth' is used later in the oath ('ye shall not enter into our said Pilgrimage for no particular profit to yourself, nor to do any displeasure to any private person, but by counsel of the commonwealth', i.e. the body of the Pilgrims)? See also the usage in the letter from the Howdenshire rebels, where 'commonwealth' seems to be the body of commons as well as their collective interest (printed above, p. 195). Or, thirdly, is it saying that the oath-taker does not enter the Pilgrimage to advance the interests of the commonwealth, but for the higher purposes then listed? If not the third, then why the negative contained in the 'not . . . but . . .' formula? This seems to maintain the point made in the earlier proclamation: that the Pilgrimage was not about taxation grievances. In fact Aske never seems to have tried to exploit the atmosphere of trepidation and fear created by rumours of taxation and confiscation although this would surely have rallied men around him.

third article of the Lincoln petition, appealing against the weight of the fifteenth, was therefore ignored. So too were the articles complaining of the Statute of Uses and asking for heretical bishops to be purged. What remained were two broad types of complaint: against religious change (including the dissolution of the monasteries) and against the evil and self-seeking councillors with whom the king was surrounded. Hence, those who swore the oath entered the Pilgrimage 'only for the love ye do bear unto Almighty God, his faith and to Holy Church militant and the maintenance thereof', and [for] 'the preservation of the king's person and his issue, to the purifying of the nobility and to expulse all villain blood and evil councillors against the commonwealth from his grace and his privy council of the same'.[84] The stakes were raised too. The rather feeble suggestion in the Lincoln articles that dissolution had reduced the availability of hospitality became a general fear for the fortunes of the 'church militant'. The councillors 'of low birth and small reputation' whose probity was suspect became men of 'villein blood', 'evil councillors' who were a threat to the king and his issue's very survival.

After Tuesday, 17 October the movement had a new oath, copies of which were distributed, but oddly no manifesto of its own, because its purpose remained that of securing the concessions first demanded at Lincoln. The question for the movement had been how it should proceed after the atrophy of the Lincolnshire rising and its surrender with its aims unachieved and its members unpardoned. Aske's solution to this quandary was to drive the movement forwards, to advance to Pontefract and besiege and take the castle with its occupants. There is a hint that this decision split the men who had been Aske's companions over the previous fortnight. Aske told Stapleton (but some weeks later) that Thomas Metham and Edward Saltmarsh 'departed from him at York disdaining that he should be over him'.[85] In a little over a fortnight Aske had been transformed from a fugitive in Lincolnshire to the leader of several thousand men, the architect of the movement's image, and its

---

[84] The reference to the privy council appears to pre-date any noticed by Professor Guy.

[85] Stapleton, 103; Dodds, *Pilgrimage*, I, 185. It may equally have been an argument over Aske's title.

strategist. Where the Lincolnshire gentry had tried to wind down the movement, Aske was a fanatic, convinced and persuaded by the manifesto he had first seen at Whitgift. If he fashioned the Pilgrimage around this document, mediated by his own preoccupations, then he did not make the rebellion in Howdenshire, Beverley, or around York, but he did draw the rebels to him, as during the following week he was to draw the Richmondshire commons into his orbit. The Pilgrimage was, and remained, a spontaneous mass movement in response to the one in Lincolnshire.

8

The 'Captain Poverty' Revolts

Earlier we saw how the risings in the East Riding and Howdenshire were responses to news of the rising in Lincolnshire. There was some interchange of personnel between the two movements. Lincolnshire sent emissaries to Beverley; Aske went to Lincoln to assess the character of the revolt. The Lincolnshire articles were circulated in Yorkshire and, in my analysis, persuaded Aske that this was a movement in which he wished to play a role. After the collapse of Lincolnshire he reshaped the ideology of the Yorkshire movement, omitting the commonwealth concerns of the Lincolnshire manifesto from his oath—'you shall not enter this Pilgrimage of Grace for the commonwealth'—and emphasizing the preservation of the church and the need for better councillors about the king.

The motivation and ideology of the risings in the North Riding, County Durham, the northern third of the West Riding, Cumberland, and Westmorland were different in character. It is far from clear that in their origins they owed anything to the example of Lincolnshire. That the rebels almost certainly knew about Lincolnshire and that their rebellion coincided with the Lincolnshire movement does not prove that they saw themselves as either allies or imitators of the Lincolnshire commons. Nor is there any evidence that they had copies of the Lincolnshire articles. Rather, the force which assembled in stages at Pontefract should be seen as a coalition of men from the eastern part of Yorkshire whose enthusiasm and purpose derived ultimately from the example of Lincolnshire, and a much larger force from the north of the county and County Durham whose ambitions were rather different. The rhetorical language of the two movements had little in common. Where Aske's movement adopted the metaphor of the Pilgrimage, the movement which started in Richmondshire claimed to act in the name of Captain Poverty, was sympathetic to the plight of suppressed monasteries, and had concerns which were overtly 'agrarian'. There was no contact between Aske and the branches of the northern movement until after the fall of Pontefract. Indeed, Aske admitted that he was ignorant of the Richmondshire rising at the time he took Pontefract.[1]

The rising in Richmondshire—broadly, the rising ground between Ripon and Richmond and the dales of Nidderdale, Wensleydale, and Swaledale—must be seen as the epicentre of a distinctive movement which spread westwards into Lonsdale and North Lancashire, north-westwards into the Lake District, and north-eastwards into Durham and beyond (Map 4). It would be wrong to read these risings as a co-ordinated effort organized by a high command in Richmond. There is every sign that the Richmondshire commons spread accounts of their revolt and demanded that the inhabitants of adjacent areas offer their support. Whilst Richmond provided the spark, the local bushfires took their colour from local preoccupations and concerns, some of which may have been active even before the rising in Richmondshire. For this reason the approach of this chapter is geographical: the evidence for each sub-movement of the Yorkshire rising will be weighed and its relationship to the rising in Richmondshire assessed.[2]

---

[1] 'The manner of the taking of Robert Aske', 335.

[2] For a very full account of the Richmondshire rising, M. L. Bush, 'The Richmondshire Uprising of October 1536 and the Pilgrimage of Grace', *NH* 29 (1993), and id., *Pilgrimage of Grace*, chs. 4–9.

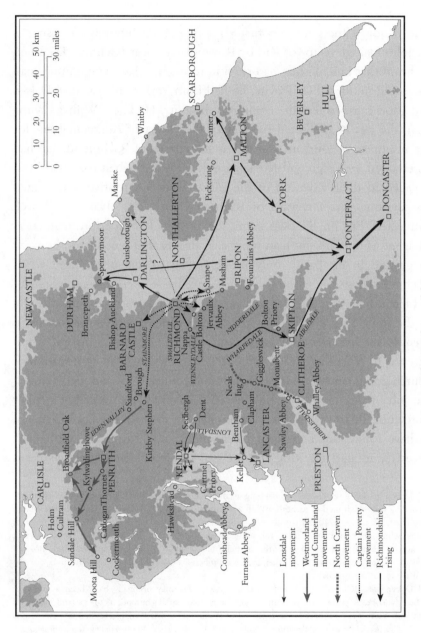

Map 4. The Richmondshire movement

I

The major witness for the first days of the Richmondshire rising is Dr John Dakyn, rector of Kirkby Ravensworth near Richmond.[3] When he heard that Lincolnshire had risen in revolt and that the commons had taken and murdered Dr Rayne, he fled from York to his parish. [4] Dakyn had good cause to fear the commons' hostility. He knew William Blithman, the newly appointed receiver of the Court of Augmentations for the bishopric of Durham and the archdeaconry of Richmond. He had entertained Dr Leigh and Mr Layton at his house when they had been engaged in their visitation of the monasteries.[5] A relative who shared his surname was a servant of Richard Cromwell's.[6] Dakyn was well connected, but on his own admission this made him triply marked as an agent of the Cromwellian regime. A deeply frightened man, he went to ground in his parish only to be forced to flee once more when Richmond rose.

In the first days of October reports reached Darcy of disturbances in the high Yorkshire dales. Crowds had gathered and sworn oaths in Wensleydale and over the Pennine watershed in Dent and Sedbergh. Their aim was to resist the closure of churches and abbeys, the confiscation of church goods, and taxation. Breyer stumbled into Dent and reported that the inhabitants mouthed wild invective against Cromwell; but neither Darcy nor the township officers Breyer spoke to at Kirkby Lonsdale seem to have found this behaviour threatening, and Darcy only thought it necessary to alert the king and the earl of Cumberland after the alarm

---

[3] Dakyn has left four separate overlapping accounts of his role in the Pilgrimage: (i) A statement, formerly a roll which has lost its head, possibly written before he was called to London in late March (cf. *LP* XII (i), no. 698), *LP* XII (i) no. 789 (= SP1/117, fos. 207r–214r); (ii) a petition to Cromwell, written whilst imprisoned, outlining his role in the Pilgrimage, ibid., no. 788 (= SP1/117, fos. 201v–206r); (iii) articles administered to Dakyn by the council (numbered 1–19), with his answers, ibid., no. 786 (= SP1/117, fos. 189r–192v); (iv) further articles (numbered 1–4) and Dakyn's answers, ibid., no. 787 (= SP1/117 fos. 193r–199v).

[4] Dakyn was BCL in 1524–5 and DCL in 1528–9. He may originally have been a monk of St Mary's York. A protégé of William Knight, archdeacon of Richmond, 1529–41 (and bishop of Bath and Wells, 1541–7), he was vicar-general of Richmond under Knight. He died in 1558. C. H. and T. Cooper, *Athenae Cantabrigiensis*, 2 vols. (1858–61), I, 181–2; Venn, *Alumni Cantabrigiensis sub nomine*; *LP* XII (i), no. 878.

[5] *LP* XII (i), no. 788.   [6] For this man leasing a monastery in 1539, SP5/2, fos. 100–115.

of Lincolnshire spread.[7] There was a qualitative difference between this simmering discontent and oath-taking and the aggressive insurrection which began on about Wednesday, 11 October. Our earliest knowledge of an insurrection comes from a letter of John, Lord Scrope written on the morning of Thursday, 12 October to his father-in-law, the first earl of Cumberland, and a deposition made in 1537 by Adam Sedber, the abbot of Jervaulx. Writing from his castle at Bolton in Wensleydale, Scrope reported that the commons of Mashamshire and Nidderdale had risen the previous day and had been at Coverham Abbey and Middleham on Wednesday evening. They had burnt beacons during the night. Scrope understood that they would come and swear him at Bolton during Thursday: he therefore intended to flee until he was certain of their intentions. (Scrope's decision to abandon his castle suggests something out of the ordinary.) On Wednesday evening a sizeable crowd of men, said to number 200 or 300, came to Jervaulx looking for the abbot, who also fled. They were led by captains called Middleton and Staveley, who can be identified as Edward Middleton and Ninian Staveley, both of Masham.[8]

By the end of Wednesday three areas were reported to have risen: Nidderdale, Kirkby Malzeard (Kirkbyshire), and Masham (Mashamshire). There are no references in any of the surviving documents to Ripon having risen; and yet it would be surprising if it had not. One would suppose that a rising over a wide and essentially rural district, such as this was, would coalesce on a neighbouring town or even be stimulated by one. One clue that may indicate that Ripon did play a role in the genesis of this movement is that Ripon Fair would have been held on the days surrounding St Wilfred's Day, 12 October.[9] Archbishop Lee had sent a proclamation to Ripon to be read at the fair announcing that the earl of Shrewsbury had set out to repress the Lincolnshire rebels. If those attending the fair had not yet heard about the disturbance further south, then Lee would have made them aware of it; but this tenuous link seems to be the only discernible connection between Lincolnshire and

---

[7] *LP* XI, nos. 563 (1–2), 564, 841.

[8] *LP* XI, no. 677; XII (i), no. 1035, the identifications from 1012.

[9] For St Wilfred's Fair, see K. L. McCutcheon, 'Yorkshire Fairs and Markets to the End of the Eighteenth Century', *Proc. Thoresby Soc.*, 39 (1940), 16, 20, 31, 136, 176.

Richmondshire.[10] Against the possibility that the rising started in Ripon, there is Dakyn: 'There were no captains about Richmond for Mashamshire were ever the first stirrers and preceded Richmond in the insurrection two days.'[11]

Whether the movement started at Ripon or Masham, it spread rapidly northwards, looking for the abbot of Jervaulx, and, it was rumoured, intending to take Lord Scrope on the Thursday. During Friday the rebels reached Richmond, raised the town, and spread the rebellion northwards and eastwards. Dakyn claimed that when he heard of the rising in Richmond he fled from his house at Kirkby Ravensworth 'onto a great moor', where he remained for the remainder of the day until he was sent word either to come in or 'be destroyed'. The following day he was escorted from his house by 500 Richmond men. When he was in Richmond on Saturday he found there 'a great multitude of Mashamshire'.[12]

Musters were held at Richmond on Friday and the commons divided into three or more groups. In a letter written on Saturday morning, Katherine Scrope, Lord Scrope's wife, told her father that one party was heading south from Richmond and then west up Wensleydale to bring in her husband, Sir James Metcalfe of Nappa or his son Christopher, and Richard Siggiswick of Walburn. A second was making its way south and east to take Lord Latimer and Sir Christopher Danby, doubtless at their houses of Snape Castle and Thorpe Perrow. The third group was striking northwards to Barnard Castle to capture the Bowes brothers and their nephew. Scrope himself had fled up Wensleydale to Thomas Blenkinsop's house at Helbeck, near Brough in Westmorland.[13] He finally arrived at the earl of Cumberland's castle at Skipton.

The party sent to Barnard Castle also fetched and swore John Dakyn as it passed Ravensworth: he mentions that they were 'of Richmond and those parts'.[14] Once at Richmond he found that Latimer and Danby had

---

[10] LP XIII (i), no. 1022 (= SP1/119, fo. 1); cf. Smith, Land and Politics, 184–5.

[11] SP1/117, fo. 196r (= LP XII (i), no. 786 (7)). It is possible that the rebellion was stimulated by the beginning of the process of assessing and collecting the subsidy, but there is no evidence to prove this conjecture.

[12] SP1/117, fos. 204 (= LP XII (i), no. 788), 207v (= ibid., no. 789).

[13] Dickens, 'Clifford Letters', 111–12.   [14] SP1/117, fo. 203r (= LP XII (i), no. 788).

already been brought in. The Mashamshire men there were in an ugly mood: 'I durst not say nothing that I should sound contrary [to] the insurgents, nor durst my Lord Latimer or Mr Danby and I perceived [?them] very quiet.' There was certainly an element of mob rule. A man called Tomlinson from Bedall, whom Dakyn had excommunicated in a matrimonial cause, threatened him with his bow bent and demanded £40 for his silence: Dakyn bought him off with 5 marks. Dakyn also reports comments in the crowd that he was one of the institutors of the new laws and a putter-down of holidays.[15]

Robert Bowes, his brothers, and Thomas Rokeby surrendered Barnard Castle to the commons on Sunday—'without a stroke', according to a hostile witness—and arrived at Richmond during the day.[16] Bowes appears to have been able to bring some order to the Richmond crowds. He started them mustering by parish, every parish choosing four men to order the others. (The similarities between Bowes's behaviour and the strategy employed by Moigne and the other gentry at Louth or Stapleton at Beverley are so self-evident they do not need to be stressed.) But during Sunday a letter was written to the county of Cleveland, perhaps by Bowes (Dakyn says he read it to the crowd), ordering them to rally with Richmondshire at Oxenfield by Darlington on the Monday. Similar letters were probably sent into County Durham.[17]

The indications are that Bowes supplanted the local leadership of the movement. These are indeed shadowy individuals, of whom we have only a handful of names and no real details. The most interesting, if anything could be learnt about him, would be the person—a 'simple poor man' —whom Dakyn saw going under the pseudonym of Lord Poverty.[18] It is significant, though, that some of the early leaders of the commons appear to overlap with the coterie of firebrands who tried to raise

[15] Ibid., fo. 207v (= *LP* XII (i), no. 789). Robert Bowes was willing to testify that Dakyn had been the subject of much hostility at Richmond: *LP* XII (i), no. 698.

[16] *LP* XII (i), no. 775. Dakyn gives the day as Sunday, but the implication is that Bowes held the castle through Saturday night. Bowes was a lawyer and long-term stalwart of the Council in the North. He died in 1555. He was steward and constable of Barnard Castle. For his life, *Hist. Parl., 1509–1558*, I, 471–3, and for an essay on his career and role in the Pilgrimage of Grace, C. M. Newman, *Robert Bowes and the Pilgrimage of Grace* (1997).

[17] *LP* XII (i), no. 789.   [18] *LP* XII (i), no. 786, sect. 18.

Richmondshire a second time in January 1537.[19] Dakyn described how Bowes stamped his discipline over the commons, and elected to raise Cleveland and lead the Richmondshire commons into County Durham. At one moment he is emphatic that the commons were beyond any man's control: 'Where any company was assembled, every man for fear of spoiling or death that was nigh they would gladly please them.' 'I think the most part of the gentlemen, although they had spoken, could have done little amongst the commons being so set.'[20] And he illustrates the commons' determination to make the gentry bend their way by their insistence that Sir Henry Gascoigne join them instead of performing the necessary obsequies for his recently deceased mother-in-law. Yet Dakyn shows that Bowes had the power to direct and divert the commons. They were glad to see him: 'and what ever he said amongst them, they in manner took it for authority.'[21]

I say that I think that the most part of the gentlemen, though they had spoken, could have done little amongst the commons being so set, yet I think that Mr Robert Bowes might have done the most of any man in those parts. He is greatly esteemed for as soon as he come in amongst them, I, being then there, perceived that all things he devised to the going forward took effect. Marry, how they would have been ordered if he had persuaded the contrary I cannot tell, but I think [that the] Richmondshire men had not gone into the bishopric had not he moved them to, for he did most and spoke most of any man at that time.[22]

Like Stapleton, Bowes threatened to withdraw if the commons would not accept his discipline, insisting that disputes amongst them be put to one side: 'Mr Robert Bowes stayed the people much that day [Sunday], which ever as they come in were in hand one to be wronged upon another for old matters and injuries, saying openly if they began on that matter, he would not meddle with them, to whose exhortation the people gave most attendance of any man.'[23] It was at Dakyn's suggestion that he insisted that all the priests with the commons be allowed to return home.[24]

---

[19] As was the case with Middleton and Staveley.

[20] SP1/117, fos. 196v, 197r (?) (= *LP* XII (i), no. 786 (ii)).

[21] Ibid., fo. 209v (?) (= *LP* XII (i), no. 789).

[22] Ibid., fo. 197r (and severely boiled down in *LP* XII (i), no. 788 to: 'The gentlemen could have done little amongst the commons. Mr Bowes was the most influential.').

[23] Ibid., fo. 209v (which *LP* XII (i), no. 789, gives as 'Bowes stayed the people who would have been revenged on each other for old grudges.').

[24] Ibid.

We do not have Bowes's own justification for his actions. It may be that he, like Aske, liked what he saw and decided to use it to further his own political aims. It may also be that he was riding the tiger, less in control than Dakyn, perhaps, appreciated, and that he felt that the rebels needed to be allowed to follow their enthusiasms until they burnt themselves out. There is also the real possibility that Bowes wanted to recruit additional gentry to strengthen his hand against the rebel host and act as a cooling, moderating force to restrain their violence; and here the preference to turn towards Durham may reflect his own network of kin allegiances. Whatever the case, Bowes's leadership was decisive in determining the direction which the revolt took.

The initial 'Captain Poverty' leadership of the movement had, however, sought to spread word of their revolt before Bowes became its major influence. At least one letter was sent to Penrith advertising their rising and offering a manifesto. Another surfaced in Alnwick. The copy seen by Sir Robert Thompson, the vicar of Brough under Stainmoor in the Upper Eden Valley, instructed the commons to assemble and swear:

to be true to God, to the faith of the church, to our sovereign lord, to the king, and to the commonwealth of this realm. And that done, that they should restore all the abbeys suppressed, with restitution of such their goods as remained within the counties. And to see such demeanour towards the Scots that no appearance of war might ensue but all to be kept in good quiet and peace. And these things done, that four substantial gentlemen should come and resort unto the commons of Yorkshire where their assembly should be to see further to be done in that matter by all their consents and counsel.[25]

According to the recollection of Bernard Towneley, the bishop of Carlisle's chancellor, who heard it read on 23 October, the letter was slightly different: 'Well beloved brethren in God, we greet you well, signifying unto you that we your brethren in Christ have [assembled] us together and put us in readiness for the maintenance of the faith of God, his laws, and his church. And where abbeys were suppressed, we have restored them again and put religious men into their houses: wherefore we exhort you to do the same.' The letter then continued to outline an agrarian programme, demanding that no man should pay 'any ingressoms [entry fines] to his landlord and [but?] a small rent for his tenement and

[25] Ibid., fo. 50v (= *LP* XII (i), no. 687 (2)).

several places to have paid no rent nor tithes but in money at their pleasure'.[26] Where Thompson and Towneley both concur is that the movement was for the maintenance of church and faith (and perhaps with a nod towards the king), and that suppressed houses were to be re-established. According to Thompson's account, there was a concern to avoid war with Scotland. It is hard to see why Richmondshire should have been concerned with this: the concern with the Borders may have been a local Cumbrian interpolation. Towneley then believed that the letter attacked rents and tithes; Thompson, that delegates should be sent to an assembly in Yorkshire. The last issue became a dead letter, for the commons moved first into County Durham and then into the West Riding. But there was an attempt to revive the commons' assembly in the very different conditions of January 1537.

Virtually none of this is reported in the limited sources outlining the revolt in Richmond and County Durham. There is no evidence of anti-landlordism (in the sense of an agitation over rents and fines) in Richmond over the weekend of 13–16 October. The evidence that there was an agitation over tenant right in Richmondshire comes from Towneley's recollection of the Captain Poverty letter, and from the Pontefract articles, collated on 2–4 December, which request that 'the lands in Westmorland, Cumberland, Kendal, Dent, Sedbergh, Furness, and the abbey lands in Mashamshire, Kirkbyshire, [and] Nidderdale may be by tenant right . . .', but this is not terribly straightforward. The way in which 'the abbey lands . . .' is placed in the text almost suggests an insertion into a pre-existing list. And if the lands of monastic houses deserved especial attention, why not also the lands of the gentry through-out Richmondshire, including those of Wensleydale and Swaledale where tenant right was also familiar?[27] The campaign against landlords seems characteristic of Westmorland, where the movement took some of its colour from pre-existing anxieties and antagonisms: it may be that Bowes's seizure of the initiative diverted the Captain Poverty movement in Richmondshire away from agrarian warfare.

[26] Ibid., fo. 46r (= *LP* XII (i), no. 687 (1)). For the letters sent to Alnwick, *LP* XII (i), no. 467, 1070 (paras. 20–1 and at very end), the last printed in J. Raine (ed.), 'The Priory of Hexham', *Surtees Soc.*, 44, 46 (1863–5), I, cxxx–cxlv.

[27] For conflicts over tenant right on the estates of Fountains and Byland, see Hoyle, 'Monastic Leasing Before the Dissolution', 122.

The Richmondshire host certainly restored the monks of St Agatha's at Easby and the canons of Coverham, although exactly when is unknown. [28] A servant of the abbot of Sawley's, travelling incognito into Northumberland shortly after Christmas, was abused by the Richmond commons for the feebleness of the commons around Sawley: 'Fye on them that dwell nigh about that house, that ever they would suffer the monks to be put out of it. And that was the first house that was put down in this country. But rather than our house of St Agatha should go down, we shall all die: and if any insurrection should happen here again, where there was but one in the same before, now there would be three.'[29]

The rising in Richmondshire created a panic amongst the gentry of the North Riding and County Durham. Some managed to escape to Scarborough Castle.[30] Sir Francis Bigod, of Mulgrave near Whitby, tried to take a boat to London, but found himself driven by the winds into Hartlepool, where the commons attempted to take him. He escaped back to Mulgrave, where he fell into the commons' hands.[31] James Rokeby, an auditor in the Court of Augmentations, took refuge in Guisborough Abbey, then at an uncle's house near the sea. As the uncle, William Rokeby, had been on the commission to survey monastic houses, he too had a particular reason to evade the rebels. Together they tried to ascertain whether they could safely make their way to Newcastle. They took refuge a second time at Guisborough, but after a letter from the rebels at Stokesley was read in the village Rokeby tried to escape but was captured by the commons. He was then forced to accompany them to his uncle William's house (?at Marske). William Rokeby agreed to come in with the rebels after they threatened to burn his house down. The host then broke into Sir John Bulmer's house at Wilton. Bulmer had already gone, but the rebels searched the house and swore his servants.[32]

Bigod and Rokeby were probably trying to flee on about Tuesday or Wednesday, 17–18 October; they may have been direct victims of the

[28] LP XII (i), no. 29.

[29] Ibid., no. 491. Sawley may indeed have been the first house to fall: above p. 80.

[30] Stapleton names Sir George Conyers, Sir Ralph Eure, Tristam Tesh, [   ] Coppindale and others. Stapleton, 92.

[31] LP XII (i), no. 578.

[32] James Rokeby is the author of the very decayed examination at LP XII (i), no. 1011 (Bush, 'Richmondshire Uprising', 67, n. 18).

Richmondshire rising, for the commons whom they feared may well have risen at the behest of the letter sent into Cleveland on Sunday, 15 October. In the bishopric there was a similar panic and flight. Lord Lumley was hare-coursing at his house at The Isle when word came from Sir Thomas Hilton that Cuthbert Tunstall, the bishop of Durham, had fled from his house at Bishop Auckland (he took refuge at Norham). Hilton urged Lumley to escape with his goods to some secure place. Lumley packed his plate and jewels and sent them with his son by night to the Maison Dieu in Newcastle. Lumley himself then came to Newcastle, where he and George Lumley stayed for two days until Hilton joined them. But Hilton judged Newcastle to be too dangerous; his servants found that the townspeople were not prepared to resist the rebels. Hilton and Lord Lumley went to Hilton's house (perhaps Hilton Castle) for refuge, whilst George Lumley went back to The Isle, where he fell into the hands of a party of soldiers from Richmondshire.[33] (Hilton was to play a prominent role in the negotiations at Doncaster with the duke of Norfolk.)

On Monday the Richmondshire host mustered at Oxenfield near Darlington. At least one piece of unfinished business remained to be completed in Richmondshire: a party of rebels were sent to Jervaulx to capture the abbot. Sedber had been spending each day hidden on Witton Fell, returning to the convent at night; but he had not been above raging about his hostility to the rebels. When the party of commons who came to get him was told that he was not at home, they demanded that the monks choose a new abbot in his place and gave them half-an-hour to do so before they began to set the house alight. The chapter bell was rung and the monks assembled, but they became deadlocked and so, out of desperation, Sedber was sent for and implored to come back to the abbey. He was first manhandled, then threatened with a dagger by Leonard Burgh, a captain of the commons, and told that he should be beheaded by one Aslaby, 'chief captain'.[34] He was sworn, then made to ride bareback through Richmond to Oxenfield, doubtless to be exhibited as a prize. George Lumley, who saw him at the muster at Bishop Auckland, reported that by then he was zealously exhorting the commons.[35]

[33] LP XII (i), no. 369, printed in full in E. Milner (ed. E. Benham), *Records of the Lumleys of Lumley Castle* (1904), 32–45. For the attitude of Newcastle, cf. pp. 428–9 below.

[34] Burgh and Aslaby were both minor local gentlemen. Bush, 'Richmondshire Uprising', 68.

[35] LP XII (i), nos. 1035, 369.

The exact chronology of the Richmondshire men's raising of County Durham is not clear. There appear to have been three musters, at Oxenfield on Monday, at Bishop Auckland, and at Spennymoor. George Lumley was taken to the muster at Bishop Auckland, where the rebels had doubtless gone in the hope of swearing the bishop of Durham. Here he witnessed Sir James Strangeways and 'young Bowes' arriving with companies of 1,000 men each, Sir Ralph Bulmer with a third company, and a knight unknown by name to Lumley with a fourth. But the two leading witnesses to events in County Durham never assign their capture or any of the other events they describe to a day of the week. It may be that the musters at Bishop Auckland and Spennymoor were held successively, but it is equally possible that they were concurrent.

Marmaduke Neville, the younger brother of Lord Latimer and so a member of a cadet branch of the Neville earls of Westmorland, was taken to the Spennymoor musters. From the context of his story, Neville was a household servant of the earl of Westmorland at Brancepeth Castle to the south-west of Durham. When the rebels came to Spennymoor, the earl received a delegation of three gentry, Robert Bowes, William Conyers of Marske in Richmondshire, and Roland Place of Halnaby in Croft-on-Tees, near Darlington. They asked the earl to join: he refused. They told Neville that unless he came in he would have his goods spoilt. Brancepeth was also visited by Sir Christopher Danby, who again asked Westmorland to come in and warned Neville that 'neither my lord my brother [Latimer] nor any other could help me'. Neville secured the earl's blessing to go to the commons, and after further requests Westmorland himself came to the rebels at Spennymoor. However, he was not compelled to go with them, Lord Neville, his son, going in his place. It was understood, however, amongst the king's forces at Doncaster that Brancepeth had been taken by the commons and Westmorland compelled to allow the commons to take his son with them. Subsequent comments reveal an appreciation that Westmorland had been betrayed by his household and forced to act as he did under duress.[36]

Neville was warned that if he did not join the common's host neither his brother, Lord Latimer, nor anyone else would be able to save him.

---

[36] Neville, *LP* XII (i), no. 29; for additional material, Hoyle, 'Thomas Master's Narrative', 62–3, 71.

Neville's anxiety was for the safety of his wife and goods. George Lumley was interrogated about the whereabouts of his father, and was told by Latimer that he should send word for him to come in or else his house would be spoilt by the commons. Lumley, after he was sworn, was called to his house at Thwing in the Yorkshire Wolds by his wife because the commons were threatening to spoil her and the house unless he appeared. The point of these warnings was not that the gentry were intimidating their fellows into joining their conspiracy, but that Neville and even the earl of Westmorland himself were being cautioned of the practical consequences of resistance: that the commons would destroy property and perhaps people too. Discipline was contingent upon their victims bending to accept the commons' will. Dakyn tells us that Bowes was able to institute some degree of discipline over the rebels at Richmond. Neville helpfully describes the next stage of the process. At Spennymoor, probably on Wednesday, 18 October, the host was divided between townships and given gentry leadership. Neville had a number of Richmondshire townships allocated to him. The abbot of Jervaulx also confirms that the host was divided into companies: equally significantly, Bowes allowed Sedber to go back to Jervaulx, the abbot, after his sub- mission, having apparently ceased to be a subject of hate.[37]

None of the witnesses tell us whether the intention was to proceed further north to Durham or Newcastle, but Neville says that after let- ters were received from Aske and Darcy calling them to Pontefract they divided into two groups. The first made its way directly to Pontefract by way of York; the second went to Skipton.[38] The abbot of Jervaulx, together with Dr Daykn and a number of elderly gentry, were employed at Jervaulx to act as a postal exchange between the two arms of the host.[39]

---

[37] *LP* XII (i), nos. 29, 1035.

[38] There appears to be no direct evidence as to the route they took to Skipton. It is normally assumed that they passed through Wensleydale and Wharfedale, but it may be objected that it was probably difficult to lead a large mounted force through an area lacking in fodder. There is a case to be made that they proceeded through the Vale of York and via Pateley Bridge. The force at Skipton included three gentlemen from around Ripon (Sir Ninian Markenfield of Markenfield, William Mallory of Studley, and John Norton of Norton Conyers), none of whom are named as being at Richmond or the Durham musters. Hence it is possible that they were picked up as the host made its way to Skipton by the more easterly route.

[39] *LP* XII (i), no. 1035. For a fuller account of the siege at Skipton, including some discussion of the gentry who undertook it, Hoyle, 'First Earl of Cumberland', 83–9.

We saw earlier how Scrope had fled to Skipton from Castle Bolton. The commons' intention in going there may well have been to tidy up more unfinished business and make a full suite of the Richmondshire landlords. The earl of Cumberland had initially been told to go to Hexham to repress the disturbance at the monastery there.[40] On 9 October he warned Cromwell of disturbances in Gilsland (Cumberland), Dent, Sedbergh, and Wensleydale, but set out for Carlisle, leaving his son, Lord Clifford, to muster troops for Lincolnshire.[41] On 12 October Cumberland was back at Skipton, when he wrote reporting that the commons of Richmondshire and Lancashire had risen and fired beacons. (This letter may well have reported the flight of his son-in-law, Scrope; but we only have a brief note of the letter.[42]) There was, at this moment, no disturbance in Craven. Subsequently Cumberland may have tried to take a force to restore order at Hexham, but Darcy understood that he had been forced to return to the security of Skipton in the company of Lord Scrope and that Craven had risen on 17 October.[43] Hamerton's behaviour on 18 October suggests that there was no general insurrection then. It was on the following day that Hamerton came to Skipton seeking Cumberland's aid on behalf of the North Craven movement.

When the detachment of the Richmondshire rebellion which travelled through the Dales to Skipton arrived there is uncertain. By this time the earl had gone some way to arranging the defence of the castle, but had lost whatever force he had assembled through defection. Christopher Aske, his receiver, who fled from the East Riding when the district began to rise, recalled that the 'earl's retinue in the king's wages' abandoned the earl and his castle to defend their own houses. Cumberland, in a letter of 26 October, told the king that the 500 gentlemen whom he had retained at his own expense against the rebels had all defected. (Had the earl attempted to mobilize his tenantry in Craven?) Aske then organized the defence of the castle with eighty household servants and forty hastily recruited youths. In a foray, he also rescued a group of Clifford women from Bolton Priory and brought them safely back to the castle.[44] There were other opportunities for heroics: as he told the king on 26 October,

---

[40] 'Letters of the Cliffords', 51–2.   [41] Ibid., 52–3; LP XI no. 742 (misdated in LP).
[42] Ibid., nos. 563–4; 'Thomas Master's Narrative', 66.   [43] LP XI, no. 760 (ii).
[44] LP XII (i), no. 1186. For the rescue of the women, see p. 444 below.

perhaps after the siege had been lifted by Robert Aske calling the Richmondshire men to Pontefract, 'The rebels . . . have summoned him [Cumberland] but he hath denied that they shall take him alive and hath defied them and set up his standard at the top of his house. They have threatened, yet for fear of his ordnance they have not yet given him the assault. He hath none with him but will live and die the king's true subject.'[45] The siege probably lasted no more than two or three days; yet whilst the earl kept himself out of the rebel's hands (and refused their overtures to go to the York conference), he was militarily impotent, trapped in his castle, his local authority collapsed, and his own tenants taking their revenge by plundering his other houses and property.[46]

The Richmondshire men who proceeded directly to Pontefract formed the vanguard in the battle formation which confronted the duke of Norfolk and earl of Shrewsbury. They were reinforced by Sir Thomas Percy's force drawn from around Malton. The rearward were the Richmondshire men who had travelled by way of Skipton. There are clues that these people had a reputation for ill-discipline, and that after the first Doncaster meeting they were far from happy to observe the truce.[47]

II

The Richmondshire commons also spread their revolt into the very east of the North Riding, to Malton and the environs of Scarborough, and were responsible for the taking and swearing of Sir Thomas Percy, the younger brother of the sixth earl of Northumberland. The evidence for this comes from Percy's examination: there is virtually no other detail about this focus of the rebellion.[48]

Percy was at his mother's house at Seamer near Scarborough when a rumour circulated that Lincolnshire had risen; he treated this with scepticism. Several days later he heard from an estate servant who brought a horse from Wressle to Seamer that Robert Aske had raised the commons and had stood at the gates of the house demanding leadership from

---

45 'Thomas Master's Narrative', 70.   46 LP XI, no. 927.
47 Ibid., nos. 945, 1045.   48 LP XII (i), no. 393.

the sixth earl. Percy then decided that it would be prudent to slip away to Northumberland. He set out either on the day after he heard of the Howdenshire rising or on the day following, disguised as one of his own servants and leading a horse. Several miles into their journey, his party was joined by a man called Percy or Percehay who asked them where Sir Thomas might be found.[49] Sir Thomas replied that he was at Seamer; the man then explained that the commons were assembling at Malton, that they lay in wait in every town to take Sir Thomas, and that if he was not to be found at Seamer the commons would spoil the dowager duchess's goods. Sir Thomas then returned to Seamer, and in the early afternoon a great number of commons arrived led by four captains. The captains entered the house and explained that the commons 'were assembled for a thing that should be for the weal of us all . . . and there be with them my Lord Latimer, My Lord Neville, Mr Danby, Mr Bowes, and divers other gentlemen and we are come to fetch you unto them and to swear you to take such part as we do'.[50] Percy was then sworn and instructed to be at a muster on the wold beyond Spittal (in Willerby parish) the following day.

Some of the detail of this account is confirmed by a servant who travelled with Sir Thomas on his abortive flight, and he, helpfully, gives the names of three of the captains who visited him at Seamer.[51] The implication of the words spoken to Percy at his swearing was that the men who came to receive him into their ranks did so as outriders of the Richmondshire insurrection: they appear to have been well informed about events in Richmond and in County Durham. But the issue is not quite as clear as this. The first matter concerns the date on which Percy was taken. His examination gives neither date nor day of the week. However, the troops he led arrived at Pontefract on Saturday, 21 October, having been in York during Friday night. Working back from this, the best estimate for the day of Percy's capture is Monday,

---

[49] The Dodds, *Pilgrimage*, I, 230–1, take this individual to be William Percy or Percehay of Ryton near Malton, a minor gentleman of a cadet line of the Percy family. This may be reasonable surmise. Percy was certainly active at the end of the week (Stapleton, 99), but there is not enough evidence to prove the identification.

[50] SP1/115, fo. 253v (= *LP* XII (i), no. 393). The draft examination also names Mr Lascelles, i.e. Sir Roger of Breckenbrough or his son: Sir Roger was a Percy estate officer.

[51] *LP* XII (i), no. 467.

16 October. This is not incompatible with a party being sent out from Richmond on the previous day. One point may be thought to undermine this. Lord Neville was not taken until at least Tuesday, and probably Wednesday. On the other hand, perhaps all we can read into this is that four months after this meeting Percy's recollection was not terribly accurate. After all, he knew who was with the rebels at Pontefract without necessarily knowing when they were brought in.

Another, more serious doubt is that none of the individuals named appear in the descriptions of the Richmondshire rising. Percy's servant gave their names as [   ] Preston, Nicholas Howburne, and William Burwell. All are elusive in *Letters and Papers*; in common with such activists, they have left few traces. However, there is probably a connection with the village of Nafferton on the other side of the wolds from Seamer. A William Burwell of Nafferton, yeoman, made his will on 1 March 1543. The administration of one Anne Preston of Nafferton, widow, was granted in 1544. Neither surname appears to be common in the East Riding. This may allow us to make a connection between the captains who swore Percy and the bailiffs of Nafferton and Kilham who were the captains of the rebels who demanded men of the prior of Bridlington.[52] Hallam, however, gives the names of the leaders of Nafferton as George Bawne and Gilbert Wedel.[53] Certainly, the high wold was included within Percy's sphere: George Lumley complained that Percy had taken all his tenants from Thwing.[54]

So it is likely that the Richmondshire commons prompted a rising in Malton on Monday, 16 October, out of which a host of commons went to swear Percy. If Percy was taken by men from Nafferton, then a different possibility suggests itself: that he was sworn by his brother's tenants, Nafferton being a Percy manor. And there is yet a third possibility. This is that the movement was spread north of the wolds by Friar Robert (Ashton or Esch), a member of the community of Trinitarians at Knaresborough. He was in Beverley in the early days of the rising there, and secured from William Stapleton a passport to go and raise Ryedale and Pickering Lythe. He was given this on Tuesday, 10 October and then disappears, only to reappear a week later outside Hull, claiming to have

---

[52] Ibid., nos. 1019, 1020 (ii).   [53] Ibid., no. 201 (iii) (at p. 90).   [54] Ibid., no. 369.

raised Malton and 'all that quarter'. Whilst there is nothing to prove that he was in Richmond, he also reported that Richmondshire had risen and taken Lord Latimer. Hence, the Malton musters may have been prompted by a freelance effort by a single enthusiast, but one who evidently had contacts with the Richmondshire host before his return to Beverley.[55]

It is ultimately not possible to select between these three possibilities. However, it is the case that there is no documented contact between Percy and the Richmondshire commons until they met at Pontefract, Percy's movement forming a discrete element within the larger movement until incorporated into the vanguard.

Having been sworn, Percy undertook to be at Spittal on the following day, where 3,000 or 4,000 men were assembled.[56] Some or all of the crowd then went to 'Mr Chamley's' house, presumably Sir Roger Cholmeley's at Roxby, between Loftus and Whitby and some 25 miles from Willerby. When, on the following day, Cholmeley, wherever he was, would not join the commons, there were demands to spoil his house. Percy would not condone this and the commons turned on him: 'strike off his head, for he will betray us. And we will have another captain.'[57] What ensued is not revealed, but Percy returned to Seamer to reassure his mother that he had not been killed before going to a second muster at Malton, to which Sir Nicholas Fairfax of Gilling was called. Percy was then instructed by Aske 'and other gentlemen's commandment' to take his men to York, then to Hull to aid the siege there, and then, after this too was countermanded, he was called to Pontefract, which had fallen to Aske before he arrived.

III

Richmondshire men were also responsible for spreading the rebellion into North Craven and Cumbria, but in both cases care needs to be taken

---

[55] Stapleton, 88, 96. The same friar is noticed in *LP* XII (i), no. 1021, and cf. *LP* XI, no. 1047. See also Cross, 'Monks, Friars and Nuns', 503.

[56] *LP* XII (i), no. 393, for what follows.   [57] SP1/115, fo. 254r (= *LP* XII (i), no. 393).

to establish exactly what these detached movements owed to the larger example. The first evidence for a disturbance in North Craven is of the 'commons'—by which is doubtless meant their tenants—restoring the abbot and monks to Sawley on 12 October. Sawley had been dissolved on 13 May under the terms of the 1536 act (although there are doubts as to whether its valuation was properly under £200). Rather than being placed under the charge of the Court of Augmentations, it had already been granted to Sir Arthur Darcy in exchange for lands in North-amptonshire.[58] After their re-entry, the monks petitioned Aske for the restitution of the church and tithes of Tadcaster, together with their possessions and rentals which Darcy had conveyed to Pontefract Castle; an oath 'to be true to God's faith, the church and the king, to expel all villain blood from the privy council' (which contains plain echoes of Aske's oath), and to pay to the abbot and convent all money due to Sir Arthur Darcy for lands belonging to the monastery, may also date from this time.[59] Whether the abbot and monks were entirely willing to return to Sawley is unclear. The abbot claimed not, upon his arrest, saying that the commons had put him in against his will.[60] The house was certainly destitute and reliant on the charity of neighbouring gentry. The monks petitioned Sir Thomas Percy for aid, received charity from Sir Stephen Hamerton and Nicholas Tempest and others, and ultimately destroyed them all.[61]

The reoccupation of Sawley by the monks was achieved before Aske issued his order in favour of the suppressed monasteries at York on 16 or 17 October. It is hard to see that their action owed anything at all to the events in Lincolnshire. The first evidence for a more general North Craven movement comes from the examination of Sir Stephen Hamerton.[62] His account of events begins with the posting of a bill on the door of Giggleswick church calling people to a muster at Neals Ing, a farm on the western edge of Malham Moor above Stainforth, probably on Friday, 20 October. Hamerton never saw this bill, for it had been taken away when he rode to see it, and his description of it is

---

[58] Above pp. 79–80.   [59] *LP* XI, nos. 784, 872 (ii); XII (i), no. 1034.
[60] *LP* XII (i), no. 506.
[61] *LP* XI, no. 785. See also Hamerton's examination on the aid he gave to Sawley, *LP* XII (i), no. 1034.
[62] *LP* XII (i), no. 1034, on which the following account is based.

correspondingly slight. But whilst returning home from his fruitless excursion he was surrounded by a crowd of armed men coming back from Neals Ing who swore him, declaring that as he had ruled them, they would now rule him. So sworn, Hamerton was made one of a party of nine who were sent to ask the earl of Cumberland to join with them. The earl demanded to know why they had risen: when they declared that it was out of fear of Bishopdale, Wensleydale, and the other northern dales, he offered to see them recompensed if they were robbed.[63] The commons rejected this as inadequate, and the earl closed the discussion by declaring: 'I defy you and do your worst, for I will not meddle with you.' The delegation then took their rejection back to a muster held at Monubent, on the unenclosed moorland north of Bolton by Bowland.

From Hamerton's rather sketchy account a few additional elements can be deduced. He offers little evidence as to who had risen. The only names he gives are those of two of the ringleaders who captured him and who may well have accompanied him to Skipton to meet with Cumberland. It is possible to identify the pair with some certainty. The first, Fawcett, was almost certainly Richard Fawcett of Over Hesleden in Littondale, a substantial tenant of Fountains Abbey. Fawcett is not a common name in Craven; this man appears in the lay subsidy returns as the richest individual in an otherwise poor township. The other ringleader is named as 'Jaks'. Individuals called Jakes (or later 'Jacques') are found only in two locations in Craven: in Buckden, or more exactly on some of the farms in Langstrothdale, and in Giggleswick. It is most likely that the Jakes in this case was of either Cray or Chapel (Hubberholme) in Langstrothdale.[64] This helps us to understand more clearly what was happening. Bishopdale is a side valley of Wensleydale, running south-west towards the head

---

[63] Bush reads the reference to the men of Bishopdale as referring to the host advancing on Skipton from the Spennymoor muster ('Richmondshire Uprising', 89–90). But only if they were lost would they have come by way of Buckden, the obvious way being to come up Coverdale and enter Wharfedale lower down the valley at Kettlewell (from where Lady Scrope's letter is dated). See e.g. Sir Arthur Darcy travelling from Barnard Castle to Sawley via Coverdale and Kettlewell in February 1537. *LP* XII (i), no. 506. The threat of Wensleydale to spoil the inhabitants of adjacent valleys is paralleled by the experience of Dent and Kendal: below pp. 234, 236. For the probable route to Skipton, n. 38 above.

[64] For Fawcett, see R. W. Hoyle, 'Early Tudor Craven: Subsidies and Assessments, 1510–1547', *YASRS* 145 (1987), 36, 49, 60, 84, 100; D. J. H. Michelmore, 'The Fountains Abbey Lease Book', *YASRS* 140 (1981), 32–3, 276–7, and Hoyle, 'Monastic Leasing', 162. For Jakes, 'Early Tudor Craven', *passim*, but esp. 86.

of Wharfedale. The modern main road from Skipton to Richmond runs up Wharfedale, then crosses the watershed to run down Bishopdale and into Wensleydale. The first place that the men of Bishopdale would come to is Buckden, but anyone wishing to travel from Wensleydale into upper Ribblesdale would probably travel by way of Buckden into Langstrothdale, cross over into the head of Littondale, go past Over Hesleden and Neals Ing, and drop down into Ribblesdale at Stainforth. Fawcett and Jakes were therefore amongst those nearest to the Bishopdale men and amongst the first to be intimidated by them (or be likely to feel their anger). Neals Ing, on the other hand, was a suitable meeting-place at which men from upper Wharfedale and Littondale could commune with those of upper Ribblesdale. Hence, the revolt was spread into Wharfedale by Bishopdale. The notice at Giggleswick was probably posted by the upper Wharfedale men, calling Giggleswick to a joint muster at Neals Ing at which Fawcett and Jakes wished to raise the large parish of Giggleswick to satisfy and buy peace from Bishopdale and Wensleydale.

The focus of the rising then drifted westwards and southwards down the Ribble valley. The holding of a muster at Monubent was doubtless intended to raise such parishes as Gisburn, Bolton by Bowland, and Long Preston. In the former, Sawley Abbey was the predominant landowner. Returning from Skipton to Monubent, Hamerton found that the commons had gone to take Nicholas Tempest of Bashall near Clitheroe, the younger brother of Sir Richard Tempest of Bowling and Bracewell. Tempest's story was that on Saturday, 21 October, whilst he was absent from his house, the commons, led by three minor gentry from higher up the valley, came into his house, spoiled his goods to the loss of £100, and seized his son, whom they threatened to kill unless Tempest surrendered himself. Tempest came in that evening and was sworn.[65]

---

[65] Tempest's examination is noted (but not printed) by *LP* XII (i), no. 1014. It is substantially printed in Mrs A. C. Tempest, 'Nicholas Tempest, a Sufferer in the Pilgrimage of Grace', *YAJ* 11 (1891). Tempest gives the names of the gentry leading the crowd which came to his house as John Catteral (of Rathmell, against whom the 1535 riots had been directed), Anthony Talbot of Halton West, Richard Hamerton (who may be the man with tenements in Bolton by Bowland in 1522), and others whose names are lost. For identifications, Hoyle, 'Early Tudor Craven', 36, 11, 32. Again, this shows how the commons were sweeping up gentry as the centre of the rising moved down Ribblesdale.

On the following day, Sunday, the commons, with Hamerton and Tempest in their company, again congregated at Monubent. Hamerton merely says that after this they dispersed; Tempest, that it was resolved that Hamerton should travel on the Monday to raise Colne and Burnley, and that Tempest himself should move down the Ribble Valley to Whalley Abbey. Tempest admitted that he had to threaten to fire the barns at the abbey before the abbot and monks would come and be sworn.[66] That evening Hamerton and Tempest met and swapped notes, but the movement then seems to have gone into abeyance for a few days, until brought back to life by Sawley to counter the threat posed to it by the earl of Derby.[67]

Derby had originally been told to mobilize against Lincolnshire, but by a letter of 20 October the king told him that he had been made aware of the rebellion on the borders of Lancashire and Yorkshire, and of the outrage that the monks of Sawley had committed by returning to their monastery. Derby was told to repress this rebellion, and to execute not only any captains of the commons who fell into his hands but also the abbot of Sawley and the monks.[68] This letter was received at Lathom on 23 October. Derby immediately replied, saying that he proposed to move against the rebels on the following Saturday, 28 October. A letter circulated on 25 October called on the earl's gentry followers to meet him at Whalley on the evening of Tuesday, 31 October with as many men as they could make, and with victual for five or six days. The abbot of Whalley was warned of his arrival.[69]

News of Derby's plan enraged the quiescent commons. They were warned by letters sent out by Sawley that the earl was planning to advance

[66] Tempest was accompanied by Edmund Lowde, William Smithies, and Richard Core. All four were named in March 1537 as 'servants of Sir Richard Tempest'. Lowde and Smithies were both of Gisburn, which confirms the view that the rebellion shifted its focus southwards and westwards along the Ribble valley. Core remains unidentified although there were persons of that name resident in Gisburn. *LP* XII (i), no. 632; Hoyle, 'Early Tudor Craven', *sub nomine*.

[67] Hamerton's examination as paraphrased by *LP* misses the words 'within a while after' between the mention of the second meeting at Monubent and the letters sent by Sawley.

[68] *LP* XI, no. 783 (draft dated 19 October); 'Derby Correspondence', 28–31. With this letter came the wide ranging commission which Derby so valued; ibid. 27–8. It is not obvious how news of the reoccupation of Sawley by the monks reached the king. It is possible that it was carried by Sir Arthur Darcy himself, who travelled south with a letter from Pontefract on 17 October. *LP* XI, nos. 784–5.

[69] 'Derby Correspondence', 32–3, 35–6; *LP* XI, no. 872 (iii).

up the Ribble and destroy Whalley, Sir Richard Tempest's house (at either Waddington or Bracewell), and Hamerton's (probably Wigglesworth). The commons again met at Monubent and resolved that they should advance along each bank of the Ribble, raising the district as they went, and camp on the Preston side of Whalley. They appear to have called a muster on Clitheroe Moor for Monday, 30 October by a summons which explicitly forbade anyone to give aid to the earl or anyone else unless it was certain that they were sworn to the commonwealth.[70] The commons sent word to the commons of Kendal, and Sir Stephen Hamerton to Walter Strickland of Sizergh near Kendal, asking for their aid, but neither request was answered.[71] The 'worshipful men' also wrote to Aske for his assistance.[72]

Forewarned of Derby's intentions, the commons occupied Whalley before the earl had even left Preston, so denying him his base for the advance on Sawley. All the ingredients seem to have been in place for a pitched battle, but the message to Aske, which was received as the commons and the royal forces were dispersing from Doncaster, alerted him to events of which he otherwise seems to have been ignorant. Aske sent word to the commons, saying that they should dissolve themselves and inform him if Derby moved against them, and asked Darcy to write to Shrewsbury with a request that Derby should be asked to honour the truce agreed at Doncaster. Word was received at Preston on Monday, 30 October, and both sides disbanded without having come into conflict.[73]

This is, then, a rather confused and semi-detached branch of the movement. The first evidence we have of any disturbance is of the monks of Sawley re-entering their conventual buildings on the commons' insistence. We cannot tell whether this was coincidental with events elsewhere or prompted by them. The larger movement came into being as a response to Richmondshire. What the Craven movement did have, which tied it into the larger movement, was the Pilgrim's oath. When they acquired it is unclear, but Aske appears to have circulated it widely after his entry

---

[70] LP XI, no. 892 (2), printed in 'Derby Correspondence', 52–3.

[71] LP XII (i), nos. 1034, 914. Hamerton had only recently entered a marriage settlement for the marriage of his daughter Margaret to Walter Strickland. D. Scott, The Stricklands of Sizergh Castle: The Records of Twenty-Five Generations of a Westmorland Family (1908), 89–90.

[72] 'The manner of the taking of Robert Aske', 338.   [73] Ibid. 338; LP XI, nos. 900, 901.

into York. It is very unlikely that either Hamerton or Tempest were sworn with it, but Tempest is quite explicit that he used Aske's oath when he swore Whalley on Monday, 23 October,[74] whilst the summons to Clitheroe Moor on 30 October, although it does not use the brand-name of the 'Pilgrimage of Grace', draws extensively on the oath. It reads as follows (with the text drawn from the oath italicized):

We desire and also charge and command you, upon pain of death and *for the love ye bear to God, his faith, and church militant, and* for *the maintenance thereof* and *for the preservation of the king's person and his issue,* for *the commonwealth* and the intent *to expulse* and *suppress all heretics and their opinions* and to avoid *all villain blood* from the king's *grace and his privy council,* that ye nor none of you give any assistance to the earl of Derby . . .[75]

Hence, it may be suggested that the events at Sawley in early October were not prompted by events in Lincolnshire. North Craven rose partly out of fear of Richmondshire, partly in solidarity with it, but having risen, there was little that could be done and the movement was only called back into existence by the threat posed by the earl of Derby. The only document it produced which has survived, the summons to Clitheroe Moor, is a reworking of the Pilgrim's oath; but the movement, whatever its origins, seems to have owed little or nothing to Aske, who was indeed ignorant of its existence. For this reason it was never called upon to supply troops to Pontefract.

IV

Events in North Craven illustrate the way in which the Pilgrimage of Grace came to overlay other, local disturbances which may have been current even before the rising in Lincolnshire. The same confusion of motivations can be seen in the movement in the Ewcross wapentake of the West Riding and the Barony of Kendal in Westmorland (where two distinct movements coalesced), and in Furness. This was an area of relatively few gentry. By the end of October two of the most significant

[74] Mrs Tempest, 'Nicholas Tempest', 253.   [75] 'Derby Correspondence', 51–2.

landowners—Lord Monteagle of Hornby and Sir Marmaduke Tunstall of Thurland Castle—had taken refuge with the earl of Derby at Preston. Sir Robert Bellingham of Burneside near Kendal was probably sworn by the commons, but made his way to the earl, whilst the abbots of Furness and Cartmell (the latter a dissolved house restored by the commons) also fled.[76]

On Saturday, 14 October two men from Dent visited Kendal to seek the advice of the deputy steward, Sir James Layborne. George Willen and William Garnett told Layborne that the commons of Cumberland, Westmorland, and Richmondshire were up and that they had warned Dent, Sedbergh, and Kendal that they should come in with them or they would be spoilt.[77] They sought Layborne's advice as to what they should do: he advised them to sit still and have no truck with them.

And yet the puzzle is that Willen and Garnett were in Kendal seeking advice as to what Dent should do because it was threatened with spoiling by Richmondshire unless it rose, when, to all appearances, Dent had already been in rebellion for ten days or a fortnight. Darcy knew of a rising in Dent, Sedbergh, and Wensleydale buttressed by mutual oath-swearing in the first days of October. He had heard that the rebels had sworn to resist further spoils, the suppression of abbeys and parish churches and demands for more money, the latter perhaps a revival of the anti-taxation disturbances of 1512–13 and 1523.[78] Breyer confirms that oaths had been sworn in Dent and a number of adjacent parishes.[79] If rumours of a thinning of chapelries were rife, then it may have had a particular resonance in Dent and Garsdale, both chapelries of Sedbergh although 5 or 6 miles distant. Our one source, the examination of William Collins, bailiff of Kendal, gives no evidence as to the objectives or motivation of either Dent or Richmondshire. The Dent men succeeded in provoking a disturbance in Kendal, but one which was entirely concerned with local grievances over tenant right, and not at all with the broader concerns of the Richmondshire rising or Pilgrimage of Grace.

---

[76] Ibid. 45–6. Bellingham was with the commons on Saturday, 29 October when Collins reports he went to the Kellet Moor muster.

[77] LP XII (i), no. 914, for the following. The parallel with Fawcett and Jakes asking Giggleswick to rise out of fear of Bishopdale and Wensleydale is striking.

[78] See above p. 52.　　[79] LP XI, no. 841.

Before they left Kendal Willen and Garnett sought Collins's advice, 'who counselled them also to be still and to make no business, saying if we might enjoy our old ancient customs here, we have no cause to rise'. Collins's comment clearly indicates that the preservation of customary tenure and the level of entry fines (gressoms) was already a matter of anxiety in Kendal. Willen and Garnett then spoke with 'divers other light persons' of the town, who, on the Sunday morning, called men from their beds and swore them by a simple oath to be true to God, the king, and their ancient customs. The crowd then decided to gather in the 'honest men' of the town, including Collins the bailiff, and compelled them all to swear oaths. If we draw a parallel with other towns—including Louth and Beverley—this might be viewed as a rising amongst the youth and artisans of the town into which the older and richer inhabitants were dragged against their wills.[80] Then the crowd went to Mr Layborne's and sought his help against their enemies (Dent?), asked him to be good to them and their customs, and required him to take their oath. He refused, but left his seal with his friends and expressed his willingness to do as other gentry did. That same night Nicholas Layborne (his brother) and Mr Strickland of Sizergh (just outside Kendal) sealed a composition with the commons concerning their customs—doubtless, in the light of what follows, an agreement not to raise fines. There then appears to have been an intermission in activity of four days. On Friday, 20 October Collins and others went to Layborne's house to petition him to be good to their customs. He was not there, but Collins reports that this was one of a number of occasions on which Layborne was approached with the request that he should respect their customs. This, then, was little more than a local dispute between the tenants of the Barony of Kendal and one or possibly two local landowners. We do not know at this stage that the crowd was motivated by religious considerations.

The movement turned into something quite different on the following day. It was reported in Kendal that Dent had risen. The men of Kendal wrote to those of Dent telling them not to meddle in the barony of Kendal and refusing to have anything to do with them. This inflamed the Dent men, who demanded that the Kendal commons should meet

---

[80] For an example of such a split within Kendal in December, see *LP* XII (i), no. 671 (2, iii).

with them on Monday morning (23 October) at Ennesmoor or else they would come and spoil them. After taking the advice of a number of gentlemen, the Kendal commons met with a much larger Dent contingent as the latter demanded, who asked the Kendal men whether they were sworn: they replied that they were. The Kendal commons admitted that their gentlemen would not come in with them, to which the Dent contingent said that 'if ye cannot rule them, we shall rule them'. The captains of the Dent men then conferred, and the vicar of Clapham read a proclamation in the name of 'Lord Poverty' instructing the crowd to reassemble on the following morning to know 'Lord Poverty's' decision.

The remainder of the week was spent in a campaign to intimidate the gentry, especially Layborne, into joining them. On Tuesday the Dent commons came to Kendal and both groups advanced towards Layborne's house at Cunswick, 2 miles west of Kendal, but turned back when they had a promise that he would come in by the end of Wednesday afternoon. On Wednesday they spoiled his house: on Thursday they agreed to spoil his 'manors', but returned home after Parson Layborne paid Sedbergh and Dent £20 for a day's grace. On Friday Layborne and a number of gentlemen surrendered themselves and were sworn at the tollbooth in Kendal. On Saturday the combined forces of Dent, Sedbergh, and Kendal, in the company of at least six gentry,[81] advanced on Lancaster, holding a muster midway at Kellet Moor, and at Lancaster they swore the mayor and the town. A proclamation was read requiring all men to attend a further muster on Bentham Moor on the following Tuesday. This may well have been cancelled after a letter was received from Aske requiring the commons to subscribe to the truce arranged at Doncaster.

The earl of Derby thought that the detachment that travelled to Lancaster probably numbered 3,000 men, although he admitted that others offered higher estimates. He sent two of his servants to Lancaster to tell the commons to disperse and offering to act as an intermediary to the king for them if they would so do. This was rejected in language which is interesting (although we only have it at second hand): Derby's servants were

---

[81] Collins names Sir James Layborne, Parson Layborne, William Lancaster, Richard Duckett, Walter Strickland, and Sir Robert Bellingham; Bellingham retired with a sore leg, but not so sore as to prevent him taking refuge with the earl of Derby at Lathom.

told that 'they had a pilgrimage to do for the commonwealth which they would accomplish or jeopardise their lives to die in that quarrel'. The earl's servants then challenged the commons either to disperse, or if they would send the earl a bill signed by twelve of their leaders promising to fight on Bentham Moor, he would meet them there and 'determine the quarrel by battle'. Again the earl was rebuffed: 'they would not fight with the said earl but if [unless] he interrupted them of their Pilgrimage.' And if he really wanted to fight them, then they would fight both him and the lord lieutenant. The use of the language of pilgrimage and their awareness of events at Doncaster suggest that by 28 October, like the Craven movement, they were in contact with Aske in at least a general way and had adopted his language, if not his leadership.[82]

Several points can be drawn out from this account. First, Dent, Sedbergh, and perhaps the district to the south around Clapham and Ingleton ('the Lonsdale Movement') had risen before Richmondshire, but in a second stage of development they claimed that they were rising in response to and out of fear of Richmondshire. And this seems to be the only connection with the latter. The second matter worthy of comment is the hostility shown by the Kendal men towards Dent and Sedbergh. The two are absolutely distinct movements. Whilst the government came to believe that Collins was complicit, the extant correspondence from November 1536 identifies one John Atkinson as the leading figure in the Dent rising: it was he, for instance, who declined the earl of Derby's challenge. He was certainly drawn from the Dent and Sedbergh focus, but otherwise remains unidentified.[83] The rising caused anxiety in Kendal and prompted a refusal to have anything to do with the rebels until the moment at which Kendal was overwhelmed by their numbers. In the hunting down of Sir James Layborne, it seems as though it was Dent and Sedbergh men who took the lead. Collins had good reasons to play down the role of his own neighbours, but he is quite explicit that it was they and not Kendal men who were paid off by the Laybornes. Thirdly,

[82] This paragraph is based on the earl's account sent to the king, *LP* XI, no. 947 (2), printed in 'Derby Correspondence', 43–4.

[83] For the identification of Atkinson as leader, see Collin's account and 'Derby Correspondence', 43–4, 66. The name is too common for Atkinson to be reliably identified from the lay subsidy materials. He was captured in April, but there is no extant examination and his fate is unknown. *LP* XII (i), no. 825.

Kendal rose at the instigation of Dent and Sedbergh, but Collins offers
no clues that the rising was prompted by religious grievances or that
the Kendal movement subscribed to the Captain Poverty ideology of
the Lonsdale movement. There was a degree of agitation over religious
innovations in the New Year, but Collins does not cite this as a concern
of the October movement. Finally, the movement came to be primarily
concerned with the question of tenure. A poem which circulated advocated
the Kendal example as one which others might follow:

> All commons, stick ye together
> rise with no great man till ye know his intent,
> keep your harness in your hands
> and ye shall obtain your purpose in all this north land.
> Claim ye old customs and tenant right to take your farms by
>   a God's penny,
> all gressums and heightenings to be laid down,
> then we may serve our sovereign lord King Henry the Eight
> God Save his noble grace
> we shall serve our lands' lord in every righteous cause with
>   horse and
> harness as custom will demand.
> Gentle commons, have this in your mind
> Every man take his lands' lord and ye have need,
> As we did in Kendalland
> Then shall ye speed.
> Make your writings, command
> them to seal to grant you your petitions as your desire.

The poem then says that if the lords would be kind to the tenants, then
they might go on Pilgrimage to maintain the faith a holy church, a clear
comment on where their priorities lay, but again perhaps a sentiment
borrowed from Aske.[84] As late as mid-January crowds were still trying
to get manorial lords to swear to the permissive custom of Kendal.[85]

Further to the west, in Furness, we find an ill-documented movement
associated to a degree with the monastic houses at Conishead and
Furness and perhaps also Cartmel. Conishead and Cartmel had both been
dissolved in 1536. Both were re-entered during October, Conishead certainly
by 16 October. A lost letter circulated by the abbot and convent

---

[84] *LP* XI, no. 892 (3); XII (i), no. 163 (2).   [85] *LP* XII (i), no. 671 (2) (ii).

of Conishead suggests that they were engineering support from amongst their tenants and neighbours by calling them to a muster on 17 October.[86] The earl of Derby understood that it was the commons of Cartmel who had restored the priory of Cartmel. The abbots of both Cartmel and Furness fled to the earl of Derby, and in the case of the latter we have some indication of the dilemma which he and the convent had to resolve when threatened with a rising of the commons.

Furness was not in any danger from the 1536 act, but it knew about its consequences at first hand because four monks from Sawley were billeted there, three of whom left for their own house when they heard it was restored.[87] By the last week of October the abbot, Roger Pyle, seems to have felt that the monastery needed to make some show of support towards the commons whilst not being seen to behave in a treasonable fashion. Pyle's solution was to flee to the earl of Derby whilst allowing the monks to align themselves with the commons by raising the monastery's tenants in their support.[88] A letter was circulated to the bailiffs and constables of Furness Fells in the name of 'our Brother Poverty and our Brother Roger [Pyle]', saying that both went forth for the aid of holy church and for the reformation of abbeys 'now dissolved without just cause'. A round robin announced a muster to be held at Hawkshead church on Saturday, 28 October, which every one was enjoined to attend 'on pain of pulling down your houses and loosing of your goods', adding that direction would be given there concerning the true faith. But the letter also drew three 'commonwealth' grievances to the recipients' attention: that baptisms would be taxed; that no man owning under £20 in lands would be allowed to eat wheat bread, white meat, or pork unless he paid for a licence; and that every ploughland would be taxed.[89] In its form and language it stands apart from the letters inspired by Aske.

Whether Pyle willingly or knowingly allowed his name to be used cannot be discovered. By the time he reached the earl of Derby's house at Lathom some of his convent had attended a muster of Swarthmore,

---

[86] Ibid., no. 849, item 29. The following section covers ground treated at greater length in Haigh, 'The Last Days of the Lancashire Monasteries', 62–3.

[87] The major sources for Furness are depositions taken in 1537: *LP* XII (i), nos. 652, 841.

[88] The fact that he wrote to Furness from Lathom justifying his actions may perhaps be read to indicate that he had deserted his brethren.

[89] 'Derby Correspondence', 49–50.

when they contributed to the commons' war chest; they then joined
with them at a rebel muster held at Dalton in Furness on 31 October
which the abbey's tenants were instructed to attend. When some of the
Dalton tenants sought advice as to what they should do, they were told
to 'agree with them [the commons] as we have done', which may perhaps suggest that the monks were anxious to reach an accommodation
with the commons. The movement seems to have been wound up shortly
afterwards, probably on the receipt of word of the truce; but when Pyle
returned he found that at least some of the monks were in close alliance
with the commons. There is no evidence that Furness Abbey prompted
the rising; rather, the house may have split between those, like Pyle, who
believed that opposition to the rebels was hopeless and that it was best
to bend with their flow, and those monks who were sentimentally—and
incautiously—attached to them.

There remains one further document which illustrates the character
of the Captain Poverty risings. This is a letter whose text was entered
in the earl of Derby's letter book without any clue as to how or when
it came into his hands. We must assume that it circulated in north
Lancashire. After a short preface outlining that this was a chain letter,
the substantive text runs:

Master Poverty, the conductor, protector, and maintainer of the whole commonalty, sendeth you all greeting in our Lord everlasting. And forsomuch as
we intend the defence principally of the Faith of our Christ Jesu under licence
of our most noble sovereign lord King Henry VIII, whose honour is entitled
to be Defender of the said Faith, and yet notwithstanding by certain heretics
of our time we see it piteously and abominably confounded, not ashaming
in open preaching to blaspheme the honour of our lord God, working most
cruelly by spoiling and suppression of holy places, as abbeys, churches, and
ministers of the same, but also rageously velipending and despising the laws and
ordinances of our Mother Holy Church, blaspheming also our Lady and all other
saints in heaven, whereby we are run in shameful slander throughout all realms
Christian to the utter confusion of all English people. Further, the said male-
factors have procured and proposed against the commonwealth certain acts of
law under the colour of parliament, which, put in execution, the estate of Poverty
can no longer bear nor suffer these premises.

Wherefore I command you all in general from sixteen years and above,
on pain of death and forfeiting of your goods, to be in arrediness to aid us in

maintaining of our said Faith of Christ and his church, of the most high honour of our sovereign lord the king and of the commonwealth of this most noble realm of England.

And ever God save the king and send him good counsel.[90]

This is not the letter sent out by Richmondshire as described by Thompson or Towneley. It is an indictment of the character of religious policy during the early Cromwellian ascendancy: the faith undermined by preaching by heretics, the suppression of abbeys, and the expected suppression of churches, and the rejection of saints in the injunctions of 1536. It acknowledges that there were then other grievances which tended to undermine the estate of the commons, but these were neither stressed nor itemized. They may well have been the kind of concerns mentioned in the call to muster at Hawkshead. The emphasis is heavily on religious rather than commonwealth grievances. It offers no agrarian programme, nor expresses anxiety about Scottish incursions. The document was impeccably loyal: the author claimed to be acting with the king's permission. He sought God's gift of good counsel to the king. The letter asked for nothing except that those who heard it should be ready to move in the defence of the church, the king, and the commonwealth. Here is Captain Poverty defending the church (rather than the commonwealth) in terms of which Aske would have approved, but without his distinctive language.

V

The final rebellion spawned by Richmondshire was in Westmorland and Cumberland, which, originating as two separate risings in the Upper Eden Valley, progressively tracked northwards towards Carlisle, mustering and recruiting as it went over a period of a fortnight.[91] At Carlisle it found that the city would not co-operate with it. Having first promised a

---

[90] Ibid. 47–9.

[91] For other accounts of the disturbances in North Westmorland and Cumberland, S. M. Harrison, *The Pilgrimage of Grace in the Lake Counties, 1536–7* (1981); Bush, *Pilgrimage of Grace*, chs. 8–9; id., 'Captain Poverty and the Pilgrimage of Grace', *Historical Res.*, 65 (1992).

boycott of Carlisle's markets, more drastic conflicts were avoided by the circulation of a proclamation announcing the truce at Pontefract and forbidding further assemblies.

The evidence for the rising comes almost entirely from the recollections of two clergymen participants, the vicar of Brough under Stainmoor, Robert Thompson, and the bishop of Carlisle's chancellor, Dr Bernard Towneley. Thompson was with the movement from Monday, 16 October onwards; Towneley from the following Monday. Although the pair co-operated during the movement, Towneley seems to have had little time for Thompson, whom he saw as one of the leaders of the revolt and the author of its ceremonial: 'the four captains with the commons had and took the same vicar as a prophet.'[92] The vicar was not some elderly hick priest but a recent Oxford graduate, a former fellow of Queen's College, who had a college living, albeit poor.[93] It is not obvious that a man of his age and education would have been sympathetic to the commons' aims. Towneley was slightly older, being made doctor of canon law in 1525. He was chancellor of the diocese of Carlisle and vicar of Caldbeck (amongst the richest of the Cumbrian livings) in 1535.[94]

Thompson began his account of the rising with an incident in Kirkby Stephen church on Sunday, 15 October, where the curate failed to include St Luke's Day in the bidding of the beads, then, following a clamour from his parishioners, announced it as a holiday.[95] (St Luke's Day was 18 October.) The attachment of the parishioners to St Luke has caused some puzzlement, but the feast and its morrow were the days of the autumn fair at Kirkby Stephen.[96] On the Monday the men of Kirkby Stephen, having heard that Yorkshire, Richmondshire, and County Durham had risen, sent word into the countryside calling people to a muster on Sandford Moor. As this meeting drew together, Thompson decided to travel to

[92] SP1/117, fo. 46v (= LP XII (i), no. 687).

[93] Thompson graduated BA in 1527 and MA in 1530. He was a fellow of Queen's College, Oxford by 1531, but resigned on his appointment to Brough (by 1535). Emden, *Biographical Register 1501–1540*, 563.

[94] He had been vicar of Horncastle, Lincolnshire, 1525–31. Ibid. 572.

[95] Most of the following is based on Thompson's examination, *LP* XII (i), 687 (2) (= SP1/117, fos. 48r–56r). Thompson's 'confession', E36/119, fos. 71r–74r, which is not printed in *LP*, is mostly material shared with the examination, but contains additional details which are cited separately.

[96] Harrison, *Pilgrimage of Grace in the Lake Counties*, 78; J. Nicolson and R. Burn, *The History and Antiquities of the Counties of Westmorland and Cumberland*, 2 vols. (1771; repr. 1976), I, 544.

his mother's house at Penrith, taking a route to avoid the rebel assembly, but he was overtaken, brought back to Sandford, sworn, and then allowed to continue on his way, but not before he promised to be with the commons again on Tuesday. During Monday there were contacts with Sir Thomas Wharton at Wharton. Thompson says that Wharton had been amongst the commons but could not agree with them, perhaps an echo of Bowes's demand for subservience. When Thompson arrived at the muster on Tuesday the crowd was minded to burn both Wharton Hall and the Musgrave's house at Hartley.[97] When they went to Wharton they found that Sir Thomas had fled, and all they could do was swear his eldest son in his place. On Wednesday they met at Kirkby Stephen and decided that they would again go up the valley, this time to Lammerside where they hoped to find Wharton, Mr Warcop, and other gentlemen. This house was empty except for servants, so they confiscated the house keys and proclaimed a day by which Wharton and Warcop were to come in or have their goods spoilt. In a field near Lammerside the commons appointed two or more of every town to bring in the goods of all the commons who would not be sworn. And they decided that on the following day Nicholas Musgrave, with 'all of his side of the water of Eden', should go down the south bank of the River Eden towards Penrith and Robert Pullen along the north bank. Musgrave set out but failed to reach Penrith, lingering around Lowther on the Thursday night in a vain attempt to trap Sir John Lowther. Pullen apparently reached Penrith and returned towards Kirkby Stephen on Friday, swearing Mr Dudley and other gentlemen at Eamont Bridge. This was a discrete movement, quite separate from the movement in Penrith (out of which the larger Cumberland movement formed), and it might be helpful to consider it further before turning to events in the town.

The movement had a local grievance—the abrogation of the St Luke's day holiday at Kirkby Stephen. However, the muster at Sandford Moor was held in response to the rumour of the rising over the Pennines. There is nothing to suggest that the commons of Kirkby Stephen had a letter out of Richmondshire, although, as we shall see, such a letter was received at Penrith. Nor did Thompson know who had first brought word of the

---

[97] A detail in the 'confession' but not in the examination. E36/119, fo. 71r.

rising out of Yorkshire: it was 'a common rumour that went abroad'. But one man who came over Stainmoor to Brough and who certainly knew of events in Yorkshire was Lord Scrope who, as we saw, fled to the Blenkinsop house at Helbeck whilst making his way to Skipton.[98] A second feature of this rising in the Upper Eden Valley was that it had a degree of gentry leadership and sought to bring in other gentry, including Wharton. Thompson names four captains at Sandford Moor: Robert Pullen, Nicholas Musgrave, Christopher Blenkinsop, and Robert Hilton. Pullen was a minor manorial lord, with a manor at Ormside. Hilton had a manor at Burton, now a deserted hamlet in the parish of Warcop. Pullen and Hilton's claim to gentility is additionally attested by their contribution of horsemen to aid Sir Thomas Wharton in 1543 (albeit only two apiece).[99] Christopher Blenkinsop was one of the churchwardens of Brough; he was also the earl of Cumberland's bailiff of Stainmoor and doubtless of the Helbeck family.[100] Nicholas Musgrave was probably drawn from the Musgrave family of Hartley in Kirkby Stephen, and so a relative of Sir William Musgrave. The identification of the latter two must remain slightly uncertain, but if it can be deduced that the captains were drawn one apiece from their respective parishes, then the proto-movement covered the four parishes of Brough, Kirkby Stephen, Warcop, and Ormside, all in all that part of the Upper Eden Valley to the south of Appleby. In Pullen the movement found its activist leader: it was he who swore Thompson, he who confiscated the keys of Lammerside Castle and ordered the commons to sequestrate their neighbours' goods. And, to anticipate matters, it was Pullen who made his way to Pontefract to witness the first meeting with the duke of Norfolk and it was he, with Musgrave, who organized and signed the petition of the commons of Westmorland. (It was also Pullen who was perceived to have betrayed the commons by Christmas.)

It seems that Penrith was visited by Pullen's column on the Thursday evening, but that the town had risen and proclaimed four captains

98 Above p. 14.

99 For Pullen, Nicolson and Burn, *Westmorland and Cumberland*, I, 516; for Hilton, ibid. 353, 612, 613. For the 1543 list, ibid., I. li. (Blenkinsop was executed in 1537 and Musgrave fled into Scotland.)

100 Harrison, *Pilgrimage of Grace in the Lake Counties*, 98. Thompson implies he was a churchwarden, SP1/117, fos. 55r–56v.

earlier in the day in response to the Richmondshire letter.[101] These captains took the names Charity, Faith, Poverty, and Piety; they were (respectively) Anthony Hutton, John Beck, Gilbert Whelpedale, and Thomas Birkbeck.[102] When Pullen returned from Penrith he ordered Thompson to go there to help the rebels, Gilbert Whelpedale being Thompson's brother-in-law. Thompson found them mustering on Penrith Fell, having already sent a detachment to Edenhall to show the letter to Sir Edward Musgrave and to raise the village and those around it. Having arrived at the Penrith muster, Thompson was proclaimed Poverty's chaplain and given the job of swearing the commons, using an oath devised by Anthony Hutton, one of the captains. From this time forwards Thompson's account is entirely concerned with the Penrith movement, and little more detail survives about events in the Upper Eden Valley.

The Penrith movement met in a series of different locations on alternate days throughout the following week, gradually drifting along the north side of the Lake District hills before holding a final muster near Carlisle. The countryside was called to its musters section by section and the gentry and clergy sworn. On Saturday they met 'five miles beyond Penrith on the fells', and the townships 'beyond Eden' were called in and sworn. On Monday, 23 October they mustered at Catlogan Thorns, where Dr Towneley, Richard Bewley, and the other gentlemen and commons around Caldbeck were sworn. Captains—two in each case —were chosen from amongst the commons of Caldbeck, the barony of Greystock, and the forest of Inglewood. On Wednesday they met at Kylwatling Howe, where they took Cuthbert Hutton and called on the vicar of Melmerby to surrender himself, 'for he and Dr Towneley, the vicar of Sowerby and the vicar of Edenhall, were proclaimed to be chaplains of Poverty and for to help the commons with their good instructions and to provide for such things as were necessary for them concerning their faith, they failing thereof, to lose their goods and lives and their heads to be set in the most famous places in all the country'.[103] On Friday the rebels met at Sandale Hill, and here the first contact

---

[101] Thompson is emphatic that 'they were gathered there before the said Pullen's coming because of a letter they had received from beyond Stainsmoor...', SP1/117, fo. 50r-v (= LP XII (i), no. 687 (2)).

[102] Ibid., fos. 50r–51v.   [103] Ibid., fo. 52r.

took place between the commons' movement and Carlisle. Messengers arrived to say that the Carlisle commons would not be sworn; in all other respects they would support them.

This greatly enraged the commons. Without the support of Carlisle, they were prone to robbery by Eskdale, Leven, and the Black Quarters, 'so that no man might take their rest in the day nor ride safely in the night'.[104] When word came that men living around Carlisle had been robbed during the day, some of the commons were allowed to go home to watch over their goods. A proclamation was made that none of the commons should sell their goods in Carlisle, and a further order issued that the commons should muster the following day at Moota Hill. Because of the poor weather (this being the day when, as we shall see, the River Don became impassable at Doncaster), the captains of Penrith lodged for the night at Cockermouth.

At Moota Hill on Saturday the abbot of Holme and Thomas Dalston of Dalston came in; both were sworn, and two captains were appointed for the lordship of Holme. Articles were drawn to be carried to Carlisle by messengers. The first asked whether the mayor and two of his brethren would attend a meeting with the commons on Monday at a muster to be held at Broadfield Oak; the second was to ask whether they 'would keep the common's enemies, meaning the Scots thieves and robbers, from them'; the third was a request that the mayor should swear his brethren. The commons charged the abbot of Holme, Towneley, and Thomas Dalston to convey the message; because they dragged their feet over this, they were denounced before the whole commons. The abbot and Towneley spent Saturday night at Dalston with Thompson; when they went to Carlisle on Sunday the city refused to admit them and they returned empty-handed to Dalston. But whilst at Carlisle they heard reports of a proclamation made in the king's name that the commons should make no further illegal assemblies.[105] Thompson was sent from Dalston to Penrith

---

[104] Ibid., fo. 52v. 'Leven' is the River Lyne; for sixteenth-century forms, see English Place Name Soc., *Cumberland*, I, 21.

[105] Thompson reports that the proclamation said that 'the matter was taken up between the king's grace and the commons and that no assembly should after that be made'. SP1/117, fo. 53v. This would seem to indicate word of the Doncaster truce, but if so, the news had carried extremely quickly. Aske sent out letters announcing the truce immediately after the duke of Norfolk left Doncaster, probably prompted by the discovery of the North Craven movement. See *LP* XI, no. 928.

carrying news of the refusal of Carlisle to negotiate, but also to seek clarification of the proclamation. No one at Penrith had heard of it, and it was decided to hold the muster as arranged.[106]

The commons met at Broadfield Oak on Monday. (Thompson says on one occasion that they numbered 15,000 men, elsewhere that there were 20,000.[107]) A delegation was sent to Carlisle, where they were shown the proclamation, and on their return to Broadfield Oak they had it read to the commons, who agreed to disperse, understanding that they would meet again on Friday, 3 November at Broadfield.[108]

Thompson took the reading of the proclamation as his opportunity to slip away: Towneley confirms that he was absent from the second muster at Broadfield Oak. Towneley did attend, as did Sir Christopher Dacre, who came armed with a promise of safe conduct, and Towneley reports that they persuaded the commons to make no more insurrection until the king's mind was known. They also insisted that the commons should lift their blockade of Carlisle. That agreed, Dacre and Towneley then went to Carlisle to request that the mayor should not take reprisals against any of the commons coming to the city, and to seek assurance from Lord Clifford that the castle garrison would not attack the commons. After both had given the required undertakings, Towneley's contacts with the rebels also ceased.

Penrith rather than Kirkby Stephen was the real dynamo of the movement in the Lake Counties. To an unappreciated degree, this involved the smaller gentry of the county who, following the normal pattern of the 1536 revolts, brought in, swore, and then co-opted into the leadership of the movement their social equals. The rebel oath was written by a gentleman of Penrith, Anthony Hutton. The larger gentry escaped. Sir Thomas Wharton fled (to where, no one knows). Sir Edward Musgrave may have been sworn, but is never noticed as being with the commons. Sir John Lowther came to the muster at Cartlogan under a safe conduct

---

[106] Towneley is exceptionally hostile to Thompson at this point, holding that he and the captains of Penrith knew of the proclamation but argued that the 'stop was but craft and falsehood', and so insisted that the muster take place, even though Towneley and the abbot of Holme were trying to spread word that the muster was cancelled. SP1/117, fo. 44r.

[107] SP1/117, fos. 73v, 53v.

[108] The text of a warrant calling Bewcastledale to this muster survives: below p. 250.

to seek men to attend the March day with him. Sir Christopher Dacre came to the final muster, again under a safe conduct, and was instrumental in persuading the commons to disperse.

Where the Eden Valley movement(s) were distinctive however, is in that they never had single gentry leader after the model of Robert Aske in the East Riding, Sir Thomas Percy in Pickering Lythe, Robert Bowes in Richmondshire and County Durham, or Sir Stephen Hamerton in North Craven. This may be a trick of the surviving documentation, in that no gentry were called upon to depose about their actions. It may also reflect the fact that the movement remained immature: that where elsewhere smaller gentry and essentially peasant captains were superseded by gentry, here authority appears to have remained much more with the captains drawn from amongst the commons. This itself seems to have been a diffuse body: Thompson refers to 'more than twenty captains, both wilful and unruly', and offers the intriguing detail that at the Catlogan muster Anthony Hutton, who had been one of the Penrith captains, walked out on the movement, saying that 'the commons would have no gen-tlemen to be their captains'.[109]

So it may be argued that the commons remained untamed by the gentry, perhaps because no suitable personality emerged: the Kirkby Stephen commons wanted Sir Thomas Wharton with them, but he ran rather than accept their rule. There were similarly ambivalent relation-ships between the movement and the clergy. The commons were con-cerned to acquire a full hand of the parochial clergy. They had a priest carry a cross before them.[110] And although they looked for instruction in the faith, they appear to have been ready to threaten and brutalize the clergy. At Catlogan the threat was made that if the parson of Melmerby did not come in, Thompson, Towneley, and the vicar of Edenhall would 'lose their goods and have their heads set on the most famous parts of all the country'.[111] Towneley reports a similar incident on Wednesday, when it was proclaimed that if the parson of Thirkeld did not come in, Towneley's head (with that of the others) would be struck off and set on the highest place of the diocese. Towneley thought that this pro-clamation was made with the procurement of Thompson.[112] When, on Saturday, 28 October, the abbot of Holme, Dr Towneley, and Thomas

---

[109] SP1/117, fos. 73r, 74r.   [110] Ibid., fo. 51r.   [111] Ibid., fo. 52r.   [112] Ibid., fo. 43r.

Dalston were dragging their feet over going to Carlisle, one Percy Simpson, with the consent of the commons, said 'that they should never be well until they had stricken off all the priests' heads, saying they would not deceive them'.[113]

Whilst Towneley's distrust of Thompson is palpable, he offers little evidence against Thompson which is not contained within one or other of Thompson's two statements, but he constantly construes his actions in the least favourable fashion. Thompson admitted that he was amongst the commons and swore them to their oath as they joined the host. He was also present at the captains' mass at Penrith. Towneley describes this (although he makes no claim to have witnessed it):

[The four captains] went in procession with the vicar of Brough at the town of Penrith openly within the parish church daily for their time after being with their four swords drawn, following the said vicar in the said procession. And after the gospel the vicar declared unto the said four captains and the commons other being [there] one of the ten commandments and that was called the captain's mass and the said four captains with the commons had and took the vicar as a prophet.[114]

Thompson's account suggests that the mass took place in this form only twice, on Wednesday, 25 October and the following day. He confirms the ritual element: that the captains followed Thompson as celebrant in procession with their swords exposed. Then, during the service, Thompson preached, declaring 'unto them one or two of the ten commandments and showed them that the breaking of those commandments was the cause of all that great trouble'. After a priest expressed doubts about having naked weapons in church, that element at least of the ceremony was abandoned, although whether the captains' mass continued is not revealed.[115]

That Thompson elected to expound the ten commandments to show how a failure to observe them lay at the root of their troubles suggests that his preaching probably made uncomfortable listening for his audience. But we have no further details to confirm this, and ultimately reach an impasse. Towneley is not a reliable witness to Thompson's actions: Thompson portrays his relationship to the commons as more subservient, more conditional on his following their demands than Towneley would

[113] Ibid., fo. 53v.   [114] Ibid., fo. 46v.   [115] Ibid., fo. 52r–v.

allow. Ironically, it was Towneley who was executed (although Norfolk was not persuaded of any great guilt), whilst Thompson appears to have survived at least into Edward's reign: he was presented to a parish in Northumberland in 1548.[116]

Whilst this reveals a great deal about the character of the movement, it does little to advance our understanding of its causes or motives. Here it is useful to employ the distinctions between precipitate causes and mature justifications and internal and external factors developed earlier. Taking the precipitants first, in Kirkby Stephen the internal cause appears to have been the suspension of the St Luke's holiday and its omission during the bidding of the beads. The external cause, and the key precipitant in Brough and Kirkby Stephen, was the breaking news of the rising in Richmondshire. In Penrith it was the receipt of the Captain Poverty letter. What may not have contributed to the rising was the ferment of rumours of confiscation and taxation circulating within Yorkshire, which are never mentioned by the limited Cumbrian sources although, as we saw, they did circulate in Lancashire over the sands.

The relationship of this movement to Richmondshire can be seen in a number of respects. There was the adoption of sobriquets for the captains of Penrith. The rebels' oath was so anodyne as not to be specific to any one locality (Thompson says he swore people to God, the faith of the church, the king, and the commonwealth and this is confirmed by Towneley).[117] The same concerns can be seen in the warrant calling Bewcastle to the Broadfield Oak muster:

To our very good neighbours and brethren in God of Banocastell [*recte* Bewcastle], Mr John Musgrave with his commons about him. We let you know that we and B [*sic*] our neighbours are assembled for the maintenance of the true faith, the king's grace, and the poor commonalty, wherefore we command you to wait upon our captains which are Charity, Faith, Poverty, and Piety to appear at Burnthwayte Auke on Friday next at ix of the clock to know more of the matter. Otherwise doing we will repute and take you [to be] enemies to God, the church, and the commonwealth, etc.[118]

As can be seen, this was not influenced by Aske's oath. Instead, we have the concerns not even of the Captain Poverty letters but of the elementary

---

[116] *LP* XII (i), no. 594. Emden, *Biographical Register, 1501–1540*, 563.

[117] SP1/117, fos. 73r, 43r.

[118] Bodl., Ms. James 27, pp. 117–8 (a reference which I owe to the great kindness of Cliff Davies).

oaths sworn in Lincolnshire which merely ask for the maintenance of the church, loyalty to the king, and solidarity amongst the commons. The use of the sobriquets for the captains—Charity, Faith, Poverty, and Piety—all suggest an attachment to the mystical world view of Piers Ploughman.[119] It is a rhetoric which is quite contrary to Aske's.

But the Penrith movement had been spawned by Richmondshire, and some wished to play a role in the latter. Robert Pullen answered the call of the Captain Poverty letter for delegates to attend a conference, and went into Yorkshire with a letter from the commons of Westmorland. He was at the first meeting at Doncaster and returned with a copy of what may have been the Lincoln articles. Using the authority of the truce, he and the commons instructed all the priests to bid beads and announce holidays after the old fashion, and convened a series of inquests where he and Musgrave drew the common's grievances into a petition which they sent to Darcy in mid-November.[120] They at least believed themselves to be part of a much wider movement in which they were anxious to play a part.

And yet one has to doubt how much the Cumberland movement owed to Richmond, apart from the original stimulus. The movement in Cumberland in its first week had more localized and immediate causes. These are represented in the proclamation which was devised by Anthony Hutton and read at every muster of the commons. Having begun by saying that they were gathered for the maintenance of the faith (and ending by asking for the old custom of bidding beads and holidays to be restored), the majority of the proclamation was concerned with the entirely secular question of thieving. That:

because the rulers of this country do not come amongst us to defend us of the robbing of the thieves and the Scots, that four captains be chosen which are called Charity, Faith, Poverty, and Pity which command you to keep your charity and peace and that no man do steal, rob, nor meddle with other men's goods and make no frays *[on] pain of death but be ready one to help another and follow the cry[121] when thieves or Scots would rob or invade us either by day or night . . .

---

[119] Bush, *Pilgrimage of Grace*, 147, n. 52, 284.

[120] *LP* XI, no. 1080, printed by Harrison, *Pilgrimage of Grace in the Lake Counties*, p. 138.

[121] The MS says *skrie*. Harrison, *Pilgrimage in the Lake Counties*, 83, reads the word as *shaw* and glosses it as warden.

We have already seen how this fear informed relations between the commons and Carlisle. There has been some fruitless debate as to whether the inadequacy of the earl of Cumberland as warden was responsible for this breakdown in civil peace. Whoever was to blame, this issue rather than the dissolution or taxation preoccupied the commons. But it did not prompt their uprising.[122]

Such fears were distinctively Cumbrian. The petition sent to Darcy in the name of the Westmorland commons in November reflected the concerns of the north of the county—the upper Eden—rather than Cumberland or the barony of Kendal in the south of the county. The grievances expressed there were not precipitants, but arose out of a more reflective process of enquiry into matters of concern. They can no more be taken to illustrate the reasons for the outbreak of the rising than the Pontefract articles can be for the Pilgrimage of Grace generally.

The petition focused on two broad groups of grievances, the first seigniorial, the second relating to absentee beneficed priests. The seigniorial grievances were three. First, they wished to have gressoms (entry fines) for poor men 'laid apart, but only penny farm, penny gressom'. This should be read as a request for fines of one year's rent, where the Pontefract articles asked for fines of two years' rent. Tithes were also to remain to every man. Secondly, they wished to have the payment of two free rents specific to the barony of Westmorland and due to the earl of Cumberland—neat geld or cornage, and sergeant food—ended. The first was paid by freeholders, the latter apparently gathered in kind from the village communities or their representatives. Exactly why these rents were so disliked is never revealed. Thirdly, they wished to have new enclosures thrown down, and indeed did this by force at the end of January. There is scattered evidence that the question of fines was settled, as in the barony of Kendal, by having the landlords enter into coerced compositions with their tenants.[123]

The second area of concern outlined in the petition concerned absentee priests. This appears in a number of contexts. The petitioners

---

[122] Westmorland and Cumberland did not pay either the subsidy or the fifteenth, hence the lack of materials with which to identify people or ascertain their levels of wealth.

[123] Both Thompson and Towneley and the poem cited on p. 238 refer to this happening, and the Pontefract articles ask for these compositions to be confirmed.

demanded that absentees contribute to taxes 'as well as them that abide with us . . .'. They desired to have Darcy's ruling as to whether it was right to sequester or evict absentees, 'for we think in our opinions that we may put in their rooms to serve God others that would be glad to keep hospitality', and then—the crux of the matter—'for some of them are no priests which have the benefice in the hand and others of them is [are] my Lord Cromwell's chaplains'. The cause of their concern may have been that the vicar of Kirkby Stephen was Peter Vannes, the king's Latin secretary, who was not in major orders. The living of Great Musgrave was held by one John Knollys who, when securing a dispensation to hold a second living in plurality in 1539, was described as Cromwell's chaplain and so was doubtless absent serving his master for some of the year.[124] Thompson, who probably wished he was an absentee, glosses this: the captains taxed the beneficed clergy to fund the commons, and obviously had difficulty extracting money from the absentees and pluralists. Both Thompson and Towneley suggest that the very principle of the great tithes (of corn) was rejected by the commons. This may be all of a piece with the roughly contemporaneous refusal of the parishioners of Brigham (Cumberland) to pay any tithe corn at all except at their pleasure.[125] The erection of a *taxation populaire* on the clergy can be paralleled elsewhere.[126] It was not of itself anticlerical but, in common with the expressed distaste for absenteeism, reflects a belief that congregations rather than patrons should choose their clergy.

VI

Although these revolts throughout the North of England were all connected to Richmondshire in some way, they shared very little in the way of common ideology, except that in some cases the captains of the commons adopted the sobriquet of Captain Poverty or some similar form. This stands in opposition to Aske's branding of the movement as

---

[124] Above, pp. 42–3.
[125] SP1/117, fos. 54r, 46r; Harrison, *Pilgrimage of Grace in the Lake Counties*, p. 58.
[126] Below, pp. 437–9.

a 'pilgrimage'. Where we find movements led by Captain Poverty, we have insurrections which are distinctively of the commons and therefore in opposition to the gentry.

In some districts the first recorded disturbances were the restoration of monks to their suppressed houses. This appears to have taken place at Coverham, St Agatha's Easby (by Richmond), and at Sawley on about Thursday, 12 October; it may have happened at Conishead a few days later. The Captain Poverty letters urged the occupation of dissolved monasteries some days before Aske issued his order in favour of monastic houses. There appears to be little evidence to show that the individual monastic communities engineered their own return. It was on to these essentially localized disturbances that the Richmondshire revolt was overlaid.

Although it may have started as a rising in support of dispossessed monks, qualitatively the Richmondshire movement was quite different. It came to encompass a much larger area: it circulated letters and articles outlining its aims; it had a leadership of some kind which called for a convention of commons, doubtless to criticize royal policy; and it developed its own branding by identifying the movement with Poverty. The dynamism of the Richmondshire rebels, their circulation of articles, and the threats they made to adjacent districts subsumed these initial risings into a larger, though inchoate movement. In its heartland this movement was captured by the gentry, and the influence of the common's captains, who may have preached social revolution, was curbed; it was likewise, in the movement in the North Wolds and around Malton. As in the Lincolnshire movement, the gentry outmanoeuvred the common's petty captains by offering a superior leadership. Elsewhere the movements remained immature because they never acquired gentry leaders. The commons laid themselves open to manipulation because of their strong instinct to capture gentry and incorporate them into their leadership. Even in Cumberland sufficient social deference remained during the rebellion for Sir John Lowther and Sir Christopher Dacre to come and address the commons' host with a safe conduct.

The movements remained dislocated, and all ended by pursuing different grievances. In North Craven the movement came to focus on the defence of Sawley Abbey, in the barony of Kendal on grievances against landlords, in the Upper Eden Valley on landlords and clerical absenteeism, but in Cumberland itself on endemic violence and thieving. Richmond-shire, north Lancashire, and perhaps Dent too all reveal a revulsion against government policy, misrepresented through rumour. In some areas the influence of Aske and the Pilgrimage can be seen—his oath was used in east Lancashire by the Craven movement, for instance—but it seems unlikely that anyone in Cumberland or Westmorland knew of him or his Pilgrimage until quite late in the day.

Throughout we see the same solidarity of the 'commons' as we found in the relationship of Beverley to Lincoln.[127] When one area rose it was appropriate for the next to rise in sympathy, even if largely ignorant of the first's aims. Where a district had not risen, though, it was entirely appropriate to demand that it did so or risk spoilation. Likewise, discipline over neighbours (or gentry) could be enforced by the confiscation of goods or threats to burn gentry houses. Hence we see both the solidarity of the commons over large areas, and also their willingness to resort to violence against their neighbours to secure compliance and cohesion. And, in their ability to formulate grievances, have these circulated in the form of letters, and their willingness to convene representative assemblies (most fully documented from February 1537), we see a polit-ical organization which existed independently of the gentry. These people did not need an Aske or a Bowes to lead them: they, however, wished to offer leadership to bend the commons to their own aims which were, as we shall see, far from identical—were even, in truth, quite opposite.

---

[127] Above pp. 142–3.

9

Misunderstanding Darcy

On the night of Saturday, 11 November, three weeks after the fall of Pontefract Castle and most of a fortnight after the truce at Doncaster, men were seen mustering in woods near Snaith. There was an alarm, beacons were fired by the quiescent Pilgrims, and the countryside rose to repel an attack by the king's forces. In fact it was Sir Brian Hastings gathering his neighbours against a rumoured rustling of his cattle.[1] In the subsequent atmosphere of misunderstanding and recrimination Somerset Herald was sent to Temple Hirst to challenge Thomas, Lord Darcy about the Pilgrims' breach of the truce. For Darcy this was an opportunity to offer his own account of his actions. Repeatedly he declared his loyalty to the king. He had tried to take Aske but failed, he had defended Pontefract for as long as possible (even when his grandchildren were held hostage against him) without hope of relief, lacking so much as a walnutful of gunpowder with which to resist. Even though he had ultimately been forced to surrender the castle, he and his fellows had done the king 'as good a service as though we had been in his privy chamber'.[2]

---

[1] *LP* XI, nos. 1059, 1117. Hastings had previously lost cattle to Thomas Maunsell, probably to feed the commons at Pontefract. Ibid., no. 1402.

[2] Ibid., no. 1086, printed in full, Dodds, *Pilgrimage*, I, 301–3.

Darcy made similar claims on at least four other occasions. He said much the same to Percival Creswell, a servant of Hussey's who was sent to Temple Hirst with letters, and repeated the claim in the letter to Norfolk which Creswell carried back with him, dated 11 November.[3] Elsewhere, in the short valedictory note with which he concluded his Letter Book (where he collected the letters he received and sent during October), he again pleaded that the reader should believe his loyalty to the king. It was not his fault that he had been forced into surrender; he had been abandoned, left without the victuals, munitions, and money which he had requested but never received.[4] As late as 14 January 1537 he could write to Henry VIII that

death of body I would choose afore the life rather than your majesty should think or find in me that I should, by any former part or of my freewill unforced and sore compelled both for lack of all furnitures of war and by the extreme compulsion and fury of the commons, enter into their companies and great follies as I have learned by sundry reports that your grace was by divers informed against me.[5]

Darcy's letter to Henry comes from a time when he was pardoned (though he clearly knew that he was under suspicion, and claimed illness as a justification for declining the king's call to court). But Darcy had also been trying to convey his loyalty to the king even during the Pilgrimage, and so we have the strange sight of one of the Pilgrims' supposed leaders declaring that he was behaving under duress even as the movement unfolded.

Historians have tended to argue Darcy's guilt on a number of grounds: his known hostility to the regime; the evidence of the 'muster book' (to which we shall turn); his surrender of the castle; the mysterious appearance of the Pilgrims' badge; and his willingness to offer the Pilgrims at least some kind of leadership—grounds which, if taken together, seem convincing, but are individually slight.[6] Much less weight has been placed on the evidence of the surviving manuscripts from October and what Darcy said to justify his actions. As he arranged and preserved many of the first

---

[3] *LP* XII (i), no. 1013; XI, no. 1045.   [4] *LP* XI, no. 929.

[5] *LP* XII (i), no. 84, printed in *St. P.* I, 524–5.

[6] For his earlier advocacy of an armed rising against Henry, above, pp. 68–70; for the muster book, below, pp. 271–3; and for some speculative comments about the badges, below, pp. 416–17.

and was anxious to present himself in the best light in the second, this material is obviously self-serving. And although he certainly made some form of deposition whilst under arrest, we have neither that nor the ensuing cross-examination, both of which might have thrown up evidence to undermine his defence of his actions. We are bound to see the events of October, to an unsatisfactory degree, through the eyes of Darcy himself.

I

The outbreak of the rising in Lincolnshire found Darcy at his house of Temple Hirst, on the River Aire south of Selby. Writing to the king on Friday, 6 October, he reported that a correspondent in Lincolnshire had written to him on the previous Wednesday describing events in Louth and Caistor. He thought that the king was probably better informed about these happenings by Shrewsbury, Burgh, and Hussey. On the Wednesday evening, however, Sir Ralph Ellerker the younger had sent word that the rebels on the south bank of the Humber were burning beacons. Ellerker proposed to take this news to the king in person, but Darcy had urged him to stay, take charge of the situation in the East Riding, and stop the passage of men over the Humber.

Darcy's reaction was impeccably prompt. On Friday he sent letters in all directions alerting others to what he knew and warning of the dangers of the situation. His son Sir Arthur Darcy was sent to the earl of Shrewsbury with a letter of credence and instructions to inform him of the reports which Darcy was hearing of unsettled conditions in Yorkshire and 'North Humberland'. Sir Arthur also carried a letter from Darcy to the king, which it was clearly intended he would deliver in person. Sir Arthur, though, 'would be no messenger when the king shall need': having found the earl of Shrewsbury mustering at Worksop against Lincolnshire, he wrote to his father saying that he would attach himself to the earl and asked for his trussing bed and harness to be sent to him. Who took the letter on to the king is unrecorded. (On 8 October Darcy was asking Sir Arthur to return, 'haste, haste you to me in any wise for my debility considered and the premises and sequels, sure I am that my said Lord [Shrewsbury] will consider that ye being with me shall be a great aid'.[7]) A third letter went to the earl of Cumberland at Skipton, warning him of the reports Darcy had received of seditious conspiracies and oath-swearing in Dent, Sedbergh, and Wensleydale.[8] A fourth letter, which appears to contain the text of a standard form, was sent to Sir Thomas Metham informing him that Sir Arthur had gone to the king and calling on Metham to persuade the country around him to 'eschew to enter into the hasty follies that others be [al]ready assembled in' and to await Sir Arthur's return.[9]

The most significant of these letters was the one directed to the king. Like Darcy's other letters to Henry VIII, this one falls into two parts, the letter itself and the 'instructions', a checklist of requests on which the king was asked to act. In the letter Darcy outlined the reports from Lincolnshire and Ellerker and those of disturbances in Northumberland and Berwick (of which little more is known). He reported that all the king's subjects in the North and West Ridings were quiet except for those in the north-western Dales, about which he had already written to Cumberland. The instructions were more specific about this peripheral movement. The rebels had sworn oaths not to permit the depredation of abbeys nor the confiscation of parish church goods. They would not pay the king any more money (presumably to the subsidy). Within Yorkshire itself, 'by reason of the insurrections in Lincolnshire and Northumberland and the murmurs and bruits spread thereof over Yorkshire, diverse quarters leaneth much unto the same touching their churches and paying of money'. And so, having warned of trouble, Darcy requested that he be supplied with ordnance, artillery, and money. He wanted to know who the king would appoint as warden-general to raise, concentrate, and lead the king's forces against the insurrection. Darcy himself was going to move to Pontefract Castle, 'after the old custom specially in times of business for surety thereof', which was the 'best and most ready place to advance the king's service'. He advised that posts be established for the rapid traffic of news. And because of his own ill-health, he asked that Sir Arthur should return, equipped with the king's instructions, to aid his father.

[7] *LP* XI, no. 605. [8] Ibid., nos. 564, 604. [9] Discussed below pp. 267–8.

The move to Pontefract Castle finally proved to be a fatal error, although
it is hard to see what else Darcy could have done—or where else he
might have gone. It was, in the beginning, an eminently sensible step.
Pontefract was much better-located than was Temple Hirst. It was nearer
Darcy's 'rooms', the Duchy of Lancaster estates of which he was steward.
It was also a more cautious distance from Lincolnshire (although allowing access to Lincoln through Doncaster) and the trouble in the East
Riding which Darcy might have anticipated. And it was defensible. The
move also had a symbolic quality: he was following the precedent set by
his predecessors as stewards in time of war, and by moving his household there he declared his intention to mobilize.[10] There seems to be
little reason to doubt Darcy when he told the king that it was 'the best
and most ready place [from where] to advance the king's service'.[11]

It was at Pontefract that royal letters were received on either Saturday
or Sunday, 7–8 October, calling on the recipients to mobilize against
Lincolnshire and to link up with the earl of Shrewsbury at Nottingham.
Sir Brian Hastings went to Pontefract to collect his letter, and in a letter to Shrewsbury written on the following Wednesday said that he and
his retinue had intended to be at Nottingham on Thursday, but having
heard on the previous evening that the East Riding had risen, he sought
advice as to what he should do. Then he told Darcy that he would meet
him with 300 men whenever or wherever he appointed. Darcy's reply rather
suggests that he had not been called on to lend men to the campaign.[12]

Darcy then received—in quick succession—letters from the king
dated 8 and 9 October. The first was a circular letter written after the
receipt by the king of the letter from Louth, reporting that the rebels
there had sued for a pardon, and that they had risen through their mistaken belief of rumours concerning the king's intentions towards church
property and the subsidy. The letter was to be publicly read so 'our good
subjects may perceive the wretched and devilish intents of those false
traitors and rebels and by the same, like true men, whereof one man is
worth twenty thieves and traitors, take the better heart and courage for
their suppression and subduing'. The letter of 9 October was specifically
a reply to Darcy's letter and instructions. It thanked Darcy for his work

---

[10] *LP* XI, no. 706.   [11] Ibid., no 563 (ii).   [12] Ibid., nos. 646, 662, 664.

in keeping the district around him quiet, but it confidently predicted that the business in Northumberland would be repressed shortly and that the preparations being made for Lincolnshire would give the rebels there 'their deserves'. If Darcy heard any man talking of the suppression of abbeys, the taking away of church goods, or the imposition of new payments, he was to be summarily imprisoned. Likewise, Darcy was to arrest any rebels found fleeing from Lincolnshire when, as the king expected, the rebellion there broke up.

This letter was not received at Pontefract until Thursday, 12 October. Darcy replied on 13 October, by which time the king's hopes for Lincolnshire were not merely prophetic but realized. (Darcy, though, almost certainly was not aware of this until Saturday or Sunday.) He, on the contrary, had daily evidence that the Lincolnshire rising was spreading through Yorkshire. Hastings had written on the evening of 10 October with news that Howdenshire and the Marshland had risen and that the rebels were intending to go to York.[13] Pontefract was increasingly acting as a refugee camp for gentry and clergy out of the East Riding. And Darcy had received an eyewitness account of events between York and Beverley from William Maunsell, vicar of Brayton, who had been held by the rebels at Howden.[14] It was probably in the light of this evidence of the rebel's intentions that Darcy wrote to the mayor of York on 11 October, warning him to expect an attack from the south-east and urging him to place the city in a state of alert, suggesting that he call on the gentlemen of the Ainsty for aid.[15]

In the light of this deteriorating situation, the king's letter offered no aid at all. Writing on 13 October, Darcy was bleak about prospects in Yorkshire. The East Riding had risen on the Monday before. The commons of the shire leant towards the same opinions as those that had sparked rebellion in Lincolnshire. A great many had already risen and more would do so. There was no prospect of any gentlemen resident

[13] Ibid., no. 646.   [14] For Maunsell, see below pp. 274–6.

[15] The letter to York (*LP* XI, no. 627) is dated 9 October in the Letter Book text. Its reports of the rebels' movements must refer to their position a day or two later and it might be a reasonable conjecture that the clerk has misread xj for ix. This seems to be confirmed by the next letter in Darcy's Letter Book, to Sir Brian Hastings (ibid., no. 664), dated 11 October, in which much the same news is retailed and where the letter to York is referred to as though recently sent. The Ainsty was the rural wapentake to the SW of York which York administered.

locally repressing the rebels. Darcy had moved to Pontefract Castle, from where he was attempting to mobilize the countryside; but he had had no answer to his earlier requests for money, ordnance, and artillery, the laying of posts, or the appointment of a lieutenant. He thought that the rebels would be at Pontefract in two or three days, but he was not certain whether they would travel by York or move directly against him. The 'instructions' detailed at greater length the extent of the rebellion and commented on the state of Pontefract Castle: 'therein not one gun ready to shoot, powder none, arrows and bows few and evil, money none, gunners none, the well, the bridge with all houses of office and other things for the defence thereof, the most out of frame that can be.'[16]

In London and Windsor the receipt of Darcy's letter on 15 October shattered the court's self-congratulation that the rebellion was over. In successive letters to Cromwell, Wriothesley (who was with the king) was able to report the surrender of the Lincolnshire gentlemen to Suffolk and guess that, for lack of news, Holderness was quiet, but then, in the next, had to report Darcy's claim that Yorkshire was up and the rebels were moving in on Pontefract.[17] What was especially unfortunate was that, as Darcy's second letter was being carried to London, it crossed with one written by the king on 13 October in which Darcy was severely admonished and, in effect, relieved of control. Henry expressed his surprise that there was an insurrection in Holderness and Howdenshire and that it remained unsuppressed. He marvelled that Darcy had not only been 'enforced to flee' to Pontefract Castle with only twelve horses, but that he had failed to tell the king. And, referring to Darcy's ill-health, the king announced that he had written instructing a number of Yorkshire gentry to raise their forces, who were to be placed under the charge of Sir Arthur under the overall command of Darcy himself. The king clearly envisaged men being raised to fight the rebels, his letter combatively looking to a resolution of the conflict either by battle or abject submission.[18]

---

[16] LP XI, no. 692, 692 (ii).   [17] Ibid., nos. 722–3.

[18] The text of the letter to Sir Arthur outlining his instructions is lost, but the general contents can be inferred from the letter to Darcy and Darcy's following letter to Shrewsbury at Nottingham (LP XI nos. 687, 739) and ibid., no. 688 (1).

If the king replied to Darcy's letter of 13 October then the text is lost, possibly because it never reached Darcy to be incorporated into his Letter Book. There was a further letter sent to him, dated 17 October, in response to a desperate message from the mayor of York and Sir George Lawson, but this never reached Pontefract.[19] Darcy, though, replied to the king's letter of 13 October on 17 October, both justifying his actions but also offering yet more detailed 'instructions'.[20] In this letter he recalled that he had written to the king advising him of events in Holderness and Howdenshire; likewise he had told him of his intention to move to Pontefract, and having done so had been active in the king's best interests.

The instructions outlined the scale of the problem. The rising now included most of the North and West Ridings. The rebels numbered 60,000 men, of whom 20,000 had entered York. Because of their speed and violence they had taken many gentlemen in their own houses (and Darcy listed eleven or so): no gentlemen could resist, 'as all the whole commons do openly favour them that do rise'. No man could trust his tenants, and household servants openly said that they would not fight the rebels. The castle itself was inadequately victualled, and Darcy had neither money, ordnance, nor artillery. Neither Pontefract nor any of the neighbouring villages would sell them any food and, in any case, the commons were blockading the castle to prevent the movement of supplies into the garrison. Despite the king's letter, Darcy was sending Sir Arthur to the king to explain the seriousness of the situation: 'that we that be in the said castle be in danger within a few days either to be taken with them and yield or else to lose our lives.' And, in conclusion: 'that by all likelihood, no possibility is it to vanquish this power of the commons with any power levied here for the causes aforesaid.'[21] As Sir Arthur took this letter in person he was outside the castle when it fell, and so his loyalty remained unimpeached.

---

[19] The letter reveals the king's poor grasp of events in Yorkshire. Sir Arthur was to take 1,000 men to hold York until either the king or Shrewsbury arrived, leaving his father with 200 men at Pontefract. York, though, had already fallen. Darcy had nothing like 1,200 men available to him. *LP* XI, nos. 749–50.

[20] Ibid., nos. 687, 760.

[21] A long section of the draft letter (SP1/108, fo. 146r–v), excluded from the copy in the Letter Book, justified sending Sir Arthur.

The correspondence between the king and Darcy points to two conclusions. Darcy, from the first letter of 6 October, never disguised the scale of the problem and, particularly in his first letter, made a number of proposals which, if implemented, might have aided the repression of the rebellion. His complaint that he never had any reply to his requests is surely correct. Of the three letters he had from the king, the first was a general circular about Lincolnshire intended to be publicly read (although one may suppose that it would have inflamed rather than soothed matters), the third an ill-informed denunciation of Darcy's behaviour. Only the second addressed the problems, but even that, as Darcy commented, was not a 'total answer but a part of the same'. Whether all Darcy's requests were practical may be doubted: but his claim that 'I was neither answered directly to my letters and instructions, nor furnished nor succoured with nothing thereof. We were all in despair and reckoned verily that the king's grace never was truly advertised thereof nor privy to the answers . . .'[22] seems not unreasonable. Perhaps the mistake was Sir Arthur's. Having decided to attach himself to the earl of Shrewsbury, whoever took his father's letter to the king in his place may have failed to impress upon him the seriousness of the developing situation in Yorkshire.

Instead—and this brings us to the second point—Sir Arthur, like the king, was preoccupied with Lincolnshire and failed to anticipate that the rebellion would spread northwards over the Humber. Indeed, the instructions received at Pontefract on 7–8 October envisaged depleting Yorkshire of troops, who would be used to drive to Lincoln from the west. Lord Clifford, Sir Richard Tempest, and Sir Brian Hastings were all gathering troops to this end on about 9–11 October.[23] On 13 October Shrewsbury, Rutland, and Huntingdon wrote with news of the collapse of Lincolnshire, and offered the view that, once cut off from its roots, the Yorkshire movement would soon wither: but this assessment, whilst not unreasonable, did not allow for Aske.[24] Even on 17 October Henry could be sceptical of the seriousness of the situation in Yorkshire. The arrival of a letter from York changed his mind, but his reaction was to order Sir Arthur to proceed to defend York, leaving his father to remain

---

[22] SP1/110, fo. 46v (= *LP* XI, no. 729) (Letter Book, conclusion to the memorandum at the end).
[23] *LP* XI, nos. 662–3, 742 (misdated).   [24] Ibid., no. 694.

at Pontefract to undertake its defence.[25] It was only on the following day that the king completely accepted how bad conditions were, but then he told Wriothesley that he did not trust Darcy.[26]

Darcy was not abandoned because the king didn't trust him, though. Rather, Henry's failure to take Darcy's situation seriously was an aspect of his general neglect of Yorkshire and his concentration on Lincolnshire. It was not until 15 October that Darcy's advice to appoint a lieutenant in Yorkshire was taken. Even then the earl of Shrewsbury did not receive his commission until early on 17 October, when he was at Newark. He was hardly able to act as a focus to opposition within Yorkshire itself.

It was in his correspondence with Shrewsbury that Darcy explored his dilemma most fully. The earl wrote on 12 October saying that he heard that Darcy's neighbours were starting to rise like those in Lincolnshire. His advice was that Darcy should 'tarry there in your country to keep the same quiet there' and, through the channel of gentlemen, distribute a proclamation along the lines of one which Shrewsbury enclosed. On 15 October Darcy, Archbishop Lee, and others taking refuge at Pontefract wrote to the earl. The greater part of Yorkshire was up; 20,000 men were before York:

And, our good lord, after your advice, here we tarry. And if we should sparpill and depart, by our faith where to go to be in surety [safety] we know not. And twice I the said Lord Darcy with the assent of the others have written to the king's grace declaring truly the feebleness of this castle and for aid, money, ordnance, artillery, powder, and gunners, for here there be none, and of it none answer nor remedy therein. And without speedy succour or comfort from his grace or from you, herein we plainly reckon us all in extreme danger.[27]

As he believed that 'policy' had done as much as it could, Darcy looked for a military end to the rebellion, but, as he constantly stressed, he was without the means to defend 'the most simple furnished [castle] that ever I think any was to defend'.[28] The next letter from Newark, written on 17 October, marked the beginning of the endgame. Shrewsbury was named lieutenant, but he, Rutland, and Huntingdon were also instructed to hold their position at Newark until the Lincolnshire rising was definitely over.[29]

---

[25] Ibid., no. 748.   [26] Ibid., no. 768.   [27] Ibid., no. 729.
[28] Ibid., no. 739.   [29] Ibid., no. 757.

There is no reply to this letter. On the following day Shrewsbury reported to the duke of Suffolk that it was impossible to deliver letters to Pontefract because of the blockade about the castle. In reality the letter of 17 October marked the end of Darcy's hope that he could hold the castle until relief arrived. The evidence, though, which is drawn both from his account and also Aske's recollections, is that he did not give in easily, and managed to string out the siege until the morning of 21 October.

II

It is too easy to hear Darcy's repeated requests for military aid (and his complaints at its failure to arrive) as an excuse for inactivity. This would be an unjustified slur. A more serious impediment than the lack of money and munitions was the lack of authority. Darcy felt himself hamstrung both by this and the failure of the king to name a lieutenant to co-ordinate opposition. He refers to this on a number of occasions, most notably in a letter of 14 October to Sir Richard Tempest. Tempest and the first earl of Cumberland were apparently devising a plan to muster troops to proceed against the rebels (either those of Hexham or Wensleydale, rather than the rising tide of the East Riding), and Tempest asked whether Darcy would be willing to join them.[30] Darcy replied:

Cousin, if my said lord and ye when ye be together have authority to assemble the king's subjects, I am here ready in your way to accompany and join with you to serve the king or his lieutenant as shall stand with his grace's pleasure and commandment with my sons and such company of my rooms and friends as I may make. Albeit as yet I have no authority nor command from the king to raise any number of his subjects.[31]

If Darcy did not feel at liberty to raise troops, he could still try to maintain order through persuasion and propaganda ('policy'), and could

[30] I infer that the rebels were those in Wensleydale, as the letter, as it is placed in the Letter Book, clearly relates to the letter Scrope sent to Cumberland on 12 October (ibid., no. 677), a copy of which was sent to Darcy by Tempest when he wrote on 13 October to invite his participation in an expedition (ibid., no. 695). Darcy, though, referred to the earl attempting to go to Hexham and being beaten back on 17 October (ibid., 760 (ii)).

[31] SP1/110, fo. 36v (= LP XI, no. 695 (ii)).

put men on standby to form an army when the appropriate authority was received. His correspondence shows him to have been active in both respects, although all his efforts finally counted for nought.

The first form of policy was propaganda. There was general agreement that accurate information acted as an antidote to seditious reports, the more so as it was acknowledged that what inflamed the commons were inaccurate rumours about royal intentions.[32] So, as we saw earlier, Henry VIII sent Darcy a circular letter on 8 October which was designed to be read publicly. Whilst repudiating the rumours, it was also drafted in inflammatory terms and, by denouncing the Lincolnshire men as traitors, would hardly have appealed to the large numbers in Yorkshire demonstrating their solidarity with those further south. Darcy's own attempts at policy had begun earlier than this and owed nothing to the royal initiative. Writing to Henry on 6 October, he explained that he had requested Sir Ralph Ellerker the younger to stay around Hull and Beverley, 'to tarry and stay your subjects of the East Riding about him, both from passing over the water of Humber into Lincolnshire and also from bruits and murmurs'.[33] Darcy's letter to Sir Thomas Metham of the same date appears to be a specimen of a more general call for calm and patience. As this letter has been read as sinister, it is worth quoting in full. It is dated at Temple Hirst and was sent 'unsealed for haste':

This shall be to advertise you that this day I have sent in post my son Sir Arthur Darcy to the kings grace by whom I doubt not to have at his return good and comfortable answers from the king's grace for me and all his true and faithful subjects concerning the reasonable griefs that they grudge with. Wherefore cousin, in all the countries and quarters nigh to you, desire ye and persuade all your loving neighbours and mine to beware and eschew to enter into hasty follies that others be already assembled in, and for a season to tarry for the return of Sir Arthur and make them fast shall be so [for] their great commodities, for I would of faith that ye and they should do no worse that I would myself. And thus our lord be all our governors.[34]

---

[32] See above pp. 88–92 (including the view of the commons at Pontefract, reported by Lancaster Herald).

[33] *LP* XI, no. 563.

[34] SP1/110, fo. 48v (= *LP* XI, no. 566). Smith thought that it announced the abortion of a planned plot because the earl of Shrewsbury had started to move against Lincolnshire. It seems unlikely that Darcy knew that when the letter was sent. Smith, *Land and Politics*, 181–2.

The aim of the letter was to play for time: its ambiguity was deliberately contrived. Sir Arthur had gone to the king to get 'good and comfortable answers . . . concerning the reasonable griefs that they grudge at'. Darcy expresses his sympathy with the rebels' complaints, even though he doubtless knew that the rumours which had provoked them were untrue. People should be dissuaded from joining in the 'hasty follies' that others were already engaged in, but should wait for the return of Sir Arthur. What had Sir Arthur gone off to see the king for? Not to seek concessions, as this might suggest, but with a shopping-list of requirements necessary to prosecute an active war against anyone foolish enough to rebel. Everyone should act like Darcy. What did he do? He went to Pontefract Castle, the symbolism of which has already been commented on. What he did not do was declare himself unilaterally against the rebels. If he had, then the immediate hostility he would have brought against himself would doubtless have clarified the historian's attitude to him, but at the cost (if the Lincolnshire parallels are recalled) of his losing whatever power of persuasion he might have possessed over the rebels. And the point must be made that this letter is not a specimen of private correspondence, but a letter to be shown and read to those whose loyalty to the Crown was wavering in the face of the feverish and exciting news coming from Lincolnshire.

This suggests that Darcy's 'policy' may have been based on a call for calm until Sir Arthur had reported back from the king, rather than a straight denial of the rumours of confiscation which were then circulating. As suggested above, the flaw in this strategy may have been that Sir Arthur allowed himself to be diverted by the thrill of mobilizing with the earl of Shrewsbury rather than proceeding southwards. Writing to Sir Arthur on 8 October, Darcy asked him to tell Shrewsbury that the 'best ways that hitherto I have found to stay the counties is by such persuasions of wisdom and letters as I do send herein a copy unto you that I have sent forth'.[35] But he had also given instructions that all assemblies of the king's subjects (including court leets) should be cancelled. On 12 October Shrewsbury was advising Darcy to use policy against the rebels by calling 'unto you some worshipful gentlemen thereabouts doo [to]

[35] *LP* XI, no. 605.

declare unto the king's true subjects a proclamation to be made in your name and the said gentlemen's', and he enclosed one which would suffice. On the following day a copy of the proclamation used in Lincolnshire was forwarded, with a testimonial as to its efficiency there. But by this time Darcy had come to recognize that the time for policy had passed. Writing to the king on 13 October, and complaining of his failure to provide direction, Darcy explained how, 'for the meantime I shall do the best I can for want of power to use policy as of late I have done, with many persuasions for the appeasing and keeping down the people and commons of this country, which by that that I see will take no further effect'.[36] On 16 October he did claim some success in a letter to Shrewsbury: 'My lords, we that be here have done our best policies whereby fourteen days they for most part have been stayed by polices and per- suasions to now, or else they had been [al]ready joined to the commons of Lincolnshire before this time.'[37] This contains a striking echo of the claim of the gentry at Lincoln, that without their persuasions the rebels would have been at Huntingdon.[38] It is impossible to gauge how suc- cessful policy was in inhibiting the rebellion. It is probably fair to say that it slowed the speed with which the countryside rose, but what it failed to do was provide Darcy with a solid body of support.

This leads to the second area of activity which it is possible to dis- cern in the correspondence. Again, when he was vindicating his actions to the king Darcy explained that, after he had gone to Pontefract, he had begun to assemble 'your subjects, the gentleman of [the honour of Pontefract], to try and know what number of men they could make and put in arrediness either forthwith or upon a certain time or an hour warning limited unto them'.[39] He was active in this way as early as 11 October, when he told Sir Brian Hastings that 'I have and am putting all my friends [and gentlemen] within my room and others in arrediness with their household servants to serve the king's grace upon an hour warning'. He would 'warn and stir them and all other good fel- lows within my rooms' only when he knew the king's pleasure 'for mine and your discharges'.[40] And he was able to tell Shrewsbury of these same arrangements on 15 October.[41]

---

[36] SP1/110, fo. 40v (= *LP* XI, no. 692). [37] Ibid., fo. 44v (= *LP* XI, no. 739).
[38] Above p. 151. [39] *LP* XI, no. 760. [40] Ibid., no. 664. [41] Ibid., no. 729.

It has to be questioned, however, what these arrangements actually amounted to. Writing to the king on 13 October, Darcy reported that he had gone to Pontefract, from where he was calling his fellows, friends, and kinsfolk; but only a few lines before he had lamented that not only were there a great number of men in arms, but 'for the repressing of the same, there is no nobleman or gentleman in these parts that can, as they affirm and have tried amongst their tenants, put any trust to your commons but only their household servants'.[42] Four days later, and again to the king, he complained 'that the cause why no resistance hath been made or can be made against them is for so much as all the whole commons openly favour them that do rise. And many of them come to them on their own courage so that no man dare trust his tenants and scarce we may trust our household servants, they said plainly they will not fight against them'.[43] That Darcy discovered that the normal reciprocal bonds between landlord and tenants had evaporated comes as no surprise in the light of the accounts we reviewed earlier, in which landlords were seen being captured by their tenants or bodies of the commons and were then, by a process of inversion, expected to lead their tenants on behalf of the larger movement. It needs to be stressed that Darcy was not alone in this. Sir Brian Hastings, whom Elton commended for his 'determined' loyalty to the king,[44] promised Darcy the use of 300 men on 10 October. A week later he wrote that 'there is no one that I dare trust but my own friends that are about me'.[45] So it was not possible to raise a tenant army to oppose the rebels in Yorkshire, and household servants also refused to fight against them.

In this light it also seems likely that Darcy was prone to talk up his ability to offer significant opposition when (or if) the king's commission of lieutenancy arrived. He told Shrewsbury and the other peers at Nottingham on 15 October that the castle contained a number of his 'fellows and friends' (enumerated in a bill we shall discuss later), with certain of their household servants, but that in addition he had a great number of gentlemen ready on an hour's warning to attend

---

[42] Ibid., no. 692.   [43] Ibid., no. 760 (ii).

[44] Elton, 'Politics and the Pilgrimage of Grace', 192.   [45] LP XI, nos. 646 [= 663(2)], 759.

with their household servants (not tenants) on either Darcy or the much-longed-for lieutenant.[46] But there are powerful grounds for doubting the very existence of this pool of individuals. Here we may review the evidence of the so-called 'muster book'. Because of its alleged date (1 October), this has been regarded as amongst the most incriminating evidence against Darcy. It has, though, never been subjected to the critical assessment that it deserves, either with regard to its date or contents. And, in truth, the evidence it contains reveals, not how Darcy was anticipating launching a rebellion at the beginning of October, but how dire his situation was in the *middle* of the month.

In form it is a paper book. On the first page it bears a title (in Darcy's own hand), then, page by page and wapentake by wapentake, a listing of gentlemen. At the end is a further list of four names. There are no totals. We may begin with the date. This was read by the compilers of *Letters and Papers* as 1 October 1536. Examination of the original manuscript shows that the single digit which they read as 'one' (first) has a line drawn over it indicating an abbreviation. Comparison with other examples of Darcy's hand shows without doubt that what he intended was not 'first October' but 'In October'.[47] Then the title, 'the names of knights, esquires, and gentlemen and their numbers of household servants promised to serve the king's grace in the company and at the leading of Thomas, Lord Darcy or his deputy, as he appoints, upon an hour's warning', clearly echoes Darcy's accounts of his activities around 11–15 October. Notice that the title refers to the number of household servants *and not tenants* which individuals could make (as in the letter to the earl of Shrewsbury of 15 October cited before). And these men were to serve the king, either under the leadership of Darcy or under such deputy as the *king* appoints, at an hour's notice: again, reflecting the preoccupation in the letters.

The muster book provides as concrete evidence of how Darcy's and the gentry's authority had disintegrated as we are likely to find. The book was drawn up by a clerk, who wrote the names of gentry down the

---

[46] Ibid., no. 729.

[47] SP1/106, fo. 234r. Anyone doubting this may wish to compare the same digit with the abbreviation four lines down in the title-page, where it reads '*in* the company of . . .'.

left-hand side of each page. It then appears from the variety of hands that the gentry themselves wrote how many men they could supply against their names. And so the appearance is that, as they came to Pontefract to be briefed and have their support solicited, they filled in the book with a declaration of how much (or how little) they could do. The muster book contains headings for seven wapentakes in the centre and south of the West Riding. One is a heading alone (Knaresborough, actually an honour rather than an wapentake, of which Darcy was steward). The other six name sixty-four gentry (excluding a handful marked 'pauper'). Of the sixty-four, roughly a third made no return—presumably they were not, or could not be, contacted. The remaining forty-four individuals could raise, in all, 130 men. Of these, sixty-one or sixty-two came from four individuals, Sir Henry Everingham (twenty-three), Sir Robert Neville (ten), Henry Rither esq. (twenty), and Sir John Wentworth (either six or seven). The remainder came in one and twos, and, in truth, many were not household servants but the gentry themselves. Entries on the lines of 'myself and one' are typical. A few individuals seem to have reduced the number of men they could offer. Charles Barneby offered ten, but this figure was cancelled and replaced by 'one of my sons or myself and one more'.

A final page of the muster book shows that Darcy had access to other forces. Here, under a heading which identifies those named as friends, suggesting that they were co-equals with Darcy rather than supporters, he listed four names, including Sir William Gascoigne the elder, who could raise 100 men, and Richard Redman (or Redmayne), who offered twenty-four. (Strangely both men came from Harewood near Otley.) In all, this supplementary list offers 130 men, making the whole force promised Darcy to be 260 men. This was a thin haul, and hardly sufficient to resist the several thousand rebels congregating around York. But where were these men? The title suggests that they were awaiting the call to travel to Pontefract, but there is evidence to suggest that by 15 October they were actually in the castle itself as either (depending on perspective) a garrison or as refugees. Talking to Somerset Herald on 14 November, Darcy complained that he had kept 260 men in the castle for fourteen days at his own charge. The coincidence in numbers between the muster book and this figure might be no more than that. Darcy, though, supplied Shrewsbury on 15 October with a list of names 'of them that be warded within the Castle'.[48] This list includes a number of people not in the muster book, including Sir George and Sir Arthur Darcy, Sir Robert Constable, and the lawyer William Babthorpe. It omits some others known to have been sheltering in there, including Archbishop Lee and Thomas Magnus (both signatories to the letter which the list accompanied), probably because they were of no military value. But the list contains Everingham, Neville, Rither, and Wentworth, the major contributors to the muster book, and, frustratingly, it then adds that there were, in addition, a further forty gentlemen in the castle. That this is approximately the number of persons who had made pledges of aid in the muster book is surely one coincidence too many.

So the muster book is not at all the document we have been led to suppose. It dates from the days around 15 October, when it had become clear that no significant number of tenants could be raised, when Pontefract had become a gathering-point for gentlemen (whose capacity to influence the turn of events had almost entirely vanished) and a small number of trusted household servants. The 260 was not the whole number of people within the castle.[49] It makes no allowance for Darcy's own household or for whatever contingents Sir George and Sir Arthur and the others of independent standing could make. But the implication of the list is that Darcy's claim that there were others in the locality who could be called out when word finally came from the king was a delusion. Darcy's friends and supporters, the men who were claimed to be mustering and priming to move at a moment's notice, were mostly sheltering in the castle and helpless.

III

When setting down his recollections of the Pilgrimage, Archbishop Lee described how: 'When word came to me in a letter from Southwell and

---

[48] *LP* XI, app. no. 11, referred to in ibid., no. 729: 'and herein be other our fellows and friends with certain of their household servants as be named in a bill here enclosed'. The Dodds read this—inexplicably—as a list of persons who met with Aske on 19 October, Dodds, *Pilgrimage*, I, 186, and were followed by Smith, *Land and Politics*, 192.

[49] Lee recalled that he had brought 30 servants with him and that the whole number of people within the castle was about 300 (although not there all at once). SP1/119, fo. 3r–v (= *LP* XII (i), no. 1022).

also by a servant of mine from my lord steward [Shrewsbury] and I suppose to my lord Darcy also that my said lord would with [a] few days
come to Pontefract Castle, the said Lord Darcy seemed very glad to hear
of his coming and afterwards seemed also sorry that he came not.' Lee
seems not to have had Darcy's confidence. Indeed, one of the points of
tension between them, as Lee himself reported, was that Darcy 'would
say that all the grudge the commons had against him [Darcy] and the
castle was for Mr Magnus and me'. Lee also records—without detail—
that Darcy 'practised with the rebels to know what they intended. And
sometime he would say that he trusted to compass that the commons
would pass by and no[t] meddle with the castle.'[50] This, it appears, is
just what Darcy tried to do. He encouraged the rising around Pontefract
and the siege of the castle in the hope that, by doing so, he could avoid
its surrender and might remain as an isolated and impotent garrison behind
the rebels' lines. The success of the strategy depended, of course, on persuading everyone that he and those who executed it on his orders had
thrown in their lot with the rebels. The disadvantage was inevitably that
observers saw that Darcy was engaged in treasonable activity.

   The chief source for Darcy's last throw of the dice was the executant
of the policy, Thomas Maunsell, vicar of Brayton near Selby. Maunsell
was quickly identified as one of the rebels' activists; he was specifically
omitted from the terms of the royal pardons, although he survived, remaining as vicar of Brayton until his death in 1555. It seems that he was well
known to the Darcy family because he was a local man. His brother,
William Maunsell, was a lawyer in Cromwell's circle who served as clerk
of the county court and under-sheriff and, by 1537, was a gentleman
usher of the chamber.[51] Thomas Maunsell has not been well served by
modern writers. The editors of Letters and Papers mangled his deposition.[52] The Dodds did him a great disservice by stating that 'the vicar
of Brayton is not a very reliable witness. There is no proof that the
earlier part of his evidence is false . . .'. R. B. Smith reduced the

---

[50] Ibid., fo. 4v (= LP XII (i), no. 1022).
[51] For William Maunsell, English and Barr, 'The Records Formerly in St Mary's Tower',
373–4.
[52] LP XI, no. 1402. The following discussion is based on a reading of the MS (SP1/113, fos. 54r–56v),
which is cited subsequently. Maunsell also incorporated a systematic error in the dating of events.

deposition to its most salient and incriminating points.[53] But Maunsell's account makes excellent sense as a further attempt by Darcy to rescue something from an impossibly weak situation.

Maunsell's story was that on Tuesday, 10 October he was travelling to Cotness near Howden to collect a debt. At Howden he was taken by the commons and held there until the following morning as a suspected spy sent by Sir George Darcy. He was sworn and released on condition that he attended the muster on Skipwith Moor. Maunsell then travelled back to Sir George Darcy (whose house was at Gateford in Brayton parish) to tell him what he had witnessed, and Sir George sent him on to his father. Maunsell offered to stay with Darcy at Pontefract, but Darcy insisted that he should go to the Skipwith Moor muster and return with an account of what happened there.

Maunsell went to the muster on Wednesday, where the 'commons had him in great mistrust and would have smitten off his head'. On leaving the muster his first instinct was to write to his brother and Leonard Beckwith, telling them to 'provide for themselves as they love their lives'. He then returned to Pontefract to tell Darcy that the commons intended to come over 'the water' (that is, strike west and south-west over the River Ouse) to the archbishop's house at Cawood and Darcy's at Temple Hirst. On hearing this Darcy instructed Maunsell to go back to Brayton. If the commons did look likely to cross the Ouse, then Sir Thomas was to raise all the people in Darcy's 'rooms'[54] to be in readiness,

that the commons might perceive them to be in readiness to go with them so that by policy thereof the commons should not come over the water. And the said Sir Thomas did say to the said Lord Darcy that and if he would send his own men out of the castle, it would cause them to raise the sooner. And so the said Lord Darcy did promise saying to the said Sir Thomas if he would do his commandment he should do the king's highness as good service as ever did any priest.[55]

---

[53] Dodds, *Pilgrimage of Grace*, I, 190; Smith, *Land and Politics*, 183–4.

[54] 'His rooms' are the manors under his control as steward. Darcy was steward of the Duchy of Lancaster's honour of Pontefract and of the estates of Pontefract Priory and Selby Abbey (Smith, *Land and Politics*, 67), and was therefore the dominant figure in the area to the east of Pontefract between the rivers Aire and Ouse.

[55] SP1/113, fo. 54r–v.

Maunsell then returned home. On Friday a party of twenty-four commons came to Brayton, where they rang the bells and raised the town. Maunsell promised them that he would raise all the towns in Lord Darcy's stewardships and then conveyed the commons back over the Ouse. He then spent Friday and Saturday spreading the rising. On Sunday afternoon he was visited by twenty of the commons conveying an instruction from Aske to lead his company to rendezvous with him at York. Maunsell played for time by saying his band of commons was too small and that he would come when it was bigger, whilst sending word to Darcy to ask what he should do. Darcy told him (through his steward, Thomas Strangeways) to proceed towards York but to go no further than Bilbrough, 4 miles short of the city itself on the road from Tadcaster, and this he did on Monday. There he heard that his brother William had refused the oath and was in some danger. Sir Thomas then rode into York, found Aske and obtained his permission to administer the oath to his brother, went to William (who would have nothing to do with him), then returned to Aske and told him that he had sworn William. He then rode back to his company at Bilbrough.

It was at Bilbrough (and, we must assume, at some time during Monday evening) that he encountered Thomas Strangeways and Gilbert Scott, going on Darcy's instruction to meet with Aske at York. (This meeting will be described below.) They told him (and we must assume that these were Darcy's instructions) to leave his company at Bilbrough, to return to Pontefract, and to raise Pontefract, Wakefield, and Doncaster. On the Tuesday morning Maunsell told the mayor of Pontefract to raise the town, and received a letter from Darcy telling him to do the same in Wakefield and the villages between Doncaster and Pontefract. This he did over Tuesday and Wednesday.

Darcy's strategy was to persuade the commons that they had no need to visit Pontefract because the area had already risen in their support. But half-measures were intended. Maunsell went around to have Darcy's men on alert (in 'areadyness') rather than have them mustered by members of the commons coming from abroad. Maunsell was to go towards York, but not to the city itself. Then, during Monday, something changed. It may have been the fall of York, or perhaps the receipt of further letters from the king urging an impractical line of action.

Whatever it was, Maunsell was told to bring out a larger area which was not immediately threatened by penetration by the commons. At the same moment Darcy sent his steward, Strangeways, to York to make contact with Aske and the Pilgrims.

Given the delicacy and danger of this mission, Strangeways was provided with written instructions, which survive. He was to go to York to get copies of the rebels' articles and their oaths and bring them back to Pontefract. He was to ascertain their numbers and report which gentlemen were in their company. And, most significantly, 'if he met any sure friend, [he was] to get them to move the captain [Aske] and commons to pass by Pontefract Castle or else delay their coming. This to give time for succour to arrive.'[56]

On Strangeway's own account, he found Aske with others at Sir George Lawson's house. He declared his message, but those who were there treated him with suspicion, telling him that they took him for a spy sent to establish their strength. Strangeways retired to his lodgings, where Christopher Monkton and Gervais Cawood brought him a copy of the Lincolnshire 'oath' and advised him—for his own safety—to leave York promptly, which he did. Aske's account, though, disagrees with Strangeways's in one important detail. He says that Strangeways came to 'know the cause of their assembly and whether they would agree to a head captain if the articles pleased him'.[57] The implications of this are tremendous. It surely points to Darcy offering to lead the Pilgrims if he could agree with their aims. Did Darcy, though, ever order Strangeways to make such an overture? Darcy's behaviour in the following few days scarcely suggests that this was his ambition. The proposal is contrary to the hope that Strangeways could find someone of influence who could divert the Pilgrims away from Pontefract. As there appears to be no further evidence to bear on the matter, it is impossible to be certain one way or another, and it may perhaps be that here, as in another incident a few days later, Strangeways was capable of taking an independent line.

Aske set out for Pontefract on Wednesday, 18 October, apparently after some dissension amongst the East Riding gentry who had been his companions over the previous week. He had with him only 300 men.[58] Aske

---

[56] *LP* XI, no. 762 (ii).   [57] *LP* XII (i), no. 852 (iii).   [58] Stapleton, 103.

was plainly well informed about the state of the castle. In 'The manner of the taking of Robert Aske' he says explicitly that the serving-men in the castle favoured him.[59] His informant may have been Strangeways; it may also have been Maunsell, for, in a later deposition, Aske claimed that Maunsell had told him (one must imagine on the Wednesday) that Pontefract had risen, and that if Aske went there the castle would soon surrender.[60] There is absolutely no evidence that Darcy masterminded this contact nor that Strangeways was acting with his approval when he told Maunsell how the castle might be entered if it were not surrendered. (He was to gather all the ladders in the town, together with several loads of whins and bracken, lay the whole at the foot of the castle gates, and burn them down.[61]) It is possible that Maunsell and Strangeways should be counted amongst the unreliable serving-men. It would also seem that the garrison was leaking away: Lee says that of the 300 men who had been in the castle, only 140 remained, 'and not all sound, but some inclining towards the commons'.[62]

So Aske was probably forewarned of what he would find at Pontefract. This, doubtless, persuaded him to risk travelling there in advance of the main body of the Pilgrims with only a relatively small force. But this pre-emptory act also suggests that he was trying to force the pace and oblige the other captains to advance beyond York. Once at Pontefract on Thursday he had Maunsell and William Acclom carry a letter into the castle demanding an immediate surrender. If this was rejected, then he promised that he would assault the castle the same evening. He also took the opportunity to outline the Pilgrims' grievances. The besieged asked that Aske himself enter the castle to speak with them. Pledges were exchanged, Sir George Darcy's eldest son being surrendered to the rebels.

The scene within the castle was almost comic, and reveals painfully how unwilling either Darcy or Lee were to deal with Aske. Aske came before them and announced 'the assembly of the commons to be for the reformation of many things that were amiss'.[63] According to his own account of his speech, he blamed the lords spiritual for failing to tell the

---

[59] 'The manner of the taking of Robert Aske', 336.

[60] Ibid. 336; *LP* XII (i), no. 852 (iii). Maunsell's own deposition makes no mention of this contact and, by the way it is framed, rather argues against it.

[61] SP1/113, fo. 55v (and omitted in *LP* XI, no. 1402).

[62] SP1/119, fo. 4v (= *LP* XI, no. 1022).   [63] Ibid.

king of the spread of heresy, and the lords temporal for hiding from him the poverty of the realm. Both were negligent. The Pilgrims had come there to induce those trapped in the castle to join them in their holy pilgrimage, but if they would not, then they would find the commons to be people without mercy. Finally he required them to surrender the castle to him.

Darcy then invited the archbishop to speak on behalf of those present. Lee politely demurred, pointing out that the castle was Darcy's charge, so forcing him to lead. Darcy told Aske that he would not deliver the castle to him, but added that as for the demand that they should join the Pilgrims, they would confer about that. If he had artillery with which to defend the castle, then Aske would have been granted neither demand. Lee then requested to be told what Aske expected him to do. Aske answered that he and Darcy were to be mediators to the king for the Pilgrims' requests and counsellors to their movement. Lee pointed out the impossibility of being both, told Aske that the only counsel he would give him was that the enterprise was unlawful, and said that if Aske would give him a safe conduct he would go amongst the commons and declare to them what he thought of their enterprise. He ended by telling Aske that whilst he could have his body, he would never have his heart in their cause.[64]

Having made his point, Aske withdrew. Darcy offered £20 for a truce until 9 a.m. on Friday morning. Aske would only allow him until 7 a.m. There was some discussion in the castle that evening as to what to do. There was patently no stomach for a siege. As Lee said, 'it was thought . . . that if any of the castle should annoy any of the commons, that none of us should escape with our lives if they took the castle'. He thought that they only had food for eight or ten days.[65] On the Friday morning Darcy requested that Aske extend the truce. Aske, perhaps knowing that the earl of Shrewsbury was at hand, would allow them no longer. As Darcy told Somerset Herald: 'I . . . being an old man of war and knowing the feats thereof, perceiving myself in that danger and could escape no otherwise with my life, for safeguard of the same did yield myself, and I promise you that if I had not wrought politically, it had cost me

[64] *LP* XII (i), no. 1022.
[65] SP1/119, fo. 4v (= *LP* XII (i), no. 1022, said in the context of a discussion of the castle's options before the arrival of Aske).

my life.'[66] That morning Aske entered the castle and swore its remaining defenders. The fall of the castle was not unexpected amongst those observing from a distance, for instance, Sir Brian Hastings, and Darcy had removed any element of surprise by warning of its inevitability if he was not relieved. The question, though, is whether Darcy was, from the beginning, the rebels' friend.

Two witnesses report that when he heard of the rising in Lincolnshire he was jubilant: 'Ah, they are up in Lincolnshire. God speed them well! I would they had done this three years past, for the world should have been better than it is.'[67] This sounds authentic. We have already seen how Darcy had convictions at odds with those which prevailed in 1536. And this was appreciated and understood by others. Shrewsbury is supposed to have withdrawn his trust in Darcy when Sir Arthur told him (on about the 6 or 7 October) that his father could raise 5,000 men 'if the abbeys stood'.[68] It sounds, of course, like Darcy pressing his own agenda, of making success contingent upon the achievement of his own political aims; but he may also have been right. There this little sign that Darcy held back in prosecuting the rebels within the considerable restraints under which he felt he was placed. He was, as we saw, desperate for some authority to muster men, and whilst it could be argued that he should simply have proceeded regardless, unlicensed mustering would surely have been regarded by contemporaries as suspicious. Was he mustering for the king or, as his previous record of political opposition to the regime would suggest, against him? This may well be the same quandary that Hussey laboured under at Sleaford: that if he mobilized it would be assumed that he was against the king, but that if he dithered, exactly the same assumption would be made. There is a clear contrast between those who merely set about raising troops, confident that their actions would not be impeached (Shrewsbury, Cumberland, Derby) and those, like Darcy, who wanted written authority before they would do so.

Strangely, the witness who was most emphatic that Darcy could not have held the castle for long was Aske. We have already seen how he

---

[66] Dodds, *Pilgrimage*, I, 302.   [67] *LP* XII (i), no. 1087, p. 497; also no. 1200.
[68] Ibid., no. 783.

was confident that the serving-men in the castle would have supported him. Pressed on the matter after his arrest, his opinion was that Darcy could have shut the gates but would not have held the castle for long, because his own gentlemen and servants would have mutinied. 'And surely it had been but death by the commons to the Lord Darcy if he had done so.'[69] His predicament was indeed severe, and this seems to have been appreciated at the time. Whilst the surviving letters contain little comment on the fall of Pontefract, it seems not to have been held against him.[70] He was, for instance, not excluded from the pardons prepared in early November and again in December. As we shall see, what did form people's opinions of his actions was his refusal to defect to the royal forces at the first Doncaster conference (which drew the comment from Norfolk, 'Fye! Fye! upon the Lord Darcy, the most arrant traitor that was ever living and both his sons true knights'[71]), and his adamant rejection of the proposal put to him in November that he should betray Robert Aske. (He also suffered a poisonous whispering campaign against him in early 1537.[72]) But Darcy also recognized that he had a credibility problem. His request in early November, made several times to Somerset Herald, was that he should be 'indifferently heard'. He believed, perhaps wrongly, that he had been surrendered up to the rebels because the king was either unaware of his real situation or was being poisoned against him by Cromwell. This may not have been so, but Darcy doubtless had some long days in which to ponder why his letters had not been acted upon. Hence he wished to convey his side of events to the king through men he trusted (and here he named Sir Francis Bryan and Sir John Russell).[73] In January 1537 he sent a book to the king which he asked might be scrutinized by some of the council, believing it would vindicate him.[74] There is no stronger contrast in the new year than the ebullient Aske believing that the king had taken his advice to secure a political reformation, and Darcy, still trying to persuade those who would listen that he had been the king's true servant throughout.

---

[69] Ibid., no. 946, answ. to Q. 117.

[70] After all, Norfolk's patent inability to hold the rebels at Doncaster by military means placed Darcy's efforts in a better light.

[71] *LP* XI, no. 909 (29 Oct. 1536).   [72] e.g. *LP* XII (i), no. 281.

[73] Dodds, *Pilgrimage of Grace*, I, 305.   [74] *LP* XII (i), no. 84.

The Confrontation
at Doncaster

We have already seen how, in the first week of October, the king's policy was one of containment to prevent the movement of the Lincolnshire rebels either southwards towards Stamford, Peterborough, and ultimately London, or westwards, over the Trent and into the east Midlands. Whilst this was being done, the Crown paid little attention to the few reports coming out of Yorkshire. It was Darcy's contention—made with some justice—that little heed was paid to his advice. It was not until the receipt of his letter of 13 October on the 15th that the gravity of the situation in Yorkshire began to dawn on the government.[1] But it was only with the receipt of a further letter from the city of York on 17 October that there was a general realization that the contagion had travelled northwards over the Humber, and that the great rejoicing and congratulation in London and Windsor when news of Lincolnshire's submission had been received was, at best, premature.[2] Even then, the royal instructions were hopelessly unrealistic. On 15 October the earl of Shrewsbury was ordered to repress the rebels in Yorkshire when he was

[1] Darcy's letter is *LP* XI, no. 692: for the reaction to it, see nos. 716, 723.

[2] The York letter is ibid., no. 704, and for reactions, nos. 748–50. On 15 October Suffolk was unaware of how grave the situation in Yorkshire was until a letter came from Darcy. Ibid., no. 728.

satisfied that the Lincolnshire rebellion had been squashed; on 17 October he was to advance against them, and Sir Arthur Darcy was told to lead 1,000 men from Pontefract to relieve the city of York.[3] Of course this was all quite hopeless: Shrewsbury lacked troops and York had been entered even before Darcy was told to lead his non-existent forces to its defence.

The military response to the Pilgrimage was conditioned by the simple failure to anticipate how the rebellion would spread. Because no one realized that the revolt had crossed the Humber, overconfidence led Henry to cancel the Ampthill muster. Troops which had gathered for Lincolnshire were sent homewards when they might have been drawn upon for a campaign against the Yorkshire revolt. Ultimately this miscalculation forced a reliance on 'policy' in order to avoid a military conflict which the Crown's local commanders were not confident of winning. This led to the consequence that the 'hot' Pilgrimage was defused at the cost of a truce which lasted for a further five weeks.

I

When news of the Lincolnshire rising broke, the king moved to hold musters at Ampthill on 16–17 October.[4] Here an army would be assembled which the king, at least momentarily, intended to lead himself.[5] The duke of Norfolk was initially told to remain in East Anglia and for a few days patrolled the counties, but on 11 October the king bowed to Norfolk's lobbying and gave him a role in the nascent army.[6] This gave Norfolk the opportunity to mobilize his tenants and *manred* in Norfolk and Suffolk, and a postal debate developed as to whether it was better for them to congregate at Cambridge or Huntingdon, or strike south to Ampthill

---

[3] Ibid., nos. 748–50.

[4] Whilst the musters are said to have been held at Ampthill, the troops were actually quite widely dispersed. On 18 October Norfolk's were at Cambridge, Exeter's at Buckingham, and the gentlemen of Gloucestershire at Stony Stratford. *LP* XI no. 775.

[5] As late as 12 October, Norfolk was planning to meet the king at Huntingdon on 18 October. Ibid., no. 671.

[6] Ibid., nos. 659, 660.

only to turn northwards in the royal army. By 12 October Norfolk was proposing to meet the king at Huntingdon on 18 October, his own forces moving directly from Cambridge.[7] As early as 13 October Henry may have been reducing the numbers of troops called to Ampthill, and even as the news of Lincolnshire's disintegration broke, the council wrote to Norfolk telling him to hold his position and advance no further. The following day his son, the earl of Surrey, who was overseeing the gathering of troops in Cambridge, told his father that he intended to disregard this instruction and hold musters as arranged until instructed to the contrary. Likewise, the marquis of Exeter had his forces trimmed on 16 October.[8] On 16 October Norfolk was querying the number of troops the king was prepared to allow him: he had only been given 5,000 men when he wanted 6,000; Exeter could hardly have fewer than 2,000 and preferably 3,000.[9] By 17 October Norfolk was warning that there were not enough horsemen available to create an additional force of 2,000 mounted troops to accompany Sir Anthony Browne to Lincoln. Yet on the same day Norfolk, having heard of the submission of the Lincolnshire rebels, was seeking clarification of whether he was still required to join the earl of Shrewsbury or whether the duke of Suffolk would join up with him once he had dealt with Lincolnshire. This drew an authoritative statement: Suffolk was to stay in Lincolnshire. Norfolk, Exeter, and a group of troops led by some Gloucestershire gentlemen were to advance to the aid of the earl of Shrewsbury with 5,000 men in total. Sir Anthony Browne was to proceed to reinforce Suffolk, but with only 560 horsemen (which was all that could be found), unless Suffolk sent word that Browne's troops were not necessary.[10]

The inability of the Ampthill musters to provide the full force required by Browne might lead to the conclusion that the decision to reduce their size in the euphoria over the fall of Lincolnshire left the men on the ground unable to meet the king's requests for troops. Where the king did have a large body of men he could call upon was at Cambridge, where the earl of Surrey was mustering the Howard forces out of Norfolk and Suffolk. The duke was clearly looking to have more men than the king

7 Ibid., no. 671.   8 Ibid., nos. 727, 737, 738.
9 Ibid., no. 738.   10 Ibid., nos. 755, 766.

would allow; whether this reflected Henry's estimation of Norfolk's needs or a desire to rein in his pretensions cannot be decided. At the same time, Henry's refusal to follow his field commander's advice about the daily wages which his troops ought to be paid suggests that he was nervous of running out of money and wished to spend as little as possible.[11]

But this was a worsening situation. As we saw, on 17 October Norfolk was asking whether it was worth going northwards at all. On the following day Henry said that it was; but the air of crisis was deepened by the receipt of letters from the earl of Shrewsbury at both London and Ampthill on Wednesday evening. The alarm had been set off by Sir Brian Hastings in a letter of Tuesday night giving precise information about the entry of the Pilgrims into York the previous day, and expressing the fear that Darcy would surrender Pontefract. Hastings placed the number of Pilgrims at above 40,000 men.[12] Sending this letter on in the early hours of Wednesday morning, Shrewsbury acknowledged that this was too big a force for him to meet in conflict: he therefore proposed to hold his position until Norfolk appeared. Commenting, Norfolk foresaw that he would not be able to make the haste required by Shrewsbury: he could not see the Ampthill contingents, although horsed, being at Doncaster before Thursday, 26 October, a prediction which events were to confirm.[13] On the following day there seems to have been a plan to reach Stamford by Saturday, 21 October, where they hoped to find money for the wages of the troops awaiting them.[14]

It was on Thursday that Norfolk finally left Ampthill. The same day, the king and council, perhaps in the light of Hastings's letter, finally realized the danger of the situation in Yorkshire. There was then a mad scramble to gather more troops from amongst those gathered at Ampthill and Cambridge. A letter reached Norfolk at Cambridge telling him to take northwards the excess of men which Surrey had gathered there the previous weekend. The Gloucestershire men were then to travel with Browne to aid Suffolk in Lincolnshire. It was too late. In an incandescent letter Norfolk reported that he had already discharged the balance of the troops. Browne had long departed northwards with his 560

---

[11] Ibid., nos. 754, 766, 772, 793, 833.   [12] Ibid., no. 759.
[13] Ibid., nos. 733, 776.   [14] Ibid., no. 793.

horsemen. Why had he been sent with so many when the rebellion in Lincolnshire had ended? 'I am apt to think that some desire great company more for glory than necessity', he added in an acidic aside.[15] Another letter calling for more troops from Ampthill caught up with Sir William Paulet and Sir William Kingston at Beaconsfield on the Friday evening. As they told the council, the Ampthill musters had been wound up earlier that day: the remaining troops were now scattered on their way homewards and there seemed little prospect of getting them back.[16]

So, on the morning of Saturday, 21 October, the duke of Norfolk was at Cambridge with 2,000 men drawn from amongst his own tenants, the remainder having been discharged. The marquis of Exeter, with 2,000 men, was somewhere behind; in addition, there was a party of 1,000 Gloucestershire men. This was a relatively light force with which to face the Yorkshire movement. As the remnants of the Ampthill musters drifted home, new letters were being sent out calling them back to a muster to be held at Northampton on 7 November.[17] And whilst the recriminations flew around the southern Midlands, Pontefract had fallen.

Norfolk's great and emerging fear, first expressed on 18 October, was that the earl of Shrewsbury would engage the rebels too soon, without adequate forces, and lose.[18] Shrewsbury's early mobilization has already been described. It was orientated towards Lincolnshire, again without recognizing that the disturbance would spread over the Humber. Hence troops were actually being gathered out of Yorkshire to reinforce Nottingham even as the rebellion took hold in the East Riding. On 5–7 October Shrewsbury was at his house at Hardwick arranging a mobilization at Nottingham on Monday, 9 October. It was Shrewsbury who sent Lancaster Herald to Lincoln and so hastened the break-up of the rebel host there, but if Suffolk expected him to march on Lincoln on 14 October, then Shrewsbury declined until he had received word of the king's response to Lancaster's petition and money to pay his troops. Shrewsbury's caution may also have arisen from the news he was receiving out of Yorkshire, both from Darcy and from Hastings.[19]

---

[15] Ibid., nos. 788, 799, 800.   [16] Ibid., no. 803.

[17] Ibid., no. 821.   [18] Ibid., no. 775.

[19] For the earl of Shrewsbury's role in the defence against the Pilgrims, G. W. Bernard, *The Power of the Early Tudor Nobility: A Study of the Fourth and Fifth Earls of Shrewsbury* (1985), ch. 2.

From the weekend of 7–8 October onwards, the earl of Shrewsbury had a significant force at his disposal at Nottingham. On 17 October he put it at 7,000 men, but the wages account for his own retinue shows that at its peak it amounted to 3,947 soldiers on horseback, under thirty-nine captains and thirty-eight petty captains. The majority of these men had enlisted by about 10–11 October; the pay records show that very few additional men joined thereafter.[20] We must assume that the earls of Rutland and Huntingdon between them had a further 3,000 men. This was too small a force with which to face the Pilgrims. It therefore makes sense of Norfolk's fears, but also shows the extreme incaution of the king's instructions of 15 October, when Shrewsbury was told to advance into Yorkshire as soon as Lincolnshire was repressed and attack the rebels from the front, the earl of Derby and Sir Richard Tempest taking their rear. The arrival of letters from Darcy describing the situation more fully and from Suffolk announcing his success made the king even more adamant that Shrewsbury should turn towards Yorkshire: 'if you think your force sufficient to give the stroke without any danger to our honour, give them the buffet with all diligence and extremity.' If there was any danger, Shrewsbury was to send word direct to the duke of Norfolk, who would come up from Ampthill with a further 5,000 troops.[21]

Shrewsbury wrote directly to Norfolk (17 October) enclosing letters which he had received from Darcy and Archbishop Lee at Pontefract. Using Darcy's estimate, he placed the rebel strength at 40,000 men and growing, and his own force at 7,000 men. He therefore begged Norfolk to advance towards Doncaster whilst Shrewsbury proposed to advance the following day: he and his troops would 'do the best we can, either to set some stay or keep them in play until you come'.[22] Norfolk was adamant that he could not make the speed Shrewsbury required, and feared, reasonably enough, that Shrewsbury might be overwhelmed by the Pilgrims.[23] Nonetheless, in a report on the Pilgrims written the following night, Shrewsbury again judged them too large a force to risk encountering: at the same moment he wrote to the duke of Suffolk asking him to release as many light horseman as he could spare to

[20] *LP* XI, no. 930.   [21] Ibid., nos. 715, 716; no. 747 may be an additional copy of 716.
[22] Ibid., no. 758.   [23] Ibid., no. 775.

reinforce the defence against Yorkshire.[24] It therefore seemed as though Shrewsbury was prepared to be prudent and keep his distance from the rebel host while Norfolk and his troops laboured up the road from the south.

Late on the evening of 20 October Norfolk sent the king his assessment of the situation. Whilst the letter is seemingly lost, its contents can be deduced from the king's reply. Norfolk advocated a two-pronged approach. The first was, sensibly, to play for time by trying to persuade the Pilgrims to disperse by 'policy'. A draft letter to be circulated amongst them had been seen and approved by the king. Should this strategy fail, then the rebels would be proceeded against by force. Shrewsbury therefore to secure the bridges at Nottingham and Newark to prevent any rebel advance over the Trent whilst keeping his distance from the rebels until Norfolk arrived.[25]

Despite Norfolk's strategic analysis, Shrewsbury advanced beyond the Trent to hold the line of the Don and established his camp at Scrooby, 10 miles to the south of Doncaster, on 22 October. His decision to do this may have pivoted on two factors. The first was the reports which he was receiving of a deteriorating military situation within Yorkshire, including, on 20 October, the surrender of Pontefract. The second was that he may have been overconfident of his power to disperse the rebels through policy. Here it may be remembered that he had scored a notable success through sending Thomas Miller, Lancaster Herald, to Lincoln. Shrewsbury tried to repeat this success by sending Lancaster to Pontefract with a proclamation to read to the rebel host on 21 October. Aske, who was perhaps aware of the herald's role in the attenuation of the Lincolnshire rising, was anxious to prevent him from addressing the rebels. Arriving at Pontefract, Lancaster was called into the castle before the incarcerated gentry, intimidated by Aske, forbidden to deliver his proclamation, and then run out of town. Aske justified his action by declaring that if Lancaster had declared to the Pilgrims that Lincolnshire had collapsed, he would have been lynched; but it is equally plausible to suppose that Aske feared to find his own movement evaporating away if Lancaster was allowed to counter the rumours of taxation and

---

[24] Ibid., nos. 773, 774.   [25] Ibid., no. 816.

dispossession which underpinned it.[26] Miller himself believed that he would have found receptive ears for his message, but his expulsion ended the attempt to talk directly to the rank and file. It may have been Lancaster's failure that persuaded Shrewsbury to make a quick advance from Newark to seize the bridges at Doncaster and Russhington.[27]

The duke of Norfolk, however, was horrified by what he believed was a major blunder.[28] By the morning of 23 October Norfolk had reached Newark, where he found a letter from the earl of Shrewsbury. Norfolk had ridden on in advance of his forces; he did not expect his men to arrive before the following day, or the marquis of Exeter's until Wednesday, 25 October. He proposed to base himself at Newark, since all he could do at Doncaster without his men was to offer advice; but it is also clear that he thought it prudent to hold the Trent lest Shrewsbury was forced into a retreat. Later in the day Norfolk reported a meeting with Lord Talbot, who had briefed him on the situation in Doncaster: Talbot was confident of holding the passages over the Don and thought that there was no desperate urgency about Norfolk's force reaching Doncaster.[29] During Wednesday night, however, Norfolk received a letter from the earl of Shrewsbury calling him to Doncaster. He set out with only a small party, but before leaving penned what he feared might be his last letter to the king.[30]

Sir, having this hour received the letter herein enclosed and [having] never heard one word from my Lord Steward [Shrewsbury] but this since Monday last at five in the morning, notwithstanding divers sent from me to him to know of his news, I being in bed and not asleep [when the letter came] . . . I have taken my horse accompanied only with my brother William and Sir Richard Page, Sir Arthur Darcy, and four of my servants to ride towards my Lord Steward

---

[26] For Lancaster's first contact with the Pilgrims, below pp. 294–5. Aske also complained that Miller had no instructions to establish the cause of their rebellion or authority to offer a pardon. 'The manner of the taking of Robert Aske', 336.

[27] Reported by the king on 24 October, drawing on lost letters. *LP* XI, no. 850. I suspect it was done by the evening of 22 October, when Shrewsbury wrote from Scrooby, 10 miles south of Doncaster, ibid., 840. Shrewsbury may have advanced because he believed the Trent was indefensible. Ibid., no. 1028.

[28] Norfolk complained about Shrewsbury's impetuous action both after the first Doncaster meeting and again in December. *LP* XI, nos. 909, 1241.

[29] Ibid., nos. 845, 846.

[30] Ibid., no. 864, here offered in a modernized text taken from the transcript in the Dodds, *Pilgrimage*, I, 259–60.

according to his desire, not knowing where the enemies be nor of what number, nor nothing more than is contained in their letter, wherein I am so far
pricked that whatsoever shall be the sequel [outcome], I shall not spare the poor
little carcass that for any ease or danger other men shall have cause to object
any *lageousness* in me.

Sir, most humbly, I beseech you to take in good part whatsoever promise I
shall make unto the rebels (if any such by the advice of others make) for surely
I shall observe no part thereof for any respect of that other might call mine
honour disdained longer that I and my company with my Lord Marquis
[Exeter] may be assembled together, thinking and reputing that none oath nor
promise made for policy to serve you mine only master and sovereign can dis-
dain me who shall rather be torn in a million pieces that to show one point
of cowardice or untruth to your Majesty.

Sir, I trust the sending for me is meant to God's purpose and if it chance to
me to miscarry, most good and noble master, be good to my sons and to my
poor daughter. And if my Lord Steward had not advanced from Trent until my
coming and that then I might have followed the effect of my letter written you
from Cambridge, these traitors with ease might have been subdued. I pray God
that hap turn not to much hurt.

The letter contains two unattractive features. If Lord Talbot had briefed
Norfolk earlier in the day, then the letter is at least highly disingenu-
ous towards Shrewsbury. Secondly, Norfolk was prepared to go to any
lengths to win the Pilgrims by policy, even, it would appear, to swear
their oath; but whatever he did could not be dishonourable if it was done
to serve the king's higher purposes. Hence the duke clearly did not expect
the king to be bound by any promises that Norfolk might make on his
behalf: nor did he accept that promises extracted by threat of force had
any binding power. The letter also makes clear the extent to which this
was a full-blown military emergency that Norfolk was not confident of
surviving: the letter is a testament, as well as a warning that extraordinary deceits might be necessary to overcome the situation.

When the king replied to the letter he explicitly permitted Norfolk
to withdraw from Doncaster, stressing that to do so would not be to his
dishonour.[31] One must ask, though, whether withdrawal was a practical
option. Whilst Norfolk had a preference for holding the line of the Trent,

---

[31] *LP* XI, no. 884.

this was to cede Nottinghamshire, and so the heartland of Shrewsbury's power, to the Pilgrims; one may appreciate all too well why this was not an acceptable policy for him. So, as Norfolk was bereft of a suitable military option, he was forced into policy. And as Lancaster Herald had already been turned away by Aske, the only alternative was a direct approach to the leadership of the movement. But what is crucial—and significant —is that the nobility and gentry of the North (as they are sometimes called) were amenable to an approach leading to a negotiated truce. All the evidence, from whatever side of the River Don, was that by sheer force of numbers and commitment the Pilgrims could have overwhelmed the much smaller royal forces. The question, then, is why they declined to do so. Stapleton makes it clear that many of the Pilgrims wished to press on and capture Doncaster, and had to be restrained from doing so.[32] The answer must lie in a more sophisticated interpretation of the Pilgrims' host than has so far been offered.

II

The final week of the October rising in Yorkshire is poorly documented. Darcy's Letter Book ends after the capture of Old Tom, and the surviving depositions gathered in 1537 tend to skate over the mustering and organization of the rebel army. Aske does provide an account in his memorial, but this is telescoped. Nowhere else in their book did the Dodds read so much into so few sources.

Having taken Pontefract Castle on the morning of 21 October, Aske appears to have set about calling down to Pontefract the other roving armies which together formed the Pilgrimage of Grace. Even before he captured Pontefract he was issuing orders to Sir Thomas Percy who, over the space of several days, was told to go to York, then to proceed to Hull, and finally, when news came that Hull was won, called to Pontefract.[33] Once at Pontefract he sent letters to the Durham and

---

[32] Stapleton, 101.   [33] *LP* XII (i) no. 393.

Richmondshire contingents and into Craven and the Yorkshire Wolds. These letters may have included the text of the oath, and this may explain how it came to be adapted for use in east Lancashire.[34] By 24 October the earl of Derby had received a letter from Aske brought to him by one of his servants who had been taken and sworn in Yorkshire. Derby forwarded it to the king unopened; sadly, it is lost.[35]

Sir Thomas Percy arrived at Pontefract during Saturday, 21 October with 10,000 men, having spent the previous night in York. William Stapleton, who led his band through York on Saturday, was told to be at Pontefract early on Sunday morning. During Sunday the Durham contingent arrived in Pontefract under lords Latimer, Lumley, and Neville; at some time either during Sunday or Monday the band which had travelled by way of Skipton Castle also arrived.[36] A council was held at Pontefract which appears to have consisted of Aske, the gentlemen who fell into his hands when Pontefract fell, and the gentlemen of the North Riding and County Durham who had arrived during the day. This council decided that Pontefract should be protected by holding the bridge at Wentbridge, about 2 miles south of the town. The Durham men were asked to take on this duty, but Robert Bowes objected, saying they were not fit to travel any further. In their place the East Riding rebels, together with the force under Sir Thomas Percy, were designated as the vanguard and advanced to Wentbridge. On Monday they took Hampole nunnery and on Wednesday Pickburn, placing them only 2 miles short of Doncaster Bridge and on higher ground. As the vanguard moved forwards, the space behind them was filled by the other contingents. By Thursday the disposition was that the vanguard at Pickburn consisted of the contingent from the Bishopric (County Durham) and the eastern part of the North Riding under lords Lumley, Neville, and Latimer, Sir Thomas Percy, and Robert Bowes; the middleward at Hampole was drawn from the East and West Ridings; and the rearward at Pontefract came largely from the North Riding dales, Richmondshire, and that part of the West Riding about Ripon and Kirby Malzeard. On

[34] 'Aske's Examination', 568–9, answ. 42. Above pp. 232–3.

[35] 'Derby Correspondence', 34–5; *LP* XI, no. 894 identifies it as Aske's work.

[36] Stapleton implies that the force who had travelled through Skipton arrived on Sunday. Stapleton, 100.

Thursday the vanguard and middleward mustered at Scawsby Lees, over-looking Doncaster, in a clear show of force. As for their numbers, it can be said that they were substantial, even when we allow for gross exag-geration. Aske supplies some details. Lords Neville, Latimer, and Lumley (the Bishopric) had 10,000 men, those from Blackamoor and Pickering Lythe (under Sir Thomas Percy) 5,000, and Yorkswold and Holderness 2,000 or 3,000. This makes 17,000–18,000 men. Aske goes on to refer to the men of the West and North Ridings but provides no figures for them, but then says at 'Stuxing Sysse' (the Scawby Lees muster) the whole force amounted to 24,000 or 25,000 men, suggesting that the unspecified West and North Ridings ran to 7,000 men between them. However, within a few lines he implies that the muster did not include the rearward under Lord Scrope, Sir Christopher Danby, and others, who amounted to another 12,000 men. The four hosts for whom he gives numbers total 29,000 or 30,000 men, with the possibility that there were a further 7,000 drawn from parts of the West and North Ridings who were not accounted for elsewhere.[37] Elsewhere Aske estimated his numbers at 30,000.[38] Marmaduke Neville estimated their numbers at 28,000 at Doncaster (that is, the vanguard and middlewards) with a further 12,000 in reserve in the rearward (at Pontefract), which agrees broadly with the figures in Aske's memorial.[39] The rearward may have been bigger still: Darcy and Sir Richard Tempest estimated it at 20,000 men, 'calling themselves 30,000'.[40] On the evidence they offered, the Pilgrims claimed that they had at least 30,000 and perhaps as many as 40,000 men under arms at Doncaster and Pontefract.[41] Norfolk appears to have accepted that he faced 30,000 men, although he had his own reasons for inflating their numbers.[42] Even if we treat these figures with some scepticism (they indic-ate that a very large proportion of adult males were in arms) and halve them, the earl of Shrewsbury, with perhaps 7,000 men at Doncaster and another 5,000 expected, still faced a vastly superior force.

[37] 'The manner of the taking of Robert Aske', 336–7.
[38] LP XII (i), no. 1175 (2) answ. 4.   [39] Ibid., no. 29.   [40] LP XI no. 928.
[41] The figures could be revised downwards. Sir Thomas Percy thought that the forces commanded by Bowes were only 3,000–4,000; his own, with those of others, amounted to 4,000 at Ferrybridge on 22 October rather than the 5,000 which Aske credited him with. LP XII (i), no. 393 (SP1/115 fos. 254v–255r).
[42] 'Thomas Master's Narrative', 71.

Aske was also prone to boast that he had good intelligence of the other side's weaknesses. He claimed under interrogation in May 1537 that the North had better scoutwatch and spies, and that the royal forces could do little without Aske knowing of it. Admittedly, he had some information from Lawrence Cook, the prior of the White Friars in Doncaster, who was sent through the lines to gather information on the rebels' numbers and location on 23 October. Aske was certainly confident that he had support in Norfolk's camp, especially amongst the troops, many of whom he expected to desert or come over to him if a battle took place ('Their commons were faint'), a view shared by Norfolk.[43] Aske also recalled a moment when Darcy, at dinner, had an unsigned letter brought to him warning that be would be captured during the night. This may have been a hoax or a further indication that the Pilgrims had their friends on the opposing side.[44]

So, in all these respects the Pilgrim's position was one of overwhelming advantage. Why, then, were they so disinclined to press it home? To understand this, we need to dispel the view that Aske and the nobility and gentry who were taken at Pontefract, and those who arrived leading armies out of the North and East Ridings or County Durham, were in any sense a cohesive leadership. It is fairly clear that Darcy and the others who had taken refuge in the castle at Pontefract cold-shouldered Aske. We have Aske's own testimony that he and Darcy were not acquainted before he went to Pontefract to call on Darcy to surrender the castle. Moreover, he also admits that they had little contact after the fall of the castle, that Lee and Magnus would not co-operate with him, and that he could not get on with Sir Robert Constable.[45]

Lancaster Herald's account of his interview with Aske on 21 October (and so within a few hours of the surrender of the castle) makes it clear that Aske was very much in control, with Darcy, the archbishop, and the others counting for little or nought. Having arrived at the castle, it was Aske, not Darcy, who summoned the Herald to a chamber where he found Aske accompanied by Darcy, archbishop Lee, and others. The

[43] *LP* XII (i), no. 1175 (ii), answ. 4; no. 854; for Norfolk's doubts, *LP* XI, no. 909. For an independent report of defections, ibid., no. 1195.

[44] Best described in the Dodds, *Pilgrimage*, I, 233.

[45] 'The manner of the taking of Robert Aske', 342; 'Aske's examination', 568–9 (answ. 41).

herald began by addressing himself to Darcy and the archbishop, but Aske, 'with a cruel and an inestimable proud countenance, stretched himself and took the hearing of my tale'. It was Aske who demanded to see the proclamation and then answered it on behalf of those assembled, 'standing in the highest place of the chamber, taking the high estate upon him'. It was Aske who outlined the purpose of the rebellion. Then, when Aske had forbidden him to give forth his proclamation, he asked Darcy to tip the Herald (surely a symbolic illustration of where power lay) and had him escorted out of town. Darcy, Lee, and the others were, at best, bystanders at this crude display of naked power.[46]

Aske appears to have expected to surrender the leadership of the movement into the hands of the nobility at Pontefract, and was disappointed when they declined to accept it.[47] But according to Lee's account of the first meeting at Pontefract (on Friday, 20 October), Aske himself was uncertain of what he sought from the nobility and gentry who had fallen into his hands. 'We desire to have you and my Lord Darcy that you may be mediators to the king's highness for our requests and for your counsel.' As Lee pointed out, the two were incompatible: 'if you would have us mediators to the king's highness for you, then convenient is that we remain as we be and not join with you, for if we join with you, we shall be no meet mediators.'[48]

Aske drew no power from the nobility in Pontefract, nor did he share his power with them. Rather Aske's authority came from his leadership of the rank and file. Even though he was a civilian, he appears to have spent the days following the fall of Pontefract mustering his forces, for it was these people and not the gentry or nobility who formed the basis of his power. He denied Lancaster Herald permission to read his proclamation from the market cross, 'nor in no place *amongst my people which be all under my guiding*' (my italics). When he gave Lancaster a copy of his oath, he said that he would 'die in the quarrel and his people with him'. And he said that he 'would have nothing put in his people's heads'.[49]

Aske may have been an almost messianic figure who was capable both of inflaming the commons and also of disciplining them. But having secured

---

[46] *LP* XI, no. 826 (= *St. P.* I, 485–70).   [47] 'The manner of the taking of Robert Aske', 343.

[48] SP1/119, fo. 5r (= *LP* XII (i), no. 1022).   [49] *St. P.* I, 486, 487 (= *LP* XI, no. 826).

their support, what did he wish to do with it? Here it is clear that the initiative was taken by Norfolk and Shrewsbury. We have already seen how Shrewsbury had sent Lancaster Herald to try to calm the body of the movement. On Tuesday he sent a letter with Lancaster Herald— it is not clear to whom it was addressed—saying that the duke of Norfolk wished to have four of the discreetest men of the north meet him at Doncaster to declare to him the causes of their rebellion so that blood-shed would be spared.[50] In fact, Norfolk was still a long way off down the Great North Road, but this was probably the line which he had urged Shrewsbury to take by letter. The Herald's proposal appears to have thrown the Pilgrims into confusion, and a council was convened. But Lancaster Herald was not given an answer to take back until the following night,[51] and it was probably only when this was received that word was sent to Norfolk at Welbeck asking him to attend quickly. Aske's account states that Norfolk was sent a counter-proposal: that 'because such persons might not be well spared, they declared how they would send four, six, eight, or twelve to meet with like number betwixt the hosts and there to declare their grieves and petitions'.[52] What exactly Norfolk found wrong with this proposal is not clear, but he appears to have sent Lancaster Herald back the following day with a further, inflammatory letter in the form of a chivalric challenge, ending:

Finally, it is now at your choice whether ye will abide the danger of battle against us, or else go home to your houses, submitting you to the king's mercy. If ye go home, ye may be assured to have us most humble suitors to his highness for you: and if ye do not, then do your worst to us, for so we will do to you. And yet we have occasion to say that we deal like honest charitable men with you to give you this warning, more gentle than your deserts doth require.[53]

It is far from clear why Norfolk was dissatisfied with the offer of a meeting between the hosts which Lancaster Herald had brought back

---

[50] Stapleton says Tuesday, and that the Herald was sent back the following night. Stapleton, 101.
[51] For this see ibid. 101.   [52] 'The manner of the taking of Robert Aske', 337.
[53] The letter is noted as *LP* XI, no. 887 and printed in *St. P.* I, 495–6. As it is signed by Norfolk and Shrewsbury, Exeter, Rutland, and Huntingdon, it cannot pre-date Norfolk's arrival at Doncaster on the morning of Thursday, 26 October. The Dodds' argument that it had been prepared by Norfolk some days before and merely sent on by Shrewsbury without thought is not convincing. Dodds, *Pilgrimage*, I, 256–7.

the previous evening, or what he hoped to gain from this letter. Certainly he was not really in a position to fight: the challenge was essentially bluster.

How Norfolk's threat was received is recounted in the only source: Aske's deposition. Aske says that some of the lords were prepared to accept it (although he gives no names), and then writes for himself a speech in which he declares to the lords and knights 'that it was no dishonour but all their whole duties, to declare their grieves to their sovereign lord to the intent the villain councillors about his grace might be know[n] and have like punishment and how they were in error of the people and how they dangered the person of their prince. And further declared what decay should ensue if battle were then'.[54] In a deposition taken whilst in prison the following May, Aske expanded on these thoughts, stressing how, if the duke had won a battle, the gentry of the North would have been 'attainted, slain, and undone and the country made a waste for the Scots', but that if the Pilgrims had achieved a victory there would have been a carnage of the nobility: 'what a loss to this realm and what displeasure to the king.'[55]

Aske, without doubt, was trying to portray himself as the conciliator, and on the basis of this slight evidence first the Dodds and later M. E. James divided the leadership of the Pilgrims between a peace party and a war party, the Dodds being quite specific: 'The Durham lords were ready to accept the new messages as a sign that all further negotiations were broken off: they advised that the challenge should be accepted and the attack should be made at once . . . Aske, however, headed a party in the council which favoured moderate measures.'[56] There is no evidence that the bishopric wished to take a hard line unless Aske's text is read exactly as identifying the 'lords' as Latimer, Lumley, Neville, and Scrope. And it is unlikely that these four were so determined on war, when they were amongst those who later negotiated a truce with Norfolk and cheerfully disbanded their army.[57] Nor is there any independent

---

[54] 'The manner of the taking of Robert Aske', 337.   [55] LP XII (i), no. 1175 (ii), answ. 4.

[56] Dodds, Pilgrimage, I, 257; M. E. James, 'English Politics and the Concept of Honour, 1485–1642', in id., Society, Politics and Culture, 350–4.

[57] It may be helpful to emphasize that there is no evidence for any dissension amongst the nobility and gentry from accepting the terms of the truce.

evidence that Aske favoured conciliation and negotiation. If anything, his behaviour over the previous fortnight argues against it, unless he really believed the rhetoric of mediation which Archbishop Lee reports. Nor do his actions over the next two days convincingly suggest that he preferred negotiation. Whatever struggle went on in the councils of the Pilgrims, Lancaster Herald was sent back with a message that the Pilgrims would negotiate on the basis of the request made on Tuesday: that four of their leaders would travel to Doncaster to outline their case to Norfolk and the earls. The four chosen were Sir Ralph Ellerker, Sir Thomas Hilton, Robert Bowes, and Robert Chaloner. Pledges were exchanged.

The decision to prefer jaw to war provoked another crisis amongst the Pilgrims. They had no articles prepared outlining their grievances. When Lancaster Herald had sought a statement from Aske as to why the Pilgrims had risen he had received a speech from Aske, but when he sought something in writing he had been fobbed off with a copy of Aske's oath in which, he said, his articles were comprehended. According to Archbishop Lee, an impromptu council was held, probably at Hampole nunnery, which the Pilgrims had commandeered as their forward base,[58] where they 'devised five or six general articles' before the quartet set out to the duke of Norfolk. Nothing was committed to paper, only to the memory of Robert Bowes. Norfolk insisted that the articles be written down.[59] Until this time there is no sign that the Pilgrims had thought about their aims: in so far as they had any, they remained the reformulation of the Lincoln articles in Aske's oath.

Pledges were exchanged and, at some time on the Thursday evening, the four representatives of the Pilgrims travelled into Doncaster. They returned at noon on Friday and reported how the duke wished to discuss the articles with a larger group of the leaders of the Pilgrimage. The Pilgrims then sent back to Norfolk the four negotiators (Ellerker, Hilton, Bowes, and Chaloner) together with others, of whom Aske names

[58] For instance, the royal pledges were conveyed to Hampole. 'The manner of the taking of Robert Aske', 337.

[59] For Lee's account, SP1/119, fo. 6v (= LP XII (i), no. 1022). Aske also referred to them as 'general articles', distinguishing them perhaps from the 'particular articles' compiled in December (p. 346 below for this usage). 'The manner of the taking of Robert Aske', 338.

lords Darcy, Latimer, Lumley, Sir Robert Constable, Sir John Bulmer, and others whose names escaped him.[60] Aske was not included: he spent the afternoon until night fell having the Pilgrims standing in array awaiting the return of the lords. This display of superiority doubtless served to remind everyone of the awful military power which the Pilgrims could call upon. But Aske also claimed that he was unaware of what was discussed at the meeting at Doncaster. He was, quite simply, cut out of the negotiations. What we may imagine was discussed was the problem of what to do with Aske.

The men who went to talk to Norfolk had universally been pulled from their beds, threatened, cajoled, or bullied into offering the Pilgrims leadership. They had at their backs a substantial army of soldiers who may well have regarded Aske rather than Latimer or Lumley or a Bowes or an Ellerker as their leader. Unless these people were actually committed to a programme which had not even been written down, but which remained the personal preference of the Grand Captain, their instinct was surely to try to persuade their tenants and servants to go home. But in order to persuade them to decamp they needed a success, something tangible. Norfolk's game, on the other hand, appears to have been to try to split the leadership of the Pilgrims from their rank and file. He surely knew all he needed to from his discussions with Ellerker, Hilton, Bowes, and Chaloner about the character of the movement and the danger that it posed. He was, after all, outnumbered. The request for a larger party to talk to him was perhaps an attempt to play for more time, but it was essentially an attempt to get the nobility and gentry to defect. Darcy was placed under pressure to do so. Somerset Herald asked him why he had not taken the opportunity, when he met Darcy in November. Darcy responded by reminding him of an adage of the late duke of Richmond: 'he that will lay his head on the block may have it soon struck off.' And he added that he had told the earl of Shrewsbury at Doncaster that if Shrewsbury was certain that Darcy would have the king's favour and be indifferently heard, then he would come in; but this had been rejected by Shrewsbury. No pardon was on offer, and who could promise that

---

[60] 'The manner of the taking of Robert Aske', 337. According to a deletion in the MS, there were 30 in all.

the king would look favourably on a man who had surrendered a royal castle, been amongst the Pilgrims, and now wanted to defect?[61]

One of Darcy's reasons was his inability to trust the king. But what surely made his—or anyone else's—defection impossible was the fact that there was a substantial armed force of uncertain discipline standing only a mile or two behind Doncaster. If the gentry had defected it is not too difficult to imagine that Aske would have led his Pilgrims down to Doncaster to annihilate Norfolk's troops. The masterstroke of what was decided at Doncaster was that it destroyed Aske's power base by dispersing his people, the Pilgrims. Both armies were to disband and disperse. Norfolk and the earl of Shrewsbury's son, Lord Talbot, were to travel with Ellerker and Bowes to the court, where they could put their case to the king in person. This resolved one problem. It ended the Pilgrimage of Grace (for the time being) as a military force, and allowed a breathing-space for the king to decide what concessions he could make. It also allowed time for a propaganda offensive to persuade the activists that there were no royal plans for confiscation afoot. But where the military victory which the king clearly sought (but which Norfolk could not possibly have delivered) might have scattered the Pilgrims, disbandment gave them the opportunity to regroup and press their case anew, and this they did in December. If we really see the gentry leadership of the Pilgrims as being an opposition force, then by the guile of policy they threw away a winning hand at Pontefract. But one may suspect that, in all truth, there was no great dissension at Pontefract about the ultimate objective, to get the Pilgrims home and to isolate Aske.

Exactly what was agreed at the first Doncaster meeting? Evidence is sparse, although something of the understanding achieved there can be reconstructed from the assumptions on which negotiations were predicated during November. First and foremost the armies gathered at Doncaster were to disperse. On the Pilgrim's side there was a belief that this included the royal army in Lincolnshire.[62] Secondly, Norfolk and Lord Talbot would accompany the Pilgrim's two representatives to court, where their articles would be presented to the king. There is no complete text of these articles drawn up at Hampole nunnery in response to Norfolk's

---

[61] Dodds, *Pilgrimage*, I, 302.

[62] For the expectation that Suffolk would withdraw, *LP* XI, nos. 1046 (3), 1049 (3), clause 3.

request. They can be reconstructed from a partially decayed set of articles carried by Norfolk (printed below, pp. 458–9) and the kings answer to them.[63] The articles were couched in extremely broad and unspecific terms as follows:

1. That the faith should be maintained.
2. That church and the liberties of the church should be maintained.
3. That the law of the realm should be as at the beginning of the realm, when 'his nobles did order under his highness'. (The king glossed this as 'the laws, the commonwealth [and] the directors of the laws under us'. The latter element became an argument over the number of nobles on the privy council.)
4. That subverters of the laws of God and the realm should be corrected, and here Cromwell, Cranmer, Lord Chancellor Audeley, and Latimer (the bishop of Worcester) were specifically mentioned, together with the 'other maintainers of the same sect'.
5. That a pardon for all offences should be granted by the authority of parliament, and so the Pilgrims called for a parliament to be held.

The possibility of a parliament was neither withheld nor conceded in the king's letter. But the request does surface from time to time. It is nearly conceded in a document of early November, which attempts to conciliate the Pilgrims and which is structured around their demands.[64] It is identified by Darcy in a letter of 11 November as one of the concessions which would most calm the commons.[65] The demand for a parliament 'kept where they [the Pilgrims] may safely come and go' was restated at the York conference. In his letters of 26 November Norfolk urged that the parliament be conceded, to satisfy a demand which had clearly been made on the occasion of the first meeting with the rebels.[66]

It was assumed that Ellerker and Bowes would return within a relatively short time—perhaps ten days or a fortnight at most—and would then present the king's answer to a meeting convened at York. That such a meeting was arranged before the Pilgrims left Doncaster seems well

---

[63] Ibid., no. 902. The king's answer is printed by the Dodds, *Pilgrimage*, I, 275–78, it was printed in late 1536 as *Answere made by the kynges highnes to the petitions of the rebelles in Yorkshire, Anno MDXXXVI* (repr. The English Experience, 872, 1977).

[64] *LP* XI, no. 1410 (4). Subsequently I suggest that its author may have been Norfolk.

[65] Ibid., no. 1045. [66] Ibid., no. 1170; 'Thomas Master's Narrative', p. 74.

established. Darcy, for instance, looks forward to Ellerker and Bowes declaring the king's pleasure to a 'council of nobles and gentlemen', but the gathering of this convention seems to have taken the king's side rather by surprise.[67]

A final matter is whether the Pilgrims were deceived at Doncaster by the duke of Norfolk feigning his support for their cause. To some degree they were most certainly taken in, for Norfolk offered the possibility of settling the Pilgrimage by negotiation, when the king looked for their annihilation by military means. But did he actually profess to agree with them, and did he thereby lead them to suppose that he was with them and against Cromwell and innovation? The supposition that he did comes first from a confused paragraph in Lord Herbert's *Life of Henry VIII*. The Dodds hoped that this might be traced back to its ur-source, and this is now possible. Thomas Master's transcript of otherwise-lost documents reveals that Norfolk denied a charge made by Darcy when the latter was imprisoned in 1537, that at the first Doncaster meeting he had allowed the rebels' articles.[68] Such an allegation was personally dangerous, but Norfolk's theatrical denial proves nothing. Even if the allegation was true, it proves nothing about Norfolk's own preferences. In his letter to the king of 25 October he made it clear that he would say anything, that no deceit was too large, if it served to persuade the Pilgrims to disperse peacefully.[69] Norfolk's record over the whole period of the 1536 rebellion shows that he preferred 'policy' to action, but only because he realized how dire the military situation was in both October and early December. Where his sympathies lay is ultimately unknown; but it is not unreasonable to assume that the Pilgrims initially thought that he was more sympathetic to them than subsequent events proved.

III

To disband without fighting could all too readily be seen as a humiliation: the Pilgrims had forced Norfolk into negotiation and had secured

---

[67] Ibid., no. 1045, 1046. For the York conference, below pp. 329–33.

[68] Dodds, *Pilgrimage*, I, 267, 'Thomas Masters' Narrative', 79.

[69] *LP* XI, no. 864 (printed above pp. 289–90).

the right to ventilate their grievances before the king. Even from the moment when the representatives of the armies each returned to their own camps, an alternative, face-saving explanation for the disbandment began to circulate on the royalist side. In the first letter which Norfolk, Shrewsbury, and the other loyalist nobles sent to the king outlining their no-score draw against Aske, they stressed the desperation of the military situation at Doncaster. The royal troops were still scattered. The rebels were determined to take Doncaster and could have come over the river by a ford no more than two feet deep, 'that 100 men might pass on a front. The rebels were in a great fury to assault the bridge, to pass the water, and to set on the camp'. Norfolk had undertaken to defend Doncaster bridge and the others their encampment. Hence, the royal forces were forced to use policy to induce the rebels to delay for a day (Thursday). During that evening Peter Mewtas, a gentleman of the privy chamber, had arrived with 100 gunners, whom Norfolk employed to defend the bridge. Then, during Thursday night, heavy rain made the river impassable. This acted as a further defence, but did not alter the overall picture. The Pilgrims controlled the countryside; the royal army was short of victual and money and could not force a battle except 'when and where [it] pleaseth them'. Hence they had agreed a treaty with the rebels and had undertaken to be suitors to the king for their pardon.[70]

Writing to the council on the Sunday morning, Norfolk elaborated on some of these points. They had been forced to disband the army because of foul weather, a lack of cover for both men and horses, and a short-age of firewood, victual, and provender, everything having been devast-ated by the enemy. Plague was rampant in Doncaster itself. '[It] was not possible to have given battle but upon apparent loss thereof. And if we should have retired in enmity, [it would have] assured ruin of our com-pany, having no horsemen . . . how at every street they should, at their will, have set on the foremost [front] or hindermost [part of the army]'.[71]

By the time Hall published his account of the Pilgrimage the story had been embellished and turned to the Crown's advantage. Here, as the royal army approached, its leaders saw how determined the rebels were to fight. So the army first practised policy to persuade them to disperse,

[70] 'Thomas Master's Narrative', 70–1.
[71] LP XI, no. 909, printed in Dodds, Pilgrimage, I, 268–9.

then, when they could find no other option than to pacify them through defeat, a day of battle was agreed upon, but on the eve of the battle the river rose so that no one could pass over it, so preventing the armies joining. This account of divine providence interfering in the follies of men (God stopping the slaughter of so many innocent persons) then has the captains coming together, the king's pardon being offered to the rebels, and an undertaking given that their articles should be placed before the king.[72] In fact no pardon was offered at Pontefract in October. And the significance of the heavy rain was not that it prevented the armies fighting, but that it washed out and doubtless further demoralized the royal forces. (Lancaster Herald was subsequently accused of sapping morale by reporting what he saw at Pontefract.[73]) Every justification Norfolk offers is doubtless fair; but it also remains the case that he had decided long before he reached Pontefract that the only way to avoid defeat was through policy, through playing for time, and this he did. The royal forces were gathered too late, were too few in numbers, too doubtful in loyalty and morale, and too poorly supplied to have held the line of the Don against 'all the flower of the North'. And so they did not try. As Norfolk said, making the best of an appalling embarrassment, 'in every man's mouth it is said in our army that I never served his grace so well as now in dissolving the army of the enemy without loss of ours'. Yet, as he also warned, there was no prospect of regrouping the dispersing royal forces.[74] Their demobilization had effectively killed any prospect of a military solution to the Pilgrimage.

Whilst Norfolk, in the company of Sir Ralph Ellerker and Robert Bowes, was making his weary way to court, anxious about his reception, the rebel host was also breaking up, although not without dissension. The rearward, 'wild people' according to Darcy, were particularly reluctant to disperse.[75] By the afternoon of 29 October Shrewsbury, Rutland, and Huntingdon could report that the rebels had all gone, and that they had dissolved the royal army and sent the king's ordnance to Nottingham.[76] As the armies dispersed Aske had word out of Lancashire

---

[72] Hall, *The union of the two noble and illustrious families* . . . , 822–3.

[73] *LP* XIII (i), no. 1311 (printed as a footnote in *St. P.* I, 487–8).

[74] *LP* XI no. 909, printed in Dodds, *Pilgrimage*, I, 268–9.   [75] *LP* XI, nos. 945, 1045.

[76] Ibid., no. 910.

of the impending conflict between the commons and the earl of Derby. The way in which this situation was defused is further indication of Aske's grasp over the movement: he wrote to the commons announcing the truce at Pontefract and calling on them to desist, while Darcy wrote to the earl of Shrewsbury asking him to communicate the settlement to Derby. Other letters asking for calm were written by Aske, one of which may have reached Carlisle by Sunday.[77] A rough-and-ready adherence to the truce was thus established throughout the North.

[77] 'The manner of the taking of Robert Aske', 338; *LP* XI, nos. 899–901, 1045, 1046 (3). For Carlisle, above pp. 246–7.

11

The Benignity of
the Prince

Ellerker and Bowes did not return to Pontefract with the king's response to the Pilgrims until 18 November. It was only on 21 November that they were able to present an account of their reception at court to an assembly of gentry and commons at York. The most remarkable feature of the intervening month was that, despite minor infringements of the truce, suspicions on both sides, and clear evidence that each was preparing for further hostilities, the truce held, such was the commons' belief in the power of an appeal to the king over the heads of his councillors. The problem for the Pilgrims was that the delay allowed the initiative to pass into the hands of the king and his circle of advisors at Windsor.

I

On the dispersal of the two armies, the Pilgrims' council also broke up. There appears to have been little contact amongst the cadre who had met with Norfolk, or between Darcy and Aske. Aske went first to York to spread word of the truce, then to Wressle where he attempted to broker a reconciliation between the earl of Northumberland and his younger brothers. Whilst the nature of the earl's illness has never been determined, he was too mentally and physically broken to be of any real assistance to either the king or the Pilgrims. Nonetheless, he continued to speak in support of Cromwell, to defy his brothers, and to curse the commons. When Stapleton warned him that his bitter complaints against the commons could place him in real danger, he replied that 'he did not care . . . he should die but once. Let them strike off his head whereby they should rid him of much pain, ever saying he would be dead.' Ultimately he surrendered Wressle to Aske, perhaps to escape from him. Then the earl retired to York, where he remained until at least the second week of December.[1] As late as 1 December he sent a ring to the duke of Suffolk for transmission to the king as a sign of his continued fealty. Suffolk understood that Northumberland was so closely guarded that he could not write.[2]

Aske was also active in Hull. The duke of Suffolk had stationed troops at Grimsby, Barton-upon-Humber (under Sir Anthony Browne, to control the ferry over the river), and all along the bank of the Trent to Gainsborough.[3] The Pilgrims were worried that the duke would use these forces to invade the East Riding through Hull. Suffolk was also regulating the flow of traffic down the Humber, which the Pilgrims held was contrary to (perhaps because it had not been provided for in) the truce at Pontefract. Aske appointed Sir Robert Constable as 'ruler' of Hull, and he set about reinforcing the fortifications and levying a garrison of 200 soldiers.[4] When the duke of Suffolk asked the mayor of Hull on about 5 November to deliver to him Anthony Curtis and the other Lincolnshire rebels who were in gaol there, he was surprised to receive in return a letter signed by Rogers the mayor, Constable, and others saying they could not act without the permission of Aske.[5] It had been agreed in the truce at Doncaster that the Lincolnshire men could trade with Hull: when Sir Anthony Browne sought to buy wine in the third week of

---

[1] Dodds, *Pilgrimage*, I, 283–5, gives a fuller account. The quotation is from Stapleton, 102–3, who is the prime source. For the earl's whereabouts in late 1536, Hoyle, 'Henry, Sixth Earl of Northumberland', 198.

[2] *LP* XI, no. 1221.   [3] Ibid., no. 1095.

[4] Dodds, *Pilgrimage*, I, 286.   [5] *LP* XI, nos. 996, 1004.

November, his servant was treated with courtesy by Sir Robert, although Browne was doubtful of the quality of the wine he bought back.[6]

Darcy retired to his house at Temple Hirst from whence he had fled a month before. From there he struck up a cordial enough correspondence with the earl of Shrewsbury, exchanging letters about the truce and supplying Shrewsbury with news from the south,[7] and a less cordial one with the duke of Norfolk. He was also visited by Percival Creswell, Hussey's servant, on 10–11 November. Creswell carried letters, but his real purpose was to propose that Darcy should prove his constancy to the king by arresting Aske. He also received a visit from Somerset Herald on 14 November. Somerset's overt reason for calling was to establish the truth about an alarm on the previous Saturday, but he too was on a mission to discover Darcy's real motives.

Darcy's position was a deeply ambivalent one. He persistently defended his actions in October and claimed that, when the facts were known, it would be appreciated how well he had served his monarch.[8] He clearly wished the truce to succeed and urged that the fastest way to wind up the revolt was to have Ellerker and Bowes return and declare the king's answer to their petitions. So, in his letter to the earl of Shrewsbury on 12 November, he argued that:

Finally and principally, all and every appointment at Doncaster is and shall be kept to the uttermost of our power that be gentlemen and else or now [i.e. or else before now] many country's commons had already been of float, for marvellously, extremely and wilfully they be banded and ready to rise and do evil acts. Surely much of the stay lies in Sir Ralph Ellerker and Bowes's return and in their discreet declaration of the king's answers at an assembly of all the barons and folks of worship of every shire and countries that hath been up.[9]

He told Norfolk that he would be 'no supporter of the commons in their evil acts'.[10] And to Sir Brian Hastings he wrote that, 'for my part

---

[6] Ibid., nos. 1075, 1095.

[7] On 12 November he sent Shrewsbury copies of the letter from Ellerker and Bowes and a copy of his reply to Norfolk's letter of 6 November. *LP* XI, no. 1049. Shrewsbury was also quick to re-establish a correspondence with Sir George Darcy. Bernard, *The Power of the Early Tudor Nobility*, 47.

[8] For instance in his letters to Norfolk (11 Nov.), Shrewsbury (12 Nov.), and Sir Brian Hastings (17 Nov.), *LP* XI, nos. 1045, 1049, and 1096, and in his conversations with Creswell and Somerset Herald.

[9] *LP* XI, no. 1049 (3), para. 8 and following.   [10] Ibid., no. 1167.

I have not meddled, nor will, further than to advise the captain to write for good stays and to avoid spoils and hope, after the coming of the two gentlemen, peace will be established' (17 November).[11] He was anxious that the Crown should also stick to the terms of the truce. The failure to return Ellerker and Bowes was a breach of its terms. He was unhappy about the Crown's continued military presence in Lincolnshire and the north Midlands.[12] He pleaded that Sir Henry Savile's antics should not be allowed to imperil the meeting with the Pilgrims.[13] As we shall see, he also knew that the Crown was cynically manoeuvring to destroy the Pilgrimage. He was put under pressure to betray Aske.[14] Overtures were made by Sir Brian Hastings to try to persuade Sir George Darcy to defect. (Unfortunately his letter fell into the hands of the rebels.[15]) He may or may not have known of contacts between Suffolk's front line and some unnamed gentlemen of the Marshland who were unhappy about the course of events in October.[16] Darcy probably had in his possession a letter from the Crown's advance camp at Nottingham which made clear the king's refusal to answer the commons' petitions or to give up Cromwell as they demanded.[17] His nervousness is revealed by his reaction to reports on 11 November that royal troops were mustering near Snaith. Darcy became hysterical, and spoke of dying a glorious death against the king's men, saying that 'he set more by the king of heaven than by twenty kings', that: 'though he might not [be able to] ride, but he might go where he would if he had a horse litter and the highest hill that he could find there would he be and he would lie in his horse litter and kneel in it and said, let them shoot guns at him and spare him not, for he could say a prayer that would preserve both him and all his servants . . .'[18] In

---

[11] Ibid., no. 1096.   [12] Ibid., no. 1050.

[13] Ibid., nos. 1122–3. As early as 2 November it was reported that Savile was threatening to hang constables who had collected money to set forth soldiers for the Pilgrims. By 19 November it was complained that Grice had sworn some of Savile's servants. During the night of 19–20 November Savile attempted to muster his tenants and this provoked fears that he was going to raid Pontefract, but he subsequently fled southwards, perhaps taking his tenants with him. This drew a complaint from Norfolk. See *LP* XI, nos. 960, 1051, 1112–4, 1122–3, 1138.

[14] Below pp. 318–20.

[15] *LP* XI, nos. 1027, 1059, 1067. Bernard, *Power of the early Tudor Nobility*, pp. 47–9.

[16] Ibid., no. 1077, 1120.   [17] Ibid., no. 1042. See below p. 324.

[18] *LP* XII (i), no. 853.

fact Sir Brian Hastings was having his neighbours walk about in white coats (the royal uniform) to deter cattle thieves—or so he said.[19]

So Darcy believed that he (and doubtless the other nobility and gentry who had been with the commons at Doncaster) had served the king well by resisting as long as they could, and had served him a second time by devising a means to have the Pilgrim host go home. But the Pilgrims had not disappeared. They remained a quiescent military force, with posts in place, watches kept over major roads, and a network of beacons. It was further alleged that new musters were taking place.[20] It was reported that Thomas Grice had seized a royal messenger at Wakefield, set him in the stocks, and taken his letter.[21] In the middle of the month Hallam's commons managed to capture a supply boat making its way to Scarborough with artillery and £100 in cash, and then recommenced the siege of the castle.[22] Doubtless all the Crown's worst fears were confirmed when Hastings reported in a letter on 8 November that the Pilgrims would attack in two columns, Darcy by way of Doncaster, whilst Aske and Constable took boats to Gainsborough and Stockwith (on the Trent) from where they would strike to Lincoln and seize the stockpiled harness of the Lincolnshire rebels.[23] That there was a plan for an offensive, should the truce collapse, is known from another witness, but whether it was the same as this apparently fantastic scheme is another matter.[24] So the king's side had good reason to factor the continuing existence of the commons into their strategy: for the most part they did not do so until late in the month, believing that they could deal with the political society of the nobility and gentry alone. The Pilgrims' leadership, however, most certainly recognized that they had to have some success with which to appease the commons, or else they would be forced to lead them into renewed war.

The first fortnight of November saw each side becoming increasingly wary of the other's good faith. The failure of the Crown to honour its part of the Doncaster compact pushed Darcy further and further into opposition. When, on 11 November, Sir Brian Hastings accidentally set off a full invasion scare, Darcy and Aske reacted by putting the honour

---

[19] Ibid., no. 1059.   [20] e.g. ibid., nos. 966, 1017, 1059.   [21] Ibid., no. 1042.
[22] Ibid., nos. 1103, 1116, 1128; XII (i), nos. 201 (ii), (iv); 202.   [23] LP XI, no. 1017.
[24] LP XII (i), no. 1186.

of Pontefract on notice to move at an hour's warning. Darcy saw himself as being party to a bargain, of which he had performed his share; the other half awaited settlement by the king. And as, with time, it seemed less and less likely that the king was grateful for—or even understanding of—Darcy's actions in October, and more and more likely that he would abrogate the Doncaster agreement, there was an inevitable slide into activities which were undeniably treasonable.

II

The duke of Norfolk, in the company of Ellerker and Bowes, arrived at Windsor on Thursday, 2 November. As late as 27 October Henry had been talking of leading an army against the rebels, should Norfolk and Shrewsbury not be able to defeat them, and there are indications that an army was being gathered towards the end of the month.[25] When word reached Windsor of the opening of negotiations at Doncaster, perhaps coupled with Norfolk's warnings of the impossibility of securing a military solution, the call for troops appears to have been countermanded.[26] By the time Norfolk and the Pilgrim's two representatives reached the court, a new strategy—of admonishment and pardon—had been decided upon.

The proclamation of a general pardon was drawn up on 2 November. Addressing itself to the rebels, it began by saying that, as the rebellion proceeded out of ignorance, the king had ordered books to be sent to them to inform them of their errors. Any person wishing to do so could sue out of Chancery a pardon for all offences committed before 1 November. There were, however, conditions attached. The pardon was conditional on the apprehension of six named ringleaders (of whom Aske was one) and four unnamed who were to be drawn from amongst the rebels of Tynedale, Redesdale, Lancashire, and Kendal. It would not apply if there was any further rebellion. All wishing to take advantage of it were to submit themselves before Norfolk (whom the king intended to

---

[25] *LP* XI, nos. 884, 885, 886, 906, 907.   [26] Ibid., nos. 918 (1–2).

appoint as his lieutenant in the North) or his deputy. If the rebels failed to become the king's true subjects and did not cease their assemblies, then the king would come with an army with which to crush them. A draft of the proclamation included the instruction that those pardoned should aid the king's commissioners to re-enter the monasteries to which the religious had been restored by the rebels, but this was dropped from the final text.[27]

This proclamation of pardon was to be taken into the North by a herald, accompanied by a trumpeter, and read by him before the commons in market-places and elsewhere. Elaborate instructions explaining how the herald was to expound the king's policy were drawn up. On his arrival in a town, the herald was to estimate the demeanour of the people and whether they were settled or 'remained in their madness'. He was then to make himself known to the mayor or chief officers and demand their assistance. Next, he was to address the inhabitants, telling them how they had been deceived into mistaken opinions, how false their grounds for rebellion were, and how their petitions showed them to have been misled. After chastising the inhabitants for their ingratitude towards the king, the herald was to continue by saying:

Surely it was a strange matter to his most noble majesty to hear of a rebellion attempted for matters of weddings, christenings, churches, eating white bread and certain other meats, marking of beasts, bringing in of money to be touched at the Tower, and such other things when neither his highness nor any of his council had, at any time in his most noble life, thought of any such matter.

Why had the commons not come to him as suitors and petitioners when such false lies started to circulate amongst them? Then they might have known from his mouth the truth of the matter and the 'detestable falsehood of them that intended to bring them to utter ruin and destruction by the stirring of them to such a grievous offence'. The subsidy did not bear on people unless they were worth £20 or more: anyone worth so much who would not pay 10s. for the advancement of the commonwealth was not a good subject. And, after much more chastising, the herald was to say that as the clerical tenth, first fruits, and the suppression of the abbeys did not bear on the commonalty, how could they

27 Ibid., no. 955 (1–3).

deny the king a source of profit which would better enable him to defend his subjects from their enemies? All the alterations in religion or observance had been determined by the clergy of the provinces of Canterbury and York to be conformable to God's Holy Word and the Testament. 'And how can simple people say the contrary?' The king preferred their preservation rather than their destruction: therefore he had retired his army from the field rather than proceed to their punishment. The proclamation of pardon was then to be read and a copy affixed to a market cross or some other place. Watch was to be kept that no one should pull it down. Finally, the herald was to gather information on the re-entry of monks and nuns into their houses.[28]

The denial of the rumours of taxation and the depredation of the commonwealth was an attempt to nail the reports which were rife in the summer and autumn of 1536. Whilst making no concessions, the herald was to educate the commons out of their wilder fears about government policy. The specific points which the proclamation answered, including the subsidy, the tenths, first fruits, and the suppression generally, appear to be drawn from the so-called York articles (that is, the articles agreed at Lincoln on 9 October), and not those compiled at Hampole to present to the duke of Norfolk. These were probably unknown at Windsor until the arrival of Norfolk, Ellerker, and Bowes on 2 November.

On arrival at Windsor, Norfolk was debriefed by the king in private. Ellerker and Bowes were then called into the king's presence and expounded the Hampole articles before him. They had to endure a royal ill-temper, especially for presuming to dictate to the king the membership of his royal council. But Henry was also magnanimous: he wished (or so he said) his subjects in the North to live in quietness rather than suffer his revenge by the sword. Calmed by the mediation of Norfolk and other councillors, the king then returned to his study to pen an answer to the rebel's petition.[29]

The first article the king answered was that touching the maintenance of the Faith.[30] 'The terms [of this complaint] be so general that hard they be to be answered.' The king claimed that he had always been minded

---

[28] Ibid., no. 956.   [29] Ibid., no. 1009.

[30] The text of the king's answer is *LP* XI, no. 957, printed in full in *St. P.* I, 506–10 and Dodds, *Pilgrimage*, I, 275–8.

to live and die 'in the purity of the same', and regretted that the rebels had given credence to 'forged, light tales' to the contrary. The second article, 'which touched the maintenance of the church and the liberties of the same', was also too general to be answered. But nothing had been done contrary to either God's law or man's; and the king regretted that the rebels should prefer 'a churl or two' to have the profits of the monasteries 'in supportation of vicious and abominable life, than I your prince for supportation of my extreme charges, done for your defence'. The third article, on laws, the commonwealth, and the council, was again rejected. The royal record was that there had never been 'so many wholesome, commodious, and beneficial acts made for the commonwealth'. The king had kept his subjects in wealth and peace. And Henry showed how there were now no fewer noblemen on the privy council than there had been at the beginning of his reign. Whilst the king declared that this was 'the truth to pull you from the blindness that you were led in, yet we ensure you we would ye knew that it appertaineth nothing to any of our subjects to appoint us our council . . .'. In the fourth article the commons had claimed that certain of the council were 'subverters both of God's law and the laws of this realm'. The king rejected these allegations: the slander was untrue, but he admitted that the report circulated widely amongst people who had never heard them preach. Again, this gave no quarter on policy.

Having answered the rebels' complaints so far as their inexactitude allowed, the king turned to what he required of them. First, he rejected entirely the right of the rebels to alter policy, or to have councillors chosen or dismissed, through insurrection. Because the rebellion had been launched out of the 'naughty nature' of the commons and a 'wondrous sudden surreption of gentlemen', a punishment other than revenge was required.

We are contented, if we may see and perceive in you all a sorrowfulness for your offences and will henceforth to do no more so, nor believe so lewd and naughty tales or reports of your most kind and loving prince and his council, to grant unto you all our letters patent of pardon for this rebellion so that you will deliver unto us ten such of the ringleaders and provokers of you in this rebellion as we shall assign to you and appoint. Now note the benignity of your prince.

The Dodds thought that the Pilgrims would receive the king's riposte as a declaration of war, and held that Norfolk and the council worked to have the text suppressed.[31] Perhaps so, perhaps not. Taken with the proclamation which Lancaster Herald was to carry, the king's letter formed a comprehensive denial of the rumours circulating about royal policy in the late summer. We need to read both together as an attempt to mould opinion out of subversion, whilst the pardon, even with its conditions, served to limit the danger to the generality of the commons whilst identifying a few individuals who could be sacrificed as a warning to future rebels. Together, they offered the sort of reassurance which had been sought by the men of Louth when they travelled to seek the advice of the subsidy commissioners at Caistor: that the rumours circulating were untrue; that royal policy was being misrepresented; that the commons' fears that the king was under the thumb of subverters of the law were unfounded. Hence, it may be argued that the royal counter-offensive, based as it was on the stark truth of military weakness, contained more subtlety than is sometimes assumed.

Here it may be worth considering an alternative approach to the problem, which, if even considered, was rejected. There survives a document headed 'Devices for appeasing and quieting the commons in the North Parts'. This is both undated and unsigned, but must date from the first few days of November before the king closed off the options it contains.[32] It may be conjectured that the author was the duke of Norfolk himself, for the 'devices' certainly encapsulate Norfolk's preference for victory through conciliation and policy. If so, they show how large the gulf was between his strategic thinking and the king's.

The key proposal was that a proclamation should be sent to every town in the North announcing that the king had heard the Pilgrims' petition from the duke of Norfolk and Lord Talbot, and that the petition had also been placed before the council in the presence of Ellerker and Bowes. It would then outline how the king, as supreme head, would continue to work for the maintenance of the church. To this end, he intended to make inquisitions to discover whether any of its doctrines were contrary to Christ's faith. A parliament might be called and, if any there could

---

[31] Dodds, *Pilgrimage*, I, 278. [32] *LP* XI, no. 1410 (4).

prove that an act of parliament or order in council passed in his reign was contrary to the laws of God and the commonwealth, the king would see it reformed. If the commons could prove that any of those they called 'subverters of the laws of God and this realm', in whom the king placed his trust, were indeed as the commons alleged, the king would proceed against them. The proclamation should also lead the commons to suppose that they could have hopes of a pardon. Besides a proclamation, the king should write to the gentry of the North to encourage them. He should prepare the cities and castles of the North to resist any new rebellion, and he should appoint a nobleman as his lieutenant of the North.

These proposals made no concessions to policy, but cast the king as a dutiful and listening monarch in the medieval mould, ready to hear and ponder the petitions of his subjects and offer correction and justice where appropriate. By doing so, the proposal addressed the Pilgrims' grievances rather than simply denying their validity. It placed on the Pilgrims the onus of proving that Cromwell and the bishops were 'subverters'. It therefore opened a way for a critique of the polices of the 1530s by inviting complaints about those who had implemented (if not devised) those policies. It ran the risk of opening a dialogue with subjects in rebellion. And this was completely contrary to the king's preferences in November 1536.

Ellerker and Bowes set out from court on Sunday, 5 November, carrying the king's reply to Yorkshire; but within a matter of hours it had been decided to call them back to Windsor. This change of heart arose from the receipt from the earls of Shrewsbury and Rutland of reports of continuing rebel activity in the North. As their letters are lost, their reports have to be reconstructed at second hand from the letter of complaint which Norfolk penned to Darcy on 6 November and Aske's reply.

Aske, it was understood at Windsor, had breached the truce in several respects. He had written to Sir Marmaduke Constable (who had been with the earl of Shrewsbury), who had then fled from Yorkshire. On Aske's account this was no more than an attempt to save him from the commons' anger at his opposition to them during October.[33] It was alleged that Aske had written to Lancashire, Cumberland, Westmorland,

---

[33] Ibid., no. 1046 (3).

and Kendal instructing them to make new commotions: in fact, as we saw, he wrote to spread word of the truce.[34]

If this was all the letters contained, then it would be worth asking whether these reports were *misunderstood* to be evidence of further offensive activity by the Pilgrims, or whether it was decided deliberately to *misconstrue* the reports in an attempt to play for time. These reports alone do not seem enough to prompt a sudden reversal of policy during Sunday, 5 November. And here it is possible to speculate that what shook the king and broke his confidence in the settlement reached at Doncaster was Hastings's letter of 3 November, in which he reported that Darcy had set the honour of Pontefract on standby and was gathering money to support soldiers. This called into question the claims— by Norfolk, Ellerker, and Bowes—that Darcy had been the Pilgrim's unwilling victim.[35] With this news, policy towards the Pilgrims passed into a new phase as the government realized that the Pilgrimage would not simply fade away with an application of propaganda.

It seems to have been accepted that the gentry had found themselves faced with a situation they could not control. They had therefore been coerced into offering leadership. Norfolk certainly held to this line.[36] So did the king, albeit with doubts.[37] It was also accepted that Darcy was probably a loyalist, whereas Aske who, it will be recalled, was expressly omitted from the general pardon, was the commons' ringleader. From this moment on it was appreciated that the movement posed a continuing threat (albeit that this assessment was based on a misunderstanding of Aske's actions). Aske was held to be the dynamic figure without whom the movement would collapse. Darcy's stock doubtless having fallen with the news that he had placed the honour of Pontefract on standby, it was decided to test his loyalty: he was made the means by which Aske might be arrested and bundled into imprisonment. Ellerker and Bowes were therefore detained at Windsor whilst contacts were made with Darcy,

---

[34] Ibid., nos. 995, 1046 (3).   [35] Ibid., no. 966.

[36] Although Norfolk was duplicitous. In his letters to Darcy his language is moderate. Writing to Cromwell on 22 November though, Darcy, Aske, and Constable were 'arrant traitors'. But that may have been what Cromwell believed and wanted to hear. *LP* XI, no. 1138. For doubts about Norfolk's soundness, pp. 339–40, 393–4 below.

[37] Cf. his comment in *LP* XI, no. 1175.

the alleged breaches of the truce being the pretext to send a messenger to him. At the same time arrangements were being made to hold the north Midlands against any new advance.[38]

Two groups of messengers set out for the North on Tuesday, 7 November and the following day. The first were servants of Ellerker and Bowes, who carried a letter from the two emissaries addressed to Darcy, outlining their reception by the king but explaining that they would be delayed in London until the breaches of the truce were investigated and explained.[39] The second was Creswell, a servant of Lord Hussey's (and so known to Darcy), who carried letters from Hussey and Norfolk. Hussey's letter to Darcy, which had been approved by the council before being sealed, was short. Hussey had been the subject of suspicion because he had been taken to be a conspirator with Darcy, but Norfolk, by appealing to the king, had relieved him from this calumny. Norfolk had told Hussey that Darcy was suspected of surrendering the castle to the rebels and, whilst Norfolk had defended Darcy so far, he could only be sure of the king's favour if he sent Aske for trial and imprisonment. One may wonder if this was not the means by which Hussey tried to expunge the doubts about his handling of Lincolnshire.[40] Creswell's second letter to Darcy was from Norfolk. The king had answered the petitions in his own hand: his answer was absolute and unanswerable. He had decided to send the answers with Ellerker and Bowes, but when word came of Aske's breaches of the truce he had decided to detain them a little longer at Windsor. Norfolk wanted details of what had been done contrary to the truce, and by whom. He warned Darcy that people at court were whispering that he had deliberately surrendered Pontefract. Norfolk, though, had 'used myself like a true friend, thinking that you delivered the castle for lack of victual and ordnance and you were forced to go with the commons like many other noblemen'. To remove all doubts, he should capture Aske.[41] Creswell was also given an oral message urging Darcy to clear his name by arresting the Grand Captain.

[38] Below pp. 323–4.

[39] *LP* XI, no. 1009. Copies of this letter may have been distributed. Five copies survive in the PRO.

[40] Ibid., no. 1007.   [41] Ibid., no. 995.

Creswell set out for the North behind Ellerker's and Bowes's servants, but arrived at Temple Hirst in their company on Friday, 10 November.[42] When he met Darcy he presented him with the two letters and told him in confidence that he had a further oral message for him. Darcy took the letters into a private room, leaving Creswell in an antechamber with a press of commons and servants. They demanded news. What was happening in London? Had Cromwell and the other ill-councillors about the king been removed from influence? Creswell said he had seen Cromwell two or so days before he set out for Yorkshire. Who was of council about the king? Creswell had seen the dukes of Norfolk, Suffolk, and Sussex, Sir William Fitzwilliam (lord admiral), Sir William Paulet (comptroller), and Sir William Kingston (vice-chamberlain). This pleased Creswell's audience. 'God save the king and them all!', he has them saying. 'For as long as such noblemen of the true noble blood may reign or rule about the king, all should be well.' Then, turning towards Darcy and the others in the inner chamber, they told Creswell that

whatsoever answer ye shall have of yonder men . . . if ye speak with the king's highness ye shall show him, or else show my lord's grace your master and other the foresaid true noble men of the council, that if the king's grace do not send and grant unto us our petitions, which we sent unto his highness by the duke's grace your master, whatsoever letter, bill, or pardon shall be sent else unto us, we shall not accept nor receive the same, but send it to his highness again.

Creswell objected that this was not a reasonable message for a subject to send the king, nor for Creswell to retail. But he was told, 'If ye be a true man, ye will report the same, for that thing which moves us to this is the faith we bear unto God, to the king's person, and [to] all his true noble blood and the commonwealth'.[43]

This conversation was brought to a close by a summons for Creswell to enter Darcy's chamber. Darcy asked the other gentlemen present to leave so he could talk privately to Creswell. Darcy then said that he had read the letters: what was the oral message? Creswell said that it was as the letters: that he should demonstrate his loyalty by having Aske sent as a prisoner to the king. The king would then not only forgive all his

---

[42] The following account is based on Creswell's examination, *LP* XII (i), no. 1013.
[43] E36/119, fo. 79v (= *LP* XII (i), no. 1013).

former anger against him, but Darcy would stand higher than ever before in his estimation.

Darcy rejected the proposal:

I cannot do it in no wise, for I have made promise to the contrary, and my coat hitherto was never stained with any such blot. And my lord grace your master knoweth well enough what a nobleman's promise is, and therefore I think that this thing cometh not of his grace's device, nor of none other nobleman's and if I might have two dukedoms for my labour I would not consent to have such a spot on my coat.[44]

The conversation then broke off, as they were called to dinner. Aske came later and was briefed by Darcy about the detention of Ellerker and Bowes at court because of the allegations that the truce had been breached. Aske denied any wrongdoing contrary to the undertakings made at Doncaster.

Creswell saw Darcy twice more. On the first occasion Darcy begged him to tell the king or the duke of Norfolk of the great service that he and the other gentlemen had done the king; that there had been no way to defend the castle, that he had received no response to his letters to the king, and that he had used all the persuasions and policies possible to save the castle from the commons. On their second meeting he desired Creswell to apologize to the king for the venom with which he and others spoke of Cromwell, 'for that should please the people best'.[45]

On Saturday evening Creswell left for the south carrying letters for Ellerker and Bowes and Norfolk, and a message for Hussey. To Ellerker and Bowes, Darcy wrote that he knew of no breaches of the truce; the allegations contained in Norfolk's letter were answered in a further letter and an accompanying bill by Aske. The delay in sending Ellerker and Bowes home again was, in itself, contrary to the agreement. Their exposition of the king's answer at a council of the noblemen and gentlemen would do more good than twenty letters.[46] The letter to Norfolk was much longer and self-justificatory. First of all, Darcy was pleased to hear that the king had devised answers to their petition. Secondly, he defended his actions after Norfolk had left Doncaster in sending letters into Lancashire and elsewhere. And he reported the problems he had

[44] Ibid.   [45] Ibid., fo. 80v.   [46] *LP* XI, no. 1046.

faced in persuading the rearward of the commons to disband. Thirdly, he denied that he had conspired with Aske before the surrender of the castle. Fourthly, he refused to betray Aske and expressed sadness that Norfolk thought he might deliver any living man in this way. He would not do it; but he was ready to serve the king to the best of his ability, and would happily serve as a kitchen-hand if this business could only be brought to a happy end. What Darcy sought more than anything else was the return of Ellerker and Bowes with the king's answers, especially his promise of a parliament.[47]

To his old friend Hussey he merely sent a message that he was sorry to hear of his trouble. He was doubtless shrewd enough to realize that the letter was not Hussey's own work, but suggested to him as a means by which he could curry favour.[48]

The Dodds considered that, in his letter to Norfolk, Darcy signed his own death warrant. 'No past service, no future pardon, could protect a man who so boldly exalted his own honour above the king's pleasure.'[49] The suggestion that he should betray Aske posed Darcy with a moral dilemma. Somerset Herald asked him about it on 14 November.[50]

Somerset: Think you my lord that if it were an unlawful act to take or kill him and send him to the king if he be a rebel as some do take him?
Darcy: Perhaps it were lawful for you and not for me, for he that promiseth to be true to one and deceiveth him may be called a traitor, which shall never be said in me, for what is a man but his promise?

What was the promise which Darcy had made to Aske which left him bound to him? Unless it was the oath which he swore when Pontefract was given up, we do not know. It is possible that the promise was not made directly to Aske, but consisted of the mutual promises made at Doncaster when the truce was agreed. Darcy's objection may well have been that, by asking him to capture Aske, Norfolk was in clear breach of the truce. Darcy was clearly committed to the Doncaster arrangement because it promised to bring peace and the end of strife to the North. A failure to honour the arrangements entered into there would prolong and inflame the rebellion, and doubtless jeopardize the nobility and

---

[47] Ibid., no. 1045.   [48] *LP* XII (i), no. 1013.
[49] Dodds, *Pilgrimage*, I, 293.   [50] Ibid. 304.

gentry who had argued for them before the commons.[51] The reality of this fear may be seen in January 1537, when the realization grew amongst the commons that they had been sold out. But in moralizing the issue, Darcy concealed an essential truth. There was no practical possibility of him, or anyone else, capturing Aske. The account Creswell gives of the temper of the household at Temple Hirst shows quite clearly that Darcy had no servants on whom he could rely to carry out a task so contrary to their inclination. Darcy was their prisoner, if not literally, then of their opinions. To require him to vindicate his record in October by an action which he found morally repugnant, politically erroneous, and impossible to fulfil in practice was a cruel entrapment.

The king's manoeuvres may also have persuaded Aske, Darcy, and Constable that there was little possibility of striking a deal with him. They may have read the delay in the return of Ellerker and Bowes as a sign that the king would never negotiate on their articles, but that he looked to pretended breaches of the truce to demonstrate the Pilgrim's faithlessness and so evade his own responsibilities. They were forced to look into the abyss: with the commons behind them, what would they do if the king refused to negotiate?

The only account of their discussions at Temple Hirst comes from Aske. They remained anxious about the defence of Hull from the duke of Suffolk. They feared that the king would move in the wintertime without considering 'their common cause or petitions', and considered how they should garrison Pontefract, Hull, and other towns. And they considered the alternative, that they should advance, in which case they would require victuals, horse provender, artillery, ordnance, and gunpowder.[52]

They also looked abroad for support. Dr Marmaduke Waldby, a canon of Ripon and vicar of Kirk Deighton, was instructed to sail to the Netherlands to open contacts with the regent (the sister of Charles V, Mary of Hungary) and to seek the supply of money, 2,000 arquebuses and 2,000 horsemen, and the pope's support. Darcy promised to send word through the Imperial ambassador in London that Waldby should

---

[51] Suffolk realized this and argued that Darcy, Constable, and Aske were those with the greatest hold over the rebels. *LP* XI, no. 1120.

[52] 'Aske's Examination', 569.

be expected. Waldby tried to evade his mission, but he was given £20 for expenses and dispatched to Hull. Before he could sail he was called home by Darcy (probably because word came of the return of Ellerker and Bowes), and never carried his message abroad. Nonetheless, it would appear that not even his reluctance could save him: he was arrested in 1537 and is last heard of in the Tower.[53] If the Pilgrim's leaders thought that the regent could do anything material to help them, they must have envisaged the rebellion stretching through the winter and into the spring.

Uncertainty and anxiety about the king's motives was therefore changing the character of the leadership. This can be seen most clearly in the case of Darcy. Simultaneously he was claiming to have done the king a great service, whilst his fear of the king's rejection was forcing him to contemplate treason in order to protect himself. Darcy had at his back not the proverbial wall, but the commons. And so, as Aske told his interrogators: 'Albeit these reasons [arguments at Temple Hirst] were but always spoken and reasoned to this intent, that if the king's highness would not grant them their pardon and petition for their commonwealth of the realm, then so to make preparation for the succour of their lives and the country.'[54]

The first part of the king's strategy devised on 5–6 November was designed to test Darcy's loyalty. The second part was a plan have in place the means to hold the north Midlands against any further advance by the Pilgrims. The earl of Shrewsbury was told to be prepared to advance to Derby to hold the rebels there. On 9 November he wrote back objecting the imposs-ibility of this, arguing that the Trent would have to be held where the road crossed the river near Derby and again at Burton on Trent. Ten thousand men would not suffice to keep the bridges and fords over the river between Nottingham and Burton.[55] The earl of Rutland was given Nottingham as his sector. He too wrote to point out the problems of

---

[53] Waldby appears to have been a linguist. His doctorate may have come from a continental uni-versity and he apparently knew some of the noblemen at the regent's court. For this episode see his examination, *LP* XII (ii), no. 1080, and for his career, Emden, *Biographical Register of the University of Cambridge to 1500*, 610.

[54] 'Aske's Examination', 569 (answ. 43).   [55] *LP* XI, no. 1028.

holding the town against an invasion from the North. The bridge over the Trent lay on the south side of the town and so could not be held without great force. Rutland asked for some professional military help to be sent to him: he was also, he told Cromwell, short of money, had substantial charges in the establishment of Nottingham Castle, and expected to receive little or none of his rents out of Yorkshire.[56] By 14 November the king admitted to Shrewsbury that the council was now persuaded that the Trent could not be held, and told him to look towards the defence of the Don using, if necessary, Sir Brian Hastings to capture Doncaster if it was held by the rebels.[57] (This may be seen as vindicating Shrewsbury's decision to advance to the Don the previous month.) Hastings was confident of holding Doncaster Bridge with 500 men and a little ordnance until he was relieved from the south.[58] At much the same moment, the duke of Suffolk had men assessing the likelihood of stopping the rebels crossing the Trent around Newark. He too reported that the task was impossible with so many fords. He was badly stretched, with only 3,600 men to defend a 50-mile-long frontier.[59]

The general situation is outlined in a letter written by Gervais Clifton, a young gentleman from Clifton in Nottinghamshire serving in Rutland's retinue at Nottingham, on 11 November. He expected that the king would pardon all the rebels except five, of whom Aske was one. (There were actually ten exemptions in the draft pardon.) He would not surrender his liberty to choose his council, nor would he 'forego my lord of privy seal [Cromwell] for any man living'. The king had ordered the earl of Shrewsbury to keep Derby, the earl of Rutland to hold Nottingham, and the duke of Suffolk to keep Newark; 'And if they [the rebels] be busy, to stop them, or else to be still: for if they stir not, we shall not [molest] them'. Clifton thought that plans were afoot to establish a garrison to hold the Don. Meanwhile the gentry were to go back home to keep the country in good frame.[60]

[56] Ibid., nos. 1037–8.   [57] Ibid., no. 1063.

[58] Ibid., no. 1026, perhaps *recte* 16 November. And cf. no. 1136.   [59] Ibid., no. 1087, 1103.

[60] Ibid., no. 1042. For Clifton see *Hist. Parl., 1509–1558*, I, 660–1. For another letter of his, 'Letters of the Cliffords', 143.

III

With the return of Creswell to Windsor carrying Darcy's letter rejecting the duke of Norfolk's overtures, and Aske's explanation of the breaches of the truce, 'policy' moved into a third stage.

A general pardon for Lincolnshire, but excluding those in gaol, Vicar Kendall of Louth, and Robert [*sic*] Leach of Horncastle (who were still at large), was sent to be read throughout the county.[61] The pardon in Yorkshire, though, was still withheld. Ellerker and Bowes were to be allowed to return to Yorkshire without either the pardon or the king's answer to their grievances, but with royal instructions as to how they were to proceed. In them the king complained that the articles brought south by Ellerker and Bowes were 'so general, dark, and obscure that it was very difficult and hard to make any certain answer unto'. Nonetheless, the instructions continued, the king would have dispatched them back earlier had it not been for the news of the breaches of the truce which Creswell had been sent to query. Since Creswell's return from the North there had been further reports of rebel activity, including an (erroneous) report of the capture of Lord Clifford, the continued siege at Skipton, the ringing of bells *in alarum*, and the interception of royal letters. In order to bring the whole matter to a conclusion, the king had decided not to make his answer known through Ellerker and Bowes, but through Norfolk, who would address 300 of the lords and gentlemen at Doncaster. Norfolk would give such a full answer as to make them grateful for the 'great clemency' of their monarch.[62]

The rebels' delegates were sent home with sweet words and the promise of more to be brought by Norfolk later in the month. The instructions given to Norfolk and Fitzwilliam flesh out the full character of royal policy at this moment.[63] They were to go to Doncaster equipped with

---

[61] *LP* XI, nos. 1061, 1062. For the text (there dated 2 December), no. 1224 (2). When Kendall was arrested is not clear: his examination shows that in mid-November he was in Coventry trying to be admitted to the Charterhouse, ibid., no. 970.

[62] *LP* XI, no. 1064 (2).

[63] The following is based on ibid., no. 1064, printed in *St. P.* I, 498–505.

a safe conduct, the text of a proclamation announcing a pardon (from which Aske and others were excluded), copies of the proclamation, and (printed) copies of the king's answer. At Doncaster they were to invite Darcy and others to hear the king's answer, assuring them of their safe passage and return. Only if they refused to accept Norfolk's verbal assurance was the written safe conduct to be employed. On their meeting, Norfolk was to tell the assembly of the king's hurt at the proceedings: that they did not petition him for the redress of the matters they held to be abuses; and that despite the agreement at Doncaster they had persisted in breaching the truce. The king of his mercy had chosen not to repress the rebellion by force but had sent his councillors. Norfolk and Fitzwilliam were then to offer those assembled a homily on the folly of rebellion. They were to tax them with rebellion against the king, with choosing a 'traitorous villain' to be their captain, and permitting him to write in the name of the whole baronage. Norfolk and Fitzwilliam were to seek to have the rebels acknowledge the same, to petition for the king's pardon, and, by their actions, to demonstrate their loyalty (presumably by surrendering up Aske and others).

In effect the king sought the rebels' unconditional surrender before he would answer their articles. The king's instructions acknowledged that Darcy and the others might wish to hear his answer at this stage, but held that this request was 'to persist in their fond and traitorous malice'. If Darcy and the others demanded to hear the king's answers, Norfolk and Fitzwilliam were to say that the king had answered the articles, but that they were only authorized to give his replies if they found the rebels conformable to his will. And if the Pilgrims wished to persist in their obstinacy, then they were to be denied sight of the articles and the king was to be informed. At this stage, if Darcy and the others were to sue for the king's pardon then it was to be offered them, initially to a select group in secret, who were to be shown the proclamation so that they might apprehend and deliver those excluded from its terms. Only then were they to be shown the king's answer and the king's proclamation of pardon publicly proclaimed. Then those seeking the pardon were to be sworn with an oath similar to that used in Lincolnshire, Darcy and the senior figures first, and again they were to be hectored both about their mistakes in the past and their conduct in the future.

If the rebels were to refuse their submission, then Norfolk was to fudge for a few days, try to persuade them of their folly, and then temporize to give the king the opportunity to recruit a new army for their repression.

So instructed, Norfolk fixed 29 November for the meeting and asked Darcy to gather the gentlemen on that date.[64] What the plans do not make clear is that, once the Pilgrims had submitted, Norfolk was to be imposed upon them as the king's lieutenant based at the castle at Sheriff Hutton. There is no explicit statement of this, but when, late in November, Norfolk is found fretting about commissions to provision Sheriff Hutton, it becomes clear that he envisaged a protracted stay in the North.[65]

The plan of action outlined here was hopelessly impractical. Norfolk and Fitzwilliam, without the support of any substantial military force, were to confront a much larger group of lords and gentlemen, many of whom had been semi-captives amongst the commons, and a few of whom may well have been radicalized by their experience, and lecture them on their subordination to the monarch.[66] They were to refuse to offer either sight of the king's answers to their articles or to bargain about the pardon until the rebels had made an abject submission and, in private, agreed to hand over one of their leaders for imprisonment and trial. There was no recognition in this strategy that the body of the Pilgrims—the 30,000 men who had come to Doncaster—were an independent force over whom the 300 nobles and gentlemen had only a tenuous and conditional control. The answer to the articles with which Norfolk had been provided gave the commons no quarter, the proclamation reminded them of the error of their ways, and the pardon omitted the pilgrim's most charismatic leader from its terms. No provision was made for debate. The king had bent not at all: he trusted that he could berate the rebels into conformity, shout down their complaints, that Norfolk could carry enough of the majesty of monarchy to subdue a rebellion. It was nonsense. There was nothing here to end the Pilgrimage of Grace, and within a fortnight Norfolk, for one, recognized this.

The Pilgrims immediately wrongfooted the whole enterprise by showing that they were a continuing political force, which sought a dialogue where the king offered a tirade. A council was convened at Temple

---

[64] Ibid., no. 1065, misdated copy no. 1014.   [65] Ibid., no. 1138.
[66] Norfolk and Fitzwilliam were travelling 'without harness'. Ibid., no. 1139.

Hirst on the arrival of Ellerker and Bowes (probably on Saturday, 18 November); those attending (so far as can be established) were Darcy, Aske, Constable, the lawyer William Babthorpe, Ellerker, and Bowes. Darcy, Constable, and Babthorpe had been amongst those who had fallen into Aske's hands at Pontefract. This was a coalition of six men, all of whom had been initially taken by force, five of whom were probably eager for the Pilgrimage of Grace to be wound up by whatever means possible, while the sixth was probably willing to ride the tiger for his own political aims. All were doubtless surprised to discover that Ellerker and Bowes had not returned with the king's answer, but merely a message that, whilst it had been written, it would only be revealed to them by Norfolk in a further ten days time. Moreover, there was the paradox that whilst the king had found their articles 'too general, dark, and obscure' to answer, he had written an answer which would offer complete satisfaction and leave them gratified by its clemency. The terms of Ellerker's and Bowes's answer, coupled with the king's pressure on Darcy (if he revealed it to the others), must have made it certain to them that Henry was not going to play by the rules. He was not going to make the concessions which they required to secure the Pilgrims' disbandment. For Aske, the course of events probably proved the futility of ever having negotiated with Norfolk at Doncaster. The council therefore seems to have taken a number of key decisions. The first was to call a meeting of the Pilgrims at York on the following Tuesday, at which Ellerker and Bowes would make their report, albeit without the king's answer.[67] The second was to defer Norfolk's meeting for five or six days until early December, and lay down terms to govern its proceedings. They would request that, at any meeting of Aske and Norfolk, hostages were to be exchanged, and that if there was no agreement at Doncaster, then there should be a truce for a further fourteen days.[68] They were forced to consider what they could do to

---

[67] It is possible that this meeting was arranged, albeit without date, at Doncaster. Aske seems to imply that the date was fixed and circulated when he and Darcy met at Temple Hirst to answer the king's first letter on 10–11 November. 'The manner of the taking of Robert Aske', 339.

[68] Norfolk had their decisions relayed to him by a letter, dated from York, which he received on Tuesday morning. *LP* XI, nos. 1126, 1138. The letter does not survive. It appears to have been signed by Ellerker and Bowes and others of the Pilgrims' command, including Aske (whose signature was placed first); quite possibly all those who met at Temple Hirst. For the contents, see *LP* XI, no. 1174, and the king's complaints about the signatories, ibid., no. 1175.

save themselves if the king either failed to produce an answer, or answered the articles in an uncompromising fashion. The stark choice was presented in a letter Aske sent to Sir Stephen Hamerton calling him to York: they would either agree with Norfolk at Doncaster, or agree upon war.[69]

The conference at York opened on Tuesday, 21 November. There appears to have been a good turnout of the nobility and gentry who had been at Doncaster in October. A letter requesting that the earl of Cumberland should attend was signed by Scrope, Latimer, Sir Robert Constable, Aske, and others.[70] Darcy did not attend, remaining at Temple Hirst. Also present were about 800 commons and gentry, the representatives of their wapentakes, including some from Cumberland whose expenses were paid by the abbot of Holme Cultram.[71] From this plenary group were chosen 200 men, who heard Ellerker and Bowes report on their reception at Windsor. The king's instructions to Ellerker and Bowes, and Norfolk's letter to Darcy, were also read (one wonders whether in full).[72] Bowes made a verbal report explaining how well inclined Cromwell was towards the rebels.[73] Sir Robert Constable then asked Bowes to withdraw, and sprang upon the conference a letter from Cromwell which had been captured in the failed attempt to run money to Scarborough Castle. The letter, addressed to Sir Ralph Eure the younger, was short but sour. After praising Eure's efforts, Cromwell explained: 'And his highness hath put everything now in such perfect order [that] if these rebels do so continue any longer in their rebellion, doubt you not but ye shall see them so subdued as their example shall be fearful to all subjects whilst the world doth endure.'[74] This represented the authentic voice of the court rather than the patient and fatherly admonitions of the king in his dealings with Ellerker and Bowes. Stapleton says—drily enough—that the contents of the letter were, 'as they took it, contrary to his said promise'.[75]

The disclosure of the letter threatened to derail the whole meeting, which turned to discussing whether it should meet with Norfolk at all.

[69] Ibid., no. 1115.   [70] 'Letters of the Cliffords', 130.   [71] *LP* XII (i), no. 466, 1259.
[72] Ibid.   [73] Stapleton, 104.   [74] *LP* XI, no. 1032.   [75] Stapleton, 104.

Constable urged that they should only negotiate from a position of strength: 'If his advice was followed, as he had broken one point in the tables with the king, he would yet break another and have no meeting, but have all the country made sure from Trent northwards: and then, he had no doubt, all Lancashire, Cheshire, Derbyshire, and the parts thereabout would join with them. Then (he said) he would condescend to a meeting.'[76] Constable's advice was not accepted. That evening Robert Chaloner was able to write to Darcy with news of the day's decisions, starting with the agreement that Darcy and the other lords should meet with Norfolk at Doncaster on Tuesday, 5 December, but should gather together at Pontefract on the previous Saturday. Darcy was asked to resolve complaints about Savile's machinations.[77]

The other issue which bedevilled the first day's meeting was the unsettled condition in Lancashire. Reports out of the county suggested that the earl of Derby was planning a new advance against the commons. There was also some anxiety that Dent and Sedbergh would advance out of the Dales and stimulate a new rising. Sir Nicholas Fairfax thought that a new rising there would be a useful way of placing the king under pressure, and Aske, in one of his depositions, seems to indicate that the conference accepted this line.[78] In fact their response was aimed at cooling the situation there whilst safeguarding their position. Darcy was asked to ensure that the earl of Derby would suspend his operations in Lancashire and conform to the terms of the truce. A second time Darcy wrote to the earl of Shrewsbury seeking his aid, and he, in turn, wrote to Derby. The earl may not have been intending to mobilize a new movement in the way it was feared at York. On 19 November he had written to London suggesting that the time was not ripe to strip the lead and melt the bells of Burscough Priory, which he was compelled to do by the end of the month.[79] The conference circulated an order that if Derby mustered Lancashire, then the surrounding districts (Craven, Kendal, Dent, Sedbergh, Lonsdale, and Furness) were to muster themselves in self-defence and notify Aske, the implication being that they were to arm, but not fight before he gave word.[80] There was a clear

---

[76] LP XII (i), no. 466.   [77] LP XI, no. 1127. For Savile see p. 309 above.
[78] Stapleton, 104–5; 'Aske's Examination', 560 (answ. 28).
[79] LP XI, nos. 1134, 1140, 1553, 1154, and 1118.   [80] Ibid., no. 1135 (1).

willingness to retaliate if the truce were broken on the king's side. Equally, there was a clear attempt to maintain discipline on the Pilgrims' side. An order was promulgated that there was to be no robbing or spoiling, nor trespassing on land, nor pulling down of enclosures before the meeting with the duke of Norfolk, except with the express permission of Aske. Nor were beacons to be burnt or bells rung 'awkward' (backwards) to raise the commons.[81]

Having agreed to meet with Norfolk, the York conference then turned to making arrangements for the meetings at Pontefract and Doncaster. Lists were compiled of men who were to represent specific areas of the north at the conferences. Within Yorkshire it was expected that the gentry and head yeomen would attend; outside the rebellion's core area, specific gentlemen were named who were to be accompanied by specified numbers of the 'tallest men'.[82] The open-ended nature of the Yorkshire lists makes it impossible to compute how many were expected.

Who first proposed that there should be a preliminary meeting—in effect, to set an agenda with which to confront Norfolk—is nowhere recorded. It may have been first proposed at Temple Hirst and then accepted by the York conference. Its purpose was clear enough. It took its cue from the king's claim that the articles sent south with Ellerker and Bowes were 'dark, general, and obscure'.[83] The Pilgrims seem to have taken this as an invitation to elaborate the simple articles prepared at Hampole nunnery. The gathering of religious grievances was to proceed side by side with the collection of purely secular complaints. Aske recalled how letters were 'to be sent to the clergy to study for the articles profitable for the faith of the church and the liberties of the same. And further that all learned counsel and wise men should bring in their learning and mind for remedy of evil laws, for the commonwealth [and] for the commodity of the country.'[84] The result of this open invitation was a complete free-for-all, as every disgruntled activist, whether gentry or common, prepared petitions outlining grievances both important and trivial. At the Pontefract conference the movement fell into the hands of pressure groups and individuals seeking favours. This had already been

---

[81] Ibid., no. 1155 (2 (ii)).   [82] Ibid., no. 1155 (1 (i)), 2 (i). See below pp. 343–4, 426.
[83] Ibid., no. 1064 (2).   [84] 'The manner of the taking of Robert Aske', 339.

the case. The York conference issued an order restoring the abbot of Guisborough to his house. The abbot of Sawley's chaplain was also in York lobbying on behalf of his house.[85]

The dynamics of the York conference are largely mysterious. It is perhaps pertinent to note that the delegates who heard Ellerker and Bowes were selected from amongst a much larger group. This may suggest that the gentry wished to filter out the more radical and volatile elements. It is not clear to whom Ellerker and Bowes actually reported. The references to the Baronage and Commonalty may refer to a single inclusive body, but might just suggest that there were two houses, in emulation of parliament. The letter to the earl of Cumberland was written in the name of both, but it was signed by a mixture of barons, knights, and esquires (and Aske); and Cumberland was asked to send word back to the baronage.[86] The commons had not gone away, though. John Hallam sent a petition to York in the name of the commons restating the Hampole articles and demanding that they be granted together with a pardon, 'or else we are fully determined to spend our lives and goods in battle as knoweth our lord God and St George'.[87] At the meeting, one of the commons' captains, called Walker, lectured the gentlemen on the need to have a pardon by act of parliament.[88]

So whilst the conference was alerted to the king's perfidy, their preference was to comply with the terms of the first Doncaster agreement and see what terms Norfolk would offer on the king's behalf for a final settlement. There is a hint that their strategy at Doncaster was to demand a free pardon before moving to the discussion of particulars. This was, in fact, the strategy employed.[89] They may have agreed that they wished to have the pardon conferred by act of parliament, and the parliament held at a place of their choosing where they might safely come and go.[90] Sir Francis Bigod understood that they had decided to demand that the first succession statute be repealed (because of the bizarre fear that the king would bequeath the throne to Cromwell), and the Princess

---

[85] *LP* XI, no. 1135 (2); Mrs Tempest, 'Nicholas Tempest', 261.
[86] 'Letters of the Cliffords', 130.   [87] 'Thomas Master's Narrative', 73.
[88] *LP* XI, no. 1170.   [89] Ibid., no. 1128 (of 24 or 25 Nov.).   [90] Ibid., no. 1170.

Mary re-legitimized.[91] Aske also commented that the commons would not be satisfied unless Cromwell was removed from power and the king agreed to rule through his nobility.[92] The meeting also appears to have discussed the military option to be employed if the Pilgrims were unable to agree with Norfolk. According to Christopher Aske, the plan was to advance in three columns which would link up somewhere south of the Trent. Aske told his master, the earl of Cumberland, of their strategy who passed the information on to the king, but no further details survive.[93] Nerves were doubtless further frayed when Robert Aske received news from the south of ships sailing from the Tower and of Cromwell's continued favour with the king. His informant claimed that the south cried out to be invaded and rescued from the king's tyranny. But passing on this discouraging news of the king's perfidy to Darcy, Aske sounded unconfident of his own position: Darcy was asked not to answer any more of Norfolk's letters until the Pontefract conference, nor to conclude any treaties with him until the general pardon had been granted.[94]

Yet the Pilgrims were unwilling to use their advantage of numbers before the meeting with Norfolk, attempts being made, for instance, to limit the numbers who might congregate at Pontefract or Doncaster during their meeting with the duke.[95] In this way they sought not advantage, but to keep their side of the bargain struck at Doncaster. The evidence is fragile, but the baronage still seem to have seen the Doncaster meeting as an occasion for reconciliation *if* Norfolk would concede their demands on the king's behalf. Once that was done, the commons would be assuaged.

IV

The news of the postponement of the Doncaster meeting reached the duke of Norfolk and Fitzwilliam in Buckinghamshire. Norfolk saw the

---

91 *LP* XII (i), no. 533 (the passage badly damaged).   92 *LP* XI, no. 1128.
93 *LP* XII (i), no. 1186.   94 Ibid., no. 849 (3).   95 *LP* XI, no. 1128.

delay as beneficial: he would inspect the castle at Nottingham, familiar-
ize himself with the fords and bridges over the Trent, and confer with
the duke of Suffolk at Newark.[96] On Wednesday, 22 November he wrote
to Darcy complaining of the delay, but particularly expressing concern
over further breaches of the truce, including the harassment and flight
of Sir Henry Savile and the reported preparations for war in Yorkshire.[97]
The delay had a further effect, but one which can be interpreted in two
ways. As Norfolk became increasingly familiar with the position in the
North, he became less and less sanguine about the practicality of the
king's instructions. Either he tried to educate the king into a new policy which, by making concessions, would be more conciliatory, or his
nerve broke.

Our ability to understand Norfolk's changing position in late November is hampered by the pilfering of his letters from the royal archives.
Whilst he was probably writing southwards on a daily or alternate-day
basis, we have only his letters written on 22 November, abstracts of those
of 26 November, and a further abstract of a letter of 30 November. Some
additional information can be gleaned from the king's replies to his letters, so far as they survive.

The first of Norfolk's letters, to Cromwell on 22 November, was chiefly
concerned with making arrangements for his widowed daughter, the
duchess of Richmond. It was only after he had dealt with that business
that he turned to the matter of the Pilgrimage. Norfolk was suspicious
of the delay of the meeting: he suspected that it was to give Darcy, Aske,
and Constable, the three 'arrant traitors', time to stir up further discontent. News had just been received of further breaches of the truce, including the flight of Sir Henry Savile to the earl of Shrewsbury: he would
take this up with Darcy.[98] There is no sign here of Norfolk chafing at
the king's instructions of 14 November, nor in Norfolk's lost letter of 24
November, written from Leicester, to which we have the king's reply.[99]

The next letters of which we have notice were written from
Nottingham on 26 November.[100] In the first, to the king, Norfolk clearly
advises him to issue both a general pardon without exceptions and to

[96] Ibid., no. 1126.   [97] Ibid., no. 1139.
[98] Ibid., no. 1138. For the letter to Darcy no. 1139, his reply no. 1167.
[99] Ibid., no. 1174.   [100] 'Thomas Master's Narrative', 74.

concede a parliament at which the Pilgrims' grievances would be aired ('which he [Norfolk] thinks necessary to be granted for the present'). If there was to be no settlement at Doncaster, then his advice was that the king should advance in person with an army of gentlemen and household servants, with enough money to pay this elite force for two months. On the same day he wrote to Thomas Cromwell, urging him to use his influence to persuade the king to 'relent and pardon these rebels and condescend to the parliament [or] else it will be wished that it had been done'.

The reasons for Norfolk's change of temper are clear enough. The decisions taken at York in a forum infiltrated by spies were never going to be terribly secret. The earl of Huntingdon had a tenant informer in York throughout the week of the conference and sent him to brief Norfolk.[101] This may not have been the first or the only knowledge that Norfolk had of the Pilgrims' deliberations and strategy. It must have been plain enough that they would not readily take their medicine from the king. As he told Cromwell, the Pilgrims had resolved that if there was no agreement at Doncaster they would renew their pilgrimage; they were sufficiently fanatical to die in the venture. There was no hope that they would willingly give up Aske. This might be the voice of the commons rather than the gentry and nobles,[102] but whichever it was, Norfolk recognized that he had not been given anything by the king which the Pilgrims would, or could, accept.

As Norfolk was begging Cromwell to persuade Henry to be flexible, the king was revealing his intransigence over the Doncaster meeting. In a letter of 27 November he refused to allow hostages to be exchanged for Aske, nor would he consent to a further truce for fourteen days if negotiations broke down.[103] On the same day he told Suffolk to work on the gentlemen and inhabitants of the Marshland (where there had been encouraging signs of discontent with the rebels), offering them pardons if they would submit. He was to make preparations to besiege Hull and to establish how many troops the Lincolnshire gentry could raise, at their own cost, for a month's campaign. Similarly, the king was

---

[101] *LP* XI, no. 1171. [102] Cf. Hallam's petition, 'Thomas Master's Narrative', 73.
[103] Ibid. 74.

enquiring of the earl of Derby to see how many troops he could muster if active hostilities were renewed.[104]

By the end of the month there are signs that Norfolk, Fitzwilliam, and Suffolk were launching a concerted campaign to influence the king's temper towards flexibility: Sir John Russell was sent to the king on 26 November carrying letters;[105] on 28 or 29 November Norfolk and Suffolk held a council of war at Newark, after which Sir Francis Bryan was sent southwards.[106] The employment of two gentlemen of the privy chamber as messengers surely suggests that men whose opinions Henry would find it hard to disregard were being sent to apply pressure. Bryan also carried a document referred to as 'Norfolk's device'. All that can be gleaned about this is that Norfolk was offering ideas for the contingency of no agreement being reached at Doncaster. He appears to have suggested that the truce should be extended and a second day of meeting arranged, and that the time gained should be employed to recruit a force of 500 or 600 horse and 200 or 300 foot in Norfolk.[107] Then Norfolk wrote to the king from Nottingham on 30 November.[108] He warned that the rebels had increased in numbers and malice. He may have estimated their numbers at 20,000 men (although on the same day Darcy denied that there was any substantial number of commons gathered at Pontefract).[109] The lords and gentlemen had lost their grip over the commons, who would not allow two or more of them to talk together in private. (Compare this with Norfolk's additional comments on 3 December: 'the people bear the rule and not the nobility, but in manner have them so suspect that they are in half captivity.'[110]) 'The rebels are so strong and our force so small, that if this meeting take no effect and war follow, we are in an ill case.' Norfolk was pessimistic about holding the line of the River Don. Again he sought more flexible instructions, if necessary to allow him to play for time until a new army could be gathered,

---

[104] *LP* XI, nos. 1176, 1178.

[105] 'Thomas Master's Narrative', 74. Russell was sent back on 2 December, carrying new instructions.

[106] *LP* XI, nos. 1197, 1207.

[107] The device is mentioned in ibid., no. 1207; for its contents, the postscript to no. 1227.

[108] For what follows, 'Thomas Master's Narrative', 75, with additional details taken from the postscript to *LP* XI, no. 1227.

[109] The number comes from the king's reply to this letter, *LP* XI, no. 1227; for Darcy's denial, no. 1209.

[110] SP1/112, fo. 96 (= *LP* XI, no. 1234).

and for a safe conduct left blank in which he could insert its duration. Norfolk was perhaps in a more optimistic mood on 2 December, when he was proposing to proceed northwards after the conference with a retinue of feed lords and gentlemen to swear York and elsewhere.[111] The barrage from the North was coupled with the advice of the council, who also believed that a pardon with omissions would not suffice.[112] The king shifted his stance and sent new instructions on 2 December.[113] It did not matter: the second agreement at Doncaster was unauthorized, but was one which the king had to swallow, then repudiate progressively.

There was another individual whose nerve seems to have been fraying in the last few days of November, and that was Robert Aske himself. This chapter has shown how he was identified as the linchpin of the movement. The assumption was made at court that it was not only within Darcy's power to arrest him, but that when that had been done, the movement would lose its impetus. The detention of Aske was, in itself, seen to be the solution to the problem of the Pilgrimage.

Aske appears to have been aware of the demand that he should be arrested. When he was called to Temple Hirst to meet with the newly returned Ellerker and Bowes, he clearly demurred until assured by Darcy of his safety. Christopher Aske, who witnessed his brother's departure for Temple Hirst, recalled that he travelled in the company of sixty commons who may have served as his private retinue or bodyguard.[114] The proposed arrest was presumably discussed at Temple Hirst; hence the request that hostages should be exchanged to ensure his safe return. It was also most certainly known amongst the Pilgrims' high command that Aske had been excluded from the pardon which Norfolk carried.[115] The king referred to him as a villain and a 'common peddler in the law', and demanded to know why the nobility of the North allowed themselves to be led by a man of servile origins.[116] (In fact Aske's ancestry was respectably gentle. He was a second cousin to the earl of Northumberland.) Aske was a marked man, held to have a special culpability for the Pilgrimage of Grace. His brother urged him to sue for a pardon at Doncaster.

---

[111] Outlined in a letter from Welbeck which is lost, but answered in *LP* XI, nos. 1237, 1242.
[112] Ibid., no. 1236.   [113] Described below, p. 341.
[114] *LP* XI, no. 1107; XII (i), no. 1186.
[115] This was reported by Clifton on 11 November, ibid., no. 1042.   [116] Ibid., no. 1175.

For this reason the following story, despite its inherent oddity, is of especial interest. On about 13 or 14 November Sir Francis Bryan sent a servant working for his friend John Knight into Yorkshire to spy. He was arrested near York, but he escaped by saying he was in the service of Sir Peter Vavasour. Arrested a second time, he was brought before Aske and recognized as Bryan's servant. So the servant (who is never named) spun a story that he was searching for a felonious chaplain of Bryan's who had absconded. Aske appears to have treated this perfectly seriously, and wrote a civil letter to Bryan, rather to his bemusement, offering to help apprehend this man if a description could be supplied.[117] Here the story would end, except for a letter of 29 November from Norfolk and Fitzwilliam to Vavasour. They had heard that Vavasour had made overtures through John Knight to see whether Bryan could secure a pardon for him. The request was that Bryan should petition the king, saying that Aske claimed he could do better service than many greater men, that there were others who were not mistrusted but who were much worse than him, and that he would gladly accept the king's pardon. Norfolk and Fitzwilliam addressed Aske through Vavasour. They would be suitors for his pardon if he gave them cause at Doncaster: his pardon would have to be justified by his actions, starting with him coming to the conference without demanding an exchange of hostages and with trust in their honour. A pardon, in short, was possible. It could be arranged. The price was Aske's defection from the commons. As it happened, Vavasour denied the report, although it is possible that this was a diplomatic disavowal.[118] In the light of subsequent events, it is not impossible that by the last days of November Aske was seeking a way into royal favour.[119]

---

[117] Ibid., nos. 1103, 1079.   [118] Ibid., nos. 1196, 1242.

[119] Aske also took the opportunity to discuss with Bryan's servant Horncliffe and Curtis, whom he said had sworn him in Lincolnshire and had then gone into Yorkshire to raise the county. Aske requested that Bryan should see them punished and volunteered that if they denied their role, he would make accusations against them in writing. It is not true that they had sworn him: what grudge Aske was settling is unclear. SP1/111, fo. 136v, which offers details not at *LP* XI, no. 1103.

12

Winding Up the Pilgrimage

At the first Doncaster meeting the gentry leadership of the Pilgrimage and the duke of Norfolk devised the means to disband the Pilgrims' army. At the second Doncaster meeting they went a stage further and wound up the Pilgrimage of Grace in return for a pardon, a number of ill-defined promises to assuage the commons, and the promise of a parliament.

I

The first few days of December continued to see differences of opinion between the king and Norfolk over the Pilgrimage. The king believed that the movement had burnt itself out. Little in the way of concessions would be needed to bring it to a conclusion. Sending Norfolk new instructions on 2 December, he argued that Norfolk had over-coloured his account of the rebels' numbers and hostility. He was surprised that the duke accepted that the Pilgrims sought a general pardon and a parliament without having met with them. If the rebels were really such a threat, why had Norfolk and the others done nothing to mobilize their own forces?[1] The king's

---

[1] *LP* XI, no. 1227.

prejudices were confirmed by the information he received from north-erners in the south. In a letter drafted on about Friday, 8 December, he held that the commons were repentant rather than inclined to a new rebellion. His sources reported no new assemblies in the north, but a weariness and a desire for a pardon. In a rebuke to his lieutenants at Doncaster, Henry told them that it was they alone who stressed the ser-iousness of the situation. At best they offered a partial account; at worst they were guilty of gross exaggeration in order to have the king agree to 'things against our honour'. Perhaps the king suspected a conspiracy against him, for he accused Norfolk of being more optimistic in his pri-vate letters to the duke of Suffolk than in those to himself.[2]

Certainly Norfolk's reports stressed the difficulties he faced. On 30 No-vember he suggested that the commons at Pontefract had the upper hand over the gentry. If no settlement could be achieved, and war followed, they could easily overrun the smaller royal forces. On 3 December he reported that the 'assembly is very great in Pontefract'. This informa-tion may have come from Lancaster Herald, who was in Pontefract dur-ing the day.[3] (A figure of 20,000 men appears in one of the king's letters and may well have come from Norfolk in a now lost letter.[4]) At the back of Norfolk's mind may have been the anxiety that he and other members of the royal delegation were entering a trap in which they would be overwhelmed by the commons. The only royal force in the district was 600 soldiers on the south side of the river at Doncaster under Sir Brian Hastings.[5]

Whilst the king was sceptical of these reports, he was sufficiently flex-ible to send Sir John Russell with revised instructions on 2 December. Russell was accompanied by a personal letter to Norfolk denouncing his faint-heartedness over the previous six weeks and enumerating all the occasions on which he had blamed others, notably the earl of Shrewsbury, for their mistakes. This drew letters back to the king and council in which Norfolk objected that he had done no more than report that which he had seen and heard. Henry's letters were an indisputable statement that the king lacked confidence in his senior men, and this

---

[2] Ibid., no. 1271.   [3] 'Thomas Master's Narrative', 75; *LP* XI, no. 1234.
[4] *LP* XI, no. 1227, also no. 1234.   [5] Ibid., nos. 1063, 1210.

surely came as a blow at the moment when they were preparing to open negotiations at Doncaster.[6]

The cold fury which Henry directed at Norfolk (in particular) may be viewed as evidence that he was, reluctantly, shifting his ground, and that he needed a scapegoat on whom he could vent his fury. The instructions of 2 December reveal that the king had listened to the reports from the North and had revised his plan of action to take account of the rebels' demands. He saw the grant of a pardon or parliament as diminishing his princely honour. Norfolk was to refuse to meet with the Pilgrims until they had dissolved their army. The heralds were to be sent to inspect the rebels' side to confirm that this had been done, and the Pilgrims were to be invited to reciprocate to check the king's good faith.

If the Pilgrims agreed to disperse their army, then the duke of Norfolk and his colleagues were to meet with the rebels' leaders. They were to open this meeting by outlining all the breaches of the truce which had occurred since they had last met, and then, when they had the Pilgrims on the defensive, were to offer the king's pardon with exceptions. If the Pilgrims' representatives refused to accept this gambit and demanded a general pardon, or if they sought the holding of a parliament or open discussion of any other articles or petitions, then Norfolk was to stall. He was to tell the Pilgrims that the grant of a comprehensive pardon or a parliament was outside his authority. The best he could do would be to join with them as suitors to the king. Norfolk was to allow six or seven days to pass, then call the Pilgrims to him and announce that the king had granted their petitions for a pardon and a parliament. The Pilgrims were then to be given the general pardon which Sir John Russell carried in reserve.

In the eventuality that the rebels insisted on discussing other articles, Norfolk was to say that the king wished to confer with other nobles, and he was to strike a truce for twenty days or more. In that time he was to raise forces and sent word to the earl of Derby and duke of Suffolk that they too were to mobilize. Norfolk was then to hold the line of the Don and wait for the king to join him with a royal army.[7]

---

[6] Ibid., nos. 1226–8, 1241–3.   [7] Ibid., no. 1227; also no. 1228.

In this way the king bent to meet Norfolk's demands for a greater freedom of manoeuvre. The duke was authorized to grant a general pardon and a parliament after a delay, but if the Pilgrims wished to proceed beyond this, then the king preferred war to further negotiation. The Pilgrims were, in no circumstances, to be allowed to present a political programme.

II

At the same moment as Sir John Russell was carrying these instructions northwards, the Pilgrims were engaged in that which the king feared most: constructing a political programme to be placed before the duke of Norfolk as the means of filling out and making concrete the obscurities of the Hampole articles. As Darcy said: 'The meeting at Pontefract is much to make and declare the first five general articles of the petitions in specialities against the meeting next or nigh Doncaster.'[8]

It had been decided at York that the Pilgrims would congregate at Pontefract two days before the meeting with the duke of Norfolk. It was anticipated that safe conducts would be received during Sunday, 3 December;[9] the first contacts between the Pilgrims' select delegation and the duke took place at Doncaster on the afternoon of 4 December. By Saturday Pontefract was filling with Pilgrims. Darcy dismissed reports that the town was already full of commons in a letter he wrote on 30 November, and further reassurances were sent to Norfolk in a letter drafted on Saturday or Sunday, which held that there were no more than 100 commons in the town. But on Sunday Norfolk said that the assembly in Pontefract 'was very great', perhaps drawing on the testimony of Lancaster Herald who had been there during the day delivering safe conducts. We have it on Aske's authority that by the end of the week there was a sizeable number of commons in Pontefract (he gives a figure

---

[8] Ibid., no. 1209. Bowyer refers to the Pontefract articles as 'articles [. . .] devised for the declaration of the generality of the articles sent to the king'. *LP* XII (i), no. 306.

[9] *LP* XI, no. 1209.

of 3,000), who had come to hear the outcome of the deliberations at Doncaster.[10]

When the Pilgrims' conference reconvened is not clear. The usual assumption is that the meeting began on Saturday, but none of the sources expressly says this. Aske's account may be read as saying that the articles were formulated in a single sitting during Sunday. The parallel opinion of the clergy was completed during Monday afternoon, by which time the lay articles were already finished.[11] Archbishop Lee was told by Lord Latimer that the Pilgrims' conference would be in council from nine o'clock on Sunday morning: it is quite possible that this is the moment at which the conference reconvened. The clergy did not receive their articles until later in the day.[12]

The exact chronology of these days—indeed, the chronology of the whole week—is therefore impossible to establish. It comes as no surprise, though, that Aske stressed in his depositions the lack of time for considered discussion.[13] The first task of the conference was to decide how many and which individuals would form the advance party to carry the Pilgrims' articles to the duke of Norfolk at Doncaster. Instructions were drafted for this party (printed below p. 460).[14] Their names had to be agreed by the commons. The conference then drafted its articles, again in two stages, these being debated and agreed by the lords and gentlemen and then placed before the commons for their approval. Finally, the conference had to agree the names of the delegation of 300 men to go to meet with Norfolk, and decide how many of them would be drawn from the commons.

That the commons were being shown the articles after they had been drafted points to the bicameral nature of proceedings at Pontefract. The conference was not, so far as we can tell, an open meeting in which the commons might carry the day, but a controlled and regulated meeting of gentry and chosen representatives of the commons. There survive two overlapping lists of gentlemen who were to be invited, named area

---

[10] Ibid., nos. 1209, 1223, 1234; 'The manner of the taking of Robert Aske', 341.
[11] LP XII (i), no. 786 (ii); 1021; 786 (ii), answ. 1.
[12] Ibid., no. 1022. Dakyn says that the clergy met over Monday and Tuesday; this seems doubtful.
[13] 'Aske's Examination', 566, answ. 29; also p. 572, answ. 102; p. 573 answ. 106.
[14] LP XI, no. 1246.

by area.[15] For some districts, notably Northumberland and Durham, only gentlemen were to be called. From Cumberland five gentlemen (three of whom were named) and eight commons were to attend. From Westmorland a mixture of gentry and commons were to be invited. The delegates from Yorkshire were a mixture of named nobles and gentry, with all the 'head yeomen' from the West Riding and 'all the worshipful men' from the East Riding. York was to send Sir George Lawson, an alderman, and six commons. The aim was to secure a wide geographical spread and not a wide social mix: the 'tallest men', 'head yeomen', and 'worshipful men' were doubtless viewed as dependable.

The decision to call a parallel clerical conference had also been taken at York, but this developed along different lines. The initial intention was that Archbishop Lee should call a meeting of clergy—exactly how many or who is never disclosed—which would consider articles placed before them by the laity. The suggestion is that their determination of these articles would aid the laity in framing their own, but the lack of overlap between the lay and the clerical articles suggests that the latter were always intended to have an independent public existence as a critique of the Cromwellian ascendancy.[16] As it happened, matters did not go according to plan. Lee refused to co-operate, and secured permission to absent himself from Pontefract. Then, a few days before the meeting, he was told that Aske expected him to draft the clerical articles; his response was that he knew of no grounds on which the clergy could complain. He was alarmed, though, by a phrase in a letter from Aske: Aske was looking in the clerical opinions for reasons 'whereupon we may damage battle'.[17] Lee refused to allow any opinion of his to be employed to justify rebellion, and decided to go in person to Pontefract. He preached in the priory church on Sunday, 3 December on two themes: the lack of any cause for rebellion against Henry VIII (which he apparently based on the king's answer), and the Pilgrims' lack of authority to draw their sword or make battle against their prince.

Lee has not had a good press from historians. The Dodds were cutting, holding that he only went to Pontefract to preach his opinions as

---

[15] Ibid., no. 1155 (i), (iii).   [16] 'Aske's Examination', 573, answers 88–92.
[17] SP1/119, fo. 7r (= LP XII (i), no. 1022), on which the remainder of the section is based.

this was less damaging than delivering them in writing.[18] Lee's own account is doubtless self-serving, but even if we give credence to Aske's view that he was physically frightened when he gave his sermon, or to Dr Pickering's opinion that he set out to support the Pilgrimage and changed direction in mid-sermon with the appearance of Lancaster Herald, it remains true that he took his opportunity to draw a line in the sand over which the Pilgrims could not pass without slipping into rebellion and treason.[19] (Aske, however, suggested that his sermon was less conclusive than Lee claimed.)

The clerical committee met in the priory at Pontefract. The majority of the members of the panel held doctorates of divinity or law, and at least moderately important preferments. They were certainly not representative of the parochial clergy.[20] They were brought the articles they were to consider by Aske. He denied their authorship, although Archbishop Lee was emphatic that they were in his hand.[21] It seems likely that their deliberations were spread over Sunday and Monday. Dr Pickering says that Aske came to see how well they were progressing on Monday afternoon and, perhaps because they were deadlocked, offered them a book by the late bishop of Rochester, John Fisher, which he thought might help them. Aske also tried to steer the committee by telling them that the pope's laws should 'have place or he would fight'.[22] Lee reports that their opinions were presented to him at about five or six o'clock on the night 'before the lords went to Doncaster'. He claimed to be revolted by what he found. He disagreed violently (he tells us) with their findings over the royal supremacy, the divorce, and the primacy of the pope. Having lectured them on their errors, he took himself off to say evensong, telling the panel that he would show them their errors in their other findings on the following morning. Lee claimed that he never saw their conclusions after that point, but Aske's testimony is that he received their opinions in the archbishop's chamber, apparently from the archbishop himself.[23]

[18] Dodds, *Pilgrimage*, I, 343.
[19] 'Aske's Examination', 572, answ. 102; *LP* XII (i), no. 1021 (i).
[20] For their identities, see Dodds, *Pilgrimage*, I, 382.
[21] 'Aske's Examination', 573, answ. 97; SP1/119, fo. 10r (= *LP* XII (i), no. 1022).
[22] *LP* XII (i), nos. 1021, 786 (ii) (2).
[23] Ibid., no. 1022; 'The manner of the taking of Robert Aske', 340; *LP* XII (i), no. 698 (3).

The duke of Norfolk began Monday, 4 December at the king's manor house at Hatfield, from where he wrote to the king, then he rode the 6 or 7 miles to Doncaster. The first contact between the Pilgrims and Norfolk took place during the afternoon. Aske says that ten knights and esquires drawn from all over the North were sent, each with three servants (making a party of forty), to receive the king's answer to their petition. Of this party, the most significant were Sir Thomas Hilton, Ellerker and Bowes, and the lawyers Chaloner and Babthorpe. Aske was not present, nor were any of the common's leaders with the possible exception of Nicholas Rudstone.[24]

From the Pilgrims' point of view, the primary purpose of this meeting was to lay down conditions for the plenary meeting and discover what concessions Norfolk was empowered to make. The instructions with which the commons' representatives went equipped show that the duke was to be reassured that the meeting would be conducted without deceit.[25] They were to receive the king's safe conduct and deliver their own to Norfolk and the other lords. They were to request a comprehensive royal pardon to cover all those implicated in the movement, and to request that in no record would they be named as rebels or traitors. They demanded that neither Richard Cromwell 'nor none of his kind nor sort' be present at the meeting. They were to receive the king's answer, establish what authority the lords had to treat with them, and discover what pledges they would offer for Aske. Only if requested were they to reveal the articles drawn up at Pontefract: 'If the particulars *of our petitions* be required, then to descend into divers particulars *thereof*'.[26] Aske implies that the articles were disclosed to Norfolk, and Thomas Master saw a letter dated 4 December from the duke which confirms that the articles were presented to him. Master, summarizing his lost source, said that the 'articles [were] far from all reason and cannot be granted'. The same source also suggests that on this occasion Norfolk offered the pardon which excluded six named and six unnamed, which 'did no good: for everyone was afraid for himself.'[27]

---

[24] *LP* XI, no. 1243 (2), gives their names, but says two servants each.

[25] Ibid., no. 1246.   [26] SP1/112 fo. 118r, text in italic from fo. 122r.

[27] 'The manner of the taking of Robert Aske', 340; 'Thomas Master's Narrative', 75. Marmaduke Neville deposed that when it was rumoured amongst the commons that they would be offered a pardon with exceptions, they said that they 'would all die on a day rather than lose the worst upon the field'. *LP* XII (i), no. 29.

III

What was in the articles which made them so obviously unacceptable? The Pontefract articles (printed below, pp. 460–3) consist of twenty-four clauses, in no obvious order, without subdivisions or subheadings.[28] The individual articles range in importance from the deeply contentious (the royal supremacy) to the really quite minor. Some articles, separated within the text, are clearly connected to others. Article 3, for instance, asks for the Lady Mary to be re-legitimized and the statute making her illegitimate to be repealed; but article 16 asks for the 'statute of the declaration of the Crown by will' to be repealed. Both clauses criticize aspects of the 1536 succession act, article 16 seeking all that was sought in article 3 and much more. Article 12 asks for a reformation in the way in which MPs were elected: article 15 asks that parliament should meet in York or Nottingham. The final articles ask for reforms in the operation of the law, and seem rather at odds with the earlier, more overtly political articles. So too do the articles concerning purely economic matters: the confirmation of tenant right, the enforcement of the anti-enclosure legislation. This jumble is no more than might be expected, given the way in which the articles were drawn together. Aske received several books of advice, one from Sir Thomas Tempest (who was absent through illness) and others from the lawyers Robert Chaloner and William Babthorpe. Others gave in 'bills', from which Aske extracted the points which appealed to him. The individual proposals for reform were then read to the assembled lords and gentlemen, and those which found favour marked 'fiat'. The whole document was then read to the commons.[29] The Pontefract articles were compiled in three stages: by soliciting proposals for reform, by Aske selecting from amongst them, and by their approval by the lords and gentry and finally the commons. Each article identifies a matter which needed reformation. There was no attempt to take these, to 'composite' them into a comprehensive programme for reform area by area. Nor was there any attempt to unify their language.

Before turning to the articles it is important to establish what they do not contain. There is no request for a pardon; nor is a parliament expressly

---

[28] It should be noted that the numbering of clauses is editorial.

[29] 'The manner of the taking of Robert Aske', 340; 'Aske's Examination', 566–7.

sought. The request for the pardon is contained in the instructions prepared for Sir Thomas Hilton. It was therefore the first request which the Pilgrims placed before Norfolk. A failure to appreciate this and an over-concentration on the twenty-four articles has disguised the fact that this was the crucial request and the articles a secondary consideration by comparison. It may also have been believed that the parliament had already been conceded at the first Doncaster meeting. Article 15 does not ask for a parliament to be held; it demands that it be held at York.[30] Moreover, there is no comment at all on the Cromwellian injunctions of July 1536, and so nothing on the subject of religious change at the parochial level. The reason for this is that consideration of these changes was referred to the pseudo-convocation which was meeting in parallel and was dealt with in its articles. The Pontefract articles (the lay articles) ought to be read side by side with the clerical articles: a concentration on the former alone has tended to unbalance our understanding of the totality of the Pilgrims' critique of the Cromwellian ascendancy. The articles look to the future. Whilst some of them call on the king to authorize changes in advance of the parliamentary session (e.g. articles 12 and 15), the majority are a programme of statutes to be enacted at the parliament (or rather, a list of legislation to be repealed) when it met. The Hampole articles looked to the king to solve the Pilgrims' grievances. The Pontefract articles show an appreciation that a new parliament would have to be employed to unravel the legislative legacy of its predecessors. Aske acknowledged his own education: initially it was thought enough to petition the king and force the articles on him, by battle if necessary; after the first meeting at Doncaster he appreciated the need for a parliament.[31]

It is possible to deduce more about the way in which the articles were composed than Aske tells us. There is a tendency for them to diminish

---

[30] The familiar text says York or Nottingham, but in the second version of the articles Nottingham has been struck out.

[31] 'Aske's Examination', 559, answ. 21. This is worth quoting in full. 'That afore they first came before Doncaster, this examinate and all the lords, gentlemen, and commons thought best to get the said statutes reformed first by petition: and therefore they first rose, if they could not so obtain, to get them reformed by sword and battle. And afterwards, upon communication had between them and my lord of Norfolk at Doncaster, the said examinate, lords, gentlemen, and commons concluded at Pontefract for a reformation to be had of the said statutes by parliament.' A comment of Darcy's also suggests that a parliament had been canvassed at the first Doncaster meeting: *LP* XI, no. 1045 (11 Nov.).

in immediate importance towards the end. Article 17, which asks for an act of indemnity for all recognisances forfeited during the 'time of commotion', seems to mark a full-stop of sorts. Articles 18–24 are all, broadly speaking, legal in their import, concerning the jurisdiction of the liberties of the church in Yorkshire (article 18), repeal of the statutes of uses and treasons (articles 20–1), a critique of chancery procedure, a request that northerners should normally be subpoenaed to appear at York and not Westminster, and a call for a 'remedy' against the fraudulent practices of escheators (articles 22–4). The unevenness of their language makes it hard to argue that articles 18–24 were drafted by a single hand or that they form a single coherent group of objections.

It is the opening eight articles which have an element of unity.[32] Seven of the eight employ the same formula, beginning 'to have' followed by the subject of the complaint and then an operative verb. The first article is especially elaborate: 'The first, touching our faith, to have the heresies of Luther . . .'. Article 6 is more typical: 'item, to have the friars observant restored to their houses again.' The early article which lacks this formula is the third: 'we humbly beseech our most dread sovereign lord that the Lady Mary may be made legitimate . . .'. This is the only occasion on which the king is directly addressed: the gravity of its language and its formula are stylistically distinct from the other articles, and this points towards an insertion. The 'to have' formula appears twice more in the articles, in articles 15 (parliament to meet at Nottingham or York) and 20 (the repeal of the statute of uses). There are, then, nine articles employing this formula and they ought to be considered to be a pre-formulated core agenda. There is one important clue which supports this deduction: when interrogated in April 1537, Aske referred to the articles made at Pontefract as the 'nine articles.'[33] After article 8 the process of drawing up articles fell into the hands of the pressure-group lobbyists. Presumably someone shouted very loud to have the localized grievance of tenant right made into article 9. Article 10, that the statute of handguns

---

[32] The eight appear together in a single text with a copy of the rider to the clerical articles which *LP* would lead one to suppose is a lost ninth article. *LP* XI, no. 1245 (iii). Another text, which *LP* says has the articles in different order, merely has the pages used in an unconventional order. Ibid., no. 1245 (ii). There are significant differences between the texts, noticed below, pp. 460–3.

[33] 'Aske's Examination', 572, answ. 102.

and crossbows be repealed, is equally a pressure-group grievance. The articles then get on track again as proposals were made or received by Aske which appeared to fill gaps or amplify the first eight articles.

Article 1 denounced heresy: the works of Luther, Wycliffe, Hus, Melanchthon, Oecolampadius, Bucer, the *Augsburg Confession*, Melanchthon's *Confessions*, the works of Tyndale, Barnes, Marshall, Rastell, St German, and other Anabaptist works were to be prohibited and destroyed. The curiosity of this list has already been remarked upon.[34] It includes some undoubted exotica. Whoever drafted it knew his heretics (even if he hadn't read them), but he then confused things by including a range of local controversialists who were by no means heretical, notably John Rastell and Christopher St German, both common lawyers. We can make sense of this list if we read it as a conflation of two: first the individuals who were seen to be a theological influence on the developing Cromwellian reformation; and secondly, a list of commentators on the law who in some way were held to be responsible for the innovations complained about in the latter clauses of the articles.

The second article requested that the supreme headship, so far as it touched the cure of souls, should be restored to the see of Rome. The bishop of Rome (he is not, in the articles, called the pope) was to have the consecration of bishops but without any payment or, at most, a pension towards the outward defence of the faith. This clause was hedged about with caution. It did not request a return to the situation of 1529. It gave the title to the king whilst taking from him an indefinable proportion of his competence. It looks as though someone strove hard to try to establish a compromise which, oddly, reads like a reverse echo of the terms by which the clergy were pardoned in 1531 when they admitted the royal claim to protectorship and supremacy with the saving clause 'as far as the law of Christ allows'. Aske claims the credit for this himself, but it also matches the distinction which Archbishop Lee offered Aske when the committee of clerics presented him with their opinions.[35]

[34] Elton, 'Politics and the Pilgrimage of Grace', 204–5. The second version of this text includes an important variant of this article. Below, pp. 460–1.

[35] 'Aske's Examination', 559, answ. 17; *LP* XII (i), no. 698 (3).

The third article sought the re-legitimation of the Lady Mary and the repeal of the succession statute of 1536 out of fear that the Crown might descend to the Stuart line. Again, this is a minimalist clause: the larger issue, that the king should not be allowed to bequeath the throne by will, was tackled head-on in article 16, perhaps because article 3 was regarded as overcautious.

Article 4 calls for the suppressed abbeys to be restored ('Item, to have the abbeys suppressed to be restored into their houses and goods'). This article was rather under-drafted and was unspecific as to how this aim was to be achieved. Article 5 calls for the tenths and first fruits to be clearly discharged 'of the same', before continuing to say, 'unless the clergy will of themselves grant a rent charge in generality to the augmentation of the Crown'. Again, the quality of the drafting leaves a great deal to be desired. On a strict reading of the clause, it should appear that it wishes to have the monastic houses whose suppression has just been reversed by article 4 freed from first fruits and tenths. The second section of the clause suggests that it is the whole clergy who should be freed, that is, the Statute of First Fruits and Tenths should be repealed in its entirety and the clergy, through convocation, invited to offer a rent charge to the Crown in lieu. The sixth article is simple by comparison. The observant friars (whose downfall had been their rejection of the royal supremacy) should be restored to their houses.

Article 7 demands that heretics, (whether) bishops or laymen, should be punished, either by burning or some other means, or they were to try their quarrel with the Pilgrims in battle. No heretics are named; nor is any definition offered as to how these individuals might be detected. This is a retreat from, say, the Lincoln articles in which six bishops are named, or the Hampole articles where Cromwell, Cranmer, Audeley, and Bishop Latimer of Worcester are identified. It may reflect a desire to avoid unnecessary conflict with the king, who had forcefully defended the orthodoxy of his bishops in his rejoinder to the Hampole articles.[36] Article 8, however, is absolutely specific. Cromwell, Lord Chancellor Audeley, and Sir Richard Rich were named 'as the subvertors of the good laws of this realm, the maintainers of the false sect of heretics, and the first inventors

---

[36] Dodds *Pilgrimage*, I, 276–7.

and bringers in of them'.[37] All were to receive 'condign [severe] punishment'; but how, whether by parliamentary attainder perhaps, is never spelt out. In sum, all the grievances of the previous seven articles were laid at their door. They had espoused heresy and allowed the works of heretical authors to circulate (article 1). They had appointed and maintained heretical bishops and maintained their sect (article 7). They were responsible for the royal supremacy which needed to be partly unpicked (article 2), the second succession statute (article 3), the statutes for the suppression of the smaller monasteries (article 4), and First Fruits and Tenths (article 5). All four articles concerned matters where parliament had extended its understood power, in three out of four cases, to interfere with the clerical estate. And the fact that the Pilgrims were committed to the traditional demarcations between church and state, parliament and convocation, is reflected not only in their suggestion that convocation might offer a perpetual tax to the king in lieu of the clerical tenths, but also in that the Pilgrims divided their critique of the Cromwellian ascendancy between these articles and the clerical articles compiled separately.

Article 8 is, then, a full-stop at the end of a group of clauses with an element of common drafting. When viewed in this light, the remaining sixteen articles may be seen for what they are: a mixture of addenda to the first eight and lobbyists' enthusiasms. Amongst the former we may include the desire that Layton and Leigh be punished for their extortion and bribery during their monastic visitations, this being another attack on members of Cromwell's circle (article 11). If the demand to have the election of MPs reformed may be read back to the critique attributed to Sir Thomas Tempest, then this too was an attack on Cromwell's ability to pack the commons (article 12). Article 19, which asks for the restoration of the liberties of the church, seeks the appeal of c. 27 Henry VIII, which absorbed liberties and franchises into the Crown. Article 14 sought the cancellation of the taxes granted in 1534. Articles 20 and 21 ask respectively for the repeal of the Statute of Uses and the treason statutes passed since 1529. All of these are tangential to the main course of the Pilgrimage. Likewise the lobbyists' clauses: of course, tenant right was

---

[37] But they were not accused of peculation and corruption, the charge made against them in the Lincoln articles.

important locally, but neither it nor the question of handguns nor the request that the (anti-) enclosure legislation be put into effect was ever any more than a sectional enthusiasm.

And yet, if it is possible to make sense of the constituent parts of the articles, the articles as a whole are puzzling. The Hampole articles tried quite hard to be anodyne: the king recognized this, and taunted the Pilgrims for their 'obscurity'. The response was to draft an elaborate list of all the legislation which the Pilgrims wished to see enacted at a future parliament, thus demonstrating their treason (although this list was drawn up under the security of an expected general pardon), but also alerting the Crown to their ambitions, and perhaps making it even more determined to ensure that the parliament never met. Perhaps the audience which the articles were intended to impress was not so much Norfolk, or even the king, but the commons. Look, they say: this is our diagnosis of the ills about which you have risen—it is now up to the king in parliament to put things right. The Pontefract articles were a gesture. They never made for practical politics.

Or were they never meant to do so? Archbishop Lee's *Declaration* contains an account of events before and during the Pontefract conference which strongly suggests that the articles were never intended to stand in the way of a settlement.[38] First of all, Lee reports a meeting between himself, Sir Ralph Ellerker, Robert Bowes, and William Babthorpe. Ellerker's and Bowes's prominence in the Pilgrimage requires no comment. Babthorpe, like Lee, had been amongst those who were captured at Pontefract. He was one of those who submitted articles to Aske in advance of the Pontefract conference, and so he may be taken to be an activist. The triumvirate asked Lee to speak to another lawyer, Robert Chaloner, 'and to exhort him to join them for the furtherance of the peace'. 'And so I sent for Chaloner, whom I found very reasonable and applying'. Ellerker, Bowes, Babthorpe, and Chaloner all met with Norfolk on 4 December. What does this tell us?

Ellerker, Bowes, and Babthorpe also requested that Lee should talk to Aske. Lee took the opportunity to do so when Aske was about to leave for Doncaster on 5 December:

---

[38] For the next two paragraphs, *LP* XII (i), no. 1022.

[I] exhorted him, as *instantly* [insistently?] as I could, to apply to the peace, and amongst other things I required him that in no wise the relief of the clergy from tenths or any otherwise, should be any let of good end to be taken, and that for monasteries, if it were true that [which] was spoken, that the king's highness would be content to take some order for them, that I thought ways might be devised, that his majesty should lose nothing although they stood. He answered that he would in all things bend himself to the peace and that he was bound to do in more ways than one. He uttered one special cause, and that they minded not to [di]minish any penny from the king's highness.[39]

All the principals seem to have been determined to achieve some form of settlement. There is, then, the deeply ambiguous behaviour of Lord Latimer. Latimer came on the Saturday night to Lee with a request that he should preach on the following morning about the illegality of rebellion against the prince. Lee does not say whether Latimer expected him to be for or against, but he either expected Lee to be against or misjudged his man. The archbishop had denied the legitimacy of Aske's rebellion when they had first met at Pontefract; his declaration itemizes other occasions when he argued, even to Aske's face, that his enterprise was illegal. He claimed that he only went to Doncaster after Aske sent him a letter which suggested that he was looking for justifications 'whereupon we may damage battle'.[40] Even if we allow for Lee's deposition portraying him in the best light, it seems most likely that his alienation from the movement could not but be well known, and that a request that he should preach could only have resulted in a sermon critical of the Pilgrimage. Aske admitted that Latimer had raised the question of whether a subject could lawfully resist his monarch, but held that Latimer did so to secure the church's licence to wage war on Norfolk if he did not satisfy their demands. Is this really so, or was Latimer asking Lee to warn the commons that, in the event of a deadlock at Doncaster, war was not an acceptable option?[41] Finally there is Darcy, with whom Lee had dinner on Sunday, 3 December. 'He [Darcy] said to me "these men have no measure in their hands. They would have me condescend to put in more articles, but I will in no wise." I said "my lord, for God's

[39] SP1/119, fo. 9v (= *LP* XII (i), no. 1022).   [40] Ibid., quotation from fo. 7v.

[41] Ibid., fo. 8v; 'Aske's Examination', 572, answ. 102; 573, answers 100, 102.

sake take such way that there be no impeachment of a good conclusion now." He answered surely, he would do his best.'[42] There seems to have been a consensus amongst the Pilgrims' gentry leaders at Pontefract. Whilst the articles betrayed an ambition to reverse the reforms of the 1530s, they were not to be allowed to stand in the way of a peaceful conclusion.

IV

When, on around Easter 1537, Dr John Dakyn was under examination, he explained how, whilst at court in the spring, he had encountered Dr Waldby who, with Dakyn, had been one of the clerical experts at Pontefract.[43] Waldby had been interviewed by Cromwell about his role in the committee. He thought that the matter was now forgotten. The same day Dr Marshall, another of the incriminated clergy, told Dakyn that he had spoken to and been well received by the king, and had explained to Henry that fear alone had led him to be involved at Pontefract. 'In truth, I believe in conscience [that] every one of us at Pontefract came thither out of fear, and when we came together every man was wary of his part and doubtful what to do.'[44]

Fearful perhaps; but the clerics' answer to the questions posed them is a trenchant document (printed below pp. 463–4), which betrays no compromise with the religious innovations of the early and mid-1530s. Throughout there is a rejection of the subordination of church to state. For men afraid they let their guard slip, preferring to tell Aske and the Pilgrims not only what they wanted to hear, but what they themselves, as clergy, felt about their political misfortunes since the fall of Wolsey.

The articles placed before the clerical committee do not survive, but the questions can generally be inferred from the answers.[45] The first asked the clerics for their opinion of the injunctions issued in the summer of 1536. They did not like them:

[42] SP1/119, fo. 8v (= *LP* XII (i), no. 1022).
[43] Dakyn was called up to London on about 22 March. *LP* XII (i), no. 698.
[44] Ibid., no. 789.
[45] They may have been drafted by Aske, above p. 345.

We think that preaching against purgatory, [the] worshipping of saints, pilgrimages, images, and all books set forth against the same or [the] sacraments or
sacramentals of the church be worth to be reproved and condemned by convocation [. . .] and that the holdings may be observed according to the laws and
laudable customs and that the bidding of beads and preaching may be observed
as hath been by old custom.

Having disposed of the injunctions, they turned to the royal supremacy.
'The king's highness nor any temporal man may not be supreme head
of the church by the laws of God, to have or exercise any jurisdictions
or power spiritual in the same, and all acts of parliament made to the
contrary to be revoked.' This left no room for the compromise over the
supremacy which the lay articles offered. The third question was about
the divorce.[46] The answer showed that at heart, the committee was composed of lawyers: 'We be not sufficiently instructed in the fact nor in
the process therein made but we refer it to the determination of the church
to whom it was appealed.' This is surely an oblique way of saying that
they rejected the Act in Restraint of Appeals and held that Henry's annulment should have been tried in Rome. The fourth and fifth opinions
allowed the committee to restate the traditional clerical privileges over
benefit of clergy and sanctuary. Article 6 touched on first fruits and tenths:
the committee held that the clergy of the northern province had never
granted nor consented to the payment of first fruits or tenths in their
convocation, nor could they make such a grant, nor could any temporal
man have authority by the laws of God to claim any tenths or first fruits.
The clerics clearly rejected the right of parliament to levy taxation on the
church, denied the right of the king to take such a tax, and doubted the
right of convocation to make such a grant. Article 7 offered the opinion
that lands given to God, the church, or religious houses could not be
taken from them. Article 8 conceded the right of the pope to make dispensations, article 9 that the pope should be taken as the head of the
church. Article 10 reserved the examination and correction of sin to the
church.

On all the points placed before them, the clergy found for the privileges and liberties of the church, the rights of convocation, and by implication the invalidity of statute when it came into conflict with the laws

---

[46] The Dodds thought that it referred to the legitimacy of the Princess Mary.

of God. They found for the papal supremacy and the right of the pope to make dispensations. This was a wholesale rejection of the innovations in relations between church and state made after 1529. But the clergy were clearly enjoying themselves. They went on. They held that the teaching of canon law should be re-established in the universities (it having been forbidden by Cromwell's reforming injunctions of 1535).[47] Clerks who had been in prison or who had fled abroad for withstanding the royal supremacy should be released and restored to their benefices. Books which argued for the primacy of the pope should be allowed to circulate freely. The use of the statutes of praemunire should be circumscribed by statute. Apostates who had left clerical orders without dispensation should be compelled to return to their orders. All first fruits and tenths due before the next parliament were to be forgiven (the expectation being that parliament would repeal the act). The statute commanding the clergy to exhibit dispensations before Michaelmas 1537 should also be repealed.[48]

This rider to the articles rather belies the claim that the clergy were coerced into their opinions. On the contrary: given the opportunity to influence matters, they not only took the most maximalist and uncompromising line over clerical privileges, but also brought into play matters which had not been drawn to their attention but about which they, as representatives of the clerical estate, felt strongly. The clerical articles reveal how unreconciled the middle-ranking clergy were to the legislation of the Reformation Parliament; equally, how eager they were to exploit a rebellion of the laity to seek the restoration of the orthodox teaching of the church and the restoration of its liberties.

V

It may be suggested that the meeting of knights and gentry negotiated a settlement which was put into effect at the plenary meeting on

---

[47] G. R. Elton, *Reform and Renewal: Thomas Cromwell and the Common Weal* (1973), 32–4.
[48] 28 Henry VIII, c. 16, 'An act for the release of such as have obtained pretended licences and dispensations from the see of Rome'.

Wednesday, 6 December.[49] Lords Scrope, Latimer, and Darcy, with Aske, together with the 300 delegates, rode to Doncaster during Tuesday, leaving lords Neville, Lumley, and Conyers at Pontefract with oversight of the gathering commons. The Pilgrims' delegation went to the Grey Friars on Wednesday morning and selected twenty knights and esquires and twenty commons to meet with Norfolk in the White Friars.[50] Once before Norfolk and the other lords, Aske made three deep bows, then he and the other Pilgrims fell to their knees and requested that Norfolk should grant them the king's free pardon. Aske does not say that the pardon was conceded at this juncture; yet, in the light of what followed, it makes sense to suppose that Norfolk did indeed grant both an unconditional pardon and a future parliament. There was some discussion over the detail of the Pontefract articles and the conclusions of the pseudo-convocation. Aske makes no comment about the discussions, except to say that he argued hard for the abbeys and in particular for the possession of the suppressed monasteries to be left with the lessees until the next parliament.[51] Norfolk was not empowered to discuss any petitions. It may be that he confronted the Pilgrims with a choice between accepting the pardon and having their articles referred to a future parliament, or a renewed mobilization. In this way discussion of the articles was deferred to another day and place. Once a settlement had been achieved (and Aske gives no indication of how long this took), Aske returned to the Grey Friars to tell the remainder of the 300 what had been decided in their name, and he then rode to Pontefract to announce the settlement to the commons assembled there.

The commons were gathered together early on Thursday morning by having the bellman call them to the market cross. From there Aske addressed them. They would receive the king's free pardon granted under the great seal. 'And the commons were then very joyous thereof and gave a great shout in the receiving of the same.' He presumably announced the concession of a parliament and a settlement over the status of the

[49] The sole account on which much of the following section is based is 'The manner of the taking of Robert Aske', 340–2.

[50] Again, this suggests a degree of bicameralism.

[51] 'Aske's Examination', 567, answ. 29. Is this what Aske really means? Surely he argued for the convents who had re-entered to remain in place?

dissolved monasteries. This done, Aske and Lord Neville returned to Doncaster.

At this moment it is worth pausing to pose a question. Was a free pardon, a promise of a parliament, and some agreement over the monasteries all that the Pilgrims of Grace had secured from Norfolk? In the light of what followed, the answer would appear to be in the affirmative. Now this may indicate that when the first face-to-face negotiations took place on Monday, 4 December (in the absence of Aske), there was a coming together on the two crucial issues on which all were agreed: how to get the commons to go home satisfied, and how to prevent the king taking reprisals against those implicated in the movement. There were certainly other matters to be resolved, but when it came to the evening of Wednesday, 6 December, Aske was apparently willing to put his name to a settlement which offered the Pilgrim gentry a pardon and the commons a short-term continuance of the smaller monasteries and the opportunity to discuss their grievances in another, future, forum.

Nonetheless, we may imagine that by about midday on Thursday there was a general satisfaction at Doncaster about how things had transpired. Certainly Norfolk was well pleased. A letter outlining the settlement was sent southwards on Wednesday evening. This letter, which would be important confirmation of Aske's account, is lost and only a part of it can be reconstructed from Henry's draft reply, in which he states his considerable dissatisfaction with Norfolk's actions in his name.[52] Norfolk clearly warned the king that the situation was so dire that he had no option but to move directly to the grant of the free and unconditional pardon, ignoring the king's preference that some should be excluded for punishment and that the pardon should be withheld for a period. He had proceeded to discuss the Pilgrim's articles against the king's express instructions, and had agreed that the dissolved monasteries should be restored in some form until an authoritative settlement could be reached. These were indeed major concessions, but substantially unrecorded: as Thomas Masters wrote a century later: 'What the treaty was, I cannot find expressly but by the guts.'[53] It may have been, literally, a gentlemen's agreement.

---

[52] *LP* XI, no. 1271.   [53] 'Thomas Masters Narrative', 76.

We can share Masters's frustration. Without Norfolk's letter we cannot discover exactly what he agreed with the Pilgrims during 4 December. Nor was there any real agreement amongst contemporaries as to what had been decided about the monasteries. If we look beyond the Doncaster meeting into December, rival interpretations circulated. Aske explains in his account how, after leaving Doncaster, he retired to his brother's house at Aughton, only stirring to join Sir Ralph Ellerker in putting the king's farmers into the abbeys of Haltonprice and Ferriby and to make an arbitration. This suggests that the Crown's lessees were to have possession of each monastery's lands, perhaps supporting the convent out of charity. John Dakyn, however, heard from Robert Bowes— who surely knew—that the dispossessed religious had been permitted to remain in their houses until parliament met; that the monks should formally surrender their houses to the king, and then be readmitted by the king's authority.[54] The monks of Sawley were also confused. Their position was rather different, Sawley having been sold rather than leased. To clarify their position, the abbot sent a messenger to Sir Stephen Hamerton who supplied a letter of introduction to Aske; his advice, given immediately before he set out for London, was that if anyone came in the king's name to put them out of possession, they should go gracefully and keep the commons about them quiet, otherwise they would be destroyed. Sir Thomas Percy, whom they next approached for advice, urged them to make no resistance if a commission came from the king for their expulsion.[55] Eighteen months later the Council of the North, some of whom had been present at Doncaster, thought that the monks had been left in place as the king's bedemen until his pleasure was known.[56]

The reason for this confusion may be simply explained by the insufficiency of the original undertakings. Aske's memoir recalls how, after he had returned to Doncaster, a letter was received from Lord Lumley at Pontefract saying that the commons were not content with Wednesday's settlement. They wanted to see the pardon. They wanted those suppressed houses which had been reoccupied by their convents to remain in existence until the time of the parliament, and they wanted the

[54] LP XII (i), no. 787. Dodds, Pilgrimage, II, 20–1, review the evidence.
[55] LP XII (i), no. 491; XI, no. 785 (which should be dated two or three days before 28 December).
[56] LP XIII (i), no. 941.

parliament to be held at York. Otherwise they would burn beacons to raise the countryside anew. 'Which letter was displeasant to all the lords and worshipful men of both parts . . .' 'Whereupon, after divers arguments and debatings amongst the said lords', Aske was sent back to the commons at Pontefract to sweet-talk them into accepting the settlement. We are not told that the Wednesday agreement was amended in the light of the common's voluble dissatisfaction, but it may have been. The implication of the commons' demand, that 'the abbots, new put in of houses suppressed, should not avoid their possession to the parliament time', implies that the original agreement was that the lessees should remain in possession until parliament had convened and legislated. What was to happen to the abbots and monks? Here it may be hazarded that, under the original agreement, they were to be supported by the lessees with *victum* and *vestitum* (sustenance and clothing). This was the king's interpretation of Norfolk's undertaking in the new year, and may have been what he was initially told had been agreed with the Pilgrims.[57] If it was thought necessary to appease the commons with a further concession, then it was certainly that the monks should go through the fiction of surrender and re-entry and the king's farmers be displaced. If this is so, then it may be seen how misunderstandings came to abound.

Aske's account suggests that the 300 returned to Pontefract on Thursday night. On Friday morning they ceremonially received the free pardon from Lancaster Herald, and probably announced what other concessions they had secured, after which the commons dispersed homewards and the lords and knights returned to Doncaster to transact the residual business.[58] Aske's account says enough to show that the commons were loath to accept the agreement at Doncaster, and that it fell to him, as the commons' leader and the man with the greatest influence over them, to sell the settlement to them. In short, he was required to mortgage his own reputation on behalf of a treaty whose terms fell well short of the Pilgrims' demands. It should not be assumed that the commons dispersed readily. Marmaduke Neville, who had been one of the

<hr />

[57] e. g. *LP* XII (i), no. 302.
[58] *LP* XI no. 902 (1), which is dated only 'Saturday' (which *LP* took to be Saturday, 28 October), appears to refer to this moment. It suggests that the Doncaster meeting finally broke up on Saturday, 9 December.

300 at Doncaster, told his interrogators that 'we thought we should be forced to divide, calling all those that we disposed to take the king's most gracious pardon to come to a side'. Charmingly, the Dodds thought that this might mean that they thought that the question was to be put to a vote.[59] In reality, Neville is telling us that the gentry thought that they might have to call on those who supported the treaty to fight those who opposed it. This is the hint that, on 7 December, the Pilgrimage nearly dissolved into those who supported the settlement and a hard-line rejectionist faction. As it happened, this split was delayed for some weeks, but the divisions and suspicions exhibited in January were present from the moment the treaty was announced.

When they returned to Doncaster the Pilgrims were taxed with a range of questions. What had happened to the king's rents? (They were ready to be collected.) When would Edward Waters and the ship sent to relieve Scarborough be handed over? After these and other questions had been answered, Aske knelt before Norfolk, demanded that no one ever call him captain thereafter, and pulled from his coat his badge of the five wounds of Christ. All the others there present likewise cast off their badges, saying 'we will wear no badge but the badge of our sovereign lord'. Norfolk then laid down an order for the putting of the king's farmers into the lands of the dissolved monasteries, and all parted. The Pilgrimage of Grace had run its course. It had gone into voluntary liquidation.

And yet . . . To say that events at Doncaster were anticlimactic is an understatement. The major concession was that all the issues which separated the Pilgrims from the king were referred to a future parliament, which would be held at York later in 1537. Together with less important undertakings to protect the monasteries until parliament met, this was enough to persuade the commons—for the moment—that they had scored a success and that they now had the means to restore the church and commonwealth to its natural state. In this sense the Pilgrimage had ended in a victory over the king. Archbishop Lee wrote to Henry on 9 December, saying he was glad 'that the king hath condescended to the pardon and to the requests of the northern men', the requests in this case doubtless being the promise of the parliament.[60] Marmaduke

---

59 Dodds, *Pilgrimage*, II, 20.   60 'Thomas Master's Narrative', 75.

Neville, Lord Latimer's brother, set out for the south after the conclusion at Doncaster. At King's Lynn he told people that the king had
granted a general pardon, to be confirmed at a parliament to be held at
Michaelmas 1537. He had reached Colchester by 16 December when he
chanced to have dinner with the justices of gaol delivery. Not only did
he boast of the setting up anew of monasteries by the Pilgrims, but also
of their success in securing a parliament to bring in reforms. Hardly sur-
prisingly, Neville was arrested, imprisoned, and ultimately executed. From
their different positions, both Lee and Neville believed that they had secured
an advantage over the king and that their deeper grievances would be
resolved in the not too distant future.[61] The same conviction comes over
from the comments of Aske and others amongst the Yorkshire gentry
in January, when they argued fiercely in defence of the Doncaster concordat in the face of its rejection by the commons. There is something
naive about the conviction that parliament could resolve their problems.
By dissolving the Pilgrimage, the Pilgrims lost their means to secure concessions from an unwilling king.

The magnitude of Norfolk's achievement at Doncaster should not be
underestimated. He had struck a deal with the leadership of the Pilgrims
which they found sufficiently satisfactory to persuade them to disband
their movement. The deal relieved them from the threat which the
commons posed to them, their families, and property. There could be
general satisfaction that a device had been found which allowed the
commons to return home with honour. The question, which cannot be
really be answered, is how many of the gentry were actually committed
to the agreement except as a cynical exercise to disperse the Pilgrims:
the speed with which they went to London to make their peace with
the king and court suggests that many were embarrassed by what had
been done in their names, and wished to stress their personal fealty to
the king. Norfolk had achieved all of this by exceeding his instructions,
it is true, and at the relatively minor cost of a free and unconditional
pardon and the promise of a parliament. The king's thirst for revenge
would have to wait a little longer. Norfolk had found the fundamental
problem—the widespread distaste for the legislation of the Reformation

[61] *LP* XI, no. 1319; XII (i), nos. 16, 28, 29.

Parliament—to be a matter beyond his power to resolve. Like a good company man, he had struck a compromise on the ground which bought time whilst referring this, the most contentious matter, to the king himself. Having dissolved itself, the Pilgrimage might have passed into a parliamentary phase: but the king's immediate aim was to ensure that that parliament never met. He doubtless found what had been agreed at Pontefract to be deeply unpalatable but, for the moment, inescapable. Henry was forced to confirm Norfolk's undertakings to Aske and others in the month following the second Doncaster meeting. Aske and Sir Oswold Wilstrop were both able to circulate open letters in the second week of January saying that the king had given them his personal undertaking that the parliament and convocation would both meet in York, where 'reasonable' petitions would be ordered. Darcy was able to tell his deputy in the honour of Knaresborough that 'there is to be a free parliament and liberty for spiritual and temporal [persons] to utter their learning and show their grief, and have justice against all who were named in the bill of the commons at Doncaster and any others of any degree so ever'.[62] But whilst the Pilgrims thought they had secured an important concession from the king, Henry's agreement to these demands was never any more than his own employment of policy. He was resilient enough to look for the means to abrogate Norfolk's treaty. It was the split within the Pilgrims that allowed him to do so.

[62] *LP* XII (i), nos. 43–5, 184.

13

The King's Love For
the North

Aske and the other Yorkshire gentry who, in January, spoke of the king's warmth to them, and his acceptance of the Doncaster settlement, would not have been so sanguine if they had been aware of a paper circulated in the court in mid-December.[1] The king, it suggested, now needed to make 'a perfect establishment of the quiet of this realm'. He should call the noblemen and gentry of the North parts to him, and

if it shall please the king's majesty of his inestimable goodness and singular clemency and wisdom by his affability and familiar conferences after their first accesses and the declaration of their troths to declare in words and countenance that he putteth their crimes passed wholly in oblivion, imputing the same rather to lightness than to any manner of malice. And by the mean his grace shall also by little and little find out the root of the matter.

The author of this paper—perhaps Cromwell—acknowledged the pardon, accepted that the king would travel into the North, and conceded that there would be a parliament. His paper, though, marked the beginning of the Crown's endeavour to recover ground and advantage.

---

[1] SP1/113, fos. 71r–73r (= *LP* XI, no. 1410 (i)).

The author of the paper was uncertain as to the rebels' aims. Would they take advantage of a parliament to 'compass the alteration of some things from their present state or take the advantage of a more propitious time to enterprise again force and violence'? The first step this writer advocated was the appointment of a lieutenant in the North 'for the administration of common justice and the training of the people again to their due obedience'. As the rebels had 'made the pretence of the maintenance of the faith one of the chief grounds and causes of their rebellion', the paper urged a preaching campaign throughout the North to establish a unity in religion. If the king was to proceed northwards to keep his parliament there, then he would need to select reliable gentlemen in the southern counties to rule in his absence. The king would need a war chest with which to face any renewed rebellion; he needed to discover where his ordnance had gone in the last rebellion so it might be readily accessible in the next. If he was minded to establish garrisons, then he should do so quickly under reliable commanders. Lastly, the author of this paper suggested that the Crown should urge the rebels' victims to launch private suits for the recovery of their goods, 'so that some of them [the rebels] shall yet come to punishment and the beginners of the rebellion do better appear'.

This paper formed the basis of a debate between the king and his council, a debate which was probably concluded by Christmas Eve, when the English ambassadors in France were told that the duke of Norfolk would be returning as the king's lieutenant with a council.[2] The conclusions of this debate, gathered together in 'a device made by the king's highness and his council for the perfect establishment of the North Parts', show how irreconciled Henry and his council were to the Doncaster settlement and how fearful they were of further disturbances.[3] Not only was Norfolk to go back as lieutenant with a salary of £2,000 to support 'an honourable table', and with 1,000 marks to employ a retinue of 200 soldiers; Suffolk was to return to Lincolnshire and the earl of Sussex was to be sent into Lancashire to aid his brother-in-law, the earl of Derby. Suffolk and Sussex were to muster and prepare the gentry of Lincolnshire and Cheshire respectively for any new outbreak of rebellion. Preachers were to be sent into both Lincolnshire and Lancashire. The lord admiral, Sir William Fitzwilliam, was to replace Darcy in all his offices in Yorkshire; he was to go to Pontefract and discipline the crown's tenants. He was to have a garrison of fifty soldiers.[4] Sir Ralph Ellerker the younger was to go to Hull with a garrison and Sir Ralph Eure to Scarborough Castle with a garrison of 100 men.[5] Sir Richard Tempest was to surrender Sandal Castle to Sir Henry Savile. The earls of Shrewsbury, Rutland, and Huntingdon were to hold their forces in readiness to move at an hour's notice. Sir John Russell, Sir Francis Bryan, and Sir William Parr were respectively given charge of Buckinghamshire, Bedfordshire, and Northamptonshire, where they were to raise troops to support Suffolk if the need arose. The earl of Westmorland was to replace the earl of Northumberland as warden of the East Marches. (Westmorland was determined to evade this responsibility.[6])

Policy was predicated on the anticipation that there might be a further rebellion in the North. A high degree of military preparedness was necessary to meet this eventuality. It needed to be backed by ample supplies of money, and a particular order was to be issued to restart the collection of the clerical tenth. Whilst there was a hope that preaching could call the people back to a state of obedience and conformity, the king and council also sought a means to spike the Pilgrim's parliamentary campaign. What this paper does not outline was the decision to call a Great Council of selected nobles and clerics. Great Councils were rare beasts in Henrician England: this one appears to have met at the end of January, but to have achieved little or nothing.[7] This document proposed that panels of divines and lawyers be convened to thrash out a response to the Pilgrim's articles in advance of the meeting of the Great Council, so that debate there could be correspondingly curtailed. By the time the Great Council met, the Doncaster settlement had collapsed into a renewed but pyrrhic rebellion, and the initiative had passed back to the king.

---

[4] Fitzwilliam already had a grant of the stewardship of Pontefract honour and the constableship of Pontefract Castle in reversion after the death of Darcy: Somerville, *Duchy of Lancaster*, I, 515, 516, also *LP* X, no. 1268. Darcy's removal was rumoured in Pontefract before Darcy was formally told of the decision: *LP* XII (i), no. 155.

[5] Evers had a garrison of 600 men in March. *LP* XII (i), no. 683.

[6] Ibid., no. 151. The story of how new arrangements for the marches were constructed in the first months of 1537 lies outside the scope of this study. See Bush, 'The Problem of the Far North'.

[7] *LP* XII (i), nos. 86, 463.

I

The days after the Doncaster concordat saw a drift of Yorkshire gentry and nobles towards the court. Marmaduke Neville asked Norfolk if he could proceed southwards, and was told that no special permission was needed.[8] It is possible that Ellerker and Bowes both returned to Windsor in the duke's entourage. Others wrote to the king or Cromwell, Lee to the king, and Darcy to the earl of Shrewsbury, Norfolk, and Sir William Fitzwilliam, whom he especially trusted.[9] Throughout the North apologies were doubtless being offered, excuses made, and fences mended.

Aske was called to the court by a privy seal of 15 December, carried to him at Aughton by Peter Mewtas, a gentleman of the privy chamber who had seen service in the king's October campaign against the Pilgrims. The king was clearly curious about his adversary: he instructed Aske to tell no one that he was called to court, and gave him a safe conduct until Twelfth Night. Aske accepted the invitation without hesitation, stopping only to send word to Darcy that he was gone.[10] Aske was the king's house guest over Christmas.[11] In that period, by the king's command, he wrote his memoir of the Pilgrimage to which he annexed his own view of what the king should do to secure the hearts of his northern subjects in advance of the return of the duke of Norfolk to the North. Aske advocated that he should return northwards equipped with a proclamation in which the king promised his subjects free elections to the forthcoming parliament and freedom of debate amongst the spirituality in convocation. He should confirm his free pardon and send word by the duke of Norfolk as to when and where the parliament would meet. Because there were so few parliamentary boroughs in Yorkshire, the king should invite burgesses from six Yorkshire towns and Kendal. Letters should be sent to Darcy and other gentlemen in Yorkshire and the North affirming

---

[8] Ibid., no. 29.   [9] 'Thomas Master's Narrative', 74; *LP* XI, nos. 1293, 1307–8.

[10] *LP* XI, no. 1306. It was alleged that Darcy advised Aske to leave posts along the road north to send word if he was imprisoned, and moreover, that Darcy volunteered to renew the rebellion even if it cost 20,000 lives. One version of this story came from Darcy's steward, Strangeways. *LP* XII (i), nos. 974, 1119, 1206. Aske did not admit this: ibid., no. 1175 (i).

[11] Dodds, *Pilgrimage*, II, 32–3 gives details.

the pardon and ordering them to maintain order until the duke's mission into the North.[12] Whether Aske or any of the other gentry about the court made any impression on the formulation of policy may be doubted, but by the time of their return to Yorkshire in mid-January, they were generally convinced of and willing to vouch for the king's magnanimity. By going to the court, they sacrificed their residual credit with the commons. One writer (perhaps Darcy) commented that 'the going up of lords, knights and gentlemen hath, and by their bruits is, likely to make the commons begin a new rebellion'.[13] Archbishop Lee was amongst those who remained at home. He thought he was under the surveillance of the commons, and told the king that he regarded himself as being their prisoner throughout December and January until the duke of Norfolk returned.[14]

Norfolk himself returned to his estates for a period of recuperation after Christmas. He had only recently arrived at Kenninghall on 6 January, but was back at court on 16 January when he received his instructions and directed letters into the North announcing his itinerary. He did not expect to reach Doncaster until 1 February or York until 3 February. Norfolk then returned to Kenninghall from where, on 27 January, he sent his will to Cromwell for safe keeping. He was there when news of Bigod's rebellion broke and, when he turned towards Yorkshire, went directly by way of Lincoln.[15] Norfolk's instructions confirm the king's unforgiving stance. The duke was to have a council along the lines suggested in the December memorandum. He was to proceed to Doncaster and offer the oath there to the gentlemen in whom he reposed the greatest trust, then proceed to Pontefract and other places, and finally to York, where he was to swear the other notable leaders and gentlemen of Yorkshire and the other northern counties, and administer the oath wapentake by wapentake. When the king's subjects came to take the oath, they were to be lectured on the king's clemency. Subjects who had lost goods to the rebels were to be allowed to petition for their restoration, although the resolution of such suits was to await the king's arrival.

---

[12] 'The manner of the taking of Robert Aske', 343–4.
[13] *LP* XI, no. 1294 (probably of about 14 Jan.).
[14] *LP* XII (i), no. 1022.   [15] Ibid., nos. 100, 101, 252, 198.

And the duke and all others of his said council shall jointly and severally travail to the uttermost of their power in all places as they shall pass secretly to ensearch and know the very grounds and causes of the late insurrection, who were the first and chief setters forth of it, and who devised every of the articles that were put in at the last assembly of Doncaster. And semblably they shall use all their wisdom and dexterity to learn and [...] what person of these parts [the south] the people of those quarters had intelligence in the time of their commotion.[16]

The duke was to expel any monastics who had re-entered their houses under cover of the rebellion, restore the king's tenants, and publicly denounce the monks as being 'very far from good religious men'. He was to investigate the enclosure of commons so that gentlemen and yeomen might ' "live together as they be joined in one body politic" under the king'. He was to be supported by preachers who would 'teach and preach the truth'. The duke and his council would administer justice twice a week; they were to progress through the North looking for any who had committed spoils or robberies since the pardon.[17]

Whilst this agenda just about stayed on the honourable side of the Doncaster Concordat, the concern to identify the ringleaders of the October movement would hardly convince the commons of the king's good faith. Nor would the oath with which Norfolk was equipped have satisfied them any further. Those coming forward to swear it were first to acknowledge their disloyal demeanour and submit themselves to his mercy. They were to declare who were the heads of the rebellion. To show their repentance, they were to be disarmed. They were to renounce all the oaths they had made in the rebellion, swear to be true subjects, and (the most bitter pill of all) they were to undertake to maintain all the acts of parliament made during the king's reign, and to aid the king or his commissioners in their execution. The oath compelled jurors to do all these things: in addition, they were to assist the king's commissioners to re-enter suppressed monasteries and to betray anyone who spoke seditious words, or slandered the king or any of his councillors, either in public or private.[18]

---

[16] SP1/114, fo. 108r–v (= *LP* XII (i), no. 98).   [17] *LP* XII (i), no. 98.

[18] Ibid., no. 98 (3): the full text of the oath may be found at PRO30/26/116, fo. 21v, concluded fo. 9r.

The purpose of the oath was to negate the Pilgrimage of Grace as a political movement: to abrogate its oath, and to compel those who had sworn it to accept the very legislation—the supremacy, the succession, and the dissolution—which they had sought to repeal. Those who refused were to be treated as rebels and punished accordingly. This was the king's policy of revanchism. It seemed certain to encourage new risings, for the oath would quickly have confirmed the commons' fear that they had been deceived at Doncaster. As it happened, the commons were already withdrawing from the Doncaster pact even before Norfolk received his commission.

The consequence of the long delay in Norfolk returning to the North was that rumour grew. Sir Ralph Sadler, writing from York on 23 January, offered the opinion that the recently repressed attacks on Hull and Scarborough had arisen out of a despair that the duke would not return. He also reported that he had been told that if Norfolk came 'to do them good, he shall be welcome, and if not, they [there] will be enough to resist him'.[19]

The acute could recognize that in several ways the Crown was not playing by the rules agreed at Doncaster. We have already noticed the uncertainties over the treatment of dissolved monasteries. The next element to shake faith in the agreement with Norfolk was the terms of the proclamation carried through the North and read in the larger towns by Clarencieux and Lancaster heralds, Clarencieux Herald starting in Wakefield and Halifax and finally taking in Penrith, Carlisle, and Lancaster; Lancaster Herald beginning in York and finally ending in Berwick on Tweed.[20] Whilst it doubtless caused offence by referring to the disturbances as a 'manifest and open rebellion', and blaming them on erroneous and false reports, the proclamation was not itself a pardon. This could only be obtained by suing in Chancery after a personal submission had been made to the duke of Norfolk, the earl of Shrewsbury, or another of the king's representatives, and giving an undertaking made not to engage in rebellion again.[21] Then, by the middle of January, printed

---

[19] St. P. I, 527–8 (= LP XII (i), no. 200).   [20] LP XI, nos. 1371, 1393.
[21] Printed in Dodds, Pilgrimage, II, 28–30. The precedent copy is PRO30/26/116, fo. 8r–v, continued fo. 21r.

copies of the king's answers to the Hampole articles were beginning to circulate. These revealed the king's authentic rage at the Pilgrims rather than the more compassionate image he was trying to present in December and January. The printed book had been overtaken by events: it still insisted on the surrender of ringleaders as a precondition to the concession of the pardon, even though this untenable position had been abandoned by Norfolk at the second Doncaster meeting; but again, the printed text showed how little the king might, or should, be trusted. It was Aske who, on his return to the North, told the king that the printed book had made men doubt whether they might have the promised pardon.[22]

A further straw in the wind showing how uncompromising the king really was came with instructions to levy the clerical tenth. Some believed that the Doncaster pact had included an agreement not to demand new taxes until they had been confirmed by the following parliament.[23] When Archbishop Lee wrote to Cromwell for the first time after the second Doncaster conference, he blamed the whole rebellion on the collection of the tenth, and added that 'no officer I have dare adventure to gather it for fear of new commotion'. Insofar as the tenth may have provided the initial flashpoint at Louth two months before, Lee may well have been right in his assessment; but his warning was overlooked in the drive to replenish the king's treasury. The 'device made by the king's highness and his council . . .' proposed that privy seals be sent to all the bishops demanding the speedy levying of the tenths.[24] To his astonishment, Lee received an instruction to proceed with the collection of the tenths at about the turn of the year. He consulted Darcy, then both wrote to the earl of Shrewsbury querying the order, with the implication that to collect the tenth was to court further disturbances. Shrewsbury would not say anything which countermanded the king's instruction, and referred the matter to Henry himself. The king drafted a letter to Lee which almost invited the clergy to resist so the king might punish them. The collection of the tenth in the diocese of York was under way by the

---

[22] *LP* XII (i), nos. 67, 102.

[23] *LP* XI, no. 1294. This had been requested by the clerics at Pontefract, above p. 357.

[24] 'Thomas Master's Narrative', 75; *LP* XI, no. 1410 (3).

beginning of February.[25] When Aske visited Beverley on 11 January to address the commons, his comfortable words about the king's love for the North and his commitment to the promises made by the duke of Norfolk were countered by Hallam: 'How happens it then, if this be true, that the tenths be gathered, for I hear say that my lord of York hath received a letter from the king's grace for the gathering of tenths or some other payment, whereas it was concluded at Doncaster that there should be no mo[re] payments gathered till the parliament time.'[26] Aske, who was unaware of the instruction, could offer no very convincing answer, and clearly lost face before the crowd.[27] In short, what the commons could see happening was at variance with the deal they had been sold at Doncaster. The pardon was less than a pardon; the king's printed book showed him rejecting the Pilgrims' complaints and bent on revenge; and the collection of the clerical tenth revealed how the king was not pre-pared to await the deliberations of the promised parliament. Both Aske and Darcy wrote to the king warning him that these various aspects of royal policy, whilst innocuous in themselves, were feeding a restless atmo-sphere amongst the commons.[28]

Then there were the rumours which circulated. It was held, for instance, that the king was moving to garrison Hull and Scarborough and use the towns as the means to subjugate the countryside. As we have seen, this contained a grain of truth, but the conviction was strengthened by the arrival at Hull of ships allegedly carrying stores for the garrison.[29] Most importantly, the commons simply ceased to trust the gentry who, it was held, were in the royal pocket. The author of one account of the state of the North (probably Darcy) wrote that: 'Seditious words and bills have been set up against all lords, knights and gentlemen, both of the South and North, "saying that under the meetings at Doncaster and now by counselling above, all is to betray them, therefore none [of the gentry]

---

[25] LP XII (i), nos. 6, 20, 39, 52, 21 (this must date from about 13–14 Jan.), 323.

[26] PRO, E36/119, fo. 21r (= LP XII (i), no. 201 at p. 88).

[27] 'Thomas Master's Narrative', 75.

[28] For Aske's letter of 12 January, LP XII (i), no. 67. Darcy wrote to the king on 14 January (ibid., no. 84): I assume that the description of the state of the North at LP XI, no. 1294 is Darcy's and can be associated with this letter.

[29] Hallam spoke of this to William Horsekey, LP XII (i), no. 201 (i). The report had also been heard by Dorothy Darcy at Gateforth near Selby and Sir Marmaduke Constable, ibid., nos. 81, 64.

they will trust unto".' [30] Aske's hold over the commons was compromised by his time at court. A bill (probably of the third week of January) claimed that he had had inducements promised him at London if he would betray the commons. This bill called on its readers to continue with their Pilgrimage of Grace, 'and ye shall have captains just and true and not be stayed by any gentleman in no wise'. Bigod's revised oath, according to one account, was the Pilgrims' oath with the addition that 'no man should give counsel to any man to sit still until such time as they had obtained their former wishes'.[31] Sadler, travelling through the countryside between Doncaster and York on 23 January, reported that there had been bills posted on church doors by night 'containing these words in effect: "commons, be ye true amongst yourselves and stick to one another, for the gentlemen have deceived you: but yet if need be, ye shall lack no captains".'[32] This was after the abortive rising in the East Riding had confirmed the breach between commons and gentry, but the distrust between the two may be traced back to Aske's need to show the pardon to the commons at Doncaster—if not earlier.

II

The renewed rising in the East Riding was the work of a renegade gentleman, Sir Francis Bigod, and a captain of the commons, John Hallam of Calkeld in Watton (to the north of Beverley).[33] Hallam's prominence in the October rising has already been noticed. He took part in the siege of Scarborough Castle; later he submitted a petition to the York conference, but it is unknown whether he attended either the Pontefract conference or the meeting with Norfolk at Doncaster. As a commons' activist, Hallam was dissatisfied with the proclamation of the pardon, thinking that it was Cromwell's work. When interrogated he said that he would rather the commons had had their petitions conceded than been granted

---

[30] *LP* XI, no. 1294.
[31] *LP* XII (i), no. 138; Dodds, *Pilgrimage*, II, 70.   [32] *LP* XI, no. 1294.
[33] A fuller account of Bigod's revolt is available in the Dodds, *Pilgrimage*, II, ch. 17.

a pardon, for they had never offended the king.[34] Hallam claimed that in the month after the conclusion of the Doncaster conference most of the commons of Holderness, Yorkswold, and Hull believed that Hull should be held for the commons until the promised parliament met. There was some debate about whether the commons should take steps to seize Hull: the bailiff of Snaith, in a message sent on about Twelfth Night, told Hallam that the commons around him believed they should, and suggested that if Hallam would lay siege to Hull (and perhaps Scarborough too), then the bailiff would lead his commons to take Doncaster and Pontefract.[35] William Nicholson of Preston in Holderness, one of the Holderness captains, was confident of raising 100 or 200 men in any venture to take Hull. Hallam also claimed to have been under pressure to rise again from the captains of the commons of Beverley and the parish clerk of Beswick, whose accusation that Hallam had lost his nerve led directly to his capture.[36] But Nicholas Rudstone, another of the Holderness captains, was later to throw in his lot with Sir Ralph Ellerker against Bigod.[37] Similarly, Sir Ralph Eure told Henry VIII that the Holderness captains generally had assisted in the suppression of Bigod's revolt. It should not be assumed that all the East Riding commons were equally energized by the rumours of deception and impeding retribution.[38]

Hallam's return to the fray was prompted by the circulation of rumours which persuaded him that the commons had been deceived. He heard that Hull and Scarborough would be fortified to allow the gentlemen a refuge and to serve as strongholds from which the countryside could be controlled. He knew that the archbishop of York had been instructed to

---

[34] *LP* XII (i), no. 201 (p. 91).

[35] I have not been able to discover to my satisfaction the identity of the bailiff of Snaith. Technically it was Darcy; we must assume that the the man implicated here was the deputy bailiff. In one source (PRO, DL1/7 G13) he is named as Oswold Grice, but I presume that he was the deputy steward. In the minister's accounts the bailiff is named as Lionel Percy (eg PRO, DL29/549/8718). He is to be distinguished from Thomas Hutton of 'Snaith', *recte* Snape, who was an activist in the first rising and author of the letter calling for the assembly at Richmond on 5 Feb. (for whom see below, pp. 387, 396).

[36] *LP* XII (i), no. 201 at pp. 85, 88. A parish or holy water clerk was 'an assistant in lower orders with an intermediary position between laity and clergy'. B. Kümin, *The Shaping of a Community: The Rise and Reformation of the English Parish, c.1400–1560* (1996), 41.

[37] Indeed, Rudstone was a turncoat: by the end of the year he was an esquire of the royal body. *LP* XII (i), no. 1311 (12).

[38] Ibid., nos. 174, 248, 466.

collect the tenth; another report circulating was that the mayor of York had received an order to disarm the commons. 'And that, as he saith, did set the people more a fire to make a new stirring.'[39]

Hallam began to turn his mind towards a new rising on Monday, 8 January. After he and a number of his neighbours had said a paternoster in Watton church, Hallam swore one of their number who had been away throughout the autumn, and then broached the subject of a new rebellion. Hull, he held, would deceive the commons, Scarborough would be fortified to resist a new siege, the gentlemen would cheat on the commons, and Hallam doubted whether the king would perform the pardon. Hallam and his neighbours agreed that they would take soundings of neighbouring gentry and that Hallam himself would go to Hull to gauge the temper of the town on Tuesday. They would meet again on Wednesday to compare notes. On this same Monday Aske received a letter from Sir Marmaduke Constable warning him that the Beverley commons had been restless over the previous few days after hearing a report that ordnance was being landed at Hull. Mr Craike (the deputy steward) had done his best to pacify them, but Constable feared that if Hallam came, then they would go to Hull and expect the Holderness commons to join them there. Constable had been in contact with Hallam to urge him to remain calm, but thought that Aske would have more chance of persuading him and the Beverley commons. Aske's response was to call an open meeting at Beverley on the following day, and he invited Hallam to meet him at Arras on the way so they might arrive together, thus recognizing Hallam's local standing.[40] Aske addressed the crowd, telling them of the king's 'great mercy and love that he beareth to his subjects, the commons of the North',[41] asserting that the king would come on progress to York and hold both a parliament and the queen's coronation there. The duke of Norfolk would also be returning with their pardons. Aske worked hard to persuade them of the king's adherence to the Doncaster agreement; but, as we saw, he had no real answer when Hallam asked him why, in that case, the king was collecting the clerical tenth and his rents contrary to the orders established there. After the meeting

[39] PRO, E36/119, fo. 28r (= *LP* XII (i), no. 201 at p. 91).
[40] *LP* XII (i), nos. 56, 64, 201 at p. 86.   [41] SP1/114, fo. 64r (= *LP* XII (i), no. 64).

Aske was dined by Mr Craike and the twelve governors. Hallam was also invited, and Mr Craike took him to one side and persuaded him not to follow those other rebel captains—William Nicholson and the bailiff of Snaith—who were threatening to rise. Hallam was persuaded of the king's good intentions and agreed not to agitate further.[42]

The spur which led Hallam to try to rise a rebellion the following week was a meeting with Sir Francis Bigod. That Bigod should have involved himself in a rebellion at this juncture has always seemed puzzling. In the October movement he tried to flee by boat from his house at Mulgrave near Whitby, but he later became Aske's captain at Scarborough, where he was almost certainly acquainted with Hallam. Bigod himself acknowledged that the commons were suspicious of him in the autumn, both for his learning and his contacts at court—and with Cromwell.[43] His motives in raising a new rebellion seem to have arisen not out of any great sympathy with the commons' aims or the Pontefract articles, but from a conviction that the king had deceived the North and that they needed to act to prevent their subjugation. As someone conversant with the court, and certainly with Cromwell, his conclusions may have been well founded on a familiarity with and understanding of the personalities involved denied to the commons and many of the gentry too. By the time he addressed a hastily convened muster at Borough on Tuesday, 16 January, convinced by rumours that the duke of Norfolk was advancing on the north with 20,000 men to seize Hull, Scarborough, and the other coastal towns. He told this crowd that the pardon was a sham, that no place had been set for the meeting of parliament (with the implication that it would not happen), and that in the proclamation of the pardon the king, quite erroneously, claimed the cure of both body and soul (a particular Bigod preoccupation).[44] Bigod's attempt to re-mobilize the commons was therefore a rebuke to those, like Aske, who had underestimated the king and consented to a worthless agreement at Doncaster. Bigod was also driven by the conviction that Richmondshire and Durham were about to rise. Exactly why he believed this is none too clear, but he had a number of link-men running to and fro, perhaps

---

[42] *LP* XII (i), no. 201 at p. 86.   [43] Ibid., no. 145.

[44] Ibid., no. 369, published in full in Milner (ed. Benham), *Records of the House of Lumley*, 32–45.

retailing reports to him which, in retrospect, were more speculative than certain. He may also have been trying to play both parties against each other, letting Richmondshire believe that the East Riding was primed to rise and vice versa. He was also relying on Sir Thomas Percy, who shows no sign of being aware of Bigod's plot.

Bigod seems to have had a general licence to interfere in the affairs of monasteries in the eastern part of Yorkshire. On 10 January he went to Watton to urge the Gilbertine monks there to elect a new prior in the place of a Cromwellian appointee who had absconded during the autumn. Hallam, a priory tenant, was also an active meddler in the affairs of the house. Over dinner at the priory, Bigod produced a copy of the proclamation of the pardon and expounded upon his doubts about it. The proclamation was in the king's name but written in the third person: was it then Cromwell's work? Was it sufficient authority to stop a sheriff seizing a man's goods? Why was it dated two days after it had been read at Pontefract? Then the conversation turned to the present situation. Bigod mistrusted the king's adherence to the Doncaster pact; he thought that the North should remain on its guard, that Hull and Scarborough should be held against the king, and that Norfolk, if he returned to the North, should be kidnapped and sworn to the Pilgrims' oath. (Hallam thought that Norfolk's reputation stood so high in the North that no one would agree to this, but held that Suffolk, whose reputation was not so great, would be resisted.[45]) Out of their discussions emerged a plot that Hallam should surprise Hull, Sir Francis, Scarborough: they would then gather a force together which would congregate at Beverley and march on Pontefract. Bigod seems to have trusted on a parallel rising in the northern Dales, the commons of which were being captained (so he claimed) by Sir Thomas Percy.

Hallam took one of his neighbours into his confidence about the plot on Thursday. On Saturday he was invited to Bigod's house at Settrington, over the wold near Malton. There, other of Bigod's informers (including a friar of St Robert of Knaresborough) brought news—exaggerated, as it turned out—of new disturbances in County Durham and the West Country. On Monday, 15 January Hallam established contacts with the

---

[45] Ibid., no. 201, p. 92.

Beverley commons and secured a promise of aid from them if he set out to take Hull. Another Beverley man was primed to make contact with Nicholson, the captain of the Holderness commons, on Hallam's word. And yet, even as Hallam was preparing the ground for rebellion, Bigod was sending word that he would seize Scarborough on the following day and that Hallam should likewise seize Hull; on Wednesday, with their forces, they were to meet at Beverley. Bigod's sudden urgency arose out of reports that Durham and Richmond were also to rise on Tuesday, but there was no realistic prospect of assembling a parallel force at such short notice. Hallam had no men to call on apart from his immediate circle of neighbours. They were persuaded to infiltrate Hull in ones and twos on the following morning and then, when Hallam arrived mid-morning, at his call of 'come hither to me all good men' they were to join him and seize the town. Hallam then started to work his contacts to raise a revolt, sending word to Nicholson that the commons of Holderness should be in Hull to aid him. It was midnight before Roger Kitchen of Beverley received a message that the plot was on for the following day. Even though he set out to alert Nicholson at six the following morning, Nicholson had gone before Kitchen could reach him. Hallam stopped off in Beverley on his way to Hull in an attempt to garner support, apparently unsuccessfully. The total force available to him to seize control of a major town was less than twenty men.[46]

Hallam's advance party was far from comfortable with their task, and by the time they reached Hull they had decided to warn the authorities. At Hull they were passed from person to person, unaware that the whole plot had already been revealed to the mayor and aldermen by one John Fowberry, a confidant of Hallam and a servant of the earl of Surrey. The city authorities immediately took steps to close and place guards on the town gates. When Hallam arrived mid-morning, he discovered that none of his contingents had reached Hull except for his own small band. He encountered William Nicholson, who was in Hull on entirely innocent business and quite unaware of the call to arms. At Hallam's suggestion, Nicholson went about encouraging his neighbours to stay in the town, 'for [it] may fortune ye shall hear of some business ere ye go. And

[46] Ibid., no. 201, at pp. 97, 93.

they asked "what business was that?" and he said he knew not.'[47] Hallam realized that there was no prospect of seizing the town, and told his accomplices to return home. He rode out of Hull even as the gates were being closed against him. As he rested his horse, he was seen by Marshall, the parish clerk of Beswick and Fowberry. 'Fie', said Marshall; 'Will ye go your ways and leave your men behind you?'[48] Hallam rode back to the (shut) gates and asked, from outside the town, that they be opened so his neighbours could leave. His name was demanded, he gave it, the authorities realized who he was, and, after a fight, he was seized. As he was led through the town Nicholson tried to start a diversion to give him the opportunity to escape. He too was captured. Bigod's letter was found concealed in Hallam's clothes, and so the whole incompetent conspiracy was exposed. His few supporters were found after a sweep of the town.

Bigod drew Hallam, Nicholson, and a small group of lesser men to their deaths. On Thursday, 18 January the mayor was able to send details of the failed conspiracy to the king and announce the capture of all the perpetrators of this adventure.[49] Bigod's own branch of the rebellion fared no better, and similarly resulted in the execution of men who were led into treason against their better instincts.

The letter which Bigod dispatched to Hallam on Monday, 15 January was one of several he sent out that day. Another went to the prior of Malton ordering him to call a muster there on the following day: a messenger carrying letters was sent into County Durham.[50] Bigod set about calling other musters, including one at Borough, which Lumley describes as being in Settrington, and a second at an unidentified location called Monyhouse. The beacon at Settrington was burnt to spread the word further.

Word of the muster at Borough came to George Lumley of Thwing on Tuesday morning.[51] Lumley's involvement in the attempted rising was accidental but cost him his life. He may be read as weak and vacillating,

---

[47] PRO, E36/119, fo. 32 (= *LP* XII (i), no. 201 at p. 95).

[48] Ibid., fo. 30v (= *LP* XII (i), no. 201 at p. 93).

[49] *LP* XII (i), no. 141.   [50] For which see ibid., no. 148.

[51] Lumley was the elder son and heir of John, Lord Lumley and so a cousin of John, Lord Scrope through his mother. In social standing he was much more than local gentry.

or confused and indecisive; but, whichever he was, he offers an authentic vision of a gentleman who was pitched into a sequence of events beyond his ability to control. When told by the constable of the 'next town' that a muster was taking place at the Borough, Lumley did not know whether it had been called for or against the king. He felt that, 'if the assembly were for the king . . . it was his duty to be there. And if it were about any new business of commotion, then he thought that it was best for him to go thither also for to stay them, or else it might be laid to his charge afterward that seeing there were few gentlemen else in that quarter that he did not endeavour himself to stay them.' And, after deliberating with his wife and the constable who brought the message, he decided to go, '. . . thinking at the least way, he could do no good amongst them, he would do no harm'.[52] At the muster he found thirty or forty men with equally little idea of the purpose of their call. Bigod, accompanied by a much larger group of horsemen, finally rode into view and made to address the commons. Having refused to talk with Lumley in private, he turned to the commons and outlined his conviction that the king had deceived them. The proclamation of pardon was read and the commons persuaded that it offered them no safeguards against their prosecution. Having worked the crowd into a frenzy against the king, Bigod and his horsemen rode off towards Hull, leaving Lumley and the excited commons to lay siege to Scarborough Castle. Lumley was also given two letters, one for the bailiffs of Scarborough instructing them to aid the rebellion, the other to the dowager duchess of Northumberland, urging her to persuade Sir Thomas Percy to declare for Bigod.[53]

On his way to Scarborough Lumley encountered the muster of Dickering Wapentake at Monyhouse, but insisted that he would only take two men from each township and sent the remainder home. A letter was sent to the prior of Bridlington asking for aid, but the prior refused and later claimed that he armed his tenants to resist Lumley if he came that way.[54] Lumley was also forced to agree that a further muster should be held at Spittal the following day to raise additional forces with which to

---

[52] SP1/115, fos 4v–5r (= LP XII (i), no. 369).

[53] Events in Scarborough are described, with local detail, in J. Binns, 'Scarborough and the Pilgrimage of Grace', *Scarborough Archaeological and History Soc.*, 33 (1997).

[54] LP XII (i), no. 1019.

occupy Scarborough. His little army of irregulars (perhaps 120–140 men in number) then entered Scarborough without opposition and perhaps even comment. Lumley insisted that all victual and lodgings should be paid for, and ordered that no one should undertake revenge attacks on those who had defended the castle in the autumn. The commons wished to take the castle, but Lumley would only allow them to picket it, arguing that it was the king's property and that they had sworn to do nothing against the king. When the opportunity arose, he sent a servant to Sir Ralph Evers to warn him that the castle was being watched and to reassure him that he would try to persuade the commons to disperse without violence.

On the following morning Lumley and the commons met with the bailiffs, who swore Bigod's new oath and agreed that the commons should mount a guard over the castle. Then he announced that he had to go home, ordered the commons to choose two of their own number as captains, and departed. One of these was a minor gentleman called John Wyvill of Osgodby, the other Ralph Fenton, perhaps of Ganton or Rudstone.[55] As he made his way back to Thwing, Lumley passed small bands returning from the muster at Spittal. He told these people that the commons had desired help for that night, but that they should return home in the morning. At Spittal he dismissed his own following of commons, promising that he would lay their grievances before the duke of Norfolk. He extracted a promise from them that they would only rise again if either he or Sir Thomas Percy required them to do so. Then he went home. On the following day he received one of the open letters which was circulating within the district to reassure the commons of the king's good intentions. He sent it on to the commons at Scarborough, repeating the assurances it contained, and giving instructions that the commons should trust the letter and return home. Lumley then went to lodge in York to be away from the commons; having taken advice from Sir Oswald Wilstrop as to what he should do, he surrendered to him and was brought before the duke of Norfolk. The commons only dispersed after Sir Ralph Eure 'retook' the town. He was satisfied merely to arrest the two captains and chastise the remainder, whom he made to promise

55 For Wyvill, ibid., nos. 409, 416 (2), and for both, Binns, 'Scarborough', 29, 39.

to be obedient in the future and to wear a cross of St George.[56] Wyvill and Fenton were, however, executed by Norfolk.

Whilst the commons were watching over Scarborough Castle in case it was used against them, Bigod's plans had gone wholly awry with Hallam's failure to secure Hull. On Thursday Bigod held a muster at Bainton, 9 miles or so north of Beverley, from where he sent three messengers to Hull to demand Hallam's release. Two were imprisoned on the grounds that they were traitors without a safe conduct; the third was sent back to Bigod by Sir Ralph Ellerker with a defiant message. From this same muster Bigod wrote to Sir Robert Constable at Holme for advice. In his reply Constable expressed surprise that Bigod had mobilized the commons when the king had signalled his acceptance of the Doncaster pact to Aske. He reassured Bigod that Norfolk was returning to the North accompanied by only his household servants and was not bringing an army of subjugation. Constable reminded the commons that their congregation was contrary to the orders taken at Doncaster, and urged them to be content to await Norfolk's return. Aske, who was with Constable at Holme, sent out his own letter to the commons disowning Bigod, saying that Bigod intended to destroy the effect of the Pilgrim's petitions granted by the king (which is, of course, exactly what he did). Aske promised to write to the king for their further pardon, stressing that he considered that they had been misled by Bigod into a foolish and unnecessary rebellion. The commons agreed that Aske should have a safe conduct to come and address them, but before this could happen Bigod moved to Beverley, invited there by the commons.[57]

The commons of Beverley seem to have rediscovered the capacity for independent action they had shown in October. The fundamental continuity between then and the middle of January may perhaps be seen by their renewed use of Woodmancy as messenger. They were said to have been close to rising at the end of the previous week, and now they did so.[58] There survives a letter in the name of the 'commons assembled there' to the dean and chapter of York asking whether they might have the chapter's support as they had in the first rising, and arguing that they fought the clergy's battles for them. This may be from Bigod's pen (as

---

[56] LP XII (i), no. 234.   [57] Ibid., no. 730 (2).   [58] Ibid., no. 64.

the Dodds assumed), but Bigod's letter to the bailiffs and commons of Scarborough was in his and Hallam's name, and signed. His letters to Durham and Sir Oswald Wilstrop were also signed.[59] This letter is unsigned, and it seems most plausible to see it as the work of the commons, whose rising was perhaps coincidental with Bigod's rather than called into being on his instructions. Once Bigod was in Beverley the tide turned against him suddenly and decisively. Sir Ralph Ellerker the younger started mustering the townships to the south of Beverley and called on Holderness to join him. A call was issued for a general mobilization. This reached as far as Bridlington.[60] Whilst Sir Ralph the younger promised his father that he would be at Beverley with his troops at noon, Sir Ralph the elder attacked at daybreak and scattered the commons, taking sixty-two prisoner. From the extant list, they were all drawn from the wolds townships: none of the Beverley commons were arrested or imprisoned.[61] Bigod himself fled, perhaps suddenly, for he left his commentary on the royal supremacy in his lodgings at Beverley; he then went to ground and evaded capture until discovered in Cumberland on 4 February.[62] The skirmish at Beverley, though, marked the end of the renewed revolt in the eastern part of Yorkshire, with nothing achieved, but with the king given an excuse not to acknowledge his side of the Doncaster agreement.

III

Bigod's mad, inept, ill-prepared rising was an enormous embarrassment to the Yorkshire gentry, but their choice was simple. They could not afford to have any truck with Bigod: they had to remain committed to the settlement they negotiated at Doncaster, to which the king had promised his adherence. Writing to the king on 18 January (before Bigod had entered Beverley), Aske reported that Sir Robert Constable had sent his letters into the wide area between the Humber and the vale of Pickering to try to stay the people. Likewise Aske had directed letters into the

[59] Ibid., nos. 143–4. Dodds, *Pilgrimage*, II, 74 (where they see the letters as indicating confusion in Bigod's aims rather than being from different people). Bigod's letter into Durham was signed: *LP* XII (i), no. 148.

[60] *LP* XII (i), no. 1019.   [61] Ibid., no. 174 (1)–(4).   [62] Ibid., nos. 401–2.

district between the rivers Ouse and Derwent, the wapentake of the Ainsty, and the city of York. He advised the early return of the duke of Norfolk, otherwise there was a danger that the people would rise, either to swear or kill the worshipful men, 'for they fear to be betrayed'. Aske acknowledged that the wide sweep of the North from Lancashire through to County Durham and the North York moors, and including Cumberland and Westmorland, was likely to rise, and that it was beyond his means to prevent it. There were no gentry to restrain the commons: they gathered around their own captains, the local equivalents of people like Hallam.[63] (Robert Bowes was active in County Durham, persuading the commons to be acquiescent.[64]) Aske was entirely correct in his assessment: during January and the first days of February there was a revival of the independent movement of the commons in Richmondshire associated in October with the name of Captain Poverty.

This was the movement of which Bigod was confident but which failed to offer him succour. He began the week by hurrying Hallam into seizing Hull to coincide with a revolt in the Dales; but he was also writing letters to Swaledale and County Durham urging rebellion. At least one of his messengers was captured en route.[65] It may be questioned whether Bigod's expected Richmondshire revolt was anything more than self-delusion; yet there was an agitation brewing throughout the highlands generally. Norfolk was aware of disturbances in the last week of January near Sheriff Hutton, in Cleveland, and near Middleham in Wensleydale. Of the first, all we know is that a man called Otterburn was arrested and executed for inciting the disturbance. A single letter fills out some details of the Cleveland disturbances. Bills calling a muster on Hambledon Hill circulated, but when a crowd gathered no one knew what to do or why they were there. Sir William Bulmer and others took the opportunity to draft and circulate a bill saying that no one should spoil or rob, but should keep the orders made at Doncaster, nor should anyone receive or circulate any unsigned bills in future. An attempt to stimulate a new rising around Barnard Castle was unsuccessful and cost one of the Richmond captains, Anthony Peacock, his life.[66]

[63] Ibid., no. 136.   [64] St. P. I, 526 (= LP XII (i), no. 200).
[65] LP XII (i), no. 139, 217, 148.   [66] Ibid., nos. 319, 416(2), 236.

The disturbances centred on Jervaulx Abbey are the best-documented and reveal the acute nervousness which existed about Norfolk's intentions. Tension was heightened by a report brought out of Lincolnshire by a servant of the abbot of Jervaulx's. He had been sent to collect the abbey's rents, but was told to linger for the duke of Norfolk's return and report on whether he was accompanied by an army. The servant returned early and reported that hangings were taking place in the county, the pardon notwithstanding. The reported hangings are not otherwise known to have taken place,[67] but they heightened fears that the duke would deal with the North after the same fashion. The departure of Lord Latimer and Sir Christopher Danby for London in mid-January was also said to have induced a nervousness in the district.[68] Amongst the bills circulating in the third week of January was one sent to Richmond on 19 January, a copy of which was secured by Sir Thomas Curwen. It ordered the commons of every township to rise and to swear all the gentlemen on pain of death to four articles. The first was to maintain 'the profit of Holy Church, which was the upholding of the Christian faith'; the second, that no lord or gentleman was to take anything of any tenant except their rent; the third, that Cromwell and his sect, 'which made the king put down praying and fasting', should be deposed; the fourth, that no gentleman was to go to London. If any gentleman refused the oath, he was to be murdered.[69] At about this time Lord Latimer, who was answering the king's call to court, heard that his house at Snape had been occupied by the commons. Darcy's information was that his house, the earl of Westmorland's, and the houses of other gentlemen who had gone up to court had been seized and inventoried by the commons.[70]

The arrival of the duke of Norfolk was therefore awaited with great trepidation in Jervaulx. The nerve of two of the younger monks, Roger Hartlepool and John Stainton, broke and, even though the monastery was under no immediate threat, they decided that they needed to mobilize against the duke. From Christmas onwards they urged Ninian Staveley and Edward Middleton of Masham 'that they should consent to gather [a] company together against the duke of Norfolk's coming, to the intent

---

[67] On this point, Dodds, *Pilgrimage*, II, 151.   [68] Ibid., no. 1012 at p. 456.
[69] Ibid., nos. 163, 185.   [70] Ibid., nos. 169, 173.

to destroy him, affirming that if he were destroyed their abbey should stand as it did, and so should Holy Church in such a state as it was in King Henry VII's days, and if he came into the country and continued there, their abbey should be put down and they should go abegging'.[71] On 28 January Staveley and Middleton's resistance broke and they agreed to help the monks. Together, they made and circulated bills calling a general muster of all men aged between 16 and 60 on Middleham Moor on the following Tuesday (30 January). Staveley and Middleton then fell out with Thomas Lobley and Lawrence Servant of Masham, who wanted to hold a muster at Richmond on the Wednesday, and from his deposition it seems that Staveley came to regret the whole matter and tried to escape from his undertakings. After they were threatened by the two monks he and Middleton agreed to see the whole matter through. When they came to the abbey with their neighbours on Tuesday the abbot refused to allow them to take the monks with them, and on Middleham Moor they found virtually no one else present. They went away wondering whether any larger group would attend the Richmond muster. At that muster, Lobley, Servant, and Thomas Hutton agreed to write to all the bailiffs and constables in Richmondshire, Durham, Cleveland, Westmorland, and the country around inviting them to send two men from each parish to meet at Richmond on the following Monday, 5 February, to agree upon a strategy towards the duke of Norfolk. Their letter reached Kendal, where it was copied and sent on. One man who saw the Kendal copy thought that it concerned tithes.[72] Norfolk sent draconian proclamations into the Dales ordering the commons not to meet. He was able to report that Richmond would have nothing to do with the parochial delegates and, in the absence of the gentry (who had gone to swear their oaths before him), the meeting broke up without any conclusion.[73]

These were confused days, marked by a desire by the gentry to hold on to the considerable gains which they, with the commons behind them,

---

[71] For what follows, see *LP* XII (i), no. 1012. The quotation is from SP1/118, fo. 258r (another copy fo. 261r). I have redated the account at one crucial moment. *LP* says that the decision to launch a muster was taken on the Sunday after Candlemas, 4 February, but this makes no sense. The first text of Staveley's confession says 'afore' Candlemas (28 January), the second 'after', and I am sure that 'afore' is right. The Dodds failed to realize this, having never used the MS: *Pilgrimage*, II, 138, n. A.

[72] *LP* XII (i), nos. 965, 671.   [73] Ibid., nos. 336, 362.

had achieved at Doncaster, whilst the commons, probably correctly, came to realize that they had been betrayed. So the leaders of the commons, their captains, who had disappeared from sight in many cases after the first Doncaster meeting, reappeared in January either as agitators wishing to resist the duke of Norfolk on his return to the North, or (in some cases) throwing in their lot with the gentry to try to preserve the Doncaster concordat, which the king appeared to have accepted. Those, like Bigod (most notably) and the more mysterious Richmondshire captains, who wished to negotiate with Norfolk from a position of strength (or even preserve their position through his assassination) did the king's work for him. They undermined the credibility of the Doncaster agreement and revealed the bad faith of those who had, allegedly, assented to it. As Norfolk wrote in 23 January in reply to a post from Thomas Cromwell, 'I received your letter containing news as I am not a little joyful to hear, trusting the rest of such ungracious promises shall come to like end. And surely my lord, if the king's affairs may be brought to good frame as this letter doth purport before my coming, I shall be as glad as any man living and nothing sorry that other men have the praise thereof.'[74]

[74] SP1/115, fo. 10r (= *LP* XII (i), no. 198).

14

The Return of the Duke of Norfolk

All men that I have talked with agree in one tale: that the only cause of this new tumult amongst the people is a certain despair, that they have conceived, that my lord of Norfolk should not come into these parts: for all men say that his coming shall stay altogether.[1]

The return of the duke of Norfolk was obviously a considerable relief to the Yorkshire gentry.[2] He arrived at Doncaster, as promised, on 1 February, where a number of the gentry and nobility had gathered to meet him, amongst them Sir Thomas and Sir Ingram Percy, the younger brothers of the earl of Northumberland. Orders had already been issued for the arrest of the Percy brothers after Northumberland had denounced them to the council, but Norfolk was happy to allow them to continue, unsuspecting, on their way to court. On 6 February it was reported that Sir Thomas was lodged in the Tower.[3]

From Doncaster Norfolk made his way to Pontefract, where he was obliged to arbitrate between Lord Darcy and Sir George Darcy over the custody of the castle. The king's decision to relieve Darcy of responsibility

---

[1] Sir Ralph Sadler to Cromwell, 23 Jan. 1537, *St. P.* I, 526 (= *LP* XII (i), no. 200).
[2] See e.g. Sir Thomas Tempest to Norfolk on 5 Feb., *LP* XII (i), no. 345.
[3] Ibid., no. 353.

led Darcy to write to Aske begging the return of munitions which he had taken from the castle during the Pilgrimage, a letter which the Crown was able to exploit after it fell into its hands.[4] It was from Pontefract that Norfolk wrote to both Cromwell and the earl of Sussex with his first reactions to the state of the North. He had been warmly received by the gentry. The gentlemen were frightened of the commons: they recognized that if the commons were not returned to obedience, then they would lose their property to them. Bills posted on church doors testified to the venom which the commons bore to them. A fear of renewed disturbances had prevented the gentry from putting the farmers of the lands of the suppressed monasteries back into possession, as had been agreed at the Doncaster conference. 'My lord, trust ye surely, the nobles and gentlemen be well afraid and of such sort that hardly I can cause them to go abouts to take the ring leaders of these new commotions.'[5]

Norfolk's arrival brought a renewed confidence amongst the gentry. The first trials and executions of the commons surely revived spirits. The duke forbade the commons to meet at Richmond on 5 February. The failure of this meeting was doubtless a fillip; the discovery of Bigod in hiding in Cumberland must have given additional satisfaction; but most of all, the smashing of the commons of Cumberland and Westmorland at Carlisle placed the gentry back in the ascendant. So too did the incorporation of some of the most prominent Pilgrims into Norfolk's council. His retinue included Ellerker and Bowes; by 9 March it also included Sir Thomas Tempest. Aske too travelled through the North in Norfolk's entourage.[6] By 14 February Archbishop Lee had gathered enough composure to send out a circular to his clergy: they were to preach on the subject of obedience to their king, to tell their congregations that the rebellion had been 'deadly sin', for which they 'were bound to make amends toward both God and his majesty for the discharging of the same', and they were to use confession to exort their parishioners to conform to the king's laws.[7] One may suspect that the greatest release of anxiety

---

[4] Ibid., no. 390.   [5] Ibid., nos. 336, 337 (= St. P. I, 534–5).

[6] For the membership of the earl's council and its relationship to the Council of the North, see App. 1.

[7] Borthwick Institute, York, D/C Inv (late AS 55), which contains five copies of the circular as sent out by the dean and chapter of York, one marked 'original'.

came when it was found that Norfolk was not leading an army of repression and that the promise of a general pardon would be honoured.

By 7 February Norfolk had reached York and had begun the task of swearing the gentlemen of Yorkshire to the pardon. He met with no dissent, but it also seems likely that he omitted to insist that the gentlemen declare all they knew about the originators of the first rebellion. By the end of the week he had conducted the first trials at York and could send to London his first list of judicial victims: two canons of Warter, for reasons which are unclear; the sub-prior of Watton, very peripherally involved in Hallam's rising; John Wyvill and Ralph Fenton, Lumley's successors as the captains of Bigod's men at Scarborough; a 'head yeoman' called Otterburn, who had tried to raise an otherwise unrecorded disturbance around Sheriff Hutton; and Anthony Peacock of Richmond, who had tried to do likewise at Barnard Castle. Others were in custody, whilst yet more were actively sought: Staveley and Middleton, for trying to launch the disturbance around Jervaulx; Marshall, the parish clerk of Beswick and Woodmansey; the serving-man from Beverley.[8] Norfolk quickly gave notice that he intended to advance on Sawley to expel the monks who had re-entered the house in October. Sawley, it will be recalled, had already been granted to Sir Arthur Darcy who, on 9 February, was asking his father to organize a force to accompany the duke on Wednesday, 14 February. Darcy wrote back wanting to know how many men were required, and whether or not with harness and in wages.[9] Norfolk was making his way towards Sawley when news came that Cumberland and Westmorland had risen anew. From Fountains he turned northwards towards Richmond and began to gather what army he could for an advance into Westmorland.[10]

When writing to Cromwell on 13 February, Norfolk had included Nicholas Musgrave and Thomas Tibbey amongst the ringleaders of the commons whom, he hoped in time, to apprehend. There had been an attempt to capture Musgrave on 6 January by Thomas Clifford—surely contrary to the pardon agreed at Doncaster—but this was in line with the instructions which Henry gave the earl of Cumberland in a letter of 1 November, 'to travail yourself all you possibly can to get into your

---

[8] *LP* XII (i), no. 416 (1)–(2).   [9] Ibid., nos. 383, 391, 408.   [10] Ibid., no. 419.

custody such as were notable traitors in this matter'.[11] Musgrave and Tibbey were warned in advance and took refuge in the church steeple in Kirkby Stephen, an impregnable stronghold, and Clifford was forced to retire empty-handed. Whether or not Norfolk ordered a new attempt to seize them, Thomas Clifford set out again on Monday, 12 February with a troop of horsemen drawn from the borders. These men were thieves and, frustrated by their inability to take Musgrave and Tibbey, who took refuge in the steeple a second time, they started to plunder Kirkby Stephen and provoked a fight with the enraged townspeople. Clifford and his troop were forced to withdraw to the safety of Cumberland's castle at Brougham, and the countryside rose in revulsion at their plundering. Musgrave and Tibbey, or someone on their behalf, started a bill circulating which claimed that Clifford and the gentlemen had slain many of their brethren and neighbours (Norfolk understood that there had been two killed). A bill calling for a muster on Tuesday morning reached Kendal, where further copies were made and circulated. On Thursday, 15 February a muster, allegedly of 6,000 men, took place at Broadfield Oak. On Friday the commons laid siege to Carlisle, perhaps consciously taking up where they had left off after word of the truce had been received at the end of October. They took the initiative, shooting arrows into the town; but, having exhausted their munitions, they withdraw for a distance to consider what to do next, and were attacked in the rear by Sir Christopher Dacre and his moss-troopers. Thomas Clifford then took the opportunity to issue from the town with the castle garrison, and the attack on Carlisle turned into a rout as the commons fled, chased by Clifford's and Dacre's mounted troops. The word in London was that 700 rebels had been killed, but Norfolk reported 700 or 800 captured, and this is surely more plausible.[12]

Norfolk was too far removed to offer any aid. Both the castle garrison and Norfolk wrote to Sir Christopher asking for his help, the duke telling him that this was a make-or-break occasion and signing himself 'your loving cousin if ye do well, or else enemy for ever'. Dacre did indeed do well and was to receive the king's fulsome thanks.[13] Norfolk

[11] 'Letters of the Cliffords', 56.   [12] *LP* XII (i), nos. 448, 492.
[13] Ibid., nos. 426, 427, 479, 492.

blamed Clifford for inciting the whole business with his ill-disciplined troops, but the duke also relished the occasion as an opportunity to prove himself. We have seen how the king thought he was too willing to make concessions to the Pilgrims in December. There were suspicions that he was soft on monasteries. He protested in one letter that he was 'neither a papist nor a favourer of traitors'.[14] So, telling Cromwell of his plans to lead an army into Cumberland, he added: 'now shall appear whether for favour of these countrymen I forbear to fight them at Doncaster.'[15]

Norfolk sent an advance party of 200 or 300 horsemen into Westmorland under Sir Thomas Wharton, with instructions to burn the rebels' houses and draw them from Carlisle. He gathered at Richmond a force of 4,000 horsemen drawn from the Yorkshire gentry, and this army had reached Barnard Castle (to cross into Westmorland by way of Stainmoor) when word reached it that the commons had been smashed.[16] Norfolk proceeded to Carlisle and declared martial law. He issued proclamations that all those involved in the attack on Carlisle were to return to the city to make their personal submission to him. Some 6,000 men came in, of whom seventy-four were selected for trial by martial law. Not only was this more expeditious, it was also guaranteed to result in conviction. Even by Norfolk's own account it was an arbitrary process:

And surely, had I proceeded by the trial of 12 men, I think that not the fifth man of these should have suffered, for the common saying is here 'I came out of fear of my life' and 'I came forth for fear of loss of all my goods', and 'I came forth for fear of burning of my houses and destroying of my wife and children'. And a small excuse will be well believed here where much affection and pity of neighbours doth reign. And Sir, though the number be nothing so great than their deserts did require to have suffered, yet I think the like of number not be heard of put to execution at one time.[17]

Those executed suffered in their own villages as a reminder to their neighbours of the dangers of rebellion. Having proceeded to make an example of the commons, Norfolk was not without sympathy for their predicament. We have already seen him critical of Clifford, but writing

---

[14] Above, pp. 339–41; *LP* XII (i), nos. 416, 381.
[15] *LP* XII (i), nos. 312, 439. See also ibid., nos. 809, 810.
[16] Ibid., nos. 439, 448. [17] SP1/116, fo. 108r (= *LP* XII (i), no. 498).

to Cromwell on 21 February, he described the commons returning home from Carlisle:

And those poor caitiffs that begun here are departed without any promise of pardon but on their good abearing. And God knoweth they may well be called poor caitiffs, for at their fleeing they lost horse, harness, and all they had upon them, and what for the spoiling of them now and the gressing [fining] of them so marvellously sore in time past and with increasing of the lord's rents by inclosings and for lack of the persons of such as shall suffer, this border is sore wrecked and especially Westmorland: the more pity they should so deserve and also that they have been sore handled in times past, which, as I and all other here think, was the only cause of this rebellion.[18]

It was the misfortune of the commons to have launched a revolt at a moment when Norfolk needed executions to vindicate his policy over the previous few months; and when the king wrote to approve of his policy, one wonders whether for him too, the mass execution of the commons was not a release of the frustration which had been building as the guilty evaded punishment by the pardon. Norfolk's return stifled any further possibility of insurrection. The difference in temperature may be seen in the end of the commons' captain from Richmond, Anthony Peacock: despite some alehouse talk of rescuing him from gaol, he was hanged without incident on 16 February, the day the Cumberland commons were routed at Carlisle.[19]

It will be recalled that when news of the rising broke Norfolk was turning towards the problem of Sawley. This was resolved without his ever being there: he wrote to the convent, which seems to have surrendered possession to Sir Richard Tempest. Sir Arthur Darcy travelled to Sawley after Norfolk's army disbanded at Barnard Castle and he managed to discover and capture the abbot.[20] Once at Carlisle, Norfolk's attention was caught by the unsettled state of Northumberland, and whilst there he received a commission to dissolve monastic houses in the North. The king's letter of 22 February also ordered him to execute under martial

---

[18] Ibid., fo. 89r (= *LP* XII (i), no. 478). This was, in part at least, an oblique criticism of the earl of Cumberland. In the spring there was an inquiry into the removal for burial of some of the bodies of Norfolk's victims. Norfolk discovered that those responsible were the wives and mothers of the deceased: again, it was insinuated that he was soft on the commons.

[19] *LP* XII (i), no. 775.   [20] Ibid., no. 506.

law any monks who had re-entered their houses, an instruction which Norfolk seems to have ignored.[21] He certainly dissolved Hexham, thus completing the unfinished business of October, and seized Prudhoe Castle for the king after the imprisonment of Sir Thomas Percy,[22] but due to a gap in the correspondence, his movements in the fortnight between his departure from Carlisle and his arrival in Durham to hold sessions on 8 March cannot be traced in detail. At Durham, Norfolk and his council discovered that they had no judicial authority in the Bishopric; and whilst he wrote urgently for a revised commission, his council decided to proceed regardless but to delay their judgement until the new commission arrived.

By 22 March he was back at York to supervise a further round of trials, probably of those implicated in Bigod's revolt. Two of these resulted in acquittals, the first of a man called Lutton,[23] the other of William Levening of Acklam. Bigod had called Levening to him on Monday, 15 January, sworn him, and then sent him to circulate word of the muster at Borough. Thereafter he had been in Bigod's company throughout the rebellion. After the rebels had been driven out of Beverley, Levening had first gone home and then surrendered himself to Constable, Darcy, and Aske, acknowledging his complicity, and they promised to plead his case to Norfolk. We have a detailed account of the jury's deliberations made for Norfolk by one its members, Thomas Delaryver. The jury split between the minority who thought Levening guilty, and the majority who were suspicious of Sir Ralph Ellerker's evidence against him, notably because it was rumoured that Ellerker had a grant of Levening's lands. Moreover, they used Lutton's acquittal as a precedent: if his involvement had been justified by coercion and duress, then why should Levening be convicted? The debate amongst the jury continued from Friday morning until Saturday evening, despite their being deprived of heat and comforts by Norfolk's servants. Finally, the deadlocked jury agreed to acquit. Norfolk was greatly angered by this decision, but on interviewing Levening he discovered that he had been harboured by Darcy, Aske, and

---

[21] Ibid., nos. 478, 479.   [22] Ibid., nos. 546, 577.

[23] This was probably Thomas Lutton of Knapton in Winteringham, assessed at £24 in lands in 1541 (PRO, E179/203/212), who made his will in 1546. *Testamenta Eboracensia*, VI, 241–2. What role he played in the rising is unrecorded.

Constable after the failure of Bigod's revolt, and this showed the way for the king to destroy them.[24]

By this time Norfolk was being instructed to arrest and send southwards an increasing number of people. Whilst at Carlisle he was ordered to send up Bigod, a friar of Knaresborough who had been captured in the mêlée, William Leach of Horncastle (who had not, in fact, been captured), Robert Thompson, the vicar of Brough, Dr Towneley, and a canon of Bridlington, Dr Pickering.[25] Norfolk sent Thompson and Towneley to London on 8 March, arguing that Thompson had done nothing indictable since the pardon except pray for the pope.[26] From Norfolk's letters we see a pattern whereby Henry appears to have latched on to individuals whose name came to his notice. Some of his victims may not have played a prominent role in the risings, but once the king took an interest in them they were lost. Such was Thomas Hutton of Snape. On 13 February Hutton was in gaol when Norfolk noted that there was no proof of offences since the pardon. On 17 March the king wanted Hutton prosecuted: he had heard that Norfolk had new evidence, besides the fact that Hutton was amongst those who called an assembly at Richmond on 5 February to prepare a supplication, but which the king held was itself treasonable. Norfolk finally had him tried in Durham, admitting that there was nothing on which a Yorkshire jury could convict.[27] Sir Robert Constable was called into the royal presence by a letter of 19 February. Why is not clear; but when he failed to start out for the south, suspicions were created and Norfolk was told to send him up under guard. He was to have a watch kept to prevent Constable escaping from Hull or Scarborough by boat. As Norfolk pointed out, he could take a boat from his own town of Flamborough without anyone being any the wiser.[28] When Constable made his way to London cannot be discovered. On 22 March Norfolk could report that he instructed Dr Dakyns and Richard Bowyer, the York notary, to go up to the court: he supplied Dakyns with a character reference from Robert Bowes, testifying to his

---

[24] For the proceeding, *LP* XII (i), nos. 730–2.

[25] Ibid., no. 479. See also the extract of the lost letter printed by Dodds, *Pilgrimage*, II, 122.

[26] Ibid., nos. 498, 594, 609.   [27] Ibid., nos. 416 (2), 666, 777, 918, 1012.

[28] Ibid., nos. 465, 594.

coercion by the commons in the first days of the Richmondshire revolt. At this time Norfolk was also encouraging Aske to go to the king and was happy to equip him with letters of commendation to both the king and Cromwell. As with Sir Thomas Percy, his method was to lull the king's victim into a sense of security so that his arrest came as a surprise.[29] Darcy travelled up to court—voluntarily—at about the same time, having told Henry in a letter of 22 March that the country was now so quiet that his presence was no longer needed.[30] At the end of the month yet more men were required by the king: Sir Stephen Hamerton, Nicholas Tempest (both caught up in the reoccupation of Sawley by its monks), and the prior of Bridlington. Norfolk thought that they were all so unsuspecting of their jeopardy that they would travel to the king on privy seals.[31]

As reports of the executions in Carlisle, York, and Lincoln circulated, it may be wondered why Aske, Darcy, Constable, and many other gentry went willingly to court during March and early April 1537. Perhaps they thought that they had no choice and that resistance was futile; but the majority of them were probably confident that, as they had not been engaged in seditious activities since the issue of the pardon, they had little to fear. The imprisonment of Sir Thomas Percy might have persuaded them otherwise. When Sir John Bulmer and his wife Margaret Cheney received a royal order to attend the king in mid-March, they chose the route of resistance rather than flight or quiet submission. Bulmer's half-baked plot was the last incident in the revolts of 1536–7.[32]

Sir John seems to have been of a generally nervous disposition. For a time, at the end of January, he was convinced that the duke of Norfolk was returning with a military force. Ralph Bulmer, his son, sent word from London that a naval flotilla of thirty ships was being prepared and that Aske and Sir George Darcy had turned king's evidence against Darcy and Sir Robert Constable. He urged his brother, Sir William, to set a watch on the coast and to prepare beacons. Bulmer was desperately anxious when he did not receive a letter from Norfolk inviting him to greet him on his entry into Yorkshire at Candlemas. This is not to say that Bulmer

---

[29] Ibid., nos. 698, 710–12.   [30] Ibid., no. 699.   [31] Ibid., no. 777.

[32] For a fuller account of Bulmer's plot, see Dodds, *Pilgrimage*, II, 96–7 and 158–63.

was any friend to the commons: during this period he seems to have been busy maintaining the peace in Cleveland at a time when bills calling for a new rising were circulating. When word came that they were to go to the king, Sir John secured permission from Norfolk to delay his journey and sought the advice of his son Ralph. When that came, it was not encouraging: 'that Sir John should look well to himself, for, as far as he could perceive, all was falsehood that they were dealt withal.' Bulmer rejected the possibility of flight, and instead, in the week before Easter, used his chaplain and domestic steward, William Staynhouse, to gauge opinions in the villages around Lastingham. Staynhouse was told to go from parish priest to parish priest to enquire of them 'if the commons would rise again, which they should know by men's confessions'. Bulmer himself went to see Lord Lumley at Kilton, near Guisborough. Lumley's son George had been imprisoned (and would eventually be executed) for his part in Bigod's revolt and the attack on Scarborough. Bulmer may have been encouraged to believe that he could strike an alliance with Lumley who, it was rumoured, had said that if he was called to London he would take 10,000 men with him. If Bulmer floated the idea of a new rising to Lumley, then Lumley rejected it and disappeared from the district. It was a matter of gossip that Lumley had victualled Kilton for Easter, but abruptly left after Bulmer had visited him. Bulmer may also have been encouraged by a letter from Sir Ralph Eure which was mildly critical of Norfolk.

Staynhouse received no encouragement from either of the priests he canvassed on Good Friday, 30 March (even though one, Thomas Franke, the vicar of Lofthouse, had played a prominent role in the first week of the Yorkshire rebellion around Howden), and it appears that they denounced Bulmer to the authorities early the next week. By 8 April Norfolk had the whole matter sewn up, and dispatched Bulmer's wife and Staynhouse to London. Sir John followed shortly after. Sir William Bulmer rode to Norfolk to try to ascertain what had happened to his brother and to see whether he was implicated by his brother's arrest. Norfolk could discover nothing to endanger him since the pardon.[33] Sir John would probably have had nothing to fear had his nerve not broken when he

---

[33] *LP* XII (i), no. 902.

received his call to London. The arrival of the Bulmers in London and the arrest of Ralph Bulmer gave the king his full hand of rebels for the trials which took place in May.

Norfolk, despite his requests to be relieved, remained in the North to supervise further trials; but the government, having by the end of the month or shortly after the principals in the Pilgrimage in its grasp, and the evidence that they had harboured Levening in the days immediately after Bigod's revolt, moved against them. On 7 April the privy council wrote to Norfolk to say that on the discovery of their association with Levening, and other matters, Aske, Constable, and Darcy had all been conveyed to the Tower to await trial. Norfolk was to circulate a report of their imprisonment amongst the people, stressing that their arrest was for crimes committed since the pardon. This he did. Their lands and goods, and in Darcy's case his papers, were seized.[34]

I

Norfolk's commission did not extend to Lancashire, perhaps out of respect for the local hegemony of the earl of Derby, whose loyalty during the Pilgrimage had been impeccable. Lancashire north of the Ribble had risen in October and had remained disturbed throughout the winter. There was as great a need for the oath to be administered throughout the county as elsewhere in the North. We saw earlier that it had been decided— probably by Christmas—that the earl of Sussex would be sent to Lancaster to assist his brother-in-law, Derby, in a parallel mission to Norfolk's. Their instructions were broadly similar to Norfolk's, but differed in detail. The chief duties were to secure the adherence to the oaths, to put the king's farmers in possession of the lands of suppressed monasteries, to investigate who had devised the Doncaster articles, discover who in Lancashire had been communicating with Yorkshire, and to intervene where lords made unreasonable demands on their tenants. It is not certain whether Sussex and Derby had a council akin to that with which Norfolk was

[34] Ibid., nos. 846, 863, 1064. For an inventory of his papers, no. 1089; 'Letters of the Cliffords', 117–8.

travelling.[35] They were supported by the chief justice of Lancaster, Sir Anthony Fitzherbert, and the second justice, Thomas Porte, and they had a commission of oyer and terminer to enable them to act judicially.[36]

The earl of Sussex was still at court on 9 February; his departure for the North was newsworthy on 18 February and he seems only to have arrived at Warrington on 26 February.[37] At Warrington he met with Derby and the other gentlemen appointed to be in commission with them. The king's instructions were read and a strategy for their implementation devised. Proclamations were made that on 28 February (being market day in Warrington) the commissioners would receive bills of complaint for offences against the king's subjects and administer the oath. The gentlemen were sworn first, then 900 or 1,000 commons, without any dissension. Sussex, Derby and Fitzherbert reported this success to the king and told him of their plan to repeat the process at Manchester, Preston, and finally Lancaster.[38] We must assume that the administration of the oath was done successfully and without difficulty throughout the county.

The next extant letters are of 11 March, addressed to Cromwell and Norfolk. We lack the key letter of this date, the news letter addressed to the king, but the letters are full of a rather different matter, the trial and execution of John Paslew, abbot of Whalley, and the trial of two monks from Whalley (one of whom was acquitted) and two from Sawley. Unfortunately, neither of the extant letters explain why Paslew was indicted, convicted, and executed in the space of two days. The calendar of the palatinate indictment rolls (which is all that remains) merely tells us that he, in combination with the other accused, was tried on five charges, and that he pleaded guilty to all five. Sussex remarked that this was a piece of good fortune, for it was unlikely that he would have been convicted by a jury.[39]

It is possible to conjecture an explanation for the trial. A much later source explains how, after the monks were evicted from Sawley a second

---

[35] The instructions never refer to a council, but *LP* XII (i), nos. 520 and 716 both do. For a discussion of the men associated with Sussex and Derby, see App. 2.

[36] For a fuller account of their mission, Haigh, 'The Last Days of the Lancashire Monasteries', ch. 7.

[37] *LP* XII (i), nos. 378, 457.   [38] Ibid., no. 520.

[39] Ibid., nos. 630–1; J. E. W. Wallis, 'The Narrative of the Indictment of the Traitors at Whalley and Cartmell, 1536–7', in *Chetham Miscellany V*, Chetham Soc., NS 90 (1931).

time, one of them, Richard Estgate, fled to Whalley where his brother was a monk and was sheltered there. The earl of Sussex was at Whalley on 6 March, having administered the oath at Preston: it is possible that Estgate was discovered there and the abbot accused of sheltering him. At the same sessions nine canons of Cartmel (three *in absentia*) and thirteen husbandmen were tried. Two of the canons were acquitted and four of the husbandmen. Again, the grounds on which they were prosecuted are unclear, but as Cartmel had been suppressed the previous summer and the canons had re-entered, we might suspect that the immediate offence was a refusal to give up possession to the Crown's farmer. The king was delighted with Sussex's summary treatment of Paslew, and in his next letter announced a significant leap in policy which had already been piloted at Barlings and Kirkstead in Lincolnshire.[40] Henry argued that the attainder of the head of the house was a forfeiture of the lands and goods of the whole house. (This was, at the very least, a constructive reading of the law.) Sussex was to seize the lands for the king and offer the monks either transfers to other houses or capacities to become regulars, that is, that they should be treated like monks belonging to houses dissolved under the 1536 statute.[41]

It also appears from Sussex's letter to Norfolk that he was making investigations in northern Lancashire to identify and capture the captains of the commons in the first rebellion. They had already interrogated (and executed) John Staines of Beetham, who had received money from his parish to attend the abortive Richmond meeting on 5 February. Sussex was interested in the role of Nicholas Tempest in spreading the Pilgrimage down the Ribble valley in October.[42] Within a few days he was beginning to accumulate evidence implicating the monks of Furness in the October rising. One Alexander Richardson, the bailiff of Dalton in Furness, made a deposition accusing the monks of, amongst other things, giving £20 to the commons. Evidence was also gathered showing how William Collins, the bailiff of Kendal, had circulated the letter calling the Richmond meeting.[43] On 21 March Sussex thought that his work was virtually complete; but the king's next letter demanded more. Sussex

---

[40] See below pp. 404–5, for events here.   [41] *LP* XII (i), no. 668 (= *St. P.* I, 540–1).
[42] Ibid., no. 632.   [43] Ibid., nos. 652, 671 (iii).

was to stay to investigate Furness further, as well as winding up matters at Whalley.

On 5 April the abbot of Furness, Roger Pyle, surrendered all his interest in the house and its lands to the king. The circumstances behind this decision are revealed in a letter written to Henry on the following day. Sussex and his fellow commissioners had examined the monks of Furness, but could find little to incriminate them in the way of misdemeanours committed after the pardon. They only had grounds for the imprisonment of two monks at Lancaster. There was a determination to seize the house into the king's hands, but no evidence on which to convict the abbot. The letter explains how Pyle was brought to Whalley and examined further, but again revealed nothing incriminating. When, however, Sussex asked him whether he would agree to surrender the house to the king, Pyle said that he would, and thought that the remainder of the monks could be persuaded to add their names to the surrender. Pyle then executed a simple surrender to the use of the king. Three of Sussex's councillors were sent to seize the house for the king, whilst Fitzherbert was consulted about the validity of this course of action. He condoned their actions, but advised that a stronger form of instrument was necessary to make the surrender fully conclusive. Accordingly a new instrument of surrender was made on 9 April, signed by the abbot and twenty-eight monks.[44] It comes as no surprise that the king was delighted by this course of action and sent his congratulations in a letter of 11 April. The work of the commission completed, it seems to have dissolved itself, and Sussex and Fitzherbert returned southwards.

The long-term significance of Sussex's creative shaping of the law has long been appreciated. At Barlings and Kirkstead the doctrine was established that an ecclesiastical corporation could be forfeited to the king by the attainder of its head. This was unexpectedly applied at Whalley and later in the spring at Jervaulx and Bridlington. At Furness it was established that the members of a corporation could, voluntarily, convey the lands and livelihood of an ecclesiastical corporation to the king. This left the way open to the non-statutory dissolution of the monasteries which began in earnest in 1538 and was completed in 1540.

---

[44] Ibid., no. 840.

There is an important distinction to be made between Sussex's and Norfolk's handling of affairs. Sussex was, without doubt, much tougher, much more determined to uncover the names of those who had been complicit in the Pilgrimage and much more eager to secure their punishment. There is no parallel in Norfolk's lieutenancy for the hanging of the abbot of Whalley (or the cynical view that it was only possible because he pleaded guilty) and the canons of Cartmel. When Levening was acquitted, Norfolk was insistent that the king should not try to punish the jury.[45] We do not see Norfolk initiating investigations of the sort which led to the identification of Collins, the bailiff of Kendal, as the linkman between Richmondshire and the lower Lake District. It was Sussex who had no hesitation about hanging people. A man called Barrett from Steeton in Craven was brought before the earl at Warrington. Barrett had been arrested for spreading a rumour that the duke of Norfolk would impose heavy taxation (of exactly the same sort as was rumoured in the autumn of 1536) on Yorkshire. He also admitted to having been at the ill-fated siege of Carlisle. Sussex's instinct was to hang, but he had (he reported) been advised by Fitzherbert that the words were not sufficient grounds for prosecution, nor could Barrett be indicted for offences committed in another county. Barrett's case was therefore referred to the king. The next time we hear of him, less than a fortnight later, he had been tried and was awaiting execution.[46] In another case, Sussex referred to the king the case of an old man who, when convicted, pleaded that he had often served the king against the Scots. The king held that his execution was especially justified, the man having accepted his wages.[47] Whilst this is illuminating of the king's personality (and his extreme hostility to anyone he thought had betrayed him), both cases illustrate a degree of cruelty not found in Norfolk, except when proving himself at Carlisle. The duke failed to take initiatives to seek out the king's enemies. His investigations were very much driven by the king's and Cromwell's demands for named individuals to be sent to them. As an example, Norfolk did nothing to try to discover the shadowy underground which wrote the Captain Poverty letters. This is to our eternal misfortune, but saved the lives of the letters' authors. The downside to Sussex's impulsive,

---

[45] Ibid., no. 1172.   [46] Ibid., nos. 520, 632.   [47] Ibid., no. 668.

no-nonsense manner may be seen in the king's request that Richard Estgate, the monk of Sawley, be sent up for further interrogation. Too late: Sussex had already had him hanged.[48] Norfolk's caution might well have been appropriate, but Sussex's bloodlust and creative construction of the law did much more to satisfy the king's need for revenge than the duke's ponderous progress through the North.

II

'The device for the . . . perfect establishment of the North Parts' envisaged that the duke of Suffolk would be sent back into Lincolnshire. Suffolk evaded the posting and Sir William Parr went in his place, equipped with a commission of oyer and terminer dated 14 February.[49] The commissioners had gathered in Lincoln by 5 March, when they indicted the most notorious of those involved in the Lincolnshire revolt, amongst them Nicholas Leach, Robert Sotherby, and Philip Trotter of Horncastle, Thomas Mackeral, abbot of Barlings, Thomas Kendall, vicar of Louth, William Morland, the monk of Louth Park, and George Huddeswell; twelve men in all, all of whom were prisoners incarcerated in the Tower. They never returned to Lincolnshire, being tried at the Guildhall on 26 March, when they were sentenced to be executed at Tyburn.[50] The trial of 100 men for their role in the revolt took place in Lincoln on 6–7 March. Moigne spoke articulately and persuasively in his defence, but was convicted regardless. Sixty-three of the condemned had their execution deferred, but thirty-four were sentenced to immediate execution, including Guy Kyme and Thomas Moigne, six secular priests (amongst them the elderly and blind Thomas Yoell), four monks of Barlings, six monks of Bardney, and the abbot and four monks of Kirkstead.[51] The abbot of Kirkstead, Kyme, and Moigne were executed immediately at Lincoln; the others were hanged

---

[48] Ibid., no. 706.   [49] This is recited in PRO, KB9/539 m. 1.

[50] LP XII (i), no. 734.

[51] One hundred were actually tried. The three missing individuals were Woodmansey, who was believed to be in prison in Yorkshire but probably always evaded capture, and Robert Carr and Leonard Bawtry, both discharged on Cromwell's instructions.

at Louth or Horncastle. At Louth, to secure the maximum terror, the executions were delayed until the town was full on market day. The other sixty-four were deemed less culpable and the commissioners petitioned for their pardon.[52] Seventeen of them remained in custody until the beginning of August, when they appeared in court to present their pardons.[53]

It had already been decided to hold that the execution of a head of house for treason was an attainder of the whole house and its lands. This policy is normally held to have been instituted after the windfall of the execution of the abbot of Whalley, but the policy was being implemented at Barlings and Kirkstead even as Paslew was undergoing trial and execution.[54] On 9 March Parr was told to make inventories of the goods and make arrangements for the lands of Kirkstead and Barlings. Parr put managers in: he asked whether the goods of the houses were to be kept or sold and, as was so often the case, suggested himself as a suitable tenant of the abbey's lands. The next post from London brought new instructions, which are never described, but on 18 March Parr sent as much plate as he had been able to discover to London, together with inventories of the abbeys' goods, and then set about tracing further plate which had been embezzled from the houses. On 22 March he was going to pay off the monks and the houses' domestic establishments. A week later he was on his way home.[55]

III

'I am here now at your pleasure: ye may do your pleasure with me.'[56] Darcy's comment to his interrogators in the Tower was a realistic statement of his predicament. He could expect no clemency: the sole purpose in keeping him alive was to establish what had actually happened during the Pilgrimage, to invite him to incriminate others, and to proceed to trial and execution. And what was true for Darcy was

---

[52] *LP* XII (i), nos. 581, 590, 591, 639.   [53] PRO, KB9/542, mm. 12–15.

[54] Paslew was tried on 9 March and executed on 10 March. The two Lincolnshire houses were amongst the six attained houses confirmed to the Crown by statute 31 Henry VIII c. 13.

[55] *LP* XII (i), nos. 639, 677, 700, 765, 768.   [56] E36/119, fo. 77r (= *LP* XII (i), no. 1120).

also true for the vast majority of others who were called to London and imprisoned.

In all, eighteen people stood trial in May for their involvement in the Pilgrimage and the post-Pilgrimage disturbances. They may be quickly named: Thomas, Lord Darcy; John, Lord Hussey; Sir Robert Constable; Sir Francis Bigod; Sir Thomas Percy; Sir John Bulmer and his son Ralph; Margaret Cheyne; Sir Stephen Hamerton; George Lumley; Robert Aske; James Cockerell, late prior of Guisborough; Nicholas Tempest; William Wood, prior of Bridlington; Adam Sedber, prior of Jervaulx; and William Thirsk, late abbot of Fountains.

The trial procedure may be quickly summarized.[57] A commission of oyer and terminer in the name of the duke of Norfolk and members of his council was issued on 28 April. A parallel commission was issued to Sir William Parr. The duke of Norfolk and his fellow commissioners issued a precept to the sheriff of Yorkshire to empanel a jury on 3 May. Darcy and sixteen others were then indicted at York, *in absentia*, on 9 May. Norfolk was supplied with duplicate bills to be placed before two separate juries: in this way the possibility of a single jury refusing to indict some or all of the accused was removed. The juries were carefully laced with the relatives of the accused. The jurors—who included John Aske, Robert Aske's elder brother—were invited to prove their loyalty by finding against their kinsmen.[58] The indictments were then transmitted to London. The Lincolnshire commission went through the same procedure: on 12 May it indicted John, Lord Hussey. Darcy and Hussey were tried by their peers on 15 May. Both pleaded not guilty; both were found guilty by all those present.[59] The remaining accused were tried by a further commission of oyer and terminer issued to the lord chancellor, Sir Thomas Audeley, on 12 May. Further juries of Yorkshiremen were empanelled, and they were tried at Westminster on 16 and 17 May. All

[57] The trial records, from the 'Baga de Secretis' are conveniently summarized in *LP* XII (i), nos. 1207, 1227.

[58] Ibid., nos. 1156, 1172 (2).

[59] *LP* XII (i), no. 1207 (16)–(21) is the record of the court convened under Henry, marquis of Exeter. It appears that Cromwell promised the lords that if they convicted Darcy, Cromwell would seek his pardon, and it may be that this weighed in their decision. *LP* XIII (ii), nos. 803, 831, which I owe to Dr Bernard.

pleaded not guilty, but before the jury returned Sir Thomas Percy, Sir John Bulmer, Margaret Cheyne, and Sir Stephen Hamerton changed their pleas to guilty. The others were all convicted, with the exception of Ralph Bulmer.

Given that trial, conviction, and execution were practically foregone conclusions, it may seem otiose to try to establish the grounds on which Darcy and the others were convicted. And yet this is important in order to understand the way in which the Crown skewered its victims whilst also paying lip service to the pardon granted in December. The formal indictment is not terribly helpful and, if it was all that survived, would be positively misleading. The seventeen indictees from Yorkshire were all accused of plotting a conspiracy on 10 October 1536 at Sherburn in Yorkshire to deprive the king of his title of supreme head and to compel him to hold a parliament and convocation, and on other days during October 1536 of making an insurrection against him. These, and all other offences committed before 10 December, had been forgiven by the king's pardon. On 17 January 1537 they had again conspired to annul statutes made for the benefit of the common weal and to depose the king, and to that end had sent messages to each other. Bigod and Lumley on 21 January and other days had assembled a great multitude against the king; the others had abetted them in their treason. Hussey was accused of conspiring at Sleaford on 1 October and afterwards with William Morland, Thomas Moigne, George Huddeswell, and others to change the laws and to depose the king: further, he abetted the others when they made war on the king on 2 October and afterwards. (Their offences had not been obliterated by the Lincolnshire pardon.)

Read literally, the indictments are absurd. Why the conspiracy in Yorkshire was said to have been launched at Sherburn is unknown: there is no indication that any of the accused were there on that day. Hussey was accused of conspiracy with a group of others, some of whom were almost certainly unknown to him and the majority of whom had already been executed. The indictments were not meant to be read as a record of what had happened: the guilt of the accused rested, not on the truth of the exact words of the indictment, but on their reputations and the evidence presented to the jury. What the Yorkshire indictment makes clear is the place of Bigod's revolt in bringing down the others, and the importance of the claim that Darcy, Constable, Aske, and others aided and abetted the revolt.

We have a digest of evidence that the Crown possessed against some of the accused and, even if this was not drawn on in the actual trial, it shows the sort of case which they believed that they could make in court.[60] Most importantly, it shows that although the Crown collected copious evidence about the events of the autumn from its prisoners, this did not play any part in their trials. Of course, the people indicted may have been selected for their actions before the pardon; but the minutes of the evidence tend to distinguish between the before and after, and the former was apparently not drawn on.[61] The nature of the case against some of the accused, such as Bigod, was self-evident. Lumley had been at Bigod's oration, had taken men from there to Scarborough, had mustered the wapentake of Pickering Lythe, and had entered Scarborough with 600 or 700 men, where he swore the officers of the town. His motivation in going to the muster at Thwing was irrelevant. But whilst Bigod and Lumley were undeniably guilty of raising a new insurrection, the majority were not. The evidence against these, arguably innocent people is more interesting, for it reveals how the Crown was prepared to redefine loyal acts as treasonable.

The evidence against Aske, Constable, and Darcy was virtually all drawn from the period of Bigod's rising. It was held against Aske that he had concealed the fact of the rising in the East Riding from the king (not true); that he had advised against the summary execution of Hallam's band (true); and that he had not apprehended the traitors in Bigod's rebellion but had undertaken to seek a pardon for them. Against Darcy, it was noted that he had tried to recover artillery taken by Aske from Pontefract. All his letters to the commons urging them to stay at peace until the arrival of the duke of Norfolk were construed as treasonous. Sir Robert Constable was likewise criticized for his letter to Bigod rebuking him for his rebellion. A letter of Constable and Aske to Hull suggesting that Bigod's messengers to the town should be released was held against

---

[60] Unless otherwise referenced, what follows is taken from *LP* XII (i), no. 1087. This is discussed at length in Dodds, *Pilgrimage*, II, ch. 20.

[61] See e.g. *LP* XII (i), no. 1020.

them; likewise their letters saying that they trusted in the king's promise to have a parliament and convocation and to redress their grievances. Together they had sheltered Levening after the failure of the rising. None of this amounted to treason. For Aske, Darcy, and Constable, no demonstration of loyalty in January could purge them of the treason of the pre-pardon period.

The Crown's case against Sir Thomas Percy was even slighter. The digest makes four points against him: that he had received the supplication from Sawley; that he had received a letter from Bigod calling on him to rise; that Lumley had deposed that Sir Thomas was the 'lock, key, and ward' of the revolt; and that Ninian Staveley and the other Jervaulx conspirators had approached him for aid. Beyond expressing politeness, he had not lifted a finger to assist any of them. Percy was clearly a marked man, if only because of his charisma and popularity amongst the commons. When Lumley said that he was the 'lock, key, and ward', he meant not that Percy was an active conspirator, but that his declaration for the commons would have been decisive, and that without it Bigod's venture was doomed.[62] Sir Stephen Hamerton had been approached by the monks of Sawley, who told him of their intention to petition Percy; Nicholas Tempest was accused of giving them victuals (out of neighbourly charity, he said). Both were prominent captains during the autumn rising, but their association with Sawley was insignificant. The evidence adduced against George Wood, prior of Bridlington, James Cockerell (quondam prior of Guisborough), and Dr John Pickering really came down to the fact that at various times they had all had contacts with Bigod. Wood admitted that he had mobilized the inhabitants of Bridlington against Lumley. He had declined to send men to aid in the expulsion of Bigod from Beverley because Sir Marmaduke Constable had advised him to hold his men close to home. This was twisted into making Wood a 'great mover' in the second rebellion, who put all his servants and tenants in harness when Lumley sent to him.[63] William Todd, the prior of Malton with whom Bigod had discussed the pardon, and whom he called upon to muster Malton, was never tried and may even have survived into the

---

[62] The comment is made in ibid., no. 369.   [63] Ibid., nos. 1019, 1020.

1560s.[64] Adam Sedber, the abbot of Jervaulx, was irretrievably tainted by his association with Staveley's failed revolt, even though it was never claimed that he was a party to its planning or that he gave it his blessing. Never can the capriciousness of the law, or the workings of the wheel of fortune, have been so clearly displayed.

For the sake of completeness, the dates of execution should be given. Bulmer, Hamerton, Tempest, Thirsk (the quondam abbot of Fountains), Cockerall, and Pickering were all executed at Tyburn on 25 May. Margaret Cheyne, Lady Bulmer, was burnt at Smithfield on the same day. Percy, Bigod, Lumley, Sedber, and Wood were executed, again at Tyburn, on 2 June. After some dithering by the king, Darcy was beheaded at Tower Hill on 30 June, after being degraded from the Order of the Garter. Hussey met a similar fate at about the same time. Constable was taken north under guard and hanged at the Beverley gate at Hull (where Hallam had been caught) on 6 July. Finally, Aske was hanged at York on 12 July. Others, like Sir Richard Tempest, who were called to London and imprisoned, remained in custody throughout the summer, Tempest dying in the Fleet gaol on 25 August. The execution of Darcy and Aske implies that the government had discovered as much as it wished to know about the origins of the Pilgrimage. Norfolk did not pursue his investigations in the North with any discernible zeal after their arrests, even though he remained there—unwillingly—until the beginning of October.[65] He, at least, accepted that the Pilgrimage had been a revolt of the commons. In June there were attempts to persuade Lord Latimer to go to court. He was reluctant, but as Norfolk told Cromwell, there was in any case no evidence against him except that he had been forced to be amongst the commons and his life had been endangered.[66] The king probably never accepted this view, but seems to have regarded the executions as drawing the matter to an end.[67]

Of course, the parliament promised at Doncaster never happened. Henry was said to have remarked in early February that if the Pilgrims had broken their promise to restore the farmers of monastic lands, then he

[64] He appears in the digest cited before: for his later life, Cross and Vickers, 'Monks, Friars and Nuns', 381–2.

[65] Dodds, *Pilgrimage*, II, ch. 21 offers a full account of Norfolk's period in the North.

[66] *LP* XII (ii), no. 14; cf. (i), nos. 131, 173.   [67] *St. P.* I, 555 (= *LP* XII (ii), no. 77).

felt under no obligation to honour his promises to them.[68] By the time Norfolk returned to the North, all probably recognized that it would be incautious to press for the parliament, and so it disappears, silently, from the records. As with so much more, Bigod may be said to have caused its downfall. The promised progress was only abandoned in June. As late as 2 May the king was still proposing to travel north to grant his general pardon in person to all except those whom Norfolk advised should be exempted (itself a withdrawal of the concession of a comprehensive pardon),[69] but first news came of the queen's pregnancy, then on 12 June the king sent word that he would not be coming that summer. He was, he said, reluctant to leave the queen, but his doctors also advised him not to travel on account of his legs. As he could not give the pardon in person, another 'personage of honour' would convey it; but this was never done.[70] Only in 1541 did Henry finally come in person to take the submission of his northern subjects.

IV

So far as we can discover what happened at the trials of the Pilgrims, it seems that they were not prosecuted for their activities in October or November 1536, but for their activities after the second Doncaster conference. The grounds for the prosecution were normally slight, and in some instances the evidence against them was twisted and deliberately misconstrued to place the accused in the worst possible light. There is certainly no evidence to support the Crown's contention that Darcy and Aske were engaged in a new conspiracy during January—certainly not when the evidence is read historically. Whilst those who were brought to trial were selected for their activities during the autumn, the question of whether those who were actually involved in a *conspiracy* in the autumn

---

[68] *LP* XII (i), no. 378.

[69] Ibid., no. 1118. In July Norfolk sent a list of names from whom the pardon should be withheld (XII (ii), no. 291 (ii)).

[70] Dodds, *Pilgrimage*, II, 259–60.

of 1536 was left unresolved by their convictions. It is the evidence for
and against an October conspiracy which we weigh here.

To begin, we turn to Aske. At first sight the man seems a paradox. He
was a youngish man, of gentry birth, probably well connected through
his service to the earl of Northumberland and cousinage to the earl of
Cumberland, who threw in his lot with a conservative religious rebellion as a popularist leader of the commons. He succeeded in forcing Henry
(through Norfolk) into making a range of damaging concessions, then
broke with some or all of the commons to defend his settlement with
the king. In the autumn he appears as a rabble-rousing charismatic; in
the spring as a boastful and naive dolt, outmanoeuvred by more seasoned
politicians like Norfolk. There is no doubt that Aske drove the Pilgrimage from his first sight of the Lincoln articles to the moment when the
Pilgrims tore off their badges and submitted to Norfolk. He devised
the very name of the Pilgrimage of Grace: he welded a set of disparate
movements into something which, temporarily at least, was a cohesive
force. It was he, and not wiser and more cautious men, who led his irregulars from York to Pontefract, so preventing the slow dissipation of the
movement on the lines of the Lincolnshire rebellion at Lincoln. Was Aske
primed to launch a rebellion in 1536? Or can we believe his own account
of stumbling into the wash from the Louth riots? In Chapter 7 I suggested that Aske's own account is plausible. He was plainly a highly political personality, very articulate, and (as his examination shows) an activist.
He needed to be involved and to believe that he was at the centre of
the movement. As his memoir shows, he was prone to boast. Norfolk
drew a pen portrait of him after Aske had spent some weeks in his entourage: 'The man is marvellous glorious, often time boasting to me that he
hath such sure espial that nothing can be done nor imagined against the
king's highness but he will shortly give me warning thereof.'[71] Norfolk
did not believe him.

Aske may well have had principled doubts about the course of royal
policy after 1529. He may have been genuinely committed to monasticism. But overall, one senses that he was a man in search of a movement, of an opportunity to fulfil a destiny. When he stumbled into the

[71] SP1/117, fo. 75r (= *LP* XII (i), no. 698).

rising in Lincolnshire his curiosity was aroused, probably because the commons he encountered at Hambleden Hill were under the direction of a social equal, the lawyer Thomas Moigne. The measure of that curiosity is that, having escaped out of Lincolnshire, his curiosity, his desire to be involved, drew him back to Lincoln. When he saw the Lincoln articles and was assured about the aims of the movement, its management by the gentry, and the coincidence of its ambitions with his own beliefs, he saw his opportunity to launch a copycat movement in support of the Lincolnshire rising. From that time onwards, although a gentleman by birth, he never played by the gentry's rules. Their strategy, employed equally by the gentry in Lincolnshire and a solitary figure like George Lumley, was to establish a hold over the commons, to reinforce their authority by drawing in other gentry, to establish the rebels as a disciplined, deferential force, and then to smother the movement through inactivity. For Aske, the rising of the commons was not a challenge to the social order which needed to be defeated, but the means by which he could secure his political ambitions. He undermined the more cautious elements and they hated him for it. He, single-handedly, was responsible for transforming a revolt of the commons over fears of confiscation into a rebellion against the king and the Cromwellian ascendancy. He led it from York, where the gentry could slowly have strangled it, into confrontation with a royal army at Doncaster. Here is Norfolk again, continuing the previous quotation: 'I cannot perceive he hath any such favour amongst the gentlemen nor honest persons, for as many as doth talk to me of him doth marvellously abhor him, every man imputing the whole beginning of this mischief to be by him. If he have any such credit or knowledge, I am sure the same is of very light persons.'[72] Aske's success was based on his willingness to do the indefensible and align himself with the commons. He refused to allow Lancaster Herald to proclaim Shrewsbury's proclamation at Pontefract, neither at the market cross 'nor in no place amongst *my people*, which be all under my guiding'.[73]

But Aske was not a conspirator. He was an example of that humbler creature, the opportunist: he too had gone through the experience of being sworn. Hence his eagerness to go and meet with Henry VIII at

---

[72] Ibid.   [73] *St. P.* I, 486 (= *LP* XI, no. 826), my italics.

Christmas 1536: the royal invitation gave him the opportunity not only to satisfy his craving for recognition, to operate on a larger stage at the very centre of the state, and demonstrate his utility to the king, but also to press his political aims on the monarch in person. In one sense there was no inconsistency for Aske in going from being a leader of the commons chastising the king's councillors to himself being a royal intimate and councillor. Both positions were equally loyal. Perhaps he saw himself as surplanting Cromwell.[74]

If Aske's fundamental opportunism is accepted, then it poses the question of what he actually sought. He started by wishing to add weight to the Lincoln articles. It was only after the Lincolnshire movement dissolved as a force that he formulated his own approach, shifting the weight of the articles in the oath away from commonwealth grievances towards the defence of the church and the cleansing of the council. So, in the letter of the baronage to the earl of Cumberland on 22 November, he states: 'the cause of our assembly which is for the maintenance of the faith of God and the right and liberty of his church militant and the destruction of heretics and their opinions and other public wealths in soul and body . . .'[75] In the first instance he believed that his aims could be secured by petitioning alone, if necessary by leading the Pilgrims to London. Petitioning was seen as the aim of the movement when he wrote to York on 15–16 October; but Aske always had the reserve position that the Pilgrims would fight if the king refused their supplication.[76] Having disentangled the Pontefract articles from their accretion of lobbyists' enthusiasms, it may be seen that Aske never really shifted in his objectives. What did alter was the means to achieve them. By the beginning of December he seemed to be satisfied that the free parliament conceded by Norfolk would be sufficient for his purposes.

As for Darcy, he never admitted any conspiracy. He had never had any reply to his letters to the king (and suspected that the king had never

[74] Remember the strange incident where he *may* have offered to defect from the Pilgrimage to royal service: above p. 338.

[75] 'Letters of the Cliffords', 130.

[76] The evolution of his thought is shown by 'Aske's Examination', 559, answ. 21. The letter to York, which also offers to fight them if they hindered their Pilgrimage, is printed below, pp. 456–7. He threatened to lead the Pilgrims to London in the interview with Lancaster Herald on 21 October. *St. P.* I, 486.

seen them); he was hamstrung by his lack of authority, by a shortage of money for wages, by having no artillery or victuals. Darcy knew that he had been deliberately sacrificed to the rebels; he had been forced to undergo the humiliation (for a soldier) of surrendering Pontefract and then being a prisoner amongst the commons. Darcy was bitter at his treatment, and understood all too clearly how his misfortune would be exploited by his enemies. The Letter Book was designed to vindicate his behaviour in October 1536; but for preference he wished to speak to the king in person or use one of his friends in the privy chamber as an intermediary. He continued to protest his loyalty, not only in a letter to Cromwell of 18 March ('I have served above fifty years the king's majesty and his father and should not in my old age enter rebellion with the commons'), but also in his private memoranda where, having welcomed the prospect of his death, he continued: 'And He [God] be my judge, never lost [a] king a truer servant and subject without any cause but lack of furniture and by false reports and pickthanks. God save the king: though I be without recovery.'[77]

And yet it might be thought that Darcy protested too much. His careful accumulation of letters, his request that the council should peruse his Letter Book, all points to man who was determined to relate and record his point of view. The most telling evidence—which Darcy never offered for audit and whose significance has remained unsuspected—is his muster book: not evidence of conspiracy, but of his inability to raise a defensive army.

Niggling doubts remain. Darcy neither planned nor encouraged the rebellion of October 1536. But he was guilty of flirting with rebellion. His discussions with Chapuys show that he had thought deeply about how the Cromwellian regime could be overturned by force. But Chapuys could deliver nothing, and Darcy perhaps had an element of the fantasist about him. Charles V was not interested in bankrolling the rebellion of elderly and alienated peers. It was Darcy's final claim that, if he had asked Chapuys for aid, he would have had it—perhaps a sort of double-bluff to prove that he had not asked, when of course he had but on an earlier occasion.[78]

---

[77] 'Thomas Master's Narrative', 79; *LP* XII (i), no. 303.
[78] 'Thomas Master's Narrative', 79.

For the one moment when the Pilgrimage looked as though it might take on an international dimension was in mid-November, when Dr Waldby was sent—then called back—on a mission to Brussels. This mission, in the long days waiting for Ellerker and Bowes to return, was prompted by a despairing conviction that the king would not negotiate, and that the leaders of the Pilgrims had no way forwards to satisfy the commons and save their own lives except through renewed rebellion. Whilst this was as clear a flirtation with treason as we can find, Darcy—surely—already knew from his contacts with Chapuys that there was no realistic possibility of Charles V sending either men, money, or munitions. The rebellion of 1536 was not the rebellion which Darcy had mused about two years before.

In two other areas doubts about Darcy's role remain. The first was his claim to Chapuys that, if he wanted to raise rebellion, he would do so by having the clergy mobilize the commons through their preaching. This is very close to what was happening in 1536. Yet no one, either contemporary or historian, has been able to demonstrate links between Darcy (or Hussey) and the renegade friar of Knaresborough, or the clergy in Lincolnshire who were anxious for their position and were prepared to spread manufactured rumours of impending confiscation. Early sixteenth-century society did not need a Darcy to start rumours or to organize the circulation of bills: the commons and the clergy were quite capable of generating their own agitators, some of whom are known to us and others not. The claim that Darcy inspired the rumours remains improbable and is certainly not proven. And, rumours or no rumours, it remains likely that no rebellion would have taken place had there not been an unfortunate conjunction of circumstances in Louth.

A second and more serious matter—which it is impossible to resolve satisfactorily—is that of the badges of the five wounds of Christ worn by the Pilgrims in October 1536. The badge was adopted, Aske tells us, after one of Robert Bowes's servants accidentally killed a Pilgrim who wore the cross of St George on his back. There was then a cry that the Pilgrims should have their own badge to distinguish them from the members of the royal host. Aske himself had a badge from Darcy.[79] The gov-

---

[79] 'Aske's Examination', 571–2.

ernment knew that to prove that Darcy had been stockpiling these badges in advance of the rebellion was their strongest card against him. When he was interrogated he was asked fourteen consecutive questions about the badges.[80] The character of these questions suggest strongly that government did not know the answers and were rather puzzled as to what had gone on. They recalled that Darcy had used this badge in his crusade against the Moors in 1511, but were they the remnants of the badges Darcy had taken to Spain or badges made more recently? If old, why had they not been disposed of, or had they been kept for the purpose of the Pilgrimage? If new, who had made them? And, most crucially: 'if you were suddenly taken by the commons, whether it is like that ye had leisure to make such badges?' Darcy's answers to these questions, if he answered them, are lost, and in an age where (in my experience at least) the devil no longer offers Faustian pacts, will always remain lost. We cannot even say whether these badges existed in dozens, hundreds, or thousands, whether they were crudely run up or as richly embroidered as the (alleged) survivor.[81] A few points may be made. This was Darcy's personal badge. It was offered to the Pilgrims accidentally to meet a particular need. It was not—and this is significant—given to Aske when he took the castle, the moment at which he might have been incorporated into Darcy's movement (or vice versa), but several days later after the arrival of the Richmondshire men before the duke of Norfolk.[82] It is implausible to believe that Darcy had had several thousand badges squirreled away since his Spanish campaign a quarter of a century earlier (or that badges would have remained in good condition for that period of time). It may be the case that Darcy had the badges prepared to be worn by his retinue in any Anglo-Scottish conflict, but the badge (as the king's interrogators were quick to appreciate) carried religious overtones which would have seemed odd in a conflict between two Christian states (though not, of course, against heretics). As his interrogators realized, the badges were telling evidence, but of what is not clear. If I was to speculate, I would suggest that they had been prepared for the rebellion Darcy contemplated in 1534–5.

[80] Ibid. 555.
[81] Familiar as the cover illustration of successive editions of Fletcher (and McCulloch), *Tudor Rebellions.*
[82] 'Aske's Examination', 571–2.

In conservative circles and at court it was probably assumed that Darcy was indeed a conspirator, albeit an incompetent one. Lord Montague held to something like this view: he thought that Darcy's mistake was that he should have gone directly to depose the king rather than trying to change the colour of his council. Montague also tacitly acknowledged that the movement was one of the commons. He thought the king's policy of deceiving them dangerous: 'if the commons do rise again, they will trust to no fair person or words.'[83] Evidence of conspiracy by Darcy eluded contemporaries. The most damaging evidence they could find came from Sir Henry Savile, who told Cromwell that Darcy circulated a letter calling the gentlemen of the western half of the honour of Pontefract to him after the castle had surrendered, and that when they arrived there they were sworn.[84] Savile's hostility to Darcy is palpable. But there is no independent confirmation of these events, and one wonders whether they were no more than a final desperate attempt to raise support with which to defend the castle. It was the opinion of the Tadcaster innkeeper with whom Sadler lodged in January 1537, not that Darcy had inspired the rebellion, but that he had not done enough against it, that he could have raised a greater force and have held the castle against Aske for longer. This man did not think that Darcy was a conspirator.[85] In fact, no one directly made the claim in 1536 that Darcy had plotted the Pilgrimage of Grace: there was a feeling, voiced by both the duke of Norfolk and the earl of Shrewsbury, that Darcy had inclined towards the commons, and this was surely so.[86] It was the authentic Darcy who was delighted when he heard that Lincolnshire had risen.[87] His unhappiness with the course of events in his declining years is beyond dispute, but there is no evidence that he did anything to stir a rebellion. Not even William Thomas, in his vindication of the king's rule, *The Pilgrim* (which is near as we have to an insider's view of events), makes the claim that there was a conspiracy to raise the commons.[88]

Against Constable, who was also arrested and tried with Aske and Darcy, there is no evidence at all that he contemplated a revolt. Indeed, he was

---

[83] Dodds, *Pilgrimage*, II, 292.   [84] *LP* XII (i), no. 281.   [85] Ibid., no. 200 (= *St. P.* I, 527).
[86] *LP* XI, no. 909; XII (i), no. 783.   [87] Above p. 280.
[88] W. Thomas, ed. J. A. Froude, *The Pilgrim: A Dialogue on the Life and Actions of King Henry the Eighth* (1861), 50–5.

only ever at Pontefract at the request of the earl of Shrewsbury, and as he told his son,

that which we did [there] was for lack of furniture and for fear of our lives, and as it was proved, we did his grace good service at Doncaster in staying of the fury of the commons whereby his grace hath his pleasure with them without battle. In the last commotion by Bigod, [he] was clearly stayed by me by persuasions both by my writings [to] my friends and sending my servants through the country with my letters, thinking that I had deserved thanks, for in good faith I trusted none other.

Nor did he admit committing treason since the pardon at his execution.[89] That said, Constable was under no illusions about his king. He was willing to supervise the garrisoning of Hull in November. He was prepared to exploit the letter found on Edward Waters to press his own view that the Pilgrims needed to negotiate from strength.

It is impossible to construct a conspiracy against Henry VIII out of these fragments of lives. It is possible to see opportunism, bravery in the face of the commons, certainly duty and loyalty. Henry was a bad master who came to regard involuntary association with the commons as evidence of collusion and conspiracy. An unknown writer assessed the defence of the abbot of Jervaulx: 'This he says was against his will, but this is no answer, for I know no man that was hurt in the compulsion thereof and he ought to have fled from them [the commons] to the king.'[90] This leads one to the conclusion that both Hussey's and Darcy's reputations would stand today without stain or ambiguity if they, like Lord Burgh, had fled to Shrewsbury at the first sign of trouble. And, in an important way, Henry forced Aske and Darcy together and fashioned the conspiracy against himself. There was, after all, little companionship between Darcy and Aske when the latter first came to Pontefract. But by his delaying of the return of Ellerker and Bowes, his playing for time and refusal to negotiate, the duplicity revealed in the letter to the Scarborough garrison, and the general suspicion of his motives, the king forced the two together into deeper treason in November. By telling the Pilgrims that the Hampole articles were so 'general, dark, and obscure' (which was,

---

[89] SP1/120, fo. 136r (= LP XII (i), no. 1225); XII (ii), no. 178.   [90] LP XII (i), no. 1036.

after all, their purpose) that he could not answer them, Henry (perhaps unintentionally) forced the Pilgrims into developing their critique further.[91] Whatever Norfolk was empowered to do at Doncaster, he was bound to make the Pilgrims's leadership into a yet more cohesive group, for if there were no concessions, then with the commons at their backs the leaders would have been forced to declare against the king; having received even minimal concessions, they were forced to co-operate with each other against Bigod and Hallam to hold on to those gains.

The story of the revolts of 1536 is, in part, the story of how the understood leaders of society reacted when their authority was challenged by a sudden, widespread disturbance, by an unexpected moment of social inversion; partly of how, with little assistance from the king, the gentry re-established their authority and brought the rising to a conclusion without massive reprisals either against them or the commons. There was no conspiracy amongst the gentry in October 1536, not even the passive conspiracy of allowing a conflagration—which they could tame and control—to take hold. Once the rebellion had started, there were a number of individuals who, for their own reasons—self-advancement, principle, fear—dabbled in treason. The other story of the loosely connected revolts of 1536–7 is that of how the commons presumed to play a role in politics. It is the society of the commons to which I now turn.

Appendix 1: The Members of the Duke of Norfolk's Council

The membership of the duke's council can be reconstructed from three sources: the signatories to two letters, and the names of the commissioners to try Thomas, Lord Darcy. This list of inferred commissioners can then be compared to the founding membership of the Council of the North under the bishop of Durham, Cuthbert Tunstall, himself one of the duke's council.

The letters are (1) of 9 March, reporting the deficiency in the commission supplied to Norfolk (*LP* XII (i), no. 615); (2) of 8 April (ibid., no. 870). The

---

[91] *LP* XI, no. 1064 (2).

commission (3) is at *LP* XII, no. 1207 (1), printing the file of indictments from the 'Baga de secretis'. Additional details of these individuals can be found in Reid, *King's Council in the North*, 490–1.

Ralph, earl of Westmorland (1, 2), of the council 1537–42. Sworn to the council 14 January (*LP* XII (i), no. 86).

Cuthbert Tunstall, bishop of Durham (1), of the council 1530–8, 1550–1, 1553–9.

Sir William Eure (1, 2, 3) later 1st Lord Eure, d. 1548, of the council from 1525.

Sir Thomas Tempest (1, 2, 3), serjeant at law, of County Durham, d. 1545, of the council from 1525.

Sir Marmaduke Constable, the elder (1, 3), not noted by Reid as a member of the council.

Sir Ralph Ellerker, the younger (2, 3), of the council from 1533. At Carlisle with Norfolk, where he acted as marshall in the prosecution of the commons (*LP* XII (i), no. 498).

Sir Ralph Eure, the younger (3), not noted by Reid as a member of the council.

Robert Bowes (1, 2, 3) of the council from 1525, d. 1555. Sworn to the council 16 January (*LP* XII (i), no. 86); acted as king's attorney in the prosecution of the commons at Carlisle (*LP* XII (i), no. 498).

William Babthorpe (3), of the council from 1525, d. 1555.

Dr Thomas Thirlby (1) successively bishop of Westminster (1540–50), of Norwich (1550–4), of Ely (1554–9), d. 1570.

Dr Richard Curwen (*Coren*) (1, 2), archdeacon of Oxford (1535–43) and Colcherter (1537–43), d. 1543.[1]

John Uvedale (1, 2, 3), secretary to the council and keeper of its signet from 1525.

Appendix 2: The Members of the Earls of Sussex's and Derby's Council

We noted earlier that the earls of Sussex's and Derby's joint instructions do not specifically mention a council, but the circle of gentry travelling with them referred

---

[1] He was bother of Hugh Coren or Curwen, archbishop of Dublin (1555–67), bishop of Oxford (1567–8), d. 1568. The Curwens were of the Cumberland family. Emden, *Biographical Register of the University of Oxford*, 1500–1540, 137–9; J. F. Curwen, *A history of the ancient house of Curwen* (1928), 255–60.

to themselves as a council on some occasions. Their membership can be broadly identified from a number of sources: a letter (1) of Sir Thomas Butler, which names a number of gentry who were clearly undertaking preparatory work for the commission (*LP* XII (i), no. 348); the signatories (2) to the inventory of Whalley Abbey, (ibid., no. 716); the witnesses (3) to the surrender of Furness by Roger Pele or Pyle, 5 April (ibid., no. 832); the signatories (4) to a letter of Henry VIII (ibid., no. 840); and the witnesses (5) to the formal surrender, 9 April (ibid., no. 880).

Sir Thomas Butler (1, 3, 5).

Sir William Leyland (2, 3, 4).

John Claydon, clerk (2, 3, 5), vicar of Middleton near Manchester, master of Attleborough College in Norfolk and a 'considerable pluralist in the London area'. (Haigh, 'Last Days of the Lancashire Monasteries', 92, n. 2). Made his will 1539, probate 1544. Asked the the earl of Sussex to serve as supervisor. PRO, PROB11/28 fos. 183v–184r.

Sir John Byron (1, 3, 5).

Sir Anthony Fitzherbert, chief justice at Lancaster (2, 3, 4, 5).

Sir John Porte, second justice at Lancaster (noted as absent on 28 February; conducting sessions at Lancaster, 6 April).

Sir Henry Farrington (2, 4, but noted as absent, 28 February).

Sir Richard Houghton (1, 5, but noted as sent with Butler and Byron to Furness, 5 April).

Sir Thomas Southworth (1).

Sir Marmaduke Tunstall (5).

Sir Thomas Langton (5).

15

The Rebellions as Commons' Revolts

The thesis which this book wishes to advance is that the revolts of 1536–7, the Lincolnshire revolt, the Pilgrimage of Grace, and the Captain Poverty risings in October, and the renewed risings in January and early February 1537 must be understood as risings of the commons which the gentry, ultimately successfully, worked to tame through the re-establishment of their authority. In their attempts to harness the commons, the gentry were hindered, first by one of their number—Aske—who saw political and personal advantage in furthering the revolts and led the commons into a stand-off with a royal force at Doncaster; and second, by the refusal of Henry VIII make concessions—notably an unconditional pardon—which would allow the gentry and commons to disperse without any fear of reprisals.

In any assessment of the revolts as risings of the commons, we need to recognize, first, that there were marked regional patterns in their character, and second, that the 'commons' were not a single, undifferentiated body of people. The revolts of 1536–7 were actually two contemporaneous but semi-independent uprisings. The first took place in Lincolnshire and east Yorkshire. It was stimulated by the riots at Louth, which spawned a copycat disorder at Horncastle, and from these two foci it developed into a localized revolt within Lincolnshire. This revolt never progressed southwards beyond Lincoln (although there were evidently disturbances in Boston); but it spread over the Humber into Yorkshire, into the East Riding, towards York, and over the Vale of York into Wakefield and the honour of Pontefract. This was a revolt stimulated by fears for parochial religion. The second revolt may owe something to reports of the disturbances in Lincolnshire, perhaps unintentionally spread by Archbishop Lee to Ripon. It started in the broad uplands between Ripon and Richmond, an area which was notoriously volatile. By sending out letters in the name of Captain Poverty, the revolt was spread westwards and northwards into Cumberland, Westmorland, northern Lancashire, and Craven, and northwards and eastwards into County Durham, Cleveland, and the North Yorkshire moors. The revolt here was concerned with agrarian discontents, with tenure, fines, and tithes, as well as the suppression of the smaller monasteries and the defence of the church. The revolt in Cumberland and Westmorland, in particular, contains a clear antagonism between tenant and landlord, which is seen at its most pointed by attempts to intimidate the landlords of the Barony of Kendal into sealing agreements over tenure with their tenants. Later in the year there were a scattering of attacks on tithe barns, perhaps even a rejection of the principle of tithes, and on enclosures.[1] There is no sign of an agrarian agitation in the Lincolnshire/East Riding movement, which is not to claim that individual landlords or their agents were not the object of hostility.[2] Because the motivations of the groups of commons and attitude to gentry were so different, the internal dynamics of their movements were also different. Contemporaries recognized that the Richmondshire men were far more radicalized than the generality of the Pilgrims of Grace. There were difficulties in persuading them to disperse

---

[1] Harrison, *Pilgrimage of Grace in the Lake Counties*, 58–9, 65.

[2] Gunn showed how, in the breakdown of law and order in Lincolnshire, the estate officials of Lady Willoughby were attacked by her tenants and criticized for the harshness of her estate policy. But there is no suggestion that her agrarian policies prompted the revolt. Gunn, 'Peers, Commons and Gentry', 60–3. Likewise one of the features of the winter disturbances in the Eden valley was the pulling down of enclosures newly made by the earl of Cumberland. *LP* XII (i), no. 687 (2). Bush claims that fining was an issue in the area of the 'Percy Host', on the basis of a comment by Sir Thomas Percy, that 'ingressum' taking was one of the causes of the revolt. But it is clear enough that Percy was answering a question about the revolt couched in the widest terms. Not even Bush can make a plausible case for agrarian issues being important in this district. *Pilgrimage*, 202–6.

from Doncaster in October; at the end of January some of their number tried to recreate the Captain Poverty movement. It should come as no surprise that the only conflict between troops and commons in the entire movement took place in Cumberland, where the distance between commons and gentry seems greatest.

As for the *identity* of the commons, there is no single occasion for which we have anything like adequate materials to undertake a social-distributional analysis.[3] We are therefore forced back on comment on the *character* of the commons, and here we must recognize that the vocabulary available to contemporaries—and perhaps, too, their interest in distinguishing the currents within the commons—was limited.[4] The commons potentially included all able-bodied adult males. When Moigne returned to North Willingham after fleeing from Caistor, he found that 'there was not a man left in this town besides my own household and those that were neither able to ride ne go'. After Beverley rose, 'no man could keep his servant at plough but that every man that was able to bear a staff went forwards towards Hunsley [Beacon]'.[5] The majority of writers simply used 'the commons' to describe an undifferentiated, apparently homogeneous, body of men. Aske, in his long account of the Pilgrimage, refers repeatedly to 'the commons'. It was, however, 'the worshipful men' who would not surrender Hull. This lack of social description is fairly typical. A few were forced to use a more differentiated vocabulary to explain their point of view. In the account of the Lincolnshire revolt in Holland attributed to Anthony Irby, the author refers to the commons: but when he and his fellow JPs worked to exercise some influence in calming the revolt, they turned to the 'honest men' of the neighbouring villages. Similarly, Moigne generally only distinguished between the commons and the 'men of worship' in his account, but when push came to shove and the JPs thought they might have to fight the commons, it was to the 'honest men' that they looked for support. Stapleton, in Beverley, was also conversant with this usage. Richard

---

[3] The only occasion on which we have a listing of the commons is when Ellerker captured 62 of Bigod's men at Beverley, *LP* XII (i), nos. (2–4). An attempt to link this to subsidy materials proved to be impossible through the severe decrepitude of the relevant subsidy returns.

[4] The same blunt terminology is used of the commons in York in the York records. R. W. Hoyle, 'Petitioning and Popular Politics in the Early Sixteenth Century' (forthcoming paper).

[5] SP1/110, fo. 151r; Hallam, PRO, E36/119, fo. 26v (= *LP* XII (i), no. 201, p. 90).

Wharton of Hull Bridge was selected because he was an 'honest and substantial man', 'of good age and gratuity', thereby associating seniority with wealth and creditworthiness.[6] Morland made plain this contrast between the 'head men of the parish' and the 'poor men of Louth', and Kendall explained what this meant in practice when he described the poor men setting out for Caistor on foot and the rich men a little later on horseback.[7] The usage of 'honest' is found elsewhere. Collins's account of the rising in Kendal distinguishes between the 'light persons' of the town who raised rebellion and the 'honest persons' whom they swore. Some of these people doubtless formed the parish vestry or Twenty-Four, who were subjected to abuse for refusing to allow the bidding of the beads about the turn of the year.[8]

It may be suggested that the use of the phrase 'honest' man was essentially urban, or, if not entirely urban, contains connotations of commercial activity. When the Pilgrims at York drew up lists of the men to be called to the Pontefract conference, they used a different vocabulary to describe the reliable individuals of less than gentry status whom they wanted to see there. One list invites 'seven of the best horsed commoners' from Cumberland; another calls for four of the 'tallest men' from Dent and Sedbergh and six or eight 'tall men' from Lancashire. Later it asks for the 'knights and esquires . . . and head yeomen' of the West Riding.[9] The duke of Norfolk used a similar phrase: in his letter to the earl of Cumberland announcing his return to the north, he told Cumberland to bring with him to York 'divers of the most substantial and head yeomen of the parts under your governance'.[10]

'The commons' was a portmanteau term covering all the men who formed the rank and file of the rebel army. But amongst them were the 'honest' or 'tall' men, whom the gentry, the 'worshipful men', could cultivate and even use against the commons as a whole. That such a distinction could be made allows us to appreciate that there were tensions within the body of the commons, between rich and poor commons, whose

---

[6] Stapleton, 87.

[7] LP XII (i), no. 380 (p. 175); SP/110, fo. 143v (not noticed in LP XI, no. 670). Aske would not allow the *footmen* to enter York, an unintended piece of social comment. 'The manner of the taking of Robert Aske', 334.

[8] LP XII (i), nos. 914, 384, 671.   [9] LP XI, no. 1155 (1, 2).

[10] 'Letters of the Cliffords', 115.

attitudes to order may well have been different. Sadler was quite clear about this:

So as the people, being of divers sorts, diversily take the matter. Some be sorry and would fain be quiet, which be of the honest sort, and be both sorry and wary of that they have done: on the other side, there is another sort that hath nothing to lose and they rejoice in mischief and desire nothing better than rumour and rebellion so that they may have thereby the better opportunity to rob and spoil the honest sort.[11]

Looking back from the vantage-point of 1538, the Council of the North commented that 'in the late commotion . . . the busiest were the poorest'.[12] It is impossible to ascertain whether they were also predominantly young; but when the commons of the upper Eden valley fell out with Robert Pullen over Christmas, it was the 'young men about Kirkby Stephen' who ransacked his house and insisted in the commons' name that he justify his actions.[13]

So the volatile commons were relatively poor, relatively powerless within their societies, and possibly also young. The events in Louth indisputably have an air of social conflict about them. The rioters on the first day of the Lincolnshire revolt were all small-town artisans who were probably excluded from the ceremony of electing the town's bailiff (which was happening elsewhere in the town). Whether there were such clear-cut antagonisms is impossible to ascertain from Stapleton's account of events in Beverley (not least because, as an outsider, he knew no one's name or trade), but the commons there acted with the same independence. There are indications that the same sorts of conflict were happening in Kendal. The 1536–7 revolts as a whole are normally thought of as a rural movement, but we may note the special significance of the urban commons in starting the revolts in Louth, and perhaps in spreading them to Horncastle and then onwards to Beverley. The revolts were actually much more urban in their character than historians have allowed.

This makes sense of a strongly anticlerical letter from Sir William Fairfax to Cromwell written in January 1537.[14] Fairfax maintained that, 'where

---

[11] *St. P.* I, 528 (= *LP* XII (i), no. 200).   [12] SP1/132, fo. 39v (= *LP* XIII (i), no. 941).
[13] SP1/117, fo. 55r (omitted in *LP* XII (i), no. 687 (2)).
[14] *LP* XII (i), no. 192; Smith, *Land and Politics*, 167.

the archbishop, bishops, abbots and spiritual persons have the rule, the people are most ready at a call' to rise in rebellion. He pointed out that the insurrection had started at Louth, the bishop of Lincoln's town, then at Howden, the bishop of Durham's town, where Sir Robert Constable was steward, and had then passed to Beverley, the archbishop of York's town, 'being worst of all'. He suggested that Otley, another of the archbishop's towns, was far from reliable. In his haste to show that the clergy were behind the Pilgrimage, Fairfax overlooked Ripon, also the archbishop's town. Fairfax evidently thought he was on to something, and so he might. Where he saw clergy pulling strings, we might see the problem of maintaining order in second-rank towns of a particular character, in which the institutions of self-government were weak, even retarded, and in which the social distance between town and country was likely to be very small.

The contrast can be made between these and the larger corporate boroughs with their panoply of mayors, aldermen, guilds—and walls. At Louth and Kendal, disturbances within the town had to be settled by the intervention of the rural JPs, which implies that the structures of power must have differed considerably from towns with their own bench and judicial powers. We are not well informed about what happened in the larger towns. Boston resisted the commons' overtures, and sent a delegation to the earl of Shrewsbury. Hull held out for a period against the commons; its mayor and aldermen appear to have been capable of taking decisive action after Bigod's attempted coup was disclosed to them. The corporation justified their surrender to the Beverley commons by the fear of starvation in the town (even though the corporation were paying the poor people wages as a militia) and rumours that it would be fired.[15] What happened at Lincoln and York is nowhere disclosed. Bowyer hints that attempts to defend York were undercut by the decision of the mayor to admit the Pilgrims.[16] Carlisle twice refused to admit the commons. Sadler was told by the mayor and aldermen of Newcastle that when the rebellion first broke out, the commons were

very unruly and as much disposed to sedition and rebellion as they of the country were and would have risen with them, yet . . . the mayor and aldermen and

---

[15] SP1/110 fo. 23 (= LP XI no. 920) Which I owe to Dr Bernard; LP XI, no. 1285.
[16] LP XII (i), no. 306.

other heads of the town did so, with wisdom and manhood, handle the commons of the same, that they did fully reconcile them, and so handled them that in fine, they were determined to live and die with the mayor and the brethren in the defence and keeping of the town, to the king's use, against all his enemies and rebels, as indeed they did.

The city had been able to mount artillery taken from ships in the harbour onto the walls. Sadler was impressed: he was also told that they had enough food stockpiled to withstand a year's siege.[17] Of course, the alliance at Newcastle between the elite and the commons was never tested by the arrival of the rebels: but one wonders whether it was not a higher degree of governmental sophistication as much as the possibility of closing the town's gates against the rebels which enabled them to even consider holding out against them.[18]

'The commons' is a shorthand term for a body of people who were not heterogeneous and who were not inevitably opposed to authority. These conclusions raise further questions: were the commons a politically informed force capable of devising a programme, or were they merely directed by higher status individuals? And did they have their own organization and leaders, or was whatever structure and discipline they had imposed by their social superiors?

I

The commons were avid devourers of news and gossip.[19] To appreciate this, we need to avoid the condescension which distinguishes between news and rumour. The distinction is false: some of the news circulating

---

[17] *St. P.* I, 532 (= *LP* XII (i), no. 259).

[18] George Lumley's examination contains material to temper this self-congratulatory account. Sir Thomas Hilton fled to Newcastle as the Richmondshire men invaded County Durham, but when he sent two servants to take soundings in the town, he discovered that [the commons'] 'minds were if the other commons came thither, not to withstand them. Saying . . . that they had laid the guns on the walls, that they would turn them when the commons came where they would'. SP1/115, fo. 214r–v (almost completely omitted in *LP* XII (i), no. 369).

[19] For a discussion of these issues in a slightly later period, A. Fox, 'Rumour, News and Popular Political Opinion in Elizabethan and Early Stuart England', *HJ* 40 (1997).

might turn out to be true, some erroneous, but those who lapped it up could not immediately tell for certain which was which. I have already argued that the rumours of confiscation which circulated in the autumn of 1536 were credible. So too were the persisting reports of the king's death which circulated almost nationally in 1537–8 and which might, oddly enough, have had their origin in the very last stage of the Pilgrimage.[20]

The appetite for news may be illustrated by Sadler's experience in Darlington on his way to Scotland in January 1537. No sooner had he gone to his lodgings than he became aware of thirty or forty people milling about in the street.

Whereupon I called unto me my host, who seemed to be an honest man, and I asked him what the people meant to assemble so together. And he answered me that when they saw or heard of any coming out of the south, they used always so to gather together to hear news. I told him I was ill suffered of them that were heads of the town to let them make such unlawful assemblies together in the street . . . he answered me, by his faith, the heads of the town could not rule them, nor durst, for their lives, speak any foul words to them. 'But,' quoth he, 'I think myself to be in some credit with them and ye shall see I shall cause them to scatter abroad, and every man to go to his home by and by.' 'Mary,' quoth I, 'if ye do well, ye should set some of them by the heals.' 'No,' quoth he, 'God defend, for so might we bring a thousand men in our tops within an hour, but ye shall see me order them well enough with fair words.' And thereupon he went to the rout in the street as they stood whispering together, and with his cap in his hand, prayed them to leave their whispering and every man to go home. And then came they all about him and asked him, who I was, whence I came, and whither I would? Mine host told them that I was the king's servant and going from his highness in embassy into Scotland. Whereunto one of them replied and said that could not be true, for the king of Scots was in France. Nevertheless, in fine, my host so pacified them that every man went his way, but much ado he had, as he told me, to persuade them to believe that I went into Scotland. And they all, with one voice, asked when my lord of Norfolk would come and with what company? And so my host came to me as a messenger from them to know the truth. And I sent them word, that he would be at Doncaster on Candlemas Even, and that he brought no more with him than his own household servants, which pleased them wondrous well, and so every man departed, and I heard no more of them.[21]

---

[20] See below pp. 431–2.   [21] *St. P.* I, 531 (= *LP* XII (i), no. 259).

These men were the commons. They posed a potential problem of discipline and needed to be handled cautiously. They were also well informed: the man who objected that James V was in France was quite right. Their curious manner is no different to Darcy's household servants quizzing Creswell when he came from London in November 1536: the acquisition of news turned on the constant questioning of travellers. Where erroneous news circulated, it sometimes brought a degree of gratification to the listener: they wanted it to be true. A splendid story circulated in January that Norfolk had defied the king over the Doncaster agreement, insisting that the commons should have their demands satisfied and that he, having promised them, should not lose honour by having them denied. Norfolk had then been committed to the Tower. When Lord William Howard, unable to secure admittance to his half-brother, encountered Richard Cromwell in Chancery Lane, he knifed and killed him. Sir Robert Constable apparently heard and believed this story, commenting that it was a shame that Lord William had killed Richard Cromwell rather than his uncle.[22] People doubtless wanted to believe this story, with its strong moral overtone that justice had been done. Other stories played on deeper fears. All the rumours of confiscation and taxation did so. Twice in the Pilgrimage word reached the North by letter that ships loaded with munitions had sailed from the Tower: these or other ships were also reported to have made landfall at Hull.[23]

The environment in which news circulated, proliferated, and probably mutated was rather like the school playground, undergraduate common room, or staff canteen. We know from our own experience that rumour can travel fast. We also know how supposed details of the private lives of one's social superiors, whether teacher, lecturer, or the managing director can be eagerly exchanged and woven into larger understandings which might well be erroneous. When it was known that Dr Palmes was going to hold a consistory at Tadcaster, and had instructed the churchwardens to bring in an inventory of the church goods, people thought it confirmed reports of impending confiscation.[24] The rumour

---

[22] Dodds, *Pilgrimage*, II, 46. For a similar tale, ibid. 291.
[23] Above, pp. 333, 376, 397.   [24] Stapleton, 82.

that the king was dead in 1537 may have started after the duke of Norfolk was seen riding fast through Newark. Why else should he be riding southwards at speed unless he had be called to court because the king had died? In fact, his haste was probably for no greater reason than that he was delighted to have been relieved of his lieutenancy.[25] The actions of the nobility were noticed and gossiped about: it was known that Lord Lumley had victualled Kilton at Easter 1537, but had suddenly changed his plans after Bulmer had paid him a visit. Questions were clearly being asked about this, and whether his meeting with Bulmer was responsible.[26] Such an example shows how the business of the gentry, episcopal, or monastic household was probably a public possession: household servants in daily contact with nobles, prelates, and gentry doubtless gossiped to their parents, siblings, and friends. The social distance might have been large, but the ability to secure privacy slight. The commons, largely excluded from the formal channels of official information, took such crumbs of information as they heard from travellers, proclamations, and household servants and rounded them out with speculation.

Most of the news and tittle-tattle which circulated was of no great importance. A little of it was judged to be dangerous or seditious and, in the acute nervousness of the 1530s, was reported to the council. Combating the rumours which circulated in the autumn of 1536 was beyond the means of government, but as the subsidy commissioners abandoned their meeting at Caistor, Moigne took time to rebut the rumours of confiscation.[27] The Crown denied their truth in the answers to the Lincoln and Hampole articles, and again in the proclamation of pardon. Lancaster Herald believed that he could have persuaded the commons to disperse homewards from Pontefract with a simple denial of the rumours of impending taxation.[28] But there was little that anyone could do to educate the commons as a whole out of powerful, but mistaken, understandings of royal policy, especially when events seemed to confirm their most alarmist fears.

---

[25] Elton, *Policy and Police*, 73–7.   [26] Dodds, *Pilgrimage*, II, 161.
[27] SP1/110, fo. 150r–v.   [28] *St. P.* I, 485.

II

The case may be made that the commons actually knew a great deal about the events of the day and were able to read them in a 'political' fashion. Whether they had anything which could be called an organization is another matter. Throughout the North, the autumn and winter of 1536 saw the appearance of 'captains'. Aske claimed primacy over these individuals by calling himself the 'Grand Captain'. The question one would like to be able to answer is whether these people always existed within small-town and rural society, or whether their appearance was a function of the rebellion. In fact virtually none of them have any existence outside the records of the revolt and even within those records most are no more than names.[29]

The first forty-eight hours of the insurrection at Louth were so chaotic that it is hard to see any one person exercising authority over his neighbours. There were wandering bands of commons moving through the countryside, ringing church bells, swearing any gentry they encountered, and calling villagers to musters. As Moigne describes the scene at Louth when he was conveyed there, the commons were an undisciplined crowd, enraged by the captured letters which identified them as rebels. Moigne is quite explicit that it was the gentry who insisted that the commons divide themselves into wapentakes, 'so that every gentlemen might resort to his wapentake and so do the most good amongst his own neighbours in the staying of them'. And, in the afternoon, 'we did come to them and severed the wapentakes ourselves and then every wapentake did appoint there to be their captain the [subsidy] commissioner which dwelled in their wapentake'. The commons, though, were not easily won over, but 'cried to go forward out of hand or else they would destroy and slay us and chose other captains'.[30] The gentry, impotent to do otherwise, acceded to their wish. Petty captains were not chosen for the Horncastle host until Friday, the fourth day of the rising.[31]

---

[29] Cf. above p. 20.   [30] SP1/110, fo. 153v.
[31] SP1/109, fo. 4r (not in *LP* XI, no. 828 (2); also *LP* XI, no. 853.

The division of the commons into wapentakes allowed the gentry to exercise a degree of control and discipline, but at the cost of making it appear that they were furthering the commons' ends. At Beverley we also see the commons milling around on the Saturday and Sunday until they alighted upon William Stapleton, an outsider to Beverley, who agreed to take on the captaincy of the commons on behalf of the 'honest men' to avoid violence. Some of the commons were, it will be recalled, reluctant to accept his authority.[32] The situation Dr Dakyn describes at Richmond seems broadly similar until the arrival of Robert Bowes: 'Whatever he said amongst them, they in manner took it for authority. He caused parishioners to divide and [?ordered] that every parish should choose four men to order the other, and so they did.'[33] The only other account we have of the appearance of captains comes from John Hallam and suggests what might happen when the gentry were not there to take a hand in the matter. After his district had risen, 'the commons about this examinate [Hallam] were without a leader or captain two or three days after and then the people named Mr Robert Hotham, Henry Newark, William Cawrser, and this examinate to be captains of all the commons from Beverley to Driffield'. But once they reached Pontefract, 'the other three named captains with him of his company slinked away by a little and little and left him alone to guide them, for the commons, as he saith, suspected them'.[34] In the January risings the dynamics were perhaps different, possibly because the commons were wise to the gentry's strategy: it was the captains (Hallam in the East Riding, Wilson and Woodmansey at Beverley, Lobley and Peacock at Richmond) whose reputations had been made by the first rising which launched the revolts.

In the first instance the commons were a crowd, thrilled by the excitement of being gathered together in large numbers, determined that anyone who opposed them should be intimidated into submission (a point I shall explore later), but unclear about tactics. At Louth, perhaps at Horncastle, certainly at Richmond, we see a struggle for control between the original agitators responsible for calling the rebels together, and the gentry whom they brought to their musters and whom, in large measure,

---

[32] Stapleton, 86; above pp. 185–6.   [33] SP1/117, fo. 209v; LP XII (i), no. 789.
[34] PRO, E36/119, fo. 26r (= LP XII (i), no. 201 at p. 90).

they probably mistrusted. The gentry shaped the revolt by offering it discipline.[35] They changed the composition of the commons by insisting that only a small number drawn from each township or parish went forwards and represented the whole. Moigne did this at Hambledon Hill, George Lumley at Monyhouse.[36] In Kett's rebellion the gentry never achieved any control over the commons. Perhaps because of the particular agrarian antagonisms within Norfolk between landlords and tenants, the gentry were the subject of much hostility and not trusted. In 1549 they were rounded up and kept under guard. One gentlemen who made overtures to the commons with food and beer was beaten up for his pains.[37] This, in turn, poses an imponderable question. Was it possible for the gentry in Lincolnshire and Yorkshire to take at least some control of the commons because the temper of social relations allowed it, or did the fact that the trick had been played once in the North made its replication impossible in East Anglia twenty years later? I suspect the former: the northern gentry answered an expectation that they would lead.

The commons did not need the gentry to tell them how to raise a revolt. Several methods could be employed. In Louth the technique was to ride around the neighbouring villages having the church bells rung and swearing the parishioners when they appeared to see what the matter was, or sending instructions that they were all to appear and muster the following day. The ringing of bells—and their ringing backwards —was a recognized alarm call which could be guaranteed to bring the population to congregate. Aske attempted to stop the Marshland from ringing their bells by telling them to wait until they heard Howden ring, and telling Howden the reverse.[38] Bills calling for a general rising could also be circulated: bills and the Captain Poverty letters from Richmond were carried to at least Penrith, Alnwick in Northumberland, and perhaps

---

[35] Dr Gunn has offered the analogy of how military commanders handled mutinies: 'When common soldiers mutinied, they could be neither ignored nor left to their own devices. Some semblence of order had to be maintained, if necessary by a partial or total concession of the mutineers' demands while the king's instructions, and pardon for any departure from orders, was obtained as a matter of urgency.' Gunn, 'Peers, Commons and Gentry', 70.

[36] SP1/110, fo. 155r; LP XII (i), no. 369.

[37] MacCulloch, 'Kett's Rebellion in Context', 44, 61.

[38] 'The Manner of the Taking of Robert Aske', 333.

into Craven and Cleveland.[39] Sir Stephen Hamerton recalled going to see a bill fastened to Giggleswick church door; two months later there was a rash of bills fastened to church doors in Craven calling on people to kill the earl of Cumberland's deer.[40] Sadler reported similar bills on church doors around Doncaster and in County Durham, placed there 'by some that do nothing else but go up and down and sow sedition amongst the people'.[41] In more settled conditions the commons could also circulate bills calling for musters through the bush telegraph of the township constables. Bigod used the constables to distribute his call to attend musters; the first George Lumley knew of the muster was when a constable brought him a bill. Likewise, in the failed Norfolk uprising of April 1537 hundred constables were to be compelled to cause the parish constables to call out the people.[42] The circulation of anonymous bills in Cleveland in January became such a nuisance that, after a meeting called by an unsigned bill (whose authors failed to appear), a bill was written by Sir William Bulmer which, amongst other things, ordered that no more anonymous bills were to be circulated.[43] Such bills were used by Staveley and the monks of Jervaulx to convene a muster, and by the shadowy captains who called the conference of the commons at Richmond on 5 February.[44] Indeed, it is an important aspect of the way in which order broke down during January that almost every activist (it seems) could circulate a bill or affix one to a church door urging solidarity against the gentry or the renewal of the Pilgrimage. They were the authentic means by which the peasant underground could make itself known.

Nor did the commons need any instruction in how to finance a rebel force. Many of them would have experience in handling money as church or guild wardens; they might also have served as parish tax-collectors or assessors. The government was curious to discover who had financed the Lincolnshire revolt, suspecting that someone had bankrolled the movement. Because of this interest, we are well informed about how Lincolnshire was funded, less so about Yorkshire.

---

[39] Above p. 217.   [40] *LP* XII (i), no. 1034; XI, no. 1299.

[41] *St. P.* I, 526, 530.   [42] *LP* XII (i), no. 1045.   [43] Ibid., no. 236.

[44] *LP* XII (i), nos. 671, 914, 959, 965. For an example of a bill circulated through Kendal, Dodds, *Pilgrimage*, II, 113 (= *LP* XII (i), no. 411).

The first source of income available to the Louth contingent was money donated by the priests present at Louth on Monday, 2 October. Some gave substantial amounts, including two gifts of £20 and one of £6 13s. 4d.: in all, six priests gave nearly £50. A number of witnesses deposed that they heard the priests say that the commons should not lack for money.[45] Four Louth men were said to have ridden about the countryside soliciting further donations from the clergy, probably with the threat of intimidation as Kendall described:

He [Kendall] saith that one Mr Chapman of Louth and Mr Etton sent to him and the priests of the church for money to pay the poor commoners their wages and that one of Louth called Robert Hertburn claimed it after a very rough fashion as who saith we had to be bounden unto it. And I told him that they was not yet master of my purse and after he went from me in anger to the other priests of the church which were contented to give money for fear than otherwise. And all they came into my house unsent for to make their bill what every man gave and so I perceived that I should have the displeasure of their army unless that I had done as all [others] did and so I sent 5s.[46]

The constable of Sotherby threatened their blind and aged vicar, Thomas Yoell, for 40s., but finally went away with 6s. 8d., given 'for fear'.[47] Church funds were also raided. Louth was said to have given £40, and at Horncastle the rebels had the church stock.[48] The Horncastle host had an unpleasant line in demanding food and lodgings from monastic houses as they passed. Barlings Abbey was virtually occupied by the host on Thursday evening. The abbot thought he had 200 men sleeping in the house that night, and he was compelled to take food to a commons' muster on the following morning.[49] The laity in Louth were also taxed. One of the commons, Thomas Noble, explained how an elderly man called Goshawk was forced to lend him a horse and a bill and to pay him wages.[50]

---

[45] LP XI, no. 968; SP1/110, fos. 162v (deposition of Thomas Manby); 163v (John Taylor); 164r (John Child), not all noticed in LP XI, no. 972.

[46] Ibid., fo. 161r; SP1/110, fo. 146r (very badly truncated in LP).

[47] SP1/110, fo. 170v (not noticed at all in LP XI, no. 973).

[48] LP XI, no. 828 (i); XII (i), no. 70 (10). Unfortunately the extant Louth churchwardens' accounts contain no disbursements for the revolt, but much of the church's money was held by the guilds and does not feature in these accounts.

[49] LP XI, no. 805.   [50] SP1/110, fo. 163r (silently omitted in LP XI, no. 973).

This money was expended on paying a daily wage to the rank and file. There are several cases of men who said that they had received small sums—normally 4*d.* a day—whilst on service. Arthur Wasshingley had wages of 2*d.* but also meat and drink. These wages are to be equated with labourers' day wages. Huddeswell thought townships had generally paid their troops. Louth went so far as to pay some of its contingent for their passage back from Lincoln.[51]

We may envisage that Yorkshire townships similarly paid their contingents. In early November it was reported that Sir Henry Savile had threatened to hang some men at Dewsbury (probably township constables) for levying taxation on their neighbours for the setting forwards of soldiers.[52] The parish of St Michael Spurriergate in the city of York paid out 25*s.* 7$^{1}/_{2}$*d.* towards the cost of equipping two soldiers to go with the commons. This included 8*s.* for the hire of a horse and 3*s.* 5*d.* for the cloth and making up of two white coats. The parish did not, however, pay wages.[53] George Lumley thought that every township gave each soldier a cash advance of 20*s.*—sixty days' wages—which seems a little unlikely.[54]

The Yorkshire Pilgrims, like the Lincolnshire rebels, also looked to the church for money. Lancelot Collins, the treasurer of York Minster, was repeatedly asked for money. First he gave £3 to Aske for his licence to stay at home. Then three captains of the commons came, and Collins gave them £10 for their commons (with a little *douceur* each) as a bribe to avoid his household being drafted into the commons' army. Then he parted with a gelding to Sir Oswold Wilstrop and Sir Nicholas Fairfax and paid various other small bribes.[55] Sir Thomas Percy said that 'every town found certain men and the gentlemen went of their own costs', but he was busy passing his charges on to the abbot of St Mary's, from whom he had 20 nobles, the abbot of Whitby (who sent a horse), and others. Sir Nicholas Fairfax thought that as the 'matter that they rose for

---

[51] e.g. *LP* XI, no. 972, 973 (not all noticed in *LP*); no. 853; SP1/110, fo. 135v (not in *LP* XI, no. 968).

[52] *LP* XI, no. 960.

[53] C. C. Webb (ed.), 'The Churchwardens' Accounts of St Michael, Spurriergate, York, 1518–1548', *Borthwick Texts and Calendars*, 20, 21 (1997), I, 181–2. The use of parish funds can be paralleled in Kett's revolt: MacCulloch, 'Kett's Rebellion in Context', 51.

[54] *LP* XII (i), no. 369.   [55] Ibid., no. 1018.

was a matter for the defence of the faith and a spiritual matter; wherefore he thought meet that the priors and abbots and other men of the
church should not only send aid unto them but also go forth in their
own persons . . .' George Lumley was sent around the abbeys of the eastern North Riding asking for men and money. Some agreed, but the order
that abbots should attend was countermanded by Aske, for whom the
notion of priests wearing armour was probably anathema.[56] Aske was
not against raising money from the church to finance his war, though.
In November he asked Archbishop Lee for a book 'of all the spiritual
promotions to be made to the intent that if good answer came not from
the king's highness, they might tax every man after the rate of the value
of his benefice or promotion'. Sir Ralph Bigod, in a rare engagement
with practicality, told the muster at Brough that they would be paid by
'the fat priests' benefices of the south that were not resident upon the
same and the money of suppressed abbeys', but then he probably had
no money with which to pay wages and had to offer the promise of the
credit of the south.[57]

The laity had access to quite significant sums through rates and in churchwardens' and guild stocks.[58] These could have supported a war for a period;
but it is perhaps only to be expected that a war in defence of the church
should have seen the taxation of the individual clergy and the church
generally as its easiest option for raising money.

III

The commons exhibited and strengthened their solidarity through the
swearing of oaths. From the first moment of the Lincolnshire rising,
a simple oath was demanded: 'for king, church, and commons'. Brown
tells us that at Louth the heads of the town were made to swear 'to be
true to God, the king, and to take the commons' part for the defence

---

[56] SP1/115, fo. 209v–210r (= LP XII (i), no. 369).
[57] SP1/119, fo. 7r (the significance of this missed by LP XII (i), no. 1022); ibid., no. 369.
[58] Kümin, *The Shaping of a Community*, is now authoritative.

of Holy Church'.[59] Sir William Skipwith was made to swear later that afternoon and the subsidy commissioners the following morning.[60] The same oath was used at Scrivelsby. One supposed eyewitness says that the oath employed at Beverley was to God, the king, and the commons and for the maintenance of Holy Church.[61] A similar oath was enjoined on the commons of Westmorland and Cumberland by the Captain Poverty letters. As Robert Thompson recorded, the commons were to swear 'to be true to God, to the faith of the church, to our sovereign lord the king, and to the commonwealth'.[62]

This oath sounds almost like a greeting which might be employed amongst the commons: 'Are you true to the king, the church, and the commons?' In Lincolnshire and Beverley it was sworn by the commons and used as a device to bind non-commons to them: the richer inhabitants of Louth, the subsidy commissioners, and Dymock's house party at Scrivelsby. When Leach made Edward Dymock swear there, Dymoke asked why. After a testy exchange, Leach said: ' "What, shall we stand here all day? Lay your hand on the book". With that the sheriff answered, "wherefore should I swear? I am sworn to the king already". With that Leach said, "Make an end, be sworn to do as we do, or else it shall cost you your life and as many as will not swear." And so the sheriff was sworn.'[63] When Aske was confronted by Huddeswell and told to swear, he too declined: 'to whom he answered that he was once sworn to the king's highness and issue and that he would not be sworn again to any other intent unless he was enforced to the same, and demanded the manner of their oath'. Having heard it, he agreed to be sworn, 'in this oath there is no treason, but standing with his first oath'.[64] Dr Towneley also argued that he was bound to God, the church, the king, and the commonwealth already, but he was forced to swear the oath regardless.[65] Sir Ralph Ellerker the younger was immediately repelled by the idea of the

---

[59] This is my reconstruction of a damaged original: SP1/109, fo. 76v (= LP XI, no. 854).

[60] For the oath being employed at Caistor, see Huddeswell's examination, LP XI, no. 853.

[61] LP XI, no. 841. This is the deposition of William Breyer. He says that the oath was administered in the name of Robert Aske, but this is not confirmed by Stapleton and seems unlikely.

[62] LP XII (i), no. 687 (2).

[63] SP1/110, fo. 137 (= LP XI no. 967 (i), printed in Gunn, 'Peers, Commons and Gentry', 55.

[64] 'The manner of the taking of Robert Aske', 332, also 'Aske's Examination', 572.

[65] SP1/117, fo. 43r, silently omitted in LP XII (i), no. 687.

oath. He held that he was sworn to the king's person and that he would not swear any further oath 'without the king's pleasure'. After the surrender of Hull, he agreed to do whatever the commons demanded except swear the oath and serve as one of their captains. His father came to Beverley to negotiate with the commons on 11 October without being sworn, for which he was most grateful.[66] When Sir William Fairfax rode through Wakefield on about 22 October, the commons demanded that he should swear the oath. He refused and rode on. The commons chased after him, broke into his house, pulled him out of his bed, and swore him in the street outside. He was then taken to Wakefield as a prisoner.[67]

In differing degrees, all these individuals tried to evade the oath. Stapleton, though, makes a fascinating, common-sense observation about it: 'he was of opinion that the oath did no good for it would make a man neither better nor yet worse.'[68] Yet, whilst for some gentry it was important to avoid taking the oath, for some of the commons it was equally important that it should be sworn. 'Be sworn to do as we do', said Leach to his gentry victim. When Hallam was ready to float the idea of a new rebellion to his neighbours, he insisted on first swearing Hugh Langdale, who had been away in the autumn and so had never been exposed to the oath. '[He, Hallam] thought it best to swear the said Langdale as others were sworn, lest he should betray them or send any word to the prior of Watton . . .' Hallam asked Langdale whether there was anything unlawful about the oath: Langdale thought not and allowed himself to be sworn. For Hallam it was a guarantee of secrecy; for Langdale it was perhaps a matter of avoiding confrontation.[69] According to depositions made in Lancashire in November, a group of men went about around midnight with their faces blacked, wearing harness, and intimidated their neighbours into swearing to God, the king, and the commons. They broke into several houses: in one they threatened their victim in front of his children. The perpetrators (one of whom was only 16) seem to have done this as an interlude between sessions in the alehouse and made rather light of it; but they also told their victims that the commons had risen towards Whalley, and it may be that they were

---

[66] Stapleton, 85, 88–9, 97, 98.   [67] Dodds, *Pilgrimage*, I, 237, citing PRO, STAC2/20/9.
[68] Stapleton, 97.   [69] *LP* XII (i), no. 201, pp. 91, 87.

in something of a panic over an erroneous report.[70] The deep ambiguities about how the oath should be treated emerge from a letter of Lord Monteagle in December. Some of his tenants had been sworn under threat of having their houses and goods destroyed. Even so, they still pledged their loyalty to the king and Monteagle and were as ready to serve as any other of his tenants. The oath hardly made any difference to them. Monteagle was not so sure: he refused to have any men who had been sworn to the commons enter his house.[71]

For some the commons' oath was essentially meaningless, almost something out of the playground. Aske recognized this, and it is a measure of the way in which he broke with (and added steel to) the commons' revolt that he wrote his own oath, a much more serious matter, which was offensive in that it demanded changes, and suggested what they might be, rather than simply defending the status quo. It was doubtless this oath rather than the commons' which so exercised the Crown. One of the drafts of the oath prepared for the duke of Norfolk contained a clause insisting that those swearing should renounce the oaths they made during the rebellion.[72] The vacuity of the common's oath was bound up with another important aspect of their understanding of their actions. They were not engaged in rebellion; they were not rebels. Moigne described the inflammatory impact of Hussey's intercepted letters, in which the commons were described as 'false and rebellious knaves' who needed to be repressed.[73] Bigod worked his crowd at the Borough by telling them that if they accepted the king's pardon they admitted that they were rebels, whilst Hallam believed that 'they had never offended' and had no need of a pardon.[74] The commons had the moral superiority of God, the king, the church, and the commonwealth behind them: they could not be rebels, for they were protesting against the destruction of church and commonwealth.

The commons also had weight of numbers and a monopoly of fervour on their side. Monteagle's tenants were not the only people who thought that it was better to bend with the commons than be broken by them. The people of Sleaford told Lord Hussey that they would serve

---

[70] *LP* XI, no. 1230, printed in full in 'Derby Correspondence', 70–5.   [71] *LP* XI, no. 1232.
[72] *LP* XII (i), no. 98.   [73] SP1/110, fo. 153r.   [74] *LP* XII (i), no. 269; 201 (iv) (p. 91).

him, but they would not take up arms against the commons. As the revolt spread through Yorkshire, Sir Thomas Tempest told his father that if he, the steward of the manor of Wakefield, reached Wakefield before the commons, the town would go with him, but 'if the commons come to Wakefield before ye come, I think that the most part of the town will go with them'.[75] The attempt by the justices of Holland to seek support amongst the 'honest persons' of their district came to nothing: 'they said they would take such part as their neighbours took and that they could not die in a better quarrel than God's and the king's'. Amongst those who decided to throw in their lot with the commons were the households and tenants of some of the major figures. Hussey was left without any local support: so too was Sir John Thimbleby.[76] The troops gathered by the earl of Cumberland defected; the household of the earl of Westmorland seems to have abandoned him in some way when he rejected the Richmondshire commons, and he was forced to surrender to Robert Bowes. Most crucially for the course of the Pilgrimage, the household servants at Pontefract leant towards the commons and Aske was confident of their support.[77] In the new year, as Sadler travelled northwards, he found that 'they let not to say, openly, in all the towns that I have passed this way, that if there be a new insurrection, they will take his part that cometh first. If the king's army comes first, they will take that part: and if the commons come first, they must needs go with them, and take their part, or else be spoiled of all they have.'[78] Hence, there were those who thought that resistance was useless. Anthony Irby, who sent word of the rising in Holland, was bleak: 'if we should withstand their rebellious commandment there were no way with us but only death, loss of our goods, and destruction of our children.' This man knew of the death of Dr Rayne; he had also heard that a Mr Etton, whom the rebels had sworn and made one of their captains, had been killed after he absconded.[79] There are one or two cases of gentry children being held

[75] *LP* XI, nos. 852, 702, and cf. the comments of the commons of Newcastle, above n. 18.

[76] PRO, E36/121, fo. 72v (= *LP* XI, no. 585); Hussey, see above, p. 162; Gunn, 'Peers, Commons and Gentry', 76.

[77] 'Thomas Master's Narrative', 62–3, 70; 'The manner of the taking of Robert Aske', 335.

[78] *LP* XI, no. 702; *St. P.* I, 528 (= *LP* XII (i), no. 200).

[79] PRO, E36/121, fo. 72r (= *LP* XI, no. 585). See p. 141 above for Mr Etton.

to ensure that their parents conformed to the will of the commons.[80] Christopher Aske reported how, after the commons had besieged Skipton for two or three days without success, they devised a plan to take hostage Lady Eleanor Clifford (Henry, Lord Clifford's wife, daughter of the duke of Suffolk and the king's niece) and other gentlewomen at Bolton Priory, 'and lead them unto the castle before the host at the assault the next day, thinking my lord would not destroy his children and thought thereby to come unto their purposes. And if not, they determined to violate and enforce them with *knaifes* [knives or knaves?] unto my lord's displeasure.' Aske was able to spirit the women into the castle with the aid of the vicar of Skipton (his spy amongst the commons).[81] There are more cases of gentle houses threatened with being ransacked or even set alight. Moigne was told that the commons would return in the morning and either pull or burn down his house; Aske claimed to have saved Sir Thomas Metham's house. Sir Thomas Percy, whilst fleeing in disguise, was told that the commons would have him or plunder his mother's house. The following day Percy was present when the commons spoiled Sir Roger Cholmeley's house at Roxby, after Cholmeley failed to answer their call to present himself. The commons threatened to torch William Rokeby's house at Marske and Sir John Bulmer's at Wilton. The same unsubtle approach was also used at Jervaulx and Whalley.[82] Lord Latimer's and other gentry houses were seized by the commons in January 1537.[83]

There was a thin line between the pillaging of houses and threats of arson to secure compliance, and the wholesale robbery of the gentry and opponents of the movement under cover of rebellion. Stapleton went to Leonard Beckwith's house at South Cave to test rumours that there was a great mass of the king's rent there (Beckwith being a receiver of the Court of Augmentations). Confronted with two locked chests, Stapleton persuaded his companions that they would only contain charters (although he admitted that it *might* have been plate), and they left them

---

[80] Mrs Tempest, 'Nicholas Tempest', 251; Sir Thomas Wharton, *LP* XII (i), no. 687 (2); Darcy, threats against his grandchildren, Dodds, *Pilgrimage*, I, 302.

[81] SP1/120, fos. 58v–59r (= *LP* XII (i), no. 1186).

[82] SP1/110, fo. 151v; 'The manner of the taking of Robert Aske', 334; *LP* XI, no. 393; Bush, *Pilgrimage*, 159; *LP* XII (i), no. 1035.

[83] *LP* XII (i), nos. 169, 173.

unopened and untouched. His hostility to robbery appears on other occa-sions.[84] Beckwith was less lucky at his other house, which seems to have been completely emptied of its possessions, down to the doors and their locks, the cattle taken out of his fields, and the fish from his ponds.[85] The first earl of Cumberland complained that the commons had broken into his houses at Barden and Carleton Park, and by December there were mass poaching expeditions against his deer.[86] The abbot of Jervaulx and John, Lord Scrope both lost sheep during the revolt.[87] Sir Brian Hastings's animals doubtless fed the commons at Pontefract.[88] Hallam com-mandeered sheep, which he sold, and distributed the money as wages.[89]

IV

Even though the commons had a cause—the defence of parish religion—money, numbers, and, in the beginning, enthusiasm, they rapidly became subservient to the gentry. The commons' revolt lasted less than ten days in Lincolnshire. The revolt in Yorkshire and the north-west in October 1536 had a much greater longevity because it was led by a renegade gentleman who relished the confrontation; the uprisings in January and February 1537 happened because the commons realized that their rebel-lion had been extinguished by guile and feared reprisals. It is hard to understand why the commons surrendered their revolt to the gentlemen. Some of the commons were doubtless persuaded that the gentlemen were furthering their best interests. Other, more reluctant rebels, perhaps drawn from the 'honest men', cleaved to the gentry as a defence against the 'light fellows', the poorer commoners, and saw the gentlemen as their best hope for getting home safely. We may suspect a conflict between the 'light fellows' and the 'honest men': perhaps the latter saw the gentry

---

[84] Stapleton, 90, 97.

[85] 'Yorkshire Star Chamber Proceedings', II, 124–33. It is not quite clear when this happened. Beckwith says 20 November, but William Acclom admitted spoiling the house and driving away Beckwith's cattle in October: *LP* XII (i), no. 536.

[86] *LP* XII (i), nos. 927, 1299.

[87] Ibid., no. 1035; Yorkshire Archaeological Soc., Leeds, MD 319.

[88] *LP* XI, no. 1402.   [89] *LP* XII (i), no. 201, p. 90.

as the means to buttress their failed authority after the fashion of their fatal day trip to Caistor. We may take it that it was the 'light fellows' who stood in Louth arguing whether the gentry should be murdered under cover of darkness: they were convinced—quite rightly so—that the gentry would deceive and betray them.[90] At Beverley, 'some light persons' argued that the gentlemen conferred together too much and 'would betray them', an obvious complaint about the commons' exclusion from authority.[91]

Most gentry accepted their incorporation into the commons' movement after it became clear that flight was not a practicable possibility. Thomas Moigne sent word that if he really had to be taken and sworn by the commons, he wished it to be done by such as would not upset his sick wife or spoil his house. The sixth earl of Northumberland, himself ill, asked Maunsell either to come and swear him himself or send 'two gentlemen of worship to take him because he would be taken with no violence'.[92] Once they were amongst the commons, the co-option of yet more gentry into the movement served further to buttress the authority of those who were already there. So small gentry swore larger gentry, and Robert Bowes (apparently) swore an earl.[93]

The gentry amongst the commons then worked hard to establish their own authority over them, mustering, appointing petty captains, and, in Lincoln, drafting petitions to the king, always working for delay. The influence of the initial urban cadre was diluted as reliable yeomen came to dominate the movement. Their objective was not to advance the defence of the church, for they probably never believed that parochial religion was under any threat in 1536; their concern was to secure a pardon, which their submission to the duke of Suffolk seemed to offer.

The Yorkshire revolt developed on different lines because of Aske, but also because the surrender of the commons' movement by the Lincolnshire gentry made the Yorkshire commons much more wary of what was being done in their name. There was, for a few days, a serious danger of a battle at Doncaster. Again, what the Yorkshire gentry wanted was a pardon. This disbandment of the rebel army at Doncaster was the first stage

[90] Above p. 148.   [91] Stapleton, 94.
[92] SP1/110, fos. 151v–152r; 113, fo. 54r–v (completely omitted in LP XI, no. 1402).
[93] LP XI, no. 945.

towards securing this, but as November passed and the pardon seemed increasingly elusive, the gentry found themselves, step by step, *at the king's invitation*, developing a deeper and more overtly political critique of the Cromwellian ascendancy. Whatever they, as individuals, thought of the development of state and religious policy since 1529 (and there are indications that many found it distasteful), they could blame it for their own predicament in October 1536. When a convincing pardon was offered it was accepted, the Pilgrims' complaints were put to one side, and the inevitable split occurred between the commons and the gentry. Of course there might have been a post-Pilgrimage, in which the Pilgrims' grievances might have been thrashed out in parliamentary forum, with who knows what result. But this never happened. It was the fear that the pardon gave less than it promised—that it was merely the cover for a repression of the commons—which provoked the secondary risings of January and February 1537. These, in effect, made void the Doncaster pact. Nonetheless, the pardon was always acknowledged, which meant that the king had to resort to a range of ruses to try to execute the leaders of the Pilgrimage. The commons' captains were deemed unimportant and largely escaped conviction, and so disappear from history.

16

Epilogue: 'to knit up this tragedy'

> . . . wherefore, considering that this matter of insurrection hath been attempted there, and thinking that as well for the example, as to see who would [groan] at their [Aske, Constable, and Darcy's] execution, it should be meet to have them executed at Doncaster and thereabouts, minding, upon their sufferance, to knit up this tragedy.[1]

There is a popular view drawn from chaos theory which holds that the beating of the wings of a butterfly in the Amazon could set in train a sequence of events which might result in a storm in the North Atlantic. Historians tend to be divided between those who favour explanations of change arising out of deep substructures within society, the historical equivalent of the formation of mountains by the grating of continental plates, and those who favour explanations based on accidents, the historical equivalent of the butterfly's wings. The former might argue that revolts occurred in 1536–7 because a politically informed and devout society was fearful about the alleged projected reform of religious observance.

---

[1] Henry VIII to Norfolk, 12 June 1537, *St. P.* I, 555 (= *LP* XII (ii), no. 77). In fact no executions took place in Doncaster.

The substructures were beginning to shift in 1536. The state's involvement in religion, not to preserve orthodoxy but to encourage reform, created a politics of religious diversity which was to endure for three, perhaps four centuries; a politics where every individual had the choice between conventional practice and reformed religion, between differing ways of achieving salvation. To historians of the latter persuasion, the revolt of 1536 was a response to reports which were untrue, to unnecessary anxieties: but within twenty years the state had acted in exactly the way men feared it was about to in the autumn of 1536. For our butterfly, the beginning of the chain of accident, chance, and mishap, we should perhaps alight upon Thomas Foster, the singing-man in Louth church, who said out loud that the church's crosses would be confiscated the following day. He was wrong. But his cry infected a town, the town a county, and from there the contagion spread throughout the northern counties with a reverberance felt throughout England. Many died in the aftermath; Foster, ironically, continued to draw his wage from Louth church for several more years.[2]

Foster is a mere bit-player in the 1530s, with an unintended moment of fame or notoriety. It is Henry VIII who permeates this book, just as he permeates the history of the 1530s as a whole. The documents tell us little about how Henry, as a person, reacted to having a major rebellion in his country. We do not know whether the letters sent out in his name reflect his preferences or the collective decision of king and council (although one may assume the former more than the latter). This is the record we can assess, and it is not a good one.

His strategic record is very poor. First, and perhaps most crucially, he ignored—or created an environment in which he did not wish to be told about—the emphatic and correct warnings which Darcy was sending from Yorkshire. His decision to wind up the army gathering at Ampthill on the dispersal of the Lincolnshire rebels was a fatal error, which determined the future shape of the Pilgrimage and compelled its defeat by policy: by negotiation, limited compromise, by playing a long game in which consideration of the Pilgrims' demands was always deferred until later. Henry always seems to have believed that the Yorkshire rebellion

[2] Lincolnshire Record Office, Louth St James 7/2.

would wind itself down after the fashion of the Lincolnshire revolt, satisfied with no more than the promise of a pardon, and the king allowed a rich picking of victims. Throughout, the king wished to treat the Pilgrims from a position of strength which he never possessed. His insistence on lecturing the Pilgrims about their disobedience to their sovereign, the offer of conditional pardons only, the willingness to mobilize afresh if the Pilgrims insisted on discussing a political programme, the pointless barbs contained in the proclamation of pardon and his printed letter to Yorkshire (where even the reference to 'rebels' in the title was a provocation), and the desire for revenge, all point towards a mind of limited flexibility and abundant overconfidence. His rejection of unfavourable reports (such as those from Darcy and Norfolk) is part of a mindset in which the certainty of divine authority and the need to secure obedience became more important than the practicalities of the exercise of political authority. Henry probably always suspected a conspiracy: he wanted to know whether the gentlemen in Lincoln winked at the rebels.[3]

The crucial compromises, which allowed the disbandment of the Pilgrims as a military force, were forced on the king by the duke of Norfolk. It was Henry's inability to compromise, his refusal to concede an unconditional pardon to people who had been unwillingly caught up in the revolt, the uncertainty about the king's motives, the general lack of trust he engendered, which extended the Pilgrimage from October 1536 into February 1537. From the moment the Pilgrims' army decamped from Doncaster, the Pilgrims were reacting to Henry: for, in sending Ellerker and Bowes to court, they passed the initiative to their monarch. Indeed, Ellerker and Bowes returned to the North with his instructions.[4] If Thomas Foster was the first begetter of the revolts, it was the king who kept them alive by refusing to allow the gentry amongst the rebels any significant concession. Royal pride, and Henry's inability to cope with what he defined as disobedience, drove royal policy.

There were two further areas in which he refused any compromise. The analysis to which the politically informed Pilgrims subscribed (and which the commons accepted) was that the normal processes of coun-

---

[3] *LP* XI no. 843.   [4] Ibid., no. 1064 (2).

sel had broken down, that the king's mind had been captured by a coterie who were forcing their own heretical religious preferences on the king and country. Parliament had failed in its duty to stop the king's excesses: it had created a situation through bogus laws in which one of the king's creatures, Cranmer, had pronounced on the king's marriage. Parliament had permitted the dissolution of the monasteries for the king's private gain, and, it was suspected, for the pecuniary advantage of his ministers. It had subordinated church to state, canon law to statute, priest to layman. Parliament had even empowered the king to bequeath the succession to the throne. Throughout the Pilgrimage there was a conviction that government was out of control. The blame for this was laid at Cromwell's door: 'Cromwell, it is thou that art the very original and chief causer of all this rebellion and mischief.'[5] Whilst Cromwell, Cranmer, Rich, Audeley, Latimer, and a handful of others were universally blamed for the state of the country, are we really to suppose that the king slumbered, unaware of what was being done in his name?

The character of the relationship between Henry VIII and Thomas Cromwell is but one aspect of the vexed question of the king's personality. Henry has been drawn as an inattentive chairman of the family firm, reluctant to be troubled with business, willing, if not anxious, to abdicate much of the work of government to two able chief executives, Wolsey and Cromwell. Some have seen him as a man of soft and malleable opinions who could be swayed against people—even his wife—by the opinions and conversations of his attendants in the privy chamber. More recently we have also had Henry the strategist, very much involved in setting a direction which Cromwell then implemented, used to dealing directly with his ministers and ambassadors.[6] It is generally agreed that he was also a committed (albeit amateur) theologian, who relished debate with, for instance, Bishop Latimer over the reality of purgatory, debate of a kind which he would have been loath to tolerate in the alehouse. The Ten Articles came directly from Henry's pen: it is inconceivable that Cromwell alone drafted the First Henrician Injunctions, or that they were issued without the king's knowledge or sanction. Cromwell was the pen,

---

[5] Allegedly said to Cromwell by Darcy when under interrogation: *LP* XII (i), no. 976.

[6] The various points of view are rehearsed in G. W. Bernard, 'Elton's Cromwell', *History*, 83 (1998).

and not the hand that held it.[7] This was the reality with which Aske was teased in the Tower.

Item, where the king's grace is a pattern of wisdom and knowledge whom it is hard for his council to seduce, was not the grudge which is pretended by the rebels to be against the said council for the said acts of parliament minded and stomached against the king's own person, albeit cloaked as aforesaid?

If it be that you thought them [the councillors] the causers of the making of the said statutes, whether you would not, if you knew the king to be the chief cause of the making of them, bear the same grudge against him?[8]

The Pilgrimage was the reaction to the Cromwellian ascendancy, but it was the king who set the tone and direction, not his minister. The Pilgrims had no idea about how to resolve a situation in which the king himself seemed, in a way, to be insane. It was possible, indeed conventional, to attack his ministers, but what was to be done when it was the head which was rotten? Lord Montague, in his tactless table-talk, saw the point: 'The Lord Darcy played the fool. He went away to pluck away the council. He should first have started with the head . . .'[9] It is to his credit that Henry made no changes in his ministers despite the barrage of complaints which they attracted, nor did he rescind the Ten Articles or the Injunctions: he stood behind both ministers and polices, because they were his own. The nearest he came to softening his policies during the Pilgrimage was in his circular to the bishops of 19 November, which forbade divisive preaching and the marriage of priests, and which encouraged Darcy, but made little in the way of concession to the Pilgrims.[10]

Nor did Henry ever deviate from the view that he was entitled to the smaller monasteries. Again we see the king driving policy in a way which was highly impolitic in the disturbed conditions of the winter of 1536–7. Where monks had re-entered their houses, he insisted on their eviction and the rapid restoration of his tenants. He wanted monks executed, and a handful were; he was clearly delighted to discover a new mechanism to seize monastic houses. There is a marked monastophobia in Henry's behaviour throughout the revolts: he despised monks for their uselessness,

---

[7] On the direction of religious policy by the king, Bernard, 'The Making of Religious Policy, 1533–46'.

[8] 'Aske's Examination', 553, question 55; LP XII (i), no. 954 (122). I owe these to Dr Bernard.

[9] LP XIII (ii), no. 804.   [10] LP XI, no. 1110, 1336.

was preoccupied with their 'abominable lives', and suspected their loyalty and obedience. It was not by chance that of the sixty-seven laymen tried at Lincoln on 6 March 1537 only fourteen were executed, but all twenty clergy convicted were executed, amongst them fourteen monks from Bardney, Barlings, and Kirkstead, whose involvement in the rebellion was, at best, inconsequential.[11]

Paradoxically, it was Henry's refusal to compromise which brought about the collapse of the Pilgrimage as a political movement and the abrogation of the concessions it secured at Doncaster. For even when a pardon had been granted, some still refused to believe that the king's mercy was intended or would be honoured. And so it was understandable that fearful men should have risen in arms anew, and as they were squashed, the promises of December were progressively withdrawn.

There is perhaps something inevitable about the rebellions of 1536. Intentionally or not, Henry set about shifting the substructures of society by recasting the understood forms of religious observance. His government, perhaps for no better reason than the need to occupy parliament and convocation, tried to do too much, too quickly. It underestimated how radical its proposals—ideas with which the king was plainly comfortable—would look to the people as a whole. It had no means of countering reports of yet more extreme innovations. For the king, the public response to his innovations was not important, for he lived in an environment of personal obedience. In the wider nation, in which the majority of the population was perplexed by the king's successive marriages, alienated from his government for its religious policies, and suspicious of its future intentions, and in which every parish contained one or more disgruntled clergyman, one singing-man was enough to start a major conflagration: if not in Louth, then somewhere else; if not Thomas Foster, then some other agent.

In retrospect, it was Henry's success in defeating the Pilgrimage that made the English Reformation possible, for this was England's War of Religion. Opposition to religious change over the next two decades was muted. The defeat of the commons owed nothing to the king, but was made possible by their manipulation by the gentry and nobility of the

[11] *LP* XII (i) no. 581.

North, many of whom were as appalled by the innovations of the mid-1530s as were the commons themselves. But one of the most striking features of that decade is the way in which the nobility and gentry exhibited solidarity with a wayward monarch. In the autumn of 1536 and the winter of 1537 they did the king a great service, in which they placed their king before their God. They were, perhaps, better servants than the king deserved.

Select Documents[1]

(i) The Lincoln Articles, 9 October 1536

The sole surviving text of the articles made at Lincoln comes from a copy apparently sent to the city of York (endorsed 'The first five articles brought to the mayor of York').

To the king our sovereign lord

[1] The suppression of so many religious houses as are at this instant time suppressed, whereby the service of our God is not well [maintained] but also the commons of your realm unrelieved, the which as we think is a great hurt to the commonwealth and many sisters be [put] from their livings and left at large.

[2] The second article is that we humbly beseech your grace that the act of use[s] may be suppressed because we think by the said act we your true subjects be clearly restrained of your [*sic*] liberties in the declaration of our wills concerning our lands, as well for payment of our debts, for doing of your grace service, as for helping and relieving of our children, the which we had by the [...] of your laws [...] the which as we think is a great hurt and [...] to the commonwealth.

[3] The third article is that where your grace hath a tax or a quindene [fifteenth] granted unto you by act of parliament payable the next year, the which is and hath been ever leviable of sheep and cattle, and the sheep and cattle of your subjects within the said shire are now at this instant time in manner utterly decayed, and [...] whereby your grace to take the said tax or quindene your said subjects shall be distrained to pay 4*d.* for every beast and 12*d.* for 20 sheep, the which would be an importunate charge to them considering the poverty that they be in already and loss which they have sustained these two years past.

[4] The fourth article is that we your true subjects think that your grace takes of your council and being about you such persons as be of low birth and small

---

[1] The texts have been prepared from existing printed texts but collated with the MSS. Names of heretics are given in their modern form. All numbering of clauses is editorial. Missing text is shown with [....]. I am grateful to Professor Diarmaid MacCulloch for help with the text of the Pontefract Articles.

reputation which hath procured the profits [of the dissolution] most especially for their own advantage, the which we suspect to be the Lord Cromwell and Sir Richard Rich, Chancellor of Augmentations.

[5] The fifth article is that we your true subjects find us grieved that there be diverse bishops of England of your grace's late promotion that hath [...] the faith of Christ, as we think, which are the bishop of Canterbury, the bishop of Rochester, the bishop of Worcester, the bishop of Salisbury, the bishop of St Davids, and the bishop of Dublin, and in especial we think that the beginnings of all the trouble of that [...] and the vexation that hath been [...] of your subjects the bishop of Lincoln.

Source: LP XI, no. 705 (i), printed verbatim in Fletcher and MacCulloch, *Tudor Rebellions*, 131 (where they are called 'The York articles').

(ii) Aske's Proclamation to the City of York, 15–16 October 1536

Lords, knights, masters, kinsmen, and friends.
We perceive that you be informed that this assembly or pilgrimage that we, by the favour and mercy of almighty God, do intend to proceed in is because the king our sovereign lord hath had so many impositions of us, we doubt not but ye do right know that to our power we have been always ready in payments and services to his highness as any of his subjects and therefore to ascertain you of the cause of this our assembly and pilgrimage is this.

Forasmuch that such simple and evil disposed persons, being of the king's council, hath not only incensed his grace with many and sundry new inventions, which be contrary [to] the faith of God and honour to the king's majesty and the commonwealth of this realm, and thereby intendeth to destroy the church of England and the ministers of the same, as ye do well know, as well as we, but also the said council hath spoiled and robbed, and further intending utterly to spoil and rob the whole body of this realm, and that as well you as us, if God of his infinite mercy had not caused such as hath taken, or hereafter shall take this pilgrimage upon them, to proceed in the same. And whether all this aforesaid be true or not, we put it to your conscience, and if you think it be true, and do fight against us that intendeth the commonwealth of this realm and nothing else, we trust, by the grace of God, ye shall have small speed, for this pilgrimage, we have [under]taken it for the preservation of Christ's church of this realm of England, the king our sovereign lord, the nobility and commons of the same, and to the intent to make petition to the king's highness for the reformation of that which is amiss within this his realm and for the punishment of heretics and subverters of the laws, and we, neither for money, malice, displeasure to no persons but such as be not worthy to remain nigh about the king our sovereign lord's person.

And further, you know, if you shall obtain, as we trust in God you shall not, ye put both us and you and your heirs and ours in bondage for ever, and further, ye are sure of the intention [*entensyon*] of Christ's curse and we clear and out of the same. And if we overcome you, then you shall be in our wills. Wherefore, for a conclusion, if ye will not come with us for the reformation of the premises, we certify you by this our writing that we will fight and die against both you and all those that shall be about towards to stop us in the said pilgrimage, and God shall judge which shall have his grace mercy therein, and then you shall be judged hereafter to be shedders of Christian blood and destroyers of your even [i.e. equal] Christians.

From Robert Aske, chief captain of the conventual assembly on pilgrimage for the same, barony and commonalty of the same.

Per me, Robertum Aske, in the name of the baronage and commonalty of the same.

The articles

First, for the suppression of religious houses; the second for the Act of Uses; the third for First Fruits; the fourth for the payment of money of the temporality; the fifth is for the base council about the king; the sixth is for the new bishops.

Source: *LP* XI, no. 705 (2), previously printed verbatim in *St. P.*, I, 466–7 and, without the articles, in Dodds, *Pilgrimage*, I, 175–6.

(iii) The Oath, ?24 October 1536

The oath of the honourable men

Ye shall not enter into this our Pilgrimage of Grace for the commonwealth but only for the love that ye do bear unto almighty God, his faith, and to holy church militant [and for] the maintenance thereof, to the preservation of the king's person [and] his issue, to the purifying of the nobility, and to expulse all villain blood and evil councillors against the commonwealth from his grace and his privy council of the same. And that ye shall not enter into our said Pilgrimage for no particular profit to yourself, nor to do any displeasure to any private person but by the counsel of the commonwealth, nor slay nor murder for no envy, but in your hearts put away all fear and dread, and take afore you the cross of Christ and in your hearts his faith, the restitution of the church, the suppression of these heretics and their opinions by the holy contents of this book.

Source: 'Derby Correspondence', printing Lancashire RO, DDF/1 (unfoliated).

(iv) The Hampole Articles, ?27 October 1536

There survives in the state papers a document which claims to be the definitive text of the Pilgrim's oath and articles sent with Norfolk on 28 October 1536. Unfortunately the document is damaged by damp and a poorly executed nineteenth-century mounting onto paper. The text is incomplete. For this reason it was largely overlooked by the editors of *Letters and Papers*, who gave it one of their more summary descriptions. The text of the oath contains clauses not found in the text of the oath in the earl of Derby's Letter Book: for this see p. (iii) above. The full text of the Hampole articles appears not to survive elsewhere, although their shape can be established from the king's letter to the Pilgrims. The document is apparently unique and hence it seems worth persevering with, despite its deficiencies.

The document is a single paper sheet with the text written across the face. From the fold-marks it seems that it was originally about 12 inches wide. Most of the left-hand 3 or 4 inches is now lost through decay. It may be inferred that the document had a wide left-hand margin (it is written to the edge of the paper on the right), so the loss is not as severe as may at first sight appear. In this transcript the losses in the oath have been filled as far as possible by interpolation from the other text of the oath, but this varies in a number ways and the match is far from complete. The possibility of filling the losses in the articles is much smaller. Text in italics is taken from the other version of the oath in the Derby Letter Book. Line-ends are shown thus: /.

The numbering employed is that used by Henry VIII in his reply to the pilgrims.

The copy of the oath and the articles sent up with the Duke of Norfolk in post to the king's grace

Ye shall not enter into this our Pilgrimage of Grace for the commonwealth but only for the love that ye bear / *unto Almighty God, his faith and the Holy Church* militant and maintenance thereof, the preservation of the king's person, his issue and / [.....] *purifying of* the true noble blood to the intent to expel all villains' blood and other being / [.....] *against* the commonwealth from his grace and the privy council of the same. And that you / *shall not enter into* our said pilgrimage for no peculiar profit to yourself nor to do no displeasure / *to any private person but* by counsel of the commonwealth nor slay nor murder for no envy or malice old or / [new] *but in your hearts put* away all fear for the premises of the commonwealth. And to take before you / *the cross of God and in your* hearts his faith to the restitution of his church and to the suppression / *of these heretics* and subverters of the just laws of God. And that ye shall not depart from / [.......] devout pilgrimage without the licence in writing of the captain / [¹/₂ line lost] and counsel of the battle and ward that ye lead or go under. / [¹/₂ line lost] nor messages but that ye shall disclose to them nor for pardon / [.......] up or return without the assent of the grand captain and/ [.....] whole contents of this book.

[1] [.......] for the maintenance of the faith of Christ.

[2] For the maintenance of the church and [liberties] of the [same].

[3] [........] the common laws and the commonwealth of this realm may be used as it hath been used / [.......] time of the beginning of his highness [reign] when his nobles did order under his highness.

[4] [.......] such as hath been the subvertors of God's laws and the laws of this realm may be corrected / [.......] according to their demerits as the Lord Cromwell, the archbishop of Canterbury, / [.......] [lord chancellor], bishop of Worcester. And diverse other the maintainers of the same sect.

[5] [.......] have done or said anything against the laws by insurrections or otherwise / [to have a pardon by act of.] parliament or otherwise as surely as can be devised for all manner [of] offences done before.

[6] [.......] their articles to the honour of God and his faith, reformation of the church militant / [.....] [preserve]ation of the king and his issue for the honour and surety of the baronage and commonwealth / [of this] realm.

Source: SP1/109, fos. 247v–248r (= *LP* XI, no. 902 (2)).

(v) The Instructions for Sir Thomas Hilton and the Pontefract Articles, 4 December 1536

The instructions and articles survive in two texts, one endorsed (on the verso of the head of the roll) 'Copy of the articles to the lords of then king's council at our coming to Pontefract'. Fletcher and MacCulloch, *Tudor Rebellions*, 135–7, print the first version (hereafter 'A') without any reference to the second 'B'. There are variations between the two texts, mostly minor; the most significant, where B contains material not in A, are printed in italics.

Instructions for Sir Thomas Hilton and other his companions

[1] First to declare to the duke of Norfolk and other the lords that the intent of our meeting of our party surely is met and thought of assured truth without any manner of deceit or malignancy [*male ingyne*].

[2] The second is [to] receive the king's safe conduct under the broad seal of England and to deliver our safe conduct and promise under our hands for the assurance of the lords there.

[3] The third to entreat of our general pardon for all causes and that all persons the which is within this realm which in heart, word, and deed assisted, joined, aided, or procured the furtherance in this our quarrel may be pardoned life, lands, and goods [*fees and offices*] and that in the said pardon nor other the king's records nor writings we be not reputed, written, nor taken as rebels and traitors nor so rehearsed in the same [*but the king's true subjects* added in another hand].

[4] The fourth that Richard Cromwell nor none of his band nor sort be not at our meeting at Doncaster but absent[*ed*] the same council.

[5] The fifth to receive the king's answer by the declaration of the lords and to certify the very intent thereof to us here.

[6] Item, to know what authority the lords hath to enter in promise with us as well of our pardon as otherwise.

[7] Item, to demand what pledge they will deliver for the captain.

[8] That if the particulars [*of our petitions*] be required, then to descend unto diverse particulars [*there of*].

[The Pontefract articles]

[1] [Text in A] The first touching our faith, to have the heresies of Luther, Wycliffe, Hus, Melanchthon, Oecolampadius, Bucer, *Confessio Germaniae* [the Augsburg confession], *Apologia Malanctionis* [Melanchthon's Apology], the works of Tyndale, of Barnes, of Marshall, Rastall, St German, and other heresies of anabaptist clearly within this realm to be annulled and destroyed.

[Text in B] *The first touching our faith, to have the heretics Luther, Wycliffe, Hus, Melanchthon, Oecolampadius, Bucer,* Confessio Germanorum, apologiae Melangto[nis] [i.e. Melanchthon's *Apology for the Angsbury Confession*, 1531], *the works of Tyndale, of Barnes, of Frith, Pandiae* [?], Unio dissidencium [an anonymous collection of Patristic texts of the late 1520s against the real presence], *the books of St German in English, of Rastall and such other heretics anabaptist clearly within this realm to be annulled and destroyed.*

[2] The second to have the supreme head of the church touching *cure animarum* to be reserved unto the see of Rome as before it was accustomed to be, and to have the consecrations of the bishops [*to be restored to the clergy*] from him without any first fruits or pension to him to be paid out of this realm or else a pension reasonable for the outward defence of our faith.

[3] Item, we humbly beseech our most dread sovereign lord that the Lady Mary may be made legitimate and the former statutes therein annulled, for the danger of the title that might incur to the crown of Scotland [*to this realm and other*], that to be by parliament [*and other to be by parliament by laudable custom*].

[4] Item, to have the abbeys suppressed to be restored unto their houses, lands, and goods.

[5] Item to have the tenth and first fruits clearly discharged of the same, unless the clergy will of themselves grant a rent charge in generality to the augmentation of the Crown.

[6] Item, to have the Friars observants restored unto their houses again.

[7] Item, to have the heretics, bishops, and temporal [men] and their sect, to have condign punishment by fire or such other[*wise*], or else [they and their partakers—added] to try their quarrel with us and our part takers in battle.

[8] Item, to have the Lord Cromwell, the Lord Chancellor, and Sir Richard Rich, knight, to have condign punishment as the subvertors of the good laws of this realm and maintainers of the false sect of those heretics and the first inventors and bringers in of them.

[9] Item, that the lands in Westmorland, Cumberland, Kendal, Dent, Sedbergh, Furness, and the abbey's lands in [*Yorkshire* deleted] Mashamshire, Kirkbyshire, [and] Nidderdale may be by tenant right, and the lord to have at every change 2 years' rent for gressom and no more according to the grant now made by the lords to the commons there under their seal. And this to be done by act of parliament.

[10] Item, the statutes of handguns and crossbows to be repealed, and the penalty thereof unless it be in the king's forest or parks for the killing of his grace's deer red and fallow.

[11] [A text] Item, that Dr Leigh and Dr Layton may have condign punishment for their extortions in their time of visitations, as in taking from religious houses £40, £20, and so to [...] sums, horses, advowsons, leases, under convent seals, bribes by them taken, and other their abominable acts by them committed and done.

[B text] *Item, that Dr Leigh and Dr Layton may have condign punishment for their extortions in their time of visitations as in bribes of some religious houses £10, £20 and so to mean sums, horses, advowsons, leases under convent seals, bribes for deposition of abbeys and priories* [i.e. abbots and priors] *such sums so extorted by them and other abominable acts by them committed and done.*

[12] Item, reformation for the election of knights of [the] shire and burgesses, and for the uses amongst the lords in the parliament house after their ancient custom.

[13] Item, statute for enclosures and intakes to put in execution and that all intakes [and] enclosures since Anno iiij H[enry] vij [Anno H[enrici] viij Anno viij] to be pulled down except mountains, forest, and parks.

[14] Item, to be discharged of the quindene and taxes now granted by act of parliament [not in B].

[15] Item, to have the parliament in a convenient place at Nottingham [*as Nottingham* deleted] or York and the same shortly summoned.

[16] Item, the statute of the declaration of the Crown by will, that the same may be annulled and repealed.

[17] Item, that it be enacted by authority of parliament that all recognisances, statutes, penalties new forfeit during the time of this commotion [*convoca'* deleted] may be pardoned and discharged as well against the king as strangers.

[18] Item, the privileges and rights of the church to be confirmed by act of parliament and priests not suffered by sword unless he be disgraced, a man to be saved by his book, sanctuary to save a man for all causes in extreme need and the church for 40 days and further according to the laws as they were used in the beginning of this king's days.

[19] Item, the liberties of the church to have their old customs as the county palatine at Durham, Beverley, Ripon, St Peter of York, and such other by act of parliament.

[20] Item, to have the statute that no man shall not will his lands to be repealed.

[21] Item, that the statutes of treason for words and such like made since Anno 21 of our sovereign lord that now is to be in like wise repealed.

[22] Item, that the common laws may have place as was used in the beginning of your [*his*] grace's reign and that all injunctions may be clearly denied [*determined*] and not to be granted unless the matter be heard and determined in the Chancery.

[23] Item, that no man upon subpoena is from Trent north[wards] [to] appear but at York or by attorney unless it be directed upon pain of allegiance and for like matters concerning the king.

[24] Item, a remedy for escheators for finding of false offices and extortionate fees, taking which not be holden of the king and against the promotors thereof.

Source: First copy ['A'], SP1/112, fos. 118r (Hilton's instructions), 119r–211r (articles, written on the recto only); second copy ['B'], fos. 122r–124v (the pages written out of order) (= *LP* XI no. 1246 (1–2)). Previously printed most conveniently (though not perfectly) in Fletcher and MacCulloch, *Tudor Rebellions*, 135–7.

(vi) The Opinions of the Pseudo-Convocation at Pontefract, 4 December 1536

The opinion of the clergy of the north parts

[1] To the first article, we think that preaching against the purgatory, worshipping of saints, pilgrimage, images, and all books set forth against the same or sacraments or sacraments of the church be worthy to be reproved and condemned by convocation, and the pain to be executed that is devised for the doers to the contrary, and process to be made hereafter in heresy as was in the days of King Henry the Fourth. And the new statutes whereby heresies now lately have been greatly nourished to be annulled and abrogated and that the holidays may be observed according to the laws and laudable customs and that the bidding of the beads and preaching may be observed as hath been used by old custom.

[2] To the second, we think that the king's highness nor any temporal man may not be supreme head of the church by the laws of God or have or exercise any jurisdiction or power spiritual by the same, and all acts of parliament made to the contrary to be revoked.

[3] To the third, we say we be not sufficiently instructed in the fact nor in the process therein made but we refer it to the determination of the church to whom it was appealed.

[4] To the fourth, we think that no clerk ought to be put to death without degradation by the laws of the church.

[5] To the fifth, we say that no man ought to be drawn out of sanctuary but in certain causes expressed in the laws of the church.

[6] To the sixth, we say that the clergy of the north parts hath not granted nor consented to the payment of the tenths or first fruits of benefices in their convocation, and also we may make no such personal grant by the laws of the church, and we think that no temporal man hath authority by the laws of God to claim any such tenths or first fruits of any benefice or spiritual promotion.

[7] To the seventh, we think that lands given to God, the church, or religious men may not be taken away and put to profane uses by the laws of God.

[8] To the eighth, we think that dispensations upon just causes lawfully granted by the pope of Rome to be good and to be accepted and pardons have been allowed by general councils of the Lateran and Vienne and laws of the church.

[9] To the ninth, we think that by the laws of the church, general councils, interpretations of approved doctors and consent of Christian people, the pope of Rome hath been taken for the head of the church and vicar of Christ and so ought to be taken.

[10] To the tenth, we think that the examination and correction of deadly sin belongeth to the ministers of the church by the laws of the same, which be consonant to God's laws.

[11] Further, we think it convenient that the laws of the church may be openly read in universities as hath been used heretofore and that such clerks as be in prison or fled out of the realm for withstanding of the king's supremacy in the church may be set at liberty and restored without damage and that such books and works as do entreat of the primacy of the church of Rome may be freely kept and read notwithstanding any prohibition [to the] contrary and that the articles of praemunire may be declared by acts of parliament to the intent no man be in danger thereof without a prohibition first awarded.

[12] And that such apostates as be gone from religion without sufficient and lawful dispensation of the see of Rome may be compelled to return to their houses and that all sums of money as tenths, first fruits, and other arrearages granted to the king by parliament or convocation and due to be paid before the first day of the next parliament may be remitted and forgiven for the causes and reasons above rehearsed.

[13] And we the said clergy say that for lack of time, instruction in these articles and for want of books we declare this our opinion for this time, referring our further determination in the premisses to the next convocation.

[14] Also we desire that the statute commanding the clergy to exhibit their dispensations granted by the pope before the feast of Michaelmas next coming may be revoked at the next parliament.

Source: SP1/112, fo. 116r–117v, also BL, Cotton Ms, Cleopatra E, v, p. 413; printed (with minor omissions) in Dodds, *Pilgrimage*, I, 383–5. Noticed (but not printed) at *LP* XI, no. 1245.

Bibliography of Printed Sources

Printed Primary Sources

BATESON, M. (ed.), 'Aske's examination', *EHR* 5 (1890), 550–73.
—— 'The Pilgrimage of Grace' [printing 'The manner of the taking of Robert Aske'], *EHR* 5 (1890), 331–43.
BREWER, J. S. *et al.* (eds.), *Letters and Papers, Foreign and Domestic, of the Reign of Henry VIII*, 23 vols. in 38 (1862–1932).
BRAY, G. (ed.), *Documents of the English Reformation* (1994).
BROWN, W. (ed.), 'Yorkshire Star Chamber proceedings', *YASRS* 41, 45, 51, 70 (1909–27).
Calendar of State Papers, Spanish.
Calendar of State Papers, Foreign, 1558–9.
CALEY J., and J. HUNTER (eds.), *Valor Ecclesiasticus, temp. Henrici VIII, auctoritate regia institutus*, 7 vols. (1810–34).
CHAMBERS, D. S. (ed.), *Faculty Office Registers, 1534–1549* (1966).
CLAY, J. W. (ed.), 'Yorkshire Monasteries: Suppression Papers', *YASRS* 48 (1912).
—— *Dugdale's Visitation of Yorkshire with Additions*, 3 vols. (1899–1917).
COX, J. C. (ed.), 'The True Confession of William Stapilton . . .', *Trans. East Riding Antiquarian Soc.*, 10 (1903), 80–106.
DICKENS, A. G. (ed.), 'New Records of the Pilgrimage of Grace', *YAJ* 33 (1937), 298–308.
—— 'Clifford Letters of the Sixteenth Century', *Surtees Soc.*, 172 (1962).
DOWLING, M., 'William Latymers Cronickille of Anne Bulleyne', *Camden Miscellany 31*, Camden 4th ser., 39 (1990).
DUDDING, R. W. (ed.), *The First Churchwardens Book of Louth, 1500–24* (1941).
FOSTER, C. W., and THOMPSON, A. H. (eds.), 'The Chantry Certificates for Lincoln and Lincolnshire Returned in 1548 Under the Act of Parliament of 1 Edward VI', *Reports and Papers of the Associated Architectural Socs.*, 36 (1922), 183–294.
HALL, E., *The union of the two noble and illustre famelies of Lancastre and Yorke* (1809 edn.).
HENRY VIII, *Answere made by the kynges highnes to the petitions of the rebelles in Yorkshire, Anno MDXXXVI* (1536), repr. *The English Experience*, 872, (1977).
HERRTAGE, S. J. (ed.), 'England in the Reign of Henry the Eighth, part 1', *Early English Text Soc.*, extra ser., 22 (1878).

Holme, Wilfred, *The fall and evil success of rebellion* (1537, pub. 1573).

Hoyle, R. W. (ed.), 'Thomas Master's Narrative of the Pilgrimage of Grace', *NH* 21 (1985), 53–79.

—— 'Early Tudor Craven: Subsidies and Assessments, 1510–1547', *YASRS* 145 (1987).

—— 'Letters of the Cliffords, Lords Clifford and Earls of Cumberland, *c.*1500–*c.*1565', *Camden Miscellany 31*, Camden 4th Ser., 44 (1992), 1–189.

Leach, A. F., 'Beverley Town Documents', *Selden Soc.*, 14 (1900).

Maddison, A. R. (ed.), 'Lincolnshire Pedigrees', *Harleian Soc.*, 50–2, 55 (1902–6).

Michelmore, D. J. H., 'The Fountains Abbey Lease Book', *YASRS* 140 (1981).

Nicholls, Sir H. (ed.), *Proceedings and Ordinances of the Privy Council of England*, 7 vols. (1834–7).

Raine, J. (ed.), 'The Priory of Hexham', *Surtees Soc.*, 44, 46 (1864–5).

Salter, H. E. (ed.), 'A Subsidy Granted in the Diocese of Lincoln in 1526', *Oxford Historical Soc.*, 63 (1909).

Speed, J., *The History of Great Britain* (3rd edn., 1632).

Statutes of the Realm, 11 vols. (1810–28).

Thomas, W., *The Pilgrim. A dialogue on the life and actions of King Henry the Eighth*, ed. J. A. Froude (1861).

Toller, T. N. (ed.), 'Correspondence of Edward, third Earl of Derby, during the years 24 to 31 Henry VIII, reserved in a ms in the possession of Miss ffarington of Worden Hall', *Chetham Soc.*, NS 19 (1890).

Raine, J. *et al.* (eds.), 'Testamenta Eboracensia', *Surtees Soc.*, 4, 30, 45, 53, 79, 106 (1836–1902).

State Papers During the Reign of Henry the Eighth, 11 vols. (1830–52).

Wallis, J. E. W., 'The Narrative of the Indictment of the Traitors at Whalley and Cartmell, 1536–7', *Chetham Miscellany V*, Chetham Soc., NS 90 (1931).

Webb, C. C., 'The Churchwardens' Accounts of St Michael, Spurriergate, York, 1518–1548', *Borthwick Texts and Calendars*, 20–1 (1997).

Wilkins, D. (ed.), *Concilia Magnae Brittaniae et Hiberniae*, 4 vols. (1737).

Williams, C. H. (ed.), *English Historical Documents, 1485–1558* (1967).

Secondary Sources

Adams, S., 'Politics', in 'The Eltonian Legacy', *Trans. Royal Historical Soc.*, 7 (1997), 247–65.

Bernard, G. W., *The Power of the Early Tudor Nobility: A Study of the Fourth and Fifth Earls of Shrewsbury* (1985).

—— 'The Fall of Anne Boleyn', *EHR* 106 (1991), 584–610.

—— 'The Fall of Anne Boleyn: A Rejoinder', *EHR* 107 (1992), 651–64.

—— 'Anne Boleyn's Religion', *HJ* 36 (1993), 1–20.

—— 'The Making of Religious Policy, 1533–1546: Henry VIII and the Search for the Middleway', *HJ* 41 (1998), 321–49.

—— 'Elton's Cromwell', *History*, 83 (1998), 587–607.

BINDOFF, S. T. (ed.), *The History of Parliament: The Commons, 1509–1558*, 3 vols. (1982).

BINNS, J., 'Scarborough and the Pilgrimage of Grace', *Scarborough Archaeological and History Soc.*, 33 (1997), 23–39.

BOWKER, M., *The Henrician Reformation: The Diocese of Lincoln under John Longland, 1521–1547* (1981).

—— 'Lincolnshire 1536: Heresy, Schism and Religious Discontent?', in D. Baker (ed.), 'Schism, Heresy and Religious Protest', *Studies in Church History*, 9 (1972), 195–212.

—— 'Historical Survey, 1450–1750', in D. M. Owen (ed.), *A History of Lincoln Minster* (1994), 164–209.

BUSH, M. L., *The Pilgrimage of Grace: A Study of the Rebel Armies of October 1536* (1996).

—— 'The Problem of the Far North: A Study of the Crisis of 1537 and its Consequences', *NH* 6 (1971), 40–63.

—— '"Up for the commonweal": The Significance of Tax Grievances in the English rebellions of 1536', *EHR* 106 (1991), 299–318.

—— 'Captain Poverty and the Pilgrimage of Grace', *Historical Res.*, 65 (1992), 17–36.

—— 'The Richmondshire Uprising of October 1536 and the Pilgrimage of Grace', *NH* 29 (1993), 64–98.

—— and BOWNES, D., *The Defeat of the Pilgrimage of Grace: A Study of the Postpardon Revolts of December 1536 to March 1537 and Their Effect* (1999).

BURTON, THOMAS, ed. J. RAINE, *The History and Antiquities of Hemingborough* (1888).

CARTWRIGHT, J. J., *Chapters of Yorkshire History* (1872).

CLARK, M., 'Kendal: The Protestant Exception', *Trans. Cumberland and Westmorland Antiquarian and Arch. Soc.*, 2nd. ser., 95 (1995), 137–52.

CONRAD, F. W., 'The Problem of Counsel Reconsidered: The Case of Sir Thomas Elyot', in P. A. Fidler and T. F. Mayer (eds.), *Political Thought and the Tudor Commonwealth* (1992), 75–107.

COOPER, C. H. and T., *Athenae Cantabrigiensis*, 2 vols. (1858–61).

CROSS, C., 'Priests Into Ministers: The Establishment of Protestant Practice in the City of York, 1530–1630', in P. N. Brooks (ed.), *Reformation Principle and Practice: Essays in Honour of A. G. Dickens* (1980).

CROSS, C., 'Monasticism and Society in the Diocese of York, 1520–1540', *TRHS*, 5th ser., 38 (1988), 131–45.

—— 'Monks, Friars and the Royal Supremacy in Sixteenth-Century Yorkshire', in D. Wood (ed.), *The Church and Sovereignty, c.590–1918, Studies in Church History,* subsidia 9 (1991), 437–56.

—— and N. VICKERS, 'Monks, Friars and Nuns in Sixteenth-Century Yorkshire', *YASRS* 150 (1995).

DAVIES, C. S. L., 'The Pilgrimage of Grace Reconsidered', *Past and Present*, 41 (1966), 54–76, repr. in P. Slack (ed.), *Rebellion, Popular Protest and the Social Order in Early Modern England* (1984), 16–36.

—— 'Religion and the Pilgrimage of Grace', in A. Fletcher and J. Stevenson (eds.), *Order and Disorder in Early Modern England* (1986), 58–91.

DICKENS, A. G., *Lollards and Protestants in the Diocese of York* (1959).

—— 'The Yorkshire Submissions to Henry VIII, 1541', *EHR* 53 (1938), 267–75.

—— 'Sedition and Conspiracy in Yorkshire During the Later Years of Henry VIII', *YAJ* 34 (1939), 379–98, repr in id., *Reformation Studies* (1982), 1–20.

—— 'Secular and Religious Motivation in the Pilgrimage of Grace', in C. J. Cuming (ed.), *Studies in Church History*, 4 (1967), 39–64; repr. in id., *Reformation Studies* (1982), 57–82.

DODDS, M. H., and R., *The Pilgrimage of Grace 1536–1537 and the Exeter Conspiracy, 1538*, 2 vols. (1915).

ELLIS, S. G., *Tudor Frontiers and Noble Power: The Making of a British State* (1995).

—— 'Tudor Northumberland: British History in an English County', in S. J. Connolly (ed.), *Kingdoms United? Great Britain and Ireland Since 1500: Integration and Diversity* (1999), 29–42.

ENGLISH, B. A., and C. B. L. BARR, 'The Records Formerly in St Mary's Tower, York', *YAJ* 42 (1966–70), 198–235, 359–86, 465–518.

ELTON, G. R., *Policy and Police: The Enforcement of the Reformation in the Age of Thomas Cromwell* (1972).

—— *Reform and Renewal: Thomas Cromwell and the Common Weal* (1973).

—— *Reform and Reformation: England, 1509–1558* (1977).

—— 'Politics and the Pilgrimage of Grace', in B. Malament (ed.), *After the Reformation* (1979), 25–56; repr. in id., *Studies in Tudor and Stuart Politics and Government*, 4 vols. (1974–92), III, 183–215.

—— 'Thomas More and the Opposition to Henry VIII', in id., *Studies in Tudor and Stuart Politics and Government*, I, 155–172.

EMDEN, A. B., *A Biographical Register of the University of Cambridge to AD 1500* (1963).

—— *A Biographical Register of the University of Oxford, AD 1501–1540* (1974).

FLETCHER, A., *Tudor Rebellions*, 3rd edn. (1983).

—— and MacCulloch, D., *Tudor Rebellions*, 4th edn. (1997).

Fox, A., 'Rumour, News and Popular Political Opinion in Elizabethan and Early Stuart England', *HJ* 40 (1997), 597–620.

Goulding, R. W., *On the Court Rolls of the Manor of Louth* (?1901).

—— *The Vicars of the Vicarage of Louth* (1906).

—— *The Building of Louth Spire, 1501–1515* (1908).

Gunn, S. J., *Charles Brandon, Duke of Suffolk, c.1484–1545* (1988).

—— 'Peers, commons and gentry in the Lincolnshire rebellion of 1536', *Past and Present*, 123 (1989), 52–79.

Guy, J., *The Cardinal's Court: The Impact of Thomas Wolsey in Star Chamber* (1977).

—— 'The King's Council and Political Participation', in A. Fox and J. Guy, *Reassessing the Henrician Age: Humanism, Politics and Reform, 1500–1550* (1986), 121–47.

—— 'The Privy Council: Revolution and Evolution', in C. Coleman and D. Starkey (eds.), *Revolution Reassessed: Revisions in the History of Tudor Government and Administration* (1986), 59–85.

—— 'Wolsey and the Tudor Polity', in S. J. Gunn and P. G. Lindley (eds.), *Cardinal Wolsey, Church, State and Art* (1991), 54–75.

—— 'Thomas Wolsey, Thomas Cromwell and the Reform of Henrician Government', in D. MacCulloch (ed.), *The Reign of Henry VIII: Politics, Poverty and Piety* (1995), 35–57.

Haigh, C., *Reformation and Resistance in Tudor Lancashire* (1975).

—— 'The Last Years of the Lancashire Monasteries and the Pilgrimage of Grace', *Chetham Soc.*, 3rd ser., 17 (1969).

—— 'Religion', in 'The Eltonian Legacy', *Trans. Royal Historical Soc.*, 7 (1997), 281–99.

Harrison, S. M., *The Pilgrimage of Grace in the Lake Counties, 1536–7* (1981).

Hicks, M. A., 'The Yorkshire Rebellion of 1489 Reconsidered', *NH* 22 (1986), 39–62.

Hilton, R. H., *The English Peasantry in the Later Middle Ages* (1975).

Hodgett, G. A. J., *Tudor Lincolnshire* (1975).

Holmes, C., *Seventeenth-Century Lincolnshire* (1980).

Hoyle, R. W., 'The First Earl of Cumberland: A Reputation Reassessed', *NH* 22 (1986), 62–94.

—— 'Land and Landed Relations in Craven, Yorkshire, c.1520–1600', D.Phil. thesis, University of Oxford (1986).

—— 'Monastic Leasing Before the Dissolution: The Evidence of Bolton Priory and Fountains Abbey', *YAJ* 61 (1989), 111–37.

—— 'Thomas Lord Darcy and the Rothwell Tenants, c.1526–1534', *YAJ* 63 (1991), 85–107.

HOYLE, R. W., 'Henry Percy, Sixth Earl of Northumberland, and the Fall of the House of Percy, 1527–37', in G. W. Bernard (ed.), *The Tudor Nobility* (1992), 180–209.

—— 'Resistance and Manipulation in Early Tudor Taxation: Some Evidence From the North', *Archives*, 20 (1993), 158–75.

—— 'The Earl, the Archbishop and the Council: The Affray at Fulford, May 1504', in R. E. Archer and S. Walker (eds.), *Rulers and Ruled in Late Medieval England: Essays Presented to Gerald Harriss* (1995), 239–56.

—— 'The Origins of the Dissolution of the Monasteries', *HJ* 38 (1995), 275–305.

—— 'The Decline of the Northern Nobility: A Case of Low Resolution Telescopy?' (forthcoming).

—— 'The Fortunes of the Tempest Family of Bracewell and Bowling Hall in the Sixteenth Century' (forthcoming).

—— 'Petitioning and Popular Politics in the Early Sixteenth Century' (forthcoming).

—— and H. R. T. SUMMERSON, 'The Earl of Derby and the Deposition of the Abbot of Furness, 1514', *NH* 30 (1994), 184–92.

IVES, E. W., *The Common Lawyers of Pre-Reformation England* (1983).

—— *Anne Boleyn* (1986).

—— 'The Fall of Anne Boleyn: A Rejoinder', *EHR* 107 (1992), 665–74.

—— 'Anne Boleyn and the Early Reformation in England: The Contemporary Evidence', *HJ* 37 (1994), 389–400.

JACKS, S., 'Dissolution Dates for the Monasteries Dissolved Under the Act of 1536', *Bulletin of the Institute of Historical Res.*, 43 (1970), 161–81.

JAMES, M. E., *Family, Lineage and Civil Society: A Study of Society, Politics and Mentality in the Durham Region, 1500–1640* (1974).

—— *Society, Politics and Culture: Studies in Early Modern England* (1986).

—— 'Change and Continuity in the Tudor North: Thomas, First Lord Wharton', *Borthwick Paper*, 27 (1965), repr. in id., *Society, Politics and Culture*, 91–147.

—— 'Obedience and Dissent in Henrician England: The Lincolnshire Revolt, 1536', *Past and Present*, 48 (1970), 3–78; repr. in id., *Society, Politics and Culture*, 188–269.

—— 'English Politics and the Concept of Honour, 1485–1642', in id., *Society, Politics and Culture*, 308–415.

JONES, B. C., 'Westmorland Pack-horse Men in Southampton', *Trans. Cumberland and Westmorland AAS*, 2nd ser., 59 (1960), 65–84.

KNOWLES, D., *The Religious Orders in England*, 3 vols. (1948–59).

KÜMIN, B., *The Shaping of a Community: The Rise and Reformation of the English Parish, c.1400–1560* (1996).

LEHMBERG, S. E., *The Later Parliaments of Henry VIII* (1977).

LIEDL, J., 'The Penitent Pilgrim: William Calverley and the Pilgrimage of Grace', *Sixteenth Century Journal*, 25 (1994), 586–95.

MACCULLOCH, D., *Suffolk Under the Tudors: Politics and Religion in an English County, 1500–1600* (1986).

—— *Thomas Cranmer: A Life* (1996).

—— 'Kett's Rebellion in Context', in *Past and Present*, 84 (1979), 36–59; repr. in P. Slack (ed.), *Rebellion, Popular Protest and the Social Order in Early Modern England* (1984), 39–62.

—— 'Henry VIII and the Reform of the Church', in id. (ed.), *The Reign of Henry VIII: Politics, Poverty and Piety* (1995), 159–80.

MCCUTCHEON, K. L., 'Yorkshire Fairs and Markets to the End of the Eighteenth Century', *Proc. Thoresby Soc.*, 39 (1940).

MARSHALL, P., *The Catholic Priesthood and the English Reformation* (1994).

MILNER, E., E. BENHAM (ed.), *Records of the Lumleys of Lumley Castle* (1904).

MORTON, C. E., 'The Walsingham Conspiracy of 1537', *Historical Res.*, 63 (1990), 29–43.

NEWMAN, C. M., *Robert Bowes and the Pilgrimage of Grace* (1997).

NICHOLSON, J., and R. BURN, *The History and Antiquities of the Counties of Westmorland and Cumberland*, 2 vols. (1771; repr. 1976).

PHYTHIAN-ADAMS, C. V., 'Urban Decay in Later Medieval England', in P. Abrams and E. A. Wrigley (eds.), *Towns in Societies* (1978).

REID, R. R., *The King's Council in the North* (1921; repr. 1975).

REX, R., *Henry VIII and the English Reformation* (1977).

RICHARDSON, W. C., *History of the Court of Augmentations, 1536–1554* (1961).

SCARISBRICK, J. J., *Henry VIII* (1968).

SCOTT, D., *The Stricklands of Sizergh Castle: The Records of Twenty-Five Generations of a Westmorland Family* (1908).

SHEAIL, JOHN, 'The Distribution of Wealth in England as Indicated in the 1524/5 Lay Subsidy Returns', *List and Index Soc.*, special ser., 28–9 (1998).

SHEILS, W., and S., 'Textiles and Reform: Halifax and its Hinterland', in P. Collinson and J. Craig (eds.), *The Reformation in English Towns, 1500–1640* (1999), 130–43.

SMITH, R. B., *Land and Politics in the England of Henry VIII: The West Riding* (1970).

SOMERVILLE, Sir ROBERT, *History of the Duchy of Lancaster*, 2 vols. (1953, 1970).

STONE, L., *The Crisis of the Aristocracy, 1558–1641* (1965).

TEMPEST, Mrs A. C., 'Nicholas Tempest: A Sufferer in the Pilgrimage of Grace', *YAJ* 11 (1891), 247–78.

VENN, J., and S. A., *Alumni Cantabrigiensis*, 4 vols. (1922–7).

Victoria County History, volumes for *Cheshire, Yorkshire, Yorkshire, East Riding*.

Index

The names of counties provided are for pre-1974 counties

Acclom, William 199–200, 278, 445
Aglionby, Henry 44
Ales, Alexander 78
Alford (Lincs.) 118
Alnwick (Northumb.) 217
Ampthill, muster at 6, 170, 173, 283–6,
    449
Ancaster Heath (Lincs.) 134, 140, 141
Aragon, Katherine of 37, 56, 57, 76
Ascue, Robert 123, 192
Ascue, Sir William 114, 115, 116, 118,
    119, 120, 147, 160, 161
Ashby, William 107, 111
Aske, Christopher 26, 45, 46, 50, 191,
    223, 333, 337, 444
Aske, John 67, 191, 406
Aske, Robert 3, 5, 6–11, 13, 67, 179, 184,
    209, 217, 222, 224, 227, 232, 236,
    248, 255, 256, 264, 266, 276, 291,
    306, 310, 316–17, 323, 328, 329, 331,
    332, 334, 335, 342–3, 344, 345, 346,
    347, 349, 350, 372, 373, 377, 383,
    390, 395, 397, 406, 416, 419, 423,
    426, 433, 435, 438, 439, 440, 442,
    444, 446, 452
  alleged letter to Beverley x, 183, 184 n.
  and Lincolnshire articles 197–8, 199,
    203, 205, 206–7
  and Pontefract conference 358–64
  apologia for monasteries 47–8
  arrest of 399
  at Doncaster conference 353–4
  career and circle of 45–6, 337
  character of 412–14
  commitment to Pontefract agreement
    373, 376–7, 384–5
  contribution to Pilgrimage 412–14
  criticizes nobility 60–1
  Darcy told to arrest him 318–21
  evidence against at trial 408
  excluded from pardons 311, 324
  executed 410
  goes to court 368
  goes to Pontefract 277–80
  in Lincolnshire 122–3, 140, 142, 144,
    148, 190–4, 210
  meets Thomas Strangeways 277
  memoir by 24–5
  overture to Norfolk 338
  powerbase amongst commons 295, 299,
    414
  proclamation to city of York, printed
    456–7
  raises Howdenshire and Marshland 187
  reformulates Lincolnshire articles
    204–7, 209
  relations with Darcy 294–5
  religious preferences of 45–8
  Skipwith Moor muster 195–6
  travels to Lincoln 193–4
  trial of 406–10
Aske, Robert, younger 195–6
Ashton (or Eshe), Robert 186, 190, 226
Atkinson, John 237
Audeley, Thomas, Lord Audeley, Lord
    Chancellor 61, 62, 63, 141, 142, 169,
    301, 351, 406, 451
Aughton (Yorks.) 193, 194, 360
Ayscough, Christopher 163

Babthorpe, William 193, 195–6, 273, 326,
    346, 347, 353, 421

Bardney Abbey (Lincs.) 404, 453
Barlings Abbey (Lincs.) 133–4, 145, 402, 404, 405, 437, 453
Barnard Castle (Dur.) 214–15, 385, 394
Barnes, Robert 350, 460
Barton upon Humber (Yorks.) 176, 191, 307
Bawne, George 178, 226
Beacons, firing of 176, 186, 187, 223, 258, 310, 331, 361, 377
Beckwith, Leonard 187, 200, 275, 444–5
Bellow, John 109, 174
bells, ringing of to raise commons 106, 111, 119, 120, 121, 125, 139–40, 148, 183, 193, 194, 331, 435
Bellingham, Sir Robert 234, 236
Bentham Moor (Yorks.) 237
Beverley 6, 7, 178, 267, 373, 379, 425, 427, 428, 434, 440
    commons of 142–3, 149, 181–2, 373, 375, 376–9, 384, 428
    description of 179–82
    rising in 183–8
Bigod, Sir Francis 33, 332, 374, 390, 396, 406, 407, 410, 419, 439
    flees commons 219
    in Pilgrimage 377
    religious tastes of 50–1
Bigod's rising 378–84, 395
Bilsby, Sir Andrew 120, 121, 145, 152
Bishop Auckland (Dur.) 8
    muster at 221
Bishopdale (Yorks.) commons of 229, 230
Birkbeck, Thomas 245
Blenkinsop, Chris. 244
Blenkinsop, Thomas 214, 244
Blithman, William 212
Bolingbroke (Lincs.) 106, 131, 132
    commissary's court at 103
Boleyn, Anne 34, 56–7
    attitude to monasteries 77–8
    fall of 75–82
    reputation of 57
Boleyn, George, see Rochford, viscount
Bolton Castle (Yorks.) 213

Bolton Priory (Yorks.) 223
Borough (Yorks.), muster at 377, 380–1, 395, 439, 442
Boston (Lincs.) 27, 112, 134, 140, 141, 142, 145, 158, 424, 428
Bowes, Sir Robert 2, 9, 10, 61, 221, 225, 248, 292, 298, 304, 306, 308, 309, 311, 320, 321, 325, 328, 329, 332, 346, 353, 360, 368, 385, 396, 416, 443, 446, 550
    at York conference 329
    held at court 316, 317
    in Norfolk's council 390, 421
    sent to Henry VIII 300, 301
    takes charge at Richmond 215–17
Bowyer, Richard 200, 396
Brancepeth (Dur.) 221
Brandon, Charles, duke of Suffolk (d. 1545) 6, 22, 151, 153, 167, 169, 179, 284, 287, 307, 319, 334, 336, 341, 366, 367, 404
Brayton (Yorks.) 261, 275, 276
Breyer, William 183, 184, 212, 234, 440
Bridlington priory (Yorks.) 226, 382, 402
    prior of, see Wood, William
Broadfield Oak (Cumb.) musters at 247, 250, 392
Brough (Westm.) 54, 249
Brougham Castle (Westm.) 392
Browne, Sir Anthony 283, 307–8
Bryan, Sir Francis 170, 171, 175, 281, 336, 336, 338, 367
Bucer, Martin 350, 460
Buckden (Yorks.) 229–30
Bulmer, Sir John 299, 406, 407, 410, 432, 444
    attempted rising by 397–9
Bulmer, Ralph 397–8, 406, 407
Bulmer, Sir Ralph 221
Bulmer, Sir William 219, 385, 436
Burgh, Thomas, third lord (d. 1550) 97, 120, 122, 148, 158, 160, 161, 162, 163, 178, 258
    see also 'Nicholas'
Burscough Priory (Lancs.) 330

Burwell, William 226
Bush, M. L. (historian) 16–17, 52, 154
Butler, Sir Thomas 422
Byron, Sir John 166, 422

Caistor (Lincs.) 5, 93, 167, 172, 164, 191
  Louth commons go to 111–16
Caldbeck (Cumb.) 245
Calverley, William 4
'Captain Cobbler', see Melton, Nicholas
Carlisle (Cumb.) 9, 11, 54, 223, 241–2,
  246–7, 371, 390, 392, 394, 428
Carr, Ralph 40–1
Carr, Robert 162, 404
Cartmel Priory (Lancs.) 238–9, 401
Catterall, John 53, 230
Cawood (Yorks.) 178, 181, 200, 275
Cawood, Gervais 195–6, 277
Cawrser, William 190, 434
Chaloner, Robert 54, 298, 330, 346, 347,
  353
Chapuys, Eustace 57, 67–9, 75, 76, 322
Charles V 67, 68, 69, 70, 322, 416
Cheney, Margaret 397–9, 406, 407,
  410
Cholmeley, Sir Roger 227, 444
church:
  liberties of 301, 352, 462
  rumoured confiscation of church goods
    88, 89–90, 157, 212
  rumoured closure of churches 90–1,
    234
Clarencieux Herald 371
Claydon, John 422
Cleator (Cumb.) 54
clergy:
  absentee 42–3, 252–3
  at Caistor 113
  at Horncastle 132–3
  at Louth 108–9, 110, 138–9
  called to prepare articles 331
  in Cumberland 248
  give money to commons 139, 437
  opinons sought at Pontefract 343,
    344–7, 355–7

rumours spread by 91–2, 416
taxation by rebels 253, 438–9
Clifford, Lady Eleanor 444
Clifford, Henry, first earl of Cumberland
  (d. 1542) 22, 32, 34, 35–6, 38, 39, 45,
  49, 53, 54, 212, 213, 223–4, 229, 244,
  252, 259, 329, 391, 394, 412, 424,
  426, 436, 443, 445
Clifford, Henry Lord Clifford, (later
  second earl of Cumberland) 38–9,
  46, 264, 325, 444
Clifford, Thomas 391–2
Clifton, Gervais 324
Clinton, Lord, see Fiennes, Edward
Clitheroe Moor (Lancs.), muster at 232–3
Cockerell, James 406, 409
Cockermouth (Cumb.) 246
Collins, Lancelot 200, 438
Collins, William 27, 234–6, 401, 426
commons:
  bills posted by 373–4, 385, 386, 390,
    435–6
  character of 425–7
  conflicts within 445–6
  interest in news 429–33
  leaders of 20, 248, 385
  letters by 20, 195, 217–18, 240–1, 435
  mustering of 222
  payment of 438
  poems by 238
  relations with gentry 140–53, 433–5,
    445–6
  reluctance to disperse from Doncaster
    304
  reluctance to accept settlement 360–2
  selection of captains by 186, 433–4
  solidarity of 255
  terminology of 425–7
Conishead Abbey (Lancs.) 238–9
conspiracy 450
  evidence for 411–20
constables 436
Constable, Sir John 188
Constable, Sir Marmaduke 53, 163, 164,
  166, 316, 376, 409, 421

Constable, Sir Robert 3, 273, 299, 307,
    328, 329, 330, 333, 383, 384, 396,
    399, 406, 408, 410, 418–19, 428, 431
  Edwin, servant of 199–200
Constable, Sir William, elder 33, 178,
    188
convocation, of 1536 82–5
Conyers, Christopher, Lord Conyers
    (d. 1538) 358
Conyers, Sir George 219
Conyers, William 221
Cook, Lawrence 294
Coppindale, [   ] 219
Coppledike, Sir John 131, 132
Cottingham (Yorks.) 185, 186
council, king's 314, 319, 418
  critique of 61–3, 204, 207, 455–6
  great council 367
  privy 60, 301
  see also counsel
counsel:
  concept of 59–63
  failure of 60–3, 450–1, 455–6
Courtenay, Henry, marq. of Exeter
    (ex. 1539) 284, 286, 406
Coverham Abbey (Yorks.) 50, 79, 213,
    219, 254
Craike, Robert 183, 376, 377
Cranmer, Thomas, archbishop of
    Canterbury 58, 61, 63, 155, 301, 351,
    451, 456
  explains Pilgrimage to Bullinger 29
Craven (Yorks.) 330
  rising in 227–33, 436
Creswell, Percival 62, 257, 308, 318–20
Cromwell, Richard 170, 171, 175, 212,
    346, 431, 460
Cromwell, Thomas Lord Cromwell 5, 10,
    26, 41, 60, 61, 62, 82, 109, 154, 155,
    157, 160, 162, 173, 262, 301, 307,
    320, 324, 329, 334, 335, 351, 365,
    368, 372, 374, 377, 386, 388, 414,
    427, 451, 456, 461
  and fall of Anne Boleyn 75–82
  as vice-regent 65, 83, 85

chaplains of 253
servant of 103
Cumberland, earls of, see Clifford, Henry
Cumberland:
  proclamation employed in 251
  rising in 8, 9, 241–2, 244–7
Curson, Richard 111, 112
Curtis, Anthony 307, 338
Curwen, Hugh 421
Curwen, Richard 421
customs 235, 238
Cutler, George 161, 163, 165

Dacre, Sir Christopher 11, 247, 248, 254,
    392
Dacre, William, third Lord (d. 1563) 34,
    35, 39, 68
Dakyn, Dr John 25, 212–16, 222, 355,
    360, 396, 434
Dalton in Furness (Lancs.) 401
Danby, Sir Christopher 214–15, 221, 225,
    293
Darcy, Sir Arthur 46, 68, 228, 231, 258,
    262, 263, 264, 267–8, 273, 289, 386,
    391, 394
  acquires Sawley Abbey 79
Darcy, Sir George 46, 68, 193, 273, 275,
    278, 309, 389–90, 397
Darcy, Thomas, Lord (d. 1537) x, 3, 7, 22,
    35, 39, 51, 62, 158, 169, 176, 178,
    200, 202, 212, 222, 223, 232, 251,
    252, 253, 282, 287, 293, 294, 299,
    304, 305, 306, 317, 316, 322, 323,
    328, 333, 334, 336, 354–5, 358, 364,
    367, 368, 369, 372, 389–90, 391, 395,
    397, 431, 449, 450, 452
  and Rothwell tenants 33
  arrest of 399
  asked to defect 299
  career of 37–8
  defence of Pontefract Castle 256–81
  discusses treason with Chapuys 68–70
  employs 'policy' 265–6, 266–9, 274–7
  evidence against 408
  executed 410

hears of Lincolnshire rising 258
his 'muster book' 257, 271–3, 415
his badges 416–17
his Letter Book 23, 257
hostility to Lutheranism 68–70
letters to Henry VIII 259–61, 263–4
maintains his loyalty to Henry VIII
    256–8
makes overtures to Aske 277
musters supporters 269–73
position after Pilgrims disperse 308–10
protests loyalty 415
religious preferences of 44
role in Pilgrimage 414–15
seeks death 309
told to capture Aske 318–20
trial of 405–10
Darlington (Dur.) 430
Davies, C. S. L. (historian) 13, 15, 97
Delaryver, Thomas 395
Dent/Dentdale (Yorks.) 8, 212, 223, 426
    commons of 330
    rising in 234–6
Dent, William 181
Derby, earl of, see Stanley, Edward
Diamond, James, 'General of the Foot'
    20
Dickens, A. G. (historian) 13
Dissolution of the monasteries 47–50, 61,
    70–4, 424, 455
divorce, the 56–8, 356
Dobson, John 67
Dodds, M. H. and R. (historians) 12–13
Doncaster (Yorks.) 8, 43, 276, 290, 419,
    446
    conference at, called by Henry VIII
    326–7; meets 357–64
    truce at 298–305
Doncaster Bridge 303, 324
Driffield (Yorks.) 190, 434
Dunne, Thomas 187, 189
Durham (city) 31
    bishop of 428; see also Tunstall,
        Cuthbert
    Norfolk at 395

Durham (county) 387
    rising in 219–22
Dymock, Sir Arthur 126
Dymock, Sir Edward (Mr Sheriff) 93, 97,
    124, 128, 130, 140, 145, 154, 175, 440
Dymock, Sir Robert 126, 128
Dymock, Thomas 128, 147, 154

Earls Colne (Essex.) 100
Eden Valley (Westm.), rising in 8, 54,
    241–5, 424, 427
Edenhall (Cumb.), vicar of 245, 248
Eglisfield, John 20
Ellerker (Yorks.) 191
Ellerker, Sir Ralph the elder 180–1, 375,
    384, 425, 441
Ellerker, Sir Ralph the younger 9, 10,
    61, 180, 183, 185, 186, 187, 191, 258,
    267, 298, 304, 306, 308, 309, 311,
    320, 321, 325, 328, 329–32, 346, 353,
    367, 368, 384, 395, 416, 440–1, 450
    at York conference 329
    held at court 316, 317
    in Norfolk's council 390, 421
    sent to see Henry VIII 300, 301
    surrenders 178
Ellerker, William 191
Elton, G. R. (historian) 14–16
enclosure 331, 347, 370, 394
    complaints about 252, 462
    riots 53, 54, 424
entry fines 217–19, 235, 252, 394, 424
Estgate, Richard 401, 404
Etton, Mr 141, 443
Eure (or Evers), Sir Ralph 10, 219, 329,
    367, 375, 382, 398, 421
Eure (or Evers), Sir William 421
'Evangelicals' 51, 64–5, 76
Everingham, Sir Henry 272, 273
Exeter, Marquis of, see Courtenay, Henry
Ewcross (Yorks.) rising in 233–8

Faircliffe, Richard 185, 186
Fairfax, Sir Nicholas 227, 330, 438
Fairfax, Sir William 427–8, 441

Farrington, Sir Henry 422
Fawcett, Richard 229–30
Fenton, Ralph 382, 391
Ferriby (Yorks.) 191, 360
Fiennes, Edward Lord Clinton (d. 1585)
    97, 159, 161, 163, 167
First Fruits and tenths 52, 71, 312, 351,
    352, 356, 357, 367, 376, 461, 463
    order to collect 372
First Henrician Injunctions 85–6, 451
    criticism of 356
Fisher, John, Bishop of Rochester
    (ex. 1534) 54, 71, 345
Fitzherbert, Sir Anthony 400, 422
Fitzroy, Henry, duke of Richmond
    (d. 1536) 32, 56, 299
Fitzwilliam, Sir William 62, 158, 170, 171,
    172, 319, 325, 327, 333, 336, 338,
    367, 368, 402, 403
Fletcher, Anthony (historian) 15
Fletcher, Bernard 147
Foster, Thomas 104, 108, 449
Fowberry, John 379–80
Franke, Thomas 195–6, 398
Frankish, Dr 5, 103, 107–9, 112
friars 44, 351, 461
    see also Knaresborough, Friary of
      St Robert
Frith, John (d. 1533) 108, 460
Frizington, (Cumb.), riots at 54
Furness (Lancs.) 330
    rising in 238–41
Furness Abbey (Lancs.) 35, 239–40, 401,
    402, 422
    see also Pyle, Roger

Gainsborough (Lincs.) 122, 162, 307, 310
Garnett, William 234–5
Gascoigne, John 195–6
Gascoigne, Sir William 40, 272
Gatton, George 120, 160
gentry:
    and commons 142, 433–5
    distrust of 369, 373–4, 386
    in Cumberland 248

role in risings 413, 446–7; in
    Lincolnshire 143–53
  threats against 125–30, 443–5
Giggleswick (Yorks.) 228, 230, 436
  riots at 53
Girlington, Nicholas 123, 148, 192
Gisburn (Yorks.) 53, 230
Green, Ralph 131
Greystock (Cumb.) 245
Grice, Oswold 375
Grice, Thomas 45, 310
Grimsby (Lincs.) 99, 307
Guisborough, Abbot of 322
Gunn, S. J. (historian) 16, 126

Halifax (Yorks.) 42, 143, 149, 371
Hallam, John 10, 24, 189–90, 310, 332,
    373, 374–7, 408, 434, 441
Hambledon Hill (Lincs.), muster at 25,
    122, 192, 435
Hambledon Hill (Yorks.) 385
Hamerton, Richard 230
Hamerton, Sir Stephen 20, 26, 45, 53,
    223, 228–33, 248, 329, 360, 397, 406,
    407, 409, 410, 436
Hampole articles 300–1, 313, 331, 342,
    353, 419
    printed 458–9
Hampole nunnery (Yorks.) 292, 298
Hartlepool, Roger 386–7
Hastings, Sir Brian 22, 194, 256, 260, 261,
    264, 269, 270, 285, 308, 309, 310,
    324, 340, 445
Hastings, George, first earl of Huntingdon
    (d. 1544) 17, 266, 304, 335
Hatfield (Yorks.) 2, 194, 346
Hawkshead (Lancs.), muster at 239
Hennage, George 159, 160
Hennage, John 5, 98, 106–9, 112, 115,
    117, 158, 164, 166–7, 193
Henry VIII 7, 44, 355, 365, 414, 418, 423
    accepts submissions, 1541 1–2
    and monasteries 452–3
    answer to the Yorkshire rebels 313–14,
    372

assessment of 449–54
attitude towards Lincolnshire rebels
  167–9
attitude towards monks 73–4, 452–3
calls Aske to him 368
criticism of 60–3, 452
dislike of Doncaster agreement 359
grant of Sawley Abbey by 79–80
inability to compromise 450–3
letter to Lincolnshire rebels 149–50
marriage and divorce from Katherine of
  Aragon 56–8
mistrusted by Bigod 378
orders Derby to repress Sawley 231
projected progress to North 365, 369,
  376, 411
progress to York, 1541 1–2, 30
religious beliefs of 64–5
role in government 55–6
rumour of death of 430, 432
sends revised instructions (2 Dec.)
  339–42
state of mind in 1536 76
statements of faith by 83–4
heralds 312
  see also Clarencieux, Lancaster, and
    Somerset Heralds
Hessle (Yorks.) 176, 186, 191
Hexham priory (Northumb.) 49, 54, 223,
  395
Hilton, Robert 244
Hilton, Sir Thomas 220, 298, 346,
  460
Hilyard, Sir Chris. 188–9
Holderness (Yorks.):
  commons of 375–6
  rising in 188–9
Holland Wapentake (Lincs.) 140, 141,
  443
Holme Cultram (Cumb.), abbot of 246,
  248, 329
Holme, Wilfred 51, 89, 92
'honest men' or 'honest persons' 141,
  425–7, 434
Hook Moor (Yorks.) 194

Horncastle (Lincs.) 6, 90, 93, 109, 120,
  156, 152, 172, 174, 405, 423, 433
  rising at 124–34
Hotham, Robert 190, 434
Houghton, Sir Richard 422
Howard, Henry, earl of Surrey (ex. 1547)
  284, 379
Howard, Thomas, duke of Norfolk
  (d. 1554) 8–9, 22, 34, 43, 62, 69,
  158, 169, 173, 220, 306, 311, 313,
  315, 316, 317, 325, 338, 348, 354,
  368, 371, 376, 378, 385, 403, 413,
  417, 418, 420, 426, 430, 431, 442,
  460
  as lieutenant 389–99
  at Doncaster conference 346, 358–64
  campaign against Pilgrims 283–305
  disbands royal army 300, 303
  doubted by Henry VIII 339–41
  his council 369, 420–1
  justifies use of 'policy' 289–90
  letter to Darcy 318
  makes way northwards 286–91
  musters troops 283–6
  persuades Henry VIII to change plans
    334–7
  returns to North 333–6
  returns 369
  to be sent into the North as Lieutenant
    366
Howard, William, Lord 289, 431
Howburne, Nich. 226
Howden (Yorks.) 193, 275, 435
  muster at Ringstone Hurst in 194
Howdenshire (Yorks.) 193
  letter from commons of 195
  rising in 194–6, 261
Huddeswell, George 111, 112, 113, 122,
  139, 140, 152, 163, 191, 404, 407,
  438, 440
Hull 11, 22, 90, 175, 178, 198, 202, 203,
  267, 307, 322, 367, 373, 375, 376,
  379, 408, 419, 428
  attempt to capture by Hallam 379–80
Hungary, Mary of ('The Regent') 322

Hunsley Beacon (Yorks.), musters at 187, 190, 425
Huntingdon 159, 166, 167, 170, 367
Huntingdon, earl of, see Hastings, George
Hus, Jan 350
Hussey, George 195–6
Hussey, John, Lord (ex. 1537) 25, 97, 114, 118, 120, 122, 152, 154, 158, 171, 257, 258, 318, 320, 321, 410, 419, 442, 443
  career of 67
  contacts with Horncastle rebels 161
  conversations with Chapuys 67–8
  role in Lincolnshire rising 159–66
  trial of 406–7
Hussey, Lady 67
Hutton, Anthony 245, 247, 248, 251
Hutton, Thomas 375, 387, 396
Hutton Cranswick (Yorks.) 190

Inglewood, Forest of (Cumb.) 245
Irby, Anthony 141, 154, 425, 443
Ives, E. W. (historian) 14

Jakes (or Jacques) 229–30
James, M. E. (historian) 14, 19, 38, 97, 126, 297
Jervaulx Abbey 386–7, 402, 419, 436, 444, 445
  abbot of, see Sedber, Adam

Kendal (Westm.) 30, 42, 368, 387, 392, 424, 426, 428
  rising in 234–6, 330
Kendal, barony of (Westm.) 252
  rising in 233–8
  commons of 232
Kendall, Thomas 97, 100, 103, 104, 105, 108, 110, 138, 325, 404, 426, 437
Kett's rebellion (1549) 19, 435
Kexby Lane End (Yorks.), muster at 199–200, 203
King, William 98, 111, 112
Kingston, Sir William 62, 286, 319
Kirkby Lonsdale (Westm.) 212

Kirkby Malzeard (Yorks.) 39
Kirkby Stephen (Westm.) 242–4, 250, 253, 392
Kirkstead Abbey (Lincs.) 133, 402, 404, 405
Kirton (Lincs.), commons of 122–3, 191
Kitchen, Roger 182, 183, 185, 379
Knaresborough, Friary and friars of St Robert 58, 92, 226, 378, 396, 416
  see also Ashton alias Eshe, Robert
Knollys, John 253
Kyme, Guy 109, 111, 116, 187, 189, 198, 404

Lambert, John 46, 53
Lammerside (Westm.) 243, 244
Lancaster 236–7, 371
Lancaster, duchy of 33, 40
Lancaster Herald 6, 23, 151, 172, 174, 286, 288–9, 291, 294–6, 298, 304, 340, 345, 361, 371
Langton, Sir Thomas 422
Langwith Lane End, muster at 133, 155
Lastingham (Yorks.) 398
Latimer, Hugh, bishop of Worcester 63, 64, 73, 77, 82, 301, 351, 456
Latimer, Lord, see Neville, John, Lord Latimer
Latymer, William 77, 78
Lawson, Sir George 263, 277
Laybourne, Sir James 234–7
Laybourne, Nich. 235
Laybourne, Parson 236
Layton, Dr Richard 3, 4, 26, 90, 212, 352, 461
Leach, Nicholas 87, 124, 146, 404
Leach, Robert 132, 325
Leach, William 90, 124, 125, 128–9, 130, 155, 396, 440
Leconfield (Yorks.) 179
Lee, Edward, archbishop of York 1–2, 26, 42, 43, 44, 53, 58, 90, 180, 181, 183, 184, 213, 265, 287, 294–5, 298, 343,

344, 350, 353, 362, 369, 372, 390, 424, 428
  flees to Pontefract 178, 200, 273–4
  preaches at Pontefract 344–5
  speaks with Aske 353–4
  surrenders to Aske 278–9
Legbourne nunnery (Lincs.) 5, 109
Leigh, Dr Thomas 3, 26, 212, 352, 461
Levening, William 395–6, 409
Leyland, Sir William 422
Lincoln 4, 6, 93, 123, 160, 198, 310, 424
  Bishop of 428; see Longland, John; his
    steward, see Hennage, John
  Chapter House at 142, 149
  mayor of 120, 122, 160
Lincoln articles 61, 63, 95, 149, 197, 203
  printed 455–6
Lincolnshire:
  JPs of 97
  Lincolnshire Rebellion 93–175, 423–4;
    geographical range of 95–6; identity
    of rebels in 136–7
  letter from commons of 186
  letter to commons at 179
  Lincolnshire Rebellion and Yorkshire
    209
  reports of executions in 386
  trials in 404–5
Littlebury, Mr 131, 132
Lobley, Thomas 387, 434
Longland, John, bishop of Lincoln 5, 63, 85, 456
Louth (Lincs.) 5, 6, 90, 116, 124, 125, 159, 172, 179, 372, 405, 423, 428, 433, 435, 437, 439, 449
  character of 98–102
  church 101–2
  clergy of 99–101, 111
  guilds of 99, 101
  identity of rebels in 135–6
  Louth men go to Caistor 111–16
  rising at 93, 102–23, 159–61
  social conflicts in 427
  spire 101–2
  vicar of, see Kendall, Thomas

Lowther, Sir John 247, 254
Lumley, George 26, 220, 221, 222, 226, 391, 406, 407, 429, 435, 438, 439
  in Bigod's revolt 380–2
  evidence against 408, 410
Lumley, John, fourth lord Lumley
  (d. 1544–5) 26, 220, 292, 293, 297, 358, 360, 398, 432
Luther, Martin 350, 460
Lutton, Thomas 395

Maddison, Sir Edward 113, 115, 117, 151–2, 153, 158, 167, 171
Magnus, Thomas 42, 273, 274
Malory, William 222
Maltby, Simon 92, 103
Malton (Yorks.) 27, 225, 226, 227
  prior of 380
Manners, Thomas, first earl of Rutland
  (d. 1543) 166, 171, 265, 304, 316, 323, 367
Markenfield, Sir Ninian 222
Market Rasen (Yorks.) 118, 119, 148, 174,
Market Weighton (Yorks.) 187, 198
Markham, Sir John, servant of 165
Marshall, Dr 355
Marshall, William 460
Marshall, parish clerk of Beswick 350, 375, 380, 391
Marshland (Yorks.) 193, 435
  gentry of 309, 335
  rising in 194–6, 261
Mary, Princess (later queen) 56, 58, 67, 82, 347, 351
Mashamshire (Yorks.), rising in 213–16
Maunsell, Thomas 196, 274–8, 446
Maunsell, William 89, 92, 261, 274–6
Melanchthon, Philipp 350
Melton, Nicholas, of Louth ('Captain Cobbler') 104, 105, 106, 111, 112, 174
Metcalfe, Chris. 214
Metcalfe, Sir James 214
Metham (Yorks) 207

Metham, Sir Thomas 194, 195–6, 198,
    202, 259, 267, 444
Mewtas, Peter 303, 368
Michell, Christopher 58
Middleham (Yorks.) 213, 385
    Middleham Moor, projected muster at
    387
Middleton, Edw. 213, 386, 391
Millicent, Thomas 109
Missenden, Sir Thomas 114, 115
Moigne, Thomas 3, 24, 88, 97, 114, 115,
    117, 118, 139, 142, 144, 152, 160,
    172, 175, 192–3, 197, 404, 407 413,
    425, 433, 435, 442, 444, 446
    flees Caistor 118
    role of in Lincolnshire rising 147–51
    sworn by commons 119
monasteries:
    Aske's order for 202–3
    at Pontefract Conference 358, 360–1
    monks re-enter 217, 254
    monks to be expelled by Norfolk 370,
    390, 394–5
    perception of 70–1
    place in northern society 46–50
    surrender and seizure of 402, 405
    sympathy for 210
    to be restored 351, 461
    visitation of, 1535 71–3
Monkton, William 195–6, 277
Montague, Lord 418, 452
Monteagle, Lord 53, 54, 234, 442
Monubent (Yorks.), muster at 229–30
Monyhouse (Yorks.), muster at 381–2,
    435
Morland, William 26, 104, 111–16, 120,
    122, 146, 404, 407, 426
Musgrave, Great (Westm.) 253
Musgrave, [   ] 251
Musgrave, Sir Edward 245, 247
Musgrave, Sir John 250
Musgrave, Nich. 243, 244, 391–2

Nafferton (Yorks.) 226
Neals Ing (Yorks.) 228–30

Neville, Henry, Lord (later fifth earl of
    Westmorland, d. 1564) 221, 225,
    226, 292, 293, 297, 358, 359
Neville, John, Lord Latimer (d. 1543) 34,
    214–15, 221, 222, 225, 227, 292, 293,
    297, 299, 329, 343, 354, 358, 386,
    410, 444, 451
Neville, Marmaduke 221, 362, 363, 368
Neville, Ralph, fourth earl of
    Westmorland (d. 1549) 34, 40, 54,
    221, 367, 386, 387, 421, 443
Neville, Sir Robert 272, 273
Neudyke, Richard 184
Newark 171, 265, 432
Newcastle upon Tyne 220, 428–9
Newcomb, John 181
Newe, Roger 89, 132
'Nicholas', Lord Burgh's servant 110, 112,
    115
Nicholson, William 375, 377, 379–80
Nidderdale (Yorks.) rising of commons of
    213–16
nobility 333
    criticism of 60–1
    households of 39
    power of 38
Norfolk 39, 435
Norfolk, duke of, see Howard, Thomas
Norris, Henry 81–2
North, the:
    character of 28–54
    council of 360, 427
    councils in 31–3
    description of 29–31
    disorders in 30, 52–4
    opposition to taxation in 52
    poverty of clergy in 42
    proposals to pacify 365–6
    religious life of 41–51
    reputation for violence 39–41
Northampton, projected muster at 286
North Cave (Yorks.) 186
North Willingham (Lincs.) 118, 119,
    425
Northumberland, conditions in 30–1

Northumberland, earls of, *see* Percy,
    Henry
Norton (Ches.) 49
Norton, John 34, 39, 222
Nottingham 347, 462
    musters at 165, 171, 194, 286–7

oath swearing 20, 191, 192, 439–42
    at Kendal 235
    in Cumberland 250–1
    in Lincolnshire 107, 109, 119, 127,
        128–9
    to king 391, 369, 370, 400
    see also Pilgrims of Grace, their oath
Otley (Yorks.) 428
Otterburn 391
Oxenfield, (Dur.), muster at 215–16, 220

papacy 356–7, 461
Page, Sir Richard 289
Palmes, Dr 91 431
pardons 311–12, 326, 334, 337, 341, 348,
        372, 374, 377, 442, 446–7, 450
    for Lincolnshire 325
    grant of 358, 359
    partial pardon offered 346
    proclamation of 371
    scepticism of 378
    requests for 117, 152, 153, 154, 161,
        171–2, 173, 460
parliament 61, 335, 341, 366
    demands for 301, 332
    of 1536 82–3
    promised 364, 368, 375, 410–11
    recalled April 1536 75
    Reformation Parliament (1529–36) 70,
        73, 79
    requested 347, 348
Parr, Katherine 34
Parr, Sir William 170, 171, 367, 404
Paslew John, Abbot of Whalley 400, 405
Paulet, Sir William 62, 286, 319
Peacock, Anthony 385, 391, 394, 434
Penrith (Cumb.) 8, 217, 243, 245, 249,
        371

Percy, Henry, fourth earl of
    Northumberland (d. 1489) 52
Percy, Henry, fifth earl of
    Northumberland (d. 1527) 33, 34,
        35, 179
Percy, Henry, sixth earl of
    Northumberland (d. 1537) 20, 32,
        34, 36, 45, 54, 68, 196, 307, 367, 412,
        446
Percy, Sir Ingram 389
Percy, Sir Thomas 26, 189, 196, 224–7,
        228, 248, 291, 292, 360, 378, 381,
        382, 389, 395, 409, 410, 424, 444
Percy or Percehay, William 225
petitions 315–16, 348
    formulation of 20–1
    see also Lincoln articles; Pontefract articles
Pickering, Dr 345, 396, 409, 410
Pilgrimage of Grace:
    place of towns in 427–9
    previous interpretations of 12–17
    regional patterns in 423–5
    sources for ix, 11, 21–7
Pilgrims of Grace:
    badges worn by 362, 416–17
    description of the movement as 20–7,
        237, 238, 253–4
    dispersal of 304
    numbers of 293
    their oath 7, 205–7, 228, 233; versions
        printed 457–8, 458–9
Plumpton, Edward 51
Plumpton, Mr 202
Place, Roland 221
'policy' 150, 151, 153, 290
    used by crown 283
    by duke of Norfolk 289–90, 302
Pontefract (Yorks.) 2, 59, 61, 224, 227,
        276, 340, 342, 358–9, 390, 413, 419,
        443
    castle 7, 178, 228, 259–60, 277–8,
        288–9
    conference at 331, 342–6; people called
        to 331, 343–4, 426
    honour of 317, 424

Pontefract articles 10, 62, 63, 72, 342
  discussion of 347–53
  printed 460–2
Porte, Sir John 400, 422
Portington, Thomas 97, 122, 191
Poverty:
  Captain Poverty 8, 22, 52, 210, 253–4,
    245, 424, 425; letter in the name of
    217, 440
  Earl of Poverty 20
  Lord Poverty 215, 236
  Master Poverty 240
  Poverty's Chaplains 245
preaching 43–4, 85–6, 366, 367, 370, 452,
  463
Preston (Lancs.) 9, 226, 232
providence 304
Prudhoe Castle (Northumb.) 395
Pullen, Robert 243, 244, 245, 251, 427
purgatory, denial of 84–5
Pyle, Roger, abbot of Furness 239–40,
  402, 422

Radcliffe, Robert, earl of Surrey (d. 1542)
  319, 366, 399–404, 421–2
Raffles, John 181
Raffles, Robert 182, 183
Rastell, John 350, 460, 461
Rayne, Dr John 6, 88, 92, 106, 112, 122,
  124, 132–3, 212, 443
Reid, Dr Rachel (historian) 52
Redman, Richard 272
Rich, Sir Richard 62, 63, 154, 155, 351,
  451, 456, 461
Richmond (Yorks.) 27, 214, 390, 434
  abbey of St Agatha at 50, 219, 254
  musters at 215–16, 387, 396
Richmond, duke of, see Fitzroy, Henry
Richmondshire (Yorks.) 90, 387, 417, 424
  earlier disturbances in 8, 52
  rising in 8, 209–55
  expectation of new rising 377–8, 385
Ripon (Yorks.) 27, 213, 424
Rising of the North (1569) 39
Rither, Henry 272–3

Rochford, George Boleyn, viscount
  (ex. 1536) 81–2
Rokeby, James 219
Rokeby, Thomas 215
Rokeby, William 219, 444
royal supremacy 58–9, 65–6, 85, 87, 350,
  356, 463
Rudstone, Nicholas 198, 346, 375
rumours 17, 46, 88–92, 103, 114, 167–8,
  169, 239, 259, 312, 375–6, 377, 403,
  416
  and news 429–32
  rebuttal of, by Moigne 114; by Henry
    VIII 117, 260, 312–13, 315, 432; by
    Lancaster Herald 89
Russell, Sir John 170, 171, 172, 175, 281,
  336, 340–1, 342, 367
Rutland, earl of, see Manners, Thomas

Sadler, Sir Ralph 176, 371, 374, 427, 428,
  430, 436, 443
St German, Christopher 350, 460, 461
Saltmarsh, Thomas 195–6, 202, 207
Sandon, Sir William 127, 130, 144
Sandal Castle (Yorks.) 367
Sandys, Lord 69
Saunderson, Chris. 181, 183, 184, 185, 186
Savage, Thomas, archbishop of York
  (d. 1507) 31, 33, 179–80
Savile, Sir Henry 33, 40, 309, 330, 334,
  367, 418, 438
Sawcliffe (Lincs.) 191
Sawley Abbey (Yorks.) 9, 50, 79–80, 203,
  219, 228, 230, 231, 239, 254, 332,
  360, 391, 394, 400, 409
Scarborough (Yorks.) 8, 9, 10, 175, 373,
  376, 408, 419
  castle 178, 219, 310, 329, 367; attempt
    to relieve 362; siege of 374;
    attempted siege 381–3
Scrivelsby (Lincs.), taking of gentry at 93,
  125, 144, 146, 147, 440
Scrope, John, eighth lord (d. 1549) 213,
  214, 223, 244, 293, 297, 329, 358,
  445

Scrope, Lady Katherine 22, 214
Seamer (Yorks.) 224–5, 227
Sedber, Adam, abbot of Jervaulx 213, 406, 410
Sedbergh (Yorks.) 212, 220, 223, 426
  commons of 330
  rising in 234–6
Selby (Yorks.) 27, 178
Settrington (Yorks.) 378
Seymour, Jane 76, 82
Shap (Westm.) 54
Sharpe, Kevin (historian) 15
Sheffield, John 118
Sherburn (Yorks.) 407
Sheriff Hutton (Yorks.) 32, 52, 327, 385
Shrewsbury, earl of, see Talbot, George
Siggiswick, Richard 214
Skip, John 77, 80
Skipton (Yorks.) 8, 9, 175, 214, 222, 223–4, 444
Skipwith, Sir William 109, 153, 440
Skipwith Moor (Yorks.), muster at 195–6, 275
Sleaford (Lincs.) 97, 159, 162, 442
Smeaton, Mark 81–2
Snaith (Yorks.) 256, 309
  bailiff of 375, 377
Somerset Herald 23, 256, 272, 279, 281, 299, 308, 321
Sotherby, Robert 125, 128, 130, 404
Southworth, Sir Thomas 422
Spennymoor, (Dur.), muster at 221
Staines, John 401
Stainton, John 386–7
Stainsby (Lincs.) 131
Stamford 170, 171
Stanes, Brian 91
Stanes, George 154, 155, 156, 197
Stanley, Edward, third earl of Derby (d. 1572) 9, 22, 23, 34, 35, 38, 39, 68, 231–3, 239, 287, 292, 305, 330, 336, 330, 341, 366, 399–400
  his council 421–2
Stapleton, Brian 45, 185

Stapleton, William 24, 91, 182, 183, 185, 198, 203, 207, 291, 292, 307, 425–6, 427, 441, 444
Starkey, Thomas 71
Statute of Uses 155, 156, 352, 455, 462
Staveley, Ninian 24, 213, 386–7, 391, 409, 436
Staynhouse, William 398–9
Steeton (Yorks.) 403
Strangeways, Sir James 221
Strangeways, Thomas 202, 205, 276–7, 368
Strickland, Walter 232, 235, 236
subsidy 168, 312
  assessors 139, 161
  at Caistor 112–14
  commissioners 191
  opposition to 259
succession (to Henry VIII) 56–8, 332–3, 347, 351
Suffolk, duke of, see Brandon, Charles
Surrey, earl of, see Howard, Henry
Sutton, Sir John 156
Sussex, 62
Sussex, earl of, see Radcliffe, Robert

Tadcaster (Yorks.) 91, 432
Talbot, Anthony 230
Talbot, Francis, Lord Talbot (later fifth earl of Shrewsbury) 289–90, 300, 315
Talbot, George, fourth earl of Shrewsbury (d. 1538) 8, 22, 34, 38, 44, 117, 152, 158, 59, 166, 171, 194, 202, 258, 282, 284, 285, 304, 308, 316, 323–4, 330, 367, 368, 372, 413, 418, 428
  advances 288–9
  and Darcy 265–6, 268–9, 280, 299
  and Hussey 163–6
taxation, complaints against 156, 212, 455
  opposition to 51–2
  rumours of 89
  see also first fruits and tenths; subsidy
Tempest, Nicholas 27, 230–1, 233, 397, 401, 406, 409, 410

Tempest, Sir Richard 33, 40, 46, 53, 54, 231, 232, 264, 266, 287, 293, 367, 394, 410

Tempest, Thomas 46

Tempest, Sir Thomas 62, 347, 352, 390, 421

Tempest, Sir Thomas (another) 443

Temple Hirst (Yorks.) 256, 258, 260, 275, 319, 337

Ten Articles (1536) 65, 83–5

tenant right 218, 347, 353, 424, 461

Tesh, Tristram 219

Tetney, Thomas 144

Thimbleby, Sir John 172, 443

Thirlby, Dr Thomas 421

Thirsk, William, late abbot of Fountains 406, 410

Thomas, William 418

Thompson, Robert 25, 26, 217, 218, 242–7, 248, 249–50, 396, 440

Thwaites, William 67, 71

Thwing (Yorks.) 222, 226, 381

Tibby, Thomas 391–2

tithes 252, 253, 424

Todd, William, prior of Malton 380, 409–10

Topcliffe (Yorks.) 52

Towneley, Dr Bernard 217, 218, 242–7, 248–50, 396, 440

Tregonwell, John 26, 88

trials:
  at Carlisle 393
  at York 395
  evidence at 407–10
  in Lancashire 400, 403

Trotter, Phillip 89, 90, 125, 126, 132, 146, 404

truce, alleged breaches of 256

Tunstall, Cuthbert, bishop of Durham 30, 43, 220, 420, 421

Tunstall, Sir Marmaduke 234, 422

Turvey, John 184

Tyndale, John 350, 460

Tyrwhit, Sir Robert 115, 160, 161, 164, 166

Uvedale, John 421

Valor Eccesiasticus 71, 80, 99

Vannes, Peter 42, 253

Vaux, Thomas, Lord 79

Vavasour, Sir Peter 338

Vavasour, William 30

Wakefield (Yorks.) 40, 202, 276, 371, 424, 441, 443

Waldby, Dr Marmaduke 322–3, 355, 416

Walker, [   ] 332

Warcop, John 243

Warrington (Lancs.) 400, 403

Warter priory (Yorks.) 391

Watton (Yorks.) 189–90, 376, 378, 391

Wedel, Gilbert 226

Wensleydale (Yorks.) 223, 230
  commons of 229
  rising in 212

Wentbridge (Yorks.) 292

Wentworth (Yorks.) 272, 273

Westmorland 32
  petition of commons of 252–3
  rising in 241–4
  renewed rebellion in 391–4

Westmorland, earl of, see Neville, Ralph

West, John, alias 'Joken Sene' 105

West, William of Alford 145–6

West, William of Louth 110

Whalley Abbey (Lancs.) 231–2, 400–1, 402, 405, 422, 441, 444

Wharton (Westm.) 243
  park at 39

Wharton, Richard 185, 186, 425–6

Wharton, Sir Thomas (cr. Lord Wharton 1544, d. 1568) 36, 243, 247, 248, 393

Wharton, Thomas (later second Lord Wharton) 46, 243

Whelpedale, Gilbert 245

Whitgift (Yorks.) 194, 197

Willen, George 234–5

Willoughby, Lady 424

Wilson, Richard 182, 183–4, 434
Wilstrop, Sir Oswold 202, 364, 382, 384, 438
Winteringham (Lincs.) 191
Wood, William, prior of Bridlington 406, 409, 410
Wolsey, Thomas, cardinal 32, 71
Woodmansey, [ ] 143, 183–4, 186, 383, 391, 404, 434
Wressle (Yorks.) 196, 224, 306, 307
Wriothesley, Thomas 155, 173, 262
Wulcye, [ ] 122, 132
Wycliffe, John 350, 460
Wycliffe, Ralph 41
Wycliffe, William 40–1
Wysse, William 182
Wyvill, John 382–3, 391

Yarborough Hill (Lincs.) 140
Yoell, Thomas 90, 92, 404, 437
York 7, 52, 282, 283, 347, 361, 371, 424, 426, 428, 462
  archbishop of, see Lee, Edward, Savage, Thomas
  dean and chapter of 383
  entered by pilgrims 199–201, 285
  letter of Aske to 203–4; printed 456–7
  mayor of 261, 263, 376
  St Leonard's hospital 42, 79
  St Michael Spurriergate in 438
  submission of (1541) 1–2
York conference 10, 224, 328, 329–32
Yorkshire:
  submission of 1–2
  trials in 406–7